TRUTH
AFLAME

T0308420

REVISED EDITION

TRUTH AFLAME

Theology *for the* Church *in* Renewal

LARRY D. HART

We want to hear from you. Please send your comments about this book to us in care of zreview@zondervan.com. Thank you.

Truth Aflame—Revised Edition

Original edition published in 1999 by Thomas Nelson, Inc.

Requests for information should be addressed to:

Zondervan, *Grand Rapids, Michigan 49530*

Library of Congress Cataloging-in-Publication Data

Hart, Larry (Larry D.)
Truth aflame : theology for the church in renewal / Larry D. Hart.-Rev. ed.
p. cm.
Includes bibliographical references and indexes.
ISBN 978-0-310-25989-3 (printed hardcover)
1. Evangelicalism. 2. Theology, Doctrinal—Popular works. I. Title.
BR1640.H37 2005
230'.04624—dc22

2005002766

This edition printed on acid-free paper.

For copyright information of other versions used, see special page at end of book.

Interior design by Beth Shagene

Printed in the United States of America

To Thea

Lovely wife
Gracious encourager
Best friend

Contents

Preface

T*RUTH* *AFLAME* WAS WRITTEN WITH A GOAL OF REVITALIZING THE CHURCH. I wanted to write a bridge-building, readable, practical, and personal book that stresses the church on mission. Theology should be doxological, devotional, and practical. The great works of the past—for example, Calvin's *Institutes*—evince these qualities. Only since the Enlightenment has the church in many quarters capitulated to the academy and made theology solely an academic discipline.

I was graced with enough Jewish *chutzpah* to attempt to write a "crossover" volume for both church and classroom settings. I trust professors will find this book useful for classroom purposes, but I also hope it reaches educated believers who wish to learn about God's calling on their lives and their place in his church.

The title reflects my own spiritual heritage. *Truth* evokes images of the evangelical emphasis on God's Word, objective truth, and the life of the mind. *Aflame* points to the Pentecostal-charismatic stress on the Spirit, the heart, and religious affections. In her best days, the church always has kept "heart religion" and "head religion" in balance and integrated. In this way, the best of premodern, modern, and now postmodern concerns are served. At the same time, the danger of conformity to *any* age, mindset, or *zeitgeist* must be acknowledged (Rom. 12:2).

I hope this work will prove to be *evangelical* in the most comprehensive sense of the term, encompassing Reformed, Arminian, Pentecostal, charismatic, and ecumenical perspectives. Utilizing insights and illustrative materials from leading popular writers, I have attempted to produce a volume that was both contemporary in style and classical in substance—a comprehensive theological survey that might actually be read! And, loving the preaching ministry as I do, I wanted to serve preachers with materials to enhance their pulpit ministries.

The fingerprints of my mentor, the late Dale Moody, can be seen all over these pages. The older I get, the more I realize how we are formed by our roots. The reader will therefore detect a distinct Southern Baptist flavor to these writings. At the same time, the influence of some forty years of associations with those of the Pentecostal-charismatic heritage can be easily discerned. My prayer is that saints from both these and other ecclesial persuasions will find relevance in these explorations of the rich, fascinating, and variegated Christian heritage we all enjoy.

Working with the editorial team at Zondervan has been one of the greatest delights of my life. At a key juncture, a brief conversation with Stan Gundry spurred me on to pursue a lifetime of ministry through writing. And Verlyn Verbrugge, who supervised this revised edition, proved to be the quintessential editor—incisive, insightful, and always the perfect Christian gentleman. We shared a joyful pilgrimage together improving and expanding the original work. Dr. Verbrugge often challenged a particular biblical interpretation or theological position, and the changes that resulted have enhanced the overall presentation. Readers of the original edition will note improvements throughout this second edition along with additional content at key points. All errors remain my own, of course.

Finally, I wish to make mention of my loving wife, Thea, to whom this volume is dedicated, and my three winsome children, Melanie, Kevin, and Jonathan. Why God would bless me with such a wonderful, supportive family is beyond my understanding. My parents, Mr. and Mrs. N. O. Hart, remain the spiritual pillars of my life. They birthed this book through their prayers and encouragement. And the kind affirmations of Myrtle Frampton, my mother-in-law, also helped make this book a reality. Many thanks to these dear saints and many others, unnamed yet most sincerely appreciated.

May all glory and honor be given to God, who continually lavishes his love on us all. Any good to be found in these pages comes from his gracious hand.

1 | Introduction
Is Theology Really Necessary?

If you point these things out to the brothers and sisters, you will be a good minister of Christ Jesus, nourished on the truths of the faith and of the good teaching [doctrine] that you have followed.

—1 Timothy 4:6 TNIV

For the time will come when people will not put up with sound doctrine. Instead, to suit their own desires, they will gather around them a great number of teachers to say what their itching ears want to hear.

—2 Timothy 4:3 TNIV

Why Didn't Someone Tell Me That I'm a Theologian?

A fine professional Presbyterian theologian once said that sex, politics, and theology were the only things worth talking about. Sex, he said, presents us with the question, "Who am I?" Politics asks, "How can we learn to live together?" But theology raises the ultimate questions about our origins, meaning, and destiny. Of the three topics, theology is the most interesting and important because it *includes* all the questions of the other two topics. *"The study of theology is by definition the quest for the ultimate truth about God, about ourselves and about the world we live in. What else is there to talk about?"*[1]

We unknowingly think about and discuss theology almost by the minute! Everyone is a theologian. If you have any opinions at all about what life is all about—what we humans are up to, what God (if you believe there is a God) is up to, and what is important in life—then you are a theologian. You have a theology whether you like it or not. Your theology is either well thought out and coherent, or it is hodgepodge and piecemeal. Even atheists are theologians!

> *We unknowingly think about and discuss theology almost by the minute! Everyone is a theologian.*

We sometimes think of theologians as professionals who specialize in esoteric, philosophical discussions about otherworldly matters that have little relevance to everyday life. Too often this idea appears accurate. In defense of the professionals, though, they have their rightful place in the scheme of things, along with specialists in other fields such as science and technology. The term *theology* can also have a bad name because there is so much bad theology out there. However, the answer to bad theology is not *no* theology, but *good* theology.

What about the Bible?

The other issue that arises when we mention theology is the Bible. Don't theologians enter into endless debate about the meanings of myriad biblical passages as they hammer out their positions (and sometimes the heads of their opponents!)? To be sure, the Bible has always played a major role in theological enterprise. Later we will evaluate what this role has been and should be.

---

[1] Shirley C. Guthrie Jr., *Christian Doctrine* (Atlanta: John Knox, 1968), 11 (Guthrie's italics).

At this juncture, however, we will simply acknowledge the central role that the Bible has had for theological discussions both inside and outside the church. The big question is then, What is the Bible all about? Jack Rogers once said that he could summarize the basic message of the Bible in ten seconds: "God made a good world and people messed it up; and God sent Jesus to put it and people back together."[2] This statement raises a number of questions—all theological in nature.

One such series of questions relates to the Bible itself: Why is the Bible so important anyway? How do we know whether its message is true? Can we be certain? Why do we accept the Bible as revelation? Theology texts address these and related issues in their prolegomena (prefatory) and methodology sections. Also, the nature of the Bible's role as revelation—its authority, inspiration, trustworthiness, and so on—arises early on in almost any thorough doctrinal work.

> *The answer to bad theology is not* no *theology, but* good *theology*

Rogers's statement raises further questions: Just who is this God who created the universe? Is the idea of a Creator God viable today in the face of the exploding body of scientific knowledge? What is the nature of the world that God made? What is the essential nature of humanity? What does it mean to be created male and female? (Now there's an interesting topic—and a profoundly theological one as well.)

Rogers's reference to our "messing things up" brings up the concept of sin. This is perhaps the most offensive doctrine of all. Are we really all sinners? What exactly does this mean?

Then mention is made of Jesus Christ. Who is Jesus Christ? What is his precise relationship to God? What was his mission? What did he do? Is he really God, as many say? Did he actually *claim* to be God? How does he "put everything back together"? Is he finished doing all this yet? Is he coming back to earth?

Get Your Thinking Straight!

These questions, and many more that can be raised, are theological. Each of us encounters them perennially throughout life. Life demands that we address these issues. Theology forces itself upon us! We are constantly working out relationships in our lives. To do this successfully, we

---

[2] *The Wittenburg Door.*

must decide what is and what should be important to us. We have to get our thinking straight about our relationships with God, with other people, with the planet we live on, and with ourselves! In the process, we wrestle with a lot of heavyweight theological questions.

There Are Theologians . . . and There Are Theologians

If we are all theologians, there must be about as many theologies as there are theologians. This is nearly true. There will be a variety of ways in which we will all approach the task—whether we are professionals or just ordinary folk. But the same fundamental questions confront us all, and unless we surrender to absolute relativism, there are only a finite number of approaches we can take.

More important than this general observation is the fact that each of us is a unique person functioning in a specific culture. Your gender, your race, your cultural heritage, your religious background, and many other factors contribute to the way you handle the theological enterprise. Because theology is profoundly personal as well as universally applicable, our mutual sharing in this exciting endeavor can be one of the most meaningful activities in which we participate.

Theology forces itself upon us!

Who Is the Theologian Who Wrote This Book?

If all these considerations are valid, then it would be helpful for the reader to know the author a little better. I hail from the Bible Belt region of the Southwest. As a Baby Boomer, I grew up around the tumbleweeds, jack rabbits, rattlesnakes, and oil wells of West Texas. My claim to fame is that I sang in a quartet with Larry Gatlin during my junior high years.

I cut my spiritual teeth on enthusiastic evangelical preaching of the Southern Baptist variety and experienced a profound conversion as a seven-year-old in the pastor's study of our hometown Southern Baptist church. The other "religion" of the region where I grew up was football. My high school football team won its first state championship my senior year and began a dynasty that continues to this day. A Pulitzer-Prize-winning author even wrote a book about these gridiron glories that has received national acclaim.[3]

[3] H. G. Bissinger, *Friday Night Lights* (Reading, Mass.: Addison-Wesley, 1990).

I must confess, however, that I grew impatient with the Sunday school discussions about the game the night before. I was on a spiritual quest to know Jesus Christ better. This quest led me into an active involvement with the charismatic renewal at the age of eighteen. Although my parents may have had misgivings, I attended a youth seminar on the campus of Oral Roberts University the summer after I graduated from high school. I was especially interested in what the two Baptist speakers at this seminar had to say.

I was impressed with the erudition of American Baptist theologian Howard Ervin. And there was also an impressive Southern Baptist gentleman by the name of Pat Robertson, who was just beginning a new television network. Robertson counseled and prayed with me the night I was "baptized in the Holy Spirit."

Needless to say, such exotic experiences did not sit well with my Baptist peers and mentors back in West Texas. Undaunted, I ended up graduating from Oral Roberts University, where I also acknowledged a divine calling to the gospel ministry. Then, to everyone's surprise, I chose Southern Baptist Theological Seminary in Louisville, Kentucky, to receive my ministerial training. While earning the M.Div. and Ph.D. degrees, I served as pastor or associate pastor in nearby Baptist churches. During this time I rediscovered the value of Southern Baptist life and the stability that this evangelical denomination affords a believer.

I continued to be a part of the charismatic movement—though not uncritically. My doctoral dissertation critiqued American Pentecostal/charismatic theology. Over the past twenty-five years I have taught systematic theology at the seminary level and both planted and pastored churches in Kentucky, Oklahoma, Texas, and Florida. My pilgrimage at Southern Seminary and in the charismatic renewal has been an ecumenical one. I can be accurately characterized as a conservative evangelical with a deep appreciation for both the renewal of the church and for the beauty of the various traditions within the church. While writing this book I have become even more poignantly aware of how deep my spiritual roots are in Southern Baptist life and thought, and yet how profoundly I have been impacted by the Pentecostal/charismatic tradition.

I hope that this introduction will help the reader to better understand why I take some of the positions that I set forth here. At the same time, there may be some surprises in store. My students in seminary often comment how difficult it is to pigeonhole me!

So What's the Strategy?

Our first task is to obtain a bird's-eye view of the entire theological scene—a kind of Christianity 101. While many of us are familiar with a few of the trees of this vast theological forest, we often get lost in the forest for lack of such an overview. We will glance back at the history of the church's thought as well as take a few soundings of contemporary theological efforts.

We will also seek to clarify the disciplines involved in doing theology. What methods will we use? What are our goals? Why has the church theologized throughout the years? What specific topics will we cover? This should be an exciting journey! Let's get started!

What, Exactly, Is Theology?

What we will explore in this book is formally known as *systematic theology*. This is what I did my seminary doctorate in and what I have taught for the last couple of decades. To me it's exciting stuff, and I hope my enthusiasm is contagious! But don't let this rather arid term throw you.

When people ask me for a layman's definition of systematic theology, I usually respond with something like this: Systematic theology takes what the Bible teaches and relates it to contemporary questions and knowledge. This description helps many overcome intimidation and confusion. In systematic theology we simply try to obtain an overall grasp of what the Bible teaches and then relate these teachings to our contemporary setting. Isn't this what diligent students of the Bible and responsible preachers of the gospel are always trying to do? Precisely! Theology is a servant of the Church. It actually has a very limited role.

> *Systematic theology takes what the Bible teaches and relates it to contemporary questions and knowledge.*

Theology is meant to help believers better understand and obey the Scriptures. It exists to engender the worship of God and the proclamation of the gospel. It also attempts to provide a sound intellectual foundation for our beliefs. It is a straightforward statement of what Christians believe about their majestic God and about his magnificent creation. It is the language *of* faith and not merely a language *about* faith.[4] Theology

[4] See Paul L. Holmer, *The Grammar of Faith* (New York: Harper & Row, 1978).

describes God's revelation of himself through the Scriptures and relates what the Bible teaches to knowledge we gain in other ways. In a real sense, theology even expresses what we *ought* to believe as it faithfully relates the teachings of the Bible.[5]

My own formal definition of systematic theology is *a coherent and comprehensive explication of the teachings of the canonical Scriptures (the Bible) in relation to contemporary questions and knowledge.* Notice how this differs from *religion,* which is the total living out of our faith. It also differs from *biblical interpretation.* Systematic theology is more comprehensive; it correlates the Bible's teachings *in their totality* with the contemporary context. In order to do this we need the help of the Holy Spirit.

The Reformers taught that the Word and the Spirit always work in tandem. Therefore, we must continually seek the help of the Holy Spirit as we do theology. The Spirit alone can interpret and apply the Scriptures for each contemporary context. Thus, spiritual discernment and devotion are also essential requirements for the theological task. No contemporary theologian has seen this reality more clearly than Donald Bloesch: "Doctrine without devotion is empty; devotion without doctrine is blind."[6] Bloesch further elaborates:

> Our goal is not merely to repeat Scripture but to apply Scripture under the guidance of the Spirit to a new situation. Doing theology is being taught by God and being formed by God into fit instruments of his service. It involves an in-depth engagement with the Word of God animated by a zeal for the glory of God.[7]

I would also like to add a renewal dimension to our definition, using categories from Richard Lovelace's classic treatment of the subject of renewal. From the perspective of the continuing renewal of the church, a truly Christian theology must be grounded in the gospel. It must be centered on Christ. It must be aware of spiritual warfare, oriented toward mission, motivated by dependent prayer, done within the Christian community, freed as much as possible from cultural binds, faithful to revealed truth (the Bible), and effectively applied to culture.[8] This is a tall order and something to be attempted with great humility!

---

[5] Compare I. Howard Marshall, *Pocket Guide to Christian Beliefs* (Downers Grove, Ill.: InterVarsity Press, 1978), ch. 1, esp. pp. 11–13.

[6] Donald G. Bloesch, *The Church* (Downers Grove, Ill.: InterVarsity Press, 2002), 18.

[7] Ibid., 23.

[8] See Richard F. Lovelace, *Dynamics of Spiritual Life* (Downers Grove, Ill.: InterVarsity Press, 1979).

Biblical, Historical, and Contemporary Theology

Three other disciplines need to be further delineated. *Biblical theology* is a separate enterprise of its own. Old Testament theologians seek to provide a comprehensive summary of the teachings of the Old Testament, and New Testament theologians do the same for the New Testament. The literature on these two specializations is massive. Systematic theology attempts to utilize and build on the results of biblical theology by demonstrating the coherence of the teachings of the Bible and by relating these teachings to contemporary knowledge.

Historical theology traces what the church has taught through the centuries. I am continually amazed at how relevant the theologians of the past can be!

Contemporary theology studies the theology of recent decades. Sometimes I am amazed at how irrelevant *these* theologies can be! There are other terms and disciplines that could be mentioned here, but these should suffice for our purposes.

Systematic theology has the audacious challenge of utilizing the results of all these disciplines and then taking the further step of providing a comprehensive presentation of the Christian faith for contemporary society. Nobody does it perfectly, and a *committee* effort would probably be more appropriate!

A Christian Theology

Jesus Christ makes systematic theology Christian. He is the center of everything: history, the Bible, our faith. A truly Christian theology must be centered in him. I have always liked the way my mentor in graduate studies, the late Dale Moody, defined theology: "A Christian theology is an effort to think coherently about the basic beliefs that create a community of faith around the person of Jesus Christ."[9]

A truly Christian theology must be centered on Christ.

Moody also pointed out that every faith has a center of reference that gives it coherence. One need only think of Moses and the Torah in Judaism, the Koran of Mohammed in Islam, Gautama the Buddha in

---

[9] Dale Moody, *The Word of Truth* (Grand Rapids: Eerdmans, 1981), 1.
[10] Ibid., 1.

Buddhism, or the social system of India that in part forms Hinduism.[10] Jesus is the center of Christian faith. This fact leads to four important observations:

First, Jesus Christ is a historical person. This fact points to the fundamental *historical* dimension of Christian theology. This dimension is the objective pole of the faith of Christians. The message we offer to the world is rooted in historical, public events that can be investigated. Christianity is not some club or cult with a privatized, esoteric faith guarded by some elite group of religionists. In the modern era, no one has better expressed this important truth than the German Protestant theologian, Wolfhart Pannenberg.

Second, Jesus Christ didn't just drop out of the sky one day to show us the Father. He emerged out of the *faith and history of Israel.* This is one of the primary reasons we often speak of our Judeo-Christian heritage. Jews and Christians are at least cousins! We pray to the same God. Our personal values and basic worldview are essentially the same. Because of the history of our respective faiths we are permanently and profoundly related.[11]

Third, we need to remember the *community of faith* that Moody referred to in his definition of Christian theology. Jesus preached the *kingdom of God* and founded the *church.* These are the controlling motifs of our faith. Much more will be said about these later. It suffices to emphasize at this juncture that we are a people called out to proclaim the reign of God—as did both Jesus and the early church. Christian theology must flow out of these realities.[12] The careful reader will note that in every chapter this dual leitmotif of kingdom and church will be sounded. It is the string on which all the doctrinal pearls we will examine have been strung.

Finally, a truly Christian systematic theology must acknowledge the *experiential* dimension of faith. There are many aspects to any functioning world religion—cognitive (a system of beliefs and a worldview), cultic (ways of expressing faith and relating together), and so forth. But as one authority on world religions has observed, the experiential dimension is essential to any living religion.[13] My own religious background has hammered this truth home to me time and again.

---

[11] See M. Eugene Osterhaven, *The Faith of the Church* (Grand Rapids: Eerdmans, 1982), 22–35.

[12] I am indebted to Stanley Grenz for this insight. See his *Revisioning Evangelical Theology* (Downers Grove, Ill.: InterVarsity Press, 1993), 137–62.

[13] Ninian Smart, *The Religious Experience of Mankind,* 2nd ed. (New York: Charles Scribner's Sons, 1976), 10–11.

Knowing God

The ultimate purpose of theology is to help us to really *know* God—not just know *about* God. This is the deepest craving of the human heart. If God is there, can I really know him? The resounding answer of saints throughout the centuries is Yes! One can enjoy in a profound, joyous, and *disturbing* way the mysterious presence of the Almighty God. In my opinion, no one addresses this issue better than J. I. Packer.[14] Evangelicals describe this as having a "personal relationship with Jesus Christ."[15] We might refer to personal experience as the subjective pole of our faith.

Much of contemporary theology has lost its audience because it has lost touch with the personal, experiential dimension of Christian faith. Some professional theologians become tongue-tied when it comes to articulating this aspect of faith. But the days of arid philosophizing are fast coming to an end. In our hurried and desperate times, people simply will not give their attention to such chaff. It is precisely at this point that I am most grateful for both my Southern Baptist and charismatic backgrounds!

> *The ultimate purpose of theology is to help us to really* know *God—not just know* about *God.*

One of Baptists' finest patriarchs, E. Y. Mullins, claimed this experiential dimension of faith as the hallmark of his theology. Mullins argued that certainty of faith comes only through a combination of the objective (historical and cognitive) and the subjective (experiential) poles. The Christian, he says,

> finds both in the religion of Christ. He finds Jesus Christ to be for him the supreme revelation of God's redeeming grace. He finds the Scriptures the authoritative source of his knowledge of that revelation. And then he finds in his own soul that working of God's grace which enables him to know Christ and to understand the Scriptures. Thus the objective and subjective elements find a unity and harmony which is entirely satisfying.
>
> Now if the opposite method is pursued and either the Bible or experience is taken alone, no such finality is possible.[16]

---

14 J. I. Packer, *Knowing God* (Downers Grove, Ill.: InterVarsity Press, 1973).

15 Tim Stafford does an excellent job of "unwrapping" this phrase for us in his *Knowing the Face of God* (Grand Rapids: Zondervan, 1986).

16 Edgar Young Mullins, *The Christian Religion in Its Doctrinal Expression* (Nashville: Broadman, 1917), 11.

Pentecostal/charismatic theologians argue that the theology of the New Testament believers was formulated in just this way. They claim as their trademark the recovery of this very element of New Testament theology. Though often critical of Pentecostal/charismatic tenets, New Testament scholar James D. G. Dunn nevertheless corroborates this understanding of early Christian theology:

> In short, as religious experience was fundamental to and creative of the earliest Christian community, so religious experience was fundamental to and creative of the earliest Christian theology. Ever-fresh religious experience, in dynamic interaction with the original witness to the Christ event, was the living matrix for NT theology. Without the latter, faith all too easily becomes fanaticism and burns itself out. But without the former, without God as a living reality in religious experience, faith never comes to life and theology remains sterile and dead.[17]

Unfortunately, theology has never been high on the agenda of many of the experientialists. On the contrary, there has too often been an actual aversion to it, resulting in the chaos we see in many quarters of American Christianity today.

Throughout the centuries the emblem of authentic Christianity has always been this balance of "heart religion" and "head religion." Our Lord himself said it would always be so: "You shall love the Lord your God with all your heart . . . and with all your mind" (Mark 12:30).

Throughout the centuries the emblem of authentic Christianity has always been this balance of "heart religion" and "head religion."

Get with the Program!

So what has God been up to all these years? This is a profound and important question. In my opinion, God has made his agenda clear to us through the Scriptures. His agenda, in simplest terms, can be stated as follows: (1) the kingdom of God and (2) the people of God.

One of the most satisfying treatments of these themes is the classic work by internationally renowned Old Testament scholar John Bright, entitled *The Kingdom of God.*[18] Bright carefully demonstrates how the

---

[17] James D. G. Dunn, *Jesus and the Spirit* (London: SCM, 1975), 361.
[18] John Bright, *The Kingdom of God* (Nashville: Abingdon, 1953).

kingdom of God is the primary unifying theme of the Bible. He further shows how the kingdom relates to the church. A systematic theologian can easily utilize Bright's insights to construct a comprehensive overview of the faith.

Even a cursory reading of the New Testament reveals that the kingdom of God was the primary emphasis of Jesus. Today we are rediscovering what he was getting at, and the church is being revitalized by the dynamic presence of the kingdom! The concept of the kingdom as a *future* hope is receiving renewed appreciation.[19] Entire schools of thought on this topic are emerging.

But with this important recovery, we must maintain the centrality of Christ and his cross. Centuries ago Martin Luther warned the church of the consequences of straying from this focus. We would do well to heed that warning today. Renewalists may be more guilty of this egregious sin than any other group within the church. False gospels such as "health and wealth" and "faith formulas" abound today. But when one sows to the wind, one reaps a whirlwind. Only a theology centered on the person and work of Christ—his incarnation, earthly ministry, atoning death, triumphant resurrection, and second coming—will adequately nourish the church in this or any age.[20]

One way to grasp more firmly the primary themes of Scripture is to search for the center of each Testament. What is the key event on which the Old Testament concentrates? If the Exodus event comes quickly to mind, then you are an astute reader of the Bible. As for the New Testament, Easter is the central event. The salvation God wrought for his people in the dramatic Exodus events were but a foreshadow of the even greater Easter events that have brought salvation to the whole world![21]

The Church's mission today is to spread the good news of the kingdom around the world. God's kingdom continues to span the globe. God's people continue to worship and serve him. They continue to serve and evangelize the world. Yet we must admit that things are clearly not—by any stretch of the imagination—ideal.

---

19 From the perspective of the revitalization of the church, the following two works are worth consulting: Don Williams, *Signs, Wonders, and the Kingdom of God* (Ann Arbor, Mich.: Servant, 1989), and Pat Robertson, *The Secret Kingdom* (Dallas: Word, 1992).

20 I can't think of a finer work to get us back on this focus than the classic work by John R. W. Stott, *The Cross of Christ* (Downers Grove, Ill.: InterVarsity Press, 1986). In relation to present discussion, see esp. ch. 1, "The Centrality of the Cross," 17–46.

21 See Moody, *The Word of Truth*, 1–6.

There Was a Time . . .

To say that the Christian scene is rather chaotic would be a mammoth understatement. Sadly, many times the greatest roadblock to the gospel's acceptance is the church itself. Today there are more "brands" of Christianity than can be counted. It seems almost incomprehensible that at one time there was only one church. At the same time, there is a kind of perverse comfort in knowing that the problems of the early church were as great as ours today. Only our head, Jesus Christ, could ever sort it all out or hold it all together.

Before we launch into our survey of the various Christian doctrines, it will be helpful to obtain further historical perspective. Again, a bird's-eye view of the theological terrain is essential.

I received my seminary training in Louisville, Kentucky, which is planted beside an impressive river, the Ohio River. The Ohio runs a course of more than 975 miles, forming several state boundaries. It is a tributary of the longest river on the North American continent and one of the world's greatest rivers—the Mighty Mississippi! These rivers provide a useful metaphor for understanding historical theology.[22]

I have already hinted that the *source* of theology is the Scriptures. Though more careful attention will be given to this position later, it is crucial to highlight this truth here in order to clarify some issues. Even the most liberal of theologies take the Bible seriously. It has always been the touchstone of Christian theological enterprise and a major focus of discussion. Generally speaking, when the church has lost sight of the full authority of Scripture or refused to obey the Bible, her greatest problems have emerged.

But there have been *tributaries* of tradition that have fed into the river of theology. How do we evaluate these? First, we must quickly admit that these tributaries are inescapable and not necessarily corruptive. The Bible itself can be seen, in part, as a collection of authoritative tradition. F. F. Bruce's *Tradition: Old and New* masterfully clarifies these issues.[23] Beware of those persons who claim to be unencumbered by tradition—who feel that they are the infallible interpreters of Scripture! These folks are usually the ones most laden with destructive, heretical teachings (traditions).

The *apostolic tradition* of the New Testament is the norm for the church universal, and the various *ecclesiastical traditions* of the churches

---

[22] I owe this river metaphor to Moody, ibid., 2–11.

[23] F. F. Bruce, *Tradition: Old and New* (Grand Rapids: Zondervan, 1970).

have either developed or distorted this truth. The major challenge the church has perennially faced is that of seeking to remain faithful to the teachings of the Bible. The Protestant Reformation was a major example of a "mid-course correction" (or corruption, depending on your point of view!). The two most significant developments of tradition are the *creeds*, which emerged from the days of united Christianity (the early centuries), and the *confessions*, which were developed in the days of divided Christianity (the various churches or denominations).[24] We need today to rediscover the beauty and usefulness of the majestic creeds of Christendom.

For some believers the mention of creeds raises all kinds of flags. Many in my own background have declared that they have a *living* faith and not a *creedal* one. Their legitimate concern is the subordination of Scripture to human traditions. Nevertheless, one must examine what is meant by a living faith. Surely such faith is not without *beliefs!* As one leading theologian from my background has argued, "The opposite of a creedal or confessional faith is a vague or contentless or undefined faith."[25]

John H. Leith has provided one of the most useful comprehensive collections of the creeds and confessions.[26] In his introductory remarks Leith points out that Christianity has always been creedal because it has always been theological. Nontheological Christianity has never been able to survive, though several such attempts have been made. Christians have always deepened their commitment through clarifying and confessing their faith.[27] The Latin *credo*, from which the word *creed* is derived, is an active verb referring to a life-commitment and not just to an intellectual consent. It indicates a confession or profession of faith. When Christians confess the creeds, as Leith explains, they are taking a stand, committing their lives, demonstrating their ultimate loyalty, and even defying every false claim on their lives.[28]

Old Testament saints confessed and communicated their faith in a creedal fashion. They continually rehearsed the Exodus events (Deut. 6:21–23; 26:5–10). Another confession centering on the attributes of the Lord dates back to Moses' great experience at Sinai (Ex. 34:6–7;

---

[24] Moody, *The Word of Truth*, 7.

[25] James Leo Garrett Jr., *Systematic Theology I* (Grand Rapids: Eerdmans, 1990), 5.

[26] John H. Leith, ed., *Creeds of the Churches*, 3rd ed. (Atlanta: John Knox, 1982).

[27] Ibid., 1–2.

[28] Ibid., 5.

Num. 14:18; Neh. 9:17, 31; Ps. 103:8; Jer. 32:18; Jonah 4:2). Jewish people to this day confess daily the great Shema (Deut. 6:4–9).

The New Testament is replete with creedal statements as well. In essence, the first Christian creed or confession was simply "Jesus is Lord" (Rom. 10:9–10; 1 Cor. 12:3; Phil. 2:6–11). The early believers literally put their lives on the line to make this confession, refusing to worship Caesar. In another creedlike statement, Paul passed along the summary of the gospel that he himself had received from others (1 Cor. 15:3–8). But perhaps the most helpful way to grasp the importance of this dimension of our faith is to return to our original marching orders as given us by the Lord himself. We refer to his words as the Great Commission:

> And Jesus came and said to them, "All authority in heaven and on earth has been given to me. Go therefore and make disciples of all nations, baptizing them in the name of the Father and of the Son and of the Holy Spirit, and teaching them to obey everything that I have commanded you. And remember, I am with you always, to the end of the age." (Matt. 28:18–20)

There will never be a more beautiful, powerful, or meaningful mandate!

The core of this passage is a call to disciple the nations. This involves two significant activities: baptizing and teaching. The historic creeds we will examine derive their teaching, confessional function, and Trinitarian form from our Lord's command. "Christian theology came into being to explain Christian baptism."[29] The church's early creeds and catechisms were formulated out of obedience to the Great Commission.

As a result, to this day there are, in my view, only two kinds of churches—dead churches and alive churches. Alive churches have the Great Commission vision and are actively pursuing it. Dead churches have been diverted in a hundred different directions. Additionally, there are only two kinds of Christians—dead Christians and alive Christians. Alive Christians take seriously their baptismal vows of obedience to Christ and faithfulness to his church. We all know what the dead Christians are doing—nothing!

I have noted sadly that many charismatic churches, which originally evinced revival fervor, have forgotten their Great Commission mandate and have become largely dysfunctional. They then fall prey to every spiritual fad that comes their way in their attempts to regain their original vitality. Our Lord would say, with tears, to these churches, "You have a

---

[29] Thomas C. Oden, *The Living God* (San Francisco: Harper & Row, 1987), 12.

name of being alive, but you are dead" (Rev. 3:1). Thus, creedal identity and spiritual vision go hand in hand in promoting vital Christianity.[30]

As we examine the major creeds that have come down to us from the days of undivided Christianity—before the myriad denominations we have today—we will find these creeds to be indispensable to our theological enterprise. These authoritative summaries of the faith provide the theological consensus that the church enjoyed in the past and so desperately needs today.

Creeds, Confessions, and . . . Confusion!

The *Apostles' Creed* is the profession of faith most commonly used by Christians around the world today. It follows the Trinitarian baptismal formula set forth by the Great Commission. In addition, it focuses on the person of the Son of God and tells a story—the gospel story of the life, death, and resurrection of Jesus Christ our Lord. It then goes on to profess belief in the Holy Spirit, the church, eternal life, and the other fundamentals of Christian faith.

Everyone loves a good story, and this is the grandest story ever told! Hear the majestic words of the most widely used and accepted creed of Christendom:

> I believe in God the Father almighty, Maker of heaven and earth, and in Jesus Christ, his only Son, our Lord, who was conceived by the Holy Spirit, born of the Virgin Mary, suffered under Pontius Pilate, was crucified, dead, and buried; he descended into hell; the third day he rose again from the dead; he ascended into heaven and is seated on the right hand of God the Father almighty; from thence he shall come to judge the living and the dead. I believe in the Holy Spirit, the holy catholic church, the communion of the saints, the forgiveness of sins, the resurrection of the body, and the life everlasting.

Perhaps, because of your church background, you can already recite these words. If not, perhaps you *should* memorize this creed. It expresses the essentials of the Christian faith—what Christians have believed since the beginning of the church. This is the "mere Christianity" that C. S. Lewis so ably defended.[31]

---

[30] Two recent works provide powerful argument for and documentation of this truth: Thomas C. Oden, *The Rebirth of Orthodoxy: Signs of New Life in Christianity* (San Francisco: HarperSanFrancisco, 2003), and Luke Timothy Johnson, *The Creed: What Christians Believe and Why It Matters* (New York: Doubleday, 2003).

[31] C. S. Lewis, *Mere Christianity* (New York: Macmillan, 1952).

Though not authored by the twelve apostles (its present form dating from about A.D. 700), the Apostles' Creed clearly reflects the apostolic tradition of the New Testament. Historically, as with all the major creeds, it has been used (1) as a confession of faith at baptism, (2) as a pattern for teaching the Christian faith, (3) as a "rule of faith" against heresies, and (4) as means of confession in corporate worship. Once again we are reminded that the Christian faith is creedal; it is theological by its very nature.

Other ecumenical creeds should be mentioned. The *Nicene Creed* (325) is used almost as widely as the Apostles' Creed. One immediately notices a shift from the individual "I believe" to the communal "We believe," as well as a stronger doctrinal tone in terms of technical language aimed at confuting heresy. Later, when further threatened by serious distortions in understanding the humanity and divinity of Christ, the church developed what has come to be known as the *Definition of Chalcedon* (451). In terms of summarizing the Christian view of Christ, we have never been able to improve on this creed, although we have had to reexpress it in every generation. Both these creeds are just as worthy of study as the Apostles' Creed.

I have always enjoyed reading the *Athanasian Creed* (c. 500). More a brief *handbook* of the faith, it has served the Western Church well as an authoritative summary of such essential doctrines as the Trinity and the Incarnation. A simple reading of the three major creeds of Christendom—the Apostles' Creed, the Nicene Creed, and the Athanasian Creed—will do more to orient someone eager to capture the essence of Christianity than consulting any other sources. Methodist theologian Thomas C. Oden has dedicated his more recent writings to introducing afresh this ecumenical consensus of the historic Christian faith.

During the past two millennia, great schisms have rent the church into three main branches. Wisdom dictates that we view each of these branches in its best light. (Churches, like people, are often viewed in their worst light!) There is a renewed appreciation today for the beauty of Eastern Orthodoxy, a significant segment of the Christian family that has until recently been largely overlooked by the West. The word *spiritual* perhaps best characterizes Eastern Orthodox theology. This theology flows out of its worship—an important lesson for contemporary theology. Eastern Orthodox believers tend to regard the Scriptures, creeds, liturgy, and other dimensions of the faith as an integral unit. For Western Christians, baffled and bewildered by the present theological chaos, Eastern Orthodoxy—which has maintained a uniformity of teaching for some twenty centuries—can be very appealing.

Equally appealing for similar reasons, it seems, is the majestic theology of Roman Catholicism. The word *sacramental* perhaps most helpfully describes Catholic theology. For Protestants suffering from a symbolically threadbare theology and worship, exposure to Roman Catholic theology can be therapeutic, though some Protestant theologies also place strong emphasis on the sacraments.

I will use the word *scriptural* to describe Protestant theology (in part, to keep the alliteration going—we Baptists are big on alliteration!). This does not, however, preempt the other two branches from placing heavy emphasis on the Scriptures. Both the Orthodox and Catholic theologies are intentionally loyal to Scripture as well. Nevertheless, the Protestant movement emerged out of a perceived need to return to the primacy of the Bible in the life and teaching of the church. Protestant theologians assert that all tradition must answer to Scripture. As a practicing Protestant, I wholeheartedly affirm this principle.

Nevertheless, being a Protestant is sometimes confusing. There are so many "brands" of us, and we all say that the Bible backs us up. The Protestant Reformation seems to have opened up a Pandora's box! In response to the disagreements among us, we have developed elaborate confessions of faith to justify and clarify our doctrinal positions. At the end of this chapter you will find a representative list of these confessions. Some of the richest theological study comes through referring back to these great confessions of faith.

The Necessity of Theology

Do all these differences of opinion demonstrate that theology itself is the problem? On the contrary, they point to the *necessity* of theology in a world awash with theological confusion. True, theology, like politics, is inherently divisive. But both are inescapable. Our only alternative is a desert island! It is important to understand the historical context that prompted the emergence of theology.

> *It was out of this missionary context that theology emerged as a necessity.*

The church of the first five centuries turned the known world upside down.

She was on mission, obeying her Lord's command to go into all the world. She had the Great Commission vision. Her God-given task was to make disciples, and this entailed both *baptizing* and *teaching*. It was out of this missionary context that theology emerged as a necessity.

Early on, the church was confronted with false teachers within its own ranks. Both Paul and John had to deal with such opponents in their churches. During the ensuing four centuries a powerful drama was played out in the church as major heresies threatened to compromise the gospel message. Theology (expressed in the creeds and pronouncements of the various councils) played an essential role in defending and preserving the faith.

Furthermore, as in any given era of church history, competing worldly philosophies and challenges had to be addressed. Emil Brunner may have been the first theologian to identify the roots of theology that emerged from this upheaval. Brunner argued that "three urgent necessities" for theology "which spring from the life of the Church itself" made the theological enterprise vital for the church's ongoing mission.[32] He named these three roots the polemical, the exegetical, and the catechetical.[33] As Dale Moody ably summarized: "The first was to refute false teachings, the second to systematize Bible doctrine, and the third to instruct young Christians before and after baptism."[34]

Brunner poignantly described the perennial need for correction of false teaching:

> The sinful self-will of man takes the Gospel—at first imperceptibly, and indeed perhaps unconsciously—and alters the content and the meaning of the message of Jesus Christ and His Mighty Act of Redemption, of the Kingdom of God and the destiny of Man. This process produces "substitute" Gospels, introduces "foreign bodies" into Christian truth, and distorts the Christian message: the very words of the Bible are twisted, and given an alien meaning, and indeed, one which is directly opposed to its purpose. The Christian church is in danger of exchanging its divine treasury of truth for mere human inventions.[35]

Then, of course, there is the natural drive toward assembling and assimilating the teachings of Scripture. Finally, new believers (as well as

---

[32] Emil Brunner, *The Christian Doctrine of God*, trans. Olive Wyon (Philadelphia: Westminster, 1950), 9.

[33] Ibid., 9–11, 93–96.

[34] Moody, *The Word of Truth*, 11.

[35] Brunner, *The Christian Doctrine of God*, 9.

veteran saints) must be taught the essentials of our faith. Thus, theology surfaces in every dimension of church life: (1) baptismal confession, (2) the teaching of new converts, (3) the summarizing of scriptural teachings, (4) refuting false teachings, (5) presenting and defending the faith, (6) corporate worship, and, sometimes forgotten, (7) preaching. Does this leave us with any doubt concerning the necessity of theology?[36]

Then Along Came Kant . . .

The church has faced many trials throughout history, yet surely the last two centuries have presented her with her most serious theological challenges. It was the so-called Enlightenment of eighteenth-century Europe that prepared the way for these mammoth upheavals.

With the onslaught of rationalism, empiricism, and skepticism among the intellectuals, the Christian faith faced a grave threat. A virtual continental divide emerged in theology that exists to this day. Since the nineteenth century, theology has been divided between two camps: (1) those who begin with man and his reason and experience, and (2) those who begin with God and his revelation.[37] The philosopher who perhaps best represents the influences that caused this division is Immanuel Kant (1724–1804).

In a sense, Kant was the first modern man. He agreed with the movement away from accepting traditional authorities, be they papal (Roman Catholicism) or biblical (Protestantism), as the source of true knowledge. He saw humankind as "coming of age" and able to determine truth and meaning for himself. No longer would appeals to creeds and dogmas—certainly not to Scripture—be acceptable. Kant's shadow has been cast over the entire two centuries that followed his death. Reason was enthroned, and the human being, rather than God, became the measure of all things. Colin Brown aptly depicts Kant's influence: "Kant personifies modern man's confidence in the power of reason to grapple

---

[36] Stanley J. Grenz and Roger E. Olson have provided an insightful book-length treatment of this issue: *Who Needs Theology? An Invitation to the Study of God* (Downers Grove, Ill.: InterVarsity Press, 1996).

[37] I use "man" in the generic sense in this section since the "God/man" contrast seems to be better highlighted thereby. Normally, throughout this volume the reader will note a moderate use of inclusive language. I will employ the traditional male-oriented language in the personal pronouns referring to God so as to avoid theological distortion. Inclusive language concerns have become an important *theological* issue in our day as well.

with material things and its incompetence to deal with anything beyond."[38]

Kant, in actuality, simply followed the lead of the rationalism of René Descartes (1596–1650). This view began with humankind's contrived philosophies and then tried to fit religion into them. German theologian Helmut Thielicke, therefore, characterizes contemporary theology as either Cartesian (what he calls Theology A), which begins with humankind and its understanding, or Non-Cartesian (Theology B), which begins with the more traditional categories of divine revelation.[39]

Whenever we try to pour our theology into a particular philosophical mold, invariably many biblical truths get left out or distorted. Such is the legacy of the philosophical liberalism that Kant bequeathed to modern theology. As a result, two battlecries still can be heard at the theological front. One group exclaims, "But the Enlightenment . . . !" The other group proclaims, "But the Bible says . . . !"

All the myriad schools of thought and theological movements of the past few centuries can be best understood and evaluated in the light of this bipolar perspective. Let's look briefly at how this dynamic has worked itself out in modern, and now postmodern, theology.

Some Said that It Was Thunder

When the Father spoke audibly to his Son at a crucial juncture in Jesus' earthly ministry, those who heard mistook it for thunder or the voice of an angel (John 12:27–30). Today a cacophony of theological voices calls for recognition. We will only mention a representative sampling.

The quest of almost all theologians during the past hundred years actually has been for *relevance.* Two horizons, past and present, must be related. Theologians try to hold together two poles in a dynamic (and hopefully creative) tension: the *historical* pole of the biblical faith of the Church and the *contemporary* pole of the present context. The challenge comes in relating these two.

William E. Hordern has pointed out that theologians, when faced with the tension between these poles, tend to become either *transform-*

---

[38] Colin Brown, *Philosophy and the Christian Faith* (Downers Grove, Ill.: InterVarsity Press, 1968), 91.

[39] Helmut Thielicke, *The Evangelical Faith,* trans. and ed. Geoffrey Bromiley, vol. 1 (Grand Rapids: Eerdmans, 1974). I have simplified Thielicke's categories.

ers or *translators.*[40] Transformers are more preoccupied with the contemporary context and with being relevant to that context. They are even willing to "modify," or transform, the content of the faith to achieve this relevance. Conversely, translators are concerned with being faithful to the given historic Christian faith and with simply "translating" that faith effectively to each subsequent generation. Both groups can become irrelevant: Transformers can lose their message, and translators can lose their audience.

Liberal theology has definitely tended toward the transforming model. If modernity can no longer swallow supernatural realities such as the verbal inspiration of Scriptures, the virgin birth of Christ, his bodily resurrection, spiritual beings such as angels or demons, miracles, signs, wonders, healings, and the like, then just jettison these outmoded ideas. Harry Emerson Fosdick (1878–1969), a gifted preacher and writer who captured the nation's ear during the first half of the twentieth century, persuasively promulgated this perspective, which became known as modernism.

Transformers can lose their message, and translators can lose their audience.

Predictably, there developed a conservative backlash to liberalism in the movement known as *fundamentalism.* The fundamentalists simply wanted to return to the Bible and hold to its supernaturalism. Unfortunately, this movement became known in many quarters as mean-spirited, obscurantist, and anti-intellectual. Nevertheless, conservative theology continued to hold forth the historic faith, and by mid-century *evangelicalism* was on the scene.

Evangelicals have often been facetiously described as "fundamentalists with Ph.D.s." Many of these new conservative theologians earned their doctorates at the elite liberal schools and armed themselves to address the challenge of modernist theology. At the same time, revivalists—the premier of whom was Billy Graham—proclaimed the evangelical faith far and near. Evangelical denominations such as my own, the Southern Baptist Convention, flourished.

Alongside these developments, a movement known as *neo-orthodoxy* emerged in Europe and spread to America. A more moderate group, they critiqued liberalism but saw fundamentalism as a dead-end street.

---

[40] William E. Hordern, *New Directions in Theology Today,* vol. 1, *Introduction* (Philadelphia: Westminster, 1966), as cited in Millard J. Erickson, *Christian Theology* (Grand Rapids: Baker, 1985), 113.

They called for a return to the orthodoxy of the Reformation and to the authority of the Bible without a compromise of intellectual integrity. In their view, the use of literary and historical methods in the study of the Bible ("higher criticism") was here to stay, and traditional understandings of the inspiration of Scripture would have to be modified. At the same time, they felt that they could remain faithful to the historic Christian faith. The giant among this group was surely the Swiss theologian Karl Barth (1886–1968).

Barth had imbibed liberal theology in his early education, but he found it unsatisfactory in the pastorate. He then embarked on a rather radical course. He decided to start preaching and teaching the Bible! Barth published his *Commentary on Romans* in 1919; as Karl Adam, a Roman Catholic theologian, said, "It fell like a bombshell on the playground of the theologians."[41] Neo-orthodoxy was launched as a journey back to the Bible, so to speak. The trouble was, according to most evangelical theologians, the neo-orthodox theologians didn't make it all the way back.

During and since those days, a broad range of *radical theologies* has emerged—from Paul Tillich to Rudolf Bultmann to "God is dead" theologians. There have also been various debates, such as the "secular city" debate (Harvey Cox), the "honest to God" debate (John A. T. Robinson), and the "myth of God incarnate" debate. Finally, there have been process theologies, eschatological theologies (such as those of Pannenberg and Moltmann, two major contemporary theologians), liberation theologies (e.g., black, Latin American, and feminist), and a (welcome) resurgence of evangelical systematic theologies. In fact, the West has been undergoing a virtual paradigm shift in recent decades, as many have become increasingly disillusioned with the legacy of the Enlightenment.

Before the so-called modern era brought in by the Enlightenment, God and the supernatural were taken for granted, so to speak. The prevailing worldview credited the supernatural realm with making sense of the natural. But, as we have already seen, the modern era proceeded to enthrone humankind and place ultimate confidence in our own rationalistic and scientific devices. Transcendent realities were pushed to the margins or simply assumed not to exist. Predictably, in our own day a *postmodern* era seems to be emerging, which challenges this humanistic optimism. Now our intuitive capacities are given greater credence. Rea-

---

[41] Cited in Moody, *The Word of Truth*, 24.

son and science have demonstrated their own limitations. Unfortunately, this "politically correct" era has capitulated to a debilitating relativism.[42] The same thing can be said for the *postliberal* response to the failed liberal experiment previously mentioned. Postliberal theologians have resigned themselves to the exploration of truths *within a given community*, generally taking a more descriptive, narrative approach and pushing the question of universal truth to the side.

In thus summarizing the modern theological scene, I have had to omit dozens of important theologians and interesting developments.[43] I will mention one, however, as a lead-in to my final comments here. Friedrich Schleiermacher (1768–1834) is considered by many to be the "father of modern theology." Influenced by Kant's critiques, Schleiermacher sought to build a theology palatable to the cultural elite of his day, based on religious experience (dependence on God, awareness of sin and guilt, and the transforming power of grace). This theology held obvious appeal, but, as with the liberal experiment in theology in general, failed to serve the church well since it lacked the strength, dynamism, and stability of a comprehensive biblical foundation.

Today the church has seen a virtual fourth branch of Christendom appear—the Pentecostal/charismatic churches, with more than a half-billion adherents.

Today the church has seen a virtual fourth branch of Christendom appear—the Pentecostal/charismatic churches, with more than a half-billion adherents. As a revival movement, it is unprecedented in the history of the church. In developing countries in particular, the rapid spread of Pentecostalism is astounding. Pentecostal churches in America, such as the Assemblies of God and the Church of God, are among the most vital and growing. Independent charismatic churches have not always fared as well.

To be sure, there are more megachurches than ever. But I have sensed and seen frustration, unrest, and decline in many quarters of the

---

[42] Millard J. Erickson has provided a thorough, trenchant analysis of postmodernosme in his *Truth or Consequences: The Promise and Perils of Postmodernism* (Downers Grove, Ill.: InterVarsity Press, 2001).

[43] Perhaps the best overview and analysis is *Twentieth-Century Theology* by Stanley J. Grenz and Roger E. Olson (Downers Grove, Ill.: InterVarsity Press, 1992).

charismatic movement. There is a fundamental need to return to sound theology. Religious experiences simply evaporate without it. In 1968 Dale Moody wrote, "Careful scholarship and the charismatic community can be united, and this is a great need of our time."[44]

Fortunately, solid scholarship is emerging rapidly. The Society for Pentecostal Studies has provided sound theological leadership for the burgeoning Pentecostal/charismatic movements for decades. And the theologies of J. Rodman Williams and Wayne Grudem have become standard texts in both evangelical and Pentecostal/charismatic seminaries.[45] Promising theological and biblical scholarship is also published in the *Journal of Pentecostal Theology* and monograph supplements to it, by Sheffield Academic Press. Finally, the numerous publications by Pentecostal theologian Veli-Matti Kärkkäinen evince not only a matured Pentecostal/charismatic theology, but also a strong ecumenical dynamic of global dimensions.

Where Do We Go from Here?

In the chapters that follow we will journey through the great doctrines of the Christian faith. I will use the categories in which systematic theology was first presented to me. These seem to be as useful today as thirty years ago—a classical progression of thought from creation to final redemption:

Revelation—How does God make himself known?
God—Who is God, and what is he like?
Creation—What does it mean to believe in God as Creator?
Humanity—Who are we, and what does it mean to be created in God's image?
Sin—What is the nature of sin, and what are its consequences?
Christ—Who is Jesus, and how does he save us?
Faith—What is the nature of the salvation God offers us?
Hope—What is Christian hope?
Love—What is God's plan for the church?

We are in for an exciting journey together!

---

[44] Dale Moody, *Spirit of the Living God* (Philadelphia: Westminster, 1968), 10.

[45] See J. Rodman Williams, *Renewal Theology* (Grand Rapids: Zondervan, 1988, 1990, 1992); Wayne Grudem, *Systematic Theology* (Grand Rapids: Zondervan, 1994).

Select List of Confessions

The following is a select list of confessions of faith and church manuals from a partial list of church traditions.

Roman Catholicism
The Council of Trent (1543–1563)
Documents of Vatican II

Anglicanism
The Thirty-nine Articles of 1563
The Book of Common Prayer (1662)

Lutheranism
The Confession of Augsburg (1530)
The Book of Concord of 1580

Calvinism
The Heidelberg Catechism (1563)
The Westminster Confession (1646)
The Book of Confessions (1967)

Methodism
The Articles of Religion (1784)
The Book of Discipline of the United Methodist Church

The Southern Baptist Convention
Abstract of Principles (1859)
The Baptist Faith and Message (1963, 2000)

2 Revelation
How Does God Make Himself Known?

And this is eternal life, that they may know you, the only true God, and Jesus Christ whom you have sent.

—John 17:3

These words of our Lord, defining eternal life, read "remarkably like a confession of faith: the eternal life, of which the Gospel speaks, consists in the knowledge of God and of Jesus the Son, the Christ he has sent."[1] And this "confession" is all the more noteworthy in that these are the words of Jesus himself. What audacity! Yet no more so than his previous announcement: "I am the way, and the truth, and the life. No one comes to the Father except through me" (John 14:6).

When the knowledgeable Nicodemus approached Jesus with what he "knew," Jesus stopped him short with his declaration that no one could either see or enter the kingdom of God without a new birth, a birth from above (John 3:1–10). In effect, Nicodemus was depending on his reason, and Jesus was saying that the Jewish leader needed a revelation. When Peter confessed his faith in Jesus as "the Messiah, the Son of the living God," Jesus replied, "Blessed are you, Simon son of Jonah! For flesh and blood has not revealed this to you, but my Father in heaven" (Matt. 16:16–17). Then Jesus went on to speak about his church and his kingdom (vv. 18–19).

The New Testament is replete with this kind of scandalous talk—a singular way into God's kingdom, Jesus as the only way to God, the promise of eternal life, actual knowledge of God through *revelation.* Our understanding of the theological concept of revelation is crucial to our task, since it affects every other doctrine we will study.

Has Something Gone Wrong?

Jesus' words that begin this chapter are some of the noblest of human language. They point to the chief end of humankind: to know God. But *can* we really know God? If so, *how*? Our secular, materialistic, hedonistic age has been blinded to such questions. The Puritans founded our first Ivy League school just eighteen years after arriving on this continent. Their concern in part was for an educated clergy, and more than half of Harvard's graduates during that century became ministers. The "Rules and Precepts" adopted in 1646 for the college included the following: "Everyone shall consider the main end of his life and studies to know God and Jesus Christ which is eternal life." Then secret prayer and twice-daily reading of Scripture are enjoined.[2] What a stark contrast to

---

[1] George R. Beasley-Murray, *John* (WBC 36; Nashville: Nelson, 1987), 296.

[2] Cited in *The Rebirth of America*, published by the Arthur S. DeMoss Foundation (1986), 41.

our educational system today! We have lost the key to knowledge, which is the fear of the Lord.

"The fear of the LORD is the beginning of knowledge," said Solomon (Prov. 1:7). "The fear of the LORD is the beginning of wisdom, and the knowledge of the Holy One is insight" (9:10). This truth was at the core of the faith that launched this nation. Has something gone wrong in America? Obviously so, and in large measure this is related to our lack of knowledge about God.

John Calvin launched his *Institutes of the Christian Religion*, a landmark work in the history of Christian doctrine, with these enduring words: "Nearly all the wisdom we possess, that is to say, true and sound wisdom, consists of two parts: the knowledge of God and the knowledge of ourselves."[3] In view of our present-day preoccupation with self-understanding and self-actualization, there is a surprisingly modern ring to this statement. Calvin argued that both are related to our knowledge of God. But why does there seem to be so little genuine knowledge of God? The Bible answers this question clearly and convincingly.

What Is Revelation?

The term *revelation* means an uncovering or unveiling. Theologians use this term to summarize a comprehensive reality—that is, how God has made himself known to us. How can the infinite God reveal himself to finite human beings? This is the age-old question. The Christian answer begins with the biblical doctrine of revelation.

> *Our knowledge of God is the result of God's gracious decision and desire to have fellowship with us.*

The Scriptures teach that God has taken the initiative in making himself known to us. He could have chosen *not* to reveal himself to us. In other words, our knowledge of God is the result of his gracious decision and desire to have fellowship with us. As we will explore later, God made us in his own image for his glory and pleasure so that we can enjoy him forever. Calvin was convinced from his study of Scripture that God's primary purpose in all his revelatory activity was *our happiness*!

---

[3] John Calvin, *Institutes of the Christian Religion*, ed. John T. McNeill, trans. Ford Lewis Battles, 2 vols. (Philadelphia: Westminster, 1960), 1:35 (I.i.1).

> The final goal of the blessed life, moreover, rests in the knowledge of God [cf. John 17:3]. Lest anyone, then, be excluded from access to happiness, he not only sowed in men's minds that seed of religion of which we have spoken but revealed himself and daily discloses himself in the whole workmanship of the universe.[4]

Calvin provides us here with an excellent introduction to the two basic kinds of revelation.

General Revelation

The revelation that Calvin refers to above is what we have come to know as *general revelation*. God has revealed himself to all people, at all times, and in all places. This divinely given revelation has been made available to humankind since its creation.

When the apostle Paul carefully laid out his gospel and theology for the Roman believers, he dealt with this doctrine:

> For the wrath of God is revealed from heaven against all ungodliness and wickedness of those who by their wickedness suppress the truth. For what can be known about God is plain to them, because God has shown it to them. Ever since the creation of the world his eternal power and divine nature, invisible though they are, have been understood and seen through the things he has made. So they are without excuse. (Rom. 1:18–20)

The RSV and the ESV both use "clearly perceived" for "understood and seen" in verse 20. Paul is referring here to the universal revelation of God in *creation*. He then turns to another dimension of general revelation:

> When Gentiles, who do not possess the law, do instinctively what the law requires, these, though not having the law, are a law to themselves. They show that what the law requires is written on their hearts, to which their own conscience also bears witness; and their conflicting thoughts will accuse or perhaps excuse them on the day when, according to my gospel, God, through Jesus Christ, will judge the secret thoughts of all. (Rom. 2:14–16)

Here the apostle identifies human conscience as a means of general divine revelation. *Creation* and *conscience*, then, are the two primary avenues of general revelation.

---

[4] Ibid., 1:51–52 (I.v.1).

Even Kant, who thoroughly critiqued arguments for the existence of God, had to admit that he was impressed with the hints of divine reality in the "starry heavens above and the moral law within." He saw clearly what many secularists have yet to see—that without belief in the reality of God there is no basis for right and wrong or law and order.

> Creation *and* conscience, *then, are the two primary avenues of general revelation.*

With the explosion of scientific knowledge we should appreciate even more the glory of God in the vast and mysterious universe he has made. Narrowing our focus to our physical bodies alone, we can be overwhelmed by the awesome design and function we find.[5] Then turning from creation to conscience, we can ask why even the most avid relativist still has a sense of right and wrong.

C. S. Lewis observed that we take full credit for our good traits and blame our bad traits on life's demands.

> These, then, are the two points I wanted to make. First, that human beings, all over the earth, have this curious idea that they ought to behave in a certain way, and cannot really get rid of it. Secondly, that they do not in fact behave in that way. They know the Law of Nature; they break it. These two facts are the foundation of all clear thinking about ourselves and the universe we live in.[6]

Here we get to the heart of what Paul is saying. But it is important to remember the *context* of his remarks on the general revelation of God in creation and conscience.

Paul's letter to the Romans could legitimately be titled "The Gospel According to Paul." Paul's concern evidently was to lay out as carefully as possible for the Roman believers a comprehensive presentation of his gospel. After his introduction (1:1–17), he depicts the basic human condition that the gospel addresses: sin (1:18–3:20). His theme verses (1:16–17) make reference to the revelation of the righteousness of God in the gospel. Then Paul refers to the revelation of God's wrath (1:18).

---

[5] Two books by Paul Brand and Philip Yancey provide impressive portrayals of our bodily nature: *Fearfully and Wonderfully Made,* and *In His Image* (Grand Rapids: Zondervan, 1980 and 1984, respectively).

[6] C. S. Lewis, *Mere Christianity* (New York: Macmillan, 1952), 21.

This section of Romans explains why general revelation is inadequate—because of our sin. We willfully "suppress the truth" (1:18) in our sinful, rebellious state. We compulsively violate our consciences. We are futile in our thinking, and our senseless minds (lit. "hearts") are darkened (1:21). As Paul wrote later to the Ephesians, people are "darkened in their understanding, alienated from the life of God because of their ignorance and hardness of heart" (Eph. 4:18).

This reality of sin, which we will explore later, is the reason why it is impossible to establish an adequate *natural theology*—that is, a theology built solely on our reason and perceptions apart from God's supernatural aid. Thomas Aquinas (1224–1274), the giant of medieval theology, made a brilliant attempt! He was convinced that truth could be compartmentalized into an upper story of verities that had to be accepted on authority and a lower realm of truths that could be demonstrated by reason alone.

Thus, Aquinas set out to prove rationally the existence of God (arguments we will examine later), the immortality of humanity, and the divine origin of the church. Doctrines such as that of Trinity, according to Aquinas, were matters of revelation to be received by faith. While often useful to believers and appealing to unbelievers, such rational arguments are never conclusive.[7] This is so in part because of how sin affects our minds.

History is often mentioned as a third dimension of general revelation. It is difficult, however, to conceive how such a revelation could be demonstrated. Perhaps a better alternative would be to point to divine *providence* (God's governance and care for his creation) as further evidence of general revelation (see Acts 14:16; 17:26–27). "Creation" and "conscience" are still the best summary terms. Numerous biblical passages refer to general revelation in all its forms.[8]

I received my first pair of glasses to correct my nearsightedness when I was in the third grade. A whole new world opened up for me. I couldn't believe how much I had been missing! In the same way, argued Calvin, the Bible helps us to see and more fully appreciate general revelation.[9] We move now to consider next the second type of divine revelation.

---

[7] Millard J. Erickson, *Christian Theology* (Grand Rapids: Baker, 1985), 157–58.

[8] By far, the most complete collection of scriptural passages on this doctrine and all other doctrines is the following excellent resource: Walter A. Elwell, ed., *Topical Analysis of the Bible* (Grand Rapids: Baker, 1991).

[9] Calvin, *Institutes,* 1:70 (I.vi.1) and 1:160–61 (I.xiv.1).

Special Revelation

Special revelation is saving revelation. Here the message of the kingdom of God hits home. Through general revelation, God makes his kingly majesty known in such a manner that we are without excuse when we refuse to acknowledge his glory and respond to him. But through special revelation, God takes a further step to fully establish his kingdom. He acts and speaks in human history. He calls out a people to himself to be a witness to all the nations. This is the most dramatic story ever told—a story found in the most influential book of all time: the Bible.

> *Special revelation is saving revelation.*

One reason I can so easily identify with evangelicals is that they emphasize telling this story. They tell the *great news* about the majesty and meaning of creation, the dignity and destiny of humankind. They tell the *bad news* about the tragic fall of humanity, and they tell the *good news* of God's saving actions in human history. This evangelical definition of special revelation serves our purpose well:

> Special revelation can be defined as that knowledge of God and his will which is given to a particular community. The revelation given to Israel and the early church and recorded in the scriptures of the Old and New Testaments constitutes the normative deposit of special revelation for evangelical theology.[10]

Notice the mention of Israel and the church. God has used these two communities of faith to spread the message and power of his kingdom to the farthest reaches of the globe. Western civilization in general, and America in particular, have benefited greatly from this Judeo-Christian heritage. Sadly, this influence can no longer be taken for granted in education, law, science, and general culture. The greatest need in an increasingly pagan America is a rediscovery of the biblical revelation that informed her ideological foundations.[11]

Let's start with a bird's-eye perspective and then zoom in on the core of special revelation. This form of divine disclosure involves a *holy land*, a *holy people*, and a *holy book*.[12] Why do we often call that portion of world geography on the eastern end of the Mediterranean the Holy Land?

---

[10] John Jefferson Davis, *Foundations of Evangelical Theology* (Grand Rapids: Baker, 1984), 89.
[11] Ibid., 97–99.
[12] Moody, *The Word of Truth*, 37–39.

Jews, Christians, and Moslems alike treasure this terrain, but why? The answer to this question lies in the revelatory events that took place there.

I have been to Israel only once, but it was a life-changing experience. Many thousands of others share this testimony. One particular incident will always loom large in my memory. We had spent most of one day in the region of Jericho—the "City of Palm Trees" and perhaps the oldest city on earth. Late that afternoon we set out to see Jerusalem for the first time. We ascended thousands of feet, approaching the mountains that surround the city (see Ps. 125:2) near the time of sunset. What happened next was a religious experience that I will never forget.

We were just topping a hill when suddenly the city of Jerusalem loomed before us. I was in a bus with about twenty United Methodist ministers. As we looked on the city for the first time, there was a simultaneous and literally audible gasp. Jerusalem! Why were we so moved? I suppose a separate book could be written to answer this question. Surely one reason is our shared appreciation for the great revelatory and saving events that have taken place there.

As we crested the hill that day and I saw Jerusalem for the first time, I suddenly felt as if I was *coming home.* I have no natural explanation for this experience. I sensed a dynamism in the spiritual atmosphere of Israel that I have experienced nowhere else on earth. Comparing notes with other pilgrims to Israel through the years, I am amazed at the similarities of experiences in this regard. Then, as one monitors world events, it becomes even more apparent how significant this area of our fast-shrinking world really is. The Holy Land—its meaning and importance are felt deeply by so many!

Then there are the people themselves who value these lands. In the Scriptures the Lord calls his people a "holy nation" (Ex. 19:6; 1 Peter 2:9). They were and are holy in the sense of being set apart to bear witness to his saving initiatives on behalf of humankind. Christians and Jews will always be a scandal to the nations because of the audacity of their revelatory claims. The Jews, in my view, witness to the reality of God by virtue of their very survival in what has so often been a hostile environment. In addition, the pervasive historical presence of the church cannot be ignored.

Christians and Jews will always be a scandal to the nations because of the audacity of their revelatory claims.

Finally, there is the holy book, the Bible—the most influential volume in human history. The Bible has withstood staunch opposition and the critical acids of literary and historical scholars. Yet millions regard it as the authoritative account of divine revelation. For Christian theology, however, we still have not reached the core of special revelation. From the Christian perspective, the only way to fully comprehend the significance of the Holy Land, God's holy people, and the holy book is to focus on the central figure of human history: Jesus Christ.

Jesus the Messiah

Toward the end of his earthly ministry Jesus asked this probing question of his Jewish opponents: "What is your opinion about the Messiah? Whose son is he?" (Matt. 22:42 REB). They responded quickly with the expected answer: The Messiah was David's son. Then Jesus quoted Psalm 110:1 and asked how David could call the Messiah "Lord" and still be his father. His point was that *he was* David's son, but he was also *more* than David's son. He was *God's* Son!

Later Paul would declare to the Roman believers that he had been set apart

> for the gospel of God—the gospel he promised beforehand through his prophets in the Holy Scriptures regarding his Son, who as to his earthly life was a descendant of David, and who through the Spirit of holiness was appointed the Son of God in power by his resurrection from the dead: Jesus Christ our Lord (Rom. 1:1–4 TNIV).

Paul's words are full of revelatory language. Notice the close link between Jewish faith and Christian faith. Paul refers to the Old Testament prophets, to David, and to the Holy Scriptures, all finding their fulfillment in Jesus Christ.

In other words, special revelation is a vastly variegated disclosure ranging from prophetic words, dreams, visions, and the like to miraculous divine interventions, such as the mighty Exodus events, to the inspired scriptural accounts of such phenomena, to the greatest revelation of all, according to Christian faith, the Incarnation. The writer to the Hebrews phrased it well:

> Long ago God spoke to our ancestors in many and various ways by the prophets, but in these last days he has spoken to us by a Son ... the reflection of God's glory and the exact imprint of God's very being. (Heb. 1:1–3)

We celebrate this central Christian mystery every Christmas. There is great reason for celebration! God himself has entered into human history to show us who he is and to save us from our sins. What better news could there be! Moreover, God has preserved this revelation for us in the Holy Scriptures.

Biblical Revelation

Biblical revelation is the foundation of Christian theology.[13] The term itself might mislead some to equate revelation with the Bible—that is, to think of revelation as *only* the Bible. But our survey thus far explodes such erroneous thinking. The Bible is not the Exodus; it is the inspired record of the Exodus. The Bible is not the Easter event; it is our God-given account of that unparalleled event. The Bible is not the Living Word (Jesus); it is the written Word of God. The Bible is not God; it is the Word of God.

Some overzealous types have fallen prey to such reductionism or into the error of bibliolatry (worship of the Bible). I have seen charismatic preachers hold up a Bible and say, "This is God!" No, it is the *Word* of God, and there is a *big* difference. However, the expression "biblical revelation" is still useful because it points to the unique role the Scriptures have in preserving and communicating divine revelation. It reminds us of the authority, inspiration, and total trustworthiness of the Bible. *"Christian theology is the articulation of the truth content implicit in divine revelation mediated in Scripture."*[14] Therefore, it is important for us to look carefully at the following dimensions of the nature of the Bible as the product and propagator of divine revelation: the authority, inspiration, infallibility, and inerrancy of the Bible.

> *Biblical revelation is the foundation of Christian theology.*

The Authority of the Bible

"The first claim to be made for Scripture is not its inerrancy, nor even its inspiration, but its authority."[15] *Biblical authority* is the first concept

---

[13] See Clark H. Pinnock, *Biblical Revelation: The Foundation of Christian Theology* (Chicago: Moody, 1971).

[14] Ibid., 16 (Pinnock's italics). Although Pinnock has altered his views somewhat since he wrote this volume, it is still one of the best statements of biblical authority in recent decades.

[15] Carl F. H. Henry, *God, Revelation and Authority*, Vol. 4: *God Who Speaks and Shows* (Dallas: Word, 1979), 4:27.

we must examine in relation to biblical revelation. Authority is not a popular subject these days. People like to talk about their *rights* more than about their *responsibilities* to authority. Personal autonomy is a cherished social value. Situational rather than principled ethics is in vogue. Impassioned protest is made for the right to choose an alternate (deviant) sexual lifestyle, to have an abortion, to publish and purchase pornographic literature—even to kill oneself.

Christians will always swim against the stream in this context. Christians believe that all of creation belongs to the Creator and is responsible to him. God, because he is God, is the ultimate authority. His kingdom transcends all other kingdoms, and his Word supercedes all human words. In simplest terms, authority refers to the right to prescribe and enforce action. When applied to the Scriptures, the word "authority" describes the distinctive role of biblical revelation. "By the authority of the Bible we mean that the Bible, as the expression of God's will to us, possesses the right supremely to define what we are to believe and how we are to conduct ourselves."[16]

The authority of the Bible is intrinsic. One need only be exposed to its message to sense its power and veracity.

The authority of the Bible is intrinsic. One need only be exposed to its message to sense its power and veracity. Additionally, the Holy Spirit bears witness to the truth of Scripture and further illumines its meaning and application. The Bible needs to be read, studied, taught, pondered, and proclaimed more than it needs to be defended. God's testimony to Scripture carries more weight than the endorsements or arguments of any theologian or church.

To be sure, there is good reason to affirm its truth and trustworthiness, but the greatest need of our day is exposure to its message. Biblical illiteracy has robbed the nation and even the church of spiritual and moral fiber. There is a famine of the Word in our land today (see Amos 8:11). I am neither a prophet nor the son of a prophet, but in these days of loss of identity and moral decay in America, I often long to shout from the housetops: "People of the United States, hear the Word of the Lord!"

---

[16] Erickson, *Christian Theology*, 241.

The Inspiration of the Bible

As we turn to consider the *inspiration of Scripture,* we will gain further insight into *why* the Bible is authoritative. One of the key scriptural passages related to the doctrine of biblical inspiration is 2 Timothy 3:16–17: "All scripture is inspired by God and is useful for teaching, for reproof, for correction, and for training in righteousness, so that everyone who belongs to God may be proficient, equipped for every good work." The phrase "inspired by God" translates one Greek word (*theopneustos*) and is better rendered "breathed out by God" (ESV) or "God-breathed" (NIV/TNIV). "Inspired" connotes that the Bible has been breathed *into,* whereas the Greek term itself is much more dramatic and direct: The Scriptures have been *breathed out* by God. They are the direct result of the breath (Spirit) and speech (Word) of God!

The Scriptures have been breathed out *by God. They are the direct result of the breath (Spirit) and speech (Word) of God!*

Carl F. H. Henry, whose magnum opus, the six-volume *God, Revelation and Authority* is surely the definitive statement on divine revelation from an evangelical perspective, describes inspiration as follows:

> Inspiration is a supernatural influence upon divinely chosen prophets and apostles whereby the Spirit of God assures the truth and trustworthiness of their oral and written proclamation. Historic evangelical Christianity considers the Bible as the essential textbook because, in view of its quality, it inscripturates divinely revealed truth in verbal form.[17]

It is important to grasp the relation and distinction between revelation and inspiration. *Revelation* refers to God's original revelatory words and deeds themselves (general and special revelation). *Inspiration* refers to the way in which the original revelation is recorded ("inscripturated") for God's people and for all peoples. The result is what we call *biblical revelation,* or "God's written Word." Closely aligned with these functions of the Holy Spirit is what we call *illumination*—the work of the Holy Spirit that enables us to understand the Scriptures and to appropriate their saving, transforming message.

---

17 Henry, *God, Revelation and Authority,* 4:129. In my opinion, this fourth volume of Henry's great work is by far the best statement on the authority, inspiration, infallibility, and inerrancy of the Scriptures available today.

The calling of the prophet Isaiah (Isa. 6) illustrates well the distinction and relation among these three concepts. Isaiah's experience of the grandeur of God is what we would call *revelation.* The inscripturated account of Isaiah's encounter came about as a result of *inspiration.* The Holy Spirit's witness to and application of this biblical narrative is what is generally called *illumination.*[18]

Theories abound as to the precise nature of biblical inspiration. Just how did the God-breathed Scriptures come to be written?

Views of Inspiration

We begin with what is undoubtedly the most "conservative" view of inspiration, the *dictation theory.* We might call this approach the "Phantom Theory." It is a phantom phenomenon because it is difficult to pin down who actually holds this view. The dictation theory argues that the Bible writers were totally passive. God simply dictated the words of the Scriptures to them, and they faithfully wrote them down. Unfortunately, this view is often used as a straw man to discredit belief in verbal inspiration.

Next we will look at some of the more "liberal" views of inspiration. These theories tend to take a more naturalistic approach, emphasizing the human side of the event. The *intuition theory,* for example, argues that the inspiration of the Bible is comparable to that of any other great literature. The Bible writers were simply people of great spiritual insight and literary ability. These gifted authors had a heightened natural understanding of religious matters. They were geniuses when it came to spiritual matters.

Similar to this view is the *illumination theory,* which again focuses on the human side of the equation. In this view the writers of Scripture are seen as having been illuminated by the Holy Spirit in the same manner that all believers experience this work of the Spirit. The difference is only one of degree, not of kind. The writers' deep spiritual experiences raise ("inspire") their normal abilities to a new level of insight. At least with this view the role of the Holy Spirit is brought into the picture. Nevertheless, with both of these theories the Bible tends to be seen as "inspired in spots"—that is, as uneven in quality and a mixture of infallible divine truth and human error.

The *dynamic theory* is cousin to the two theories described above. Here again, the Holy Spirit is active but only in the sense that he has

---

[18] See Davis, *Foundations of Evangelical Theology,* 173–74.

influenced the *thoughts* of the Bible writers. The writers themselves choose the actual *words* they apply. This description of inspiration accounts for the fact that the personality of the writers does seem to come through in their writings.

Another theory views the Bible as merely a witness to revelation. The Scriptures are simply a record of the special revelatory events in history; no supernatural "inspiration" was needed to chronicle these events. As we have already noted, however, revelation consists of considerably more than historical events. Also, surely the events themselves require divine interpretation in order to be fully revelatory.

Though none of the above theories proves adequate as a definitive statement on inspiration, each has a kernel of truth. As a rule, the Bible writers were very gifted individuals. Surely they did experience the illumination of the Holy Spirit, including the guidance of their thoughts. And the Bible does witness to revelation—but it is more than merely a witness. In recent years James Barr's neo-liberal view has been given wide circulation. Barr is tolerant of a number of approaches, including theories we will examine later. He even allows in part for verbal inspiration. But he strongly rejects biblical inerrancy and subsumes the Bible under the church's authority.[19]

Neo-orthodoxy improved little, if any, upon these views. Karl Barth believed that the Bible was probably written like any other book—no inspiration was needed. According to Barth, God gave us the Scriptures to facilitate a personal encounter with him. The Holy Spirit continually "inspires" this revelatory encounter by illumining the Scriptures. The Bible *becomes* revelation for us when, for example, it is preached and its message is illumined to us by the Spirit. Ironically, Barth's theology is characterized by detailed exegesis of the Scriptures; he took them very seriously. Barth truly was a "preacher's theologian" and loved to preach the Bible.

Emil Brunner also saw revelation as an "I-Thou" encounter. The Bible for Brunner was only a witness to revelation, and he belittled any concept of verbal inspiration. At the same time, there is a warmth to the theological writings of both Barth and Brunner. They believed that people could know God, and they saw the Bible as central to the Christian tradition. But, as evangelicals observe, their journey back to the Bible was incomplete.

---

[19] See, e.g., among his many books, *Beyond Fundamentalism* (Philadelphia: Westminster, 1984), 13.

William J. Abraham contends that we should take a second look at the word *inspire.* Perhaps, he explains, we should understand the dynamic of inspiration by means of a different model. Much as a good teacher inspires her students, so God by his revelatory and saving acts and personal dealings with the authors of Scripture inspired their writings. Being a teacher myself, this theory has a personal appeal. Unfortunately, it breaks down. Clearly, Abraham is basing his view on the English usage of the word *inspire* rather than on the Greek term (recall 2 Timothy 3:16). One must ask Abraham whether he regards the writings themselves as inspired or only the writers.[20]

> *Evangelicals generally espouse a verbal inspiration view of Scripture.*
> *The actual writing of the Scriptures entailed a flowing together of both divine and human activity.*

Paul J. Achtemeier's view of biblical inspiration is much broader than that of Abraham. He sees God's influence on the entire process of the composition of the Bible—from the history of the collected traditions all the way through to the actual reading and interpretation of Scripture today. Achtemeier has sort of homogenized the doctrines of inspiration, divine providence, and the illumination of the Scriptures. More precision is needed.[21] One can learn much from the works of Abraham and Achtemeier, but their respective personal theories of inspiration leave something to be desired. They back away from the full evangelical view of the verbal inspiration of the Bible.

The Broad Evangelical View of Biblical Inspiration

Evangelicals generally espouse a verbal inspiration view of Scripture. Sometimes called the *verbal plenary* view of biblical inspiration, this approach emphasizes the inspiration of both the writers *and* the writings. It is a *verbal* inspiration in that the Holy Spirit has influenced not merely the ideas of the biblical authors but their very choice of words. In contrast to the dictation view, however, the influence is generally more indirect and providential. God was actively involved in the writ-

---

[20] William J. Abraham, *The Divine Inspiration of Holy Scripture* (Oxford: Oxford Univ. Press, 1981).
[21] Paul J. Achtemeier, *The Inspiration of Scripture* (Philadelphia: Westminster, 1980).

ers' lives from the very beginning, preparing them for the task to which they had been selected.

The actual writing of the Scriptures entailed a flowing together of both divine and human activity. The technical terms for this dynamic are *concursive* or *confluent.* The Bible writer's own vocabulary and literary style are evident, and he might not even be directly aware of divine direction. But the final result is the very choice of words that God desires. Decades ago J. I. Packer aptly described this divine/human confluence:

> We are to think of the Spirit's inspiring activity, and, for that matter, of all His regular operations in and upon human personality, as (to use an old but valuable technical term) *concursive*; that is, as exercised in, through and by means of the writers' own activity, in such a way that their thinking and writing was *both* free and spontaneous on their part *and* divinely elicited and controlled, and what they wrote was not only their own work but also God's work.[22]

This model is helpful in many areas of theology. When the scientist explores the origins of the universe or the historian researches the Exodus events, they are viewing their subject matter from the only vantage point available to them—the human perspective. The theologian, on the other hand—on the basis of biblical revelation—describes the creation of the universe and the Exodus in somewhat different terms (from the divine perspective, so to speak). These descriptions need not be contradictory, but rather are complementary.

In the same way, Luke, for example, can be seen from one perspective as having carried on the very human activity of collecting historical materials in order to write his "orderly account" (Luke 1:1–4). At the same time—perhaps even without Luke's awareness—God mysteriously directed his every choice of words. Decades prior to this, God's guiding hand had been at work preparing Luke to write this Gospel with his own distinctive style and theological perspective. Is anything too difficult for God (see Luke 1:37; cf. Gen. 18:14; Jer. 32:17, 27)?[23]

Divine/human concursive action may also be described as a *synergism.* Rather than God's doing and causing everything (*monergism*), we see a

---

[22] J. I. Packer, *"Fundamentalism" and the Word of God* (Grand Rapids: Eerdmans, 1958), 80 (Packer's italics).

[23] See I. Howard Marshall's excellent treatment of this dynamic in *Biblical Inspiration* (Grand Rapids: Eerdmans, 1982), 40–42. Also Abraham, *The Divine Inspiration of Holy Scripture*, 3–5.

flowing together of divine and human activity. Later we will see how this synergy applies to providence and redemption, for example. God's sovereignty is so powerful that he does not need to micromanage to have everything under his control and working toward his chosen ends. As with the biblical writers, God is free to exercise his influence to the degree of control that he freely chooses. Thus, some Old Testament prophecies are dictated directly to, say, an Isaiah or a Jeremiah (whose books also contain historical materials as well), while Luke gathers his own sources and writes his historical accounts under a more indirect influence. In either case, the words written are precisely the ones God wants written.

Finally, the term *plenary* points to the fact that the totality of the Bible is inspired by God, not just portions of it. Evangelicals regard the entire canon (the authoritative collection of books included in the Bible) as the divinely inspired norm and source for theology. Furthermore, there are no *degrees* of inspiration, only degrees of revelation. Although more of God may be revealed in John than in Judges, both books are equally "inspired by God and useful for teaching the truth, rebuking error, correcting faults, and giving instruction for right living" (2 Tim. 3:16 GNB).

Word and Spirit

In 2 Timothy 3:16, Paul focuses on the inspiration of the *writings* of Scripture. Peter draws attention to the inspiration of the *writers:*

> Above all, you must understand that no prophecy of Scripture came about by the prophet's own interpretation of things. For prophecy never had its origin in the human will, but prophets, though human, spoke from God as they were carried along by the Holy Spirit. (2 Peter 1:20–21 TNIV)

Notice how the role of the Holy Spirit is highlighted. The Bible writers were "carried along" (*pheromenoi*) by the Holy Spirit.

For too long the key role of the Holy Spirit has been neglected—even among evangelicals. Clark Pinnock's *The Scripture Principle* goes a long way toward correcting this error.[24] Pinnock notes an excessive rationalism among both liberals and conservatives, which can be remedied only by a return to a full-orbed doctrine of the Spirit.[25] J. I. Packer notes the Spirit's involvement in the inspiration, canonization, preser-

---

[24] Clark Pinnock, *The Scriptural Principle* (San Francisco: Harper & Row, 1984).

[25] Pinnock's presentation is marred, however, by such statements that the story of Peter's getting the coin from the mouth of the fish (Matt. 17:24–27) has "the feel of a legendary feature" (ibid., 125). Such "rationalism" is uncharacteristic of the general tenor of Pinnock's writings.

vation, translation, authentication, illumination, and interpretation of the Scriptures. This just about covers it all, doesn't it? Packer is, as usual, concisely and precisely to the point.[26]

The Word and the Spirit always work in tandem. At the very beginning, the Spirit hovered over and swept across the face of the dark waters like a mighty wind, and then God *spoke* (Gen. 1:1–3). At Jesus' baptism the Holy Spirit descended on him in bodily form like a dove, and then the Father spoke (Luke 3:22). "A sound like the rush of a violent wind" accompanied the descent of the Spirit on the disciples at Pentecost, resulting in their praising God in other tongues and Peter's boldly proclaiming the Word of God (Acts 2:1–36). Examples abound in Scripture of this dual action of the Word/Spirit of God.

The Reformers were strong on this point. They viewed as spurious any so-called revelation that divided the Word and the Spirit. On the one side, they opposed Romanism for contending that the church rather than the Spirit could authenticate the Scriptures. On the other side, they opposed the enthusiasts for appealing to the Spirit apart from the Scriptures as the authority for their new revelations. Reportedly, Luther once confronted this error in typically dramatic fashion. Certain heretical prophets were exclaiming, "the Spirit, the Spirit," in support of their false teachings, to which Luther responded disdainfully, "I slap your spirit in the snout!" He knew that it was certainly not the *Holy* Spirit inspiring their unscriptural revelations. Calvin, in his *Institutes*, was equally strong on this point.[27]

How relevant this truth is to the contemporary church! Evangelical rationalists, on the one hand, seek to substitute the Word for the Spirit. "Charismaniacs," on the other, credit the Spirit for bizarre teachings that have no relation to Scripture. Do we ever quit repeating the mistakes of history?

Once all the evidence is in—the relevant passages studied, the Scriptures as a whole inductively observed, the Spirit prayerfully sought and heeded, historical and contemporary theology consulted, and reason reverently applied—the doctrine of the verbal inspiration of the Bible is found to be compelling and essential.[28] Moreover, the Scriptures in

---

[26] J. I. Packer, *Keep in Step with the Spirit* (Old Tappan, N.J.: Revell, 1984), 239.

[27] The classic statement on the Reformers' teaching on the inseparability of the Word and the Spirit and the contemporary relevance of that teaching is Bernard Ramm's *The Witness of the Spirit* (Grand Rapids: Eerdmans, 1959).

[28] See Erickson, *Christian Theology*, 207–9 for an insightful treatment of methodological considerations in arriving at a theory of inspiration.

their totality, when observed phenomenologically, present the reader with a prophetic (i.e., verbal) model of inspiration.

A quick perusal of the Bible from Genesis to Revelation yields the impression of direct divine speech: The Scriptures are God's sermon to humankind! The revelation of God's law to Moses at Sinai is introduced: "Then God spoke all these words" (Ex. 20:1). Similarly, the prophets received specific, saving revelation in terms of "the word of the LORD" (see Amos 3:1; 4:1; 5:1; Hos. 4:1; 5:1; Mic. 1:2; 3:1; 6:1). That the prophets' words were seen as *God's* words is reflected, for example, in Jehoshaphat's exhortation, "Listen to me, O Judah and inhabitants of Jerusalem! Believe in the LORD your God and you will be established; believe his prophets" (2 Chron. 20:20). Old Testament wisdom literature also bears witness to verbal inspiration: "Every word of God proves true" (Prov. 30:5). David, the psalmist, agrees: "The promise of the LORD proves true" (Ps. 18:30). This small sampling from the Hebrew Scriptures could be expanded into hundreds of references.

The New Testament writers held to the same concept of inspiration. Matthew, for example, sees Isaiah's prophecy of the virginal conception (Isa. 7:14) as "spoken by the Lord through the prophet" (Matt. 1:22–23). When replacing Judas prior to Pentecost, Peter reminded the one hundred and twenty that "the scripture had to be fulfilled, which the Holy Spirit through David foretold concerning Judas" (Acts 1:16; cf. Ps. 109:8). Paul reminded his Roman readers that "the Jews were entrusted with the oracles of God" (Rom. 3:2) and that the gospel was promised by God himself "through his prophets in the holy scriptures" (Rom. 1:2). Already, in Peter's day, at least some (if not all) of Paul's letters were included with "the other scriptures" (2 Peter 3:16).

Thus, the broad evangelical view of the Bible's inspiration simply continues the basic understanding held by the saints in biblical times on through to the modern period. Only since the Enlightenment has this consensus been challenged. Since that time, however, theological warfare has raged over this foundational issue. In addition, if the inspiration of Scripture has been a perennial topic of debate, its corollaries of infallibility and inerrancy have been even more hotly contested.

The Infallibility and Inerrancy of the Bible

Over the last two millennia the vast majority of Christians have embraced the inspiration and infallibility of Scripture. But during the last two centuries, scholars have debated these issues, and varying positions have gradually filtered down to the grassroots level. More recently, evangelicals themselves have suffered internecine struggles over biblical *infallibility*.

The bottom-line question is whether we can trust everything the Bible says. This is a rather modern concern in terms of a basic distrust of and irreverence toward Scripture. For centuries the teachings of the Bible were accepted without question. St. Augustine's position—that if he ever came across a problem in Scripture he would assign it to a faulty manuscript, a translation error, or to Augustine's own inadequate understanding—was typical of the church's reverence for the Bible.

The term inerrancy *may be modern, but the concept is as old as the people of Bible days, including Jesus himself.*

The term *inerrancy* may be modern, but the concept is as old as the people of Bible days, including Jesus himself: The Scriptures are *the* authority, and you can trust what they teach! John Gerstner's historical conclusions are typical: "The evidence shows that the overwhelming general consensus of the church and the teaching of her greatest theologians in all branches of her communion has been inerrancy. . . . Most official Christian declarations of the last two millennia have affirmed it."[29] To the consternation of many, even evangelical theologians in recent years have challenged these conclusions.

Jack Rogers and Donald McKim, for example, seek to qualify this picture of biblical accuracy by separating off scientific and historical matters from theological and ethical ones. They argue that the church has in the main always done this. In a position that they seek to document in *The Authority and Interpretation of the Bible*,[30] they assert that infallibility can be ascribed only to the theological and ethical teachings of the Bible. One's first impression is that a high view of Scripture is still being advocated in this book. The Bible was never purported to be a scientific textbook anyway, and Rogers and McKim dismiss what historical blemishes

[29] John H. Gerstner, "The Church's Doctrine of Biblical Inspiration," in James Montgomery Boice, ed., *The Foundation of Biblical Authority* (Grand Rapids: Zondervan, 1978), 50–51.

[30] Jack B. Rogers and Donald K. McKim, *The Authority and Interpretation of the Bible* (San Francisco: Harper & Row, 1979).

there may be in the Bible as rather inconsequential. They still affirm its basic message as reliable. Many of their evangelical colleagues, however, have responded, in effect, "The church has already been down that road, and it is a treacherous one!"

Because our "original sin" problem inclines us toward increasing skepticism, the lesson of history—for example, the liberal experiment notes above—is that we never stop where Rogers and McKim do. Ultimately we will jettison greater and greater portions of biblical teachings. Furthermore, this position doesn't fit the facts. John Woodbridge set about to critique this new so-called evangelical position. In my opinion, he embarrassed these otherwise accomplished scholars by demonstrating their faulty methodology and grossly inaccurate documentation.[31]

A separate volume could be written chronicling the drama of this evangelical debate and the roles of the leading advocates of the various positions. In the seminary classroom I often bring a suitcase full of books to class to recount the positions and "war stories" of this evangelical family dispute. But I will avoid the temptation to go further here.

Initially (and historically), *infallibility* and *inerrancy* were used interchangeably, but gradually a distinction has come into vogue. Among evangelicals, "infallibilists" are those who take a position like that of Rogers and McKim. "Inerrantists" hold to the historic position of the entire accuracy of the Bible. Perhaps evangelicals owe Carl F. H. Henry the greatest debt for sorting out these issues and providing the comprehensive statement on biblical authority.[32]

Henry applies the term *infallibility* to the *copies* of the Scriptures (the only thing we have—and good copies as well, in comparison with other ancient literary works). He defines this term as "not prone to err." In other words, since we have only copies of the *autographs* (the original writings; e.g., Paul's letters), some apparent discrepancies may remain unresolved. Nevertheless, these copies demonstrate that we can fully trust the Bible. Henry then assigns the term *inerrancy* to the autographs, which are totally without error.[33]

Henry also acknowledges that the biblical writers did not use the exact same historiographic methods we use today, nor did they possess our modern scientific worldview. Nonetheless, through God's supernatural guidance and inspiration the teachings of the Bible are totally

---

[31] John D. Woodbridge, *Biblical Authority: A Critique of the Rogers/McKim Proposal* (Grand Rapids: Zondervan, 1982).

[32] Henry, *God, Revelation and Authority*, vol. IV.

[33] See, e.g., ibid., 220, n. 1.

trustworthy in all areas—faith, practice, science, and history. This is my position exactly. Henry is an *irenic* (peace-loving) *inerrantist.* Unfortunately, not all inerrantists have been as skilled at constructive dialogue.

Evangelical Bloodshed over the Bible

Henry found himself having to disagree with his successor to the editorship of *Christianity Today,* Harold Lindsell. Lindsell's volumes, *The Battle for the Bible* and *The Bible in the Balance,* raised a furor within the evangelical community.[34] Lindsell did not hesitate to name names and throw down the gauntlet. Most of his information was accurate. (I say *most* because I know personally a few of the men Lindsell attacked, and I find him patently unfair in his treatment.) He was accurate in his argument that a degenerative process sets in when inerrancy is abandoned. His method of reconciling apparent biblical discrepancies was questionable at points, but it was his overall strategy that Henry regretted.

Early on, Henry warned about making "inerrancy a theological weapon with which to drive those evangelicals not adhering to the doctrine into a non-evangelical camp," and about invalidating their otherwise valid scholarly contributions.[35] My own denomination, the Southern Baptist Convention, has been riddled with controversy—and still is, though an uneasy calm now prevails. Wounds and scars abound, as civil wars are always the bloodiest. SBC leaders such as R. Albert Mohler Jr., David S. Dockery, and Timothy George have provided an informed, scholarly perspective.[36] Hopefully, Henry's irenic spirit and sound theological perspective will prevail among evangelicals in general and Southern Baptists in particular.

As unfortunate and unfair as the warfare has sometimes been, the issue of inerrancy is nevertheless a crucial one. The church in America is at a crossroads, faced with the choice of two fundamentally different paths into the future. One is an invitation to continue the failed liberal experiment of accommodation to the spirit of the age. The other is a clarion call to faithfulness to biblical revelation and to the faith once and for all delivered to the saints.

---

[34] Harold Lindsell, *The Battle for the Bible* (Grand Rapids: Zondervan, 1976); idem, *The Bible in the Balance* (Grand Rapids: Zondervan, 1979).

[35] See his article in *Christianity Today* (May 7, 1976), 24.

[36] See Robison B. James and David S. Dockery, eds., *Beyond the Impasse?* (Nashville: Broadman, 1992); Timothy George and David S. Dockery, eds., *Baptist Theologians* (Nashville: Broadman, 1990); and David S. Dockery, *Christian Scripture* (Nashville: Broadman & Holman, 1995).

Some eighty years ago a liberal British biblical scholar, Kirsopp Lake, saw clearly the lines of demarcation. Unfortunately, from my perspective at least, he chose errantly himself. Still, his words manifest an eerie prescience. (Keep in mind that liberals tend to label all inerrantists [somewhat pejoratively] as fundamentalists.)

> It is a mistake often made by educated persons who happen to have but little knowledge of historical theology, to suppose that fundamentalism is a new and strange form of thought. It is nothing of the kind; it is the partial and uneducated survival of a theology which was once universally held by all Christians. How many were there, for instance, in Christian churches in the eighteenth century who doubted the infallible inspiration of all Scripture? A few, perhaps, but very few. No, the fundamentalist may be wrong; I think that he is. But it is we who have departed from the tradition, not he, and I am sorry for the fate of anyone who tries to argue with a fundamentalist on the basis of authority. The Bible and the *corpus theologicum* of the Church is on the fundamentalist side.[37]

Affirming biblical authority is only half the battle, however. There are still intractable Bible difficulties to deal with. More importantly, the whole issue as to how the Bible is to be interpreted and utilized in theology and in the life of the church must be addressed.

What Do We Do with the Bible We Have?

As far as the issue of inerrancy is concerned, there are five basic positions. The *absolute* or *detailed inerrancy* position of, for example, Harold Lindsell and Francis Schaeffer seems to be that all discrepancies can be resolved (even if the cock has to crow six times at Peter's denial of the Lord to blend the biblical narratives [Lindsell]!).

The more moderate *full inerrancy* view of Carl Henry, Millard Erickson, and many other evangelical scholars is more nuanced, balanced, and comprehensive. It modestly admits, for example, that some Bible difficulties still stump us (though if all the data were in they could be resolved). This view was expressed in *The Chicago Statement on Biblical Inerrancy* issued by The International Council on Biblical Inerrancy, a ten-year joint evangelical project.

The *complete infallibility* view of Jack Rogers, David Hubbard, and others asserts that the Bible inerrantly achieves its saving purpose, even

---

[37] Kirsopp Lake, *The Religion of Yesterday and Tomorrow* (Boston: Houghton, 1926), 61.

though there may be scientific and historical blemishes. In relation to the inerrancy question, faith and practice are distinguished from science and history. The scholars in both the full inerrancy and complete infallibility camps agree on a constructive use of biblical criticism (the historical and literary methods), but differ as to how biblical criticism affects one's view of inerrancy.

Partial infallibility or *limited inerrancy* is the rubric for scholars such as Dewey M. Beegle and Stephen T. Davis, who argue that one can still have a high view of Scripture and humbly admit that there are errors (even theological and ethical ones) in the Bible.

Finally, liberals and neo-orthodox scholars *reject* biblical infallibility and inerrancy outright.[38]

Even with a basic evangelical commitment to biblical authority, challenges remain. Given the diversity of the evangelical community and the varying views on the precise meaning of infallibility and inerrancy, it is not surprising that evangelicals use the Bible in theology in different ways. Robert K. Johnston has provided an interesting and instructive sampling of approaches (written by the individual scholars themselves).[39] At an even more basic level, however, every Christian and Christian theologian faces the complex issue of *biblical hermeneutics* (interpretation).

"Do You Understand What You Are Reading?"

Philip's question to the Ethiopian eunuch has relevance today. Through communication from an angel of the Lord and the Spirit himself (all revelatory experiences), Philip found himself asking the eunuch whether he understood the words of Isaiah (Acts 8:26–31). The eunuch learned that day the messianic significance of the ancient prophecy and came to faith in Christ.

Today we still need help to understand the Scriptures. It is not enough merely to assert biblical authority. The Bible must be rightly interpreted and explained (2 Tim. 2:15). Many cults believe in the inerrancy of Scripture, but this conviction does not keep them from misinterpreting what the Bible teaches.

---

[38] See Erickson, *Christian Theology*, 222–24, and Robert K. Johnston, *Evangelicals at an Impasse* (Atlanta: John Knox, 1978), 15–47.

[39] Robert K. Johnston, ed., *The Use of the Bible in Theology/Evangelical Options* (Atlanta: John Knox, 1985).

While I must keep my comments brief, I must address this issue. After establishing a sound approach to the authority of Scripture, the International Council on Biblical Inerrancy set out to tackle the difficult issue of biblical hermeneutics. Their published results are tremendously important and helpful.[40]

The fundamental challenge of biblical hermeneutics is that of relating the ancient text to the modern scene. A maxim of sound interpretation has been first to ask: What *did* the text mean? Who wrote it? To whom? When? Why? What did the writer intend his hearers to understand by what he wrote? This objective pole of the hermeneutical task must be the controlling one. Then one may ask the second question: What *does* it mean? Here we seek to understand the contemporary significance of the text. Too many people want to short-circuit this process, bypassing the first question and going immediately for the contemporary meaning of the text. Too often they project their subjectivity onto the text in a sort of inkblot-test approach.

Hermeneutics can become quite complex. Consider philosophical hermeneutics, a distinct literary discipline, for example. One surefooted guide through this maze is Anthony C. Thiselton's *The Two Horizons.*[41] Thiselton maintains that we must always hold the past and the present together in tension while at the same time pursuing the goal of the "fusion of horizons" to understand the contemporary significance and impact.[42]

When we read and study the Scriptures, we constantly ask the Spirit to help us understand and apply the text. We look first for the straightforward significance of the passage in its historical context (the grammatical/historical approach). We compare Scripture with Scripture. We utilize the best study aids available to us. We study with other believers and pool our insights—and sometimes our ignorance! This is an exciting and demanding task. A helpful resource for this approach is *How to Read the Bible for All Its Worth,* by Gordon D. Fee and Douglas Stuart.[43]

Having said this, I still maintain that our greatest need today is to simply read widely in the Scriptures and expose ourselves to them on a

---

40 Earl D. Radmacher and Robert D. Preus, eds., *Hermeneutics, Inerrancy, and the Bible* (Grand Rapids: Zondervan, 1984).

41 Anthony Thiselton, *The Two Horizons* (Grand Rapids: Eerdmans, 1980).

42 Ibid., 314–19.

43 Gordon D. Fee and Douglas Stuart, *How to Read the Bible for All Its Worth,* 3rd ed. (Grand Rapids: Zondervan, 2003). See also by the same authors: *How to Read the Bible Book by Book* (Grand Rapids: Zondervan, 2002).

day-to-day basis. It takes about ten minutes per day to read through the entire Bible once a year. This is about half the time many of us devote to the daily newspaper. Furthermore, we need to acquire the habit of making use of the numerous excellent translations of the Bible available to the English-speaking reader. Perhaps our goal should be to read completely through a different translation of the Bible each year. It's amazing how much our theology can be straightened out simply by reading the Bible![44]

Revelation Is Truly Divine

Having surveyed the doctrine of revelation, we can see how crucial this tenet of our faith is to the rest of our beliefs. In my opinion, no one has done a better job of presenting this doctrine than Carl F. H. Henry. Henry offers these fifteen theses on divine revelation. They provide a breath-taking overview of the topic:[45]

1. Divine revelation comes by divine initiative. God freely chose to disclose himself to us.
2. Furthermore, God did it for our benefit, offering us personal fellowship with him in his kingdom.
3. This blinding revelation does not exhaust God's transcendent glory and mystery.
4. Because God is one living God, his revelation is a unified one.
5. It is also, however, a diversified manifestation of his divine reality.
6. It is a personal revelation in both its content and its form.
7. It is a historical revelation, involving God's mighty acts in human history.
8. The ultimate disclosure of God is in the miracle of the Incarnation; Jesus Christ is truly "God with us," Immanuel!
9. Christ, as God's eternal Word, is the mediating agent of all divine revelation.
10. Revelation is rational-verbal; that is, it is conveyed in intelligible words and thought.
11. The Bible is the source and channel of divine truth.

---

[44] On the task of selecting and using serviceable translations of Scripture, see Fee and Stuart, *How to Read the Bible for All Its Worth*, ch. 2 ("The Basic Tool: A Good Translation"), 33–53. On the translation task itself, see Glen G. Scorgie, Mark L. Strauss, and Steven M. Voth, eds., *The Challenge of Bible Translation* (Grand Rapids: Zondervan, 2003).

[45] See Henry, *God, Revelation and Authority*, vols. II (1976), III (1979), and IV (1979).

12. The Spirit inspired the Scriptures and illuminates their meaning.
13. The Spirit also enables us to appropriate the saving message of Scripture and regenerates us.
14. The church, as an instrument of the kingdom, mirrors the redemptive message of divine revelation.
15. The greatest revelation of God is yet to come. At the end of the age, Christ will appear to judge the earth, subdue evil permanently, and bring forth a new heaven and earth.

The Pattern of Authority

We should briefly consider two other matters before moving on to the doctrine of God: the pattern of authority and the issue of continuing revelation. These two concerns are interrelated.

What or who is the ultimate authority for theology? We have answered this question in part, and yet we have also skirted the issue somewhat. This chapter has emphasized biblical authority. Now we must stress that the authority of the Bible is derived or delegated. Who would question the assertion that if God is God, then *he* must be the ultimate authority? This truth becomes even more apparent when we study the doctrine of God. Moreover, we should recall the words of Jesus: "All authority in heaven and on earth has been given to me" (Matt. 28:18). Christ is the head of his body, the church. On these two matters virtually all Christians can agree.

When we take the next step, however, and try to ascertain the authority of the Bible, differences emerge. Robert S. Paul helps to clarify the issues. Generally speaking, churches will emphasize one of three channels of Christ's authority. One group stresses the authority of the church itself, subordinating the Bible to the church. Another group elevates the authority of the Spirit. A third group places the Bible above the traditions of the church as well as above any revelation someone might believe they have received from the Spirit. I'm sure you can think of examples of all three approaches.[46]

The Scriptures, the saints, and the Spirit—how do we relate these three channels of Christ's authority? The Protestant instinct to elevate the authority of the Bible above the church and its traditions, and all claimed revelations from the Spirit, seems to fit best with the entire pat-

[46] Robert S. Paul, *The Church in Search of Its Self* (Grand Rapids: Eerdmans, 1972).

tern of divine revelation. The church can easily go astray, developing traditions and practices that distort, rather than develop, the apostolic tradition deposited in the New Testament and the very gospel message itself. Too often, sincere saints have received so-called revelations from the Spirit that prove to be spurious. The Bible must be the norm.

At the same time, the Bible should be read and taught in the context of accountability to the church. And the Spirit is the very life breath of the church—the only true illuminator of the Scriptures. So there is an integral relationship among the three. No one has better explicated this dynamic than Bernard Ramm. His volume *The Pattern of Religious Authority* remains a classic on the pattern of authority.[47]

Robert S. Paul asserts that we must also evaluate the one "non-theological" factor, reason itself. After all, have we not employed reason throughout our entire exploration of divine revelation? Here an examination of what is known as the Wesleyan Quadrilateral—Scripture, tradition, reason, and experience—is in order. One of the geniuses of the Wesleyan tradition has been the highlighting of these four dimensions of the theological enterprise. Surely all four are in play whenever we do theology. But how do we prioritize them? The pattern we saw earlier points the way: Scripture must be the touchstone.[48]

> *The Protestant instinct to elevate the authority of the Bible above the church and its traditions, and all claimed revelations from the Spirit, seems to fit best with the entire pattern of divine revelation.*

In the early years of Youth for Christ, Billy Graham and Chuck Templeton were the two leading evangelists of the day. In fact, many saw more promise in the dynamic and eloquent ministry of Templeton than they did in Graham's ministry. When Templeton began to doubt the veracity of the Scriptures because of questions he was encountering in seminary, Graham could not adequately respond to the problems his friend raised. For about a

---

[47] Bernard Ramm, *The Pattern of Religious Authority* (Grand Rapids: Eerdmans, 1959).

[48] See Donald A. D. Thorsen, *The Wesleyan Quadrilateral* (Grand Rapids: Zondervan, 1990). Davis also provides an insightful analysis of these dynamics in his *Foundations of Evangelical Theology*, chs. 4–7. Donald G. Bloesch provides a trenchant analysis of authority in *The Church: Sacraments, Worship, Ministry, Mission* (Christian Foundations; Downers Grove, Ill.: InterVarsity Press, 2002), 82–98.

year Graham struggled with the issue of the authority of the Bible. Finally, he knew that he must resolve the issue once and for all. At a student retreat center Graham went apart to pray. Seated on a rock with his Bible open before him on a tree stump, Billy Graham confessed: "Oh, God, I cannot prove certain things. I cannot answer some of the questions Chuck and some of the other people are raising, but I accept this Book by faith as the Word of God."[49]

The whole world knows the rest of the story. Templeton ultimately left the ministry. To this day, the phrase most associated with the dynamic and authoritative ministry of Billy Graham, arguably the greatest evangelist in the history of the church, is, "The Bible says. . . ." Graham's inspiring ministry and testament of faith provide a lesson for us all.[50]

Continuing Revelation?

When one does a simple word study on the term "revelation" in the Bible, something disturbing often happens. The term *revelation* is used in the New Testament in a way we have yet to consider. Paul, for example, prayed that God would give the Ephesians "the Spirit of wisdom and revelation [*apokalypsis*], so that you may know him better" (Eph. 1:17 NIV). His advice to the Corinthian church was, "When you come together, each one has a hymn, a lesson, a revelation [*apokalypsis*], a tongue, or an interpretation. Let all things be done for building up" (1 Cor. 14:26 NRSV). Is there a present-day dimension of revelation? Without a doubt there is, even though many hesitate to acknowledge it for fear of denigrating biblical revelation.

This fear is not ungrounded in view of the abuses evident in the contemporary church. Nevertheless, as Clark Pinnock asserts:

> Revelation has not ceased. A phase of it has ceased, the phase that provided the gospel and its scriptural witness, but not revelation in every sense. If it had, we could not know Christ as Lord, because we would be left to our own cognitive powers. We have in us "the spirit of revelation," which causes the letter of the Bible to become charged with life and to become the living voice of God to us. The Spirit did not withdraw from

---

49 William Martin, *A Prophet with Honor* (New York: William Morrow, 1991), 112.

50 Lee Strobel contrasts Graham and Templeton, providing a glimpse into Templeton's agnosticism in a haunting interview: *The Case for Faith* (Grand Rapids: Zondervan, 2000), 7–18.

> the church after the canon was completed but remains in the church speaking through the Scriptures, revealing Christ to us afresh. Indeed, indications are that the Spirit continues to address us through one another, through gifts like prophecy, for example.[51]

Wayne Grudem's thorough treatment of the gift of prophecy has received a wide welcome throughout the evangelical community.[52] God did not suddenly become mute after the canon was closed. Literally millions of saints testify that God still speaks today. (Recall how the Spirit spoke to Philip [Acts 8:29].)

To limit the Spirit's communication to merely emotions devoid of cognitive content is ludicrous. Yet one of evangelicalism's leading communicators has done just this in an interview with *Christianity Today*.[53] Perhaps there is a semantic difficulty here, as Chuck Swindoll clearly has as intimate a walk with the Lord as anyone could desire. We all desperately need one another to sort these things out!

Rightly understood, the prophetic, revelatory activity of the Spirit can actually enhance the Bible's authority. If the task of biblical hermeneutics is to complete the circuit between the ancient texts and our contemporary setting, then a functional charismatic dimension of church life can release the Spirit to apply the Scriptures in an even more direct and vivid manner.

For example, a prophetic exhortation to a deeper discipleship of our Lord can strengthen the biblical injunctions. These kinds of utterances in corporate worship do not have to be delivered in a "spooky," otherworldly manner. Grudem has helped both evangelicals and charismatics by explaining that prophecy in a contemporary church is simply someone's relating *in his or her own words* something that the Lord has brought spontaneously to mind. Through expressions such as this, the Spirit can more easily prevent our merely "playing church" and can wield his sword (Eph. 6:17) in our midst. Only as the Spirit and the Word work in tandem can we truly hear the word of the Lord.

It should be emphasized that the type of revelation referred to here is clearly subordinate to Scripture. In fact, the primary way in which the Spirit communicates to us is through the Bible. All other perceived communications from him should be gauged by Scripture and by the

---

[51] Pinnock, *The Scripture Principle*, 163.

[52] Wayne Grudem, *The Gift of Prophecy in the New Testament and Today* (Westchester, Ill.: Crossway, 1988).

[53] See "Dallas's New Dispensation," *Christianity Today* (October 25, 1993), 14–15.

spiritual discernment of seasoned saints. J. Rodman Williams gives this sage advice:

> There is *nothing more to be added* [to special revelation]: God's truth has been fully declared. Accordingly, what occurs in revelation within the Christian community is not new truth that goes beyond the special revelation (if so, it is spurious and not of God). It is only a deeper appreciation of what has already been revealed, or a disclosure of some message for the contemporary situation that adds nothing essentially to what He has before made known.[54]

The growing evangelical/charismatic consensus in this delicate area is truly exciting! The Spirit is not through teaching us yet!

In the final analysis, we are forced to acknowledge the limits of our understanding and to accept confidently by faith the divine revelation so graciously offered us by our Triune God. Then, paradoxically, everything begins to make sense for the first time. Let us turn now to a study of this majestic God who has revealed himself to us and lavished his love upon us.

---

[54] J. Rodman Williams, *Renewal Theology*, 3 vols. (Grand Rapids: Zondervan, 1988), 1:44 (Williams's italics).

3 | God
Who Is God, and What Is He Like?

How Do We Find God?

God IS

God's Essence

God's Name and God's Names

The Attributes of God

- God's Holiness
- God's Power, Constancy, Eternity, Glory, and Wisdom
- God Is Love
- God's Mercy, Grace, Patience, Kindness, and Faithfulness
- God's Goodness and Knowledge

The Triunity of God

The Doctrine of the Trinity in Biblical, Historical, and Contemporary Theology

The Experience of God

Appendix: Arguments for the Existence of God

- Five Bases for Faith
- Arguments for the Existence of God

Lord, you have been our dwelling place in all generations. Before the mountains were brought forth, or ever you had formed the earth and the world, from everlasting to everlasting you are God.

—Psalm 90:1-2

Source, Guide, and Goal of all that is—to him be glory for ever! Amen.

—Romans 11:36 NEB

And without faith it is impossible to please God, for whoever would approach him must believe that he exists and that he rewards those who seek him.

—Hebrews 11:6

DEALING ADEQUATELY WITH THE DOCTRINE OF GOD is like trying to empty the ocean with a teaspoon. It is rather comical to think that a finite creature can say anything of significance about an infinite God.[1] Indeed, laughter and joy are marks of the people of God: "For the kingdom of God is . . . righteousness and peace and joy in the Holy Spirit" (Rom. 14:17). When C. S. Lewis was, as it were, dragged—kicking and struggling—into theism and then into the kingdom, he was "surprised by joy."[2]

But to *know* God, one has to come by the way of the cross. Human wisdom falls infinitely short. "As God in his wisdom ordained, the world failed to find him by its wisdom, and he chose by the folly of the gospel to save those who have faith. . . . We proclaim Christ nailed to the cross" (1 Cor. 1:21–23 REB). Jürgen Moltmann was true to the mark when he wrote, "Christian faith stands and falls with the knowledge of the crucified Christ, that is, with the knowledge of God *in* the crucified Christ."[3] We do not boast of our faithful religious practices. We shun the glory of our vain philosophies. We refuse to exult in our mystical experiences. Rather, with the apostle Paul we say, "May I never boast of anything except the cross of our Lord Jesus Christ" (Gal. 6:14).

> *Dealing adequately with the doctrine of God is like trying to empty the ocean with a teaspoon.*

How Do We Find God?

As Paul instructed the Corinthians in the verses quoted above, we can only find God through *the gospel*, through *faith*, through *Christ and his cross*. Blaise Pascal incessantly hammered this truth home:

> We only know God through Jesus Christ. . . . Apart from him, and without Scripture, without original sin, without the necessary Mediator who was promised and who came, it is impossible to prove absolutely that God exists, or to teach sound doctrine and sound morality. But through and in Jesus Christ we can prove God's existence, and teach both

---

[1] See Thomas C. Oden, *The Living God* (San Francisco: Harper & Row, 1987), 1. Oden is amused by the thought of "human beings thinking about God."

[2] C. S. Lewis, *Surprised by Joy* (New York: Harcourt Brace Jovanovich, 1955).

[3] Jürgen Moltmann, *The Crucified God*, trans. R. A. Wilson and John Bowden (London: SCM, 1974), 65 (Moltmann's italics).

> *We can only find God through* the gospel, *through* faith, *through* Christ and his cross.

doctrine and morality. Jesus Christ therefore is the true God of men.[4]

Pascal felt that it was vain and audacious to use the so-called metaphysical proofs to convince people about God. These arguments were fine for believers, "for those with living faith in their hearts can clearly see at once that everything that exists is entirely the work of the God whom they worship."[5] But as Pascal knew so well, it is far too easy for prideful, wretched humanity to simply walk away from the most brilliant of philosophical arguments.

God IS

First, we must believe that God is, and that he rewards those who diligently seek him. It is impossible to approach him or please him without faith (Heb. 11:6). The truly Christian doctrine of God begins with the *fact* that God is, that he is the living God. He is the *I AM* of biblical revelation. For Christians "there is one God, the Father, from whom are all things and for whom we exist, and one Lord, Jesus Christ, through whom are all things and through whom we exist" (1 Cor. 8:6).

King Darius finally came to acknowledge the sovereign God to whom Daniel prayed faithfully. When he saw that God was able to deliver Daniel from the lions, he called Daniel "servant of the living God" (Dan. 6:20). He further decreed "that in all my royal dominion people should tremble and fear before the God of Daniel: For he is the living God, enduring forever. His kingdom shall never be destroyed, and his dominion has no end" (Dan. 6:26).

God is the *living* God, and his kingdom can never be destroyed. He is the God who is *there*, to use Francis Schaeffer's favorite declaration. And no one knows him "except the Son and anyone to whom the Son chooses to reveal him" (Matt. 11:27). Jesus said that no one can come to God, the Father, except through him [Jesus] (John 14:6).

Clearly then, the Christian doctrine of God is based on a proper understanding of who Jesus is. His disciples learned this in a poignant

---

[4] Blaise Pascal, in James M. Houston, ed., *The Mind on Fire: An Anthology of the Writings of Blaise Pascal* (Portland, Ore.: Multnomah, 1989), 147.

[5] Ibid., 151.

fashion at Caesarea Philippi. First, Jesus asked what others were saying about him. Then he singled out his own:

> "But who do you say that I am?" Simon Peter answered, "You are the Messiah, the Son of the living God." And Jesus answered him, "Blessed are you, Simon son of Jonah! For flesh and blood has not revealed this to you, but my Father in heaven. And I tell you, you are Peter [*Petros*], and on this rock [*petra*] I will build my church, and the gates of Hades will not prevail against it. I will give you the keys of the kingdom of heaven, and whatever you bind on earth will be bound in heaven, and whatever you loose on earth will be loosed in heaven." (Matt. 16:15–19)

Our own personal answer to Jesus' question—"Who do you say that I am?"—is crucial to our understanding of God!

Peter responded that Jesus was "the Messiah"—this was the first instance of such a startling declaration. Jewish hopes for centuries had been centered on the coming of the Messiah. Then Peter added, "the Son of the living God." Peter saw Jesus as uniquely related to "the living God" as "Son." Jesus responded by saying to Peter that his "Father in heaven" had "revealed" this to Peter. Immediately, Jesus talked about building his church and about the keys to the kingdom of heaven.

Thus, the Christian doctrine of God is fundamentally based on the following: (1) that Jesus is the *Messiah* of Jewish hopes; (2) that he is the *Son* of the living God; (3) that God is his *Father;* (4) that the *church* is Christ's special creation; and (5) that in the *gospel* lie the keys for entrance into the kingdom. All these truths, according to Jesus, come by *revelation.*

> *Just as we know that Jesus is the Messiah, we know that the God of Jewish faith is also the God of Christian faith.*

Just as we know that Jesus is the Messiah, we know that the God of Jewish faith is also the God of Christian faith. The Christian Bible has both an Old Testament and a New Testament. The latter would be incomprehensible without the former. A fundamental definition of God is that he is "the God and Father of our Lord Jesus Christ" (2 Cor. 1:3; Eph. 1:3; 1 Pet. 1:3). To embrace Christian faith one must, among other things, receive the revelation of God, accept the gospel of God (Rom. 1:1), confess the Son of God, submit to the reign of God, and enter the church, which is the household of God (Eph. 2:19; one of many such New Testament metaphors). To become a Christian (echoing the words of the Reformers), you must accept God, through Christ, as your Father, and the church as your "mother."

Instead of bowing to feminist fads and tampering with biblical revelation, contemporary theologians would do better to follow the lead of Luther and Calvin. Inclusive God-language has become a watershed issue in the church today, but the end result can be a doctrine of God that bears little resemblance to the God of biblical revelation.[6] Would it not be better to explore the doctrine of the church in terms of feminine metaphors? Calvin's strong doctrine of the church accomplishes this masterfully:

> For there is no other way to enter into life unless this mother [the visible church] conceive us in her womb, give us birth, nourish us at her breast, and lastly, unless she keep us under her care and guidance until, putting off mortal flesh, we become like the angels [Matt. 22:30].[7]

The vital importance of membership in a local, visible church must be recovered in our day if America is to catch anew a transforming vision of our majestic God. Substitution of private piety and televised church for personal involvement in and accountability to a local church leads to a cheapened view of God.

God's book, the Bible, is about God. He is a God who always has been and always will be. He is a God who creates, loves, judges, and saves. He is an awesome King, who evokes the utmost respect. Yet he is also a tender, compassionate parent, who cares about the smallest need.

> *The true and living God, the God of the Bible, is a saving God who calls us into his* kingdom *to be the* people of God.

The Bible has a unifying theme evident from start to finish. "It is a theme of redemption, of salvation; and it is caught up particularly in those concepts which revolve about the idea of a people of God, called to live under his rule, and the concomitant hope of the coming Kingdom of God."[8] As we move through this exposition of Christian theology, we will be con-

---

[6] See Donald G. Bloesch, *The Battle for the Trinity* (Ann Arbor, Mich.: Servant, 1985).

[7] John Calvin, *Institutes of the Christian Religion*, 2 vols., ed. John T. McNeill, trans. Ford Lewis Battles (Philadelphia: Westminster, 1960), 2:1016 (IV.i.4).

[8] John Bright, *The Kingdom of God* (Nashville: Abingdon, 1953), p. 10.

tinually aware of the unity of God's truth. Notice in John Bright's statement how the doctrines of revelation, God, and redemption are interrelated. His summary is helpful not only to the student of the Bible, but also to systematic theologians.

The true and living God, the God of the Bible, is a saving God who calls us into his *kingdom* to be the *people of God*. These themes appear constantly throughout this systematic theology. In my opinion, God can be clearly understood only in terms of this "agenda," which he has disclosed to us through biblical revelation.

Millard Erickson has aptly stated: "If the doctrine of Scripture is the foundation of faith, then the doctrine of God is its superstructure, within which much of the rest of what we believe fits."[9] It is important that we be extremely careful about the ideas we form about God. The effects of these notions are far-reaching—not only in terms of the "precision" of our theology, but also in how we live our lives. Carl Henry, in his typically trenchant style, shows how the statement "God *is*" provides an apt summary of the doctrine of God:

> If we give the subject "God" and the predicate "is" their true and full sense, we must speak of God's essence, names, attributes, and triunity, and do so expressly on the basis of his revelatory self-disclosure addressed to his created and fallen creatures.[10]

Because of the simplicity of God (his undivided nature, see below), Henry says that "the statement 'God is'—if we know what we are saying—exhausts all that a course in theology can teach concerning him."[11] Therefore, we will follow the outline provided for us in Henry's statement. We will study, in turn, God's (1) essence, (2) names, (3) attributes, and (4) triunity.

Before doing so, let me draw attention to a theologian in the New Testament who sums up these categories of the doctrine of God perhaps better than anyone else, either within or outside the Scriptures: the apostle John. In seminary we first began translating the Greek New Testament from the writings of John because of the simplicity of the vocabulary, grammar, and syntax of these New Testament books. We discovered that John's writings contain some of the most sublime and profound theology in all the Bible! Three simple statements in John's writings aptly sum up the doctrine of God:

---

[9] Millard J. Erickson, *Does It Matter What I Believe?* (Grand Rapids: Baker, 1992), 35.

[10] Carl F. H. Henry, *God, Revelation and Authority* (Dallas: Word, 1982), 5:131.

[11] Ibid., 5:131.

1. "God is spirit" (John 4:24)—God's *essence*
2. "God is light" (1 John 1:5)—God's *holiness*
3. "God is love" (1 John 4:8, 16)—God's *love*

God's holiness and love are the two rubrics under which we will summarize the *attributes* of God. John is also the consummate theologian of the *triunity* of God in the Bible. That just about covers it all, doesn't it!

God's Essence

The woman of Samaria experienced one of the greatest privileges any human being could ever enjoy: She was taught personally by Jesus Christ himself who God really is and who the Messiah is! Jesus referred to God as "the Father" and as one who seeks "true worshipers" (John 4:21–23). He told her straightforwardly that he was the Messiah: "I am he, the one who is speaking to you" (4:26). He also stated the nature of God in three simple words: "God is spirit" (4:24).

God as Spirit is not limited to a physical body as we are. As Spirit he infinitely transcends the created order. As spirit he is present everywhere within the created order. As Spirit he is also invisible. John says in his opening prologue: "No one has ever seen God." Then he adds: "It is God the only Son, who is close to the Father's heart, who has made him known" (John 1:18). We are speaking of an infinite, eternal mystery. We stand in awe of such an Exalted One. The only proper response is to reverence and worship him:

> To the King of the ages, immortal, invisible, the only God, be honor and glory forever and ever. Amen.
>
> He . . . is the blessed and only Sovereign, the King of kings and Lord of lords. It is he alone who has immortality and dwells in unapproachable light, whom no one has ever seen or can see; to him be honor and eternal dominion. Amen. (1 Tim. 1:17; 6:15–16)

To understand the spirituality of God it is important to maintain the biblical balance between his *immanence* and *transcendence.*

We have already referred to these concepts. *Immanence* denotes God's being "everywhere present" within the created order. This is not to be understood pantheistically: God is *not* the universe. But he *is* intimately related to it in an omnipresent fashion. Paul argued this before the philosophers at Athens (Acts 17:27–29). As One who is *transcendent,* God is "wholly other" than—and "outside"—the created order. Perhaps there is even a human analogy to this reality. Just as we transcend our physical bodies in our spirits—albeit in a finite manner—so God infinitely transcends the universe.

> *To understand the spirituality of God it is important to maintain the biblical balance between his* immanence *and* transcendence.

The Lord himself bears witness to the truth of these two realities: "Am I a God near by, says the LORD, and not a God far off? Who can hide in secret places so that I cannot see them? says the LORD. Do I not fill heaven and earth? says the LORD" (Jer. 23:23–24). God is both "near by" and "far off." He "fills heaven and earth." Yet this Exalted One relates in a very special way to the humble:

> For thus says the high and lofty one
> who inhabits eternity, whose name is Holy:
> I dwell in the high and holy place,
> and also with those who are contrite and humble in spirit,
> to revive the spirit of the humble,
> and to revive the heart of the contrite. (Isa. 57:15)

To speak of the holiness of God is to speak, in part, of his transcendence. Today there has been a tragic loss of the sense of the transcendence of God, both in theology and in the life and worship of Christians. This is a fundamental loss of insight into the very nature of God.[12]

God in his essence is uncreated, uncaused, independent, and self-sufficient. Here our finite, time-bound language (not to mention the limits of intellect) fails us. Everything in our existence is contingent. Everything in the universe merely exists and is caused by something else. *But God is.* To "exist" is to be finite, caused, dependent. Someone who asks, "Who made God?" does not understand God's essence. God is, by his very nature, self-existent, and he causes all other existence. We call this quality God's *aseity* (from *a se,* of himself, or, underived existence). God's covenant name, "I AM" (Yahweh), communicates this aspect of

---

[12] Stanley J. Grenz and Roger E. Olson are able to effectively evaluate modern theology as a whole in terms of the dynamics of immanence and transcendence: *Twentieth-Century Theology* (Downers Grove, Ill.: InterVarsity Press, 1992).

his nature. Again he says of himself, "Before me no god existed, nor will there be any after me" (Isa. 43:10 REB).

A correlate of this truth is the *simplicity* of God. God is simple in that he is not a composite of parts, but is undivided. He is one God, indivisible. "Since God is one, not composed of parts, God is completely, not partially, present in all of God's activities."[13] This doctrine will be important to our understanding of the Trinity further on in our study.

God simply *is*. Whatever God was or will be, he always has been. He is eternally present to all of time and space. He "experiences" all temporal events simultaneously. In contradistinction to the concept of God in process theology, God *never changes* in his essence. "For I the LORD do not change" (Mal. 3:6). Now we are in reality mentioning attributes of God: Because he is one in his essence, this delightful fact is unavoidable!

God's Name and God's Names

God in his essence is also a personal God. Francis Schaeffer always liked to refer to the *infinite-personal* God. In view of all the distortions of understandings of God, his two-word description was a needed correction. So far, we have primarily been considering God in his infinity. Now we must see him in his personality.

Over the centuries humankind has had the audacity to ascribe its own names to God rather than to accept God's divinely revealed names.

That God is personal is made crystal clear by the fact that he has given us names by which to call and know him. Unfortunately, over the centuries humankind has had the audacity to ascribe its own names to God rather than to accept God's divinely revealed names. How would we feel if someone decided that our name, which we happen to like very much, was unacceptable and changed it—refusing to address us by the name we disclosed to them? This is exactly what we have, at times, done to God.

Philosophers have generally assigned impersonal names to God, based on their impersonal conceptions of him. He has been referred to

[13] Oden, *The Living God*, 57.

as "the One," "the Absolute," "the Infinite," "the Prime Mover," "the First Cause," and so on. These barren, impersonal appellations are not worthy of God. Theologians have often committed the same offense. But as Carl Henry has stated: "Sinful man adequately knows God's true nature only through remedial redemptive revelation in which God has taught us his first, and middle, and last names."[14]

In ancient Near Eastern thought, one's name stood for the essence of that person. It was not merely a label of identification; rather, it revealed the inner nature and character of the person. When God dealt with a person—when he called and changed that person—he often changed the person's name as well. Remember, for example, Abram and Jacob in the Old Testament and Simon Peter in the New Testament. Parents also chose names for their children that reflected their perceived character. Thus, the names of God in biblical revelation bear great significance for the doctrine of God.

Let us begin, however, with a consideration of the *name* (singular) of God. The third commandment says: "You shall not take the name of the LORD your God in vain" (Ex. 20:7 RSV). Our Lord taught us to pray: "Our Father in heaven, may your name be hallowed; your kingdom come" (Matt. 6:9–10 REB). John's Gospel is replete with references to the divine name. Jesus was not accepted by his own people, but to all who accepted him, "who believed in his name, he gave the right to become children of God (John 1:12 NIV).[15] Jesus said, "I have come in my Father's name" (5:43). In his high priestly prayer for the disciples, Jesus stated, "I have made your name known to those whom you gave me from the world" (17:6). John wrote his Gospel so that we might "believe that Jesus is the Messiah, the Son of God, and that through believing" we might "have life in his name" (20:31).

Emil Brunner saw the name of God as the center of the biblical doctrine of revelation. Further, he was convinced that this concept contained "the meaning of the whole Biblical doctrine of God." Brunner delineated four points with reference to the name of God and the biblical doctrine of God. (1) He stated that "God is known only where He Himself makes His Name known." (2) He emphasized the personal nature of God conveyed in this concept. (3) He then stressed that God's name was given for the purpose of establishing "a personal relation and

---

[14] Henry, *God, Revelation and Authority*, 2:175.

[15] The REB accurately conveys the meaning of the words "who believed in his name" with "who put their trust in him."

communion." (4) Finally, he aptly pointed out how our self-sufficiency is set aside by God's self-revelation in his name. The disclosure is initiated by God, not by us![16]

Let us look at a few of the names of God. As Henry says, "Nowhere does systematic theology, as a discipline of study, move nearer the heart of the Bible than when it expounds the revealed names of God."[17] The names (note the plural) of God indicate the various facets of his one divine nature. By studying these names we are better able to grasp the riches and depth of God's self-revelation to humankind. God accommodates our limitations by communicating to us in anthropomorphic terms. His divine revelation is both personal and propositional. We encounter him personally and learn *about* him as well—a common dynamic in all interpersonal relations.

The name *El* is the general Semitic name for God. Israel adapted this term to her monotheistic faith. The name connotes God's strength, power, and majesty. It points to God's might and his transcendence. The stories surrounding the births of Ishmael and Isaac and the circumcision of Abraham illustrate the significance of the name in ancient Near Eastern culture and in divine revelation.

The angel of the Lord told Hagar to name her son Ishmael, "God hears." Hagar responded by calling the Lord *El Roi,* "the God who sees" (Gen. 16:7–14). He truly is the God who sees our every need and responds with compassion. Next, God changed Abram's name to Abraham—from "exalted father" to "father of a multitude." He also changed Sarai's name to Sarah, both names apparently meaning "princess" (17:1–16). Their son was named Isaac, "he laughs," because of the ages of Abraham and Sarah and because of Sarah's laughter (17:17–18:15). In restating the covenant to Abraham, God referred to himself as *El Shaddai,* God Almighty (17:1). God Almighty is the creator and sustainer of the universe as well as the keeper of covenant. This name evidently derives from the term "mountain," connoting strength, stability, and permanence. The only permanent reality in our lives is God, who is *our* strength and stability amid the ever-changing exigencies of life.

Earlier, during Abram's mysterious encounter with Melchizedek, God is referred to as *El Elyon,* "God Most High" (Gen. 14:17–24). God's omnipotent supremacy is highlighted by this name. Are we aware in

---

[16] Emil Brunner, *The Christian Doctrine of God,* trans. Olive Wyon (Philadelphia: Westminster, 1950), 119–26.

[17] Henry, *God, Revelation and Authority,* 2:172.

America of how far we have drifted from a proper reverence for our exalted God? The way we use his name in our culture would puzzle and appall the patriarchs. A secularized society holds literally nothing as sacred. At Beer-sheba Abraham called on the name of the Lord, *El Olam*, "the Everlasting God," or "the God of Eternity" (21:33). This name signifies that God's sovereignty continues from age to age. One is reminded of the majestic words that began this chapter (Ps. 90:1–2) and of Isaiah's words: "The LORD is the everlasting God, the Creator of the ends of the earth. He does not faint or grow weary; his understanding is unsearchable" (Isa. 40:28).

Elohim is the first name for God that we encounter in the Bible: "In the beginning God [*Elohim*] created the heavens and the earth" (Gen. 1:1 RSV). This is a plural noun, used regularly with a *singular* verb or adjective—a practice unknown in Semitic languages. We will examine this phenomenon later in relation to the Trinity. (*Eloah* is the singular vocative form related to the plural *Elohim.*) "In the Bible, *Elohim* is uniquely the one God who concentrates in himself the being and powers of all the gods, comprehending the totality of deity in himself."[18] The true God encompasses all the powers and attributes ascribed to the false gods and eclipses these nonexistent deities. Israel used *Elohim* in this manner. Again, only God (*Elohim*) *is*!

Among the many names by which God revealed himself to Israel, the supremely important one was, of course, the covenant name *Yahweh.* Exodus records God's own introduction of this hallowed name to Moses:

> But Moses protested, "If I go to the people of Israel and tell them, 'The God of your ancestors has sent me to you,' they will ask me, 'What is his name?' Then what should I tell them?"
>
> God replied to Moses, "I AM WHO I AM. Say this to the people of Israel: I AM has sent me to you." God also said to Moses, "Say this to the people of Israel: Yahweh, the God of your ancestors—the God of Abraham, the God of Isaac, and the God of Jacob—has sent me to you.
>
> This is my eternal name,
> my name to remember for all generations. (Ex. 3:13–15 NLT rev. ed.)

> And God said to Moses, "I am Yahweh—'the LORD.' I appeared to Abraham, to Isaac, and to Jacob as El-Shaddai—'God Almighty'—but I did not reveal my name, Yahweh, to them." (Ex. 6: 2–3 NLT rev. ed.)

[18] Ibid., 2:185.

The basic meaning of this name would be "he who is" or "he who is truly present." It is the third person singular of the Hebrew verb "to be." After the Exile the Jews, in reverence for this holy name, refused to pronounce it and chose to substitute *Adonai* ("Lord") wherever it occurred. This practice continues in synagogues to this day. Most modern English translations of the Bible use *Lord*, or *Lord*, to translate Yahweh—continuing this ancient tradition.

A translation, however, that has confused the picture somewhat is the well known and popular name *Jehovah*. The Hebrew alphabet does not contain vowels; words are comprised solely of consonants. Vowel sounds must be supplied by the reader. To indicate the proper pronunciation of words, a series of markings called vowel points were added centuries after the Hebrew Scriptures were written. The rabbis wrote the vowels of Adonai under the consonants YHWH to indicate that the name Adonai should be spoken. Some Christians erroneously began to pronounce this combination as "Jehovah." But this is not a Hebrew word; the accurate rendering of the holy covenant name written as YHWH is *Yahweh*.

Yahweh is God's proper name, as it were. It occurs more than 6,800 times in the Old Testament, exclusively in reference to the God of Israel.[19] It is also combined with other terms to form compound names. *Yahweh-Jireh*, "the Lord will provide [also, who sees ahead]" (Gen. 22:14), was the name Abraham gave to the place where God provided the substitute for Isaac. *Yahweh-Rapha*, "the Lord who heals" (Ex. 15:26), was given by the Lord himself as a promise that if Israel would heed his Law, then he would prevent any of the diseases of Egypt from coming upon them. *Yahweh-Shalom*, "the Lord is peace" (Judg. 6:24), was the name that Gideon gave to the altar he built after the angel of the Lord issued God's call to him. *Yahweh-Tsidkenu*, "the Lord is our righteousness" (Jer. 23:6), was the name of the future Messiah, according to the Lord's promise through Jeremiah. Other edifying examples could be given. And provision, healing, peace, and righteousness are still available to God's people in the name of the Lord!

Theos is by far the most prominent New Testament name for God, with more than a thousand occurrences. This name is the equivalent of *El* and *Elohim* in the Old Testament. *Kyrios* (Lord) is a name of comparable importance. The Bible of the early church was the Septuagint, the

---

[19] Ibid., 2:210.

Greek translation of the Hebrew Scriptures. In the Septuagint, *Kyrios* translates both *Adonai* and *Yahweh.* In the New Testament, both the Father and the Son are referred to as *Kyrios.* As we noted in the introductory chapter, the earliest Christian confession is that Jesus is *Kyrios* (Lord). As Paul instructed the Roman believers: "If you declare with your mouth, 'Jesus is Lord,' and believe in your heart that God raised him from the dead, you will be saved" (Rom. 10:9 TNIV).

The New Testament believers came to understand both Jesus' uniqueness and their own relationship with God in terms of the name Father.

Note too the culmination of Peter's message on the day of Pentecost: "Therefore let the entire house of Israel know with certainty that God has made him both Lord and Messiah, this Jesus whom you crucified" (Acts 2:36). In this forceful statement we see a juxtaposition of key names and concepts. God himself is said to have designated Jesus as Lord (*Kyrios*)—and not only Lord but also *Messiah* (the Greek word for this is *Christos*). It was the resurrection of the crucified Christ that expressed and authenticated this reality. Jesus is portrayed here in a unique relation with the Father. Ultimately, the church would need a full-fledged doctrine of the Trinity to articulate and guard the truth and meaning of this relationship.

The name *Father* also played a major role in the New Testament doctrine of God. It was Jesus who placed this name at the forefront. The New Testament believers came to understand both Jesus' uniqueness and their own relationship with God in terms of the name Father. Jesus used the most intimate form of address to God in the endearing word *Abba* ("Daddy"; see, for example, Mark 14:36). Perhaps no one has expounded the full significance of Abba more helpfully than Joachim Jeremias:

> The complete novelty and uniqueness of Abba as an address to God in the prayers of Jesus shows that it expresses the heart of Jesus' relationship to God. He spoke to God as a child to its father: confidently and securely, and yet at the same time reverently and obediently.[20]

Furthermore, the early believers also experienced the work of the Holy Spirit in this distinctive dimension. The cry "Abba, Father" also

[20] Joachim Jeremias, *New Testament Theology* (New York: Charles Scribner's Sons, 1971), 67.

rang in their own hearts and from their own lips, assuring them of their redemption (Rom. 8:15; Gal. 4:6)—all made possible by the Lord Jesus Christ himself!

As should be abundantly clear, the names of God in Scripture are indispensable to a complete doctrine of God. They point to God's personality, spirituality, sovereignty, majesty, unity, holiness, and love. Perhaps the best way to illustrate and document this fact is to revisit Moses' awesome encounter with God when the new stone tablets were given. This is also the perfect entrance to the cathedral of the divine attributes.

The Attributes of God

Israel had sinned grievously against the Lord—even as he was giving the law to Moses on Mount Sinai. Moses interceded for God's people. Then a vivid revelation of the holy love of God took place. In fact, the phrase "holy love" perhaps best summarizes *all* of the divine attributes. The *holiness* of God and the *love* of God are the two categories under which all the attributes of God will be organized. One is reminded again of the summary statements of John: God is light (holiness) and God is love (love).

God in his holiness was ready to consume Israel (Ex. 33:3, 5). Later Joshua would warn God's people that the Lord "is a holy God" and that if they went after foreign gods, the Lord, "a jealous God," would "consume" them (Josh. 24:19–20). With the second giving of the tablets, God reminded his people of who he was: "the LORD, whose name is Jealous, is a jealous God" (Ex. 34:14). The people were in awe of the holy God who manifested his glory (through the pillar of fire) when he spoke with Moses in the tent of meeting (33:7–11).

> *Those who follow this God will find themselves spontaneously worshiping him as they study his attributes!*

God, who emphasized to Moses that he knew Moses "by name" and who had given Moses his favor, promised his presence with Moses as he led Israel onward (Ex. 33:12–17). Then Moses prayed for the Lord to show him his glory. The Lord responded, "I will make all my goodness pass before you, and will proclaim before you the name, 'The LORD'; and I will be gracious to whom I will be gracious, and will show mercy on whom I will show mercy" (33:19). "But," he went on to say, "you cannot see my face; for no one shall see me and live" (33:20). Notice that the revelation came through the *name*, Yahweh, and that both God's holiness (cf. "glory"; "no one shall see me") and love ("goodness"; "gracious[ness]"; "mercy") were manifested.

God instructed Moses to cut two new stone tablets and go up Mount Sinai. God would hide Moses in the cleft of the rock and allow Moses to see only his back. The narrative from this point is truly majestic:

> The LORD descended in the cloud and stood with him there, and proclaimed the name, "The LORD." The LORD passed before him, and proclaimed,
>
> "The LORD, the LORD,
> a God merciful and gracious,
> slow to anger,
> and abounding in steadfast love and faithfulness,
> keeping steadfast love for the thousandth generation,
> forgiving inquity and transgression and sin,
> yet by no means clearing the guilty. . . ." (Ex. 34:5–7)

Surely this was one of the most extraordinary manifestations of God's holiness. At the same time, it provides us with a rather comprehensive list of the attributes of God's love ("merciful," "gracious," "slow to anger," and so forth).

There are numerous ways to go about listing and categorizing the divine attributes. I have adapted to my own use the presentation of my mentor in doctoral studies, the late Dale Moody. Moody enumerates seven properties of God's holiness and seven properties of God's love.[21]

> *The properties of God's holiness:* (1) wrath, (2) righteousness, (3) power, (4) constancy, (5) eternity, (6) glory, and (7) wisdom.
>
> *The properties of God's love:* (1) mercy, (2) grace, (3) patience, (4) kindness, (5) faithfulness, (6) goodness, and (7) knowledge.

Those who follow this God will find themselves spontaneously worshiping him as they study his attributes!

---

[21] Dale Moody, *The Word of Truth* (Grand Rapids: Eerdmans, 1981), 94–115.

God's Holiness

When Isaiah was convicted, cleansed, and commissioned as God's messenger (Isa. 6:1–9), he saw "the Lord sitting on a throne, high and lofty" (v. 1) and heard the words of the seraphs: "Holy, holy, holy is the LORD of hosts; the whole earth is full of his glory" (v. 3). And in the heavenly worship around the throne of God in John's Revelation, the four living creatures sing day and night: "Holy, holy, holy, the Lord God the Almighty, who was and is and is to come" (Rev. 4:8). These are both visions of the Holy One in his transcendent majesty, worthy of eternal praise and adulation.

The Song of Moses asks: "Who is like you, O LORD, among the gods? Who is like you, majestic in holiness, awesome in splendor, doing wonders?" (Ex. 15:11). Hannah exults in her song of praise: "There is no Holy One like the LORD, no one besides you" (1 Sam. 2:2). All of these expressions of worship acknowledge the holiness of God in one of its fundamental dimensions. This is God's essential, majestic holiness—his "otherness," his transcendence, his separateness from all that he has made. This is a foundational dimension of divine holiness.

The other dimension is what might be called God's ethical, moral holiness. Habakkuk addresses God in reverential awe: "O LORD my God, my Holy One," and declares, "Your eyes are too pure to behold evil, and you cannot look on wrongdoing" (Hab. 1:12–13). These dimensions combine to prompt reverential fear of the Lord and repentant, grateful worship. Reading R. C. Sproul's classic, *The Holiness of God*,[22] elicits the same response today.

Because God is simple and a unity, his attributes are infinite and integrated within the one divine nature. They are never contradictory. In Hosea, for example, the Lord expresses his tenderness toward his people:

> How can I give you up, Ephraim?
>   How can I hand you over, O Israel? . . .
> My heart recoils within me;
>   my compassion grows warm and tender.
> I will not execute my fierce anger;
>   I will not again destroy Ephraim;
> for I am God and no mortal,
>   the Holy One in your midst,
>   and I will not come in wrath. (Hos. 11:8–9)

---

[22] R. C. Sproul, *The Holiness of God* (Wheaton, Ill.: Tyndale, 1985).

Too often we tend to pit God's holiness against his love, his wrath against his mercy—as if God were contradictory or even schizophrenic. Some theologians dismiss attributes such as wrath, seeing them as "beneath" God and conflicting with his grace and mercy. This position simply distorts and denies the biblical picture of God.

Habakkuk's prayer more accurately represents God's majestic nature: "O LORD, I have heard of your renown, and I stand in awe, O LORD, of your work. In our own time revive it; in our own time make it known; in wrath may you remember mercy" (Hab. 3:2). Therefore, we will be *comparing* the properties of God's holiness and love as we proceed in order to demonstrate the unity and majesty of the divine nature.

The first property of God's holiness we will consider, therefore, is his *wrath*. Divine wrath is "the settled and active opposition of God's holy nature to everything that is evil."[23] Paul's letter to the Romans, a careful and systematic presentation of the Christian faith and gospel, is an excellent place to turn for a thorough treatment of this attribute.

Paul's theme verses (Rom. 1:16–17) refer to the revelation of the righteousness of God in the gospel. Then the apostle writes, "The wrath of God is being revealed from heaven against all the godlessness and wickedness of human beings" (1:18 TNIV). The word wrath (*orge*) is found thirty-six times in the New Testament, twenty-one of which are in Paul's letters. Twelve of those twenty-one occurrences appear in Romans, and all twelve refer to the divine wrath.[24] The verb "revealed" appears in the present continuous tense in both verses 17 and 18. The gospel is a revelation of both the grace of God in the gift of righteousness and the wrath of God against *all* (v. 18) sin. The wrath of God is, in part, the *reason* for the gospel. We need salvation because of our sin and the wrath and judgment of God against our sin.

Leon Morris explains Paul's meaning:

> We should not overlook the further fact that the revelation of the wrath of God is in this context linked with the gospel. We see some revelation of the divine wrath, it is true, in the suffering, frustration, and sheer disaster that are so often the consequences of sin. But Paul is saying rather that it is the cross that shows us the measure of God's wrath. It is in the events of the gospel that the revelation occurs. Forgiveness is no cheap gesture. It is as costly as the cross. It is meaningless without the wrath. . . .

---

[23] Leon Morris, *The Epistle to the Romans* (Grand Rapids: Eerdmans, 1988), 76.

[24] Ibid., 75, n. 189.

> Unless there is something to be saved from, there is no point in talking about salvation.[25]

Notice also in these verses that God's wrath is a *revealed* wrath and that it is being revealed in the present historical (and personal) situation.

Paul then describes the eschatological (end-time) wrath of God. He warns about "the judgment of God" (Rom. 2:3), about "the day of wrath, when God's righteous judgment will be revealed" (v. 5). He points out that God's "kindness and forbearance and patience" are intended to lead us to repentance (v. 4). Finally, note the *personal* quality of God's wrath: "But by your hard and impenitent heart you are storing up wrath for yourself on the day of wrath, when God's righteous judgment will be revealed. For he will repay according to each one's deeds" (vv. 5, 6).

> *The key to a true understanding of God's wrath is to view it in the light of the cross.*

The testimony of Romans is more than sufficient to establish the doctrine of divine wrath. The Scriptures, however, are replete with this teaching. The key to a true understanding of God's wrath is to view it in the light of the cross. In the gospel, Paul announced (Rom. 1:16–18), there is a revelation of *both* "the wrath of God" (judgment) *and* "the righteousness of God" (salvation). Jesus said exactly the same thing (John 3:14–17). Just as the serpent represented both judgment and salvation in the wilderness (Num. 21:4–9), so the cross is the means of both God's judgment on our sin and our (God-given) salvation from sin and its consequences!

A second property of God's holiness is the r*ighteousness* of God. Martin Luther hated the phrase "the righteousness of God." He struggled to apprehend the message of Romans, but that ominous phrase stood in the way "because I took it to mean that righteousness whereby God is righteous and deals righteously in punishing the unrighteous."[26] What he ultimately discovered would change his life and the course of history:

> Night and day I pondered until . . . I grasped the truth that the righteousness of God is that righteousness whereby, through grace and sheer mercy, he justifies us by faith. Thereupon I felt myself to be reborn and to have gone through open doors into paradise.[27]

---

[25] Ibid., 76–77.

[26] Quoted in F. F. Bruce, *The Epistle of Paul to the Romans* (TNTC; Grand Rapids: Eerdmans, 1963), 59.

[27] Ibid.

Luther finally understood how Paul linked the righteousness of God in his holiness and the grace of God in his love! Righteousness and salvation are virtually equated in certain biblical passages. God's own personal testimony is this: "There is no other god besides me, a righteous God and a Savior; there is no one besides me" (Isa. 45:21). He further comforts his people: "But my salvation will last forever, my righteousness will never fail"—a Hebrew parallelism equating salvation and righteousness (Isa. 51:6 NIV).

At the same time, righteousness can be used of God in the sense of punishment or judgment. The Lord warned Judah of impending exile for her greed and self-indulgence: "But the LORD of hosts is exalted by justice, and the Holy God shows himself holy by righteousness" (Isa. 5:16). Additionally, God's people are expected to keep God's righteous law because he is righteous and his law is righteous (cf., e.g., Ps. 119:137–44). These three dimensions of God's covenantal righteousness (saving, punitive, and mandatory) are a distinctive Baptist theology.[28]

Our righteous God is a God of justice and righteous judgment. As Abraham interceded for Sodom for the sake of the righteous, he argued, "Shall not the Judge of all the earth do what is just?" (Gen. 18:25). The prophet Amos warned those who "turn justice to wormwood, and bring righteousness to the ground" (Amos 5:7). He called to repentance those "who afflict the righteous ... and push aside the needy" (v. 12). The Lord, the God of hosts, was weary of the empty ceremony of the Israelites; the God of righteousness laid bare his heart of compassion and concern for social justice with words and sentiment that echo today: "But let justice roll down like waters, and righteousness like an everflowing stream" (v. 24).

In his Sermon on the Mount, Jesus exhorted his disciples not to be anxious about the necessities of life: "But strive first for the kingdom of God and his righteousness, and all these things will be given to you as well" (Matt. 6:33). John Stott explains that God as King has the "right to rule in the lives of his creatures" and that "one of God's purposes for his new and redeemed community is through them to make his righteousness attractive (in personal, family, business, national, and international life), and so commend it to all men."[29] There is clearly a social dimension to the gospel in that God's righteous people are to mirror

[28] James Leo Garrett Jr., *Systematic Theology I* (Grand Rapids: Eerdmans, 1990), 232–33.

[29] John R. W. Stott, *Christian Counter-Culture: The Message of the Sermon on the Mount* (Downers Grove, Ill.: InterVarsity Press, 1978), 170–71.

his compassionate heart for justice while at the same time announcing the good news of his offer of the forgiveness of sins and eternal life through faith in Jesus Christ.

The heart of "The Gospel According to Paul" is Roman 3:21–26. Here we gain access to the heart of God's righteousness. Paul announces that the righteousness of God has been revealed through the gospel, the righteousness from God that comes "through faith in Jesus Christ for all who believe" (v. 22). Believers in Christ are justified (declared righteous) as a gift (*dorean*), by his grace,

> through the redemption that is in Christ Jesus, whom God put forward as a sacrifice of atonement by his blood, effective through faith. He did this to show his righteousness, because in his divine forbearance he had passed over the sins previously committed; it was to prove at the present time that he himself is righteous and that he justifies the one who has faith in Jesus. (Rom. 3:24–26)

The *righteous* God is also a *gracious* God, who gives righteousness as a gift to all who acknowledge the atoning death of his Son, Jesus Christ, and put their trust in him. Thus, "the righteousness of God" in Romans and in Paul's theology in general is (1) an *attribute* of God, as he truly is a *righteous* God; (2) an *activity* of God, as he rescues us from sin through the cross of Christ; and (3) an *achievement* of God, as he *gives* to us *his* righteousness and thereby a right standing with him.[30] Surely a *Hallelujah!* is appropriate here. Only through the atoning death of Christ announced in the gospel could God be both just and the justifier!

God's Power, Constancy, Eternity, Glory, and Wisdom

Closely related to the righteousness of God is his *power.* Psalm 97 demonstrates this relationship: "The LORD is king! . . . Righteousness and justice are the foundation of his throne. . . . The mountains melt like wax before the LORD, before the LORD of all the earth" (Ps. 97:1–5). The Bible gives abundant testimony to the *omnipotence* of God. The biblical doctrine of the creation of the universe (*creatio ex nihilo*) alone would be enough to establish God's unlimited power. Our minds cannot conceptualize such power; we have no analogy for it.

God also manifests his power in redemption. Through Ezekiel he promised to regather his people after the Exile for the sake of his "holy

---

[30] John R. W. Stott, *Romans: God's* Good News *for the World* (Downers Grove, Ill.: InterVarsity Press, 1994), 63.

name" and to "display [his] holiness before their eyes" (Ezek. 36:21–23). The Exodus itself was an awesome display of God's power. And the resurrection of Christ from the dead was the greatest historical demonstration of that power known to humankind. Again, the Bible is replete with passages referring to the power of God in these events. The gospel itself is "the power of God for salvation to everyone who has faith" (Rom. 1:16). Here the paradox of God's power expressed in apparent weakness comes to the fore, as Paul sought to explain to the triumphalist Corinthians (1 Cor. 1:18–25; 2 Cor. 12:9–10; 13:4).

For God, literally nothing is impossible or too difficult or too wonderful (Gen. 18:14; Num. 11:23; Job 42:1–2; Jer. 32:17, 27; Matt. 19:26; Luke 1:27). At the same time, God has freely chosen to restrain and limit his power to allow for a real but limited freedom of choice for his finite creatures. Acknowledging this fact helps prevent us from fanciful flights into speculative philosophy or into a deterministic fatalism.

God in his infinite power created space and time. As the Lord of time he stands above time, yet relates intimately with it. As mortals, we live within time and perceive that the only constant in life is change. We are continually amazed at how we change—how our friends and family change. Sometimes people change for the better, sometimes for the worse. Human history fascinates us because of all the intriguing changes that take place. *God never changes!* He is the one constant in life. His constancy and changelessness provide a stable foundation for our lives. This truth is especially meaningful in an era of such rapid change![31]

The psalmist observed that the universe wears out like a garment, but "you [God] are the same, and your years have no end" (Ps. 102:26–27). God says of himself to his people: "For I the LORD do not change" (Mal. 3:6). James says that all good things come from God: "These good gifts come down from the Creator of the sun, moon, and stars, who does not change like their shifting shadows" (James 1:17 NCV). God is dependable, reliable, and trustworthy. Furthermore, God's constancy is descriptive of his other attributes. In fact, we often distort this divine attribute when we isolate it from the other attributes. God can be mistakenly seen as remote, static, and impersonal.[32] Sometimes theologians import this caricature of God from Platonic philosophy.

Process theologians and open theists rightly protest this static, impersonal, and uncaring portrayal of God as one who is impervious to our

---

[31] Compare Brunner, *The Christian Doctrine of God*, 266.
[32] Oden, *The Living God*, 111.

pain.[33] Unfortunately, the god of process thought is limited and changing—a sometimes pathetic deity who lacks many of the majestic attributes of the God of biblical revelation. Students of Scripture at the grassroots level rarely make this mistake, however, as the Scriptures explode such inferior concepts of deity.

Sometimes we are thrown off by the anthropomorphisms of Scripture—for example, descriptions of God's "repenting" or changing his mind, relenting, or being sorry for a decision or action (1 Sam. 15:35; Jer. 42:10; Amos 7:3, 6). God does "change" in his *attitude* (Gen. 6:6; Isa. 54:8; 64:7; Jer. 3:12) and *actions* (see the verses cited in first sentence of this paragraph), but never in his *character* (Num. 23:19; Ps. 102:27; Mal. 3:6; James 1:17) or *counsel* (Ps. 33:11; Heb. 6:17).[34] Actually, it is humans who change, not God. God is merely relating to us in terms of the space-time continuum in which we live and in personal terms. As Erickson observes:

> Some apparent changes of mind are changes of orientation that result when humans move into a different relationship with God. God did not change when Adam sinned; rather, humankind had moved into God's disfavor. This works the other way as well. Take the case of Nineveh. God said, "Forty days and Nineveh will be destroyed, unless they repent." Nineveh repented and was spared. It was humans who had changed, not God's plan.[35]

Because God is Lord of time, he is not only changeless, but also eternal. The *eternity* of God means that he is:

> (1) *Before* time: "Before the mountains were brought forth, or ever you had formed the earth and the world, from everlasting to everlasting you are God" (Ps. 90:2).
>
> (2) *Above* time: "For thus says the high and lofty one who inhabits eternity, whose name is Holy" (Isa. 57:15).
>
> (3) *Ahead* of time: "May the God of hope fill you with all joy and peace in believing" (Rom. 15:13).[36]

Because our thinking is rooted in time, it is difficult for us to conceptualize God's being prior to time—but no more difficult than thinking

---

[33] More will be said later on open theism.

[34] Moody, *The Word of Truth*, 99–100.

[35] Millard J. Erickson, *Introducing Christian Doctrine*, ed. L. Arnold Hustad (Grand Rapids: Baker, 1992), 87 (Erickson's italics).

[36] Moody, *The Word of Truth*, 100–101.

about what was prior to the Big Bang! Knowledge of the eternity of God strengthens our cosmology.

We must not forget God's immanence and transcendence in this discussion: Our transcendent God who *created* time is independent of the changes of time, yet intimately involved with time in his immanence. Only such a God could both see the drama of history as a *completed* reality and at the same time *walk through* that drama with us![37]

Perhaps acknowledging God's being *above* time, inhabiting eternity, is easier to contemplate, but it was the theologians of hope (Moltmann and Pannenberg) who helped us see that God is also *ahead* of us in time! He is the God of the future. He is the God of hope. All three concepts of God's relation to time (before, above, and ahead) are essential, however, in order to accurately envision how God relates to time. The incarnational model also helps us to understand how the Eternal One relates to time. As Thomas Oden has pointed out, this approach is a classical one, and helpful for many reasons.[38] God does not have to cease to be God in order to interact with time.

Millard Erickson expresses well how the eternal God relates to time:

> There is a successive order to the acts of God and there is a logical order to his decisions, yet there is no temporal order to his willing. His deliberation and willing take no time. He has from all eternity determined what he is now doing. Thus, his actions are not in any sense reactions to developments. He does not get taken by surprise or have to formulate contingency plans.[39]

Because even Christians forget this dimension of God's sovereignty, there is often an unnecessary (and unacceptable) anxiety in our hearts and minds: God has everything under control!

The *glory* of God is his manifested presence. Glory is the immanent disclosure of God's transcendent holiness. "The glory of God signifies his splendor, majesty, and radiance, particularly as these make an impression upon the world of the creature."[40] God's glory and his revelation are closely aligned. "He glorifies himself by revealing himself. God's glory is the shining of his light in the darkness of this world."[41]

---

[37] See Millard J. Erickson's excellent presentation of the various views of God's eternity (and his own creative synthesis, which I have adapted here) in *God the Father Almighty: A Contemporary Exploration of the Divine Attributes* (Grand Rapids: Baker, 1998), 114–40.

[38] Oden, *The Living God,* 63.

[39] Millard J. Erickson, *Christian Theology* (Grand Rapids: Baker, 1985), 275.

[40] Donald G. Bloesch, *Essentials of Evangelical Theology,* 2 vols. (New York: Harper & Row, 1978), 1:37.

[41] Ibid., 1:38.

Isaiah's vision of enthroned deity included the announcement, "The whole earth is full of his glory" (Isa. 6:3). The psalmist exulted, "The heavens declare the glory of God" (Ps. 19:1 NIV). The Scriptures promise that one day "the earth will be filled with the knowledge of the glory of the LORD, as the waters cover the sea" (Hab. 2:14). Humankind exists to reflect and declare that glory, but has fallen short (Rom. 3:23). God's glory is everywhere, and we don't see it! His universal glory became incarnate in Jesus Christ, and we still didn't recognize him (John 1:14). Sin has blinded humankind to God's glory. We are adulterous and idolatrous. We "traded the glory of God who lives forever for the worship of idols" (Rom. 1:23 NCV). Therefore, the *knowledge* of the glory of the Lord is still lacking in every generation. Only God's own people truly (albeit imperfectly) acknowledge his glory.

> *The* glory *of God is his manifested presence. Glory is the immanent disclosure of God's transcendent holiness.*

God's plan, however, will not be frustrated. He still sits on his exalted throne, and he *will* be glorified. The prophet Micaiah was not impressed with the kings of Israel and Judah (Ahab and Jehoshaphat) "sitting on their thrones, arrayed in their robes" (1 Kings 22:10). He mocked the false prophets and announced, "I saw the LORD sitting on his throne" (v. 19). Only a similar vision of our majestic God in his sovereign glory will strengthen us to proclaim boldly God's Word today.[42] As Packer aptly describes, God will glorify himself "by establishing his kingdom and exalting his Son, by creating a people to worship and serve him, and ultimately by dismantling and reassembling this order of things, thereby rooting sin out of his world."[43] This divine agenda *will* be accomplished. And we have the choice of either cooperating with it and being blessed or resisting it and being judged.

The glory of God also refers to what theologians call the *omnipresence* of God, already alluded to in the description of God's universal glory. God's glory is closely connected to his goodness. Moses asked the Lord to show him his glory, and the Lord immediately replied, "I will make all my goodness pass before you" (Ex. 33:18, 19). The Hebrew term for *glory* refers to something that has "weight" or importance. (In earlier parlance the term "heavy" was used to mean profound or significant.)

---

[42] James I. Packer, *Hot Tub Religion* (Wheaton, Ill.: Tyndale, 1987), 54.
[43] Ibid., 25.

Paul clearly has this Old Testament concept in mind when he speaks of the "eternal weight of glory" that awaits us (2 Cor. 4:17).

Perhaps the most significant perspective on God's glory is found in what has been called "The Gospel of Glory," John's Gospel. The prologue contains these majestic words: "The Word became a human and lived among us. We saw his glory—the glory that belongs to the only Son of the Father—and he was full of grace and truth" (John 1:14 NCV). John's Gospel is replete with references to glory and glorification. But, significantly, John leaves out the dramatic account of Christ's transfiguration that is found in the first three Gospels (Matt. 17:1–13; Mark 9:2–12; Luke 9:28–36). Surely this event was the most spectacular manifestation of the glory of Christ during his earthly ministry. Why didn't John even mention this glorious event, much less explore its full significance, especially in view of his emphasis on glory?

The answer becomes clear when we look carefully at how John presents the subject of glory in his Gospel. The first instance is the statement that the Word lived or dwelled among us (John 1:14). John specifically alludes to the *Shekinah* glory of Old Testament times—the glory of the pillar of cloud and fire (Ex. 13:21–22), the glory of Sinai (19:16–25), and, most importantly for understanding John 1:14, the glory of the tabernacle (Ex. 40:34–38). *This* is the glory, John says, that "tabernacled" among us in the Incarnate Word!

However, the glory John describes in his Gospel is unique. He portrays a lifestyle of lowly service to humankind and the agonizing and humiliating death of the cross. The Rubicon-event of the raising of Lazarus was definitely a manifestation of the "glory of God" (John 11:40), but so was the *cross* (12:23). The *humility* of God's glory is what shocks prideful humanity. But those who truly understand it will boast only in the cross of Christ (Gal. 6:14).[44]

In Jesus' high priestly prayer we have a glimpse into the inner sanctum of the Godhead (John 17). Jesus is preparing to be "glorified" in the cross; he mentions the glory he had with the Father before the world existed (vv. 1–5). He then prays for his disciples (vv. 6–19), saying that he has made God's name known to them (cf. Ex. 33:19, where the Lord proclaims his name while he reveals his glory to Moses!). Jesus also says he has been glorified in his disciples (John 17:10). In his prayer for the church universal (vv. 20–26), he petitions for unity: "The glory that you

[44] Leon Morris provides a masterful treatment of this subject in *Reflections on the Gospel of John*, 2 vols. (Grand Rapids: Baker, 1986), ch. 3, 2:17–26.

have given me I have given them, so that they may be one, as we are one" (v. 22; note also v. 23). He then prays, "Father, I desire that those also, whom you have given me, may be with me where I am, to see my glory, which you have given me because you loved me before the foundation of the world" (v. 24). The prayer culminates with these words: "I made your name known to them, and I will make it known, so that the love with which you have loved me may be in them, and I in them" (v. 26).

When we are privileged to hear such intercessory words from the mouth of our Lord, "the Lord of glory" (1 Cor. 2:8; James 2:1), our immediate response is to glorify God for his grace and goodness—that he would want to share his very life with us! This is the secondary meaning of the glory of God, namely, the glory that we ascribe to him in our worship and gratitude. "Ascribe to the LORD the glory of his name; worship the LORD in holy splendor" (Ps. 29:2). Thus the psalmist praises the Lord who shows his glory in the thunderstorm. The Bible is filled with similar expressions with which God's people glorify his name.

We are to glorify God with our entire lives (Matt. 5:16; 1 Cor. 6:20; 10:31). Furthermore, we have the "hope of glory," which motivates us in everything we do and makes us eternally optimistic (Rom. 5:2; 8:18–25; Col. 1:27). Even our sufferings are linked to his glory (1 Peter 4:12–16). Finally, we await our glorification at the end of the age, when we enter into the fullness of God's glory (Rom. 8:28; Phil. 3:21).

Glory and goodness are two of the most comprehensive attributes of God. We have, therefore, devoted extended space to them. The answer to the first question of the Westminster Shorter Catechism is surely correct: "Man's chief end is to glorify God, and to enjoy him forever." Jesus Christ, who is the "radiance of God's glory" (Heb. 1:3 REB), has made it possible for us to do just this! With the Christmas angels we exult: "Glory to God in the highest heaven" (Luke 2:14). Our doxology (from the New Testament term *doxa,* meaning "glory") is the overflow of the divine glory. *SOLI DEO GLORIA!*

Closely related to the glory of God is the *wisdom* of God. In correcting the Corinthian triumphalism, Paul emphasized the message of Christ and his cross as the wisdom of God (1 Cor. 1:18–2:16). He declared: "But we speak God's wisdom, secret and hidden, which God decreed before the ages for our glory. None of the rulers of this age understood this; for if they had, they would not have crucified the Lord of glory" (2:7–8). Corinthian pride had led to divisions for a number of reasons. They boasted about the leaders who had baptized them (1:10–17). They were enamored with mere worldly or human wisdom (vv. 18–31). Evidently, pride had also entered into their experience of spiritual gifts (1 Cor. 12–14).

Paul always pointed the Corinthians back to Christ and his cross. Instead of stumbling after miraculous powers and knowledge, whether through "revelations" or prideful intellectualism, the Corinthians were exhorted to center on Christ, who is "the power of God and the wisdom of God" (1 Cor. 1:24; see also v. 30). "For God's foolishness is wiser than human wisdom, and God's weakness is stronger than human strength" (v. 25). Since Jesus Christ is our wisdom, righteousness, sanctification, and redemption, then our boast should be in the Lord (v. 31). Only by the Spirit of God can we transcend human wisdom and receive the things of God (2:6–16). Paul's message was Christ and the cross, "with a demonstration of the Spirit and of power, so that your faith might rest not on human wisdom but on the power of God" (2:1–5).

Human wisdom is too often founded on faulty values and limited knowledge. The wisdom of God is "that attribute of God by virtue of which he always acts with full knowledge and correct values."[45]

> God has access to all information. So his judgments are made wisely. He never has to revise his estimation of something because of additional information. He sees all things in their proper perspective; thus he does not give anything a higher or lower value than what it ought to have. One can therefore pray confidently, knowing that God will not grant something that is not good.[46]

Furthermore, God's Word contains what is known as wisdom literature in Job, Proverbs, Ecclesiastes, and elsewhere. Here we find wonderful teachings "concerned with the art by which right thought issues in appropriate action."[47] True wisdom, according to the Bible, always finds its source in God. Our God is personally knowledgeable and palpably practical.

God's wisdom is seen in his *creation*: "O LORD, how manifold are your works! In wisdom you have made them all" (Ps. 104:24). God gave Job a firsthand account of his divine wisdom in creation (Job 38–41). The evidence is abundant both in Scripture and in the universe itself that

---

[45] Millard J. Erickson, *Concise Dictionary of Christian Theology* (Grand Rapids: Baker, 1986), 67.
[46] Erickson, *Introducing Christian Doctrine*, 85.
[47] Moody, *The Word of Truth*, 103.

God's wisdom permeates his creation (Prov. 3:19; 8:22–31; Jer. 10:12). *Christ* himself is the supreme revelation of divine wisdom (1 Cor. 1:24, 30). In him "are hidden all the treasures of wisdom and knowledge" (Col. 2:3). We have already seen the wisdom of God in the *cross* (1 Cor. 1:18–3:3). Finally, perhaps to the surprise of many, the wisdom of God is revealed through the *church.* In Ephesians Paul explains God's wise plan—formerly hidden—of uniting Jew and Gentile through the gospel. This "hidden purpose" of God "lay concealed for long ages with God the Creator of the universe, in order that now, through the church, the wisdom of God in its infinite variety might be made known to the rulers and authorities in the heavenly realms" (Eph. 3:9–10 REB).

Christ *himself is the supreme revelation of divine wisdom.*

God Is Love

Having looked at the properties of God's holiness, we find ourselves reaching the same conclusion as the writer to the Hebrews: "Therefore, since we are receiving a kingdom that cannot be shaken, let us give thanks, by which we offer to God an acceptable worship with reverence and awe; for indeed *our God is a consuming fire*" (Heb. 12:28, italics added). We find here again a straightforward statement concerning God's nature: Our God is a consuming fire! He is a holy and majestic God, who deserves our worship and gratitude, reverence and awe.

We have studied God's essence as spirit: "God is spirit" (John 4:24). We have examined the attributes of his holiness: "God is light" (1 John 1:5). Now we come to the very heart of God's nature according to biblical revelation. "God is love" (1 John 4:8, 16). Let us read this programmatic statement in its full biblical context:

> Beloved, let us love one another, because love is from God; everyone who loves is born of God and knows God. Whoever does not love does not know God, for God is love. God's love was revealed among us in this way: God sent his only Son into the world so that we might live through him. In this is love, not that we loved God but that he loved us and sent his Son to be the atoning sacrifice for our sins. Beloved, since God loved us so much, we also ought to love one another. No one has ever seen God; if we love one another, God lives in us, and his love is perfected in us.

> By this we know that we abide in him and he in us, because he has given us of his Spirit. And we have seen and do testify that the Father has sent his Son as the Savior of the world. God abides in those who confess that Jesus is the Son of God, and they abide in God. So we have known and believe the love that God has for us.
>
> God is love, and those who abide in love abide in God, and God abides in them. (1 John 4:7–16)

This passage has to be one of the simplest and yet most profound statements in all the Bible, not only concerning the nature of God but also concerning the essence of Christian faith and life and the assurance of salvation.

John provides in these verses a threefold test for authentic faith. The three characteristics of a genuine Christian are: "possession of the Spirit, confession of Jesus as the Son of God, and living in the love of God. On this basis there can be erected a firm foundation for Christian hope."[48] According to I. Howard Marshall, the statement that God is love "is simply the clearest expression of a doctrine of the nature of God" in Scripture. Marshall observes: "Since love is a personal activity, the statement stresses the personality of God to the fullest extent."[49] Neither the language nor the context permit us to reverse the words to "love is God," as is the tendency in process theology. God is not some impersonal principle—even one as noble as love. He is the living, personal God, who sovereignly rules the universe and who alone has revealed the true nature of love.[50] Ultimately, love can only be defined in relation to God because his very nature, and his alone, is love.

Virtually all commentators point out that these verses recall perhaps the best-known verse in John's writings, if not the entire Bible: "For God loved the world so much that he gave his only Son, so that everyone who trusts in him may not perish but have eternal life" (John 3:16; author's translation). C. H. Dodd notes the dynamic quality of these Johannine statements: "The Word of God to men is love; the coming of His Kingdom is an act of love. Hence, if we ask, What is God's nature? the answer must be given in terms of love."[51] To say "God is love" is to say much more than merely "God loves." To say "God is love"

---

[48] I. Howard Marshall, *The Epistles of John* (NICNT; Grand Rapids: Eerdmans, 1978), 222.

[49] Ibid., 213.

[50] Stephen S. Smalley, *1, 2, 3 John* (WBC 51; Dallas: Word, 1984), 239–40.

[51] C. H. Dodd, *The Johannine Epistles* (Moffatt NT Commentary; London: Hodder & Stoughton, 1946), 108.

> implies that all His activity is loving activity. If He creates, He creates in love; if He rules, He rules in love; if He judges, He judges in love. All that He does is the expression of His nature, which is—to love. The theological consequences of this principle are far-reaching.[52]

God judges in love, but he also loves in justice. As John R. W. Stott observes: "He who is love is light and fire as well. Far from condoning sin, His love has found a way to expose it (because He is light) and to consume it (because He is fire) without destroying the sinner, but rather saving him."[53] All of this comes by way of the cross.

We see clearly and receive fully God's love only in the cross of Christ. John hammers this truth home in these passages we have been considering. Karl Barth, perhaps the greatest theological mind of the twentieth century, while giving a public lecture at one of America's premier educational institutions, was asked by a student what was the most profound thought he had ever considered. Barth silently reflected for a long time. He then replied, "Jesus loves me. This I know. For the Bible tells me so."[54] Jesus himself said: "No one has greater love than this, to lay down one's life for one's friends" (John 15:13). I came to a saving knowledge of Jesus Christ as a seven-year-old when I realized that he died for me *personally*. The Father's love enveloped me then through the presence of the Holy Spirit, and God has proven his faithfulness as a love that will never let me go.

We see clearly and receive fully God's love only in the cross of Christ.

God's love is a *covenant* love. He calls us, in his gracious offer of salvation, into a *community* of love. He further joins us to his *kingdom* mission of spreading (and living) the message of his love. Thomas C. Oden has captured the centrality of divine love:

> It is impossible to speak of Christian teaching without speaking of God's love. To make clear what God's love means is the central task of Christian preaching.... The music God makes in creation is not a dirge but a love song to, for, and through creatures.[55]

With the grandeur of this vision before us, we turn now to consider the properties of God's love.

---

[52] Ibid., 110.

[53] John R. W. Stott, *The Epistles of John* (TNTC; Grand Rapids: Eerdmans, 1964), 160–61.

[54] James Montgomery Boice, *Foundations of the Christian Faith* (Downers Grove, Ill.: InterVarsity Press, 1986), 331.

[55] Oden, *The Living God*, 118.

God's Mercy, Grace, Patience, Kindness, and Faithfulness

We began our study of the divine attributes by referring to Moses' encounter with God on Mount Sinai at the renewing of the covenant (Ex. 33–34). The Lord's revelatory words to Moses became central to the faith of Israel (34:6–7; see also Num. 14:18; Neh. 9:17, 31; Pss. 86:15; 103:8; 145:8; Jer. 32:18; Joel 2:13; Jonah 4:2; Nah. 1:3; also Ex. 20:5–6; Deut. 5:9–10). We have in these words (Ex. 34:6) what Dale Moody has called "the five points of Yahwism":[56]

The LORD, the LORD,	
a God merciful	(1) *mercy*
and gracious,	(2) *grace*
slow to anger,	(3) *patience*
and abounding in steadfast love	(4) *kindness*
and faithfulness	(5) *faithfulness*

To complete the biblical teaching on the love of God, we must add God's (6) *goodness* and (7) *knowledge.*

The Bible is full of rejoicing in the *mercy* of God. "Blessed be the God and Father of our Lord Jesus Christ! By his great mercy he has given us a new birth into a living hope through the resurrection of Jesus Christ from the dead" (1 Peter 1:3). Where would we be without God's mercy? We want mercy for ourselves, but often we refuse to offer it to others. One sure sign that we have entered God's kingdom is that we begin to break free from this syndrome (Matt. 5:7, 43–48; 6:12–14; 7:1–5; Luke 6:27–36, esp. v. 36). Our hope is anchored in the mercy of God:

> But this I call to mind,
> and therefore I have hope:
> The steadfast love of the LORD never ceases,
> his mercies never come to an end;
> they are new every morning;
> great is your faithfulness.
> "The LORD is my portion," says my soul,
> "therefore I will hope in him." (Lam. 3:21–24)

The biblical writers found no difficulty in linking God's wrath with his mercy. Recall Habakkuk's prayer: "In wrath remember mercy" (Hab. 3:2 RSV). To disloyal Israel God "was merciful; he forgave their iniquities

---

[56] Moody, *The Word of Truth,* 104.

and did not destroy them. Time after time he restrained his anger and did not stir up his full wrath" (Ps. 78:38 NIV).

There can be no more poignant picture of God's mercy than the relationship between the prophet Hosea and his "wife of whoredom," Gomer (Hos. 1:2). Again, the Lord pledges his loyalty to his people: "And I will take you for my wife forever; I will take you for my wife in righteousness and in justice, in steadfast love, and in mercy. I will take you for my wife in faithfulness; and you shall know the LORD" (2:19–20). Wrath and mercy are not contradictory attributes; but mercy does "qualify" wrath, so that "it is never possible to say that God is wrath, as one may say that 'God is love.'"[57]

"Divine *mercy* is the disposition of God to relieve the miserable, salve the wounds of the hurt, and receive sinners, quite apart from any works or merit."[58] At the same time, God often calls his people to repentance. He calls them to forsake sin and to seek him (Deut. 4:29–31; Isa. 55:6, 7; Jer. 3:11–13). Micah praised God for his mercy: "Who is a God like you? . . . You do not stay angry forever but delight to show mercy" (Mic. 7:18 NIV). He was confident that the Lord knew how to restore his people. Only by God's grace and mercy are we enabled to repent. The tax collector, rather than the Pharisee, went home justified because he prayed, "God, be merciful to me, a sinner!" (Luke 18:13). Those who pray this "Sinner's Prayer" today can receive the same mercy and salvation.

> *Divine mercy is the key to a full understanding of God's plan of salvation.*

"The mercy of God is always a picture of the condition of man, on the one hand, and of the compassion of God on the other."[59] To the Ephesians, for example, Paul describes our desperately lost condition and then adds those two wonderful words "But God": "But God, who is rich in mercy, out of the great love with which he loved us even when we were dead through our trespasses, made us alive together with Christ—by grace you have been saved" (Eph. 2:4–5; see vv. 1–10). And to Titus Paul writes, "For we ourselves were once foolish, disobedient, led astray . . . despicable." But God saved us "according to his mercy" (Titus 3:3–5).

---

[57] Ibid., 105.
[58] Oden, *The Living God,* 126 (Oden's italics).
[59] Moody, *The Word of Truth,* 105.

Divine mercy is the key to a full understanding of God's plan of salvation. The apostle Paul sought to understand the role of his own people Israel in this plan—after all, as a whole they had rejected Jesus as Messiah. Had God failed to fulfill his promises? Could the church find itself in the same spiritual straits someday? Would God's plan of redemption ultimately triumph? The divinely given answers to these and other questions are given in Romans 9–11. These chapters—often debated and misunderstood—must always be taken as a unit in order to avoid the Scylla of arbitrary election on the one side and the Charybdis of universalism on the other.

Again, divine mercy is the key to correct interpretation. C. E. B. Cranfield perhaps explained it best:

> We shall misunderstand these chapters, if we fail to recognize that their key-word is "mercy." Paul is here concerned to show that the problem of Israel's unbelief, which seems to call in question the very reliability of God Himself, is connected with the nature of God's mercy as really mercy and as mercy not just for one people but for all peoples; to show that Israel's disobedience, together with the divine judgment which it merits and procures, is surrounded on all sides by the divine mercy—and at the same time to bring home to the Christian community in Rome the fact that it is by God's mercy alone that it lives.[60]

Cranfield adds that it is the church's failure to understand the message of divine mercy here in Romans that often leads to the mistaken idea that God has totally rejected Israel.[61]

The mercy of God also gives us the strength to endure (James 5:7–11; Jude 17–25). As the writer to the Hebrews exhorts:

> Since therefore we have a great high priest who has passed through the heavens, Jesus the Son of God, let us hold fast to the faith we profess. Ours is not a high priest unable to sympathize with our weaknesses, but one who has been tested in every way as we are, only without sinning. Let us therefore boldly approach the throne of grace, in order that we may receive mercy and find grace to give us timely help. (Heb. 4:14–16 REB)

It is a *throne of grace* that we approach to receive mercy. Our sovereign, holy God is also a God of grace.

---

[60] C. E. B. Cranfield, *Romans: A Shorter Commentary* (Grand Rapids: Eerdmans, 1985), 215.
[61] Ibid., 215–16.

If we were to choose *one term* to sum up the Christian gospel, the gospel of the kingdom, it is *grace.* Grace is one of the most important words in the Bible. It is a word of good news. As an attribute of God, how should grace be defined? Thomas Oden defines grace as follows:

> Grace is the favor shown by God to sinners. It is the divine goodwill offered to those who neither inherently deserve nor can ever hope to earn it. It is the divine disposition to work in our hearts, wills, and actions, so as actively to communicate God's self-giving love for humanity.[62]

The first prerequisite for understanding grace (and experiencing it) is an awareness of sin and a willingness to admit one's *need* of grace. We must acknowledge that we are spiritually bankrupt and helpless to do anything about it. Jesus congratulates those who have come to this place of felt need: "Blessed are the poor in spirit, for theirs is the kingdom of heaven" (Matt. 5:3).

If we were to choose one term *to sum up the Christian gospel, the gospel of the kingdom, it is* grace.

"Grace is an overarching term for all of God's gifts to humanity, all the blessings of salvation, all events through which are manifested God's own self-giving."[63] Grace is God's *stooping* down in lowly service to his fallen creatures.[64] "Grace is God's way of empowering the bound will and healing the suffering spirit."[65] It is a one-word definition of salvation.[66]

We have already encountered the grace of God in numerous biblical passages previously cited. It is an attribute found in both Old and New Testaments. The Hebrew noun *chen* means grace or favor. But the key Old Testament terms are the adjective "gracious" (*channun*) and the verb "to be gracious" (*chanan*). In our programmatic passage for this section (Ex. 34:6), the Lord announces he is gracious. Usually, the word is also linked with the phrase "full of compassion" (see Pss. 111:4; 112:4; 145:8). Jonah was angry when Nineveh repented. He admits to God, "I

---

[62] Thomas C. Oden, *The Transforming Power of Grace* (Nashville: Abingdon, 1993), 33, 206.
[63] Ibid., 33.
[64] Henry, *God, Revelation and Authority*, 4:15.
[65] Oden, *The Transforming Power of Grace*, 15.
[66] I started to name the last three chapters of this volume Grace, Kingdom, and Church, rather than Faith, Hope, and Love, because the former terms more precisely designate the contents of those chapters. (The Grace/Faith chapter deals with the doctrine of salvation.) Nonetheless, I stayed with the Pauline trilogy of faith, hope, and love because of their familiarity and obvious relationship.

knew that you are a gracious God and merciful, slow to anger, and abounding in steadfast love, and ready to relent from punishing" (Jonah 4:2). Notice the contrast between Jonah's anger (4:1, 9) and God's compassion (4:9–11). The Lord "waits to be gracious" (*chanan*) to us (Isa. 30:18)!

The New Testament word for grace is *charis.* Jesus Christ, the Incarnate Word, is described by John as "full of grace and truth" (John 1:14). "From his fullness we have all received, grace upon grace. The law indeed was given through Moses; grace and truth came through Jesus Christ" (1:16–17). Paul admonished those who turned from faith in Christ back to legalism (requiring circumcision): "You who want to be justified by the law have cut yourselves off from Christ; you have fallen away from grace" (Gal. 5:4). Paul knew all too well the bondage of trying to achieve salvation by observance of the law. Through his life-transforming encounter with Christ, Paul became the grace theologian *par excellence* of the New Testament. In fact, it can be argued that "Paul was the first and greatest Christian theologian."[67] James D. G. Dunn's classic presentation of Paul's theology summarizes best Paul's distinctive contribution:

> Among the most innovative features which shaped Christian theology for all time are the key terms which Paul introduced. Above all we should think of "gospel," "grace," and "love"—gospel as the good news of Christ focusing in his death and resurrection, grace as epitomizing the character of God's dealings with humankind, love as the motive of divine giving and in turn the motive for human living. Between them, in their specialist Christian usage, these words sum up and define the scope and character of Christianity as no other three words can. And that specialist Christian usage, in each case, we owe entirely to Paul.[68]

Paul's *experience* of grace determined in large measure his *doctrine* of grace. For the apostle, grace was God's saving *action.* The words "grace," "Spirit," and "power" (esp. "grace" and "Spirit," which can be virtually interchanged in many Pauline passages without altering their meaning) are closely aligned. "For Paul grace means *power,* an otherly power at work in and through the believer's life, the *experience* of God's Spirit."[69] Grace is seen, in Paul's letters, as God's dynamic action. The believer's

---

[67] James D. G. Dunn, *The Theology of Paul the Apostle* (Grand Rapids: Eerdmans, 1998), 2.
[68] Ibid., 733.
[69] James D. G. Dunn, *Jesus and the Spirit* (London: SCM, 1975), 202–4 (Dunn's italics).

entire life becomes an expression of God's grace. "Grace gives the believer's life its source, its power and its direction. All is of grace and grace is all."[70]

In Paul's explanation of "the gospel of God" (Rom. 1:1), we are "justified by his [God's] grace as a gift, through the redemption that is in Christ Jesus, whom God put forward as a sacrifice of atonement by his blood, effective through faith" (3:24–25). The cross was the means of God's grace to us all. It is through our Lord Jesus Christ that we have "access to this grace" (5:2). The grace of God and "the grace of the one man, Jesus Christ" (5:15) triumphed immeasurably over the sin and judgment introduced into the race through Adam (5:12–21). Our salvation is by sheer grace—a gift from God (Eph. 2:8–9). It is the result of the gracious action of our Triune God through which we are justified, reborn, and given eternal hope (Titus 3:4–7).

Largely through a rediscovery of Paul's testimony to the grace of God, Luther was reborn and launched (almost inadvertently) the Protestant Reformation.

This glorious gospel had almost been eclipsed by human traditions and legalistic "salvation" in Martin Luther's day. Then, largely through a rediscovery of Paul's testimony to the grace of God, Luther was reborn and launched (almost inadvertently) the Protestant Reformation. Dorothy and Gabriel Fackre describe well this event:

> Luther was overwhelmed by this Good News: God accepts the unacceptable! God loves the unlovely! Those pointing fingers of Christ that he saw as he looked up were *really* outstretched hands at the end of open arms, reaching to lift us up. Christ so welcomes us with infinite tenderness. The hard Work done on Calvary is all there, right now, for us. All we have to do is accept it in trust. And so we are declared righteous before God—justified by grace through faith. What a different view of things! It changed the church, re-forming its ranks. So came the Reformation, with its accent on salvation by grace through faith, and "evangelical" Christianity.[71]

---

[70] Ibid., 205. Dunn's treatment of Paul's doctrine of grace in this volume is nothing short of masterful.

[71] Dorothy and Gabriel Fackre, *Christian Basics: A Primer for Pilgrims* (Grand Rapids: Eerdmans, 1991), 93–94 (Fackre's italics).

Each new generation must, so to speak, rediscover the grace of God. Indeed, the entire pilgrimage of the believer is a continual discovery of God's grace. Even evangelicals need to be reoriented from time to time. Philip Yancey, Scott Hoezee, Chuck Swindoll, and Jerry Bridges have provided the evangelical community—and all Christians, for that matter—with life-transforming treatments of the liberating truth of the grace of God to help us in that process.[72] Ours truly is "the good news of God's grace" (Acts 20:24)!

Paul's testimony to Timothy was that "the grace of our Lord overflowed for me with the faith and love that are in Christ Jesus" (1 Tim. 1:14). He continues:

> The saying is sure and worthy of full acceptance, that Christ Jesus came into the world to save sinners—of whom I am the foremost [Grace!]. But for that very reason I received mercy, so that in me, as the foremost, Jesus Christ might display the utmost patience, making me an example to those who would come to believe in him for eternal life. To the King of the ages, immortal, invisible, the only God, be honor and glory forever and ever. Amen. (1:15–17)

It is to this "utmost patience" that we will shortly turn our attention.

Paul reminded the Corinthians: "For you know the grace of our Lord Jesus Christ, that though he was rich, yet for your sakes he became poor, so that you through his poverty might become rich" (2 Cor. 8:9 NIV). The Incarnation, what C. S. Lewis calls "the Grand Miracle," is the greatest expression of the grace of God:

> In the Christian story God descends to re-ascend. He comes down; down from the heights of absolute being into time and space, down into humanity . . . He had created. But He goes down to come up again and bring the whole ruined world up with Him. One has the picture of a strong man stooping lower and lower to get himself underneath some great complicated burden. He must stoop in order to lift, he must almost disappear under the load before he incredibly straightens his back and marches off with the whole mass swaying on his shoulders. Or one may think of a diver, first reducing himself to nakedness, then glancing in mid-air, then gone with a splash, vanished, rushing down through green and warm water into black and cold water, down through

---

[72] Philip Yancey, *What's So Amazing About Grace?* (Grand Rapids: Zondervan, 1997); Scott Hoezee, *The Riddle of Grace* (Grand Rapids: Eerdmans, 1996); Charles R. Swindoll, *The Grace Awakening* (Dallas: Word, 1990); Jerry Bridges, *Transforming Grace* (Colorado Springs, Colo.: NavPress, 1991).

> increasing pressure into the deathlike region of ooze and slime and old decay; then up again, back to colour and light, his lungs almost bursting, till suddenly he breaks surface again, holding in his hand the dripping, precious thing that he went down to recover. He and it are both coloured now that they have come up into the light: down below, where it lay colourless in the dark, he lost his colour too.[73]

If in his grace God stoops to rescue us from our sin and its consequences, in his *patience* he waits untiringly for us to accept his grace. Millard Erickson rightly calls this attribute the *persistence* of God.[74]

God lovingly gives us "space" and time to respond to his gracious offer of redemption and fellowship. He refuses to coerce us to accept his gift of righteousness. Rather, he "woos" us to himself. Even though we deserve divine judgment, God restrains his power to pass sentence on us.[75] He is "slow to anger" (Ex. 34:6).[76] The key New Testament term for God's patience *(makrothymia)* means literally "long-tempered," which can legitimately be contrasted with our English concept of being short-tempered.[77] God is patient with us because he wants to save us. "Bear in mind that our Lord's patience is an opportunity for salvation, as Paul, our dear friend and brother, said when he wrote to you with the wisdom God gave him" (2 Peter 3:15 REB). He was patient in Noah's day (1 Peter 3:20), and he has delayed final judgment until now, "not wanting any to perish, but all to come to repentance" (2 Peter 3:9).[78]

If in his grace God stoops to rescue us from our sin and its consequences, in his patience *he waits untiringly for us to accept his grace.*

Paul echoes this same theme. In the past, God, in his forbearance (*anoche*), passed over people's sins (Rom. 3:25; see also Acts 14:16), but now in view of the atonement of Christ that same forbearance is also a call to repentance (Rom. 2:4, which refers to God's patience and kindness as well; cf. Acts 17:30). God "has endured with much patience" (Rom. 9:22) Israel's unbelief, but there is still hope (ch. 11). Paul also refers indirectly to God's patience (1) when he describes *agape* (1 Cor.

---

[73] C. S. Lewis, *Miracles: A Preliminary Study* (New York: Macmillan, 1947), 115–16.

[74] Erickson, *Christian Theology*, 296–97.

[75] See Moody, *The Word of Truth*, 107.

[76] Cf. Num. 14:18; Neh. 9:17; Pss. 86:15; 103:8; 145:8; Joel 2:13; Jonah 4:2; Nah. 1:3.

[77] William Barclay, *Flesh and Spirit* (Nashville: Abingdon, 1962), 91.

[78] The verb "to be patient or long-suffering" (*makrothymeo*) is used in this verse.

13:4) as a love that "is patient" (*makrothymeo*) and (2) when he lists patience as an aspect of the fruit of the Spirit (Gal. 5:22).

Emil Brunner aptly observes that God's patience has made human history possible. God had every right to end the human story at any time from the Fall onward. Instead God mercifully "gives this breathing-space to the human race" as an opportunity for repentance and redemption.[79]

Dale Moody sees the attribute of divine patience as the basis for belief in the *passibility* of God, that is, that God is able to suffer with his creation.[80] Though this particular attribute may not be the actual basis for belief in a suffering God, it is at least one aspect of such a foundation. Traditionally, many theologians have argued for divine *im*passibility to guard the doctrine of God's constancy. But surely God, out of the fullness of his being as perfect love, is able to enter vicariously into the sufferings of his creation. Does not his being personal and relational imply this truth? Does not love itself require it? Surely the Incarnation implies in part that God can so enter into the human experience![81] The God revealed in the writings of the Old Testament prophets virtually explodes with divine passion. Philip Yancey has highlighted this phenomenon: "Hosea is one of the most emotional books in the Bible, an outpouring of suffering love from God's heart."[82] The doctrine of the impassibility of God as traditionally understood must be seen as an accretion from philosophy, not a teaching of holy Scripture.

The fourth property of God's love is his *kindness*. Returning to Exodus 34:6, we read that the Lord abounds "in steadfast love." The Hebrew word translated "steadfast love" is *chesed*, one of the most important words of the Old Testament. Various translations have been used: lovingkindness, covenant love, steadfast love, or even simply, love. Each of these terms has merit. The word *chesed* communicates God's love, and that love is a steadfast, enduring, and faithful love. It is a love characterized by kindness. Most important, it is a covenantal love. God establishes and keeps covenant with his people.

When God gave the Ten Commandments at Sinai, he forbade idolatry and described himself as "showing steadfast love [*chesed*] to the thousandth generation of those who love me and keep my commandments" (Ex. 20:6; Deut. 5:10; cf. Deut. 7:9). Psalm 136 celebrates the lovingkindness of the

---

[79] Brunner, *The Christian Doctrine of God*, 274–75.

[80] Moody, *The Word of Truth*, 108.

[81] See Garrett, *Systematic Theology I*, 249–51; Moltmann, *The Crucified God*, 230; H. P. Owen, *Concepts of Deity* (New York: Herder & Herder, 1971), 23–25, 145–46.

[82] Philip Yancey, *A Guided Tour of the Bible* (Grand Rapids: Zondervan, 1989), 138.

Lord, which "endures forever." God's lovingkindness truly is "better than life" (Ps. 63:3).

The New Testament word that corresponds with *chesed* is *chrestos*, kindness. We have already seen that God's kindness is meant to bring us to repentance (Rom. 2:4). Peter states that every authentic believer has "tasted" the kindness of the Lord (1 Peter 2:3). Paul puts divine kindness in an eternal perspective ("in the ages to come") in Ephesians 2:7. In his teaching on the law of love and the Golden Rule, Jesus says that "the Most High ... is kind to the ungrateful and the wicked" (Luke 6:35). Finally, Paul refers to the appearance of the "loving kindness [*philanthropia*] of God our Savior" (Titus 3:4). God's holy constancy and his lovingkindness are, in the final analysis, twins.

Next we read of God's *faithfulness* (Ex. 34:6). Just as Hosea remained faithful to Gomer, so the Lord promises redemptive love as a faithful spouse: "I will take you for my wife in faithfulness [*ʾemunah*]" (Hos. 2:20). "It is God himself who called you to share in the life of his Son Jesus Christ our Lord," Paul assures the Corinthians, "and God keeps faith" (1 Cor. 1:9 REB).[83] Furthermore, he assures them that God, in his faithfulness, will not allow them to be tested beyond their strength (10:13). Again and again the Scriptures attest to God's faithfulness.

God's Goodness and Knowledge

I experienced a theological revolution as a junior high student when I read the words of an Oklahoma healing evangelist by the name of Oral Roberts. It was a simple yet life-transforming sentence of merely five words: *God is a good God.* I wanted desperately to believe those words. However, I had developed a concept of God that, upon later reflection, I realized was somewhat vindictive. For example, every time I had a bad basketball game, I thought God was punishing me for my sins. From this perspective, God was not even as good as most of the deacons at the church—and my dad was chairman of the deacons!

Actually, Oral Roberts was highlighting one of the most important teachings about God in the entire Bible. The *goodness* of God, as we will see, encompasses all the other attributes of God. God truly is a good God!

Moses prayed, "Show me your glory," and the Lord responded, "I will make all my goodness pass before you" (Ex. 33:18–19). Carl F. H. Henry writes:

---

[83] "God keeps faith" is literally, "God is faithful."

> Two New Testament texts provide a useful introduction to the goodness of God; in one Jesus affirms that "no one is good but God only" (Mark 10:18), in the other Paul affirms of mankind that "there is none good, no not one" (Rom. 3:12; cf. Ps. 14:1, 3). What is this *agathos* that characterizes the living God, this *chrēstotēs* that man as sinner fails to reflect in thought, word or deed?[84]

To these two Greek words for goodness should be added the Hebrew term *tob.* "O taste and see that the Lord is good; happy are those who take refuge in him" (Ps. 34:8). The prophet Nahum praises both God's wrath and goodness: "The LORD is . . . wrathful. . . . The LORD is slow to anger but great in power. . . . The LORD is good, a stronghold in a day of trouble" (Nah. 1:2–3, 7). But what precisely is the goodness of God?

The goodness of God is the benevolence of God. Charles Hodge describes it as "the disposition to promote happiness."[85] Karl Barth adds: "We understand by goodness the sum of all that is right and friendly and wholesome: the three taken together."[86] James I. Packer sees God's goodness as his generosity:

> Generosity expresses the simple wish that others should have what they need to make them happy. Generosity is, so to speak, the focal point of God's moral perfection; it is the quality which determines how all God's other excellences are to be displayed.[87]

If God were presented more in these terms today, many more would desire to know him! The good God of biblical revelation is neither a "Sugar Daddy" nor an austere, aloof judge. He is generous beyond our comprehension. He is a loving Father who delights to bless his creatures. Jesus taught: "If you then, who are evil, know how to give good gifts to your children, how much more will your Father in heaven give good things to those who ask him!" (Matt. 7:11). His brother James wrote: "Every generous act of giving, with every perfect gift, is from

---

84 Henry, *God, Revelation and Authority,* 4:251.

85 Charles Hodge, *Systematic Theology,* 1:427; cited in Jack Cottrell, *What the Bible Says about God the Ruler* (Joplin, Mo.: College Press, 1984), 290. This is volume two of a three-volume work that in many ways is the most thorough and satisfying treatment of the doctrine of God to appear in recent years. Cottrell interacts broadly with theological scholarship and provides a rich analysis of the relevant biblical texts throughout his presentation. See also *What the Bible Says about God the Creator* (1983) and *What the Bible Says about God the Redeemer* (1987), both published by College Press of Joplin, Mo.

86 Karl Barth, *Church Dogmatics* (London: T. & T. Clark, 1936), II/2, 708; cited in Moody, *The Word of Truth,* 111.

87 J. I. Packer, *Knowing God* (Downers Grove, Ill.: InterVarsity Press, 1973), 146–47.

above, coming down from the Father of lights, with whom there is no variation or shadow due to change" (James 1:17). (Notice how closely related are the Fatherhood of God and the goodness of God.)

Perhaps the most majestic presentation of divine goodness comes from the seventeenth century. Stephen Charnock's classic, *The Existence and Attributes of God,* contains a discourse on the goodness of God of some 147 pages! Charnock defines God's goodness as his bounty. He asserts that this attribute comprehends all the divine attributes.[88] Even after three centuries, Charnock's words enable us to enter into the beauty of this doctrine:

> This is the most pleasant perfection of the Divine nature; his creating power amazes us; his conducting wisdom astonisheth us; his goodness, as furnishing us with all conveniences, delights us; and renders both his amazing power, and astonishing wisdom, delightful to us. As the sun, by effecting things, is an emblem of God's power; by discovering things to us, is an emblem of his wisdom; but by refreshing and comforting us, is an emblem of his goodness; and without this refreshing virtue it communicates to us, we should take no pleasure in the creatures it produceth, nor in the beauties it discovers. As God is great and powerful, he is the object of our understanding; but as good and bountiful, he is the object of our love and desire.[89]

Charnock's imagery reminds us that God manifests his goodness both through and toward the natural order.

Psalm 145 is one of the greatest psalms that celebrate the goodness of God. David extols the King and blesses his name (v. 1). He speaks of God's mighty works being praised from one generation to the next (v. 4). He continues:

> They shall celebrate the fame of your abundant goodness,
> and shall sing aloud of your righteousness. . . .
> The LORD is good to all,
> and his compassion is over all that he has made.
> All your works shall give thanks to you, O LORD,
> and all your faithful shall bless you.
> They shall speak of the glory of your kingdom,
> and tell of your power. . . .

---

[88] Charnock, *The Existence and Attributes of God,* 2 vols. (repr. Grand Rapids: Baker, 1979), 2:218–19.

[89] Ibid., 2:219.

The eyes of all look to you,
    and you give them their food in due season.
You open your hand,
    satisfying the desire of every living thing.
        (Ps. 145:7, 9–11, 15–16)

Commenting on these verses, J. I. Packer states:

> The psalmist's point is that, since God controls all that happens in His world, every meal, every pleasure, every possession, every bit of sun, every night's sleep, every moment of health and safety, everything else that sustains and enriches life, is a divine gift. And how abundant these gifts are![90]

And Charnock observes:

> All things are not only before his eyes, but in his bosom. . . . The whole world swims in the rich bounty of the Creator, as the fish do in the largeness of the sea, and birds in the spaciousness of the air. The goodness of God is the river that waters the whole earth.[91]

Indeed, the river is an excellent metaphor for divine goodness!

Author Norman Maclean was raised in the same Presbyterian tradition as Charnock and Packer. Maclean's father, a Presbyterian minister, deeply appreciated the goodness of God in nature—a reality that apparently could be best entered into fly-fishing! Norman Maclean recalls how he spent his Sunday afternoons. After his brother, Paul, and he had spent an hour in the study of The Westminster Shorter Catechism, they would walk the hills near their western Montana home with their father as he sought restoration between the morning and evening services. He always asked them the first question of the catechism, and they would dutifully reply: "Man's chief end is to glorify God, and to enjoy him forever."[92]

The brothers and their father spent many hours fly-fishing together in the beautiful trout rivers of that majestic region. The father gave them as much instruction in the art of fly-fishing as he did in religion. Once while they were fishing, Norman noticed that his father was reading John 1 about the Word. Asked what he was reading, his father replied, "I used to think water was first, but if you listen carefully you

---

90 Packer, *Knowing God,* 147.
91 Charnock, *The Existence and Attributes of God,* 2:296.
92 Norman Maclean, *A River Runs Through It* (Chicago: Univ. of Chicago Press, 1976), 1.

will hear that the words are underneath the water.... The water runs over the words."[93]

On the final page of his story Maclean writes: "Eventually, all things merge into one, and a river runs through it."[94] In view of the goodness and beauty of God that permeates Maclean's land and lore, I choose to interpret that river as the goodness of God. Both the movie and the book powerfully communicate the goodness of God as seen in the awesome beauty of nature, the simple dignity of human beings, made in God's image, and the enduring truths of the Christian religion. Unmistakably, God's goodness and God's glory cover the earth.[95]

Time and again, as we study the divine attributes, we are reminded that God is a *personal* God. Nowhere is this fact more important than when we consider the *knowledge* of God. God, according to Scripture and classical theism, is *omniscient*, all-knowing. It is always tempting to revert to impersonal concepts whenever we consider anything related to the infinity of God. We pervert omnipresence into pantheism; omnipotence becomes a pan-causalism, a sort of theistic determinism. The pantheistic error compromises *God's* personal nature, while determinism compromises *our* personhood. In both distortions the personal relationship God desires us to have with him is diminished.

> *It is always tempting to revert to impersonal concepts whenever we consider anything related to the infinity of God.*

Therefore, the first thing to be said is that God's knowledge is a *personal* knowledge. As Brunner expresses it: "His knowledge is not that of a record office, but it is the knowledge of Him who wills to glorify Himself in this Creation, and to have fellowship with it."[96] There is a decisive difference between a cosmic computer and a heavenly Father!

Psalm 139 provides a classic statement of God's personal, infinite, and loving knowledge of his creation:

---

93 Ibid., 95–96.

94 Ibid., 104.

95 I will leave open the question of which worldview (monistic, dualistic, or theistic) is reflected in Maclean's words "all things merge into one." We will deal with worldviews in part in the next chapter.

96 Brunner, *The Christian Doctrine of God*, 265.

> Lord, you have examined me
> and know all about me [NRSV: "have searched me
> and known me"]. . . .
> You know my thoughts before I think them. . . .
> You know thoroughly everything I do.
> Lord, even before I say a word,
> you already know it. . . .
> Your knowledge is amazing to me;
> it is more than I can understand. (139:1–4, 6 NCV).

David then describes the omnipresence of God in verses 7–12. He follows this with a moving description of God's creation of David in his mother's womb (vv. 13–18): "You knit me together in my mother's womb" (v. 13). He goes one step further and refers to God's *fore*knowledge of David's life: "In your book were written all the days that were formed for me, when none of them as yet existed" (v. 16).

With these verses, another dimension of God's knowledge begins to emerge: His knowledge is a *loving* knowledge. As Dale Moody states: "God's knowing is God's loving."[97] Moody points out that in biblical thought "knowing" had the background of the sexual relation between a man and a woman. Adam "knew" his wife, and the Virgin Mary "knew not" a man (Gen. 4:1, 25; Luke 1:34 KJV). The Lord's words to Israel were: "You only have I known of all the families of the earth" (Amos 3:2). Moody remarks: "The Lord, of course, was not ignorant of other families in the sense of omniscience, but knowledge is a covenant relation of love and loyalty."[98]

Jesus often alluded to this kind of divine knowledge: (1) "Your Father knows what you need before you ask him" (Matt. 6:8); (2) "Indeed your heavenly Father knows that you need all these things [food, drink, and clothes]" (6:32); (3) "And even the hairs of your head are all counted" (10:30). Paul wrote to the Corinthians: "But anyone who loves God is known by him" (1 Cor. 8:3). Real knowledge of God is evidenced by love. We can have exalted spiritual revelations and our intellects can be crammed with the thoughts of the greatest theologians past and present, and yet we may not really know (= love) God. God doesn't merely know *about* us; he *knows* us. He wants us not to merely know about him, but to know him.

---

[97] Moody, *The Word of Truth,* 111.
[98] Ibid., 112.

Psalm 147 weaves together many of God's attributes:

He heals the brokenhearted,
    and binds up their wounds.
He determines the number of the stars;
    he gives to all of them their names.
Great is our Lord, and abundant in power;
    his understanding is beyond measure. (147:3–5)

The God of infinite knowledge ("his understanding is beyond measure") and power is also a gracious God (147:1), who "lifts up the downtrodden" (v. 6), sustains the life of the planet (vv. 7–11), and cares for his people (vv. 12–14). Truly God's knowledge is a loving knowledge.

God knows every person personally, lovingly, and exhaustively: "And before him no creature is hidden, but all are naked and laid bare to the eyes of the one to whom we must render an account" (Heb. 4:13). He knows our past, present, and future. He foreknows everything that is going to take place. The atoning death of Jesus transpired "according to the definite plan and foreknowledge of God" (Acts 2:23). Those whom God "foreknew he also predestined" for salvation (Rom. 8:29).[99] God can foreknow our decisions without determining them. As we will see later, there are some things that God desires and God determines, other things that God desires and we determine, and finally things that we desire and God permits.[100]

> *Real knowledge of God is evidenced by love.*

Here are two notions that, in my opinion, are simply the result of muddled thinking: (1) that God must determine everything in order to be truly sovereign, and (2) that his foreknowledge of our decisions determines them. Through his *infinite* knowledge and power God can be in complete control of everything and still give us authentic freedom of choice. He is also able through his infinite knowledge and his transcendence of time to know the contingencies of the future as *contingencies* and to foreknow our free choices.[101] Of course, only his grace can enable our decision to receive his offer of forgiveness and salvation. But there is still a divine-human reciprocity: He does not coerce this decision, and it is an authentic choice.[102] God will not violate our personhood. By far,

---

[99] We will consider this much-debated doctrinal issue later.

[100] Cottrell, *What the Bible Says about God the Ruler*, 299–329 (again, more on this later).

[101] See Brunner, *The Christian Doctrine of God*, 262.

[102] I first heard Oral Roberts use the phrase, "divine-human reciprocity." I have found it to be very useful in a number of areas.

the most satisfying treatment of divine omniscience and foreknowledge that I have found has been that of Thomas C. Oden.[103]

Open theism challenges these notions about God's knowledge. Beginning with a new metaphysic—that the future must be open for there to be authentic freedom within the creation—open theists argue that God has chosen to limit his knowledge of the future so that we can have authentic choice. Immediately, we see that the extremes of both Calvinism and Arminianism are based on the same fallacy, namely, that foreknowledge requires foreordination.

Extreme Calvinism argues that God knows the future perfectly because, and only because, he has predetermined it. By contrast, open theism, an extreme form of Arminianism, maintains that God does *not* know the future perfectly precisely because it is not predetermined. The premise is exactly the same: God's perfect knowledge of the future requires his predetermining the future. It is a false premise, and St. Augustine himself addressed it centuries ago:

> The conclusion is that we are by no means under compulsion to abandon free choice in favor of divine knowledge, nor need we deny—God forbid!—that God knows the future, as a condition for holding free choice (*City of God*, 5.10).[104]

The theological and pastoral results of open theism are devastating. The entire construct flies in the face of the sovereign workings of God throughout the Scriptures and throughout history. It robs the Christian of confidence and security. Why would we want to entrust our lives to a God whose counsel cannot be trusted, since he often second guesses even himself?[105]

The Triunity of God

Having considered God's essential nature and having surveyed the majestic attributes of God, we have yet to give full attention to the most

---

103 Oden, *The Living God*, 69–74. For a balanced treatment of grace, foreknowledge, election, predestination, and related matters see Oden's *The Transforming Power of Grace.*

104 Cited in Norman Geisler, *Chosen But Free* (Minneapolis: Bethany, 1999), 165.

105 One way to access the debate is to compare Gregory A. Boyd's *God of the Possible: A Biblical Introduction to the Open View of God* (Grand Rapid: Baker, 2000) with Bruce A. Ware's *God's Lesser Glory: The Diminished God of Open Theism* (Wheaton, Ill.: Crossway, 2000). Ware's volume, in my view, provides the soundest perspective; it is truly an edifying volume. Millard J. Erickson's *What Does God Know and When Does He Know It?* (Grand Rapids: Zondervan, 2003) is arguably the fairest and most comprehensive analysis of the entire open theism debate to date.

important thing that Christians believe about God. Biblical revelation points to a foundational truth about God that sets Christianity apart from all other religions. It is a mystery, to be sure—but it is a mystery not of darkness but of *light.* I am speaking of the triunity of God: the Holy Trinity.

Growing up in the Baptist church, I heard pastors countless times repeat these words (or something similar) in the church baptistry just prior to baptizing someone, and I have used this formula myself many times since: *In obedience to the command of our Lord and Savior, Jesus Christ, and upon your public profession of faith in him, I baptize you now, my sister, in the name of the Father, and of the Son, and of the Holy Spirit. Amen.* The command referred to is, of course, the Great Commission (Matt. 28:18–20).

Christian worship services are often concluded with Paul's majestic benediction: "May the grace of the Lord Jesus Christ, and the love of God, and the fellowship of the Holy Spirit be with you all" (2 Cor. 13:14 NIV).

We sing to God: "Holy, holy, holy, merciful and mighty! God in three Persons, blessed Trinity." We confess our faith: "I believe in God the Father Almighty . . . and in Jesus Christ his only Son our Lord . . . I believe in the Holy Spirit. . . . " We pray (1) in the Spirit, (2) through the Son, and (3) to the Father (see Eph. 2:18). An ancient Christian doxology still in use today, the *Gloria Patri,* reads: "Glory be to the Father, and to the Son, and to the Holy Ghost: as it was in the beginning, is now and ever shall be, world without end. Amen."

> *The doctrine of the Trinity is a* practical *teaching with far-reaching implications.*

Clearly the Christian faith is a Trinitarian faith. "Everything the whole of Christian theology has to say about God and man and the world is nothing but an attempt to understand what it means to believe in God the Father, Son and Holy Spirit."[106] As difficult as this is to accept intellectually, the doctrine of the Trinity is a *practical* teaching with far-reaching implications. Because what we believe always determines how we behave, whether we affirm and fully appreciate this truth about God becomes crucial to our faith and life.

When he was dying of tuberculosis, Oral Roberts was told that God had put the debilitating disease on him. He was also told that Jesus loved him. The teen-aged Roberts grew to hate God and to love Jesus.

---

[106] Shirley C. Guthrie Jr., *Christian Doctrine* (Atlanta: John Knox, 1968), 89–90.

Through his miraculous healing and subsequent study of the Bible, he came to appreciate the infinite love of our Triune God. Many people today have a distorted view of the atonement along these same lines: "God is mad at us and wants to get us, but Jesus loves us and keeps him from it." The doctrine of the Trinity explodes this popular myth by demonstrating the unity of the loving Godhead in the saving events of Calvary.

> *In actuality, belief in the Trinity sprang from the* experience *of God's people.*

Many people hold to a sort of "swing shift" Trinity. First, the Father created, then the Son came to save us, and finally the Spirit came and now stays here with us. God is a heavenly committee of finite beings—like three peas in a pod. This heresy, albeit seemingly unintentional and benign, is in effect a reversion to a polytheism in which the gods come and go at will. It rightly discerns the flow of redemptive history, but it loses sight of the unity of the Godhead. It is valid to affirm the threeness of God as long as we do not compromise his unity.

In actuality, belief in the Trinity sprang from the *experience* of God's people. The first disciples believed as all Jews confessed: "Hear, O Israel: The LORD our God, the LORD is one" (Deut. 6:4 NIV). Jesus himself affirmed this belief (Mark 12:29). However, after the resurrection of Christ especially, the early disciples began to fully appreciate the divinity of Christ. Also, the gift of the Holy Spirit, for which Jesus himself had prepared them, contributed to their Trinitarian understanding of God. Perhaps it was the gift of the Holy Spirit more than anything else that sealed this doctrine in their hearts and minds.

Two charismatic utterances, as it were, issue from the heart of every true believer in Christ: (1) "Jesus is Lord" (1 Cor. 12:3) and (2) "Abba! Father!" (Rom. 8:15–17; Gal. 4:6–7). Both utterances, according to Scripture, are prompted by the Holy Spirit. Thus, the Christian stands at the base of a Trinitarian triangle—indwelled by the Spirit and looking heavenward, with one hand extended to God the Father and the other to Jesus the Lord.[107] At the same time it must be quickly added that, according to the Johannine testimony, the coming of the Paraclete (the Spirit) means that both Jesus and the Father have come to make their home in our hearts as well (John 14:15–24, esp. v. 23).

---

[107] Dunn, *Jesus and the Spirit,* 326.

The evangelical testimony to the saving grace of God is patently Trinitarian. The church proclaims the evangel, or good news, of the kingdom of God. In "receiving Christ" new believers, through the work of the Spirit, experience Jesus as Lord and God (see John 20:28) and God as Father. Our water baptism, "in the name of the Father and of the Son and of the Holy Spirit," is further testimony to our Trinitarian experience. We are members now of the "household of God" (Eph. 2:19), the church—on mission to spread the good news of the kingdom across the globe. The Spirit himself, as the very life-breath and Lord of the church, leads and empowers that mission.

The Doctrine of the Trinity in Biblical, Historical, and Contemporary Theology

The actual doctrine of the Trinity, including the term itself, developed during the patristic era (the first five centuries of the church), primarily in response to heresies that threatened to distort the gospel and teachings of Scripture. Though the biblical ingredients were already established, the early fathers and councils were forced to carefully formulate this doctrine in order to guard against distortions of the biblical revelation.

Geoffrey W. Bromiley provides these helpful comments regarding the Trinity:

> Although not itself a biblical term, "the Trinity" has been found a convenient designation for the one God self-revealed in Scripture as Father, Son, and Holy Spirit. It signifies that within the one essence of the Godhead we have to distinguish three "persons" who are neither three gods on the one side, nor three parts or modes of God on the other, but coequally and coeternally God.[108]

With this definition before us, let us survey quickly the biblical materials on which this doctrine is based.

The primary contribution of the Old Testament, not surprisingly, is the emphasis on the *unity* of God (Deut. 6:4). Both Judaism and Christianity are monotheistic faiths. The Lord will not tolerate any other "gods" (Ex. 20:3–5). Christianity is monotheistic, but not unitarian. It is

---

[108] G. W. Bromiley, "Trinity," in *Evangelical Dictionary of Theology*, ed. Walter A. Elwell (Grand Rapids: Baker, 1984), 1112.

Trinitarian, but not tritheistic. It is as important to believe in the unity of God (contrary to much popular piety) as it is to believe in the triunity of God (contrary to much contemporary theology). Biblical monotheism is a major contribution of the faith of Israel to the Christian faith.

However, there are other Old Testament "preparations" for the doctrine of the Trinity, even with regard to the threeness of God. The very first verse of the Bible reads, "In the beginning God created the heavens and the earth" (Gen. 1:1 RSV). The word for God in this verse is *Elohim*— which is *plural* and is linked with a *singular* verb. Some have tried to explain this phenomenon as a "plural of majesty." However, it is doubtful that the Hebrew language has such a construct. Could this be a foreshadowing of the plurality of the Godhead? Many exegetes, both ancient and modern, have believed so.

> *Christianity is monotheistic, but not unitarian. It is Trinitarian, but not tritheistic.*

The second half of the next verse reads: "and the Spirit of God was moving over the face of the waters" (Gen. 1:2 RSV). Here *God* and the *Spirit of God* are distinguished. The Spirit of God is mentioned often throughout the Old Testament (e.g., Ex. 31:3; 35:31; Num. 11:24–26; 1 Sam. 16:13–15; Job 33:4; Ps. 104:30; Isa. 11:2). Thus, the groundwork was being laid for a full-orbed doctrine of the Spirit as a coequal member of the Godhead, a doctrine that awaited the completion of the New Testament.

Genesis 1:3 begins: "Then God said. . . . " The *Word of God* is alluded to here: "By the word of the LORD the heavens were made, and all their host by the breath of his mouth" (Ps. 33:6). John wrote, "In the beginning was the Word. . . . All things were made through him" (John 1:1, 3 RSV). Thus, the first three verses of the Bible refer to God, the Spirit of God, and the Word of God. The *Wisdom of God* is closely aligned with God in the Old Testament as well. For example, in relation to creation, the Wisdom of God is seen "at the beginning" with God (Prov. 8:22–31). The concepts of both the Word of God and the Wisdom of God were preparatory for the New Testament doctrine of the person of Christ.

Another Old Testament preparation for the doctrine of the Trinity also appears in Genesis 1: "Then God said, 'Let us make humankind in our image, according to our likeness'" (Gen. 1:26; cf. 3:22; 11:7; Isa. 6:8). To whom does the word "us" refer in these passages? Certainly the heavenly King could be addressing his court. But, again, could this also be an allusion to plurality within the Godhead?

The *angel of the Lord* is another preparation for the triune concept of God. The references are numerous and the stories intriguing (e.g., Gen. 16:7; 21:17; 24:7, 40; Ex. 14:19; 23:20; 33:2; Num. 20:16; 22:21–35; 1 Sam. 29:9; 2 Sam. 14:20; 19:27). What about the heavenly messengers of Genesis 18 and 19? The Lord himself seems to be tangibly present in these narratives concerning Abraham and Lot.

Two fascinating Old Testament passages have attracted special attention down the centuries for their Trinitarian patterns: Isaiah 48:16 and Haggai 2:1–7. Isaiah 48:16 reads: "'Come near me and listen to this: From the first announcement I have not spoken in secret; at the time it happens, I am there.' And now the Sovereign LORD has sent me, with his Spirit" (NIV). If the speaker is the Lord's Servant and Messiah, which is possible, then there is an implicit Trinitarian pattern in this statement: (1) the Sovereign Lord, (2) the Messiah or Servant, who is speaking, and (3) the Spirit, who has been sent with the Servant.

Haggai 2:1–7 is less certain. Haggai delivers the word of "the LORD Almighty," who promises: "And my Spirit remains among you" (vv. 4–5). Then the Lord says that "the desired of all nations will come" (v. 7 NIV). Ancient Jewish commentators took the phrase "the desired of all nations" to refer to the Messiah. The accompanying plural verb, however, suggests that most modern translations are correct in not capitalizing "desired." Nevertheless, from the standpoint of *Jewish* biblical hermeneutics, the triadic pattern is clear.[109]

The New Testament, in contrast to the Old, is filled with Trinitarian patterns. To be sure, no formal doctrine of the Trinity per se is presented, but all the ingredients for that doctrine are clearly in place. Triadic formulas abound, but abstract terms such as "nature," "substance," "person," or "circumincession" are predictably absent. Such language, of course, is derived from philosophy, while the Bible is refreshingly concrete in its teachings and predominantly narrative in its presentation.

The Synoptic Gospels provide a glimpse of the triunity of God early on, in the account of the baptism of Jesus. The Spirit descends in the form of a dove on Jesus, and the Father's voice from heaven announces that Jesus is his beloved Son (Matt. 3:13–17; Mark 1:9–11; Luke 3:21–22). On the Day of Pentecost Peter phrases his "invitation" in Trinitarian fashion:

---

[109] Oden, *The Living God*, 190.

> "Repent, and be baptized every one of you in the name of Jesus Christ so that your sins may be forgiven; and you will receive the gift of the Holy Spirit. For the promise is for you, for your children, and for all who are far away, everyone whom the Lord our God calls to him." (Acts 2:38–39)

Notice the words: "Jesus Christ," "the Holy Spirit," and "the Lord our God." Peter also refers, at the outset of his first letter, to his readers' having been: (1) "chosen and destined by God the Father and [2] sanctified by the Spirit [3] to be obedient to Jesus Christ and to be sprinkled with his blood" (1 Peter 1:2). From this pattern alone it becomes evident that the New Testament evinces a markedly stronger Trinitarian flavor than that of the Old Testament.

Paul's letters develop this triadic pattern even further. For example, the Trinity is seen in bas-relief in these seven key passages: (1) the gifts of the Holy Spirit (1 Cor. 12:4–11); (2) the closing benediction (2 Cor. 13:13); (3) the opening praise and prayer (Eph. 1:3–23); (4) Paul's description of the church (Eph. 2:18–21); (5) another prayer (Eph. 3:14–21); (6) the seven great unities of the church (Eph. 4:4–6); and (7) the infilling of the Spirit (Eph. 5:18–20). Such powerful and profound passages are truly edifying! The apostle also points clearly to the deity of the Father (see 1 Cor. 8:4–6), the Son (Phil. 2:9–11), and the Holy Spirit (2 Cor. 3:17).

John brings us to a new level of insight and awe by allowing us a peek, as it were, into the inner life and dialogue of the holy Trinity.

John brings us to a new level of insight and awe by allowing us a peek, as it were, into the inner life and dialogue of the holy Trinity. We have already seen his strong Trinitarianism in our exploration of the love of God (1 John 4:7–15). But it is in John's Gospel that we receive the most intimate portrait of the Godhead. A good place to focus our attention is the five so-called "Paraclete sayings" of Jesus in his upper room discourse with the disciples (John 14–16).

The word "Paraclete" was John's (actually Jesus') special name for the Holy Spirit as the "one called alongside to help us," our "Counselor." Each of Jesus' sayings highlights an aspect of the ministry of the Holy Spirit, while at the same time providing insight into the nature of the

Trinity.[110] (1) *Helper* (John 14:15–24): Through the Father's giving us the Spirit the Trinity takes up residence within us. (2) *Teacher* (14:25–26): The Father will send us the Spirit to continue Jesus' teaching ministry among us. (3) *Witness* (15:26–27): Jesus sends the Spirit from the Father to empower our witness. (4) *Judge* (16:4–11): Jesus leaves the earth bodily in order to send the Spirit, who will convict the world of sin. (5) *Guide* (16:12–15): The Holy Spirit guides us into all truth, the things of Jesus and the Father. An entire book could be devoted to these sayings alone.

Let us look now at the historical developments of the doctrine of the Trinity. The coming of Jesus Christ into history introduced a fundamental theological question: How can Christians claim to believe in one God and worship Jesus Christ as God? Three foundational tenets of Christianity are held in a dynamic tension: (1) the unity of God (monotheism); (2) the divinity of Christ; and (3) the distinction between Jesus and God. Human intellect being what it is, heresies were almost inevitable. The church responded to these threatening distortions of the faith in a fourfold manner: the development of *creeds*, a *canon* (Old and New Testament Scriptures), *church organization* (bishops and church councils), and a carefully thought-out *Christology* (doctrine of the person of Christ). The culmination of this process was the authoritative doctrine of the Trinity, which has been passed down to us today.

John's depiction of Christ as the Logos, the Word, became an important tool in communicating and defending the gospel. Jaroslav Pelikan summarizes well what happened:

> The climax of the doctrinal development of the early church was the dogma of the Trinity. In this dogma the church vindicated the monotheism that had been at issue in its conflicts with Judaism, and it came to terms with the concept of the Logos, over which it had disputed with paganism.[111]

The heresies combated by the church generally denied one of the three foundational tenets mentioned above, ostensibly to dissolve the intellectual tension and to make the faith more "acceptable"—a perennial pattern in the history of Christian thought. *Dynamic Monarchianism* (adoptionism) denied the second tenet: the full divinity of Christ. Later an even

---

[110] See Dale Moody, *Spirit of the Living God* (Philadelphia: Westminster, 1968), 164–75.

[111] Jaroslav Pelikan, *The Christian Tradition: A History of the Development of Doctrine: 1. The Emergence of the Catholic Tradition (100–600)* (Chicago: Univ. of Chicago Press, 1971), 172.

more formidable foe, *Arianism*, would do the same. *Modalistic Monarchianism* (Sabellianism or modalism) rejected the third tenet: the distinction between Jesus and God, ultimately between the Father, the Son, and the Holy Spirit.

Monarchianism (meaning "sole sovereignty") was an honest, albeit misled, attempt to explain the meaning of Christ and God. Around A.D. 190, a tanner by the name of Theodotus introduced the idea that Jesus was just an ordinary man prior to his baptism, at which point he was adopted by God as his Son. Theodotus even believed in the virgin birth of Jesus. Nevertheless, he thought that Jesus was still only a man—a man who received God's power (*dynamis*) at his baptism. He "received Christ," or the power of the Spirit, and went out to do the miraculous works of God. Later Paul of Samosata (fl. 268–69) held a similar view. He denied that Jesus was the Logos, claiming that the Logos was the command of God, not the person of Christ. Paul of Samosata did, however, allow for applying the name of God to Christ in the sense that he received the title as a reward for his obedience. Both positions were a blatant denial of John 1:1 (". . . and the Word was God"), and both were ultimately rejected by the church.

Modalism was the other (more widespread) monarchian heresy. Also known as Sabellianism, because this heresy was introduced by Sabellius (fl. 198–222), this doctrine denied the distinction between Christ and God. Other adherents to this position were Praxeas (fl. 180–198) and Noetus (d. c. 250). According to this view, there is only one God, the Father. Christ is God, so Christ must be the Father. The Father, Son, and Holy Spirit are merely *names* for God, not distinctions within the Godhead. Sabellius taught that God came first of all in the *prosopon* (person) of the Father and Creator. Then he came as Son to redeem us. Finally, he came as Spirit to give us life. God was seen as one person with three names and activities. He successively played the "roles" of Father, Son, and Holy Spirit.

It was Arius (c. 256–336), however, a presbyter of the church in Alexandria, who promulgated the heresy that most threatened the doctrine of the Trinity. The argument of *Arianism* is that both Jesus and the Spirit are creations of God. Arius held an exalted view of Christ, nonetheless. He saw Christ as the creator of the world and as supreme above all other creatures, including the angels. Christ was created by God out of nothing as the perfect image of the Father, and he became the Creator. But he was not the Logos; he was not himself divine. According to Arius, there was a time when Christ did not exist.

The hero of the long struggle against Arianism was Athanasius (c. 295–373). He argued powerfully for the central importance of the Incarnation and the Trinity. He taught that Christ was of "one substance" (*homoousios*) with the Father. Trinitarianism won the day, and the Councils of Nicea (325) and Constantinople (381) basically authorized the position hammered out by Athanasius. The great Cappadocian theologians—Basil, Gregory of Nazianzus, and Gregory of Nyssa—further refined the orthodox position. Centuries later, John of Damascus (c. 675–749), the last of the Greek church fathers, contributed the full-orbed concept of *perichoresis* (Gr. term; Lat. *circumincessio*), describing the interpenetration of the infinite persons of the Godhead, the inner-Trinitarian relations of God.

The resultant doctrine of the Trinity affirms: (1) the unity of God; (2) the triunity of God: the three distinct Persons of Father, Son, and Holy Spirit; and (3) the equality of the Persons of the Godhead. A definition of the Trinity, therefore, is as follows: *The Triune God is one God who exists eternally as three infinite, eternal, interpenetrating Persons: Father, Son, and Holy Spirit.* He is one God: monotheism. He is three divine Persons: Trinitarianism. Each Person of the Godhead is infinite and eternal: God is not a "committee" of finite, independent persons. The Persons of the Trinity are interpenetrating (*perchoresis*)—that is, God cannot be divided. When one experiences one Person, one experiences all three Persons of the Trinity. God is both an *economic* Trinity (i.e., revealed as triune by his *actions*) and an *immanent* (essential, ontological) Trinity (i.e., triune in his very *being*). The former reveals the latter. Historical revelation manifests the reality of God's being as one triune God.

> *The Triune God is one God who exists eternally as three infinite, eternal, interpenetrating Persons: Father, Son, and Holy Spirit.*

The formula for the Trinity that emerged from the Council of Constantinople (381) was: one substance (*ousia*) in three persons (*hypostases*). Both substance and persons are problematic to many modern theologians. Substance is questioned because of a general loss of the transcendence of God. Moderns tend to want to see God only *within* the natural and historical processes (usually in some sort of evolutionary mode). And the term *persons* is also scrutinized. Clearly, *hypostasis* did not mean finite personality in the modern psychological sense, but it did mean *personal* and definitely served to differentiate between the Persons of the Godhead.

But does Person mean "center of consciousness," as we think of it today? There is no consensus of opinion on this question. Is God one "thou" or three "thous"? Claude Welch rejects the notion of three centers of consciousness and prefers to understand God as one subject, one "thou," who subsists as three modes of being.[112] Leonard Hodgson, by contrast, welcomes the concept of three complete persons in the modern sense. He argues for an *organic*, rather than a mathematical, unity—a unity that has no earthly analogy.[113] Welch's position is perhaps more prominent today, but the concept of a *social* Trinity has been on the ascendency in recent years. Jürgen Moltmann is one of the key influences in this direction.

The general pattern historically has been that the Western Church tends to begin with the oneness of God and then go on (hopefully) to affirm the threeness of God. The Eastern Church, in contrast, tends to start with the threeness and proceed to the oneness. The Father is seen as the "source" of the Son and the Spirit (eternally generating the Son and spirating the Spirit). Finally, in my opinion, we in the West have begun to catch on. We are beginning to learn two things from Eastern Orthodoxy: (1) that our theology should flow out of our worship, and (2) that the threeness of God is not something to shy away from, but it is, rather, a wondrously edifying mystery!

The twentieth century witnessed a virtual renaissance of Trinitarian theology. Perhaps it was the neo-orthodox theologian, Karl Barth, who led the way in his massive *Church Dogmatics*, the entire structure of which was Trinitarian. Barth represented well the Western, Augustinian tradition, which has guarded the unity of God and sought assiduously to avoid tritheism. Karl Rahner (1904–1984), the giant of twentieth-century Catholic theology, also helped revive the doctrine of the Trinity. He bequeathed to us what has come to be known as "Rahner's Rule," that the economic Trinity and the immanent Trinity are one and the same. Rahner also represented well the Augustinian tradition, rejecting the idea of three centers of consciousness in the Godhead.

---

[112] Claude Welch, *In His Name: The Trinity in Contemporary Theology* (New York: Charles Scribner's Sons, 1952).

[113] Leonard Hodgson, *The Doctrine of the Trinity* (Digswell Place: James Nisbet, 1943).

It took Jürgen Moltmann to shock us out of our latent unitarianism or modalism. Taking the Eastern approach, Moltmann develops a social doctrine of the Trinity and depicts what he calls the "Trinitarian history of God." The heart of the Christian faith, according to Moltmann, is Jesus' Godforsaken death on the cross. Calvary reveals the pain in the heart of God. In this event God cut himself off from himself, sacrificed himself. In the Father's giving up the Son, the cross happens to God. There is a cross at the heart of the Godhead. If this sounds like patripassianism (the so-called heretical belief that the Father was crucified and suffered), so be it, says Moltmann. Many times Moltmann communicates in a shocking manner, ostensibly to capture our attention. Moltmann does not say that the Father was literally crucified. But he does say that God suffers for us and that the cross was a Trinitarian event. From my perspective, this position is valid.[114]

At the very opposite end of the continuum is the unitarianism of G. W. H. Lampe. Lampe sees God as the creating and saving Spirit, who fully indwelt Jesus and through him saved us, and who indwells us. To Lampe, there is no need for—nor indeed any substantive meaning to—the classical doctrine of the Trinity.[115] Such a simple yet intriguing view of the divine appeals to our rationalism, which is always uncomfortable with paradoxes and mysteries; but it does little justice to the biblical texts that vibrate with the Trinitarian mystery.

One of the more dynamic conceptions of the Trinity in recent years has been put forth by John Macquarrie. Macquarrie refers to the Father as "primordial" Being—God as the source of all being, Creator. The Son is "expressive" Being—the agent of creation, communication, and redemption. The Holy Spirit is "unitive" Being—proceeding from the Father and the Son and uniting the creation back to God.[116] Macquarrie's existential/ontological model of "God as Being" may seem somewhat fuzzy to many minds, but it can also be viewed as a very dynamic depiction of the triune God. God speaks and breathes forth his creation, communicates with it and redeems it, and unites it back to himself—

---

[114] See Jürgen Moltmann, *The Trinity and the Kingdom*, trans. Margaret Kohl (San Francisco: Harper & Row, 1981), and *The Crucified God* (1974). Royce Gordon Gruenler is also developing this social or community approach to the Trinity in promising ways: *The Trinity in the Gospel of John* (Grand Rapids: Baker, 1986).

[115] G. W. H. Lampe, *God As Spirit* (Oxford: Clarendom, 1977), 225–27. One wonders how far James D. G. Dunn is leaning in this same direction. See *Jesus and the Spirit*, 326.

[116] John Macquarrie, *Principles of Christian Theology* (New York: Charles Scribner's Sons, 1966), 182–93.

three dynamic and ongoing movements, as it were. At least this is how I have utilized Macquarrie's model. Wolfhart Pannenberg, using a Hegelian historical model oriented toward the future, accomplishes a similar dynamism.[117] Pannenberg also keeps ever before us the kingdom of God—a necessary emphasis in our time.

Catherine Mowry LaCugna, by demonstrating the inseparability of the doctrines of the Trinity and redemption, has shown in a powerful way how practical and relevant the doctrine of the Trinity (as a community of divine persons) is to the life of the church. Unfortunately, the immanent or ontological Trinity may have been somewhat eclipsed by her strong emphasis on the relational/redemptive economic Trinity. Also, her feminism, though moderate to most, may result in less than a full appreciation for the traditional rubric of God's Fatherhood. Nonetheless, Donald Bloesch effectively incorporates LaCugna's insights into his masterful presentation of the biblical doctrine of God.[118] John D. Zizioulas, an Eastern Orthodox theologian, and Leonardo Boff, a Brazilian Catholic theologian, each develop powerful social concepts of the Trinity as well, showing the relevance of this approach for the life and mission of the church.[119] And evangelical theologians Kevin Giles and Gilbert Bilezikian utilize this model to defend an egalitarian view of women in ministry.[120]

Millard Erickson summarizes well the Bible's portrayal of the Trinity, utilizing the insights of this Western rediscovery of the Eastern Church's grasp of the "threeness" of God:

> The Trinity is a community of three persons, three centers of consciousness, who exist and always have existed in union with one another and in dependence on one another. Each is dependent for his life on each of the others. They share their lives, having such a close relationship that each is conscious of what the other is conscious of. They have never had any prior independent existence, and will not and cannot

---

[117] See the helpful summary provided by E. Frank Tupper: *The Theology of Wolfhart Pannenberg* (Philadelphia: Westminster, 1973), 247–49.

[118] Catherine Mowry LaCugna, *God for Us: The Trinity and Christian Life* (San Francisco: HarperSanFrancisco, 1991); Donald G. Bloesch, *God the Almighty* (Christian Foundations 3; Downers Grove, Ill.: InterVarsity Press, 1995).

[119] See John D. Zizioulas, *Being As Communion: Studies in Personhood and the Church* (Crestwood, N.Y.: St. Vladimir's, 1984), and Leonardo Boff, *Trinity and Society*, trans. Paul Burns (Maryknoll, N.Y.: Orbis, 1988).

[120] See Kevin Giles, *The Trinity and Subordinationism: The Doctrine of God and the Contemporary Gender Debate* (Downers Grove, Ill.: InterVarsity Press, 2002), and Gilbert Bilezikian, *Community 101: Reclaiming the Local Church as Community of Oneness* (Grand Rapids: Zondervan, 1997).

have any such now or in the future. Each is essential to the life of each of the others, and to the life of the Trinity. They are bound to one another in love, *agapē* love, which therefore unites them in the closest and most intimate of relationships. This unselfish, *agapē* love makes each more concerned for the other than for himself. There is therefore a mutual submission of each to each of the others and a mutual glorifying of one another. There is complete equality of the three. There has been, to be sure, temporary subordination of one member of the Trinity to the other, but this is functional rather than essential. At the same time, this unity and equality do not require identity of function. There are certain roles that distinctively belong primarily to one, although all participate in the function of each.[121]

In my view, this contemporary approach to the doctrine of the Trinity is the wave of the future. Beginning with the Trinity of the Persons of the Godhead in perichoretic communion incorporates the best of both the Eastern and Western traditions. The heretical tendency of this view would, of course, be tritheism. But the Greek, or Eastern, view, beginning with the Father as the source and origin of all divinity (Son begotten, Spirit proceeding), could also tend toward the heresy of subordinationism; and the Latin, or Western, view, beginning with the one divine nature that is equal in all three Persons, could tend toward the heresy of modalism.[122] My personal conviction is that the social model is the most biblical and practical, and Millard Erickson has provided the best overall presentation of Trinity from this vantage point in his *God in Three Persons.*[123]

Having said all this about the Trinity, as Barth would add, "we have said nothing."[124] We quickly run up against our limits when we consider such an awesome mystery. And yet the effort is all-important, for the doctrine of the holy Trinity is at the heart of the Christian faith. There is today what might be called a "Trinitarian crisis" in contemporary theology. Just as opponents of orthodoxy redefined the terms in the patristic era, and just as the cults do today, much contemporary theology has redefined this crucial doctrine or jettisoned it altogether. An honest

---

121 Millard J. Erickson, *God in Three Persons* (Grand Rapids: Baker, 1995), 331.

122 See Boff, *Trinity and Society*, 234–35.

123 See also Roger E. Olson and Christopher A. Hall's *The Trinity* in the Guides to Theology series (Grand Rapids: Eerdmans, 2002), which may be the best place to begin one's explorations into this glorious doctrine.

124 Barth, *Church Dogmatics*, I/1,422.

return to the authority of biblical revelation is a beginning step. Perhaps the next step is a renewed appreciation for the church fathers. The "mere Christianity" of the historic orthodox faith still carries tremendous power—because it is the truth! The work of Thomas C. Oden particularly helps us to take these two steps.

At the same time, we must not back away from the task of expressing afresh these important doctrines to each new generation. In our day we need to rediscover the full divinity of the Holy Spirit, both in our doctrine as well as in our experience. Certainly our Christologies, which have tended to be totally functional (Christ as a man uniquely used *by* God, rather than Christ *as* God), could be balanced out with an ontological perspective of Christ as the preexistent divine Being. Perhaps we need also to recover the Fatherhood of God.

> *Authentic Christianity has always been a Trinitarian movement.*

We have seen a "Jesus movement" in our country. The charismatic renewal is cast as a "Holy Spirit" movement. Both movements have revitalized American Christianity. But we need to remember that biblical Christianity has been, and always will be, a "Father movement." The Spirit's work is to bring us *through* the Son *to* the Father (Eph. 2:18). Authentic Christianity has always been a Trinitarian movement. Thomas Smail's insightful volume, *The Forgotten Father*, makes these points masterfully.[125] The Spirit's work is to draw people to Christ and his church, to bring God's rebellious subjects into his kingdom and back to his family. The Father's mission is a mission of love, and the focal point of his message is the crucified and risen Savior, through whom he beckons the world back to himself.

The Experience of God

In order for our doctrine of God to be sound, our experience of God must be vital. And in order for our experience of God to be vital, our doctrine of God must be biblical. God is infinitely more than a doctrine. He is a living reality. Too much modern theology is nothing more than esoteric philosophizing.

125 Thomas A. Smail, *The Forgotten Father* (Grand Rapids: Eerdmans, 1980).

> Over against all this cloudy vagueness stands the clear scriptural doctrine that God can be known in personal experience. A loving Personality dominates the Bible, walking among the trees of the garden and breathing fragrance over every scene. Always a living Person is present, speaking, pleading, loving, working, and manifesting Himself whenever and wherever His people have the receptivity necessary to receive the manifestation. . . .
>
> A spiritual kingdom lies all about us, enclosing us, embracing us, altogether within reach of our inner selves, waiting for us to recognize it. God Himself is here waiting our response to His Presence. This eternal world will come alive to us the moment we begin to reckon upon its reality.[126]

Such devotional writings as this by Tozer will do much to enrich and correct our doctrine of God. Moreover, we should always approach our studies devotionally!

Spiritual disciplines and sound scholarship should go hand in hand. Richard Foster's classic on prayer describes the spiritual dynamics of this process:

> We are exiles and aliens until we can come into God, the heart's true home. Pride and fear have kept us at a safe distance. But as the resistance within us is overcome by the operations of faith, hope, and love, we begin moving upward into the divine intimacy. This in turn empowers us for ministry to others.[127]

In order for our doctrine of God to be sound, our experience of God must be vital. And in order for our experience of God to be vital, our doctrine of God must be biblical.

Again, our theology and ministry flow out of our worship.

I am drawn again and again back to the simple, yet profound words of the apostle John: God is Spirit. God is light. God is love. God is Father, Son, and Holy Spirit. He is a wonderful mystery—a God of holy love whom we can trust. The following words from a sermon preached by Marguerite Shuster at Knox Presbyterian Church in Pasadena, California, on May 29, 1988 form a fitting conclusion to this chapter:

---

[126] A. W. Tozer, *The Pursuit of God* (Harrisburg, Penn.: Christian Publications, 1948), 50, 52.

[127] Richard J. Foster, *Prayer: Finding the Heart's True Home* (San Francisco: HarperCollins, 1992), 80.

> The Trinity will remain incomprehensible in the sense that we will never succeed in encompassing God in the little circle of our own understanding. But the mystery itself gives us the clue we most need to the nature of God—that he truly is the God who is love—the God who (1) loves us, (2) gives himself for us, and (3) enables us to love him. We can trust him because he is who he reveals himself to be.[128]

Appendix: Arguments for the Existence of God

Can we *know* there is a God? The Christian answer is yes. But as has already been pointed out, faith is a prerequisite for such knowledge (Heb. 11:6). If we begin with ourselves—our reason and experience—we will only get so far, no matter how intelligent we may be. If, by faith, we are willing to begin with God and his revelation, we can come to an assurance not only that God exists, but we can come to know who he is and what he is like.

Natural theology, apologetics, and the philosophy of religion deal with the relation of reason and experience to divine revelation. Does divine revelation contradict reason? Ultimately, the answer is no. In fact, the only reason we can use reason is that God exists and has freely chosen to reveal himself. In my opinion, humankind is faced with only two logical choices: faith in God or nihilism. Nietzsche realized this and, without faith, went insane. Existentialist philosophers have merely exerted their wills, but the haunting reality of their faithlessness is inescapable. What are we without faith, hope, and love?

> *Humankind is faced with only two logical choices: faith in God or nihilism.*

The fashion today is to buy into some sort of supernaturalism (usually of a New Age variety). Spiritual confusion abounds. Is Christianity right and every other worldview wrong? There are tenets of the Christian faith that are definitely an affront to human reason. But how can we know the *truth*? The Christian answer is that *truth is personal.* It is rooted in the self-revealing God himself. It is related to him who claimed to be "the way, and the truth, and the life" (John 14:6). It is related to the inscripturated truth of God's Word, the Bible. Christianity stood at

---

128 Marguerite Shuster, "The Oldest Math," in *God, Creation, and Revelation* (Grand Rapids: Eerdmans, 1991), 331.

the forefront of the development of educational institutions because of its conviction that *all truth is God's truth.*[129] Again, we *can* know there is a God, but it will always be a pilgrimage of faith. We are all on a journey. But for the Christian this is a *journey into light!*[130]

The very modest purpose of this appendix is simply to lay out in summary form an approach to the "case for Christianity" in general, and for belief in the existence of God in particular. We will only look at an outline. I have relegated this section to an appendix because we are dealing with apologetics proper here (which would require at least a one-volume treatment!) and also because the "God of the philosophers" does not compare with the "God of the patriarchs" (Moody).[131] Only through biblical revelation can we get the full picture!

Five Bases for Faith

My favorite brief presentation in this area is Clark H. Pinnock's *A Case for Faith.*[132] I will use Pinnock's presention to lay out "Five Bases for Faith." Then I will survey the theistic arguments per se. We will set forth our case in much the same way as does a lawyer. The cumulative evidence is, in my opinion, quite convincing!

The first basis for faith is the *pragmatic* basis. What is the foundation for belief in the dignity and worth of humankind? How do we find meaning in life? How do we decide what is right and wrong? How do we find healing for the hurts of life? What about sin and guilt? Christianity offers substantive answers to all such questions. Francis Schaeffer was a master at demonstrating that the Bible is the only adequate basis for belief in the dignity of humankind. Only because God is really there and has spoken, argued Schaeffer, are we able to affirm truth and values. Kant even argued that if there were no God, we would have to posit one in order to uphold moral and ethical norms. The gospel of Jesus Christ brings ultimate meaning to one's life.

---

[129] Arthur F. Holmes, *All Truth Is God's Truth* (Grand Rapids: Eerdmans, 1977). This little gem is a good beginning point for a study in this field. See also Holmes's *Contours of a World View* (Grand Rapids,: Eerdmans, 1983).

[130] Emile Cailliet, *Journey into Light* (Grand Rapids: Zondervan, 1968). Cailliet, a former Princeton philosopher and theologian, provides a poignant testimony of his journey out of unbelief into Christian faith through his discovery of the Bible as the book that "understood" him.

[131] I owe these phrases ("God of the philosophers" and "God of the patriarchs") to Dale Moody. See *The Word of Truth,* 78–89.

[132] Clark H. Pinnock, *A Case for Faith* (Minneapolis: Bethany, 1980). My favorite overview of approaches to Christian apologetics is Gordon R. Lewis, *Testing Christianity's Truth Claims* (Chicago: Moody Press, 1976).

The *experiential* basis is actually a potent argument for faith in the God and Father of our Lord Jesus Christ. Concerning the existence of God, Hans Schwarz observes: "The first and most obvious concern must be to investigate whether God is somewhere experienced as a living reality."[133] The answer is obvious. Literally millions upon millions of people throughout the centuries have claimed an experience of the presence of the living God. Humankind is incurably religious. In Western society secular eras are inevitably followed by a religious resurgence. We cannot seem to stand a religious vacuum. In fact, only those religions that have an experiential dimension survive (cf. my introductory chapter).[134] John Calvin held to the axiom "There is within the human mind, and indeed by natural instinct, an awareness of divinity."[135]

Additionally, the Christian experience of the Holy Spirit as a personal and life-transforming presence is another cogent evidence for the faith. The Pentecostal/charismatic tradition has brought to the church of the twentieth and twenty-first centuries a greater appreciation for the person and ministry of the Holy Spirit. The Bible teaches that the Holy Spirit bears witness to the truth of the gospel—often apart from any of our sustained arguments for belief.

We have already touched on the *cosmic* basis for faith in the chapter on revelation. General revelation, according to Scripture, is God's supernatural disclosure of himself through what he has made—a disclosure to all people, at all times, in all places. The ordered and designed creation all about us, and the conscience within us, together point to the reality of God. Later we will look more closely at the theistic arguments related to this biblical truth (the teleological, cosmological, and moral arguments). The cosmic basis for faith, therefore, appeals to our minds, which seek to discern truth and fact. We ask the question: How could the intellectual, personal, and moral dimensions of humankind (assuming there is no Creator God) emerge out of a cold, meaningless, impersonal, amoral universe? It definitely requires a sacrifice of intellect—or at least a blind faith—to hold to such a notion. There is good reason to believe that the universe is filled with meaning and that our thinking, feeling, and deciding personalities are *not* the product of a mindless, meaningless process![136]

---

133 Hans Schwarz, *The Search for God* (Minneapolis: Augsburg, 1975), 15.

134 Ninian Smart, *The Religious Experience of Mankind*, 2d ed. (New York: Charles Scribner's Sons, 1976), 10–12.

135 Calvin, *Institutes,* 1:43 (I.iii.1).

136 Lee Strobel presents these ideas effectively and attractively in *The Case for a Creator* (Grand Rapids: Zondervan, 2004).

The *historical* basis for faith continues the discussion of the biblical doctrine of revelation—this time in relation to special revelation. God has, according to the Bible, revealed himself personally in history. This took place in the holy history of the tiny, miraculous nation of Israel, but supremely in the incarnation of God's eternal Son, Jesus Christ. God spoke his creative word, and the universe sprang into existence. He gave his prophetic word, and revelatory and saving events transpired within human history. He sent the living Word, Jesus Christ, to save us through his atoning death and resurrection. Finally, he gave us his written Word, the Bible. All of this revelatory activity is available for public inspection! None of this was "done in a corner" (Acts 26:26). How does one explain away the empty tomb and the disciples' readiness to die for their belief in the *resurrected* Christ?

> *There is good reason to believe that the universe is filled with meaning and that our thinking, feeling, and deciding personalities are* not *the product of a mindless, meaningless process!*

The greatest need is for Christians simply to spread this good news. Paul was convinced that the gospel carries its own power. He said that the gospel *is* the power of God for the salvation of everyone who believes (Rom. 1:16). God's purpose in giving us the Bible was primarily to provide us with an authoritative record of all these revelatory and saving events. Pinnock expresses this well:

> The gospel in essence is a newscast. It concentrates its attention upon what God has done in history for the salvation of mankind. That is why it contains little of what we have called natural theology. It is not that the Bible is against sincere efforts to make sense of belief in God in terms of his revelation in nature and the world, but that it is so much more interested in God's revelation in human history. The fullness of truth is revealed according to Hebrew thinking through what *happens* rather than what *is*, and this explains the emphasis.[137]

The most loving thing any Christian can do is to share the good news of Jesus Christ with a world desperately in need of him.

Pinnock's final circle of evidence may surprise some, but in my view it is a crucial though neglected insight. He argues that there is a *com-*

---

[137] Pinnock, *A Case for Faith*, 74 (Pinnock's italics).

munity basis for faith in the church. Jesus said, "By this everyone will know that you are my disciples, if you have love for one another" (John 13:35). Christian orthodoxy must lead to Christian orthopraxy (loving service to God and humankind). We are to model the kingdom of God. As studies of cults have shown, people join themselves to a group more because they are loved and cared for by that group than because they are convinced of the group's beliefs. Beliefs *are* important, however; and tragedies often occur within cults precisely because of false beliefs and practices.

We are by nature social creatures. We need to belong to a family. We need to belong to God's family, the church. And the church is called to reflect Christ's lifestyle of loving service to humankind.

Arguments for the Existence of God

Now let us consider the formal theistic arguments—arguments for the existence of God. We begin with one of the most intriguing arguments, an *a priori* argument that takes a deductive approach, reasoning from self-evident propositions. In one sense it is not an argument at all, at least in comparison to the arguments to follow. Anselm of Canterbury (1033–1109) worked from the Augustinian premise of *faith seeking understanding*. He precedes his *ontological* argument with a statement that well summarizes his approach: *Credo ut intelligam*—"I believe in order that I may understand." This priority of faith and divine revelation sets Anselm's argument apart from the arguments to follow, which tend to place philosophical argumentation before faith.

Philosophical speculation can only take one so far. At the most, one can achieve a degree of confidence in the probability of God's existence. Which God it is that exists, and what he is like, are questions that can only be partially addressed through philosophy. The Christian approach should be to present the God of biblical revelation and *then* to address the question whether this particular God—the God of the patriarchs, the God and Father of our Lord Jesus Christ, the God of infinite, holy love, the Triune God—exists.[138] Placing philosophical speculation before biblical revelation confuses the picture.

Anselm did not shy away from speculation, but the prevailing tenor of his argument is that of a prayerful meditation—which at the same time brilliantly establishes a rationale for belief in the existence of

[138] Oden, *The Living God*, 134–36.

God.[139] Anselm's argument is at once both the simplest and the most profound of all the theistic arguments. It is built on humankind's innate awareness of God—the conviction that everyone possesses intellectually an inherent idea of God. Anselm begins by defining God as a being "than which nothing greater [more perfect] can be conceived."[140]

It is self-evident that we have such an idea in our minds. The question that must be asked is how such a conception of absolute perfection could ever derive from our limited, imperfect intellects. The very idea that God is "that than which nothing greater can be conceived" implies that God exists. For if God, as the ultimately perfect one, only existed in our minds, then he would not be the being "than which nothing greater can be conceived." Therefore, God most certainly exists!

Gaunilo, a French monk, gave the obvious rejoinder. He said that he conceived the most perfect island. Therefore, that island, because it is the most perfect island, must exist.[141] Anselm replied by pointing out that God and islands belong in two different categories. An island is not the most perfect thing conceivable. Only God is "that than which nothing greater can be conceived." To be sure, this is an intellectual teaser, but Anselm was not using philosophical sleight of hand. Rightly considered, this is a profound statement of the majesty of God as necessary being—a powerful argument for the existence of God. Anselm first defined God as the most perfect being conceivable, and then described the *aseity* of God (the fact that God exists in and of himself, *a se*). As a good Augustinian, Anselm simply used philosophical argument to elucidate a biblical doctrine.

As a good Augustinian, Anselm simply used philosophical argument to elucidate a biblical doctrine.

René Descartes (1596–1650), the father of modern philosophy, would later utilize the ontological argument on a totally philosophical basis. Descartes observed in the human mind an idea of God as an infinite, eternal, omniscient, omnipotent, immutable, independent substance who created everything that exists. How, Descartes asked, could our finite minds ever conceive of such a being unless he actually exists?

---

139 We will examine Anselm's other major theological contribution, on the atonement, in a later chapter.

140 *Proslogion,* chs. 2–4.

141 Actually, Gaunilo used "islands" (plural).

Only the perfect God could give us the notion of his perfection and reality.

Immanuel Kant (1724–1804), again working solely from a philosophical basis, challenged Descartes' argument simply by noting that conceived existence does not necessarily entail actual existence. A triangle can only be defined in a certain way, but that does not necessarily mean that a given defined triangle actually exists. The person actually carrying a hundred dollars in her purse has a hundred dollars more than the person who only conceives of them. Also, Kant points out, existence per se is not an *attribute* or predicate of anything. Grammar and logic are two different considerations: Existence might be a predicate grammatically, but not necessarily logically. Nevertheless, Anselm would again simply point out that we are not dealing with finite realities here. The concept of God belongs in a different category.

Underneath the ontological argument is the conviction, dating back to Aristotle, that whatever emerges at the end of a process must have been there from the beginning. The question as to how humankind could have ever conceived of God without his actually existing has yet to be adequately answered by those who deny God's existence.[142]

I have devoted more space to the ontological argument than to the arguments that follow, simply because of its spiritual and aesthetic beauty.[143] Tragically, sin too often blinds us to the truth so elegantly expressed in the ontological argument. It is a neglected argument, but one that has been revived in new forms in recent years. It balances itself on the razor's edge of the limits of human language and logic. It also forces the fundamental religious questions that face each generation.

More than four centuries before Christ, the Greek philosopher Parmenides asked perhaps the most profound question of all time: Why is there something and not nothing? The two fundamental responses to this question are: (1) that the universe simply exists on its own, or (2) that God created the universe. The first position is even more difficult to hold today in view of what scientists are now learning about the physical universe (but this is to anticipate our upcoming discussion of the doctrine of creation). The second position is, of course, taught in biblical revelation, but it has also been argued by philosophers for centuries. Aristotle, in his *Metaphysics,* posited a *cosmological*

[142] I gained this insight from Eric C. Rust when I took his philosophy of religion class in seminary.
[143] See also Oden, *The Living God,* 174, 179.

argument for the existence of God as the Prime Mover. But it was the great Doctor of the Church, Thomas Aquinas (1225–1274), who presented this argument in its classic form.

Aquinas, probably the greatest philosopher and theologian of the medieval period, actually rendered four versions of the cosmological argument. In his *Summa Theologiae* (1265–1273), which runs to about sixty volumes, Aquinas attempts in one section to prove God's existence in what are known as the Five Ways. The first four of these "ways" are in reality the cosmological argument in variant forms. This is an *a posteriori* argument—derived inductively by reasoning from observed facts of the universe. Aquinas argues: (1) from motion and change to a Prime Mover; (2) from the causal nexus of the universe to a First Cause; (3) from contingency in the natural order to a noncontingent ground of existence, God as Necessary Being; and (4) from a gradation of values and perfections to Absolute Value, the Supremely Perfect Being.

> *More than four centuries before Christ, the Greek philosopher Parmenides asked perhaps the most profound question of all time: Why is there something and not nothing?*

In simplest language this argument reasons as follows. The universe is in constant change and motion. Yet nothing changes or moves itself; it is, rather, acted upon externally. How could this process have ever begun without a Prime Mover? Every effect has a cause; nothing ever causes itself. How then could this reality exist without a First Cause to initiate the process? Everything in the observable universe is contingent. Everything is caused to exist by something else. Nothing ever causes itself to exist. How then could anything exist at all unless there is a noncontingent reality to cause existence—God, who is self-existing, Necessary Being. Only a being of absolute perfection could cause the relative perfections that we perceive in the created order (e.g., truth, goodness, and nobility).

Kant, that theistic argument iconoclast, simply noted that there might be an endless chain of causality. In fact, the argument for an uncaused cause runs counter to our experience of the universe. But *is* the universe "alive" on its own, or does its cause need to be accounted for in view of its contingency? Modern science pokes holes in Kant's critique: The prevailing Big Bang cosmology *begs* for a causal explanation!

Kant did correctly observe, however, that behind these cosmological arguments lies the ontological argument. That there is an integral relation between the two should not surprise us if God truly exists and there is, therefore, such a thing as absolute truth.

The cosmological argument is actually a rationale for the biblical doctrine of creation, as is the *teleological* argument, Aquinas's fifth way. Again, we are looking at an argument of inductive reasoning based on the observed facts of the universe (*a posteriori*). The teleological argument is in reality an extension of the cosmological argument. It asks the obvious question: How could a universe of such majestic, intricate design have come about by accident? This is probably the most popular argument, precisely because of the mystery, beauty, and apparent design of the universe.

It is an *old* argument, dating back to such ancient philosophers as Anaxagoras, Pythagoras, Plato, and Aristotle. The best-known modern presentation of this argument is that of William Paley (1743–1805), an Anglican theologian and an Archdeacon of Carlisle Cathedral in England. His *Natural Theology* (1802) is still a popular exposition of this attractive argument.

The essence of Paley's argument is the analogy of a watch. If I were walking in a desert place (similar to the West Texas plains in which I grew up) and came upon a rock, I could easily attribute its existence to such natural forces as wind, rain, heat, and the like. However, if I came across a watch, it would be much more difficult to attribute its existence to such forces. Even if I had never seen a watch before, or if the watch did not work, or if I did not know all the constituent parts of the watch, I would still conclude that an intelligence of some sort had designed the watch.

One can easily make the transition from such an artifact to the natural order. The regular function of the solar system, the seasons of our planet, the awesome design and function of the human brain, or even simply the human eye—the examples are myriad—all point to a Divine Designer. Combined with the knowledge of the biblical doctrine of general revelation (and I am going beyond Paley here), the study of the natural sciences becomes a delight to the Christian believer as one discovers just how impressive the design and order of the universe really is!

Ironically, the skeptical response to Paley's argument had already been published twenty-three years earlier in David Hume's *Dialogues Concerning Natural Religion* (1779). Given unlimited time and a finite number of constituent particles in random motion, Hume argued, a stable order will ultimately emerge and persist precisely because of its stability. The universe is *bound* to appear ordered. Besides, the natural order is more like an organism such as a plant or an animal than it is an artifact such as a watch.

In defense of Paley, it is important to note that he examined specific phenomena *within* the created order rather than focusing on the whole. Darwin, probably in response to Paley, later exploited the weakness of this approach with his theory of evolution, in terms of continuous variations and natural selection. F. R. Tennant, however, in his *Philosophical Theology* (1930), has demonstrated that a teleological argument can be constructed precisely from a holistic and evolutionary perspective.[144]

Hume's third criticism, that even if Paley's argument were convincing it would not thereby demonstrate the existence of the God of the Bible, is valid, however. Kant added that Paley's argument could only prove an Architect for the universe, not the divine Creator of the universe. Kant, nevertheless, held a tremendous respect for this argument.

The bottom line is that there are limitations to such arguments. The deity proven might just as easily be conceived as the clockmaker God of deism or the solely immanent God of pantheism. But, again, combined with the biblical doctrines of general revelation and creation, this argument carries enormous appeal. There really does seem to be a *telos*, an end, goal, or purpose to everything. And Kant was right to show the integral relation of all three of these theistic approaches—the ontological, cosmological, and teleological arguments.[145] For Kant, however, the surest argument for God is the *moral* argument, to which we now turn.

With the moral argument we return to *a priori*, deductive reasoning. Here we ask, What is the source of our moral notions? If there is no transcendent norm, why do we instinctively think and behave as if there were? In his argument for miracles, C. S. Lewis points out the inconsistencies of the socially sensitive and activist naturalist who continually gives passionate appeal for justice and compassion, when all along his worldview provides no basis for determining such. Lewis sees this built-in sense of right and wrong (conscience) as God-given and as evidence for God and the supernatural.[146]

---

144 F. R. Tennant, *Philosophical Theology*, 2 vols. (New York: Cambridge Univ. Press, 1928–1930).

145 The Intelligent Design movement adds scientific, mathematical, and philosophical evidences and arguments to Paley's original work, although the actual intent of the movement itself is more modest. See William A. Dembski's *The Design Revolution* (Downers Grove, Ill.: InterVarsity Press, 2004) for an apt introduction to this exploding field of research.

146 Lewis, *Miracles*, 34–39. See also his *Mere Christianity* (New York: Macmillan, 1952), chs. 1–5. The moral argument was one of Lewis's favorites, and few can match his eloquence and persuasion.

It is natural for Christians, with an inherent moral and religious orientation, to utilize such arguments. But Kant attempted to do so totally from a philosophical base. In his *Critique of Practical Reason* Kant sought to argue for the existence of God solely on the basis of reason that emanates from our moral consciousness. Kant held a strong conviction about humankind's sense of duty. Unfortunately, our highest good—consisting of the combination of virtue and happiness—is never fully realized in this life. What motivates us in this direction is the ultimate fulfillment of this ideal in the life to come. Therefore, Kant hypothesized, we must hold to three fundamental concepts: God, freedom, and immortality. God, of course, is the transcendent source for moral norms. Freedom is necessary for there to be authentic responsibility. And immortality is required for there to be the ultimate righting of all wrongs and the achievement of final virtue and happiness. Liberal theology sought to combine this perspective with a general Protestant tradition in an attempt to translate the faith to modernity. The experiment has largely failed. Nevertheless, the moral argument has perennial appeal because of the God-given conscience within humankind.

A fifth theistic argument can be summarized under the rubric of *historical* or *experiential*. The history of humankind gives ample testimony to our religious nature and the widespread reality of belief in the divine. This approach is more an observation than an argument. Nevertheless, this observation argues convincingly for itself. We too often underestimate the power of religious experience. Most people are not satisfied with pragmatic or philosophical arguments. If God is really there, they want to know him, not merely know about him.

Blaise Pascal was transformed by a fiery encounter with God, the testimony to which he kept sewn into the lining of his coat. This experience informed everything he wrote. Even the brilliant Aquinas ultimately considered the dozens and dozens of tomes of philosophical and theological writings he produced as *chaff* in comparison with the encounter he experienced with God later in life. I vividly remember my mentor, Dale Moody, sharing with us in his classes such experiences as his overwhelming encounter with the presence of God in the library of Oxford University. He was accused of being a mystic, but I think he was just experiencing normal Christianity. Moody always reminded us seminarians that although we might excel many of our parishioners in our sharpened *conceptions* of God, there would be many a simple saint who would far exceed us in their *perceptions* of God!

We have hardly exhausted the arguments for the existence of God. For example, we could return for another look at humankind in terms of our minds as well as our total personal makeup. Just how did mind and personality develop from a seemingly mindless and impersonal universe? The historical argument mentioned above could be expanded to include historical evidences for the Christian faith, such as the resurrection of Jesus Christ from the dead. A careful and honest study of the person and work of Christ can be disconcerting to the unbeliever. Reason is on the side of faith. Reason and historical evidence will never prove conclusively to an unbelieving mind the reality of God, but they can clearly be used by the Holy Spirit to prepare one for the divine/human encounter.[147]

All truth really is God's truth!

Thomas C. Oden has summarized well how the theistic arguments should be seen:

> Despite limits, the classical theistic arguments for God's existence have a cumulative effect when taken seriously.... No one argument can be sufficient for so great a reality. Any single argument may be found lacking in this or that way, but taken together they have been held by the tradition to be sufficient to bind the inquiring, rational, self-critical mind to the sure knowledge that this caring God exists.[148]

At the very least, I hope this brief survey has whetted your appetite for further study in this rewarding field of research, argumentation, and continuing exploration. All truth really *is* God's truth!

---

[147] Among the myriad excellent evangelical works in this arena, the penetrating and insightful volumes by former atheist Lee Strobel deserve special mention: *The Case for Christ* (Grand Rapids: Zondervan, 1998), *The Case for Faith* (Grand Rapids: Zondervan, 2000), and *The Case for a Creator.*

[148] Oden, *The Living God,* 139.

4 Creation
What Does It Mean to Believe in God as Creator?

On June 22, 1633, the long trial finally ended. The last session took place in Santa Maria Sopra Minerva, a Dominican convent in the center of Rome, built on the ruins of an ancient temple dedicated to the goddess of wisdom. The defendant, dressed in the white robe of a penitent, was led in. Shaking beneath the folds of his loose-fitting robe, Galileo Galilei knelt before the ten judges of the Inquistion to hear his sentence.

—Charles E. Hummel[1]

[1] Charles E. Hummel, *The Galileo Connection* (Downers Grove, Ill.: InterVarsity Press, 1986), 9.

GALILEO'S TRIAL EPITOMIZES THE CONFLICTS that have perennially emerged between the church and the academy. Notice I did not say between science and Scripture. The actual battle has always been one of *interpretation*: How does one interpret the Bible? How does one interpret the scientific evidence?

Galileo himself saw no conflict between the Bible and the discoveries of science. We often call Galileo the father of modern science precisely because of his overall approach to his discipline. As a scientist, Galileo did not trouble himself with the metaphysical questions of the philosophers and theologians. He was perfectly content to combine theory and experiment in order to explore humbly the workings of the universe.[2] As a devout Catholic, Galileo honored the authority of the church and accepted implicity the doctrines of Scripture. His perspective on the relation between science and the Bible is expressed succinctly in his assertion: "The Bible tells us how to go to Heaven, not how the heavens go."[3]

> *The doctrine of creation proves itself not only viable but also essential to a full-orbed comprehension of the meaning of the created order.*

Nevertheless, Galileo found himself in trouble with the Roman Catholic Church precisely because of his published scientific findings. His *Dialogue on the Two Principal World Systems* (1632) subtly challenged the centuries-old consensus that the universe was geocentric (i.e., revolved around the earth). It appeared that Galileo agreed with Copernicus. Galileo had the audacity to call into question the authoritative viewpoint of the venerable Aristotle and the great doctor of the church, Thomas Aquinas (not to mention the pope). Galileo, sixty-nine years of age and in poor health, humbly recanted, but history would record that he had also joined the Copernican revolution.

It is with the biblical doctrine of creation that systematic theology truly becomes *systematic*—that is, it accepts the responsibility of relating the teachings of the Bible to contemporary questions and knowledge. Although challenged and questioned as never before in this scientific age, the doctrine of creation proves itself not only viable but also essential to a full-orbed comprehension of the meaning of the created order.

---

[2] See Ian G. Barbour, *Issues in Science and Religion* (New York: Harper & Row, 1966), 24–26.

[3] Cited in Hummel, *The Galileo Connection*, 9.

As we will see, the focus of Scripture is more on the Creator than on the creation. The Bible is a God-centered book that yields a portrait of God as the great King and Creator of the universe. At the same time, his handiwork itself is also an awe-inspiring reality. And there are numerous implications to the fact that the universe is God's *creation* and not just a brute fact. Closely related to this truth is the doctrine of humanity's having been created in God's image. The fall of the human race and God's redemptive plan are also closely tied to the doctrine of creation. There truly is an organic relation among the various doctrines of Scripture.

The Importance of the Doctrine of Creation

Langdon Gilkey, in his classic work on the doctrine of creation, *Maker of Heaven and Earth*, shows how the doctrine of creation is fundamental to everything else the Scriptures teach.

1. "The idea that God is the Creator of all things is the indispensable foundation on which the other beliefs of the Christian faith are based. It affirms what the Christian believes about the status of God in the whole realm of reality: He is the Creator of everything else. On this affirmation logically depends all that Christians say about God, about the world they live in, and about their own history, destiny, and hope."
2. "The idea of creation expresses that fundamental relation between God and the world within which the Gospel of redemption is both important and viable, and so this conception provides the indispensable framework within which the Christian faith speaks its message of love."
3. "The idea of creation, therefore, provides the most fundamental, if not the most characteristic, definition of God in the Christian faith. Among all the activities of God, creation is that activity or attribute which sets him apart as 'God.'"
4. "As the foundation upon which all that is Christianly significant about God is based, the idea of the Creator is an indispensable and primary element in any Christian theology."[4]

---

[4] Langdon Gilkey, *Maker of Heaven and Earth* (Garden City, N.Y.: Doubleday, 1959), 15, 16, 79, 101.

The Christian gospel has ultimate meaning because the God who saves us is the One who claims us and rules us—*because he created us*! It is *his* judgment, love, and promise with which we are confronted, and not that of some lesser reality.[5] We need constantly to be reminded that God created us and that we exist for his glory and pleasure, not he for ours.

The Christian gospel has ultimate meaning because the God who saves us is the One who claims us and rules us—because he created us!

Carl F. H. Henry rightly asserts: "The doctrine of creation is the bedrock foundation of every major doctrine of the church."[6] And Robert Webber is true to the mark when he observes: "The failure to affirm the doctrine of creation results in an inability to come to grips with history and the meaningfulness of life."[7] This is precisely the Gordian knot that secularized Western society has been unable to solve. As George Marsden has noted, "One way to describe the history of modern Western thought is as a rejection of the doctrine of creation and its systematic exclusion as a consideration in academic study, outside of theology itself." The implications of this "politically correct" approach—not only in the natural sciences, but in the social sciences and humanities in general—are staggering.[8] By excluding the Creator God from our worldview we have become what the Bible describes as *fools*!

The first affirmation of the Apostles' Creed is: "I believe in God the Father Almighty, Maker of heaven and earth." John Calvin entitled Book 1 of his *Institutes of the Christian Religion* "The Knowledge of God the Creator." Karl Barth in his *Church Dogmatics* devoted 2,337 pages to the doctrine of creation, including 428 pages to "The Work of Creation" alone. The opening words of Scripture are: "In the beginning God created the heavens and the earth" (Gen. 1:1 RSV). During the Apollo 14 lunar mission astronaut Edgar Mitchell placed on the moon a microfilm packet containing the entire Bible and also containing one verse from the Bible in sixteen languages. The verse was Genesis 1:1.[9]

---

[5] See ibid., 16.

[6] Carl F. H. Henry, *God, Revelation and Authority*, Vol. VI: *God Who Stands and Stays*, Pt. 2 (Dallas: Word, 1983), 119.

[7] Cited in Henry, ibid., 119.

[8] George M. Marsden, *The Outrageous Idea of Christian Scholarship* (New York: Oxford Univ. Press, 1997), 84.

[9] Ronald F. Youngblood, *The Book of Genesis: An Introductory Commentary*, 2d. ed. (Grand Rapids: Baker, 1991), 22.

Every other biblical doctrine is informed by the doctrine of God as the Creator of the heavens and the earth. This doctrine in its fullest expression is an important distinctive of Christianity—a distinctive that sets it apart from every other world religion and philosophical outlook. The rise of modern science and the debate among Christians themselves (including evangelicals) over how one relates the Bible's teachings in this area to modern knowledge make the study of this doctrine imperative.

Every other biblical doctrine is informed by the doctrine of God as the Creator of the heavens and the earth.

The Definition of Creation

One can define creation both in terms of the product and the act. E. Y. Mullins provides a simple definition in terms of the product: "By creation is meant all that exists which is not God." He then adds: "This includes nature and man and all other forms of being other than God himself."[10] A. H. Strong defines creation in terms of act: "By creation we mean that free act of the triune God by which in the beginning for his own glory he made, without the use of preexisting materials, the whole visible and invisible universe."[11] In his description of the great tribulation period, Jesus predicts suffering "such as has not been from the beginning of the creation that God created until now, no, and never will be" (Mark 13:19). This unusual verse refers to creation both as product ("the creation") and as act ("that God created").[12]

Bruce Milne provides another useful definition: "Creation is that work of the triune God by which he called all things that exist, both material and spiritual, into existence out of non-existence."[13] Then, almost as a passing remark rather than a formal definition, Paul K. Jew-

---

[10] Edgar Young Mullins, *The Christian Religion in Its Doctrinal Expression* (Nashville: Broadman, 1917), 251.

[11] Augustus Hopkins Strong, *Systematic Theology* (Valley Forge, Pa.: Judson, 1907), 371. Perhaps Strong's definition could be sharpened by referring to *acts* (plural) rather than act in view of the viability of progressive creationism, but this is something to be considered later.

[12] See James Leo Garrett Jr., *Systematic Theology* (Grand Rapids: Eerdmans, 1990), 1:291.

[13] Bruce Milne, *Know the Truth: A Handbook of Christian Belief* (Downers Grove, Ill.: InterVarsity Press, 1982), 72. Milne goes on to say: "The biblical view of God as creator includes his continuous, unbroken sustenance and renewal of the world" (73). He is referring to the concept of continuing creation, which will also be considered later.

ett provides further help: "Creation describes a miracle freely wrought by the transcendent will and power of the living God."[14] Each of these definitions adds an ingredient that enriches and clarifies what is meant by creation in the Bible.

A full-orbed definition of creation also includes the biblical concept of "a new creation," brought about by God's redemptive work through his Son, Jesus Christ (see, e.g., 2 Cor. 5:17; Gal. 6:15; Rev. 21:1). Again, this demonstrates the organic unity of Christian doctrine.

Broadly speaking, the biblical doctrine of creation explicates two important truths related to God and the universe: (1) the *distinction* between God and his creation, and (2) the *relation* between God and his creation. Perhaps the best way to illustrate this distinctive of revealed religion is to contrast biblical theism with two other dominant and competitive perspectives: dualism and monism.

According to *dualism*, there are two eternal realities: spirit and matter. Spirit, which is good, is always limited by matter, which is evil. Creation is *ex materia*, that is, from preexistent, eternal matter. God is, therefore, limited by this eternal material reality. Since matter is eternal, evil is also eternal; we are locked into an eternal conflict between good and evil from which there is no escape. There is no ultimate hope. This is the perspective of the *Star Wars* films. The reason we can be upbeat about the dualism of Luke Skywalker and friends is that they inevitably win. Unfortunately, in real life it doesn't always work that way, and evil is many times almost intolerably oppressive. (More precisely, the dualism of *Star Wars* is a metaphysical dualism, with both a good side and a dark side of "the Force" [God].)

> *A full-orbed definition of creation also includes the biblical concept of "a new creation."*

According to *monism*, creation is *ex deo*; that is, creation emanates from God's own being. We are a "chunk" of God, as it were. Moreover, creation takes place by necessity. God does not choose for the process to take place. Our very finitude is the source of evil, which, of course, is inescapable. It is a lack of good and is a necessary part of the process of creation. Again, there is no ultimate hope.

According to theism, creation is *ex nihilo*, out of nothing. The Big Bang cosmology (more precisely, cosmogony), which appears to rule the day at present, confronts us with this reality. Our finite intelligence

---

[14] Paul K. Jewett, *God, Creation, and Revelation* (Grand Rapids: Eerdmans, 1991), 453.

does not want to accept it, but there was a "time" when there was nothing. The first moment of the universe was a sudden appearance of light. There was no atmosphere for a big *bang*![15] God simply said, "Let there be light" (Gen. 1:3)—and that was before the sun, moon, and stars. But what does "before" mean in this context? At any rate, according to theism, God *freely* chooses to bring forth the universe out of nothing. He continues to preserve and interact with his creation. He allows evil, but for an ultimately good purpose. He will conquer evil in the final analysis. We have tremendous hope!

Metaphysics asks the same questions as theology.

Arthur F. Holmes, to whom I am indebted for the broad distinctions between dualism, monism, and theism presented above, summarizes well the implications of the biblical doctrine of creation:

> Monism loses the *distinction* between God and creation, either absorbing the creation into God (as with neo-Platonism, pantheism, and some Eastern religions) or else losing God in the creation (as with materialism, philosophical naturalism, and secular humanism). On the other hand, dualism confuses the *relationship* by affirming the coeternality of God and matter, or spirit and matter, and so denies that God is an almighty maker of all, who acts with full freedom in his creation. The God-creation theme thus differentiates Christian theism from other world views and is crucial to thinking Christianly about anything at all.[16]

These descriptions of worldviews illustrate how philosophical considerations are inescapable when doing theology.

This is partly the case simply because metaphysics asks the same questions as theology. Also, systematic theology must by definition relate to contemporary philosophical concerns. Finally, all thinking is to some degree philosophical in nature. With the resurgent hodgepodge of New Age ideologies, "worldviewish" thinking is even more imperative.[17] Having noted the importance of the doctrine of creation and having broadly defined it, we must now explicate the biblical doctrine of creation.

---

[15] I owe this insight to Marguerite Shuster's excellent sermon on the doctrine of creation. Ms. Shuster credits Lewis Thomas for this perspective (see Jewett, *God, Creation, and Revelation,* 511).

[16] Arthur F. Holmes, *Contours of a Worldview* (Grand Rapids: Eerdmans, 1983), 58 (Holmes's italics). For the broad delineations mentioned above, see pp. 8–10.

[17] See James W. Sire, *The Universe Next Door,* 2nd ed. (Downers Grove, Ill.: InterVarsity Press, 1988).

The Biblical Doctrine of Creation

Studying creation should be one of life's most exciting enterprises. Take a moment to look around. What is there to see? That anything is there is an amazing fact on its own. Reflecting on what is *there*—including "the God who is there," to use Schaeffer's favorite phrase—is what contemplating the doctrine of creation is all about. We must study both the Creator (which we have already begun to do in our previous chapter) and the creation, including ourselves. Remember Calvin's axiom that all true wisdom consists of the knowledge of God *and* of ourselves. Surely the study of the natural order should also be factored into the equation. One of the most astute observers of God's majestic creation is Annie Dillard, whose *Pilgrim at Tinker Creek* is a masterful description of the beauty and mystery of creation.[18]

> *God's* Logos *(thought, word, message . . . Son) brings forth the creation, orders it, and holds it together.*

Dillard is amazed, for example, at the intricacy of the created order. Thinking back to beginnings, she writes, "The lone ping into being of the first hydrogen atom *ex nihilo* was so unthinkably, violently radical, that surely it ought to have been enough, more than enough. But look what happens. You open the door and all heaven and hell break loose." She continues, "This is the truth of the pervading intricacy of the world's detail: the creation is not a study, a roughed-in sketch; it is supremely, meticulously created, created abundantly, extravagantly, and in fine detail." Then she invites the reader to look around: "Look, in short, at practically anything—the coot's feet, the mantis's face, a banana, the human ear—and see that not only did the creator create everything, but that he is apt to create *anything*. He'll stop at nothing."[19]

In Western thought we once described the universe as being like a machine. Then we came to view it more as an organism. Then "Sir James Jeans, British astronomer and physicist, suggested that the universe was beginning to look more like a great thought." Dillard adds, "But if the thinker's attention strays for a minute, his simplest thought ceases altogether."[20] We are on the right track. God's *Logos* (thought, word,

---

[18] Annie Dillard, *Pilgrim at Tinker Creek* (New York: Harper's Magazine Press, 1974).
[19] Ibid., 131, 134–35 (Dillard's italics).
[20] Ibid., 145.

message . . . Son) brings forth the creation, orders it, and holds it together (John 1:1–3; Col. 1:15–17; Heb. 1:1–4).

But the universe seems so dynamic. There is so much flux, so much change. It almost overwhelms us with its complexity and diversity. Was there a plan? *Is* there a plan? We would only know it if God told us. And he has: "I made the earth, and created humankind upon it; it was my hands that stretched out the heavens, and I commanded all their host" (Isa. 45:12). It is something we know only by faith: "By faith we understand that the universe was formed by God's command [lit., the word of God], so that the visible came forth from the invisible" (Heb. 11:3 REB).[21] But what of his plan? Did God build the universe the way we build a house—beginning with a lot of detailed plans? This is worth investigating.

God's Plan

One of Pat Robertson's best books came on the heels of his devastating defeat in his run for the presidency. The book was simply titled *The Plan*.[22] The Four Spiritual Laws begin with these encouraging words: "God loves you and has a wonderful plan for your life." *Does* God have a wonderful plan for our lives? One Calvinist friend of mine said he could not in good conscience use this presentation of the gospel because he didn't necessarily believe that statement. Is God's plan for the "nonelect" good? He was raising an important question. Does God simply write a script and determine everything, or is there real freedom in the universe?

I have a distinctive bias in this regard. My thinking is decidedly marked by a dominant strand of Southern Baptist theology that elevates the importance of freedom. Perhaps the key Baptist patriarchs who have influenced me are E. Y. Mullins and Herschel Hobbs. These theologians, I believe, have captured both the spirit and the letter of the Scriptures in relation to God's sovereignty and humankind's freedom. This is a mindset that stands in sharp contrast to much Reformed theology, which has dominated evangelical theology over the decades and is reflected in the writings of such respected scholars as J. I. Packer, Millard Erickson, Carl F. H. Henry, R. C. Sproul, and others. At the same time, it is essentially harmonious with the Reformed theology of Donald Bloesch.

---

[21] See Jewett, *God, Creation, and Revelation*, 453–54.

[22] Pat Robertson, *The Plan* (Nashville: Thomas Nelson, 1989).

The more I study and reflect on this issue, the more I am convinced that this is the genius of Baptist theology: (1) that God has given us real freedom; (2) that he elects us all in Christ; (3) that Christ died for all of us and each of us; (4) that tragically we can resist his grace because he has given us a choice; and (5) that God knows how to keep us and finish what he starts in our lives. (In other words, God really does have a wonderful plan for our lives!) Calvinists can only *fully* agree with that fifth point. This wonderful concept of freedom is a key ingredient to understanding the sovereign reign of God over the cosmos.

The prevailing opinion, led by such historical theological giants as Augustine and Calvin, has been that God has *decreed* everything that happens before the creation of the universe. The instinct to guard the biblical truth of God's sovereign freedom, control, purpose, plan, and will is valid. What is not valid is the belief that God must determine everything that happens in order to be able to control it. As Mullins and Hobbs say: "A holy and loving God *permits* some things that he does not *perpetrate.*"[23]

This wonderful concept of freedom is a key ingredient to understanding the sovereign reign of God over the cosmos.

Nevertheless, Scripture is replete with teaching that God's sovereign purpose and plans, his counsel and will, prevail. We see it in the natural order. Job, in his final reply to his friends, points the way to divine wisdom. He says to look to the doctrine of creation. God alone knows the way to wisdom, Job insists,

> For he looks to the ends of the earth,
> and sees everything under the heavens.
> When he gave to the wind its weight,
> and apportioned out the waters by measure;
> when he made a decree for the rain,
> and a way for the thunderbolt;
> then he saw it and declared it;
> he established it, and searched it out.
> And he said to humankind,
> "Truly, the fear of the Lord, that is wisdom;
> and to depart from evil is understanding." (Job 28:24–28)

---

[23] Herschel H. Hobbs and E. Y. Mullins, *The Axioms of Religion*, rev. ed. (Nashville: Broadman, 1978), 64 (Hobbs's and Mullins's italics). Hobbs revised and updated this classic of Baptist theology, originally written by Mullins.

In another wisdom passage we are told that God "gave to the sea its decree, that the waters should not pass his commandment" (Prov. 8:29 KJV). The Lord again asserts this same truth that the sea's boundaries have been set in the sand "by a perpetual decree," no matter how much the waves may toss and roar, and that, therefore, we should fear the Lord (Jer. 5:22 NKJV). Nature itself gives abundant testimony to the order God has established in his sovereign control. He has decreed the paths of the stars and planets. He has sovereignly ordered the inner workings of the atom. Our universe—more accurately, *his* universe—works reliably according to the design and decree of its maker.

History also is under God's sovereign control. As Hezekiah prayed, "O LORD, God of Israel, enthroned between the cherubim, you alone are God over all the kingdoms of the earth. You have made heaven and earth" (2 Kings 19:15 NIV). Everything in heaven and earth is God's, and the kingdom is his alone. He is exalted as head over all and is the ruler of all things (1 Chron. 29:11, 12). He is "the great King over all the earth ... [who] reigns over the nations ... [and] is seated on his holy throne.... The kings of the earth belong to God" (Ps. 47:2, 8–9 NIV). "He changes times and seasons, deposes kings and sets up kings" (Dan. 2:21). "He does as he pleases with the powers of heaven and the peoples of the earth" (Dan. 4:35 NIV). As the psalmist says: "Our God is in the heavens; he does whatever he pleases" (Ps. 115:3).

God's will, plan, and purpose ultimately prevail.

God's will, plan, and purpose ultimately prevail. "The human mind may devise many plans, but it is the purpose of the LORD that will be established" (Prov. 19:21). Paul says that in Christ "we were also chosen, having been predestined according to the plan of him who works out everything in conformity with the purpose of his will" (Eph. 1:11 NIV). "But the plans of the LORD stand firm forever, the purposes of his heart through all generations" (Ps. 33:11 NIV). Isaiah exalts the Lord and praises his name "for in perfect faithfulness you have done marvelous things, things planned long ago" (Isa. 25:1 NIV). The Lord says, "I make known the end from the beginning, from ancient times, what is still to come. I say: My purpose will stand, and I will do all that I please" (Isa. 46:10 NIV). "Who can speak and have it happen if the Lord has not decreed it?" (Lam. 3:37 NIV).

Paul K. Jewett, writing from a Reformed perspective, adds these cautionary words:

> To trace the world back to the decree of God is to say that the world is not here by accident but by the resolve and purpose of an all-wise Creator. Yet our concurrence with "decretal theology" is not without reservation. The doctrine of the divine decree is easily stated in such a way that the relationship between God and the world becomes a static rather than a dynamic one. Such a static view threatens not only one's doctrine of creation, but also one's doctrine of providence, by undercutting the reality of human freedom, the seriousness of human responsibility, and the significance of human history.[24]

The error Jewett warns against has unfortunately been evident time and again among those who rightly seek to guard the doctrines of God's grace and sovereignty.

The Reformed teaching of the divine foreordination of everything that happens is the prime example of the error Jewett cautions against (although I am sure that Jewett would not couch the problem in the same terms that I am about to use). Although every effort is generally made to avoid the appearance of determinism, the end result is the same: Authentic human freedom is sacrificed on the altar of divine sovereignty. It is well known that Calvin taught that God *decreed* Adam's fall, not just permitted it. Somehow people think that the only way God can be supremely sovereign is to, in effect, cause everything to happen. Reformed theologians often try to smooth this over. But the end result is the same—a theistic determinism that, in my opinion, goes far afield from the Scriptures.

Jack Cottrell has expressed the issue well:

> In many ways this reduces to a disagreement not over the basic nature of God, but over the basic nature of the *creation.* What kind of *creation* did God purpose to make? One that has no capability of acting independently of God in any way whatsoever? One in which he must predetermine every specific motion, no matter how minute? Or one that has been freely endowed with a measure of freedom concerning individual movements, decisions, and actions? I, along with most non-Calvinists, have opted for this latter model. But if this was the kind of world God decided to make, then this *was* his decree, and it was a *sovereign* decree. This is the kind of world he wanted; so this is the kind of world he decreed and made.[25]

---

[24] Jewett, *God, Creation, and Revelation,* 452.

[25] Jack W. Cottrell, "The Nature of the Divine Sovereignty" in Clark H. Pinnock, ed., *The Grace of God, the Will of Man* (Grand Rapids: Zondervan, 1989), 107 (Cottrell's italics). See also Cottrell's excellent volume, *What the Bible Says About God the Ruler* (Joplin, Mo.: College Press, 1984).

Cottrell's point is well taken. This area needs clarification on the present evangelical scene.

The reality of our freedom in no way diminishes God's majesty and sovereignty:

> This granting of freedom to man is not an evidence of weakness in God but of strength. An absolute dictatorship shows its weakness in denying any freedom to its subjects. Liberty granted to its subjects is evidence of democracy's strength.
>
> God is not in the business of building robots, but of developing self-conscious and responsible human beings.[26]

Furthermore, the Arminian doctrine of divine foreknowledge also fits the biblical pattern well. But even Millard Erickson accepts the fuzzy thinking of Calvinistic determinists when he asserts that foreknowledge implies determination.[27] A little Southern Baptist common sense goes a long way in this regard:

The reality of our freedom in no way diminishes God's majesty and sovereignty.

> But foreknowledge of events does not necessarily mean that God causes them. At the finite level you may know that two cars are going to collide at an intersection. But this does not mean that you cause it. Because of his omnipresence God knows all things simultaneously, without need of reason or thought processes. But it is contrary to the Bible's presentation of God's nature as holy, righteous, and loving to attribute to him the evil that transpires in the world.[28]

This issue will surface again when we consider divine providence. At this juncture, the important point is that God's sovereign purpose and control do not entail the foreordination of all events. Rather, while God is in *control* of the entire natural and historical processes, he at the same time allows authentic freedom.

In the Beginning . . .

The two most important chapters in the Bible for understanding the *Christian* doctrine of creation are Genesis 1 and John 1. Both chapters start with the same words, "in the beginning." "The first word about cre-

---

[26] Hobbs and Mullins, *The Axioms of Religion*, 113–14.

[27] Millard J. Erickson, *Christian Theology* (Grand Rapids: Baker, 1985), 360.

[28] Hobbs and Mullins, *The Axioms of Religion*, 63.

ation is Genesis 1, but the final word is John 1."[29] In Genesis we have a majestic account of the creation of everything that is. In John the doctrines of creation and redemption are woven into a seamless fabric, with the focal point being the Incarnate Word, who brings grace to the world. Both the *great news* of creation and the *good news* of redemption overshadow the *bad news* of the sin of humankind. Genesis 1 is the old creation. John 1 is the new creation, which, as we will see, provides the analogy for the old. A truly Christian doctrine of creation always holds the two together. "Hence, in the Christian understanding of creation, Genesis 1 is always interpreted in the light of John 1."[30]

The Bible's first words are:

> In the beginning God created the heavens and the earth. Now the earth was formless and empty, darkness was over the surface of the deep, and the Spirit of God was hovering over the waters.
>
> And God said, "Let there be light," and there was light. God saw that the light was good. (Gen. 1:1–4 NIV)

In these opening verses of Scripture we have almost every major theme of the Christian doctrine of creation.

The Hebrew verb for "create" (*baraʾ*) is distinctive in Scripture; it is used only of divine activity, never of human activity. We human beings must always have existing matter in order to create; God, however, creates matter itself. The phrase "the heavens and the earth" means "the universe" in modern parlance. God *speaks* the universe into existence (cf. Ps. 33:6, 9; 148:5; Heb. 11:3). This is *creatio ex nihilo,* creation out of nothing. And he pronounces everything he creates *good* (culminating with "very good" in Gen. 1:31).

The Holy Trinity creates the universe. The "Spirit of God was hovering over the waters" (Gen. 1:2 NIV; see also Job 26:13; 33:4; Ps. 33:6; 104:30; Isa. 40:12–13). The picture is that of a great bird hovering over her nest as well as (perhaps) a mighty wind sweeping over the waters. God the Son was also involved in the creation, as the prologue of John's Gospel testifies. Here again, we encounter with some of the most beautiful words in the Bible:

> In the beginning was the Word, and the Word was with God, and the Word was God. He was with God in the beginning.

---

[29] Jewett, *God, Creation, and Revelation,* 494.

[30] Ibid., 445.

> Through him all things were made; without him nothing was made that has been made. In him was life, and that life was the light of all people. The light shines in the darkness, and the darkness has not overcome it. (John 1:1–5 TNIV)

The prologue to Hebrews expresses the same truth concerning God's Son:

> When in times past God spoke to our forefathers, he spoke in many and varied ways through the prophets. But in this the final age he has spoken to us in his Son, whom he has appointed heir of all things; and through him he created the universe. He is the radiance of God's glory, the stamp of God's very being, and he sustains the universe by his word of power. (Heb. 1:1–3 REB)

The writer of Hebrews also applies Psalm 102:25 to Jesus Christ: "In the beginning, Lord, you founded the earth, and the heavens are the work of your hands" (Heb. 1:10).

Paul's letter to the Colossians gives the same testimony: "In [or by] him all things in heaven and on earth were created, things visible and invisible ... all things have been created through him and for him. He himself is before all things, and in [or by] him all things hold together" (Col. 1:15–17). And to the Corinthians Paul wrote: "Yet for us there is one God, the Father, from whom are all things and for whom we exist, and one Lord, Jesus Christ, through whom are all things and through whom we exist" (1 Cor. 8:6).

Viewing these passages contextually further corroborates the close relation between creation and redemption. The gospel *is* related to the doctrine of creation. Paul explained to the Ephesians that he was a servant of the gospel and "the plan of the mystery hidden for ages in God who created all things; so that through the church the wisdom of God in its rich variety might now be made known" (Eph. 3:9–10). The gracious plan of redemption was given by God the Creator to the *church.* It is through redemption that God's purpose in creation *will* be fulfilled. "The biblical theme which embodies the story of how God is carrying out his cosmic purpose is the *Kingdom of God.* ... All history is moving toward the day when God will establish with finality the universal acknowledgment of his lordship (Isaiah 45:23)."[31]

We enter that kingdom and his church through becoming a new creation. "Let there be light" happens afresh when one enters the kingdom

---

[31] Cottrell, *What the Bible Says About God the Creator,* 159 (Cottrell's italics).

(see 2 Cor. 4:6; Eph. 5:14). "So if anyone is in Christ, there is a new creation: everything old has passed away; see, everything has become new!" (2 Cor. 5:17). *Ex nihilo,* God brings forth the new creation—just as he did the old! But we must first humble ourselves and admit our need. As Martin Luther poignantly said: "It is God's nature to make something out of nothing. This is why God cannot make anything out of him who is not yet nothing."[32]

And God Said . . .

Returning to Genesis, we next seek to discern the pattern and purpose of the original account of creation. Our primary focus in this chapter will be on Genesis 1; Genesis 2 we will save for the ensuing chapter on humanity. It is notoriously difficult to treat these verses adequately. We are always looking for ways to make the Scriptures "fit" modern science, or conversely we try to come up with a "science" that fits the Scriptures. Our goal should be to allow the Bible to speak for itself.

I will be taking a literary approach to Genesis. Working from the conviction that the Bible must first be understood in its historical context, I see the initial clue to properly apprehending the Genesis message is to probe the type of literature we are dealing with in these opening chapters. Those who have a penchant for the prosaic (wooden literalists) always have a difficult time with the first and last books of the Bible. The powerful symbolism of apocalyptic literature—as seen in Revelation—and the equally powerful symbolic language of ancient Near Eastern literature—the milieu out of which Genesis comes—are both problematic to superficial literalism.

A careful initial observation of Genesis 1 reveals a number of characteristics. We have here neither a scientific treatise nor a straightforward historical narrative. This is a stylized piece that treats origins—things that transpired long before there could be any sort of journalistic or historical account as we know them. These majestic, programmatic passages perfectly introduce both the patriarchal narratives that follow as well as the entire Bible. This is *poetic prose*: neither straightforward Hebrew poetry nor historical narrative. They have a hymnic ring and strong symbolic content. They tell the *who, what,* and *why* of creation, but very little about the *when* and *how* (thus, our divergent conclusions today; see below).

---

[32] Cited in Helmut Thielicke, *How the World Began,* trans. John W. Doberstein (Philadelphia: Muhlenberg, 1961), opening page of quotations.

Genesis is ancient Near Eastern literature. It must therefore be interpreted in much the same way that we interpret other ancient Near Eastern literature. When compared with this literature, Genesis surprises us with its similarities, but even more with its dissimilarities. While the style is similar, the content is significantly contrasting. Genesis is in part a critique of Mesopotamian polytheism; it serves just as well today as a critique of modern paganism (secularism).[33] The opening verses evince a beautiful literary framework, which I would like now to present.[34]

The descriptive words "formless and empty" in verse 2 (NIV) provide the framework for the entire passage (Gen. 1:1–2:3). The first three days of creation are days of forming: God *separates* and *gathers*. The next three days are days of filling: God *makes* and *fills*. (He also commands to *be fruitful* and *increase*.) Days 1/4, 2/5, and 3/6 correlate.[35] The framework of the six days of creation in Genesis 1 can be displayed as follows:[36]

Days of forming	*Days of filling*
1. "light" (v. 3)	4. "lights" (v. 14)
2. "water under the expanse . . . water above it" (v. 7)	5. "every living and moving thing with which the water teems . . . every winged bird" (v. 21)
3. a. "dry ground" (v. 9)	6. a. "livestock, creatures that move along the ground, and wild animals" (v. 24); "man" (v. 26)
b. "vegetation" (v. 11)	b. "every green plant for food" (v. 30)

What is formed in Day 1 is filled in Day 4; what is formed in Day 2, is filled in Day 5; and so on. Obviously, no strict chronology is being followed. In Hebrew the only day that has the definite article *the* before it is Day 6. The others are literally translated "one day," "a second day," "a third day," and so on.

---

[33] See William Sanford LaSor, David Allan Hubbard, and Frederic Wm. Bush, *Old Testament Survey* (Grand Rapids: Eerdmans, 1982), ch. 7. The authors provide the most helpful introduction to these opening chapters of Genesis that I have been able to discover.

[34] The reader is referred to the following, from which I have adapted my overview of Genesis: Youngblood, *The Book of Genesis*, 21–32; Kenneth Barker, gen. ed., *The NIV Study Bible* (Grand Rapids: Zondervan, 1985), 6–8, for which the study notes to Genesis were provided by Youngblood. I will also be referring to: James I. Packer, "The Challenge of Biblical Interpretation: Creation," in *The Proceedings of the Conference on Biblical Interpretation: 1988* (Nashville: Broadman, 1988), 21–33. It is to Kenneth A. Matthews's response to Packer that I owe the remark concerning the who, what, why, how, and when questions related to creation (*Proceedings*, 39–40).

[35] It is a fascinating exercise simply to go through the NIV text, marking these words and following this pattern.

[36] *NIV Study Bible*, 6.

At the same time, it must be emphasized that *nonchronological* does not mean *nonhistorical.* The *fact,* not the *myth,* of creation is being communicated, albeit in a more liturgical fashion. J. I. Packer's remarks are helpful at this point. This framework or literary view—"a total poetical picture of the fact of creation, that is, a total pictorial presentation of the reality of God bringing the world into being"—"is the only viable one," according to Packer. One need only note that light is created on Day 1, while the sun, moon, and stars are not created until Day 4. Packer ultimately concludes that this majestic passage is "a celebratory presentation of the fact of creation for purposes of doxology, and basic instruction made in the form of a picture of a week's work." Packer adds: "There are many pictorial presentations of God at work in Scripture. This is one of them."[37]

Packer also delineates three didactic purposes, one polemical concern, and one nurturing purpose. The first teaching purpose is the knowledge of God: "What he is saying is not meet the creation, as if you have never seen the sun and the moon and the stars and the animals and human beings before, but meet the Creator." Next, the passage communicates knowledge of ourselves as made in God's image and as stewards of the creation. Finally, it teaches the divinely established Sabbath rest. The polemical concern is that of polytheism, magic, and superstitious cults. And the nurturing purpose is one of worship, rest, and the cultural mandate. We honor God with our worship and our work in a weekly cycle, which includes one day of rest.[38]

William LaSor, David Hubbard, and Frederick Bush provide a useful summary of this literary approach to the opening chapters of Genesis:

> Recognizing the literary technique and form and noting the literary background of chs. 1—11 does not constitute a challenge to the reality, the "eventness," of the facts portrayed. One need not regard this account as myth; however, it is not "history" in the modern sense of eyewitness, objective reporting. Rather, it conveys theological truths about events, portrayed in a largely symbolic, pictorial literary genre. This is not to say that Gen. 1—11 conveys historical falsehood. That conclusion would follow only if it purported to contain objective descriptions. The clear evidence already reviewed shows that such was not the intent. On the other hand, the view that the truths taught in these chapters

---

[37] Packer, "The Challenge of Biblical Interpretation: Creation," 29–30.

[38] Ibid., 27–28.

> have no objective basis is mistaken. They affirm fundamental truths: creation of all things by God; special divine intervention in the production of the first man and woman; unity of the human race; pristine goodness of the created world, including humanity; entrance of sin through the disobedience of the first pair; depravity and rampant sin after the Fall. All these truths are facts, and their certainty implies the reality of the facts.[39]

This helpful perspective on the biblical materials will also clarify our considerations of the doctrines of humanity and sin that follow in subsequent chapters.

Summary of Theological Assertions

Here, then, is a brief list of the salient biblical truths we have discovered thus far. These are the major theological tenets of the doctrine of creation:

1. *creatio ex nihilo*: The universe was created by God out of nothing; there was no preexisting material; God is both totally distinct from, yet intimately related to, the created order.
2. *divine freedom*: God did not bring forth the universe by necessity but by a free and loving choice.
3. *all inclusive*: God made everything that is: *ta panta* in the Greek New Testament—often translated "the universe" in REB (Eph. 3:9; Col. 1:16; cf. Eph. 1:10; cf. also Rev. 4:11).
4. *the goodness of creation*: God repeatedly pronounced everything he made good (Gen. 1:4, 10, 12, 18, 21, 25; in 1:31, "very good").
5. *humanity in God's image*: Humanity is the crowning achievement of God's creation.
6. *rejection of polytheism*: There is only one God.
7. *rejection of dualism*: Nothing is eternal but our good God.
8. *rejection of deism*: God is no clockmaker deity who "wound up" the universe and now lets it run on its own.

Volumes could be—and have been!—written on each of these points. It is readily apparent that the doctrine of creation is one of the major teachings of Scripture, a teaching that informs every other doctrine of the Bible.

---

[39] LaSor, Hubbard, and Bush, *Old Testament Survey*, 74.

Implications of the Doctrine of Creation

What are some implications of the doctrine of creation? We begin with the fact that the meaning of the creation is, in the final analysis, found only in the knowledge of the Creator. We must quickly add that one can fully enter into the *enjoyment* of creation through this loving knowledge. Too often Christianity has been offered as some sort of asceticism, when the opposite is true. Jesus' Jewish opponents said John the Baptist (an ascetic) had a demon, but they accused Jesus of being "a glutton and a drunkard" (Matt. 11:19; Luke 7:34). Jesus broke all the restricting religious molds. He entered fully into life and enjoyed it to the hilt. He was a careful observer of nature. He took great delight in children. He enjoyed friendships, even with persons of the opposite sex. He attended social gatherings and in general enjoyed the pleasures of daily life. Jesus was no ascetic.

The goodness of creation means that every dimension of it has been designed by God. Human sexuality was God's idea. The joys of marriage and family were God's idea. We are literally inundated with the beauty and pleasures of the created order that surrounds us. Work and the other creative expressions of human culture are a part of God's design. Christians who rightly apprehend the biblical doctrine of creation are not world-denying sorts. They oppose the sinful perversions of worldly pleasures, but not the pleasures themselves. C. S. Lewis maintained that the disdain of enjoyment "crept in from Kant and the Stoics and is no part of the Christian faith." Our hunger for joy and happiness is not the problem, he adds. The problem is that "we are far too easily pleased."[40]

John Calvin saw colors, smells, beauty, music, food, drink, clothing, and other earthly pleasures as good gifts from a good God.[41] In fact, for all the bad press they have been given, the Puritans showed this same sort of *joie de vivre.* Believe it or not, they were actually the social progressives of their day![42] Evangelicals need to rediscover their Puritan heritage. Even more important, we must apprehend more fully the biblical doctrine of creation with all its ramifications.[43] One thing that has

---

[40] C. S. Lewis, *The Weight of Glory* (Grand Rapids: Eerdmans, 1949), 1–2.

[41] Cf., e.g., John Calvin, *Institutes of the Christian Religion,* 2 vols., ed. John T. McNeill, trans. Ford Lewis Battles (Philadelphia: Westminster, 1960), 1:719–21 (III.x.1–2).

[42] See Leland Ryken, *Worldly Saints: The Puritans As They Really Were* (Grand Rapids: Zondervan, 1986), for an engaging, yet objective, portrayal of the Puritans.

[43] Cf. Shirley C. Guthrie Jr., *Christian Doctrine* (Atlanta: John Knox, 1968), 159–65; and John Piper, *Desiring God: Meditations of a Christian Hedonist* (Portland, Ore.: Multnomah, 1986).

attracted me—and millions of others—to the writings of Chuck Swindoll down through the years is this same authentic, earthy spirituality that is able to laugh and enjoy God's creation and God's creatures. It is here that we also see the close link between creation and the Incarnation. The Incarnation itself is an affirmation of the doctrine of creation.

Finally, any reader of this tome probably does not need to be reminded that the doctrine of creation is also an affirmation of the mind. Jesus said that we should love God with all our heart, soul, *mind*, and strength (Mark 12:29–30). Some experientialists may have missed this: Our minds matter to God![44] There is a dangerous zeal that is not according to knowledge (see Rom. 10:2), but apart from this there is simply an impoverishment of our spiritual lives that results from neglecting this dimension of our being. One area in which our minds have definitely had to be engaged is that of relating modern science to the biblical doctrine of creation.

Science and Scripture

Too often today Christian students from the elementary grades through graduate studies are presented with a dilemma: to accept either (1) naturalistic evolution or (2) so-called "scientific creationism"—as if those are the only too options. On the one hand, the universe is depicted as a brute fact of matter, motion, and chance with no ultimate meaning or purpose. On the other hand, students are given the option of accepting an extravagant theory that the world only *appears* to be old because of a universal flood. In addition, it is often implied or even stated explicitly that any so-called Christian who questions this latter theory is theologically or even spiritually suspect. They are accused of not believing the Bible, when in reality it is only a particular *interpretation* of the Bible and of the scientific evidence that they question.

With this context in mind, I would like to provide the reader with at least seven different options for correlating biblical and scientific data that relate to the doctrine of creation. These varied theories can be delineated as follows:

1. The gap theory
2. The flood theory

[44] See John R. W. Stott, *Your Mind Matters* (Downers Grove, Ill.: InterVarsity Press, 1972).

3. The pictorial or revelatory day theory
4. The appearance of age theory
5. Progressive creationism
6. Theistic evolution
7. Intelligent design

(1) *The gap theory* argues that there is a "gap" between Genesis 1:1 and 1:2 of perhaps billions of years. The first verse describes an original creation aeons ago. Then Satan fell, and the world was ruined (probably by God's judgment). The earth *became* formless and empty (v. 2). Verses 3–31 are, therefore, actually an account of the *reconstruction* or re-creation of the world.

The Scofield Reference Bible (1909) popularized this theory among conservatives for a number of generations. It is actually an ingenious interpretation, allowing for geological ages as well as a recent creation (actually *re*creation) some six thousand years ago in six twenty-four-hour periods. Unfortunately, this is a form of *eisegesis*—that is, a "reading into" the text content that simply is not there. Neither the immediate context nor any other biblical passages support this so-called "gap" between verses 1 and 2. One scientific question that remains is the radical difference between our present forms of life and those we see in the fossil records. How can we legitimately call this a reconstruction with such a disparity.[45] Even a Jurassic Park could not compensate for this inadequacy!

(2) By far, the theory that has received the most attention in recent years is the *flood theory*. Go into the average Christian bookstore and ask for help on books about science and Scripture, and you will more than likely be pointed toward literature that represents this viewpoint. Hundreds of local churches across the country have sponsored conferences in which a representative of this theory will overwhelm the listeners with "scientific" evidence supporting this theory. It is the theory defended by the Creation Research Society. Perhaps the most influential book in this school of thought is *The Genesis Flood*, by John C. Whitcomb Jr. and Henry M. Morris,[46] although hundreds of other volumes are available. Two other well-known proponents of this view are Duane T. Gish and

[45] See L. Duane Thurman, *How to Think about Evolution* (Downers Grove, Ill.: InterVarsity Press, 1978), 121. Dr. Thurman's excellent analysis of the various Bible-science controversies is still well worth consulting. He also provides a concise overview of most of the theories presented here.

[46] John C. Whitcomb Jr. and Henry M. Morris, *The Genesis Flood* (Philadelphia: Presbyterian & Reformed, 1961).

Thomas G. Barnes. Advocates of this position usually insist that this is the only legitimate understanding that remains faithful to the Bible (read in a literalistic fashion). This position is self-named as "creation science" or "scientific creationism."

At its humble beginnings, one finds the revelations and writings of Ellen G. White (Seventh-day Adventism), which definitely influenced George McCready Price, one of the early popularizers of creationism. White claimed to have been taken back in a vision to the original week of creation. It was a literal week of twenty-four-hour days. Now the entire fascinating history of scientific creationism is available in the prize-winning volume by Ronald L. Numbers: *The Creationists: The Evolution of Scientific Creationism.*[47] Scientific creationism has attracted hundreds of scientists with earned doctorates and is a formidable movement in contemporary Christianity.

In simplest terms the flood theory is a flood geology. The explanation for the apparent age of the earth is the universal flood of Noah's day. During that cataclysmic flood the more motile and complex organisms were buried in sediment closer to the top. The less motile organisms would, of course, be found in lower strata. Scientific creationists have never been able to adequately explain, however, how plants, which are *not* motile, could reach the higher levels.[48] Also, it is imperative to accept the concept of a universal flood, which has difficulties both biblically and scientifically. Finally, this view definitely requires a wooden, literalistic reading of Genesis 1 as a virtual scientific description of creation. Most evangelical theologians today view this theory as sincere but misinformed.

There are as many problems with flood geology as there are with naturalistic evolution, and the militarism of the creation science movement sometimes produces more problems than it solves. Nevertheless, it will continue to thrive, if for no other reason than the fact that its adherents continue aggressively to promote the theory at the grass roots level.

(3) *The pictorial* or *revelatory day theory* argues that the six days of Genesis 1 are days of *revelation,* not days of creation. God revealed that he is the Creator to Moses in six consecutive days; he did not actually create the universe in that time period. Of course, the obvious difficulty with

---

[47] Ronald L. Numbers, *The Creationists: The Evolution of Scientific Creationism* (New York: Knopf, 1992). The information on Ellen G. White and George McCready Price can be found on pp. 73–75.

[48] See Thurman, *How to Think about Evolution,* 122.

this approach is that a straightforward reading of the text seems to indicate that creation, not revelation, is in purview (although we have received this knowledge of divine creation by revelation—the Scriptures themselves).

(4) *The appearance of age theory* is even more ingenious. Since Adam and Eve very probably had navels, trees had rings, and so forth—all pointing to a past that never actually existed—so the earth also was brought forth with an apparent antiquity that never existed. Although irrefutable (and somewhat amusing), the theory raises serious questions. Is not God portrayed as somewhat deceptive in this theory of creation? Could not the universe, by this same argument, have been created *five minutes ago*? And, on a more humorous note, how do we know that Adam and Eve had navels? Perhaps a modicum of humor, humility, and tolerance is needed in all our conversations about our beginnings. After all, none of us was there to see how it all transpired.

Progressive Creationism

(5) *Progressive creationism* probably has the greatest acceptance among evangelical scholars. The two dominant forms of this theory are the *day-age theory* and the *literary framework view. The day-age theory* notes that the Hebrew word for day (*yom*) can also refer to an extended period of time. Therefore, it poses, the biblical account actually describes a series of divine creative acts over a long period of time, and this description also correlates with the geological and fossil record. Millard Erickson provides this helpful definition of progressive creationism:

> The teaching that God created *de novo* in several steps; that is, he created the first member of each "kind," which then developed (or evolved). The kinds, then, have not evolved from one another in an uninterrupted causal chain. This view, which is sometimes called microevolution (evolution within kinds) as opposed to macroevolution (evolution across kinds), puts emphasis upon the fact of creation rather than upon evolution. God created man *in toto*, fashioning both the material and immaterial aspects of human nature *de novo*; he did not use an existing being that had evolved physically and modify it into a human.[49]

Clearly, this position accords better with the findings of natural science, allowing for the antiquity of the universe and humankind. The

[49] Millard J. Erickson, *Concise Dictionary of Christian Theology* (Grand Rapids: Baker, 1986), 39.

major question that must be raised, however, is whether the biblical days of creation can be that easily correlated with the geological eras.

The literary framework view was expounded in-depth earlier, when we explored the Genesis 1 creation account. The study notes on this passage in *The NIV Study Bible* reflect this view. It offers a natural handling of the Scriptures in their historical and literary settings, and it allows for an old earth cosmogony. This observation leads us naturally into a consideration of the final theory evangelicals have put forward in relating the Scriptures to modern scientific knowledge.

Theistic Evolution

(6) *Theistic evolution* has gained popular acceptance, even in evangelical circles. The Bible tells us *who* created the universe, and evolution tells us *how*, according to this theory. At first blush, it sounds appealing; the war is over! But, of course, it isn't. At the very least, humanity still must be seen as unique in the created order, which requires some form of divine intervention in the natural processes. This is not problematic for Christian theologians, but it is a faith perspective not shared by naturalists.

Other questions must also be raised. Does the concept of natural selection match up with the biblical tenet of a *good* creation? Is there really conclusive evidence for *macroevolution*, that is, of development from one species or kind to another? *Microevolution*, development *within* kinds, is generally accepted by all, but macroevolution is still strongly theoretical.[50] We must also remind ourselves that science is continually in flux. What we have today are evolutionary *theories*. Where will we be five years from now? It is never wise to put all one's eggs in one basket in this regard.

Nonetheless, the evolutionary model prevails today, and many Christians committed to biblical inerrancy are able to reconcile this concept with the scriptural doctrine of divine creation. Many in the American Scientific Affiliation (ASA), an evangelical Christian organization that promotes research in this area, espouse theistic evolution. Since the ASA focuses more on dialogue among scholars than on making their findings known to the general public, their work is largely unknown at the grass roots level—in contrast to the work of the Creation Research Society. Perhaps the leading advocate of this position is Howard J. Van Till.

---

[50] Thurman, *How to Think about Evolution*, passim (esp. 124–25).

Van Till does not like the label *theistic evolution* because it seems to put the accent on the natural processes of the creation rather than on the Creator himself. He prefers to call his view *the creationomic or fully gifted creation perspective.* His view can be seen as closely related to progressive creationism: Both theories argue for an old universe, the antiquity of humankind, and development within the creation. Both positions are solidly committed to the inerrancy of Scripture. They differ, however, in their interpretations of Genesis and perhaps of certain scientific data. Howard J. Van Till has provided one of the best expositions of this approach in his volume, *The Fourth Day: What the Bible and the Heavens Are Telling Us about the Creation.*[51]

Van Till approaches Genesis 1 in the same manner in which I presented this chapter earlier.[52] Just as Youngblood, Packer, and others have said (including the notes of *The NIV Study Bible*), Genesis 1 is a literary introduction to the Creator and the *fact* of creation. It was not intended to provide a chronological and scientific account of precisely *how* God brought forth the universe. Thus, there is no need to attempt to correlate the days of creation with the epochs of geological development, for example.

In addition, the evolutionary model of modern science can be accepted *with some modifications.* Primarily, the nuance that differentiates Van Till's perspective from naturalistic evolution is the emphasis on divine activity rather than natural process. Van Till, for example, refuses to call his position *theistic evolution* (though in actuality it is) because of this very problem. "Theistic evolution" seems to connote natural processes that God manages to take over and use for his purposes, as if these processes were independent from God. "Divine action ought always to be the matter of primary importance, with natural process as the secondary or contingent reality."[53] Van Till continues:

> This emphasis on the primacy of divine action should not, however, be interpreted as implying that God deterministically causes every event that occurs in his Creation. This Creation is no mere puppet, and its Creator is not some sort of divine puppeteer whose control eliminates the possibility for responsible freedom of action on the part of his creatures. Within the dynamic order of the divinely governed Creation and

---

[51] Howard J. Van Till, *The Fourth Day: What the Bible and the Heavens Are Telling Us about the Creation* (Grand Rapids: Eerdmans, 1986).

[52] See ibid., ch. 5.

[53] Ibid., 265.

> its divinely directed history there appears to be a remarkable balance between predictable regularities and meaningful contingencies. Natural history is permeated with events that are contingent on circumstance and with occasions in which choice must be exercised by responsible creatures. As we noted earlier, the Creation of which we are a part is a fitting context for human responsibility.[54]

Van Till has collaborated with other scholars to provide fascinating perspectives on the labyrinthian paths of contemporary discourse on this subject in *Portraits of Creation: Biblical and Scientific Perspectives on the World's Formation.*[55] Van Till has also contributed to a recent volume that addresses the dilemma with which I began this section: the necessity to choose between naturalistic evolution and scientific creationism. Those are *not* the only options![56]

Finally, this perspective also provides a needed emphasis on *continuing creation.* The biblical doctrine of creation repudiates deism. The Bible portrays God as intimately involved with everything that happens both in nature and in human history. Even Christians look at a terrifyingly beautiful thunderstorm in naturalistic terms, when in reality they should be perceiving the glory of God (see Psalm 29). When we tell our children that God made them, we should not be embarrassed. It is procreation, but it is also creation (Ps. 139:13–18). Continuing creation is really divine providence, in which God upholds, preserves, and governs that which he has made.

However, having said all this, serious cautions are in order. As Van Till has continued to clarify his position, some potentially fatal flaws in his theory have surfaced, in the opinion of competing theorists.[57] His use of the literary framework approach to the Genesis materials is not problematic. In fact, progressive creation advocates often take this approach. As one listens closely to Van Till's argument, it becomes clear that he seems to be speaking out both sides of his mouth. On the one hand, he attempts to depict the evolutionary process as the result of God's "gifting" his creation. But is that the picture actually offered by the evolutionary model? Far from it! It is a tooth and claw, wasteful, and ulti-

---

[54] Ibid.

[55] Howard J. Van Till, Robert E. Snow, John H. Stek, and Davis A. Young, *Portraits of Creation: Biblical and Scientific Perspectives on the World's Formation* (Grand Rapids: Eerdmans, 1990).

[56] Howard J. Van Till, Davis A. Young, and Clarence Menninga, *Science Held Hostage: What's Wrong with Creation-Science AND Evolutionism* (Downers Grove, Ill.: InterVarsity Press, 1988).

[57] See J. Moreland and John Mark Reynolds, gen. eds., *Three Views on Creation and Evolution* (Grand Rapids: Zondervan, 1999), esp. ch. 3, in which Van Till presents and defends his view.

mately meaningless process, at least according to the traditional model. Van Till can't have his cake and eat it too.

On the other hand, the process Van Till depicts is so seamless as to be almost deistic. The creation seems to be evolving according to a predetermined "giftedness" with which it was endowed at its inception. One wonders whether the whole theistic evolution experiment will ultimately fail. Design theorists, our final perspective, have little doubt that it will fail.

Intelligent Design

(7) Two landmark publications, Phillip E. Johnson's *Darwin on Trial* and Michael J. Behe's *Darwin's Black Box: The Biochemical Challenge to Evolution,* alerted many to a new theory on the block: the *intelligent design movement.*[58] A roaring revolution may be in the offing—a perspective that may provide the broadest basis for cooperative efforts among the major Christian theorists (young earth and old earth advocates alike) as well as the strongest challenge to naturalistic evolution. Phillip Johnson, a Berkeley law professor, is perhaps the major spokesperson and apologist for the movement. His numerous volumes and his spirited lectures and debates have helped spread the word that a major challenge to Darwinism is on the scene. William A. Dembski is the scientific systematician for the movement, and he defines the movement in this way:

> Intelligent design is three things: a scientific research program that investigates the effects of intelligent causes; an intellectual movement that challenges Darwinism and its naturalistic legacy; and a way of understanding divine action. Intelligent design therefore intersects science and theology.[59]

In simplest terms, intelligent design is "the science that studies signs of intelligence."[60]

For the Christian community, intelligent design offers "a theory of creation" (thus, I have listed it as the seventh alternative in our list) that "puts Christians in the strongest possible position to defeat the common enemy of creation, to wit, naturalism."[61] It is a bridge-building enterprise—

---

58 Phillip E. Johnson, *Darwin on Trial* (Downers Grove, Ill.: InterVarsity Press, 1991); Michael J. Behe, *Darwin's Black Box* (New York: Free Press, 1996).

59 William A. Dembski, *Intelligent Design: The Bridge Between Science & Theology* (Downers Grove, Ill.: InterVarsity Press, 1999), 13.

60 William A. Dembski, *The Design Revolution* (Downers Grove, Ill.: InterVarsity Press, 2004), 21, 33.

61 William A. Dembski, ed., *Mere Creation: Science, Faith & Intelligent Design* (Downers Grove, Ill.: InterVarsity Press, 1998), 13–14.

between science and theology and between competing factions in the Christian community.[62] The foundational question—before we get into all the details—is *whether God is really there or only a figment of our imaginations.*[63] Naturalism is the real challenge to the biblical doctrine of creation.

Therefore, of all the major creation theories, design theorists are the most critical of theistic evolution. They see Van Till's arguments as a losing proposition for all parties in the debate. To the Darwinian secularists, the word "theistic" before the word "evolution" indicates that Christian theorists have simply introduced God into a process that's working just fine without him, thank you. To design theorists the term "evolution" points to a random, wasteful, meaningless process that can in no way reflect the creative hand of God; in fact, it precludes such a possibility, which was Darwin's precise point.[64]

The exploding intelligent design movement is doing for the contemporary scientific community (both secular and Christian) what Paley's natural theology did for the philosophical community of his day—and what Paul's appeal to general revelation did for the Christians of Rome (Rom. 1:19–20). All point to the Creator God, who can be "clearly perceived, ever since the creation of the world, in the things that have been made" (1:20 ESV). But we must remember that Paul's teleological argument is immersed in his rather dismal depiction of human sinfulness. Sinful humanity continues to "suppress the truth" (1:18) and defiantly deny the evidence for God all around us. No amount of scientific evidence or rational argument can counteract this recalcitrance. Only the Holy Spirit, through the message of the gospel of grace, can break through the hardened human heart. But respect for the image of God in humanity and the need to consolidate believers in the teachings of Scripture suggest that such efforts are worthwhile and even essential.

The Road Ahead

What bodes for the future? The young earth and theistic evolution views seem to have the greatest weaknesses—either in the seemingly

---

62 See Nancy Pearcey's foreword to Phillip E. Johnson's *The Right Questions* (Downers Grove, Ill.: InterVarsity Press, 2002), 7–25.

63 See Phillip E. Johnson's *Reason in the Balance* (Downers Grove, Ill.: InterVarsity Press, 1995). In this sense, Johnson has simply picked up the call of Francis Schaeffer to a previous generation—the call to acknowledge the God who is really there.

64 Dembski, *Intelligent Design,* 109–14; cf. Cornelius G. Hunter's fascinating *Darwin's God: Evolution and the Problem of Evil* (Grand Rapids: Brazos, 2001).

artificial explanations for the "apparent" age of the cosmos offered by young earth advocates or the capitulation to naturalistic methodology on the part of theistic evolutionists. Some form of progressive creationism will most likely prevail, combined with the ever new and exciting insights and evidence from the intelligent design movement. But the questions and debates continue.

What we all have in common is the instinct to see God's order in what he has made. As Alister McGrath observes: "The Christian faith holds that the patterning and regularity of the world are not imposed upon that world by an order-seeking mind, but are inherent to nature itself."[65] Indeed science itself was birthed out of this Judeo-Christian perspective. "The resonance between reason, the world, and God," continues McGrath, "is no accident; it is an integral aspect of the Christian doctrine of creation."[66] Darwin offered his best explanation of the world, knowing full well he could not prove it conclusively. Christians do the same, but with greater confidence in our perspective, having welcomed divine revelation on the matter in the Scriptures.[67]

As we interact with one another we should keep our common goals in mind. If the theistic evolutionist can demonstrate a compatibility with the biblical portrait of image of God in creation, Christ, and the Christian, so be it. Van Till is giving it a valiant effort. If the flood geologist can further substantiate his case, so be it. And if progressive creationism wins the day, as I predict here, it won't be without the help of all the believers in the discussion.

In broadest terms, evangelicals tend to take one of three approaches to the creation/science problem. Some emphasize miracle only, in a literal six-day creation some ten thousand years ago. Others combine miracle and process over a long period of time, as in progressive creationism. Still others put even further stress on process, as in theistic evolution.[68] The last two of these three approaches are the most closely aligned, but all three share a strong conviction concerning God as the Creator and humankind as created uniquely in God's image. In short, all seven theories outlined above can be considered as "evangelical" (even though

---

65 Alister McGrath, *The Reenchantment of Nature: The Denial of Religion and the Ecological Crisis* (New York: Doubleday, 2002), 11.

66 Ibid., 22.

67 Ibid., 180.

68 Adapted from Walter L. Bradley and Roger Olsen, "The Trustworthiness of Scripture in Areas Relating to Natural Science" in *Hermeneutics, Inerrancy, and the Bible*, eds. Earl D. Radmacher and Robert D. Preus (Grand Rapids: Zondervan, 1984), 285–317; cf. esp. chart, 311.

the appearance of age theory may be somewhat tongue-in-cheek!). While we aspire to be intellectually rigorous, we should at the same time seek to be personally generous. Tolerance has never been our long suit. When a modern scientist refers to the Big Bang and the Christian recites the words of Genesis 1:1–3, they may be saying two different things—but they are also surely referring to the same mysterious moment: that awesome epoch when God by divine fiat literally *spoke* the universe into existence.

Divine Providence

Closely related to the biblical doctrine of creation is the doctrine of divine providence. Providence is one of the most edifying and comforting teachings of the Bible. John Calvin certainly saw it this way. Under the heading, "Creation and providence inseparably joined," we read the following words from his *Institutes of the Christian Religion*:

> Moreover, to make God a momentary Creator, who once for all finished his work, would be cold and barren, and we must differ from profane men specially in that we see the presence of divine power shining as much in the continuing state of the universe as in its inception. For even though the minds of the impious too are compelled by merely looking upon earth and heaven to rise up to the Creator, yet faith has its own peculiar way of assigning the whole credit for Creation to God. To this pertains that saying of the apostle, to which we have referred before, that only "by faith we understand that the universe was created by the word of God" [Heb. 11:3]. For unless we pass on to his providence—however we may seem both to comprehend with the mind and to confess with the tongue—we do not yet properly grasp what it means to say: "God is Creator." Carnal sense, once confronted with the power of God in the very Creation, stops there, and at most weighs and contemplates only the wisdom, power, and goodness of the author in accomplishing such handiwork. (These matters are self-evident, and even force themselves upon the unwilling.) It contemplates, moreover, some general preserving and governing activity, from which the force of motion derives. In short, carnal sense thinks there is an energy divinely bestowed from the beginning, sufficient to sustain all things.
>
> But faith ought to penetrate more deeply, namely, having found him Creator of all, forthwith to conclude he is also everlasting Governor and Preserver—not only in that he drives the celestial frame as well as its several parts by a universal motion, but also in that he sustains, nour-

ishes, and cares for, everything he has made, even to the least sparrow [cf. Matt. 10:29].[69]

In my opinion, this is one of the most beautiful and profound statements on divine providence ever penned. Calvin's classic is replete with such statements. And in contrast to much modern theology, Calvin does not hesitate to speak doxologically, devotionally, and personally in his theological writings. He was writing for the saints, not just for the scholars.

Calvin's statement is comprehensive. God is *not* a "momentary Creator" as in a deistic perspective. Part of what it means to say "God is Creator" is to include the doctrine of providence. God's divine power is continually at work upholding, preserving, and governing his creation. He "sustains, nourishes, and cares for" his creation "even to the least sparrow," as Jesus taught.

But providence is another one of those doctrines, like the Holy Trinity, in which the term itself (*providence*) is not a biblical term, but is used as a comprehensive concept to point to a teaching that is found on virtually every page of Scripture. Providence means that God *sees ahead* and, therefore, makes wise *provision* for his creation. He is a supremely competent manager, overseer, and ruler of his creation. He is both Father and King. He has both a kingdom and a family. He values highly the material planet he has created. He has assigned humankind with the *ecological* responsibility to care for this incredible planet. He orders literally everything, yet allows real (though limited) freedom to his creatures.

The workings of nature, the ongoing events of human history, and, yes, our individual lives are under his divine care and supervision. This again is the *great news* of Scripture that believers have the responsibility and privilege to communicate to the world. (We will deal with the *bad news* of sin and evil shortly—as well as how the *good news* of Jesus Christ addresses these realities!)

By its very definition providence is oriented to the future. It strongly implies *purpose*. Everything has been created for a purpose. Every*one* is created for a purpose. History has meaning; it is going somewhere. It is not an endless cycle. Each of us as individuals was created for a purpose, and God works to assure the fulfillment of that purpose. Especially with the entrance of sin and evil into the picture, the cosmic story is dramatic,

---

69 Calvin, *Institutes*, 1:197–98 (I.xvi.1). My attention was first drawn to this statement in Cottrell's preface to his own masterful treatment of providence, *What the Bible Says About God the Ruler*, 7.

tragic, yet even sometimes comic. For everything to reach completion, there must be a second coming of Jesus Christ, the consummation of the kingdom, the general resurrection, and the final judgment.

There are two fundamental dimensions to divine providence. Though they should not be artificially divided so as to destroy the *unity* of divine providence, they must nevertheless be differentiated. Biblically speaking, providence is seen as *preservation* and *government*. The first has more to do with the material dimension of the universe, while the second relates to the personal/historical realm—God's fulfilling his purposes for the creation.

Psalm 104 is one of the most beautiful expressions of the creating and sustaining work of God in the Scriptures. It is also exalted praise and worship. It *teaches* worship and gratitude as the proper response to the Creator and *enables* us to express properly such adoration. Psalm 139 moves us from the natural realm to the personal dimension. The depth of God's intimate involvement in our lives—past, present, and future—as presented in this psalm is nothing short of astonishing!

Jesus echoed these same themes in his Sermon on the Mount and elsewhere. As disciples, we can be confident that the Father already knows what we need even before we ask him in prayer (Matt. 6:8). (Nevertheless, we *are* to ask him: God's sovereignty and omniscience do not preclude prayer.) As we strive for God's kingdom and righteousness, we do not need to be anxious about anything; God will supply all our needs (6:25–34; see also Phil. 4:6–7, 19). He takes care of the sparrow and has counted the very hairs of our head (Matt. 10:29–31). God's loving care extends to all persons, "for he makes his sun rise on the evil and on the good, and sends rain on the righteous and on the unrighteous" (5:45).

Without God's creating and sustaining hand none of us could exist: "You are the LORD, you alone; you have made heaven, the heaven of heavens, with all their host, the earth and all that is on it, the seas and all that is in them. To all of them you give life, and the host of heaven worships you" (Neh. 9:6). Notice how all life is a divine gift and that the worship of God is the proper response to this fact. Christ himself holds all things together (Col. 1:17) and "sustains all things by his powerful word" (Heb. 1:3). The Creator is minutely involved with his creation—from atoms to galaxies. If he withdrew his sustaining presence from the universe, it would immediately fall back into the nothingness from which it came.

We are especially aware of God's providential care for his covenant people. Who cannot but be moved by the Joseph narratives in Genesis 37–50? Joseph was powerfully aware of God's sovereign plan and provision both for himself and his people (45:5–8; 50:20). The life of Moses also abounds with examples of providence. One of the major themes of Daniel is the sovereignty of God and his faithfulness to his people. Clearly Israel knew and rejoiced in divine providence.[70]

New covenant saints are also vividly aware of God's sustaining, preserving presence. John 10 assures us that we are under the constant care of the good Shepherd and that no one can snatch us out of God's hand (John 10:28–30). Romans 8 joyfully announces that the future is bright for God's people and that absolutely nothing can separate us from the love of God (Rom. 8:18–39). God's power is at work within the church, and he *will* be glorified "in the church and in Christ Jesus throughout all generations, for ever and ever!" (Eph. 3:21 NIV).

The Kingdom of God

God not only preserves his creation; he also *governs* it. We are again made aware of the dominance of the kingdom of God in all the teachings of the Bible. James Leo Garrett Jr. aptly summarizes the Scriptures' testimony to God's universal reign over his creation:

> The Old Testament presents Yahweh as the king of Israel (Num. 23:21; Deut. 33:5; 1 Sam. 12:12b), and even Solomon was said "to sit on the throne of the kingdom of God over Israel" (1 Chr. 28:5 NIV; see also 1 Chr. 29:23; 2 Chr. 9:8; 13:8). But in the Psalms, the hymnbook of Israel, Yahweh's kingship is repeatedly affirmed as universal (Ps. 103:19). He rules over all the earth (Ps. 47:2, 7; 97:9), over the kings of the earth (Ps. 47:9; 97:1, 5), and over the nations (Ps. 96:10; 99:1–2). He foils the plans and purposes of peoples and nations (Ps. 33:10–11), and his rulership is eternal (Ps. 66:7; 93:2; 146:10). This universal kingship does not rule out Israel's being chosen by Yahweh (Ps. 47:3–4). Yahweh frustrated Pharaoh and resisted Sennacherib's attack on Jerusalem but employed Cyrus as his servant. The numerous pronouncements of divine judgment on Israel's neighbors made through the prophets constitute further confirmation of this universal rulership.[71]

---

[70] See Walter A. Elwell, ed., *Topical Analysis of the Bible* (Grand Rapids: Baker, 1991), 201–207, which contains almost six double-columned pages of biblical references to divine providence at work in the life of God's people Israel

[71] Garrett, *Systematic Theology*, 1:326–27.

The Christian church also sees God's kingly reign as the clue to understanding divine providence. The whole of this reality is centered in the person of Jesus Christ.

As Jesus began his earthly ministry, he "came into Galilee proclaiming the gospel of God: 'The time has arrived; the kingdom of God is upon you. Repent, and believe the gospel'" (Mark 1:15 REB). The time *was* fulfilled; it had "fully come" (Gal. 4:4 RSV). Our Creator and Redeemer was on the scene in person! The incarnate, teaching, preaching, healing, crucified, risen, glorified, and reigning Savior became the center point of human history.[72] God's purpose is to "bring everything together under Christ, as head, everything in the heavens and everything on earth" (Eph. 1:10 NJB). The second-century father Irenaeus of Lyons built virtually his entire theology on this one verse with its concept of recapitulation, or the summing up and unifying of the universe under the headship of Christ.

This same Christ Jesus will come again to raise our bodies from the grave: "After that will come the end, when he will hand over the kingdom to God the Father," and God will be "all in all" (1 Cor. 15:24, 28 NJB). Thus, God's providential rule is comprehensive—from creation to consummation, from "the heavens and the earth" (Gen. 1:1) to "a new heaven and a new earth" (Rev. 21:1).

This understanding of the sovereign reign of God both comforts us and, in all honesty, puzzles us. It is comforting to know that God is in control, but we are also vexed by the presence of evil. People of mature faith learn to trust God even when evil seems to prevail. Jerry Bridges has written a classic on this subject entitled *Trusting God* (subtitled *Even When Life Hurts*).[73] Bridges' thorough treatment of divine sovereignty and providence and their practical implications should be required reading for all believers, for inevitably we are all confronted with the choice to trust God in difficult times or to capitulate to unbelief and fall apart. One of the troublesome questions that always emerges is whether God's will is always done.

Thy Will Be Done

Jesus taught us to pray in this way:

---

[72] Cf. Oscar Cullmann, *Christ and Time: The Primitive Christian Conception of Time and History*, trans. Floyd Filson, rev. ed. (London: SCM, 1962).

[73] Jerry Bridges, *Trusting God: Even When Life Hurts* (Colorado Springs: NavPress, 1988).

> Our Father in heaven,
> may your name be hallowed;
> your kingdom come,
> your will be done,
> on earth as in heaven.
> Give us today our daily bread.
> Forgive us the wrong we have done,
> as we have forgiven those who have wronged us.
> And do not put us to the test,
> but save us from the evil one. (Matt. 6:9–13 REB)

This is a prayer for providence. We are taught to pray for God's kingdom to come and his will to be done. Is God's will always done?

Indeterminism says that God is not in control and, therefore, his will is not done. *Determinism* says that God's control is so absolute that in effect human freedom and responsibility are canceled. *Omnicausality* says that God does everything and his creation does nothing. *Chance* says that no personal or rational power is in control. And *fate* says that the ultimate power is not necessarily benevolent.[74] What does the Bible say?

Jack Cottrell has provided an almost exhaustive answer to this question in his volume, *What the Bible Says About God the Ruler* (1984). I will adapt aspects of Cottrell's excellent presentation.[75] God's will can be summarized under three rubrics: (1) There are some things that God desires and God determines. (2) There are some things that God desires and we determine. (3) There are some things that we desire and God permits.

(1) There are some things that God decides will happen, and they do happen. Our God is a God of plan and purpose. Even though he has given us freedom of choice in many matters, he is still working out his divine plan. "People may plan all kinds of things, but the LORD's will is going to be done" (Prov. 19:21 TEV). God's ultimate purposes *will* prevail (Ps. 33:11; Isa. 14:27). Creation itself fits into this category. The twenty-four elders worshiped God and confessed, "for you made the whole universe; by your will, when it did not exist, it was created" (Rev. 4:11 NJB). God decided that there would be a universe, and there was a universe. Redemption also fits into this category. On the day of Pentecost Peter announced that Jesus' crucifixion took place "according to the definite plan and foreknowledge of God" (Acts 2:23).

---

[74] Adapted from Thomas C. Oden, *The Living God* (San Francisco: Harper & Row, 1987), 277–78.
[75] See Cottrell, *What the Bible Says About God the Ruler*, 304–17.

The prayer meeting recorded in Acts 4:23–31 is a creation/providence passage through and through. After Peter and John were released from the Jewish council, they went to their friends and reported all that had happened. The people prayed, "Sovereign Lord, who made the heaven and the earth, the sea, and everything in them" (v. 24). They continued: (vv. 27–30).

> "For in this city, in fact, both Herod and Pontius Pilate, with the Gentiles and the peoples of Israel, gathered together against your holy servant Jesus, whom you anointed, to do whatever your hand and your plan had predestined to take place. And now, Lord, look at their threats, and grant to your servants to speak your word with all boldness, while you stretch out your hand to heal, and signs and wonders are performed through the name of your holy servant Jesus." When they had prayed, the place in which they were gathered together was shaken; and they were all filled with the Holy Spirit and spoke the word of God with boldness. (4:27–31)

This passage refers (a) to God as creator, (b) to God as "Sovereign Lord," (c) to the events of the crucifixion as taking place according to what God had planned and predestined, (d) to prayer, and (e) to miracles—"signs and wonders." Every one of these themes is traditionally treated in systematic theology as aspects of the doctrine of creation.

(2) There are things that God desires, but he allows a decision on our part. Often he patiently waits for us. He even allows us to say no to him.

> Here is something, dear friends, which you must not forget: in the Lord's sight one day is like a thousand years and a thousand years like one day. It is not that the Lord is slow in keeping his promise, as some suppose, but that he is patient with you. It is not his will that any should be lost, but that all should come to repentance. (2 Peter 3:8–9 REB)

God "desires everyone to be saved and to come to the knowledge of the truth" (1 Tim. 2:4). Jesus lamented over Jerusalem:

> Jerusalem, Jerusalem, the city that kills the prophets and stones those who are sent to it! How often have I desired to gather your children together as a hen gathers her brood under her wings, and you were not willing! (Matt. 23:37)

Notice that God desires to save us all, but he allows a decision on our part. Later we will discover how he even aids us in such decisions. Compare, for example, Paul's words to the Philippians: "Work out your own salvation with fear and trembling; for it is God who is at work in you, enabling you both to will and to work for his good pleasure" (Phil. 2:12–13). There is a divine/human reciprocity here.

God's will is also that we be holy, that we progress in sanctification (1 Thess. 4:3), but we obviously do not always cooperate fully with him in this process. So God desires some things that do not always happen—including the salvation of every single human being he has created.

(3) Finally, there are some things that we desire and God permits. There *is* such a thing as the permissive will of God (Acts 14:16; 16:7; 18:21; 1 Cor. 4:19; 16:7; Heb. 6:3; James 4:13–15). God evidently allows us a circle of freedom on certain matters of indifference. He permits certain things that we desire and decide. There are myriad daily decisions that come under this category: what toothpaste we use, what dress we choose to wear, whether we buy a foreign or domestic automobile, what tie we choose to wear. However, there may be times when God becomes specific about even such matters as these.

I remember vividly a story I heard as an eighteen-year-old at a youth seminar on the campus of Oral Roberts University. Pat Robertson shared how the Lord directed him to wear a certain tie; later on the plane a gentleman commented on Robertson's tie. In the ensuing conversation, Robertson had the privilege of leading this man to a saving knowledge of Jesus Christ. This is part of the adventure of following Jesus Christ!

God's will is not some rigid blueprint in which one wrong decision ruins his plan for us for the rest of our lives. God is more like a master chess player who is about a million games ahead of us. As we desire to please him and diligently seek to obey—even with our imperfect knowledge of him, his ways, and his will—God knows how to get us where he wants us. He knows how to complete his purposes for our lives. He can even turn our blunders into good. His is truly Amazing Grace! There is a *freedom* in following Christ.[76]

God's guides us by:

1. *Faith*: "The just shall live by faith" (Rom. 1:17 NKJV). Too often we want to know beforehand what God desires so that we can decide

[76] See Jerry Sittser, *The Adventure: Putting Energy into Your Walk with God* (Downers Grove, Ill.: InterVarsity Press, 1985), esp. ch. 16, "Guidance and Freedom." Sittser's book is one of the best I have read on the Christian life. I often enthusiastically recommend it to others!

whether we want to do it. But the order is always trust and obey. Faith and obedience are two sides of the same coin. We must be willing to obey *beforehand*; then God's guidance comes.

2. *Facts*: The Holy Spirit will never impress on us something contrary to God's Word. Also, most of God's will for our lives has already been revealed to us in the Bible. If we do not trouble ourselves to ascertain just what that is, why should God grant us guidance on other matters?
3. *Feelings*: There *is* a personal guidance from the Holy Spirit available to every believer (Rom. 8:14; Gal. 5:16, 18, 25). We Westerners often have a tough time with the intuitive side of things, but that does not exempt us from the responsibility of a sensitive, obedient walk with Christ in the Spirit.
4. *Friends*: Christ has made the members of his body interdependent. Often he will use the wise counsel of others as a means of guiding us.
5. *Fences*: God often guides through circumstances. He can shut a door that no one can open, and he can open a door that no one can shut.

Many times God will dovetail two or more of these avenues in guiding us down his chosen path for us. The Christian walk truly is a great adventure!

The Spirit World

As a college student I was strongly influenced by the life, works, and ministry of Francis Schaeffer. One parable he related, entitled "The Universe and Two Chairs," made an indelible impression on me. His key point is that there is an unseen half of the universe, a supernatural dimension, that impinges on the seen half. The invisible God hears and answers our prayers. It is this life of faith, to which we as believers in Christ have been called, that will be as much a testimony to the reality of God as any of our intellectual arguments and answers. Schaeffer notes: "We can say we believe in a supernatural world, and yet live as though there were no supernatural in the universe at all."[77]

Christianity, Schaeffer goes on to say, is much more than intellectual assent to the tenets of the faith. Christianity is also a *life* of faith. He

[77] Francis A. Schaeffer, *Death in the City* (Downers Grove, Ill.: InterVarsity Press, 1969), 133.

observes, "Many Christians I know seem to act as though they come in contact with the supernatural just twice—once when they are justified and become a Christian and once when they die."[78] Biblical restorationism was the burden of Schaeffer's heart—a restoration that entailed reformation and revival.

Reformation refers to a restoration to pure doctrine; revival refers to a restoration in the Christian's life. Reformation speaks of a return to the teachings of Scripture; revival speaks of a life brought into its proper relationship to the Holy Spirit.

> The great moments of church history have come when these two restorations have simultaneously come into action so that the church has returned to pure doctrine and the lives of the Christians in the church have known the power of the Holy Spirit. There cannot be true revival unless there has been reformation; and reformation is not complete without revival.[79]

Schaeffer not only lectured about these matters; he *lived* them. Edith Schaeffer, Francis's wife, wrote a moving account of how God supernaturally answered prayer time and again in the establishing of their international ministry, L'Abri.[80]

The doctrine of creation continually reminds us of the supernaturalism of our faith. There is a *Secret Kingdom* that constantly impacts the visible world.[81] There truly are *Kingdoms in Conflict*.[82] An invisible drama is going on behind the scenes. The invisible creator God of the unseen dimension answers prayer in the visible realm. Schaeffer's illustration in the parable mentioned above was God's answer to prayer in starting two engines of a DC4 on which he was a passenger in 1947. Had this miracle not occurred, the plane would have crashed into the dark waters of the Atlantic, over which the plane was virtually skimming. The pilot could give no explanation of how the impossible happened. Schaeffer could: It was simply answered prayer.[83]

Francis Schaeffer epitomizes classical evangelical Christianity, which perennially has sought a biblical restorationism. Puritanism, Pietism,

---

[78] Ibid., 134.

[79] Ibid., 12 (Schaeffer's italics).

[80] Edith Schaeffer, *L'Abri* (Wheaton, Ill.: Tyndale, 1969). Later she relates their life stories in *The Tapestry* (Dallas: Word, 1981).

[81] Pat Robertson, *The Secret Kingdom* (Dallas: Word, 1992).

[82] Charles Colson, *Kingdoms in Conflict* (Grand Rapids: Zondervan, 1987).

[83] Schaeffer, *Death in the City*, 131–32.

Methodism, and Revivalism form the historical roots of the Pentecostal/charismatic revival of this century in particular and of the total evangelical movement in general. All four religious movements were characterized by this serious-minded, warm-hearted effort to approximate the vitality of New Testament Christianity.[84]

Such a restorationism in our day entails in part a life of faith, prayer, miracles, angelic activity, and spiritual warfare with the unseen forces of darkness. The doctrine of creation points us not only to nature, but also to human nature (which we will study in the following chapter) and to supernature.[85] We are confronted with the spirit world—an often mysterious, yet real creation of God.[86] In concluding our survey of the doctrine of creation, then, it is appropriate to consider briefly the following topics: (1) prayer, (2) miracles, (3) angels, and (4) Satan, demons, and evil.

Prayer

The trend among American seminaries in recent years has been away from activism and toward quietism. Spirituality and spiritual formation are high on the agenda of many of these institutions, and rightly so.[87] Among the many other tasks the ministry entails, surely prayer is a fundamental function of ministry and of the community of faith and should be taught and practiced during one's seminary pilgrimage. If spirituality can be described as "those attitudes, beliefs and practices which animate people's lives and help them to reach out towards super-sensible realities,"[88] then prayer is a primary means of dealing with the supernatural realities one faces. And prayer should, therefore, be understood and practiced from a biblical perspective.

Prayer is prominent in both the Old and New Testament Scriptures. Alan Richardson effectively summarizes the theology and practice of prayer as found in the Old Testament:

---

[84] See Stanley J. Grenz, *Revisioning Evangelical Theology* (Downers Grove, Ill.: InterVarsity Press, 1993), ch. 2, "Revisioning Evangelical Spirituality," 37–59. I have traced these historical precedents for contemporary evangelical/charismatic Christianity in an unpublished doctoral dissertation: Larry Douglas Hart, "A Critique of American Pentecostal Theology," The Southern Baptist Theological Seminary, 1978, 63–68, 84–85.

[85] See Dorothy and Gabriel Fackre, *Christian Basics* (Grand Rapids: Eerdmans, 1991), 5–17.

[86] I owe the title of this section ("The Spirit World") to the title of ch. 17 of James Montgomery Boice's *Foundations of the Christian Faith* (Downers Grove, Ill.: InterVarsity Press, 1986), 167.

[87] See Grenz, *Revisioning Evangelical Theology*, 40–41.

[88] Gordon S. Wakefield, "Spirituality," *The Westminster Dictionary of Christian Theology*, ed. Alan Richardson and John Bowden (Philadelphia: Westminster, 1983), 549. I was alerted to this definition by Grenz, *Revisioning Evangelical Theology*, 42.

> Since the earliest days of Israelite religion, prayer to Israel's God was spontaneous, natural and unaffected, however formalized it may have become in later Judaism. The God to whom Israel prayed was the saving, protecting and judging God of prophetic religion. The Psalms exemplify the direct approach of Israel to God: the Israelite, whether individually or corporately, poured out all his concern to God—for his safety, his harvest, his sins and failures, his joys and sorrows, his thanksgiving and praise. Such spontaneous address was possible only because God was essentially "Thou," the one who called forth the response of those who knew his name.[89]

Prayer is so abundant in the Old Testament, as well as the New, that the Bible can be called a prayer book. Early in Genesis we find Abraham interceding for Sodom (Gen. 18:16–33). Abraham's servant (probably Eliezer) had a dramatic experience of miraculous answer to prayer in seeking out Isaac's wife (24:12–15). Who can forget Jacob's wrestlings in prayer as he prepared to meet Esau (32:9–12, 24–32)?

Moses is depicted as a mighty man of prayer throughout the Exodus events and in intercession for rebellious Israel (Ex. 32:11–14; Num. 14:13–19). Hannah rejoiced to see God's response to her humble request (1 Sam. 1:9–18, 26–28; 2:1–10). David was submissive in his prayers (2 Sam. 7:18–29; 12:16–23). Solomon prayed for wisdom and received that and much more (1 Kings 3:3–15; see also his prayer at the dedication of the temple: 8:22–53).

Elijah's prayer on Mount Carmel was dramatically answered to the glory of the one true God (1 Kings 18:36, 37). When James, our Lord's earthly brother, taught about the prayer of faith for the sick (James 5:14–18), he used Elijah as an encouraging example: "Elijah was a human being as frail as ourselves—he prayed earnestly for it not to rain, and no rain fell for three and a half years; then he prayed again and the sky gave rain and the earth gave crops" (5:17–18 NJB; cf. 1 Kings 17:1; 18:41–46).

Jehoshaphat and all Judah saw God's deliverance because of humble, dependent prayer (2 Chron. 20). Ezra's prayer preceded reformation and revival (Ezra 9–10). Daniel's prayer of confession for God's people resulted in the appearance of Gabriel (Dan. 9). These examples of fervent prayer and divine intervention far from exhaust the pattern and power of prayer depicted in the Old Testament.

---

89 Alan Richardson, "Theology of Prayer," *The Westminster Dictionary of Christian Theology*, 457.

In the New Testament Jesus himself is both the exemplar and the expositor of prayer. The writer who best communicates this is Luke, who is the theologian of prayer in the New Testament. In his two-volume account of the life of Jesus and the early church, Luke is careful to point out the central role of prayer at all the key junctures of the mission of both Jesus and the church. The people prayed outside while inside the temple Zechariah received Gabriel's announcement concerning John the Baptist (Luke 1:10). The prophetess Anna, who received revelation concerning the Christ child, had spent her time continually fasting and praying in the temple (2:36–38).

Luke is the only Gospel writer who tells us that it was *while Jesus was praying* that the Spirit descended in bodily form like a dove on him when he was baptized by John the Baptist (Luke 3:21). Although the crowds continually sought out Jesus, he often withdrew to an isolated place to pray (5:16). Jesus spent the entire night in prayer before appointing the Twelve (6:12). Again, only Luke tells us that it was while Jesus was praying that Peter made the great confession and Jesus was transfigured before Peter, James, and John (9:18, 29). "At one place after Jesus had been praying, one of his disciples said, 'Lord, teach us to pray, as John taught his disciples'" (11:1 REB), and Jesus gave the model prayer (11:2–4). Jesus' disciples might well have asked Jesus to teach them how to teach and preach as he did, how to heal the sick, how to lead and influence people. But they had already learned the secret to Jesus' life and ministry: prayer. A song I once heard in a seminary chapel service asks: If Jesus needed to pray, how about you?

Jesus agonized in his prayer at Gethsemane, submitting to the Father's will (Luke 22:39–45). He prayed, "Father, forgive them; for they do not know what they are doing," when his executioners crucified him (23:34). His last words before he died were, "Father, into your hands I commend my spirit" (23:46). Jesus lived a life of prayer from start to finish.

The disciples constantly devoted themselves to united prayer in preparation for their empowerment for mission at Pentecost (Acts 1:14). On the day of Pentecost about three thousand persons were added to the church. "They devoted themselves to the apostles' teaching and fellowship, to the breaking of bread and the prayers" (2:42). Churches today that center on (1) the teaching and preaching of the Scriptures ("the apostles' teaching"), (2) body-life in the Spirit ("fellowship"), (3) worship centered in the Lord's Supper ("the breaking of bread"), and (4) prayer ("the prayers") are vital churches. We have already looked at the mighty prayer meeting of Acts 4:23–31, which resulted in the disciples' being filled with the Holy Spirit and speaking the Word of God with boldness. Numerous additional examples can be given. Clearly, the key to powerful prayer is to heed Jesus' teaching on prayer and then *do it.* Prayer is more caught than taught!

One of the keys to effective prayer is simply *persistence.* Jesus taught us to keep on asking, keep on seeking, and keep on knocking—fully assured of our heavenly Father's eagerness to give us good things (Matt. 7:7–11). Luke's Gospel includes Jesus' parable that illustrates this point (Luke 11:5–8) and refers to the Father's eagerness to give us *the Holy Spirit* (rather than "good things," as in Matthew; see Luke 11:13). Jesus teaches the church that concerted, united prayer yields amazing results (Matt. 18:19–20). He also emphasized the powerful effect of *believing* prayer (Matt. 21:21–22; Mark 11:20–25). Jesus' parable about the persistent widow concludes with these haunting words: "But when the Son of Man comes, will he find faith on earth?" (Luke 18:8 REB). James also emphasized how crucial faith is, asserting that doubt and double-mindedness nullify prayer and stable Christian living (James 1:5–8). John Calvin also strongly emphasized the role of faith in prayer.[90]

In his Upper Room discourse, which centered primarily on the person and ministry of the Paraclete, the Holy Spirit, Jesus repeatedly stated that the disciples should ask and receive from the Father (John 15:7, 16; 16:24). Jesus himself is the Paraclete (advocate) with the Father who intercedes for us (1 John 2:1–2). Jesus' intercessory ministry on our behalf is a salient feature of the New Testament (John 17; Rom. 8:34; Heb. 7:24–25). Moreover, the Holy Spirit helps us in our prayers, interceding for us according to the will of the Father (Rom. 8:26–27) and empowering our prayers (Eph. 6:18). We are not to be anxious, but rather to rejoice and to present our petitions to the Lord (Phil. 4:4–6). We are to pray constantly (1 Thess. 5:17).

The Lord's Prayer (Matt. 6:9–13; Luke 11:2–4), which is really the Disciples' Prayer, is our pattern for prayer. In the Sermon on the Mount Jesus said, "when you give alms . . . when you pray . . . when you fast" (Matt. 6:2, 5, 16 REB). He did not say *if* you do these things. Jesus *assumes* that we will give to the poor, pray, and fast. But how much do we actually do these things? And we wonder why the church is often powerless

[90] Calvin, *Institutes,* 2:863–64 (III.xx.11).

and ineffective. Also, Jesus said that we must not make a show of our prayers (6:5–6) or "go babbling on like the heathen, who imagine that the more they say the more likely they are to be heard" (6:7 REB).

The Lord's Prayer is a *church* prayer, centered on *God* and the *kingdom.* It begins by affirming God's *immanence* ("Our Father") and *transcendence* ("in heaven"). First, we focus on God's name, kingdom, and will. Then we ask for provision, forgiveness, and protection. We begin with reverence, worship, and submission—concern with God's having *his* way. Then we present our petitions for daily sustenance, forgiveness, and safety. God is pleased that we depend on him for our daily necessities. He also instructs us that we must be willing to forgive others the wrongs they have done to us if we are to experience his forgiveness (reenforced in Matt. 6:14–15). Instead of prideful carelessness and overconfidence we are to exhibit humility, fear of the Lord, and dependence ("And do not put us to the test" [6:13 REB]). Finally, we are to ask the Father to "save [deliver, rescue] us from the evil one" (6:13 REB). Our battle with Satan and evil is real and is an aspect of God's providential care. Some manuscripts add: "For yours is the kingdom and the power and the glory, forever. Amen" (6:13 REB).

Thus, this prayer begins and ends with adoration and includes thanksgiving, intercession, petition, and confession—all the basic forms of prayer. The five most fundamental kinds of prayer, therefore, are (1) worship, (2) thanksgiving, (3) intercession, (4) petition, and (5) confession. As Dale Moody often emphasized in his systematic theology class, if a person would simply devote one minute to each of these kinds of prayer daily, that would be five minutes more than most of us devote to formal prayer each day. But if we discipline ourselves to such a full-orbed prayer life, that five-minute span will soon extend to ten, fifteen, twenty minutes and beyond as we begin to practice authentic prayer.

If theology itself is not an act of prayer, it is not true Christian theology. Perhaps the greatest sin of the church today is prayerlessness. Where are the theologians who emphasize prayer in the manner of the giants of previous centuries, such as John Calvin? Calvin's arguments for the necessity of prayer need to be heard again in our generation.[91] It is time that we "dig up by prayer the treasures that were pointed out by the Lord's gospel, and which our faith has gazed upon."[92]

---

[91] Ibid., 2:851–53 (III.xx.2–3).

[92] Ibid., 2:851 (III.xx.2).

The real dividing line for contemporary Christianity is not so much liberal/conservative as it is believing/unbelieving.[93] Authentic Christianity is supernatural Christianity. Answered prayer should be the norm. Pat Robertson reports that Christian Broadcasting Network has "seen tens of thousands of answers to prayer," and that George Gallup told him a few years back that "at least 7.5 million Americans have reported some kind of miraculous answer to prayer, primarily in relation to physical healing."[94] I believe them both.

Richard J. Foster has written a book already acknowledged as a classic on prayer. *Prayer: Finding the Heart's True Home* is virtually an exhaustive study that provides rich historical and theological perspectives as well as eminently practical, helpful, and encouraging teaching on the life of prayer.[95] I cannot imagine a better source for help in this vital area.

Miracles

To believe in providence is to believe in miracles. It is to practice the life of prayer. It is to interact with the realm of the supernatural, acknowledging the reality of angels as well as engaging in spiritual warfare with the unseen forces of evil that oppose God's good creation.

During my college years I played basketball in a home arena that had these words emblazoned in large script on the sides of the court: *Expect a Miracle!* And sometimes the Oral Roberts University basketball team needed a miracle to pull out a win. (Unfortunately, at times the divine response to our prayers was *no.*) Oral Roberts taught us that God always answers prayer: sometimes yes, sometimes wait, and sometimes no; but he always answers prayer. In my opinion, this is a good theology of prayer.

I type these words the day after I have had the privilege of hearing J. I. Packer preach on the Exodus events. Packer pointed out how most of the signs Moses performed could be understood in terms of the supernatural *timing* of natural events—what he called *providential* miracles, in contrast to such *creative* miracles as the death of the firstborn. Packer emphasized how God demonstrated his infinitely superior power over

---

[93] See also Richard J. Coleman's excellent delineation of these issues in his chapter "Prayer, Providence, and the World," in *Issues of Theological Warfare: Evangelicals and Liberals* (Grand Rapids: Eerdmans, 1972), 145–65.

[94] Robertson, *The Secret Kingdom*, 46–47.

[95] Richard J. Foster, *Prayer: Finding the Heart's True Home* (San Francisco: HarperCollins, 1992).

that of the hardhearted pharaoh of Egypt. It is this central truth of the sovereignty of God—that his *kingdom* reigns supreme—that informs the biblical doctrine of miracles.

Miracles are signs of the kingdom of God. Jesus said, "But if it is by the finger of God that I cast out the demons, then the kingdom of God has come to you" (Luke 11:20). Jesus was echoing the words of Pharaoh's magicians, who during the Exodus events could not duplicate the miracle of the gnats. They exclaimed, "This is the finger of God!" (Ex. 8:19). Christ's redemptive rule is attested by miracles, according to Gordon R. Lewis and Bruce A. Demarest.[96] Embracing this vision of the kingdom requires the adoption of an entirely different worldview. Don Williams, a dynamic biblical scholar, describes it well:

> God is king. He reigns enthroned in glory with a sea of flaming angels bowing low before him and rising to shout his praises. From his throne he speaks and the galaxies are hurled into space. From his throne he orders the molten, gaseous stars, and directs the planets circling them. From his throne he places our earth into its orbit and rules the ages of our geological and historical life. From his throne he upholds all things and judges all things. Moreover, on the awesome final day each of us will stand before his throne and give an account of our lives to him.[97]

Williams goes on to indicate how God wants to direct our lives as his people and to spread his reign in the lives of others across the globe. He continues: "Only when we have been established in this biblical worldview, both intellectually and experientially, will we be rid of our bias against miracles."[98]

Unwittingly, Western Christians have been brainwashed by an Enlightenment mentality that, in its unbelieving rationalism and skepticism, is an offense to the Spirit of Christ. No one has alerted us to this problem more effectively than Charles H. Kraft, professor of anthropology and intercultural communication at Fuller Seminary. His groundbreaking volume, *Christianity with Power: Your Worldview and Your Experience of the Supernatural,*[99] shows how we have cut ourselves off from the supernatu-

---

[96] Gordon R. Lewis and Bruce A. Demarest, *Integrative Theology*, (Grand Rapids: Zondervan, 1990), 2:104 (section heading).

[97] Don Williams, *Signs, Wonders, and the Kingdom of God* (Ann Arbor: Vine Books, 1989), 1.

[98] Ibid., 21.

[99] Charles H. Kraft, *Christianity with Power: Your Worldview and Your Experience of the Supernatural* (Ann Arbor: Vine Books, 1989), see esp. ch. 4, "Enlightenment Christianity Is Powerless," 37–49.

ral and often substituted a Christianity of mere words for an authentic faith with attended kingdom power.

However, those who believe in the creating and sustaining God of biblical revelation "are not much troubled about miracles, for they see the effects of supernatural power in everything around them."[100] In the broadest sense of the term we are surrounded by miracles. The universe itself is a miracle. Certainly its coming into existence by fiat creation is a miracle. The central tenets of our faith all involve miracle: *creation, incarnation, resurrection, consummation.* One thinks of the clusters of miracles surrounding the Exodus, the ministries of Elijah and Elisha, the life of our Lord Jesus Christ, and the militant New Testament church.[101] Moreover, miracles have accompanied the historic church throughout her history and have abounded in the Pentecostal/charismatic revival of recent decades. Christianity is rife with supernaturalism.

In the strictest sense, however, miracle is a prescribed term both in Scripture and in Christian theology. "By miracle we mean those special supernatural works of God's providence which are not explicable on the basis of the usual patterns of nature." This is how Millard Erickson defines miracle. He further describes miracles as "those striking or unusual workings by God which are clearly supernatural."[102] The four biblical terms that refer to miracles are *powers, wonders, signs,* and *works.* These four—*taken together*—define what the Bible means by miracle.

Miracles are dramatic manifestations of the *power* of God. They evoke our *wonder* and amazement. They are *signs* of the rule and reality of our sovereign Lord. Jesus, in John's Gospel, describes his miracles as the *works* the Father had given him to do and as witnesses to his divine sonship. Miracles do not *violate* the "laws" of nature. The so-called laws of the natural order are in actuality observances of the normal ways God has chosen the universe to operate. In his sovereign freedom God can choose at any moment to supercede these laws with the higher law of his infinite power. When a massive jetliner lifts off the runway and soars into the brilliant blue skies, it is not "violating" the laws of gravity. Gravity is still very much in force—a fact failed engines would readily verify! Rather the laws of aerodynamics have simply superceded the law of gravity. So it is with the miracles of God.

---

[100] Henry Stob, "Miracles," in *Basic Christian Doctrines,* ed. Carl F. H. Henry (Grand Rapids: Baker, 1962), 82.

[101] See Lewis and Demarest, *Integrative Theology,* 2:104–5.

[102] Erickson, *Christian Theology,* 406.

Miracles reflect the freedom, love, and power of God.[103] Their reality is based on these divine attributes. Our sovereign God is free to do "whatever he pleases" (Ps. 115:3). The omnipotent Lord of glory "is able to do immeasurably more than all we ask or imagine" (Eph. 3:20 NIV). Furthermore, in his infinite love he often intervenes to meet human need. Theologians who try to spiritualize Jesus' miracles by avoiding this fact of divine compassion have forgotten that God is love. Jesus healed the sick because they were sick. God freely chooses to manifest his loving supernatural power on behalf of suffering humanity.[104]

God performs his miracles selectively, however, and for clear kingdom purposes. He will not be dictated to, even by some overwrought religious zealot. We cannot *schedule* his miracles in our vain attempts to market our ministries. Christian triumphalism is shallow and ultimately cruel. God's power is centered in the cross and is perfected in our weakness (2 Cor. 12:9). God must surely be tired when we pridefully "strut our stuff" in many charismatic healing meetings. Authentic Christian healing will evince the Holy Spirit's "love, joy, peace, patience, kindness, generosity, faithfulness, gentleness, and self-control" (Gal. 5:22). A circus atmosphere works against the humble, servant attitude that should characterize our ministry to one another and to those outside the church. We should be permitted, however, to celebrate God's gracious goodness toward us in meeting our needs. It is *all* to *his* glory—this is the primary purpose of all miracles.

I will never forget the opportunity I had to meet Joni Eareckson Tada while I served as chaplain at Oral Roberts University. I had invited her to speak to the entire campus in a voluntary chapel service (the only one we could schedule). The chapel was crammed to the rafters. Sterling saints such as Joni, as she is affectionately known by millions, are our champions of faith. Too often charismatic Christians are embarrassed by those who haven't been healed. But it takes *greater* faith to continue trusting, thanking, praising, and serving the Lord when the healing doesn't come as we desire. Joni shared privately with me how she has had to help many a precious saint "pick up the pieces" after attending a healing meeting.

---

[103] J. Rodman Williams provides an insightful analysis of miracles utilizing these three rubrics: *Renewal Theology* (Grand Rapids: Zondervan, 1988), 1:144–48.

[104] This assertion does not ignore the mystery of God's will in allowing human suffering, but even here he has an ultimate good in store—even if we must enter the next life to fully appreciate this fact.

We need a theology of suffering as well as a theology of miracles. We will reach a point of balance in the body of Christ when evangelicals have healing testimonies at their evangelistic rallies and charismatics have suffering testimonies at their public meetings. God can be glorified in both. We must desire to know Christ *both* in the power of his resurrection and in the fellowship of his sufferings (see Phil. 3:10).

Signs and Wonders

On the day of Pentecost Peter confronted the Jews with the message of Christ:

> You that are Israelites, listen to what I have to say: Jesus of Nazareth, a man attested to you by God with deeds of power, wonders, and signs that God did through him among you, as you yourselves know—this man, handed over to you according to the definite plan and foreknowledge of God, you crucified and killed by the hands of those outside the law. But God raised him up. (Acts 2:22–24)

It was a simple, straightforward message: You killed Jesus; God raised him. Our sins took Jesus to the cross; God vindicated him by his bodily resurrection.

Jesus was "attested" by God—that is, God showed forth his Son, singled him out, displayed him, commended him, "accredited" him (NIV), and made it clear who Jesus really was. And how did God do this? He did it "with deeds of power, wonders, and signs that God did through him among you." He also "raised him up." All of this took place according to God's sovereign plan. Notice the important place Peter gives to *miracles* as signs of attestation to Jesus.

The phrase "deeds of power" translates the Greek word *dynamis*, rendered "miracles" in numerous other modern English translations. The word itself does means "power." It is a key word in the New Testament. Jesus returned from his wilderness testing "in the power of the Spirit" (Luke 4:14 RSV). A short while later, Luke, the "charismatic theologian" of the New Testament, again notes the divine power at work in the ministry of Jesus: "One day, while he was teaching, Pharisees and teachers of the law were sitting near by ... and the power of the Lord was with him to heal" (5:17). When the woman with hemorrhaging touched Jesus' clothes, he immediately was "aware that power had gone forth from him" (Mark 5:30). Her touch of faith had tapped into the power of God. Back in his hometown of Nazareth the people were amazed at his wise teaching in the synagogue as well as his miracles: "What deeds of power are being done by his hands!" (6:2). Yet Jesus was "amazed at their unbelief" (6:6) and "could do no deed of power there, except that he laid his hands on a few sick people and cured them" (6:5). Does our unbelief often hinder the power of Christ in our midst today? Too often we simply do not expect him to do anything among us when we meet together in his name.

At any rate, miracle after miracle was manifested in the ministry of Jesus and the early church, as any concordance will indicate. Jesus promised his disciples that they would "receive power when the Holy Spirit has come upon you" (Acts 1:8), and they did! Their lives and ministries showed forth radiantly the power of God. But to complete the biblical picture we must note the nature of this power. It stands in sharp contrast to power as manifested in the world.

The apostle Paul, whose own ministry was authenticated "by the power of signs and wonders, by the power of the Spirit of God" (Rom. 15:19), saw the gospel message itself—the story of Christ nailed to the cross for our sins—as "the power of God for salvation to everyone who has faith" (1:16). He emphasized strongly to the Corinthians that "the message about the cross . . . is the power of God" (1 Cor. 1:18). The message of "Christ crucified" may be scandalous and foolish to many, but Christ *is* "the power of God" (1:20–24). "God's weakness is stronger than human strength" (1:25).

With this same motif Paul contrasted authentic spiritual power with the false miracles of the "super-apostles" who opposed him. God's power is perfected in our *weakness* (2 Cor. 12:9; cf. chs. 10–12). Fleshly power always corrupts because our corrupt human natures become puffed up with pride. But genuine spiritual power humbles us. It is most often released in moments of humiliation and weakness as we acknowledge our dependence on God and our complete helplessness.

I will never forget when Billy Graham spoke in a chapel service during my seminary days. Dr. Graham said that there was no excuse for a man or woman of God to become puffed up with spiritual pride. The closer we are to God, the more aware we become of how utterly iniquitous we are, and we are humbled. Graham said that at those moments when he has been tempted to such pride, God has a way of kicking him down a notch or two and reminding him whose power it is. Power is always dangerous. This is why God links his power to the message of the cross.

Peter also mentioned "wonders" and "signs" in his Pentecost sermon. Our English word "miracle" is derived from the Latin word *mirari*, meaning "to wonder at." We often refer to something dramatic, beneficent, and inexplicable as "wonderful." The word "sign" is perhaps the most helpful term in expressing the nature of miracle. A miracle is a sign of the kingdom of God; it points beyond itself to a transcendent reality, purpose, and *person* (God). Miracles do not happen randomly. God is deliberate and purposeful in his miracles. Jesus' opponents often requested signs from him to authenticate his ministry, but Jesus refused to oblige them (see Mark 8:11–13). In his Olivet Discourse Jesus warned that false messiahs and false prophets would perform misleading signs and wonders (Matt. 24:24; Mark 13:22). Perhaps this is why the Synoptic Gospels (Matthew, Mark, and Luke) never apply the terms "sign" or "signs and wonders" to Jesus' miracles.[105]

Signs, however, play a major role in John's presentation of Jesus' ministry. In fact, they are integral to his purpose in writing this Gospel:

> Now Jesus did many other signs in the presence of his disciples, which are not written in this book. But these are written so that you may come to believe that Jesus is the Messiah, the Son of God, and that through believing you may have life in his name. (John 20:30–31)

John builds his Gospel around seven signs and seven "I am" sayings. The first twelve chapters can be titled "The Book of Signs." John also uses the word "works" (*ergon*) to describe Jesus' miracles. Although many did not see the *sign* in the miracle (John 6:26), and still others demanded "signs and wonders" (4:48)—and John has his stated purpose in utilizing historical accounts of Jesus' miracles—miracles have a limited role. One must believe in Jesus in order to grasp the full significance of his miracles.[106]

Ironically, the Bible's miracle narratives evince one disconcerting pattern: Those times when God did the most miracles—and the most dramatic miracles!—were seemingly the times when even his own people were the most rebellious and unbelieving. As Philip Yancey has observed: "With remarkable consistency, the Bible's accounts show that miracles—dramatic, showstopping miracles like many of us still long for—simply do not foster deep faith."[107] Yancey illustrates this point by

---

[105] Williams, *Renewal Theology*, 2:150.

[106] See Leon Morris, *New Testament Theology* (Grand Rapids: Zondervan, 1986), 242–43.

[107] Philip Yancey, *Disappointment with God* (Grand Rapids: Zondervan, 1988), 117.

reminding us how the incredible Transfiguration event did not transform the faith of Peter, James, and John; they still forsook Jesus when he needed them most. Yancey's volume *Disappointment with God* is a welcome balance to the miracle-mongering that goes on in many quarters today.

Nevertheless, "signs" (Heb. *ʾot*; Gk. *semeion*) and "wonders" (Heb. *mopet*; Gk. *teras*) play a major role in biblical revelation.[108] Jesus even made this mind-boggling assertion: "Very truly, I tell you, the one who believes in me will also do the works that I do and, in fact, will do greater works than these, because I am going to the Father" (John 14:12). Paul taught that God distributes and appoints "workings of miracles" in the church as part of its ongoing ministry (1 Cor. 12:10, 28–29). Their limited role and the possibility of counterfeits are no excuse for shying away from them.

Surely God has raised up the Pentecostal/charismatic revival (more than a half-billion strong—astonishing in view of the fact that no such movement even existed at the turn of the twentieth century) as a desperately needed corrective for a church that has too often depended on human wisdom and eloquence rather than a gospel message accompanied "with a demonstration of the Spirit and of power" (1 Cor. 2:5). Could it be that the primary reason we have come up with our elaborate cessationist arguments is to rationalize our own spiritual deficiencies? It is time to open our minds—and our hearts—afresh to God's miracle-working power![109]

The Biblical Balance

I have engaged in this extended discussion of miracles because we need an honest appraisal of this subject from all sides. Signs and wonders are *not* the basis for unity in the body of Christ. Surely our unity is in Christ himself—the work of his Spirit, based on the authoritative teachings of the Scriptures. Miracles, strictly speaking, are *not* everyday occurrences, but rather extraordinary events that bring glory to God and point people toward his kingdom. There *is* a danger of counterfeits. But this should no more discourage us from embracing present-

---

[108] Again, any serviceable concordance will provide the copious references.

[109] J. Rodman Williams has provided an excellent treatment of miracles from both biblical and contemporary perspectives in his *Renewal Theology*, 1:141–68; 2:375–80. See also the engaging volume by Jack Deere, a former Dallas Seminary professor: *Surprised by the Power of the Spirit* (Grand Rapids: Zondervan, 1993).

day miracles than counterfeit evangelism should discourage us from authentic evangelism. Based on my own study of the Bible and my own observation and experience, I believe that God is still working miracles today. As we listen to and learn from one another in the body of Christ, our Lord will bring us to the place of biblical balance in this area as in many other areas.

Clark Pinnock exemplifies this sort of openness and balance. He communicates well his vision of what God desires for the church in his little book *Three Keys to Spiritual Renewal.*[110] Here he challenges God's people to scriptural reformation, spiritual renewal, and ethical action. With reference to present-day miracles, Pinnock shared sound biblical guidelines and vivid personal experience in Billy Graham's *Decision* magazine:

> In 1982 I faced the prospect of blindness. I had developed senile macular degeneracy: a fissure had opened in the retina near the center of vision, allowing blood to pass into my eye. Because I had already lost sight in my other eye in 1967, the situation was grave. If the opening did not close, I would be blind in both eyes.
>
> My home church did not practice a regular ministry of praying for healing from God, but they responded wonderfully to this emergency. In a few days it became apparent to my doctors that the condition had been halted, then reversed. The hole in the retina had scarred over, no longer threatening my sight. I believe that I experienced an act of God that day in response to the prayers of my congregation, and I was blessed with the gift of continuing sight.
>
> Evangelicals everywhere are reporting a power dimension in faith that is new to their experience. As in the Apostle Paul's day, the Gospel is going forth not only in human effort "but in demonstration of the Spirit and power" [1 Cor. 2:4 RSV]. God's Word is being accompanied by God's deeds, "by the power of signs and wonders, by the power of the Holy Spirit" [Rom. 15:19 RSV].
>
> As a result of these experiences, we are developing a new openness to God in all areas of our lives. We are becoming skeptical of those who rule out the supernatural work of God, and we are learning to take God's power more seriously. Gradually we are becoming more natural with the supernatural.[111]

---

[110] Clark Pinnock, *Three Keys to Spiritual Renewal* (Minneapolis: Bethany, 1985).

[111] Clark H. Pinnock, "Does God Have to Give Us—A Miracle a Minute?" *Decision* (May 1993), 12–13.

Pinnock goes on to present a biblically balanced perspective on miracles, healing, and the supernatural with which most would wholeheartedly agree.

A friend of mine from seminary days, Southern Baptist missionary Dr. Ralph Bethea, has recounted in hundreds of Southern Baptist churches across the nation the incredible signs and wonders—some of the most dramatic I have ever heard or read about—that accompanied an historic breakthrough in the predominantly Muslim African nation of Kenya. This outpouring of the Spirit resulted in more than 120,000 converts and 200 new churches. Dr. Bethea's lovely wife was martyred in that land. It all started when this humble missionary and twelve other ordinary saints sought God in desperate prayer for a spiritual breakthrough with the gospel in their field of labor. Astounding miracles resulted from the ensuing outpouring of God's Spirit, and the Lord added to his church daily. Could it be that God is preparing his people even now for an end-time missionary harvest unparalleled in Christian history? Only *he* knows, but we can certainly pray for this to happen! We are likely to perceive increased angelic activity as well.

Angels, Angels, Angels

The subject of angels has become extremely popular in contemporary culture. *Time* magazine ran a cover story with these words on the front: "The New Age of Angels: 69% of Americans believe they exist. What in heaven is going on?"[112] Inside, the magazine relates some very interesting facts and stories:

> There are angels-only boutiques, angel newsletters, angel seminars, angels on *Sonya Live.* A *Time* poll indicates that most Americans believe in angels. Harvard Divinity School has a course on angels; Boston College has two. Bookstores have had to establish angel sections.... In *Publishers Weekly*'s religious best-seller list, five of the ten paperback books are about angels.
>
> This rising fascination is more popular than theological, a grass-roots revolution of the spirit in which all sorts of people are finding all sorts of reasons to seek answers about angels for the first time in their lives.[113]

What should be noted, however, is that there is probably more interest in angels in the New Age religions than there is among Christians.

---

[112] *Time,* December 27, 1993 (cover).

[113] Nancy Gibbs, "Angels Among Us," *Time* (December 27, 1993), 56.

It is mandatory, therefore, that the church be clear about what the Scriptures teach concerning angels, so that we can better evaluate contemporary beliefs and events.

Although there are numerous references to angels, the Bible mentions them almost incidentally. They are mysterious in part because of the paucity of information provided about them. The church historically has swung from an extreme of preoccupation with angels, bordering on worship, to a categorical denial of their existence. The latter group must often be reminded that the same arguments they use against belief in the existence of angels can be used against belief in the existence of God. In relation to angelology (i.e., the doctrine of angels), we are definitely dealing with "the spirit world."

Angels are spiritual beings created by God as his servants and messengers. They also serve God's people. The primary biblical terms (Heb. *malak*; Gk. *angelos*) denote literally "messenger" and are used of both human and supernatural messengers. We are, of course, focusing on the supernatural beings known as angels. "By angels we mean those spiritual beings that God created higher than humankind, some of whom have remained obedient to God and carry out his will, and others of whom disobeyed, lost their holy condition, and now oppose and hinder his work."[114] This definition of angels by Erickson points to the existence of both good and evil angels. We will consider good angels first and then turn our attention to evil angels.

We have about as much innate knowledge of angelic existence as dogs have of human existence. John Macquarrie, on the basis of philosophical existentialism, argues for a "hierarchy of beings" in creation, with humankind at the pinnacle of earthly beings, and the angelic order of beings above humankind.[115] This order of the creation as revealed in Scripture should humble us. There *are* powers and intelligences higher than ours, and these angelic beings are to be respected and appreciated. Humankind is not the measure of all things. Because of biblical revelation we do have more knowledge of angelic existence than animals have of our existence.

---

114 Millard J. Erickson, *Introducing Christian Doctrine*, ed. L. Arnold Hustad (Grand Rapids: Baker, 1992), 145–46. God's sovereign purposes cannot ultimately be "hindered" in terms of being prevented; but it is clear biblically that God has allowed this powerful opposition to his good purposes for an ultimate good.

115 John Macquarrie, *Principles of Christian Theology* (New York: Charles Scribner's Sons, 1966), 215. Macquarrie mentions a cat rather than a dog when pointing to our natural limitations in understanding angelical existences.

When the writer of Hebrews argues for the superiority of Christ to the angels, he also helps us to define more exactly who angels are: "Are not all angels spirits in the divine service, sent to serve for the sake of those who are to inherit salvation?" (Heb. 1:14). Angels are "spirits," not corporeal beings. They are "in the divine service," and they are "sent," in part, to help us. Evidently, angels were created by God prior to his creation of the physical universe. The Lord asked Job where he was when the Lord created the universe, "while the morning stars sang together and all the angels shouted for joy" (Job 38:7 NIV). The word "angels" translates the Hebrew "sons of God," one of the terms for angels. Just as God spoke the worlds into existence, so the angels also came to be: "He commanded and they were created" (Ps. 148:2, 5).

In Roger Elwood's imaginative fable, *Angelwalk*, an angel named Darien remembers his creation:

> I yet recall my first moment of existence—from nothingness to awareness, looking up into the very face of God, knowing that though He had created ten thousand upon ten thousand of us, each was special to Him, each as though the only one. God reached down and took my wings and breathed into me the power of life, of flight, the reality of immortality. He first created my very self, and then He gave that self life everlasting.[116]

Although the reference to wings can be questioned (it is not clear that all the angelic creations have wings like the cherubim and seraphim), Elwood's mythical account may not be far from reality. God alone is by nature immortal (1 Tim. 6:16), but he created the angelic hosts—a vast number (see Deut. 33:2; Ps. 68:17; Matt. 26:53; Heb. 12:22; Rev. 5:11)—and gifted them with immortality (Luke 20:36). Divine love extends to these majestic creatures just as to the rest of creation.

The power and appearance of angels can be frightening. On the first Easter morning there was a sudden earthquake; an angel of the Lord descended from heaven, rolled the stone back from the entrance to the tomb, and sat on it. "His appearance was like lightning, and his clothing white as snow. For fear of him the guards shook and became like dead men" (Matt. 28:1–4). So awesome and powerful are the angels that people have tended to worship them. Even John, who received such great revelations concerning end-time events (much of which was given by angels), fell into this error:

---

[116] Roger Elwood, *Angelwalk* (Westchester, Ill.: Crossway, 1988), 23–24.

> I, John, am the one who heard and saw these things. And when I heard and saw them, I fell down to worship at the feet of the angel who showed them to me; but he said to me, "You must not do that! I am a fellow servant with you and your comrades the prophets, and with those who keep the words of this book. Worship God!" (Rev. 22:8–9)

Paul had to deal with those who promoted a false spirituality that included the worship of angels (Col. 2:18). He combated this syncretistic faith in part with the doctrine of creation, reminding the Colossians that in Christ God created "all things in heaven and on earth ... visible and invisible, whether thrones or dominions or rulers or powers" (1:16). Here the apostle uses further terminology descriptive of the angelic order (cf. Rom. 8:38; 1 Cor. 15:24; Eph. 6:12; Col. 2:15).

The exact organization of angels is unclear, but there do seem to be different categories. An archangel's call will accompany the return of Christ (1 Thess. 4:16). We have the name of one archangel, Michael (Jude 9), who is described as a "prince," "a great prince," and "one of the chief princes" (Dan. 10:13, 21; 12:1). Michael and his good angels defeat Satan ("the dragon") and his evil angels (Rev. 12:7–9). Gabriel is the other angel named in the Bible. He is mentioned in Daniel 8:16; 9:21 and is the messenger both to Zechariah and to Mary (Luke 1:19, 26).

Isaiah saw seraphim (Heb. pl.) or seraphs (modern parlance) in his heavenly vision and describes them (Isa. 6:2–3). Cherubs or cherubim (Heb. pl.) or their images are mentioned often in the Scriptures (Gen. 3:24; Ex. 25:18–20; 1 Kings 6:23–35). Just as the Lord promised his presence above the mercy seat, over which were extended the wings of the cherubim of hammered gold (Ex. 25:22), so he is also described elsewhere as being enthroned on the cherubim (1 Sam. 4:4; 2 Sam. 6:2; 2 Kings 19:15; 1 Chron. 3:6; Isa. 37:16). The "four living creatures" of Ezekiel were cherubim (Ezek. 1:5; 10:1–22). Angels are also called "holy ones" (e.g., Ps. 89:5, 7), "watchers" (Dan. 4:13, 17, 23), and "the assembly" or "council" (Ps. 89:5, 7). The shepherds on the night of Jesus' birth saw a "multitude of the heavenly host" (Luke 2:13).

What do God's angels do? "The good angels praise God continually, communicate his message to us, minister to us, execute judgment on his enemies, and will participate in the second coming."[117] Isaiah, Daniel, and John were given glimpses into the heavenly worship of the angels (Isa. 6:1–3; Dan. 7:9–10; Rev. 7:11–12). We have already noted

---

[117] Erickson, *Introducing Christian Doctrine*, 147.

numerous instances of angels announcing God's messages to people. It is comforting to know that angels minister to God's people as well—delivering from peril (Acts 5:19; 12:6–11) and serving our needs at God's behest (Heb. 1:14). God promises us that "he will command his angels concerning you to guard you in all your ways. On their hands they will bear you up, so that you will not dash your foot against a stone" (Ps. 91:11). Billy Graham has said that he believes in angels because of the Bible's testimony and because he has sensed their presence in his life at special times.[118] Many Christians can say amen to Graham's testimony.

Angels are given enormous powers to execute God's judgment (see, e.g., 2 Sam. 24:16; 2 Kings 19:35; Rev. 8:6–9:21). Their activity was prominent in the life and ministry of Jesus and the early church, and they will appear with Christ at his second coming (Matt. 25:31).

Finally, "the angel of the Lord" should be mentioned (see Gen. 16:7, 9; 22:11, 15; Ex. 3:2; Num. 22:22–27, 31–35; Judg. 2:1, 4; 5:23; 6:11, 12, 20–23; 13:3, 13, 15–23; 2 Kings 1:3, 15; 19:35; 1 Chron. 21:12, 15–30; Ps. 34:7; 35:5–6; 37:36; Zech. 3:1–4:14; 12:8). Exactly who the angel of the Lord is has been one of the most tantalizing mysteries in Scripture. Probably Dale Moody is right to explain this angel as "the personal presence of the Lord."[119] Actually the entire topic of angels has an air of mystery about it. We have only scratched the surface in these few sentences. But we must now turn to perhaps an even greater mystery, "the secret forces of wickedness" that are at work in God's creation (2 Thess. 2:7 REB) and the intractable problem of evil that challenges belief in providence.

Satan, Demons, and Evil

To mention Satan is to point to the entrance of unspeakable evil, rebellion, and destruction into God's good creation. Rather than being an embarrassment for evangelical saints confronted with modern skepticism, the biblical teaching about Satan is a key piece to the puzzle of human existence.

On the basis of biblical authority, Christianity teaches that personality is at the heart of all reality. Carl Henry expresses this well:

---

[118] Billy Graham, *Angels: God's Secret Agents* (Garden City, N.Y.: Doubleday, 1975), 15.

[119] Dale Moody, *The Word of Truth* (Grand Rapids: Eerdmans, 1981), 166–67; see Henry, *God, Revelation and Authority*, 6:232.

> God did not create the vast space-time universe as a continuum populated by creaturely life only on planet Earth. Only where scholars negate the universal presence of God and ignore the fact of his creation of angelic hosts does the notion thrive that personality counts very little in the immensities of the universe. In Scripture the key to interpreting all of reality is the personal dimension. When Scripture speaks of the heavenly expanses it does so not in terms of purposeless fireballs, dead stars, burnt craters, moon rocks and planetary rings; it suggests rather that personal beings populate the universe, beings who are continually oriented to the plan and purpose of the Creator.[120]

Furthermore, evil itself is portrayed in Scripture as having its ultimate origins in a personal reality and not in some impersonal dimension of an unfinished creation, sociological or psychological phenomena, or political powers. It is important to add quickly that this personal evil originates among God's *creatures* and is not an "alter ego" of God locked in eternally unresolved conflict.

A chief actor in the biblical drama, Satan is "a fallen spirit from the angelic world, a demonic creaturely intelligence who impinges dramatically on the course of human events."[121] While secular scientism continues to construct its own mythologies of "nonhuman intelligences on other planets" and the like, "Christian theology considers the modern repudiation of the reality of angels, and especially of Satan, as an aspect of man's spiritual revolt."[122] Disbelief in the existence of the devil fits his strategy well: "Satan is most successfully present where he is denied, forgotten, unexpected or unnoticed."[123] He equally relishes excessive interest (as well as worship).

In his classic *The Screwtape Letters*, C. S. Lewis warned of both errors (disbelief or unhealthy interest). Satan and his demons "hail a materialist or a magician with the same delight."[124] Calvin Miller rightly names Satan "World Hater" in his mythic trilogy, *The Singer, The Song,* and *The Finale.*[125] The devil hates God and his creation. He opposes the kingdom of God and his people. As Christ's kingdom expands, Satan's dominion diminishes. Human history is the story of kingdoms in conflict. But to grasp the full significance of the human drama, we need

---

120 Henry, *God, Revelation and Authority*, 6:229.
121 Ibid.
122 Ibid., 6:230.
123 Ibid., 6:250.
124 C. S. Lewis, *The Screwtape Letters* (New York: Macmillan, 1961), 3.
125 All three published by InterVarsity Press (Downers Grove, Ill.), 1975, 1977, 1979.

biblical revelation with its accurate portrayal of the creation, both visible and invisible.

Satan appears both at the beginning and the end of the biblical story and at numerous points in between. He seduces the first couple into rebellion in the garden: "Now the serpent was more crafty than any other wild animal that the LORD God had made. He said to the woman, 'Did God say . . . ?'" (Gen. 3:1). But he is finally and permanently removed at the end of the age and the consummation of the kingdom of God. The Revelation of John describes our enemy's ultimate defeat, indicating precisely his identity: (1) the "great dragon . . . that ancient serpent, who is called the Devil and Satan, the deceiver of the whole world"; (2) "the dragon, that ancient serpent, who is the Devil and Satan" (Rev. 12:9; 20:2). He is a formidable foe; yet, since Calvary, he is defeated.

His name "Satan" means "adversary." He is "the Devil" (*diabolos*) and "the accuser of our comrades" (Rev. 12:9, 10). He dominates the ethos of human culture; he is alienated from God worldwide and so is called the "prince" or "god of this world" (John 12:31; 14:30; 16:11; 2 Cor. 4:4; 1 John 5:19). He is "Apollyon" ("destroyer," Rev. 9:11) and "the tempter" (Matt. 4:3; 1 Thess. 3:5). He is Beliar (Gk.) or Belial (Heb.), the personification of lawlessness and wickedness—a troublemaker and scoundrel (2 Cor. 6:15; cf. Deut. 13:13: see *NIV Study Bible* note). Peter warned, "Like a roaring lion your adversary the devil prowls around, looking for someone to devour" (1 Peter 5:8). The devil is "a murderer," "a liar," and "the father of lies" (John 8:44). "The picture is one of unimaginable meanness, malice, fury, and cruelty directed against God, against God's truth, and against those to whom God has extended his saving love."[126]

Contrary to popular imagery, Satan "disguises himself as an angel of light" (2 Cor. 11:14), which accounts for the plethora of false world religions and cults. Even as he tempted Jesus (Matt. 4:1–11; Mark 1:12–13; Luke 4:1–13), so he seeks to deceive us as he did Eve and to lure us away from Christ (2 Cor. 11:3). We should not be "ignorant of his designs" and "outwitted by Satan" (2:11). We should "put on the whole armor of God" (Eph. 6:11–18), submit to God, and resist the devil; he will then flee (James 4:7; 1 Peter 5:6–10). We can overcome "because God's Spirit, who is in you, is greater than the devil, who is in the world" (1 John 4:4 personal trans.).

---

[126] J. I. Packer, *Concise Theology* (Wheaton, Ill.: Tyndale, 1993), 69.

We must remember that the devil is a creature of God, albeit with powers for which in our own strength we are no match. But Satan is no match for God; "his rebellion ends in sure defeat and unmitigated judgment."[127] At the second coming of Christ the "basic weakness of Satan since the cross will then be made manifest"; "he cannot and has not frustrated God. God has frustrated him once and for all at Calvary."[128] The devil is not omnipotent, omniscient, or omnipresent, as is God. He is ruled by God just as is the rest of creation. At present, however, God allows him to rule over "the domain of darkness" (Col. 1:13 REB; cf. Acts 26:18). Satan's dominion is populated with angels who joined his rebellion, known as demons (Gk. *daimon, daimonion*).

The activity of the devil and his demons was frantic during the life and ministry of Jesus—and for obvious reasons. Their defeat was at hand. Jesus constantly cast out demons, who clearly recognized who he was (Mark 1:25), and Jesus gave his disciples this same power (Luke 9:1; 10:17). One such encounter aptly illustrates the dynamics of these kingdoms in conflict. A demonized man, blind and mute, had been brought to Jesus, and Jesus cured him. The amazed crowds wondered if this could be their long-awaited Messiah. But the Pharisees said, "It is only by Beelzebul, the ruler of the demons, that this fellow casts out the demons" (Matt. 12:24). Jesus identified Beelzebul—the Greek form of the Hebrew *Baal-zebub,* meaning "lord of the flies," a term of derision (see 1 Kings 1:2)—with Satan, then concluded: "But if it is by the Spirit of God that I cast out demons, then the kingdom of God has come to you" (Matt. 12:28). The Spirit and the kingdom are closely aligned in the Scriptures. The Spirit routs the demons and establishes God's kingdom!

Having been cast out of heaven with Satan, the demons too await God's judgment (2 Peter 2:4; Jude 6). Though allowed some movement and power, they "drag their chains wherever they go and can never hope to overcome God."[129] Packer continues: "As the devil is God's devil (that is Luther's phrase), so the demons are God's demons, defeated enemies (Col. 2:15) whose limited power is prolonged only for the advancement of God's glory as his people contend with them."[130]

There is still a mystery to the spirit world. Students of Scripture will undoubtedly continue to debate whether Isaiah 14:12–20 and Ezekiel

---

[127] Henry, *God, Revelation and Authority,* 6:236.

[128] G. C. Berkouwer, "Satan and the Demons," in *Basic Christian Doctrines,* 74, 73.

[129] Packer, *Concise Theology,* 67, citing "Calvin's picturesque phrase."

[130] Ibid., 68.

28:12–19 refer not only to historical figures but also to the fall of Satan.[131] Do passages like 1 Timothy 4:1–5 and 2 Timothy 3:1–9 indicate increased demonic activity just prior to Christ's return? If so, then perhaps this could explain the rise of incidences of the casting out of demons in evangelical ministry today. Certainly there is a place for the sage advice offered by George Mallone in his *Arming for Spiritual Warfare.*[132]

We are called to vigilance, as our Lord taught us: "Rescue us from the evil one" (Matt. 6:13). Satan is "the evil one" (*ho poneros*; cf. Matt. 13:19; Eph. 6:16). We need the Lord's daily protection and deliverance, realizing that in ourselves, apart from Christ's authority, we are no match for the evil one. Yet in Christ we can have a daily victory:

> No, in all these things we are more than conquerors through him who loved us. For I am convinced that neither death, nor life, nor angels, nor rulers, nor things present, nor things to come, nor powers, nor height, nor depth, nor anything else in all creation, will be able to separate us from the love of God in Christ Jesus our Lord. (Rom. 8:37–39)

God has given to us the dramatic account of the defeat of the great dragon in Revelation 12 "to assure those who meet satanic evil on earth that it is really a defeated power, however contrary it might seem to human experience."[133]

Questions remain, however. Why did God allow Satan in the first place? And why did God permit him to tempt Adam and Eve? The implication of the biblical picture of God is that he had an ultimate good in mind, although we may not be able fully to perceive it. It is widely speculated that the reason we were given the possibility of redemption and the devil and his demons were not is that we were tempted to do evil from an external, deceptive force, and the fallen angels were not.

Nevertheless, we have not dealt with another form of evil that confronts humankind almost daily: *natural evil.* If God is a loving, all-powerful God, then how do we explain all the suffering on this planet as a result of hurricanes, tornadoes, floods, earthquakes, debilitating diseases, and the like? Moreover, moral evil is also a problem because we often suffer as a result

---

[131] See Harold Lindsell's interesting notes on these passages in the *NRSV Harper Study Bible: Expanded and Updated,* ed. Verlyn D. Verbrugge (Grand Rapids: Zondervan, 1991). Lindsell's note on Ezekiel 28:12 is an excellent summary of the biblical doctrine of Satan.

[132] George Mallone, *Arming for Spiritual Warfare* (Downers Grove, Ill.: InterVarsity Press, 1991).

[133] George Eldon Ladd, *A Commentary on the Revelation of John* (Grand Rapids: Eerdmans, 1972), 171.

of the sins of others. In addition, why do the innocent suffer? Why do bad things happen to good people? *There are no easy answers to such questions.* Any easy answers are no answers at all. Volume upon volume has been written addressing these types of questions, and we will only skim the surface in these few paragraphs.

The issue at its simplest is as follows: (1) God is great; (2) God is good; (3) there is evil.[134] The third statement seems to contradict the first two. There is a tension here that our intellect screams to have resolved. If this were only a theoretical/theological problem, things would not be so bad. But we are faced, without exception, with a personal/religious problem as we all suffer things that seem so unjust. And we see so much of this kind of suffering elsewhere. As with other paradoxes of the faith, superficial answers simply deny one or more of the three truths listed above.

Some deny God's greatness. They claim that God would like to alleviate our suffering and evil, but he simply cannot because his power is limited. Others deny his goodness because he allows such evil. There have even been those who deny the reality of evil itself. Some, for example, assert that the material world is illusory and evil. Only the realm of the mind or spirit is considered real and good. One can overcome the physical with the mental or spiritual. When such a person gets a headache, it is tempting to say: Never mind, no matter! But that is a cruel joke to play on a probably sincere individual.

The Bible does not allow us any easy outs, but it does give us some clues to the problem of evil. We have already looked at some of them. There *is* such a thing as transcendent evil. I cannot personally account for some of the evil I read about in the newspaper without this category. Humankind is tragically fallen and sinful (as we will consider later), but there are some evil acts that simply must be inspired by the destroyer himself. However, the devil and demons get blamed for many things that are simply the result of our free choices. We are literally enslaved to sin, and we create much of our misery, inflicting suffering on one another. Thus far we have mentioned the moral free will of humankind and the devil and demons.

A third factor is the righteous judgment of God. Time and again the Old Testament depicts God's judgment of a nation or an individual *within history*. Our sins do have consequences. But we must be cautious

---

[134] See Erickson, *Introducing Christian Doctrine*, ch. 15: "Evil and God's World: A Special Problem," 138–44.

about deciding that God is judging someone in a given situation. This was the theology of Job's friends, and God himself corrected them. In this regard, it is helpful to return to the story of the Fall. One of God's curses was on the *ground* because of Adam's sin (Gen. 3:17). The physical universe itself has been affected adversely by the sin of humankind.

The apostle Paul deals with this reality in a profound way in Romans 8:18–30. He poignantly depicts the suffering that surrounds us, saying in effect that there is "a whole lot of groaning going on." Creation groans as it awaits the revelation of the children of God. We groan as we await our full redemption, which includes our resurrection bodies. The Spirit helps us in our prayers with unutterable groanings. It helps to focus on that first groaning as we contemplate suffering.

Paul says that the creation has been "subjected to futility," longing to "be set free from its bondage to decay" (Rom. 8:20–21). In other words, God allowed the fall of humankind to impact the created order. This in part accounts for much of the suffering in nature. The real answer Paul gives us, however, relates to the end times to which he refers. There *will* be a judgment where all wrongs will be righted. The creation was subjected to futility "in hope" (v. 20). One day there will be a new heaven and a new earth (Isa. 65:17; 66:22; 2 Peter 3:13; Rev. 21:1). The biblical doctrines of final judgment and cosmic redemption are important factors in the problem of evil. Paul could say: "I consider that the sufferings of this present time are not worth comparing with the glory about to be revealed to us" (Rom. 8:18). That's a part of the good news that the church has to share with the world![135]

While we should exert every effort to avert the destruction of this beautiful planet and the injustices that plague every society, even our most sterling endeavors will always fall short. *But there is hope!* Jesus Christ has given us hope, so we keep on working: "Christ in you, the hope of glory" (Col. 1:27). This kind of heavenly mindedness has always resulted in much earthly good.

God IS in Everything

So God in his providence refuses to make us puppets of his will. He permits evil for ultimately good purposes, many of which we will never know in this life. "For now we see in a mirror, dimly, but then we will see face to face. Now I know only in part; then I will know fully, even as I

[135] See Moody, *The Word of Truth*, 557–75.

have been fully known" (1 Cor. 13:12). Many of the answers await us in heaven. Life in Jesus Christ is truly abundant (John 10:10), but we are not exempt from suffering. We must always remember that there is someone who has suffered infinitely more than any of us: Jesus Christ. On his cross of redemption and atonement he revealed not only God's righteous anger against our sin, but also the suffering heart of our loving God.[136]

Catherine Marshall encountered the school of suffering many times during her lifetime—including the loss of her husband, Peter Marshall, in the prime of their lives. The first chapter in her book *Something More*, entitled "Yes, God Is in Everything," deals profoundly with the question of providence and evil. Her words form a fitting climax to our consideration of divine creation and providence:

> But the Gospel truly is good news. The news is that there is no situation—no breakage, no loss, no grief, no sin, no mess—so dreadful that out of it God cannot bring good, total good, not just "spiritual" good, if we will allow Him to.
>
> Our God is the Divine Alchemist. He can take junk from the rubbish heap of life, and melting this base refuse in the pure fire of His love, hand us back—gold.[137]

---

[136] I can think of no better books that deal with suffering in its totality—physical, mental, and spiritual—than those of Philip Yancey: *Where Is God When It Hurts* (Grand Rapids: Zondervan, 1977), and *Disappointment with God* (Grand Rapids: Zondervan, 1988).

[137] Catherine Marshall, *Something More* (New York: McGraw-Hill, 1974), 7.

5 Humanity

Who Are We, and What Does It Mean to be Created in God's Image?

O Lord, our Sovereign,
how majestic is your name in all the earth!
You have set your glory above the heavens.
Out of the mouths of babes and infants
you have founded a bulwark because of your foes,
to silence the enemy and the avenger.
When I look at your heavens, the work of your fingers,
the moon and the stars that you have established;
what are human beings that you are mindful of them,
mortals that you care for them?
Yet you have made them a little lower than God,
and crowned them with glory and honor.
You have given them dominion over the works of your hands;
you have put all things under their feet,
all sheep and oxen,
and also the beasts of the field,
the birds of the air, and the fish of the sea,
whatever passes along the paths of the seas.
O Lord, our Sovereign,
how majestic is your name in all the earth!

—Psalm 8

What better way to begin our study of the doctrine of humanity than with this majestic hymn celebrating the glory of our Creator and our own God-given dignity! Divine majesty and human dignity go hand-in-hand in the Scriptures. Humankind is only comprehensible in relation to its Creator. To be truly human is to be related to God. Only knowledge of God enables knowledge of humanity. One is reminded again of the words with which the young genius, John Calvin, began his magnum opus, *Institutes of the Christian Religion*: "Nearly all the wisdom we possess, that is to say, true and sound wisdom, consists of two parts: the knowledge of God and of ourselves."[1] David skillfully weaves together the doctrines of divine revelation, of God, and of creation with the doctrine of humanity in this eighth psalm.

God is revealed in his names, and two of the most important begin this psalm: *Yahweh* and *Adonai.* Yahweh is, of course, the covenant name God revealed to his people; and Adonai, meaning Sovereign, King, Absolute Ruler, is voiced in place of Yahweh in the Jewish synagogue to this day in order to avoid pronouncing the divine covenant name. Then the psalmist mentions the majesty of God's name in the earth and his glory in the heavens. He sees the glory of God in the starry heavens and in children's spontaneous songs of praise (Ps. 8:1–3).

In comparison to God's vast universe we can feel insignificant. How much more so today with our knowledge of just how big the universe actually is! "What are human beings that you are mindful of them, mortals that you care for them?" (Ps. 8:4). "Mortals" translates the Hebrew *ben ʾadam* ("son of man"), a title used of the Messiah in, for example, Matthew 10:23 and Hebrews 2:5–8. Yet, the Bible tells us, we are "a little lower than God" (Ps. 8:5). The word "God" here is *ʾelohim,* which could also refer in this context to the heavenly beings or angels. God has crowned humankind with "glory and honor" and has given us "dominion" over all his works (8:5–6). Our dignity and purpose is God-given. But the question that still confronts us is: "What are human beings?" (8:4). Many answers to this question have been offered.

What Is Man?

Only a few years ago this question would not have raised any eyebrows. But today using the word "man" instead of "humanity" or "humankind"

[1] John Calvin, *Institutes of the Christian Religion,* 2 vols., ed. John T. McNeill, trans. Ford Lewis Battles (Philadelphia: Westminster, 1960), 1:35 (I.i.1).

causes problems for many. Using the word "man" in a generic sense is considered sexist language in many quarters. Therefore we generally will avoid doing so. However, from this writer's perspective something is lost by avoiding the generic use of the word "man"—especially in terms of contrasting humankind with God in succinct (and, one might add, biblical) language. Nevertheless, one of the fundamental questions about our identity is raised by this very issue: What does it mean to be human *as male and female*? We will look at this important dimension of our humanness shortly.

Some see humanity as solely a *biological* phenomenon. Viewing human beings from the perspective of the natural order, Charles Darwin (1809–1882) developed his theory of natural selection in *The Origin of the Species* (1859) and *The Descent of Man* (1871), and in effect challenged the biblical view of our distinctive position in the created order. Ironically, at one time Darwin professed Christian belief and accepted the biblical doctrine of the uniqueness of humanity. Today millions of people espouse Darwin's perspective on the human race.

If we are solely biological creatures, no different from any other life forms on this planet, then all our traditional values are challenged.

The implications of this viewpoint, however, are far-reaching. If we are solely biological creatures, no different from any other life forms on this planet, then all our traditional values are challenged. Suppose, for example, someone is driving down a residential street and both a child and a dog dart in front of the automobile. If the driver has time to avoid only one of the two, which should she choose? Our natural response would be, of course, to save the child's life. But if we are not different from the animals and if we are not a higher order of creation, how can we continue to maintain this position? Clearly, contemporary society values human life less today in large measure because of this very problem.

Nevertheless, there is a kernel of truth to this perspective. We do share a kinship with the natural order. We are *creatures* who are born, eat, sleep, reproduce, age, and die just as the animals do. Given our biblical responsibility for the earth, we can view animals as our "cousins," as it were, and even enjoy our similarities. Richard P. McBrien has expressed it well:

> We cannot easily overestimate the importance of Darwin's work. No longer can any serious person reflect on the meaning of human existence as if each one of us lived in an environmental or cosmic vacuum. We are not disembodied spirits. We are bodily creatures, materially linked with the rest of creation, and especially with other living beings. Reason may indeed set us on a qualitatively different level of reality, but so, too, do our will, our emotions, our sexuality, our esthetic sense, and our total bodiliness.[2]

Solely at the biological level we are "fearfully and wonderfully made" (Ps. 139:14), as Paul Brand and Philip Yancey demonstrate so well in their volume by the same name.[3]

Karl Marx (1818–1883), another highly influential voice on the modern scene, defined humanity in relation to the social order. This *sociological* perspective dominated the lives of more than a third of the world's population in the twentieth century. Marx saw the individualism of capitalist societies as creating much of the misery of humankind. He sought to subordinate the individual to society and to eliminate the differences between the "haves" and the "have-nots." This vision of each of us contributing according to ability and receiving according to need was appealing. Unfortunately, it failed to take into account the sinfulness of humanity and the need for individual initiative. As a social experiment Marxism was a dismal failure, and many so-called liberationist theologians were left with egg on their faces, having sought to construct a doctrine of redemption almost solely on a political basis, combining Christianity with Marxism.

However, capitalism can be as materialistic as socialism, and we are faced with an even greater crisis now that the communist empire has fallen. The modern-day prophet Alexander Solzhenitsyn warned us of this danger years ago. Western society is literally pulling apart at the seams because of the moral chaos that dominates virtually every social institution. Our only hope lies in a spiritual revival more powerful than this world has yet seen.

Again, there is a kernel of truth to be acknowledged from the sociological perspective. The Scriptures themselves define humanity in social and relational terms. The difference, however, is that the biblical sense retains the vertical dimension of our relationship to God. We are by biblical definition social creatures.

---

[2] Richard McBrien, *Catholicism* (Minneapolis: Winston, 1981), 105. I am indebted to McBrien for many of the perspectives on humankind described in this section.

[3] Paul Brand and Philip Yancey, *Fearfully and Wonderfully Made* (Grand Rapids: Zondervan, 1980).

Our present-day sensualism suggests that millions of us see ourselves primarily as *sexual* creatures. This perspective can be traced back in large measure to the massive influence of Sigmund Freud (1856–1939). Freud saw humankind driven by an unconscious conflict related to proper sexual gratification. He took a totally materialistic view, in which religion is seen as simply wish-fulfillment that prolongs an immature status and is destructive. Unfortunately, Freud seemed to portray humankind at its worst rather than at its healthiest and best, and the result was a pessimistic view of humanity.

The Bible does makes it clear, of course, that God created us as sexual beings (Gen. 1:27). Sexuality was God's idea, not Hollywood's (or some sort of psychological determinism). Sexuality was one of God's good gifts to us, and all of us—female and male—are created in the divine image (again, more on this later).

Perhaps the strongest philosophical influence in the contemporary search for human significance has been that of *existentialism.* Humankind is challenged to face honestly its mortality and to take responsibility for achieving meaning in life in spite of death. From a nonreligious view philosophers such as Friedrich Wilhelm Nietzsche (1844–1900), Jean-Paul Sartre (1905–1980), and Albert Camus (1913–1960) told us simply to exert our wills and assert what is true and important from our own perspective, apart from any so-called revealed norms. According to this perspective there is no divinely revealed truth, as there is no God. This is a dark and tragic view of humankind. It is easy to see why New Age teachings have in large measure succeeded existentialism by offering hope for life beyond the grave and the continued perfection of humanity.

It is a strongly biblical counsel, however, to face our mortality honestly and to live life from the perspective of eternity. Søren Kierkegaard (1813–1855) made this one of his lifelong projects. First, he says, we lose ourselves in the crowd. Then, perhaps, we can move to the aesthetic stage of seeking enjoyment—only to come to despair in that pursuit. The ethical stage is next, where we find true freedom in our moral responsibility—again, only to end in despair. Then we may move to a religious stage. It may be a natural, humanistic religion, or it may be authentic faith. In authentic Christian faith and human existence we encounter God, acknowledge our fear and guilt, surrender our sovereign egos, and submit to the Unconditioned, Wholly Other God.[4]

---

[4] I have depended on notes from Eric Rust's philosophy of religion course, which I received during my Southern Baptist Theological Seminary pilgrimage, for this description of Kierkegaard's thought—my own highly simplified account, to be sure!

The existentialist philosophy of Martin Heidegger (1889–1976) has exerted perhaps the greatest influence on modern theology. Heidegger analyzed human existence in terms of polarities. There is the polarity of freedom and finitude. Our existence is limited by certain given facts such as intelligence, race, temperament, heredity, and environment. We are both rational and irrational. We are responsible and yet often impotent in seeking to do what we perceive to be right. We have both anxiety and hope. We exist both as individuals and as social creatures. Death is the boundary, limit, or framework of human existence. Authentic human existence faces this reality head-on and derives therein a sense of urgency and responsibility. As an atheist Heidegger believed that beyond death lies nothingness.[5]

Major modern theologians such as Rudolf Bultmann (1884–1976), Paul Tillich (1886–1965), and John Macquarrie (b. 1919) have made large use of Heidegger's philosophy. Among these three, perhaps Macquarrie has come the closest to the warmth of the ethos of the biblical perspective. In his discussion of "Human Existence" (ch. 4 in his *Principles of Christian Theology*), Macquarrie concludes that a person makes sense of these polarities of human existence only when he or she is grasped by a God-given faith.[6]

The list of modern theological concepts of humanity is virtually endless. Karl Barth (1886–1968) saw humankind as God's covenant-partner—even after our irrational choice of sin against our Creator. Jürgen Moltmann (b. 1926) sees value in biological anthropology, cultural anthropology, and religious anthropology as they provide insights into the nature of human existence. But he rightly argues for a Christian anthropology based on the God-man, the crucified Christ, who "belongs to no one nation, race, or class."[7] Wolfhart Pannenberg (b. 1928) sees our *openness* to the world as that which distinguishes us from animals. The cultural environment is more fundamental than the natural environment. Language is crucial in terms of mastering our environment, and imagination is even more important as we face the future. Imagination is to humankind what instinct is to animals. Ultimately, it is our openness to God that sets us apart: "What the environment is for animals, God is for man. God is the goal in which alone his striving can find rest and his destiny be fulfilled."[8]

---

[5] McBrien, *Catholicism*, 116–17.

[6] John Macquarrie, *Principles of Christian Theology* (New York: Charles Scribner's Sons, 1966), 74.

[7] Jürgen Moltmann, *Man: Christian Anthropology in the Conflicts of the Present*, trans. John Sturdy (Philadelphia: Fortress, 1974), 20.

[8] Wolfhart Pannenberg, *What Is Man?* trans. Duane A. Priebe (Philadelphia: Fortress, 1970), 13.

William Shakespeare wrote in *Hamlet*: "What a piece of work is a man! How noble in reason! how infinite in faculty! in form, in moving, how express and admirable! in action how like an angel! in apprehension how like a god!" G. K. Chesterton observed: "Man is not a balloon going up into the sky, nor a mole burrowing merely in the earth; but rather a thing like a tree, whose roots are fed from the earth, while its highest branches seem to rise almost to the stars."[9] It is the biblical testimony itself that best expresses the grandeur of humankind as created in God's image (and, as we will study later, the tragedy of humankind because of sin).

"Let Us Make Humankind . . ."

Genesis 1:26–28 tells us the seven most important truths we need to know about the essence of humanity (again, apart from the fact of sin):

> Then God said, "Let us make humankind in our image, according to our likeness; and let them have dominion over the fish of the sea, and over the birds of the air, and over the cattle, and over all the wild animals of the earth, and over every creeping thing that creeps upon the earth."
>
> So God created humankind in his image,
> in the image of God he created them;
> male and female he created them.
>
> God blessed them, and God said to them, "Be fruitful and multiply, and fill the earth and subdue it; and have dominion over the fish of the sea and over the birds of the air and over every living thing that moves upon the earth."

God's crowning creative achievement is portrayed in these majestic words.

Seven foundational truths about humankind are asserted through the words used in this passage:

- *God*: In Scripture humankind is always defined in relation to God.
- *make*: We are creatures with a finite existence.
- *humankind*: We are the culmination of God's creative acts.

---

[9] Shakespeare and Chesterton are cited in Paul Brand and Philip Yancey, *In His Image* (Grand Rapids: Zondervan, 1984), 16.

- *image/likeness*: Our uniqueness lies in our having been made in the divine image.
- *dominion*: This divine image is expressed in the dominion God has given us to rule and care for the created order.
- *male/female*: Human sexuality is a part of God's design for humankind, and both sexes are made in God's image.
- *blessed/be fruitful*: God personally and lovingly blessed and ordained our role in his creation, commanding us to fill the earth and subdue it in a loving nurture. This blessing is a powerful reality attested in Scripture.

These truths about humanity can only be fully known through biblical revelation. Any attempt to define humankind apart from our fundamental relationship with God is futile. Even a natural theology falls far short at this point. The Bible provides the only adequate basis for belief in the dignity of humanity.

> *The Bible provides the only adequate basis for belief in the dignity of humanity.*

The Scriptures begin with God's creating humankind in his own image and giving us dominion over the earth. We are only creatures to be sure, but we stand apart from the rest of creation by virtue of the unique relationship we have with God. We were made to know God, to love God, to glorify God, and to serve God. Humankind is *wonderful.* Christians might be embarrassed to make such a statement, but it is true.

Francis Schaeffer once said, "I am convinced that one of the great weaknesses in evangelical preaching in the last few years is that we have lost sight of the biblical fact that man is wonderful." In resisting humanism, Schaeffer explained, we have emphasized our lostness and reduced humankind to a nonentity. He continued, "In fact, only the biblical position produces a real and proper 'humanism.'"[10] In their apologetic, *Christianity: The True Humanism,* J. I. Packer and Thomas Howard sharply delineate the issues:

> Humanism tells us to think of ourselves as having no environment save that which science—physical, psychological, political, social, economic—studies; no life beyond heartstop day; and no rational goals beyond self-discovery, pursuing pleasure, and lessening others' misery here and now.

[10] Francis A. Schaeffer, *Death in the City* (Downers Grove, Ill.: InterVarsity Press, 1969), 80.

> Christianity teaches us to view God as our ultimate environment; to know him in and through the persons, things, and values that surround us; and to see ourselves as immortal beings of infinite worth whose calling for all eternity is to adore the God who has made us and loved us, to love him and our fellowman in return, and to experience joy in so doing. Each view sees the other as ruinously wrong-headed.[11]

Not only is the biblical vision of humanity more attractive than that of humanistic secularism, it is also true.

Adam and Eve in Eden

The parallel account of the creation of humankind in Genesis 2 adds color and detail to the statement of the first chapter. Whereas Genesis 1 was a more formal, programmatic, hymnic, and liturgical passage, Genesis 2 provides a prose narrative with a number of interesting details. We see the forest in the first chapter, the trees in the second chapter. And we are introduced to the primal couple, Adam and Eve:

> Then the LORD God formed man from the dust of the ground, and breathed into his nostrils the breath of life; and the man became a living being. And the LORD God planted a garden in Eden, in the east; and there he put the man whom he had formed....
>
> Then the LORD God said, "It is not good that the man should be alone; I will make him a helper as his partner." ... So the LORD God caused a deep sleep to fall upon the man, and he slept; then he took one of his ribs and closed up its place with flesh. And the rib that the LORD God had taken from the man he made into a woman and brought her to the man. Then the man said,
>
> "This at last is bone of my bones
> and flesh of my flesh;
> this one shall be called Woman,
> for out of Man this one was taken."
>
> Therefore a man leaves his father and his mother and clings to his wife, and they become one flesh. And the man and his wife were both naked, and were not ashamed. (Gen. 2:7, 8, 18, 21–25)

Some exciting details relating to the creation of humankind appear here. Genesis 1:1–2:3 form a majestic introduction to the entire book

[11] J. I. Packer and Thomas Howard, *Christianity: The True Humanism* (Dallas: Word, 1985), 14.

of Genesis. Genesis 2:4 introduces the first of its ten major sections. The key word is "generations" (*toledot*): "These are the generations of the heavens and the earth when they were created" (cf. 5:1; 6:9; 10:1; 11:10; 11:27; 25:12; 25:19; 36:1; 37:2). Notice that the first section deals with "the heavens and the earth when they were created." The verses we are looking at not only complement what we have already read in the previous chapter, but also set the stage for the account of the fall of humankind.

The time is thousands of years ago. The place is the ancient Near East. (We have never been able to determine precisely the location of Eden, although the mention of the Tigris and Euphrates rivers narrows the focus somewhat.) God's most important creative activity is about to take place. We must remind ourselves that Moses' account is topical rather than chronological, yet he is describing an event that took place in space and time. The Lord God (now the redemptive covenant name for God, *Yahweh,* is included) forms (*yaśar*) the man (*ʾadam*) from the dust of the ground (*ʾadamah*). God forms or fashions the man much as a master craftsman, a potter, forms a piece of clay. The man is made from the earth—he is an earthly creature, tied to the planet by divine design.

> *We are* unitive *beings. We are dust plus breath. We are animated mud, as it were. God himself gives us life.*

Then God breathes into the man's nostrils the breath (*nešamah*) of life, and he becomes a living soul (*nepeš ḥayyah*). The man receives life by God's breathing into him. What could be more personal? (John shows how the new creation begins in much the same way [John 20:22].) The man becomes a living soul, just as the animals are living souls—the exact same words are used (cf. Gen. 1:20, 24; 2:19). The point is that we are *unitive* beings. We are dust plus breath. We are animated mud, as it were. God himself gives us life. To the original reader of the Hebrew text these words were (typically) *concrete* and clear: If one has breath, he or she is a "living soul"; if God takes away one's breath, he or she is a "dead soul." In the most fundamental sense we don't *have* souls, we *are* souls.[12]

Then God places Adam in the Garden of Eden to care for it. God notes that it is not good that the man is alone and declares that he will

---

[12] This statement will have to be qualified later, when we consider the constitution of man. Nevertheless, the overriding testimony of Scripture is that man *is* a soul, a unitive being.

make someone who corresponds to the man as a life partner—"a helper as his partner" (Gen. 2:18). (The note about the animals in vv. 19–20 sets humanity apart from animals in a pagan context in which animals were worshiped; humankind is fundamentally different from the animals even though made physically from the same substance.) God causes the man to fall into a deep sleep, takes one of his ribs, and "builds" (*banah*) a woman. As the "father of the bride," he brings her to the man. Notice she came from Adam's *side*, not from his head to lord it over him, nor from his feet to be trampled upon and dominated—"but out of his side to be equal with him, under his arm to be protected, and near his heart to be beloved."[13]

Adam breaks into song (Gen. 2:23). It is a song of joy, exuberance, delight, recognition, and gratitude. There is a beautiful play on words. Woman (*ʾiššah*) is taken out of Man (*ʾiš*). Bone of my bones, flesh of my flesh (cf. "one flesh" in v. 24). Every happily married person knows exactly what Adam was singing about that day! This is additional evidence of the goodness of God. Verse 24 sums up the dynamics of marriage in three key words: leaving, cleaving, and becoming one flesh. Leaving involves the establishing of a new family unit. Cleaving points to the permanence of the marriage commitment. It means "to stick like glue," a union that can be torn asunder only at a great cost to both parties. And "one flesh" indicates the most intimate personal unity known to humankind, expressed, of course, in sexual union.[14]

> *Adam is every man, yet Adam is also a historic person with descendants.*

The following chapter contains the tragic story of the Fall and God's judgment, which we will examine later. One comment is made, however, that should be noted. We are told that the "man named his wife Eve, because she was the mother of all living" (Gen. 3:20). As the NRSV marginal note explains, in Hebrew "*Eve* resembles the word for *living*." Finally, Genesis 5 begins a new section with an interesting choice of words related to humankind: "When God created humankind [*ʾadam*], he made them [lit., him] in the likeness of God. Male and female he created them, and he blessed them and named them 'Humankind' [*ʾadam*], when they were created" (5:1–2). The following verses further

[13] From Harold Lindsell's note on Gen. 2:22 in the *NRSV Study Bible: Expanded and Updated*, ed. Verlyn D. Verbrugge (Grand Rapids: Zondervan, 1991), 6 (Matthew Henry's comment).
[14] See Walter Trobisch, *I Married You* (New York: Harper & Row, 1971).

illuminate the picture: "When Adam had lived one hundred thirty years, he became the father of a son in his likeness, according to his image, and named him Seth. . . . Adam lived . . . nine hundred thirty years; and he died" (5:3–5).

It is important to note that Adam and Eve are seen as both symbolic and historical in these opening chapters, as the verses we have looked at clearly indicate. *Adam* is translated both as generic man and as a proper name. Genesis 5:1–5 illustrates these usages precisely. Adam is every man, yet Adam is also a historic person with descendants. Eve's name is symbolic, yet at the same time it denotes that humankind issues forth from her. This raises the questions: Are we to see the entire human race as having come from the first couple, Adam and Eve? How do we relate the biblical materials with modern anthropology and paleontology? Just how old *is* humankind?

The Antiquity of Humanity

For the Christian theologian, the age of humankind is in many ways a much more difficult problem to address than the age of the universe. The Scriptures tell us everything we need to know to make sense of human existence, but scientists keep digging up fossil remains that raise new questions concerning the origin of humanity. Since systematic theology relates what the Scriptures teach to contemporary questions and knowledge, it is imperative that we examine this information and come to at least some tentative conclusions.

We are aware immediately that no one has all the answers; there is much speculation in all quarters, both scientific and theological. As Christians committed to the authority of the Bible, however, seeking an integration of knowledge is both a serious and intriguing pursuit. What we do know through biblical revelation is crucial. What we don't know is puzzling, but not devastating. Surely in this area of research, above all others, a modicum of humility and tolerance is appropriate.

In 1974 Donald Johanson discovered in the mud of a lake shore of East Africa the fossil remains of a tiny female creature dated at more than three million years old. These remains were given the name "Lucy," after the Beatles' song "Lucy in the Sky with Diamonds." "Lucy" revolutionized the scientific quest for knowledge of human origins.[15] How do

---

[15] Michael D. Lemonick, "The Origin of Our Species," *Time* (February 28, 1994), 62.

we evaluate such discoveries, theories, and conclusions of modern anthropology and paleontology in the light of the biblical narratives?

For more than a century archaeologists, anthropologists, and others have participated in the discoveries and assessments of skulls, jaws, teeth, thighs, and arms that they have attributed to human beings and that they have dated by use of geological evidence and of fluorine. Notable among these were the Neanderthal man in Germany (1857ff.), the Cro-Magnon man in France (1868), the Java man (1891ff.), the Piltdown man in England (1912ff.), the Peking man (1921ff.), and more recent discoveries in southern and eastern Africa.[16] Where do we find Adam and Eve in all this?

Lest the church make the same mistakes it made with Copernicus and Galileo, it is important to check our interpretation of Scripture as well as the scientific facts. Often we discover that it is our understanding of what the Bible teaches that is the problem rather than a conflict between the Bible and scientific data. The Bible does not teach that the universe is geocentric, but for centuries most Christians believed it did. The problem was not with the Bible but with its interpreters. This fact must be balanced from the other side by reminding ourselves that scientific opinion is continually changing as well. In the final analysis, since God's revelation is unified and noncontradictory, what is revealed in both nature and Scripture will coincide.

In Genesis 4 we are confronted with the fact that "the man" (*haʾadam*), from whom God made Eve is Adam (*ʾadam,* without the definite article *ha*). Now we must see Adam and Eve as historical personages—parents who give birth to Cain and Abel and later Seth. Furthermore, the cultural picture one derives from this same chapter is probably that of the Neolithic (New Stone Age) period. This would mean that Adam and Eve lived from ten to twelve thousand years ago. How does this picture fit with scientific research that places North American Indians back some twenty-five thousand years—much less the fossil remains that may place humankind back a half million years ago or more?

Dale Moody's statement that "among conservative evangelical Christians the question of the relation between the Adam of the Scriptures and the first men described in scientific anthropology is far from answered"[17] is an understatement. Moody's approach is to accept

---

[16] James Leo Garrett, *Systematic Theology* (Grand Rapids: Eerdmans, 1990), 1:407.

[17] Dale Moody, *The Word of Truth* (Grand Rapids: Eerdmans, 1981), 198.

(almost uncritically) modern science and biblical criticism. Modern science sees humankind evolving from hominids millions of years old. Biblical criticism posits JEDP theories, which Moody uses to suggest three Adams: "(1) Individual Adam in the J source of Genesis 4, (2) Representative Adam in the JE source of Genesis 2:4b–3:24, and (3) Collective Adam in the P source of Genesis 1:1–2:4a."[18] Thus, humankind could be dated back hundreds of thousands of years (Moody guesses about four hundred thousand years), and one can still allow for a historical Adam, whose wife was Eve and whose sons were Cain, Abel, and Seth. He also argues for polygenism, the belief that God created many other humans besides Adam and Eve (which would explain, among other things, where Cain got his wife).[19]

As creative and ground-breaking as Moody's proposal is, it suffers two fundamental weaknesses: his use of the highly tentative JEDP theories and his positing of polygenism. One could argue for a multiple use of *ʾadam* in the opening chapters of Genesis without resorting to JEDP speculations (critical theories die hard). And positing multiple human origins creates all sorts of difficulties, not the least of which is how to interpret the biblical doctrine of sin. Few evangelical theologians have had the courage to confront the scientific realities as honestly as Moody. As we all must, however, Moody acknowledges limitations of knowledge: "It may be that all men have descended from a primal pair, but it matters not if that was 20,000,000 years ago or more recently."[20]

There is nothing close to a consensus among evangelical scholars on the antiquity of humankind.

There is nothing close to a consensus among evangelical scholars on the antiquity of humankind. Scientific data is itself inconclusive. Can it be proven that the Indians of North America go back twenty-five thousand years? What do we know for certain about characteristics of the hominids of millennia past? Much still surely lies in the arena of conjecture. Nevertheless, scientific data must be taken seriously. On the basis of Scripture can it be established beyond doubt, for example, that a Neolithic period is being described in Genesis 4? How many "Adams"

---

[18] Ibid., 200.

[19] Ibid., 198–212. Moody's presentation in this section, entitled "Adam: Man and Mankind," is colorful and informative, evincing a broad scientific knowledge.

[20] Ibid., 172. Now that Dale Moody—a trusted friend and mentor—is with the Lord, he may have solved all these mysteries!

exactly are there in Genesis? And are we required to hold to a primal pair as the source of the entire human race? And, again, just how old is humankind?

Tool-making goes back a half million to two million years ago. Is this the beginning of humankind? It probably is not, in view of the fact that chimpanzees use tools today. If the use of fire is the criterion for determining human life, then humankind could go back some four hundred thousand years. (Proponents of this theory usually conclude that some sort of primitive verbal communication is also operative.) Neanderthal "man" (40,000–100,000 years ago) buried their dead: Could humankind be dated back to this period? The tools and art of Cro-Magnon "man" of some 25,000 years ago is impressive. Does human language go back 30,000–40,000 years or does it come much later? The evidence is still inconclusive. Where does this maze leave us?

Millard Erickson concludes that humankind is perhaps 30,000–40,000 years old, going back to the Cro-Magnon period (and assuming that language was operative then). Perhaps the domestication of animals and plants goes back to this late period, or perhaps we have read too much into Genesis 4 as far as seeing a Neolithic culture is concerned. Erickson admits that there is still much uncertainty in this area and that "much additional study" is needed.[21] Gordon Lewis and Bruce Demarest take seriously the overtones of the Neolithic period in Genesis 4 and date humankind at some 10,000–12,000 years ago.[22] Then, to illustrate how varied Christian opinion is, we should consider the conclusions of Lutheran theologian Hans Schwarz. Schwarz, a theistic evolutionist, sees the human family evolving most immediately from Cro-Magnon "man" at a relatively late date in comparison with our previous considerations.[23]

It appears that the fossil remains are of Pre-Adamites, that the Scriptures do teach that as a race we go back to Adam and Eve, and that our origins could be as late as 10,000 to 12,000 years ago or perhaps as early as 40,000 years ago. Erickson is right about the need for further study. Nor can we forget that the catastrophe theory of the Creation Science school of thought has argued for a late date for humankind all along—

---

[21] Millard J. Erickson, *Christian Theology* (Grand Rapids: Baker, 1985), 484–87.

[22] Gordon R. Lewis and Bruce A. Demarest, *Integrative Theology* (Grand Rapids: Zondervan, 1990), 2:30.

[23] Hans Schwarz, *Our Cosmic Journey: Christian Anthropology in the Light of Current Trends in the Sciences, Philosophy and Theology* (Minneapolis: Augsburg, 1977), 81.

as well as for a young earth. For many, however, scientists have uncovered too much data that contradicts this position. Still, Christians should be tolerant of differences of opinion in this difficult area of study. In one sense, the antiquity of humanity is one of the most fascinating subjects one could ever explore. But in many respects, God's ways are always beyond finding out.

The Image of God

We come now to a central tenet of the Christian faith. It is one of the most important teachings of the Bible. It is one of the major contributions of Christianity to human culture, and it is at the core of the biblical doctrine of humanity. The Scriptures teach that humankind has been created in the image of God: *imago Dei.* God said, "Let us make humankind in our image, according to our likeness; and let them have dominion" (Gen. 1:26). This understanding of humanity is fundamental to belief in our dignity and purpose. Human life is of supreme significance because each of us is created in the divine image.

To be created in the image (*ṣelem*) of God is to be made "according to [his] likeness [*demut*]." In other words, humankind is Godlike. In our very *substance* we are like God. This *fact* of our Godlikeness has important implications concerning our *purpose.* We were made for God, and we were made for one another. We were made to love and to be loved. And we were made to care for this beautiful planet on which we have been placed. We are to have *dominion* over the created order. Millard Erickson states the matter succinctly and accurately: "The image itself is that set of qualities of God which, reflected in humans, make relationships and the exercise of dominion possible."[24]

We were made for God, and we were made for one another. We were made to love and to be loved.

Getting a handle on the image of God in humanity, however, can prove to be a somewhat slippery endeavor. One major reason is the fact of sin, which must be related to the doctrine of humanity. Again, Erickson's remarks are helpful:

---

[24] Millard J. Erickson, *Introducing Christian Doctrine,* ed. L. Arnold Hustad (Grand Rapids: Baker, 1992), 168.

> If we investigate the Bible's depiction of humanity, we find that people today are actually in an abnormal condition. The real human is not what we now find in human society. The real human is the being that came from the hand of God, unspoiled by sin and the fall. In a very real sense, the only true human beings were Adam and Eve before the fall, and Jesus. All the others are twisted, distorted, corrupted samples of humanity. It therefore is necessary to look at humans in their original state and at Christ if we would correctly assess what it means to be human.[25]

Because of the sinfulness and fallenness of humankind, we are actually less than fully human. This fact does not mean, however, that the divine image has been lost. When someone sins, we often say, "He's only human." We should say, "He's *less* than human." Sin distorts our humanity and our Godlikeness. We must consider this tragic reality as well. A comprehensive grasp of the divine image entails the study of (1) the image of God in *creation,* (2) the image of God in *Christ,* and (3) the image of God in the *Christian.*[26]

The Image of God in Creation

We have already referred to the programmatic passage in the opening account of creation (Gen. 1:26–27). There God's Word plainly states that *all* of humankind, male and female, has been created in the divine image and given dominion over the earth. Psalm 8, with which we began this chapter, reiterates this same truth. Dale Moody is impressed with the precision and comprehensiveness of this psalm in relation to the doctrine of humanity:

> Man's dominion under God could hardly be stated with greater clarity. This applies to Everyman, not just to the First Man. More than the creatures and less than the Creator: that is man's glory and honor. To mix ancient and modern ideas, man is less than the angels and more than the apes.[27]

We are neither angels nor animals. We are the Godlike creatures God has made in part to care for the animals. In the *totality* of our beings we reflect God's image. We are creatures, to be sure—creatures made from the dust as were the animals, creatures who are tied to the earth in terms of our daily sustenance. Yet we are a *special* creation of God: "Let us make

---

[25] Ibid., 162.
[26] Cf. Moody, *The Word of Truth,* 226–34.
[27] Ibid., 228.

humankind," rather than "Let the earth bring forth" (contrast vv. 26 and 24).[28]

Having been made in God's image bestows on humankind dignity and privilege as well as responsibility and identity. We are indeed "God's offspring" (Acts 17:28–31), but we also have the responsibility of stewardship over this planet. Moreover, it is important to stress in this secularized and paganized age that we *belong* to God. "The earth is the LORD's and all that is in it, the world, and those who live in it" (Ps. 24:1). When the Jewish rulers maliciously sought to entrap Jesus concerning the payment of taxes to the emperor, Jesus not only silenced them with his wise reply, he also affirmed the principle of ownership in the divine image. Just as the image of the emperor on the denarius indicated what was owned by the emperor, so God's image in us is his stamp of ownership on us (Matt. 22:20–21). In fact, we are *twice* God's, through both creation and redemption (see also 1 Cor. 6:19–20).

Furthermore, as John Stek has documented, both primeval and patriarchal histories are permeated with the metaphor of divine kingship, as are the Scriptures. As human beings created in God's image, we are his royal stewards on this planet. We symbolize his ownership of the creation. We are extensions of divine rulership of planet earth. Creation theology is kingdom theology.[29] Thus, when the king himself, Jesus Christ, appears in history, the message of the kingdom of God again comes to the fore. As a race we humans are simply rebellious subjects and stewards. What is even worse, we are often impervious to this fact. God himself has to get our attention. These three truths of biblical revelation should be shouted daily from the housetops: (1) We are *creatures*; (2) we are *Godlike* creatures; (3) and we are *responsible* creatures—responsible to God and for one another. We were made to love God with all our heart, soul, mind, and strength and to love our neighbor as ourselves (Mark 12:29–31).

Genesis 5:1–2 reiterates 1:26–27, mentioning only "the likeness of God." However, a new concept is introduced in the ensuing verse. Seth is described as being in Adam's "likeness, according to his image" (5:3). Comparing Scripture with Scripture, it is interesting to place 1 Corinthians 15:45–49 alongside this passage. Paul uses an Adam/Christ typology or analogy in arguing for the resurrection of Christ and of Christians.

---

[28] Derek Kidner, *Genesis* (TOTC; Downers Grove, Ill.: InterVarsity Press, 1967), 50.

[29] John H. Stek, "What Says the Scripture?" in *Portraits of Creation* (Grand Rapids: Eerdmans, 1990), 232–58.

The apostle states: "Just as we have borne the image of the man of dust, we will also bear the image of the man of heaven." Christ is "the last Adam" and "the second man." A new humanity, as it were, begins with him. As "living souls," all persons share the image of the "first man, Adam." We are "from the earth" and made "of dust." Even though each of us has the divine image as did Adam, we also are going to die physically because of our sin (as did Adam). However, in Christ we have the hope of resurrection to eternal life with a resurrection body like that of Christ himself.

God places an infinite value on each human life.

God places an infinite value on each human life. The whole world does not compare in value to one human life (see Luke 9:25). Thus, God requires a "reckoning for human life":

> Whoever sheds the blood of a human,
> by a human shall that person's blood be shed;
> for in his own image
> God made humankind. (Gen. 9:6)

The death penalty has this passage in part in its background. But there are other important implications. Surely, if there is any possibility at all that the life in a mother's womb is human life, we should avoid medical abortions if at all possible. The multi-million-dollar abortion industry—which has performed millions of "convenience" abortions—is slaughtering innocents as sacrifices to the pagan idols of our day. God will hold us accountable.

To the Corinthians Paul wrote that a man "is the image and glory of God; but the woman is the glory of man" (1 Cor. 11:7 NIV). This is a difficult passage. Paul *is* saying that there needs to be a differentiating of the sexes in the life of the church (and, by implication, in society). Paul is *not* saying that women are inferior to men, that women do not have the divine image, that women cannot be fully functioning members of Christ's body, or that women exist only for men. Again, comparing Scripture with Scripture, the Genesis passages simply will not allow this twisting of the text—and neither will the Pauline context of this passage. Many abuses can result from poor exegesis. Paul delicately balances the unity and diversity of the sexes, as he does the spiritual gifts. Women and men are one in their humanity but different in their sexuality. As J. I. Packer observes:

> The ideology of "unisex," which plays down the significance of the two genders, thus perverts God's order, while the French tag on gender distinction, "*vive la différence!*" (Long live the contrast!) expresses the biblical viewpoint.[30]

The testimony of Scripture is clear and consistent: All persons are made in God's image. Therefore, as James exhorts, we need to be careful how we speak to one another. We use our tongue "to bless the Lord and Father, but we also use it to curse people who are made in God's image [lit., likeness]" (James 3:9 NJB).

The Image of God in Christ

Paul is explicit in his writings that Christ is the image of God (*eikon tou theou*; 2 Cor. 4:4; Col. 1:15). The Colossians passage is even more expressive: "He is the image of the invisible God" (Col. 1:15). The writer of Hebrews says of Christ, "He is the radiance [*apaugasma*] of God's glory, the stamp [*charakter*] of God's very being" (Heb. 1:3 REB). At the culmination of his opening prologue John writes, "No one has ever seen God; God's only Son, he who is nearest to the Father's heart, has made him known" (John 1:18 REB). The phrase "has made him known" translates the Greek term *exegesato*: Christ "exegetes" the Father for us; he interprets, explains, and describes him. When Philip asked Jesus to "show us the Father," Jesus said in part, "Whoever has seen me has seen the Father" (John 14:9). Thus, Jesus Christ himself becomes the key to a complete understanding of the divine image in humankind.

Francis Schaeffer liked to refer to the God of biblical revelation as the personal-infinite God. An infinite chasm exists between God in his infinity and all else. In that sense, we are no closer to God than animals, plants, or machines. On the personal side, however, there is a chasm between us and all else (i.e., animals, plants, and machines). Made in the personal divine image, humankind has a unique kinship with God. "The reasonableness of the incarnation, and the reasonableness of communication between God and man, turn on this point, that man, as man, is created in the image of God."[31] Indeed, authentic Christian faith is incarnational in its very essence. This fact implies in part that the doctrine of humanity must be informed by the incarnation, must even be based on it, to be faithful to divine revelation.

---

[30] J. I. Packer, *Concise Theology* (Wheaton, Ill.: Tyndale, 1993), 76.

[31] Francis A. Schaeffer, *The God Who Is There* (Downers Grove, Ill.: InterVarsity Press, 1968), 94–95.

Only in God is our humanity complete. That is why we must look at Jesus Christ, the God-Man, for a picture of humanity in perfection. It is precisely *because* Jesus was God Incarnate that his humanity was complete. Dale Moody states it well: "The fullness of humanity is found only in the fullness of deity. True man is man truly indwelt by God. That Jesus Christ was, and in him the fullness of our humanity is realized." Then Moody cites Colossians 2:9–10: "For in him the whole fullness of deity dwells bodily, and you have come to fullness in him, who is the head of every ruler and authority."[32] Although the image of God has been "marred" by sin, it has not been lost. Nevertheless, only through Christ can the divine image in us be restored and perfected.

The Image of God in the Christian

The restoration of the divine image in humankind is at the center of God's plan through the ages. John R. W. Stott expresses it well:

> If we had to sum up in a single brief sentence what life is all about, why Jesus Christ came into this world to live and die and rise, and what God is up to in the long-drawn-out process both BC and AD, it would be difficult to find a more succinct explanation than this: *God is making human beings more human by making them more like Christ.* For God created us in his own image in the first place, which we then spoiled and skewed by our disobedience. Now he is busy restoring it. And he is doing it by making us like Christ, since Christ is both perfect man and perfect image of God.[33]

The apostle Paul laid out God's agenda as follows: "For those whom he foreknew he also predestined to be conformed to the image of his Son, in order that he might be the firstborn within a large family" (Rom. 8:29). It was God's gracious decision, made before the creation of the world, that we would have the divine image restored to us in Christ.

> *It was God's gracious decision, made before the creation of the world, that we would have the divine image restored to us in Christ.*

As C. E. B. Cranfield, a renowned authority on Romans, has observed, behind this passage is the fact of our being created in God's image (Gen. 1:27) and of Christ's being eternally

---

[32] Moody, *The Word of Truth*, 419.

[33] John Stott, *Focus on Christ* (New York: Collins, 1979), 140–41 (Stott's italics).

the image of God (2 Cor. 4:4; Col. 1:15). Paul is referring to a life of progressive conformity to the image of Christ (sanctification), culminating in our glorification when that process will be completed at Christ's return.[34] The power behind this process is the Holy Spirit himself:

> Now the Lord is the Spirit, and where the Spirit of the Lord is, there is freedom. And all of us, with unveiled faces, seeing the glory of the Lord as though reflected in a mirror, are being transformed into the same image from one degree of glory to another; for this comes from the Lord, the Spirit (2 Cor. 3:17–18).

The glory of the law is fleeting, but the Spirit brings *freedom* and *transformation* (lit., metamorphosis). It is also striking to note the close association between image and glory—a phenomenon often seen in the Scriptures. What an exhilarating vision! As God's children, there is much we do not yet know. "What we do know is this: when he is revealed, we will be like him, for we will see him as he is. And all who have this hope in him purify themselves, just as he is pure" (1 John 3:2–3).

One day we *will* again bear the full divine image—in our resurrection bodies (1 Cor. 15:49). Meanwhile, we must put off the old life and be clothed with Christ: "This is the new being which God, its Creator, is constantly renewing in his own image, in order to bring you to a full knowledge of himself" (Col. 3:10 GNB; see also Eph. 4:24). One means of cooperating with the Holy Spirit in this process is to study the life of Christ in the New Testament.

What, then, was Jesus like? He is what the Father wants us to be like. We look into the mirror of Scripture and glimpse his glory. We see a person who lived totally for God and for other persons. We see a man who esteemed women and children far beyond the custom of his day. We notice how observant and appreciative he was of nature. We are poignantly aware of his preoccupation with the kingdom of God. He was totally committed to doing the will of the Father. He based his life on the principles of the Scriptures. He lived a life of prayer. He was a people person. He showed great compassion for people in need. He lived in total dependence on the Father in the power of the Spirit. He did signs and wonders. He confronted and conquered satanic forces. The description could go on and on.[35]

---

[34] C. E. B. Cranfield, *Romans: A Shorter Commentary* (Grand Rapids: Eerdmans, 1985), 205.

[35] In addition to the standard studies of the life of Christ, the following volumes provide additional help: Michael Green, *Who Is This Jesus?* (Nashville: Thomas Nelson, 1992); C. H. Dodd,

However, to the authentic believer Jesus is more than a historical figure; he is our contemporary. One of the ministries of the Holy Spirit is to reveal Jesus to us (see John 16:14). He also wants daily to conform us into Christ's image. What precisely does he want to do? James D. G. Dunn provides an insightful answer to this question:

> If the Spirit attests his activity above all by love, then we should recall that *the* expression of love for Paul is Christ dying for sinners (Rom. 5:8). Thus we might legitimately infer that Paul intends the "hymn to love" and the "fruit of the Spirit" (1 Cor. 13:4–7; Gal. 5:22) as "character sketches" of Christ. In that case it follows that for Paul the distinguishing and delimiting mark of the Spirit is again the image or character of Jesus; *to be spiritual is to be like Christ.*[36]

To the authentic believer Jesus is more than a historical figure; he is our contemporary.

Again, "this comes from the Lord, the Spirit" (2 Cor. 3:18). We cannot simply *imitate* Christ. But we can certainly *actively* cooperate with the Spirit in his transforming work. Ultimately the Christian life is *allowing Christ to live his life through us* (John 15:1–17; Gal. 2:19–20)!

Imago Dei: A Theological Summary

Staying as close as possible to the Scriptures, how can we best summarize the biblical doctrine of the image of God in humankind? It is helpful to return to the initial statements in the Bible related to this subject:

> Then God said, "Let us make humankind in our image, according to our likeness; and let them have dominion. . . .

The Founder of Christianity (New York: Macmillan, 1970); Marcus J. Borg, *Jesus: A New Vision* (San Francisco: Harper & Row, 1987); R. T. France, *I Came to Set the Earth on Fire: A Portrait of Jesus* (Downers Grove, Ill.: InterVarsity Press, 1975); John Pollock, *The Master: A Life of Jesus* (Wheaton, Ill.: Victor, 1985); Donald Guthrie, *Jesus the Messiah* (Grand Rapids: Zondervan, 1972); Robert H. Stein, *Jesus the Messiah: A Survey of the Life of Christ* (Downers Grove, Ill.: InterVarsity Press, 1996); Ben Witherington III, *The Jesus Quest*, 2d ed. (Downers Grove, Ill.: InterVarsity Press, 1997); Philip Yancey, *The Jesus I Never Knew* (Grand Rapids: Zondervan, 1995); Darrell L. Bock, *Jesus according to Scripture: Restoring the Portrait from the Gospels* (Grand Rapids: Baker, 2002); James D. G. Dunn, *Jesus Remembered* (Christianity in the Making 1; Grand Rapid: Eerdmans, 2003); Larry W. Hurtado, *Lord Jesus Christ: Devotion to Jesus in Earliest Christianity* (Grand Rapids: Eerdmans, 2003).

[36] James D. G. Dunn, *Jesus and the Spirit* (London: SCM, 1975), 321 (Dunn's italics).

> So God created humankind [ʾ*adam*: man] in his image,
> in the image of God he created them [lit. "him"];
> male and female he created them.
> God blessed them, and God said to them, "Be fruitful and multiply, and fill the earth and subdue it; and have dominion. . . ." (Gen. 1:26–28)

Although the image of God is not formally defined in this passage or any other, all the ingredients for a definition are provided both within the text itself and in its context.

Historically, the Church has differentiated between image and likeness. It has defined "image" as the personal/rational functions of humanity, and "likeness" as the moral/spiritual dimension. The Fall erased the latter, but it is being progressively restored through redemption and sanctification. However, the Scriptures do not actually permit such an interpretation. The phrases "in his image" and "according to our likeness" must be seen exegetically as parallel and synonymous—the latter, to all effects, defining the former. One is still puzzled, therefore, as to precisely what the divine image might be.

Millard Erickson helpfully summarizes three basic approaches to this question: (1) substantive, (2) relational, and (3) functional.[37] The *substantive* approach looks for those Godlike qualities in the nature of humanity that constitute the divine image. Reason has often come to the fore in this school of thought, especially among theologians who major on the ratiocination of the faith! But as important as reason is, it is only one dimension of both the divine and the human. A broader concept is needed. The *relational* approach emphasizes the vertical and horizontal relationships of humanity as constituting the divine image. Usually theologians in this school of thought—such as Barth and Brunner—argue from an existentialist base. The *functional* approach highlights the word "dominion" in the text cited above. We are in God's image in that we are given dominion over the planet.

Each approach contains a kernel of truth. The substantive view must be seen as primary because the image of God is presented in Scripture as something we *are,* not merely as something we do. It is imperative, therefore, that we search out those Godlike qualities that constitute his image in us. The relational approach also helps us delineate the *purpose* for which God made us: to love. We were made for God and for each other (Mark 12:29–31). The functional view is also legitimate, for the

---

[37] Erickson, *Christian Theology,* 498–512.

text above mentions *twice*, and in close proximity, that God gave humankind dominion over the creation. How should we, then, correlate these positions?

We have already indicated that the substantive concept is primary. However, it is difficult to keep the other two emphases separate. At this juncture a cultural critique is imperative. When someone in America asks, "Who is Mary Jones?" the answer is most often given in terms of what Mary Jones *does.* "Mary Jones is executive vice-president of Freedom Bank." In other cultures, however, this question would be asking for personal traits: "What is Mary Jones *like*? What is it like to relate to Mary Jones? What kind of person is she in her interpersonal relations?" There is a deeper dimension to a person than the functional or relational dimensions, however. Who we are at the core of our being, in our essential nature, is foundational to how we behave functionally and relationally.

Applying this insight to the image of God in humanity, we must take a holistic approach to do justice to the biblical picture of humanity. Made in the image of God, we are personal, relational, and spiritual creatures. We are also moral creatures. We are also competent creatures with God-given abilities to rule over and care for this planet. Because we have all these qualities, we are able to serve as God's representatives on earth. God is a God of holy love. He is personal, spiritual, relational, and holy. He is love. We too are personal, spiritual, and relational. The reality of sin forbids us from saying we are holy. We do have a conscience, however, which further witnesses to the divine image. But sin has affected us in our totality.

> *Being created in God's image means that we reflect Godlike qualities personally, intellectually, volitionally, emotionally, morally, spiritually, relationally, and functionally.*

Because of sin we are now *less* personal, less spiritual (spiritually *dead,* according to Scripture), less relational (alienated from God, each other, and even our very selves), and less competent—in short, less human. Because we have forgotten our Creator, we suffer spiritual amnesia. We simply do not know who we are because we do not know who God is. (Again, recall Calvin's words concerning knowledge of God and knowledge of self.) Once, while speaking at an Ivy League school, Billy Graham was asked by a seminarian: "Who am I?" Many laughed nervously, but Graham took the young man's question seriously. We cannot fully know ourselves unless we know God. Theologically, we must remember that our doctrine of God informs our doctrine of humanity. As Dale Moody observed, "Likeness to God is the image of God, but one's view of God determines the view one holds of the image."[38] Thus, we have tried to correlate the two in the above remarks.

Utilizing Packer's succinct summary, a holistic statement of the image of God in humankind could be enunciated as follows:

> God's image in man at Creation, then, consisted (a) in man's being a "soul" or "spirit" (Gen. 2:7, where the NIV correctly says "living being"; Eccles. 12:7), that is, a personal, self-conscious, Godlike creature with a Godlike capacity for knowledge, thought, and action; (b) in man's being morally upright, a quality lost at the Fall that is now being progressively restored in Christ (Eph. 4:24; Col. 3:10); (c) in man's environmental dominion. Usually, and reasonably, it is added that (d) man's God-given immortality and (e) the human body, through which we experience reality, express ourselves, and exercise our dominion, belong to the image too.[39]

Packer adds that the body only indirectly reflects God's image in the instrumental sense of exercising dominion and relating to others. Christ's incarnation, of course, informs this concept.[40] Being created in God's image means that we reflect Godlike qualities personally, intellectually, volitionally, emotionally, morally, spiritually, relationally, and functionally.

As our opening psalm reminds us, we have been given "dominion over the works of [God's] hands," and he has made us "a little lower than God" and has "crowned [us] with glory and honor" (Ps. 8:5–6). Moody's remarks are again apropos:

> The very words "glory and honor" summarize man's likeness. Man was made to make present the reality of God. The glory of God is the Presence of God, and man is the reflector of this glory even more than the glory of the heavens. The soul, not the stars, is the summit of God's creation. Man, not the majesty of the earth, is the crown of all creation.[41]

Surely there could be no higher or healthier (or more realistic) view of humankind than what we find in the Bible!

---

[38] Moody, *The Word of Truth*, 226.
[39] Packer, *Concise Theology*, 72.
[40] Ibid.
[41] Moody, *The Word of Truth*, 228.

Of What Do We Consist?

One final important question must be addressed: What is the constitutional nature of the individual person? Are there constituent "parts" to our makeup, or are we an indivisible unity? More important than what the philosophers and social scientists say is what the Scriptures say. The multiplicity of descriptive terms in the Bible is somewhat overwhelming. Our focus, however, will be on the various ways of interpreting our constitutional makeup rather than on an exhaustive treatment of all possible descriptive terms related to humanity.

If Annie Dillard is an exegete of nature, Paul Brand is an exegete of the human body. This world-renowned hand surgeon and expert on leprosy has a gift for revealing how we are fearfully and wonderfully made by the Creator's hand and for illustrating spiritual principles for the life of the church. In one of his books Dr. Brand describes the wonders of the human brain:

> The brain contains imagination, morality, sensuality, mathematics, memory, humor, judgment, religion, as well as an incredible catalog of facts and theories and the common sense to assign them all priority and significance. In the human head, concludes Nobel laureate Roger Sperry, "there are forces within forces within forces, as in no other cubic half-foot of the universe that we know." There is nothing on the earth so wonderful.[42]

We are continually amazed by our brains. One of the ways that God has marked us off from the hominids that preceded us was in the size of our brains. So much of our personality is knit into the fibers of this fascinating organ tucked safely inside our skulls.

But what is the mysterious force that activates our brains? There is some immaterial dimension of our being that, when absent (at death), renders our brain powerless. The writers of the Scriptures and theologians down through the centuries have called this aspect of our being the "soul" or "spirit." Yet there is such an integral relation between the material brain and the ethereal spirit that either can impact the other. For example, an automobile accident or a stroke can damage the brain and alter the personality of an individual. A person may have never used profanity in her life, yet be heard utilizing words her family and friends never thought she even knew as a result of a brain injury. Has her spiritual character changed? No, her brain is simply malfunctioning.

---

[42] Brand and Yancey, *In His Image*, 128–29.

Medical doctors have known for many years that the spirit of a person is often the key to his or her physical recovery. Are there two natures within an individual—the physical body and the soul or spirit? The consensus of the church has been that there are. Jesus himself taught this distinction: "Do not fear those who kill the body but cannot kill the soul; rather fear him [God] who can destroy both soul and body in hell" (Matt. 10:28). The apostle Paul characterized his Christian walk and ministry with these words: "So we do not lose heart. Even though our outer nature is wasting away, our inner nature is being renewed day by day" (2 Cor. 4:16). Paul knew that in Christ the believer has a foretaste of the powers of the age to come: "But if Christ is in you, though the body is dead because of sin, the Spirit is life because of righteousness" (Rom. 8:10).

We may die before Christ returns, and our bodies may return to the dust from which they came. But we know that to "be away from the body" is to be "at home with the Lord" (2 Cor. 5:8). Jesus promised the thief on the cross: "Truly I tell you, today you will be with me in Paradise" (Luke 23:43). Two things happened to the thief that day. His physical body died and was buried. His soul or spirit went to be with Christ in Paradise. Even though his body was decaying in a grave on earth, the thief himself was in heaven with the Lord!

From a prison Paul wrote these revealing words to the Philippians:

> For to me, to live is Christ and to die is gain. If I am to go on living in the body, this will mean fruitful labor for me. Yet what shall I choose? I do not know! I am torn between the two: I desire to depart and be with Christ, which is better by far; but it is more necessary for you that I remain in the body. (Phil. 1:21–24 NIV)

Paul believed that leaving his body (in death) and being with Christ (in heaven) was "better by far." How many of us actually live our lives from this perspective? "For to me, to live is Christ and to die is gain." Passages like this reveal just how *materialistic* we are.

At the same time, we must quickly add that Paul was no Platonist who despised his material body, saw it as evil, and longed to escape it. He viewed the intermediate state as incomplete—as being "unclothed"—and longed for his resurrection body (2 Cor. 5:1–5). Nevertheless, the point is that the Bible portrays humankind in the dichotomist terms of soul/spirit and body and further elucidates this reality in its teaching about the intermediate state.

Most of the time in the Bible, "soul" refers to the whole person, beginning with Genesis 2:7. It can also signify a person's life as well as his or her inner person. For example, Jesus asks what profit there is in gaining the whole world and forfeiting one's soul or life (*psyche*; Matt. 16:26). But, as we have already seen, Jesus also uses "soul" to refer to the inner person that survives death (10:28). Many times "soul" and "spirit" are used interchangeably, as, for example, in Mary's words in The Magnificat: "My soul magnifies the Lord, and my spirit rejoices in God my Savior" (Luke 1:46–47). Most interpret the two clauses as parallel and thus regard soul and spirit as coterminous. Again, within the one human life are two fundamental dimensions: material and immaterial, physical and spiritual. The liberal tradition has at times sought to "substitute" belief in the immortality of the soul for the resurrection of the body. This position is impossible for anyone who accepts the inerrancy of Scripture. The Bible does not offer us that option.[43]

It is misleading, however, to imply that dichotimism has gone unchallenged within Christian circles. The monistic view has been encapsulated in the classic statement by H. Wheeler Robinson: "The Hebrew idea of personality is an animated body, and not an incarnated soul."[44] In this view of humanity we are an indivisible unity. Since we do not transcend our bodies, as in the dichotomist view, then when we die we must simply await the resurrection of our bodies for the continuation of conscious existence. There is no disembodied intermediate state. Body and soul are synonymous, and there is no immortality of the soul.[45] Bodily existence is the only *human* existence. Existing apart from the physical body is "unthinkable."[46] The instinct in monism to guard the *unity* of the human person is scripturally valid. Unfortunately, this view "runs past the truth" in denying our spiritual transcendence and ability to exist apart from our physical bodies.

In many conservative circles today the trichotomist view is popular. Here the human is seen as comprised of three parts: spirit, soul, and body. The two key passages on which this teaching is based are 1 Thessalonians 5:23 and Hebrews 4:12. Probably the most influential writing

---

43 Cf. Erickson, *Christian Theology*, 522–24.

44 H. Wheeler Robinson, "Hebrew Psychology," in *The People and the Book*, ed. Arthur S. Peake (Oxford: Clarendon, 1925), 362.

45 To be clear: The statement "the soul is by nature immortal" is Platonic, *not* scriptural. According to Scripture, God alone is *by nature* immortal. However, God can and does give the gift of immortality to humankind.

46 Erickson, *Christian Theology*, 525.

that has promulgated this doctrine is Watchman Nee's *The Spiritual Man.*[47] Trichotomism is popular at the grass roots level of the charismatic movement. It argues that the spirit is the innermost aspect of the human. At the new birth the spirit is regenerated. It becomes indwelt by the Holy Spirit and sanctified by his presence. The soul is comprised of three dimensions: intellect, will, and emotions. The body, of course, is the physical organism in which dwell the soul and spirit.

According to one form of this teaching, sanctification is the process wherein the Holy Spirit is gradually gaining control of the soul and body as he has already gained control of the spirit. One can see here a number of dangers. First, how can it be asserted that the soul is comprised of mind, will, and emotions? There is not one scrap of scriptural evidence that the soul should be understood in these terms. This form of trichotomism has simply poured the nineteenth-century psychological concepts of the cognitive (mind), conative (will), and affective (emotions) dimensions of the human personality into the biblical term "soul." This teaching can also be dangerous.

A form of "superspirituality" emerges when the intellect is disdained as impure and the spirit is seen as a superior receptor of "revelation knowledge." Paul's words to the Corinthians are germane: "Since we have these promises, beloved, let us cleanse ourselves from every defilement of body and of spirit, making holiness perfect in the fear of God" (2 Cor. 7:1). The biblical doctrine of sin clearly indicates that we are defiled in our entire being, *including our spirit,* as the above passage states unequivocally. J. I. Packer expresses it well:

> Biblical usage leads us to say that we *have* and *are* both souls and spirits, but it is a mistake to think that soul and spirit are two different things; a "trichotomous" view of man as body, soul, and spirit is incorrect. The common idea that the soul is an organ of this-worldly awareness only and that the spirit is a distinct organ of communion with God that is brought to life in regeneration is out of step with biblical teaching and word usage. Moreover, it leads to a crippling anti-intellectualism whereby spiritual insight and theological thought are separated to the impoverishing of both, theology being seen as "soulish" and unspiritual while spiritual perception is thought of as unrelated to the teaching and learning of God's revealed truth.[48]

[47] Watchman Nee, *The Spiritual Man,* 3 vols. (New York: Christian Fellowship, 1968).
[48] Packer, *Concise Theology,* 74–75.

These dangers must be acknowledged and confronted. At the same time—as is often the case—there is a kernel of truth in the trichotomist approach. Humankind does stand in three fundamental relationships: to God, to others, and to the physical world. Each relationship is distinct. Also, the verses previously mentioned are not easily dismissed (though one should hesitate to build a major doctrine on two or three passages). In 1 Thessalonians 5:23 Paul simply uses a Greek idiom, "spirit and soul and body," to refer to the whole person. In Hebrews 4:12 the author "is not concerned to provide here a psychological or anatomical analysis of the human constitution, but rather to describe in graphic terms the penetration of God's word to the innermost depth of man's personality."[49]

But Paul introduces some new ingredients into biblical psychology in his explanation of speaking in tongues. In seeking to balance out the Corinthian overemphasis on speaking in tongues, the apostle acknowledges: "I thank God that I speak in tongues more than all of you; nevertheless, in church I would rather speak five words with my mind, in order to instruct others also, than ten thousand words in a tongue" (1 Cor. 14:18–19). Paul sought not to exterminate tongues but rather to regulate them. He also explains the nature of tongues: "For if I pray in a tongue, my spirit [*pneuma*] prays but my mind [*nous*] is unproductive" (v. 14). The apostle then goes on to refer to praying and singing "with the mind" and "with the spirit" (v. 15). There is a clear distinction here between the mind and the spirit. How does one evaluate this distinction?

In modern psychological parlance we might say that praying with one's spirit in a tongue is prayer from the unconscious or subconscious mind. But does this terminology actually address the question raised by Paul's description in the Corinthian letter? In this instance, Paul would be lending his weight to what we know as depth psychology today. There definitely is a difference between the mind and the spirit in this instance, but this phenomenon alone does not serve as a basis for a strict trichotomism. At best one could refer to spirit, *mind,* and body, rather than spirit, soul, and body. One also thinks of the biblical references to the heart and of Christ's love commandment: "You shall love the Lord your God with all your heart, and with all your soul, and with all your mind, and with all your strength" (Mark 12:30). Are there four com-

[49] Philip E. Hughes, *A Commentary on the Epistle to the Hebrews* (Grand Rapids: Eerdmans, 1977), 165.

partments, then, to our makeup? Also, should we differentiate between soul and mind on the basis of this passage? Try as we may, it is all but impossible to come up with three neat divisions of a human being.

There are parallels between the mystery of humanity and the mystery of the Trinity. To be faithful to biblical revelation, we must affirm one God in three persons. In relation to the Incarnation, as we will discover, it is necessary to acknowledge one person with two natures. In relation to humankind, we perceive (1) one unitive person, (2) with two natures (physical and spiritual), and (3) three fundamental relationships (God, humanity, and the world). We must never lose sight of the unity of the human person. At the same time, we must acknowledge a material and an immaterial nature. There are not three natures or substances comprising an individual—spirit, soul, and body. But there are three relational dimensions to human life. And at least with respect to prayer and praise, one can differentiate between the mind and the spirit.[50]

What a joy and privilege to be God's image-bearing creatures!

What a joy and privilege to be God's image-bearing creatures! The Bible provides the only solid foundation for belief in the dignity and destiny of humanity. Nevertheless, we have thus far looked at only half of the story of our race. The other dimension of the human story is a tragic tale of sin and failure. Fortunately, our sovereign God anticipated this part of the story as well and has provided a powerful remedy in the person of Jesus Christ.

---

50 By far the most satisfying and complete treatment of this subject in particular, and of the doctrine of humanity in general, that I have been able to discover is that of Gordon R. Lewis and Bruce A. Demarest: *Integrative Theology*, Vol. 2, 123–180. Millard Erickson's overview is also quite valuable and insightful: *Christian Theology*, 519–39.

6 Sin

What Is the Nature of Sin, and What Are Its Consequences?

The first thing . . . God does when He makes anyone a new creature in Christ, is to send light into his heart and show him that he is a guilty sinner.

—J. C. Ryle

It is not possible to know Christ without knowing both God and our wretchedness.

—Blaise Pascal

The line separating good and evil passes not through states, nor between classes, nor between parties either—but right through every human heart—through all human hearts.

—Aleksandr Solzhenitsyn[1]

---

[1] These opening quotations are taken from J. C. Ryle, *Holiness* (Welwyn, Eng.: Evangelical Press, 1979), 1; James M. Houston, ed., *The Mind on Fire: An Anthology of the Writings of Blaise Pascal* (Portland, Ore.: Multnomah, 1989), 149; Aleksandr I. Solzhenitsyn, *The Gulag Archipelago 1918–1956,* trans. Thomas Whitney (New York: Harper & Row, 1975), 612, cited in Charles W. Colson, *Loving God* (Grand Rapids: Zondervan, 1983), 102.

PRISON IS EVIDENTLY A GOOD PLACE for us to learn that we are sinners. Both Alexander Solzhenitsyn and Chuck Colson thank God for their prison experiences because it was there that they discovered the important fact of their own sinfulness.[2] The usual progression is that we are mad, then sad, and then glad. Our pride causes us to reject any notion of a serious moral problem in relation to God. That is someone else's problem. There are always worse sinners to whom we can point. *They* are the ones who should be worried. It's the liberals or fundamentalists or chauvinists or bigots or terrorists or whoever who are culpable. They are the evil ones, the bad guys. It angers us that anyone should suggest that *we* are sinners. Then, by God's grace, we finally confront our own iniquity with a godly sorrow leading to repentance. Then comes the *joy*!

By God's grace, we finally confront our own iniquity with a godly sorrow leading to repentance. Then comes the joy*!*

While doing research for his book *Loving God*, Chuck Colson could find little contemporary writing on the topic of sin. He recalls:

> After a long search, however, an unlikely source—Mike Wallace of "60 Minutes"—furnished just what I was looking for.
>
> Since Christians are not accustomed to gleaning theological insights from network TV, I'd better explain.
>
> Introducing a recent story about Nazi Adolf Eichmann, a principal architect of the Holocaust, Wallace posed a central question at the program's outset: "How is it possible . . . for a man to act as Eichmann acted? . . . Was he a monster? A madman? Or was he perhaps something even more terrifying: was he normal?"
>
> *Normal?* The executioner of millions of Jews *normal?* Most self-respecting viewers would be outraged at the very thought.
>
> The most startling answer to Wallace's shocking question came in an interview with Yehiel Dinur, a concentration camp survivor who testified against Eichmann at the Nuremburg trials. A film clip from Eichmann's 1961 trial showed Dinur walking into the courtroom, stopping short, seeing Eichmann for the first time since the Nazi had sent him to Auschwitz eighteen years earlier. Dinur began to sob uncontrollably, then fainted, collapsing in a heap on the floor as the presiding judicial officer pounded his gavel for order in the crowded courtroom.

[2] Cf. Colson, *Loving God*, 102.

> Was Dinur overcome by hatred? Fear? Horrid memories?
>
> No; it was none of these. Rather, as Dinur explained to Wallace, all at once he realized Eichmann was not the godlike army officer who had sent so many to their deaths. This Eichmann was an ordinary man. "I was afraid about myself," said Dinur. "I saw that I am capable to do this. *I am . . . exactly like he.*"
>
> Wallace's subsequent summation of Dinur's terrible discovery—"Eichmann in all of us"—is a horrifying statement; but it indeed captures the central truth about man's nature. For as a result of the Fall, *sin is in each of us*—not just the susceptibility to sin, but sin itself.[3]

We must return, therefore, to the early chapters of Genesis—to the primeval history of humankind and the account of the entrance of sin and evil into the created order—to the story of the Fall.

The Fall

Besides the announcement of the Sabbath rest in Genesis 2:1–3, Genesis 1 culminates with: "God saw everything that he had made and indeed, it was very good" (1:31). The description "very good" encompasses the entire universe, including humankind, both male and female. Furthermore, we are informed that we bear the divine image and that we, as God's regents, have dominion over the earth. The most basic question—Why?—has been answered. We know why the universe is here, and we know why we are here.[4]

The next two chapters of Genesis move from the ideal of the past to the real of the present. If the world is "very good," then why are sin, evil, and ruin rampant? What has gone wrong with the world, and especially with humankind? Genesis 2 and 3 are devoted almost solely to these questions. According to God's inspired Word, the world's number-one problem is summed up in one three-letter word: *sin.* Thus, the rest of this primeval history (chs. 2–11) explicates and illustrates this fact.

Genesis 2 describes the paradise in which Adam and Eve lived prior to the Fall. Indeed, Eden becomes symbolic in Scripture for cosmic redemption, as paradise lost reverts to paradise regained. Eden, mean-

---

[3] Charles Colson, *Who Speaks for God?* (Westchester, Ill.: Crossway, 1985), 136–37.

[4] The following analysis is indebted to these sources: William Sanford LaSor, David Allan Hubbard, and Federic William Bush, *Old Testament Survey* (Grand Rapids: Eerdmans, 1982), 80–82; Henricus Renckens, *Israel's Concept of the Beginning,* trans. Charles Napier (New York: Herder & Herder, 1964), 156–58.

ing perhaps "delight," is "the garden of the LORD" or "the garden of God" (Isa. 51:3; Ezek. 31:8–9; Joel 2:3). The city of God, to use Augustine's phrase, will be like Eden, only bigger and better. It will make the lush and delightful parks of Walt Disney World look like slums (see Rev. 21–22).

The Lord God himself planted the first garden in Eden and placed the man there "to till it and keep it" (Gen. 2:8, 15). The park was perfect—no thorns or thistles. The man's work was creative and fulfilling. God gave the woman to the man as his life-partner, and they exulted together in an uninhibited, guilt-free relationship of love and fellowship—a social and sexual relationship of deep meaning and beauty: "And the man and his wife were both naked, and were not ashamed" (2:25).

> *The world's number-one problem is summed up in one three-letter word:* sin.

"Out of the ground the LORD God made to grow every tree that is pleasant to the sight and good for food, the tree of life also in the midst of the garden, and the tree of the knowledge of good and evil" (Gen. 2:9). The tree of life conferred eternal life (3:22; see also Rev. 22:2, 14, 19). Neither of the primal couple partook of this tree (God made sure of that after their fall into sin). God only stipulated that "of the tree of the knowledge of good and evil you shall not eat, for in the day that you eat of it you shall die" (Gen. 2:17). The man received this command and evidently related it to the woman after her creation, or perhaps God himself did so. It was only one command: a test, not a temptation. God had good purposes in mind. But then enter the serpent, with malevolent designs of almost unimaginable proportions.

"Now the serpent was more crafty than any other wild animal that the LORD God had made" (Gen. 3:1). Although this mysterious creature is almost incidental to the story, the focus being primarily on the man and the woman and their responsible decisions, the serpent is nevertheless crucial to the narrative for several reasons. First, we can infer that there must have been a transcendent fall in the heavenlies prior to the fall of Adam and Eve. The serpent is clearly portrayed as pursuing evil intentions. Sin already existed prior to the fall of humankind. The serpent symbolizes sin and temptation. We learn from the last book of the Bible that this ancient serpent is none other than the great dragon, the devil, Satan, the deceiver of the whole world (Rev. 12:9; 20:2). The talking snake is a personification of the evil one. The Fall account in Genesis informs us of the entrance of sin into the human race, not of the origin of sin itself, which took place in the spiritual realm when Satan and his angels rebelled.

We see this wily creature, the serpent, sowing doubt and suspicion in the woman's mind. He twists God's words and attempts to get the woman to doubt God's Word: "Did God say. . .?" (Gen. 3:1). (He does the same today.) He tries to deceive the woman to believe that God is holding out on her by prohibiting partaking of the tree of the knowledge of good and evil. Since wisdom in the ancient mindset entailed the ability to discern good and evil (see 2 Sam. 14:17; Isa. 7:15), the temptation portrayed here is to personal autonomy in determining what is morally right and wrong. Do we not do so today?

Society has decided that sexual unfaithfulness, promiscuity, and perversion are all right, while God has revealed in his authoritative Word that he abhors these destructive sins. We think our eyes are open, that we are wise, that we are equal to God, and that we can decide for ourselves what is good and evil (see Gen. 3:5), when actually we are spiritually blind and morally bankrupt. New Age spiritualities promulgate personal divinity, a lie that goes straight back to Eden: "You will be like God [or gods]" (v. 5).

Eve was beguiled into doubting God's goodness through a threefold temptation—a pattern repeated in the life of Jesus (see Luke 4:1–13) and in the life of the Christian as well (1 John 2:16). Christ countered the devil's lies with the truth of the Scriptures, however, and refused to disobey his Father. Unfortunately, our first parents did not, and we have suffered the results ever since. Eve "took . . . and ate" (v. 6)—a simple act with horrible results. Only as God himself took on himself our poverty and death could the words "take and eat" become tokens of salvation.[5]

The devil lied blatantly: "You will not die" (Gen. 3:4). Thus Jesus describes him in these words: "He was a murderer from the beginning and does not stand in the truth, because there is no truth in him. When he lies, he speaks according to his own nature, for he is a liar and the father of lies" (John 8:44). Anyone who fails to take these words with utmost seriousness is foolish.

The woman gave some of the forbidden fruit to the man, and he ate. Immediately, cataclysmic changes began. Their eyes were opened, as the

[5] Derek Kidner, *Genesis* (TOTC; Downers Grove, Ill.: InterVarsity Press, 1967), 68.

serpent had said, but what they saw was not what they had anticipated. The serpent had lied. It was like a bad LSD trip in which the horrors of hell are revealed rather than the beauty of heaven. Fear and shame, foreign to the primal couple, now consumed them.[6] Each saw himself or herself and the other in a completely different light. "They recognize their lost condition and realize from what a high estate they have fallen."[7] They seek to hide themselves from each other and from the Lord (Gen. 3:7–8).

Did Adam and Eve die? Spiritual death was immediate. Physical death came later. Again, a half-truth from the evil one had tricked them. Augustine in *The City of God* rightly asserted that the death against which God had warned them was threefold: spiritual, physical, and the second death of final judgment.[8] This same comprehensive conundrum of death confronts humankind to this day.

Through a series of probing questions the Lord God confronts the man and the woman with their sin (Gen. 3:9–13). The sense of tragedy in these exchanges is almost unbearable. Innocence is lost. Fellowship with God is broken. Guilt hovers like a specter over the primal couple. Barriers of shame separate the man and the woman from each other. A spiritual schizophrenia, as it were, invades their souls. One wants to weep while reading this story. Even the pain in God's heart is evident here.

Immediately the couple attempt to rationalize their sin. The man blames both the Lord God and the woman: "The woman whom you gave to be with me . . ." (Gen. 3:12). The woman blames the snake (v. 13). God's judgment descends on them all. He pronounces a curse on the serpent and then informs the woman and man in turn what the consequences of their actions will be. The woman will have much pain in childbirth and will be subject to her husband. The man will work himself to death tilling the recalcitrant soil to which he will return at death (vv. 14–19).

But there is also a note of grace in the narrative. When the Lord God cursed the serpent, he announced a permanent enmity between humankind and the serpent (Gen. 3:15). Historically, the church has

---

[6] Cf. Gerhard von Rad, *Genesis*, trans. J. H. Marks (OTL, rev. ed.; Philadelphia: Westminster, 1972), 91.

[7] Edward J. Young, *Genesis 3: A Devotional and Expository Study* (London: Banner of Truth Trust, 1966), 68.

[8] Cited in Kidner, *Genesis*, 69.

applied a canonical interpretation to this text, calling it the *Protoevangelium*—the first announcement of the gospel. Jesus Christ—"born of a woman" (Gal. 4:4), born of a virgin (Isa. 7:14; Matt. 1:23)—would ultimately, through his cross and resurrection, defeat the evil one. The church, even with all its problems, would finally triumph, becoming "wise in what is good and guileless in what is evil" (Rom. 16:17–19). Her slogan would become: "The God of peace will soon crush Satan under your feet" (16:20 NIV, NJB). James D. G. Dunn observes:

> Above all, the slogan, with its echo of Gen. 3:15, effectively ties together the whole sweep of salvation-history: God's purpose is nothing less than the complete destruction of all the evil which has grown like a large malignant cancer within the body of humankind and the restoration of his creation to the peace and well-being he originally designed for it.[9]

Even in the midst of judgment that fateful day in the garden, the Lord God remembered mercy. He furthermore clothed the couple with animal skins to cover their shame (Gen. 3:21). Henri Blocher rightly sees this as a beautiful portrayal of God's grace covering our sin and degradation.[10]

> *Even in the midst of judgment that fateful day in the garden, the Lord God remembered mercy.*

Nevertheless, the dye had been cast. In order to prevent the man and woman from eating from the tree of life and living forever in their fallen state, the Lord God drove them from the garden and placed cherubim and a flaming sword "to guard the way to the tree of life" (Gen. 3:23–24). There is a finality to this act. Nothing would ever again be the same. David L. Smith, in his excellent treatment of the doctrine of sin, *With Willful Intent: A Theology of Sin*, provides this apt summary of the biblical account of the Fall:

> This Fall was a time and space event perpetrated by a literal pair of human beings, the first originally created by God. It is no myth. That the story is recounted in highly figurative language does not remove it from the realm of actual historical occurrence.
>
> That our first parents were tempted by an external sinful agent does not remove them from the sphere of accountability. Satan's power is

[9] James D. G. Dunn, *Romans 9–16* (WBC 38b; Dallas: Word, 1988), 907.

[10] Henri Blocher, *In the Beginning*, trans. David G. Preston (Downers Grove, Ill.: InterVarsity Press, 1984), 191.

not—nor has it ever been—irresistible. The reason for this original sin was a conscious, active decision on the part of those who committed it.

The sin of Adam and Eve had calamitous results both for them and for all human beings since. Sin brings to human beings alienation from God, one another, and all of creation. It engenders guilt within the transgressor and makes one liable to God's condemnation and punishment. God's wrath, poured out upon these human rebels, leads to spiritual death.[11]

The Avalanche

Genesis 4–11 document just how "calamitous" this fall of the primal couple was. It immediately sets into motion a catastrophic series of events that prove beyond any doubt that humankind is a corrupted species.[12] There is fratricide in the very next generation. Jealous Cain kills righteous Abel, even though he had been warned by the Lord himself that sin, like an evil demon, was crouching at his door (4:7). Again the probing question is asked: "Where is your brother Abel?" (4:9; cf. 3:9: "Where are you?"). Cain replies impudently, "Am I my brother's keeper?" (4:9 REB). In judgment the Lord curses the ground Cain would normally till and sends him out as a fugitive and wanderer. In grace the Lord puts a mark of protection on Cain so that no one will kill him.

> *Increased violence has always typified cultures in their last stages of decadence. (Should Americans take notice?)*

The next half of Genesis 4 culminates with Lamech's "Song of the Sword" (4:23–24). It is chilling to read how Lamech boasts of taking vengeance into his own hands and wantonly destroying human life.[13] The development of human culture depicted in 4:17–24 illustrates an important fact of human civilization: Even the most sophisticated of cultures can evince barbaric cruelties (witness Nazi Germany). Social, cultural, and economic advance does not diminish the corruption of the human heart.

---

[11] David L. Smith, *With Willful Intent: A Theology of Sin* (Wheaton, Ill.: Victor, 1994), 356–57.

[12] Marguerite Shuster observes that just as there is salvation history (*Heilsgeschichte*) in the Scriptures, so there is also a death history (*Todesgeschichte*). We see these histories intertwined both in Gen. 4–11 (which I refer to here as the "Avalanche") and throughout the Scriptures.

[13] See Ronald Youngblood's note on Gen. 4:23 in *The NIV Study Bible*, gen. ed. Kenneth Barker (Grand Rapids: Zondervan, 1985), 13.

The enigmatic story of the intermarriage of "the sons of God" and "the daughters of men" (Gen. 6:2 RSV) can be interpreted in a number of ways, but the overall message is clear. The rampant spread of sin and evil—perhaps now including more prevalent demonic powers—has resulted in a world "filled with violence" (6:11). Indeed, increased violence has always typified cultures in their last stages of decadence. (Should Americans take notice?) Verses 5–8 culminate this series of stories and introduce the Flood story. Now the pain in God's heart is made explicit. An unprecedented historical judgment is about to be rendered:

> The LORD saw that the wickedness of humankind was great in the earth, and that every inclination of the thoughts of their hearts was only evil continually. And the LORD was sorry that he had made humankind on the earth, and it grieved him to his heart [cf. NIV: "The LORD was grieved . . . and his heart was filled with pain."]. So the LORD said, "I will blot out from the earth the human beings I have created—people together with animals and creeping things and birds of the air, for I am sorry that I have made them." But Noah found favor in the sight of the LORD.

The ensuing story of "Noah's Ark" has become *too* familiar to us. We often view it as a sort of Disney adventure on the high (very high) seas. But this story was intended to convey a terrifying account of the fierce judgment of God on the heinous sins of humankind. Even here, however, a note of grace rings loud and clear. Because Noah found grace or favor in the eyes of the Lord (Gen. 6:8), God preserved the race—even though it was utterly iniquitous. After the flood, when Noah had offered pleasing burnt offerings, "the LORD said in his heart":

> I will never again curse the ground because of humankind, for the inclination of the human heart is evil from youth; nor will I ever again destroy every living creature as I have done.
>
> As long as the earth endures,
> seedtime and harvest, cold and heat,
> summer and winter, day and night,
> shall not cease. (8:21–22)

God then blessed Noah and his sons, commanded them to repopulate the earth (cf. Gen. 9:1 with 1:28), and designated the rainbow as a sign that he would never again judge the world by a flood (9:1–17). Sin, however, continued to plague humankind. The very next scene depicts Noah drunk and lying uncovered in his tent (9:20–28).

The primeval prologue culminates with the story of the Tower of Babel (Gen. 11:1–9). Jacques Ellul, in his groundbreaking study *The Meaning of the City*, effectively explicates the full significance of this story.[14] Ellul proposes that in the Scriptures—as well as in the history of human civilization—the city is a primary symbol of sinful humanity's defiance and rebellion against God. It all begins with Cain. He goes away from the presence of the Lord and builds a city (4:17). "The entire history of the city has its beginning in Cain's act."[15] Both Cain and Nimrod (10:8–12) build cities that express by their very names humankind's vaunted independence from God. The land of Shinar (roughly, modern Iraq) becomes a central focus of the drama. Ellul sums up the significance of this territory in simple terms: "Shinar, the land of sin. No other interpretation is possible. And, after Cain, it is the cradle of urban civilation."[16]

The people migrate to "the land of Shinar" (Gen. 11:2), where they say: "Come, let us build ourselves a city, and a tower with its top in the heavens, and let us make a name for ourselves; otherwise we shall be scattered abroad upon the face of the whole earth" (11:4). Ellul explains:

> To make a name for oneself has nothing to do with the modern expression referring to a reputation; it means becoming independent, and that is what their attempt at building meant. The people wanted to be definitively separated from God. They knew well that in spite of their revolt they were still tributary to God, that God was still their Lord, that God was still the one naming them, "calling them by their name," just as Adam right after the fall. Like it or not, they still belonged to God. And that is what the people wanted to eliminate. . . . It is much more than taking over God's power. It is the desire to exclude God from his creation. . . . And the sign and symbol of this enterprise is the city they wanted to build together.[17]

God says, in effect, "That won't do!" He confuses their language and scatters them over the face of the earth (Gen. 11:6–9). Was this judgment or mercy?

Gerhard von Rad sees this as judgment. God acts so decisively that one wonders whether he has had it with humankind. What is next? Is

---

[14] Jacques Ellul, *The Meaning of the City*, trans. Dennis Pardee (Grand Rapids: Eerdmans, 1970).
[15] Ibid., 10.
[16] Ibid., 14.
[17] Ibid., 16.

there any hope for humanity? Then follows the patriarchal narratives, beginning with Abraham, which unfold God's saving plan for his people and for the entire world.[18] Ellul, by contrast, sees mercy in God's act of confusing our language and scattering us across the globe. For humankind to break off relations with God is for them to die. God simply refuses to let that happen. He sovereignly scuttles their proud plans.[19]

Ellul's thesis seems to be on target. God plants a garden paradise. Humankind defiantly builds a city. God takes this proud symbol of our rebellion and makes of it the emblem of our salvation (see Rev. 21–22). He begins with Abraham, who "was looking forward to a city with firm foundations, whose architect and builder is God" (Heb. 11:10 REB).

The writers of the New Testament often turned to these Genesis accounts of sinful humanity in presenting their own teachings on sin. John, for example, provides a profound theology of sin, salvation, and sanctification in 1 John 3. Defining righteousness and sin in terms of love and hate, John points to Cain as the paradigm: "We must not be like Cain who was from the evil one and murdered his brother. And why did he murder him? Because his own deeds were evil and his brother's righteous" (1 John 3:12). If Genesis 6:1–4 deals with the demonic, then surely Mark is the New Testament theologian who utilizes this motif to the maximum in his Gospel in his frequent reference to Jesus' exorcisms. In his portrayal of sin, judgment, and redemption, Peter refers back to "the days of Noah, during the building of the ark," to Noah, "a herald of righteousness," and to "a flood on a world of the ungodly" (1 Peter 3:18–22; 2 Peter 2:5).

In everything we have seen thus far, "where sin increased, grace abounded all the more."

Luke, historian and theologian,[20] alluded to the Tower of Babel story when he described the events of Pentecost—the descent of the Spirit and the spread of the kingdom. John R.W. Stott expresses it well:

> Nothing could have demonstrated more clearly than this the multiracial, multi-national, multi-lingual nature of the kingdom of Christ.

---

[18] Von Rad, *Genesis*, 153; cited in LaSor et. al., *Old Testament Survey*, 86.

[19] Ellul, *The Meaning of the City*, 17.

[20] See I. Howard Marshall's excellent study, *Luke: Historian and Theologian* (Grand Rapids: Zondervan, 1970).

> Ever since the early church fathers, commentators have seen the blessing of Pentecost as a deliberate and dramatic reversal of the curse of Babel. At Babel human languages were confused and the nations were scattered; in Jerusalem the language barrier was supernaturally overcome as a sign that the nations would now be gathered together in Christ, prefiguring the great day when the redeemed company will be drawn "from every nation, tribe, people and language [Gen. 11:1–9; Rev. 7:9]. Besides, at Babel earth proudly tried to ascend to heaven, whereas in Jerusalem heaven humbly descended to earth.[21]

In everything we have seen thus far, "where sin increased, grace abounded all the more," as the apostle Paul exults in Romans 5:20. It is imperative that we turn next to his writings, for only in doing so can we fully grasp the biblical doctrine of sin. The apostle thoroughly explores the full implications of the fall of our first parents. His Adam/Christ typology (see, e.g., 1 Cor. 15:22) profoundly communicates the dismal results of Adam's sin as well as the saving victory of Christ's obedience. How is it that Adam's sin came to infect the entire human race? Are we all guilty because of Adam's sin; and, if so, why? These difficult questions have been debated down the centuries, and Paul—almost inadvertently—raises them himself in his own "systematic theology," his letter to the Romans. Would that he had addressed them directly!

The One Man

Romans is a gospel book. Yet, because the gospel is good news for people ensnared in what is patently bad news—sin—the apostle also addresses that subject. He is also concerned about the living out of the gospel, the life of sanctification. Therefore he must deal with the sin question from that vantage point. In the process, the distinctly Pauline perspective on the faith is given unique expression.

The passage that deals specifically with the results of Adam's sin (Rom. 5:12–21) is well known and hotly debated. Some of the greatest and godliest of minds have disagreed about aspects of this complex passage. Modesty and tolerance are definitely in order. At times, however, it seems that we have missed the forest for the trees. Paul's overall point is unmistakable.

---

[21] John Stott, *The Spirit, the Church, and the World: The Message of Acts* (Downers Grove, Ill.: InterVarsity Press, 1990), 68.

After his introduction (Rom. 1:1–15) and statement of his theme (1:16–17), Paul devotes an extended section (1:18–3:20) to the universality of sin among both Gentiles and Jews. "Jews and Gentiles alike are all under sin," and "the whole world [is] held accountable to God" (3:9, 19 NIV). The following six verses (3:21–26) are Romans *in nuce*—the heart of Romans and a convenient summary of the essence of the Pauline gospel: justification by faith. Paul adds that since we are "justified by his [God's] grace as a gift" (3:24), all boasting is excluded (3:27–31). Abraham is then adduced as the prime Old Testament example of this principle and as our father in the faith (ch. 4).

Chapters 5 through 8 form a unit that describes the Christian life as one of (1) having peace with God (ch. 5), (2) sanctification (ch. 6), (3) freedom from the condemnation of the law (ch. 7), and (4) indwelling by the Holy Spirit (ch. 8). Chapters 9–11 explicate Israel's role in God's plan of redemption, and the rest of the letter is Paul's practical and ethical application of the faith in the life of the church and of the individual believer (chs. 12–16).[22]

It is important to obtain this bird's-eye view of Romans in order to understand 5:12–21 in their proper perspective. That Paul is centering on the person of Christ in this section is made clear by the way he brackets his material with the phrase "through our Lord Jesus Christ" (or something almost identical; cf. 5:1, 11, 21; 6:23; 7:25; 8:39). In 5:1–11, Paul describes how formerly helpless, ungodly sinners, the enemies of God, now have peace with God because of reconciliation. He then extends the picture beyond the boundaries of the church to encompass the entirety of humankind. Paul shifts from the first person plural in 5:1–11 to the third person plural in 5:12–21. He wants to make an important point.

> *Sin is universal in scope. But* what Christ has accomplished is universal in scope as well!

Sin is universal in scope. Paul has already fully established this fact in 1:18–3:20. Now he seeks to emphasize an even more important fact: *What Christ has accomplished is universal in scope as well!* He utilizes an Adam/Christ analogy or typology in order to explicate this central truth of the faith. In this regard, these verses (5:12–21) are similar in importance to 3:21–26.

---

[22] See C. E. B. Cranfield, *The Epistle to the Romans*, 2 vols. (ICC; Edinburgh: T. & T. Clark, 1975), 1:28–29. I am indebted to Cranfield for much of the analysis that follows.

Twelve times the apostle uses the word "one." The *one man* Paul really wants us to notice, however, is not Adam, but *Christ.* "For certainly Christ is much more powerful to save than Adam was to ruin," commented John Calvin.[23] Nevertheless, it is true that "by a man came death" and "by a man has come also the resurrection of the dead"; "for as in Adam all die, so also in Christ shall all be made alive" (1 Cor. 15:21–22 RSV). Through one man sin and death entered the world. But through Christ, "the last Adam" and "the second man" (15:45, 47), righteousness and life are made available to all. Christ *is* "our peace" and has created "in himself one new humanity" (Eph. 2:14–15).

Here in a nutshell is Paul's message in Romans 5:12–21: What both Adam and Christ did has affected *all* of us; what Christ did, however, is infinitely greater and more powerful than what Adam did. As Chrysostom stated: "Sin and grace are not equivalents, nor yet death and life, nor yet the devil and God; but the difference between them is infinite."[24] What Gordon Fee has written concerning Adam in 1 Corinthians 15:21–22 applies to Romans 5:12–14 as well: "In saying that 'all die in Adam,' Paul means that this common lot of our humanity is the result of our being 'in Adam,' that is, being born of his race and thereby involved in the sin and death that proceeded from him (cf. Rom. 5:12–14, 18–19)."[25] It is the nature of this involvement that has often been the point of contention.

The incomplete sentence with which Paul begins this section (Rom. 5:12) has been a much-debated verse: "Therefore, just as sin came into the world through one man, and death came through sin, and so death spread to all because all have sinned." Sin and death are personified as powers that make their entrance into the world through Adam. That much is clear. The fact that death has spread to all is also self-evident. It is that final clause that is disputed. Should it be translated "because all sinned" (NIV) or "because all have sinned" (NRSV; cf. "for that all have sinned" in KJV)? Did we all sin "in Adam" and, therefore, die? Or do we inherit a sin nature from Adam and die "because of our own sins"? In other words, do we inherit Adam's *guilt*?

One approach is to see Adam as our *federal* head. Because he is our divinely designated representative, what Adam did implicates us all. Both his sin and guilt is imputed to us. Since this precise formulation is

---

[23] Cited in F. F. Bruce, *Paul: Apostle of the Heart Set Free* (Grand Rapids: Eerdmans, 1977), 329.

[24] Cited in Cranfield, *Romans,* 1:273.

[25] Gordon D. Fee, *The First Epistle to the Corinthians* (NICNT; Grand Rapids: Eerdmans, 1987), 751.

nowhere explicitly stated in Scripture, another approach is to see Adam simply as our *natural* head, the ancestor of us all. Nevertheless, both his sin and his guilt are viewed as being imparted to us through heredity (Augustine).

Paul does seem to speak in universalistic terms in this paragraph. For example, in completing his thought from 5:12, he writes these summary comments:

> Therefore just as one man's trespass led to condemnation for all, so one man's act of righteousness leads to justification for all. For just as by the one man's disobedience the many were made sinners, so by the one man's obedience the many will be made righteous. (5:18–19)

Paul is saying that sin is universal. But there is no universalism of *guilt* (Augustine) or *salvation* (Origen).[26] Just as Christ's righteousness is imputed to us conditionally on the basis of our faith in him, so guilt must be seen as imputed to us conditionally on the basis of our own volitional sin.[27] Thus, children who die before the age of accountability or the mentally retarded, for example, are not prevented from heaven because of inherited guilt. The question that remains, however, is just how we inherit our sin natures. Before using Romans 7 to personalize the doctrine of sin even more, we will briefly consider this question.

Inherited Sin

The doctrine of original sin, which we have been exploring, is not a popular one, and understandably so. We do not like to be confronted with God's law. We do not like to be reminded that we are "outlaws." This very resistance to the truth, as we have already seen, is evidence of our problem. Judaism and Christianity are perennially scandalous because of their teachings concerning sin. Commenting on Romans 5:13–14, C. E. B. Cranfield observes: "It is only in the presence of the law, only in Israel and in the Church, that the full seriousness of sin is visible and the responsibility of the sinner stripped of every extenuating circumstance."[28]

Blaise Pascal described our condition as "one of inconsistency, of boredom, and of anxiety."[29] We are notoriously inconsistent. It is amaz-

---

[26] Cf. Dale Moody, "Romans" (Broadman Bible Commentary 10; Nashville: Broadman, 1970), 197–98.

[27] See Millard J. Erickson, *Christian Theology* (Grand Rapids: Baker, 1985), 639.

[28] Cranfield, *Romans*, 1:282.

[29] See Houston, ed., *The Mind on Fire*, 51.

ingly easier to see iniquities in others than to see our own. We are too often bored with life, while deep inside we are convinced that life was meant to be an exciting adventure. Ecclesiastes is as precise a depiction of contemporary humanity as can be found: All is meaningless. We are also an anxious lot. Reinhold Niebuhr built his entire psychological theory of original sin on this common experience of anxiety.

According to Niebuhr, we have a dual nature. We are finite creatures, and yet we are able spiritually to transcend our limitations somewhat and to aspire to a perfection that is always beyond our reach. This inevitable tension between freedom and finitude, between our spirituality and our mortality, leads to an anxiety that is the occasion for sin. We seek to overcome our anxiety in one of two ways: We either lose ourselves and "drown" our anxieties, as it were, in sensuality (in alcohol, sex, etc.), or we seek to overcome through pride.

We may yield to a pride *of power*, in which we attempt to control people and situations. Abuse of power is one of the salient sins of humankind. Or we might, in pride *of knowledge*, refuse to acknowledge our intellectual limitations and seek to absolutize our worldview. Somehow, if we can convince others that we know more than they, we feel more secure and righteous. This is a besetting sin of seminarians who try to bolster their own positions by demonstrating that they are better read and generally superior in knowledge to their peers. This points us to the third manifestation of pride, the most dangerous of all: pride *of virtue or religion*. The Pharisees of Scripture are a prime example of this sin. Attempting to prove our spiritual and moral superiority is one of the most destructive and dangerous sins of all.[30]

Niebuhr's analysis is brilliant. It is an accurate depiction of how sin *might* manifest itself in our lives. It is *not*, however, a biblical explanation of the origin or essence of sin. Anxiety is only one dynamic dealt with in the Bible, and it is never portrayed as the original seedbed of sin. Nevertheless, many a relevant sermon may be derived from Niebuhr's honest and penetrating analysis of the human situation.

Others have attempted to trace the source of sin to our social and economic struggles or to our supposed animal ancestry, but none of these theories does justice to the biblical picture. Almost inevitably we end up discussing *symptoms* of our fundamental sin problem rather than the problem itself. We are looking at various sins rather than at sin in its

---

30 See Reinhold Niebuhr, *The Nature and Destiny of Man*, vol. 1 (New York: Charles Scribner's Sons, 1964).

essence. In the final analysis, we must return to the Garden of Eden, to the sin of our first parents, and to that mysterious *fact* of the transmission of sin from generation to generation.

One concept that seems to fit the biblical picture and to help us comprehend the situation is *traducianism.* Traducianism teaches that our parents hand on to us our *spiritual* natures as well as our physical natures. Even genetic studies seem to suggest this, as certain personality orientations and susceptibilities to addictions have been traced to heredity. Augustine was correct in this regard, although he was never able personally to break free from a biblically unworthy "low" view of sexuality. His preconversion struggle to give up his mistress evidently marked his later theology, and it is often true for all of us that past experiences may distort our present perceptions and conceptions.

> *Our parents hand on to us our* spiritual *natures as well as our physical natures.*

Paul evidently had Adam's natural headship in mind when in Romans 5 he depicted the spread of sin and death. David L. Smith uses a powerful contemporary analogy to communicate this biblical truth:

> Sin may be compared to the HIV virus. It lurks seemingly dormant within its human host; but at some point it suddenly explodes into AIDS, and its destructive power becomes evident to all. Ultimately, it causes death. Sin is seemingly inactive in one ignorant of the law (as in a child), but when knowledge of the law dawns, guilt over transgression occurs and sin kills spiritually as one becomes cognizant of one's real condition before God.... Until there is an awareness of guilt (that is, of having transgressed the law), the penalty of eternal death is not imputed. It is mitigated by the Savior's atonement.
>
> We see that guilt is charged against the sinner only on account of his or her own personal transgression, not because of Adam's. Because all transgress, all are guilty. In this way there is a solidarity of all human beings with Adam.[31]

The apostle Paul calls the fallen nature that we inherit from Adam "the flesh." And it is this same apostle, almost certainly because of his prior failed pharisaical quest for righteousness by keeping the law, who shows the fascinating relationship between the law and sin already alluded to in Romans 5:20.

[31] Smith, *With Willful Intent,* 369.

Romans 7 almost haunts us with its poignant depiction of the power of sin over our lives. Without the help and hope afforded us in chapter 8, we would succumb to despair. But because of Christ there is hope for us both in this life and in the life to come. Nevertheless, it is imperative that we look honestly at the message of Romans 7. Here the apostle gets personal.

Let's Get Personal

In Romans 5:12–21 "Paul presents the history of humanity as a drama in two parts—two epochs dominated by the two figures, Adam the tragic hero, and Christ the redeemer hero."[32] The apostle deals in a profound way with the doctrine of original sin in relation to Christ's victorious redemption. All human beings are seen as under the power of sin and death. Those outside the law die as a *consequence* of their sin, and those who have willfully broken God's law ("transgression") die in *punishment* for their sin. But all die because all sin.

> In short, Paul could be said to hold a doctrine of *original sin,* in the sense that from the beginning everyone has been under the power of sin with death as a consequence, but not a doctrine of *original guilt,* since individuals are only held responsible for deliberate acts of defiance against God and his law.[33]

In Romans 7 Paul takes us a step further in our understanding of sin. Verses 7–13 in particular *personalize* the Garden of Eden story in such a way that we all perceive our fallenness and culpability before God.

The role of the law in the life of the church was of paramount importance to Paul. Had he not guarded the gospel from legalism as well as antinomianism, the church would have suffered a tremendous loss. "Some things" in Paul's letters may be "hard to understand" (2 Peter 3:16), but God's sovereign wisdom in including them in the canon is obvious. Thanks to Paul, in large measure, the church did not lose the gospel.

The law is "holy and just and good" (Rom. 7:12); but it also brings condemnation, and is powerless to rescue us from the dominion of sin. Sin and death, as malevolent powers, have utilized the law literally to kill us (7:11). The story of Adam and Eve is the story of every person.

---

[32] James D. G. Dunn, *Romans 1–8* (WBC 38a; Dallas: Word, 1988), 288.
[33] Ibid., 291 (Dunn's italics).

It is interesting that the apostle singles out the one commandment—"You shall not covet"—that deals with a totally *inward* reality, an attitude of the heart (Rom. 7:7). As a practicing Pharisee, Paul had been able to uphold external appearances of keeping the law. "But sin, seizing an opportunity in the commandment, produced in me all kinds of covetousness" (v. 8). Notice the echoes of the Genesis Fall story in his ensuing comments:

> Apart from the law sin lies dead. I was once alive apart from the law, but when the commandment came, sin revived and I died, and the very commandment that promised life proved to be death to me. For sin, seizing an opportunity in the commandment, deceived me and through it killed me. (vv. 8–11)

The law is not sin, and the law did not bring death: "By no means!" (Rom. 7:7, 13). The law is holy and good. "It was sin, working death in me through what is good, in order that sin might be shown to be sin, and through the commandment might become sinful beyond measure" (v. 13).

Paul then goes on to describe the nature of human life as lived in the "flesh," our fallen nature inherited from our first parents (Rom. 7:14–25). Only "the law of the Spirit of life in Christ Jesus" can set us free from "the law of sin and death" (8:2). (We will explore this dynamic in the doctrine of sanctification later.) These verses are notoriously difficult, but the overarching description of the moral bondage of humankind is indisputable. They denote perfectly what is meant (or at least should be meant) by *total depravity*.

But there is a definite parallel between what happened to Adam and Eve in the garden and what happens to every one of us. At some tragic point we lose our "innocence," as it were, and we sin highhandedly. We consciously embrace our sin nature and deliberately transgress God's law. Our bondage to sin at that point becomes painfully obvious. Only the cross of Christ, applied in our lives personally by the power of the Spirit, can liberate us from this downward pull. The Scriptures are poignantly realistic about sin and its consequences, as well as positively optimistic about the power of the gospel (Rom. 1:16–17) to rescue us from this dreadful morass. At this juncture it is helpful to clarify the exact nature of sin and its universal scope.

The Nature and Universality of Sin

In introducing his gospel, Paul states that the good news reveals a righteousness from God that comes through faith (Rom. 1:17). Then he immediately points out that God's wrath has been revealed from heaven against all the ungodliness (*asebeia*) and unrighteousness (*adikia*) of humankind (1:18). These two words provide a comprehensive summary of what the Bible means by sin. They point to the essence of sin.

Human life consists of two fundamental personal relationships: One is vertical—our relationship with God; the other is horizontal—our relationships with other human beings. In the law of God known as the Ten Commandments these two dimensions are precisely delineated. The first four commandments concern our relationship with God, and the last six deal with human relations. When Jesus was asked by a lawyer among the Pharisees which was the greatest commandment, he cited Deuteronomy 6:5 and Leviticus 19:18. We are to love God with our whole being and to love our neighbor as ourselves (Matt. 22:37–39). Then Jesus added: "On these two commandments hang all the law and the prophets" (22:40). *All* the Scriptures are "suspended" from this love command! That is truly a momentous statement. If sin is the transgression of God's law (or "lawlessness" [*anomia*], 1 John 3:4), then we are near the very core of sin when we perceive it as failure in relation to the love command.

> *The ungodliness* (asebeia) *and unrighteousness* (adikia) *of humankind point to the essence of sin.*

First and foremost, we are *ungodly*. A godly person is humbly reverent toward God. An ungodly person arrogantly refuses to acknowledge and glorify God.[34] As ungodly persons we do not live according to faith but rather in unbelief, which is sin (Rom. 14:23). Our fundamental relationship with God is broken. We have other gods besides the true and living God. We make idols. We wrongfully use God's name, and we ignore the Lord's day, failing to "keep it holy" (Ex. 20:1–8). We simply do not love God with all our heart, soul, mind, and strength.

In this passage of Romans, Paul depicts this ungodliness that characterizes us all as ignorance (Rom. 1:18–23) and idolatry (1:24–25).[35]

---

[34] Smith, *With Willful Intent*, 314.

[35] In much of the analysis which follows I am indebted to the two following sources: Dale Moody, *The Word of Truth* (Grand Rapids: Eerdmans, 1981), 275–79, and David L. Smith, *With Willful Intent*, 314–26.

In our willful ignorance we "suppress the truth" (v. 18), but God's general revelation of himself leaves us "without excuse" (vv. 19–20). Humankind simply refuses to acknowledge God: "For although they knew God, they neither glorified him as God nor gave thanks to him, but their thinking became futile and their foolish hearts were darkened" (v. 21 NIV; cf. Eph. 4:17–19). Ours is a false wisdom (Rom. 1:22), a problem that goes back to the garden (Gen. 3:6). In a cynical age unbelief is viewed almost as a virtue, when in reality, according to Scripture, it leads only and ultimately to ignorance. Romans 1:23 forms a transition to the next aspect of ungodliness (idolatry): "And they exchanged the glory of the immortal God for images resembling a mortal human being or birds or four-footed animals or reptiles." Such a trade can only be described as ignorance.

Three times here Paul says, "God gave them up" (Rom. 1:24, 26, 28). This is a terrifying prospect! Humankind left to itself is its own worst enemy. The results are the grossest forms of idolatry (1:24–25). Luther derives from this passage four stages of perversion or perdition through which humanity goes: ingratitude, vanity, blindness, and idolatry—each leading to the other.[36] *Der Mensch hat Gott oder Abgott,* Luther would say. Humankind has either God or an idol. Or, as Bob Dylan would sing in our own day, "You gotta serve somebody; may be the devil, may be the Lord—but you gotta serve somebody." We are by nature creatures who worship. If we refuse to worship God, who alone is worthy of our praise, we will worship something or someone else.

Because sin is fundamentally an offense against God, we have already begun to see its essence. "Sin is the displacement of God," says Millard Erickson.[37] He is precisely correct. Years ago I read a sermon by Billy Graham (which I now am unable to locate) entitled "Let God Be God." I have never been able to forget those words. Our "failure to let God be God" is "the essence of sin."[38] Sin is failing to acknowledge God as God. "Idolatry in any form, not pride, is the essence of sin."[39] Erickson also highlights *unbelief* as "the major factor in our failure to love, worship, and obey God."[40] This description of the essence of sin is nothing more than a summary of Paul's words in Romans 1:18–25.

---

[36] Martin Luther, *Commentary on the Epistle to the Romans,* trans. J. Theodore Mueller (Grand Rapids: Kregel, 1954), 45–46.

[37] Millard J. Erickson, *Introducing Christian Doctrine,* ed. L. Arnold Hustad (Grand Rapids: Baker, 1992), 181.

[38] Ibid., 580.

[39] Ibid., 580. See also Smith, *With Willful Intent,* 326.

[40] Erickson, *Christian Theology,* 580.

Many would want to elevate *pride* to the position of the primal or essential sin. Pride is certainly a major sin addressed in Scripture. C. S. Lewis's chapter "The Great Sin" in *Mere Christianity* is a devastating analysis of this pervasive sin.[41] Any serviceable Bible concordance will readily attest to the gravity and predominance of this particular sin. But it is nevertheless not the essence of sin. Jesus pointed out that pride is one of many sins that proceed "from within, from the human heart" (Mark 7:21–23). Upon reflection, it becomes clear that pride has idolatry at its base: Pride is a refusal to let God be God.

Second, Paul continues his examination of sin by looking at examples of sin as *unrighteousness*: sins of the human flesh (Rom. 1:26–27) and sins of the human spirit (1:28–32). Among the sins of sensuality, the apostle singles out homosexuality (vv. 26–27). He would be highly controversial in doing so today. But for those who acknowledge the authority of Scripture—and who carefully observe the course of the rise and fall of human civilizations—Paul is correct in emphasizing the seriousness of this sin. First, he calls it *sin*, not a sexual preference or an alternate lifestyle. Second, he points to the destructive nature of this sin. Homosexuality tends to increase in a culture as its deterioration accelerates and its collapse nears. America should take notice. It is one of the few sins described in the Bible as an abomination (*tôʿebah*) and in the Old Testament was punishable by death (Lev. 18:22; 20:13). According to Scripture, homosexuality is loathsome, abhorrent, and nauseating to God.[42] It should be to us as well. Practicing homosexuals are listed by Paul as among those who will not inherit the kingdom of God (1 Cor. 6:9–10).

The Christian attitude is, of course, one that hates sin and loves the sinner. Jesus exemplified this principle when he associated with those whom the religious world shunned. In fact, the sins of the human spirit that Paul lists next (Rom. 1:28–32) are often more destructive to a local church than many of the cultural sins often emphasized. How wide is the trail of destruction of human life left by gossips and slanderers in the church (vv. 29–31)! Our *selective* analysis of sin is a major crippling factor in church life.

Paul is unrelenting in his depiction of the sin problem of the human race. Both Jew and Gentile are under the power of sin and in need of the gospel (Rom. 2:1–3:20). Sin is *universal*. In order to drive home this

---

[41] C. S. Lewis, *Mere Christianity* (New York: Macmillan, 1943), 108–14.

[42] See John Jefferson Davis, *Evangelical Ethics* (Phillipsburg, N.J.: Presbyterian and Reformed, 1985), 117; Erickson, *Christian Theology*, 575.

point, Paul presents a collection of Old Testament texts that poignantly depict human sinfulness in thought (3:10–12), word (3:13–14), and deed (3:15–18). Eugene Peterson renders this passage effectively in a contemporary paraphrase:

> There's nobody living right, not even one,
> nobody who knows the score, nobody alert for God.
> They've all taken the wrong turn;
> they've all wandered down blind alleys.
> No one's living right;
> I can't find a single one.
> Their throats are gaping graves,
> their tongues slick as mud slides.
> Every word they speak is tinged with poison.
> They open their mouths and pollute the air.
> They race for the honor of sinner-of-the-year,
> litter the land with heartbreak and ruin,
> Don't know the first thing about living with others.
> They never give God the time of day.[43]

"Since all have sinned" (Rom. 3:23), all have need of the gospel (3:23–26).

The Results of Sin

Just as we have touched on the universality of sin at numerous points throughout our exploration of the biblical doctrine of sin, so we have also noted the results of sin at several junctures. In a word, the result of sin is *death.* In one of the best-known verses in all of Paul's letters—and indeed in all the Bible—the apostle summarizes the human situation and the gospel message that addresses that situation: "For the wages of sin is death, but the free gift of God is eternal life in Christ Jesus our Lord" (Rom. 6:23). Another excellent modern translation brings out the contrast Paul is drawing here: "For sin pays a wage, and the wage is death, but God gives freely, and his gift is eternal life in union with Christ Jesus our Lord" (REB). Charles Haddon Spurgeon expressed it well: "Here you have both the essence of the gospel and a statement of that misery from which the gospel delivers all who believe."[44]

---

[43] Eugene H. Peterson, *The Message: The New Testament in Contemporary Language* (Colorado Springs, Colo.: NavPress, 1993), 308–9.

[44] Charles Haddon Spurgeon, "Death and Life: The Wage and the Gift," in *Metropolitan Tabernacle Pulpit* (London: The Banner of Truth Trust, 1971), 31:601; cited in James Montgomery Boice, *Romans* (Grand Rapids: Baker, 1992), 2:706.

The gospel of the kingdom as preached by both Jesus and Paul presents us with *a choice of two.* For example, in the Sermon on the Mount (Matt. 5–7) Jesus presents us with a series of twos:

- two kinds of righteousness (5:20–48) in terms of avoiding anger (vv. 21–26), sexual purity/adultery (vv. 27–30), marital fidelity/divorce (vv. 31–32), honesty in speech (vv. 33–37), nonretaliation (vv. 38–42), and active love (vv. 43–48)
- two kinds of piety (6:1–18) in relation to giving to the poor (vv. 2–4), prayer (vv. 5–15), and fasting (vv. 16–18)
- two treasures: earth/heaven (6:19–21)
- two persons: blind/sighted (6:22–23)
- two masters: God/money (6:24)
- two gates, roads, and destinies (7:13–14)
- two kinds of prophets or teachers (7:15–20)
- two houses/foundations (7:24–27)[45]

In similar fashion, Paul, in his "gospel" known as Romans, also presents us with a choice of two. There are the wrath of God (Rom. 1:18; 2:5–10) and the righteousness of God (1:17; 3:21). There are the Adam/Christ and law/grace dichotomies of chapter 5. Chapter 6 offers a choice of slavery, "either of sin, which leads to death, or of obedience, which leads to righteousness" (6:16). It is a choice of death or eternal life (6:20–22). In 6:23 it is: sin vs. God, death vs. eternal life, and sin's wages vs. God's gift—God's grace leaves us with a choice.

Sin, personified as a slave owner, is depicted as paying the allowance or pocket money that was traditionally paid slaves in Roman society. This "wage" that sin pays is death. In contrast, God gives us a "free gift" (*charisma*)—"eternal life in Christ Jesus our Lord."[46] Sin is deceitful. It promises freedom, but gives bondage. It promises life, but ends in death. Insidiously, sin works against all meaning, purpose, and fulfillment in life. "Eternal life," however, speaks of a quality of life as well as unending life. It is life lived in relation with the one who made us and who saves us (see also John 17:3). It is life filled with meaning and purpose.[47]

The Lord God stated plainly to Adam what the consequence of disobedience would be: "You shall die" (Gen. 2:17). Death is the comprehensive

---

45 See John R. W. Stott, *Christian Counter-Culture: The Message of the Sermon on the Mount* (Downers Grove, Ill.: InterVarsity Press, 1978).

46 See C. E. B. Cranfield, *Romans: A Shorter Commentary* (Grand Rapids: Eerdmans, 1985), 146.

47 See Leon Morris, *The Epistle to the Romans* (Grand Rapids: Eerdmans, 1988), 267.

> *Death is the comprehensive biblical term for the results of sin: physical death, spiritual death, and eternal death.*

biblical term for the results of sin: physical death, spiritual death, and eternal death. For most of us the first form of death of which we are aware is *physical* death. Original sin is verified empirically at funeral homes every day throughout the country. Every funeral procession we see reminds us that humankind is sinful and that everyone ultimately faces physical death. In his book *Facing Death and the Life After*, Billy Graham writes:

> Death is perennial. During World War II, C. S. Lewis pointed out that war does not increase death; death is total in every generation. It takes every one of us. George Bernard Shaw wryly wrote, "The statistics on death are quite impressive. One out of one people die."[48]

Physical death is our last great enemy: "The last enemy to be destroyed is death" (1 Cor. 15:26). Christians look forward to the day when God himself "will wipe every tear from their eyes. Death will be no more; mourning and crying and pain will be no more, for the first things have passed away" (Rev. 21:3–4).

Death is also a *spiritual* reality. Adam and Eve died in a spiritual sense on that fateful day in the Garden of Eden. They became alienated from the Lord God with whom they had previously enjoyed unbroken fellowship. They ran and hid from him in guilt and shame (Gen. 3:8–10). Humankind has been alienated from God ever since. God is seen as an intruder, a "party pooper." There is an enmity with God (Rom. 5:10). All people are "alienated from the life of God because of their ignorance and hardness of heart" (Eph. 4:18). Humankind is "estranged and hostile in mind, doing evil deeds" (Col. 1:21). Again, the dismal picture of Romans 1:18–32 comes to mind. We are also alienated from one another—person against person, male against female, race against race, nation against nation, and even church against church. Furthermore, we are alienated from ourselves, divided within our own persons—tormented by our own personal dis-ease. Sin pays an awful wage.

This spiritual death entails a spiritual blindness as well. Our minds are darkened. Our hearts are hardened (Rom. 1:21; Eph. 4:17–19). All people stubbornly refuse to listen to God; they have "closed their minds

---

[48] Billy Graham, *Facing Death and the Life After* (Dallas: Word, 1987), 17.

and made their hearts as hard as rock" (Zech. 7:11–12 GNB). "Who can understand the human heart? There is nothing else so deceitful; it is too sick to be healed" (Jer. 17:9 GNB).

Spiritual death also means moral servitude. Humankind is enslaved to sin, as Romans 6:17–19 describes explicitly (see also 1:18–32). Our natural instinct is to flee from God rather than pursue him (Gen. 3:8; Ps. 53:1–3; Isa. 65:1; Rom. 3:11). We are helpless to change ourselves (Jer. 13:23; Hos. 5:4). Jesus himself said: "Very truly, I tell you, everyone who commits sin is a slave to sin" (John 8:34).

Paul reminded the Romans that "the mind that is set on the flesh is hostile to God; it does not submit to God's law—*indeed it cannot*. . . . But you [believers] are not in the flesh; you are in the Spirit" (Rom. 8:7–9, italics added). Everyone in Adam's race is "in the flesh"—completely unable to fulfill God's moral law. *We are free to choose many things in this life, but we are not free to choose holiness. Only God's grace can enable that choice.*[49] As Paul said: "I am of the flesh, sold into slavery under sin" (Rom. 7:14). This is a poignant and personal confession of moral servitude and total depravity.

Total depravity means that throughout our entire being we are tainted with sin, in moral bondage, and completely unable to save ourselves. It does not mean that we are as bad as we possibly could be. The image of God has not been totally annihilated; even unregenerate persons are capable of noble motives and actions.[50] But the pressures of life inevitably bring out the worst in us at some point. One of the best books to illustrate and document this truth is Langdon Gilkey's *Shantung Compound: The Story of Men and Women Under Pressure.*

As a young American teacher in China during World War II, Gilkey was placed, along with many others, in a Japanese internment camp for two and a half years. It was a sort of human civilization in miniature, as people from virtually every walk of life were thrown together and forced to create afresh their own new society. Gilkey's liberal belief in the innate goodness of humankind was exploded. He was amazed at how even the most religious persons could rationalize their self-interest. One refreshing exception to this pattern was a young missionary named Eric Liddell (Eric Ridley in the book—Gilkey changed all names, for obvious reasons). Liddell consistently gave of himself in loving, sacrificial

---

[49] See Donald G. Bloesch, *Essentials of Evangelical Theology* (New York: Harper & Row, 1978), 1:98–101.

[50] See Erickson, *Christian Theology*, 628–31.

service to others (especially to the young people). This Olympic hero, whose life was beautifully portrayed in the movie *Chariots of Fire*, died of a brain tumor while in that camp.[51]

The final result of sin is *eternal death*. It is what the Bible calls "the second death" (Rev. 20:6, 14). Whether we want to hear it or not, sinful humanity faces wrath, judgment, and hell. God's wrath is already being revealed (Rom. 1:18), and there awaits humankind "the day of wrath, when God's righteous judgment will be revealed" (2:5; see also 2:6–11; 3:5; 5:9). The crucial issue here is Jesus Christ: "Whoever believes in the Son has eternal life, but whoever rejects the Son will not see life, for God's wrath remains on him" (John 3:36 NIV). Humankind is "dead through trespasses and sins ... children of wrath." But God, by his grace, can make us "alive together with Christ" (Eph. 2:1, 3, 5). We have already studied the wrath of God, and we will explore further the doctrines of salvation, judgment, and hell in subsequent chapters.

Jesus Christ is humankind's *only hope for deliverance from sin.*

As Spurgeon said, we are all like the dry, dead bones in Ezekiel's valley: "Mortal, can these bones live?" (Ezek. 37:3). Yes, they can! But only God can conquer death and cause us to *live*.[52] Christians can exult with Paul: "The sting of death is sin, and the power of sin is the law. But thanks be to God, who gives us the victory through our Lord Jesus Christ" (1 Cor. 15:56–57).

America today is inundated with societal ills. Crime is rampant. Violence stalks the halls of our schools. A long list of intractable problems could be compiled. The only way for us to regain our mental and moral stability is to acknowledge our number one problem: sin. America has a sin problem. Karl Menninger's book asks the right question: *Whatever Became of Sin?*[53] Until we deal with this root issue we can only put a temporary bandage on our problem. Jesus Christ is America's only hope.

Jesus Christ is *humankind's* only hope for deliverance from sin. Because of who he is and because of what he has done, salvation from sin and its results is a gift now offered to humankind. Therefore, we will turn next to the enriching study of the person and work of Christ—to what is known in theological parlance as Christology and atonement.

---

[51] Langdon Gilkey, *Shantung Compound: The Story of Men and Women Under Pressure* (New York: Harper & Row, 1966), 192–93.

[52] Spurgeon, "Death and Life: The Wage and the Gift," 612; cited in Boice, *Romans*, 2:711–12.

[53] Karl Menninger, *Whatever Became of Sin?* (New York: Bantam Books, 1978).

7 Christ
Who Is Jesus, and How Does He Save Us?

(continued on next page)

Christ Crucified
- Why Christ Died
- For God So Loved . . .
- Advocate, Atonement, and Example
- The Gospel According to Paul
- But Now . . .
- Sacrifice
- Covenant
- Redemption
- Reconciliation
- Propitiation
- Justification
- Victory

Historical Theories of the Atonement

One Solitary Life

He was born in an obscure village, the child of a peasant woman.

He grew up in still another village, where he worked in a carpenter's shop until he was thirty.

Then for three years he was an itinerant preacher.

He never wrote a book. He never held an office. He never had a family or owned a house. He did not go to college. He never visited a big city. He never traveled two hundred miles from the place where he was born. He did none of the things one usually associates with greatness.

He had no credentials but himself.

He was only thirty-three when the tide of public opinion turned against him. His friends ran away. He was turned over to his enemies and went through the mockery of a trial. He was nailed to a cross between two thieves. While he was dying, his executioners gambled for his clothing, the only property he had on earth. When he was dead, he was laid in a borrowed grave through the pity of a friend.

Nineteen centuries have come and gone, and today he remains the central figure of the human race, and the leader of mankind's progress.
All the armies that ever marched, all the navies that ever sailed, all the parliaments that ever sat, all the kings that ever reigned, put together, *have not affected the life of man on this planet so much as that one solitary life.*

—Michael Green[1]

---

[1] Michael Green, *Who Is This Jesus?* (Nashville: Oliver-Nelson, 1992), 2.

Who Is Jesus?

It is more appropriate to ask "Who *is* Jesus?" than to ask "Who *was* Jesus?" for Jesus of Nazareth is *both* "a historical figure" and "our eternal contemporary."[2] And when he comes into someone's life, he inevitably changes that person's life.

When Bill Hull first stepped onto the basketball court, I looked carefully at him and made two quick judgments: It would be a long process in his becoming a Christian, and he would have a difficult time making the team with all that beer fat hanging off him. But within three weeks he was a committed Christian, and he proved to be one of the best players the university has ever produced. We became roommates in the athletic dorm. Subsequently, Bill entered the ministry. His numerous books on discipleship and his dynamic leadership within his denomination have prompted speaking engagements in seminaries and conferences across the country. This whole process began when he encountered Jesus Christ personally.

> *When Jesus comes into someone's life, he inevitably changes that person's life.*

Earlier I told the amazing story of Ralph Bethea, a Southern Baptist missionary to Kenya. Frustrated with the meager results from their efforts in evangelism and discipleship, Bethea and twelve of his friends earnestly sought God for a spiritual breakthrough. How could they ever effectively communicate the reality of Jesus Christ among a people who had been so blinded to the uniqueness of Christ for centuries? God gave them a strategy. They simply went throughout the community asking people, "What can Jesus do for you?" They began to see miraculous answers to prayer. Signs and wonders comparable to those of the New Testament began to occur. The result was more than 120,000 converts and two hundred new churches—perhaps the greatest impact among Muslims in the history of Christian missions. Jesus Christ, our eternal contemporary, had shown himself powerful!

There is a great advantage in knowing personally the person about whom one is writing. I first saw Jesus in my godly parents. I first met Jesus

[2] F. F. Bruce, *Jesus: Lord and Savior* (Downers Grove, Ill.: InterVarsity Press, 1986), 13.

Christ as a seven-year-old in the pastor's study of a Southern Baptist church in Fort Stockton, Texas. He has been my constant life-companion ever since.

It may shock some people and appear somewhat audacious to speak of Jesus in such direct and personal terms. But it is the way the believers of the New Testament era—as well as millions of other Christians through the centuries—have spoken of their relationship with Jesus Christ. Sadly, theologians too often have made Jesus out to be a "problem." They speak and write as if the Jesus of history and the Christ of faith are two different persons. One wonders at times if some of them really *know* the one about whom they are writing.

The person and work of Christ are an indissoluble unity.

Nevertheless, it is important at the outset of our study of the person and work of Christ to remind ourselves of the nature of our subject. He is the living Christ, who is still the most powerful influence in the world today, both historically and *personally*! Luke Timothy Johnson reminds us that it makes a great deal of difference whether we think Jesus is dead or alive: Studying the *living Jesus*, who is risen and reigns on high, is an altogether different enterprise from the study of a dead historical figure.[3]

The person and work of Christ are an indissoluble unity. Distortions and even heresies inevitably develop whenever one is subordinated to the other.[4] For the purpose of analytical study, the logical progression is to examine first the person of Christ and then his work. Historically speaking, however, it was the other way around. People were first confronted with the historical Jesus in action, and then they developed their confessions of faith concerning him.[5] The three programmatic questions we will consider are: (1) Who is Jesus? (2) What has he done for us? and (3) How can we know him? This third question is essential if we are to avoid separating our doctrine from our discipleship.[6]

---

[3] Luke Timothy Johnson, *Living Jesus: Learning the Heart of the Gospel* (San Francisco: HarperSanFrancisco, 1999), 3–6.

[4] See H. D. McDonald, *Jesus—Human and Divine* (Grand Rapids: Zondervan, 1968), 106–8.

[5] See Reginald H. Fuller, *The Foundations of New Testament Christology* (New York: Charles Scribner's Sons, 1965), 15.

[6] See Douglas D. Webster, *A Passion for Christ: An Evangelical Christology* (Grand Rapids: Zondervan, 1987).

In plainest terms, the distinctive Christian claim is that Jesus Christ was and is *God incarnate.* Jesus was crucified for making this claim. If this claim is not true, then Christianity is exploded. It is simply another world religion. *But if it is true,* this is the most important news anyone could ever learn![7] Furthermore, Christ came not only to show us the Father, but also to save us from our sins. This is what God's good news, announced beforehand in the sacred prophetic writings, is all about:

> It is about his Son: on the human level he was a descendant of David, but on the level of the spirit—the Holy Spirit—he was proclaimed Son of God by an act of power that raised him from the dead: it is about Jesus Christ our Lord. (Rom. 1:2–4 REB)

John wrote his majestic Gospel for this very personal reason: "that you may come to believe that Jesus is the Messiah, the Son of God, and that through believing you may have life in his name" (John 20:31). Scholars have produced myriad recondite tomes explicating John's theology, but people of all ages have simply sat down and read the apostle's straightforward, yet profound, Gospel and encountered for themselves, by faith, the Savior whom John exalts![8]

What Sort of Man Is This . . . ?

Jesus' personal presence and power continually prompted the query as to his identity. When he stilled the storm on Lake Galilee, his disciples "were amazed, saying, 'What sort of man is this, that even the winds and the sea obey him?'" (Matt. 8:27). Clearly Jesus was *more* than a man, for no ordinary man ever commanded such authority!

Jesus' triumphal entry brought a similar response:

> When he entered Jerusalem, the whole city was in turmoil, asking, "Who is this?" The crowds were saying, "This is the prophet Jesus from Nazareth in Galilee." (Matt. 21:10–11)

The question that rang through the streets of Jerusalem that day "suggests the universal quest of the human heart."[9] And the answer given by the crowds was correct as far as it went. Jesus *was* a prophet, but he was also priest and king—the traditional rubrics for describing his saving work on behalf of humankind.

---

[7] See John R. W. Stott, *Basic Christianity* (Grand Rapids: Eerdmans, 1958), 7.
[8] See Leon Morris, *New Testament Theology* (Grand Rapids: Zondervan, 1986), 225.
[9] Herschel H. Hobbs, *Who Is This?* (Nashville: Broadman, 1952), 4.

Perhaps the most revealing of such occurrences was Peter's confession at Caesarea Philippi, which we have noted in an earlier chapter. In this instance, Jesus himself poses the questions. First, he asks his disciples what others are saying about him: "Who do people say that the Son of Man is?" (Matt. 16:13). One immediately notices Jesus' favorite self-designation: *Son of Man.* The veiled reference to the exalted one (in Daniel's "night visions," Dan. 7:13–30) who was given "an everlasting dominion" is inescapable. The disciples respond that Jesus has been identified as John the Baptist or Elijah or Jeremiah or one of the prophets (Matt. 16:14).

> *"What sort of man is this?"* He is the incomparable Christ!

Then Jesus presses his disciples for their own response: "But who do *you* say that I am?" (Matt. 16:15; "you" is emphatic in the Greek). Peter gives his divinely revealed answer: "You are the Messiah, the Son of the living God" (v. 16). Jesus is the Messiah of Jewish hopes. He is the eternal Son of God. Peter has received this insight by revelation from the Father (v. 17). Jesus announces his kingdom/church plans (vv. 18–19) and his impending crucifixion (vv. 21–23), renews his universal call to discipleship (v. 24), and predicts the end-time return of the Son of Man (vv. 27–28). Son of Man. Messiah. Son of God. Revelation. Kingdom. Church. Discipleship. Second Coming. All are essential ingredients in the Christology of the New Testament.[10] (We also note again the organic unity of the teachings of Scripture.) Unless we view Jesus in relation to these crucial components of New Testament revelation, we do not see him clearly. Indeed! "What sort of man is this?" *He is the incomparable Christ!*

Jesus and the Gospel

In a real sense Jesus *is* the gospel. Paul uses the phrase "the gospel of Christ" a number of times (Rom. 15:19; 1 Cor. 9:12; 2 Cor. 2:12; 9:13; 10:14; Gal. 1:7; Phil. 1:27; 1 Thess. 3:2). Christ is both the *source* and the *subject* of the good news.[11] In Jesus we see that the gospel is literally a life and death issue. "For the wages of sin is death, but the free gift of God is eternal life in Christ Jesus our Lord" (Rom. 6:23). The "law of

---

[10] Christology is the doctrine of Christ, the comprehensive subject-matter of this chapter.

[11] See Millard J. Erickson, *Christian Theology* (Grand Rapids: Baker, 1985), 1063.

the Spirit of life in Christ Jesus" has set us free from "the law of sin and of death" (Rom. 8:2)!

Death, like a pall of darkness, covers humanity. Billy Graham expresses it well:

> Death casts its shadow over the land. On every continent, in every nation, and through every city, town, village, and hut, death rides unfettered. It brings hardship, suffering, and sorrow wherever it goes. . . . Death is an accomplished master of destruction, and his credentials precede him: abortion, abuse, addiction, brutality, crime, disease, drugs, hatred, lust, murder, neglect, pestilence, racial conflict, rape, revenge, starvation, suicide, violence, and war. These are his calling cards.[12]

But as Matthew reminds us in his Gospel, Jesus brought light into this darkness. His Galilean ministry was a fulfillment of Isaiah's messianic prophecies: "Land of Zebulun, land of Naphtali, on the road by the sea, across the Jordan, Galilee of the Gentiles—the people who sat in darkness have seen a great light, and for those who sat in the region and shadow of death light has dawned" (Matt. 4:15–16). Matthew's very next words are: "From that time Jesus began to proclaim, 'Repent, for the kingdom of heaven has come near'" (v. 17).

Into this dark and dying, sin-sick world comes the message of light and life—the message of Christ.

John's Gospel sounds the same note: "In him was life, and the life was the light of men. The light shines in the darkness, and the darkness has not overcome it" (John 1:4–5 RSV). Light came into the world, said John, but we loved darkness rather than light because our deeds were evil (3:19). The purpose of his Gospel was in part that we might "have life in his [Jesus'] name" (20:31). Sin brought darkness and death. Christ brings light and life: "I am the bread of life" (6:35); "I am the light of the world" (8:12); "I am the resurrection and the life" (11:25); "I am the way, and the truth, and the life" (14:6).

Into this dark and dying, sin-sick world comes the message of light and life—the message of Christ. William Tyndale, in his *Prologue to the New Testament*, characterizes the ethos of the gospel as "good, merry,

[12] Billy Graham, *Storm Warning* (Dallas: Word, 1992), 225.

glad and joyful tidings, that make a man's heart glad, and make him sing, dance, and leap for joy."[13] Again, Billy Graham says it well:

> What a glorious life we have to offer through the Gospel to those who are searching for purpose and meaning in life; or to those who have been crushed by oppression or circumstances; or to those who have found that materialism and sensual pleasure are not the answer to the deepest yearnings of their heart.[14]

Jesus said, "I came that they may have life, and have it abundantly" (John 10:10). And only he can give us that kind of life—the quality of life for which we all long.

Matthew summarizes Jesus' Galilean ministry with these words: "And he went about all Galilee, teaching in their synagogues and preaching the gospel of the kingdom and healing every disease and every infirmity among the people" (Matt. 4:23 RSV; see also 9:35). Predictably, these three dimensions of ministry—teaching, preaching, and healing—also characterized the ministry of the early church. They should likewise characterize the church's ministry today.

Peter presented the gospel of Christ in similar terms at Cornelius's house:

> You know the message he [God] sent to the people of Israel, preaching peace by Jesus Christ—he is Lord of all. That message spread throughout Judea, beginning in Galilee after the baptism that John announced: how God anointed Jesus of Nazareth with the Holy Spirit and with power; how he went about doing good and healing all who were oppressed by the devil, for God was with him. We are witnesses to all that he did both in Judea and in Jerusalem. They put him to death by hanging him on a tree; but God raised him on the third day and allowed him to appear, not to all the people but to us who were chosen by God as witnesses, and who ate and drank with him after he rose from the dead. He commanded us to preach to the people and to testify that he is the one ordained by God as judge of the living and the dead. All the prophets testify about him that everyone who believes in him receives forgiveness of sins through his name. (Acts 10:36–43)

This is about as full an account of the apostolic preaching of the gospel as one can get; it is also an excellent paradigm for our own gospel preaching. We should notice that Peter refers both to Jesus' Galilean

[13] Cited in Robert H. Mounce, "Gospel," *Evangelical Dictionary of Theology*, ed. Walter A. Elwell (Grand Rapids: Baker, 1984), 472 (spelling in quotation modernized).

[14] Billy Graham, *A Biblical Standard for Evangelists* (Minneapolis, MN: World Wide Publications, 1984), 49–50.

ministry of preaching, teaching, and healing and to his Judean ministry, which culminated with his death and resurrection.

Dale Moody characterizes the earliest evangelism in these words:

> It has been said that apostolic preaching fed the flock with a three-pronged fork! Each sermon had three points: (1) the Old Testament promise was fulfilled; (2) the story of the life, death, resurrection, and exaltation of Jesus was the *fulfillment*; and (3) the call was repent and believe this good news, the gospel about Jesus Christ.[15]

One notices immediately the stress on the resurrection. Just as the Exodus was the center of Old Testament faith, so Easter is the center of New Testament faith. As Paul wrote to the believers in Rome, justification through faith is God's gift to us "who believe in him who raised Jesus our Lord from the dead, who was handed over to death for our trespasses and was raised for our justification" (Rom. 4:25).

> *The four Gospels themselves are really expansions of apostolic gospel preaching.*

The four Gospels themselves are really expansions of this apostolic gospel preaching. All authentic Christian proclamation is Easter proclamation! We have good news to announce: Christ is risen! We have been reconciled to God through his death and are saved by his resurrection life (Rom. 5:10)! I am typing these words on Easter Sunday. Earlier, our family celebrated Christ's resurrection with about 2,400 other believers in a beautiful service of worship. After returning home, we learned by phone of the impending death of a loved one. In such circumstances, Easter faith makes all the difference.

The strength of the church in which I was raised—the Southern Baptist Convention—is the gospel preaching that has been its hallmark. Paul knew well that the gospel carries its own power: "It *is* the power of God for salvation to everyone who has faith" (Rom. 1:16, italics added). Millard Erickson is right when he asserts that the gospel is the heart of the entire ministry of the church.[16] In simplest terms our message is as follows: "that Christ died for our sins in accordance with the scriptures, that he was buried, and that he was raised on the third day in accordance with the scriptures, and that he appeared [to many]" (1 Cor. 15:3–5). Ironically, while growing up I heard more gospel preaching from the Pauline letters than from the Gospels themselves. George R.

---

[15] Dale Moody, *The Word of Truth* (Grand Rapids: Eerdmans, 1981), 6 (Moody's italics).

[16] Erickson, *Christian Theology*, 1059–67.

Beasley-Murray's little volume, *Preaching the Gospel from the Gospels,* has been a help to many a preacher in correcting this imbalance.[17]

> *Because of Jesus Christ there is hope for* everyone.

The ultimate evidence of our profound sin problem is how we resist this good news. Jesus' own hometown synagogue almost killed him after his inaugural sermon based on the messianic prophecies of Isaiah. In part this rejection was because of his assertion that the gospel was for all—both Jew and Gentile (Luke 4:16–30).[18] Even to this day people resist receiving the very best news anyone could ever hear: Because of Jesus Christ there is hope for *everyone.*

The centrality of Christ to the totality of Christian theology becomes immediately evident. He *is* the supreme revelation of God. He *is* the Creator and Sustainer of the cosmos. He *is* the only complete human being. And he *is* our salvation, our hope, and our sovereign, the head of his church. Every doctrine we will study is centered in him in a profound way. The historic creeds and confessions of Christendom evince this same characteristic. Before exploring in more depth just who Jesus is in his divinity, humanity, and unity and what he has done for us to save us from our hopeless sinful condition, we should examine this centrality further in terms of the church, the kingdom, the Spirit, and the Father.

Jesus and the Church

One can hardly overemphasize the close relation in the Scriptures between Christ and the church. Not only is Jesus Christ the image of the invisible God and the Creator and sustainer of the universe, he is also "the head of the body, the church" (Col. 1:15–18). He told Peter, "I will build my church" (Matt. 16:18).

In comparing the church to the human body, in order to bring home his point about the church's unity within its diversity, the apostle Paul makes an interesting statement: "For just as the body is one and has many members, and all the members of the body, though many, are one body, so it is with Christ" (1 Cor. 12:12). In this context one would expect Paul to write, " . . . so it is with *the church.*" But Paul, closely identifying Christ with his church, writes, "so it is with Christ." One will recall

---

[17] George R. Beasley-Murray, *Preaching the Gospel from the Gospels* (London: Epworth, 1956).

[18] See Charles Colson, *Kingdoms in Conflict* (Grand Rapids: Zondervan, 1987), 81–88, for a dramatic retelling of this momentous event and an exploration of its significance.

that during his Damascus Road encounter with Christ, Paul was confronted with his persecution of the church: "Saul, Saul, why do you persecute me? . . . I am Jesus, whom you are persecuting" (Acts 9:4–5). Surely Paul never forgot those words.

The apostle penned an entire letter[19] that can aptly be entitled, "Christ and the Church": Ephesians.[20] One can hardly find a more exalted view of the church. This is precisely the case, again, because of Christ's close relationship with his people. God has made Christ "the head over all things for the church, which is his body, the fullness of him who fills all in all" (Eph. 1:22–23). As believers, our very life and purpose is wrapped up in Christ (2:1–10), as well as our unity as "members of the household of God" (vv. 11–22). We are "a holy temple in the Lord," and Christ himself is "the cornerstone" (vv. 20–21). God's intention is "that through the church the wisdom of God in its rich variety might now be made known to the rulers and authorities in the heavenly places. This was in accordance with the eternal purpose that he has carried out in Christ Jesus our Lord" (3:10–11).

> *We cannot understand the church apart from Christ,* nor *can we fully understand Christ apart from the church!*

Our goal in "building up the body of Christ" is that "all of us come to the unity of the faith and of the knowledge of the Son of God, to maturity, to the measure of the full stature of Christ" (Eph. 4:12–13)—thus, the importance of studying the person and work of Christ. We are to "walk in love, as Christ loved us and gave himself up for us, a fragrant offering and sacrifice to God" (5:2 RSV). Paul compares the union between husband and wife and the union between Christ and the church (vv. 21–33). The "one flesh" relationship between husband and wife (Gen. 2:24) is a profound mystery; and, Paul explains, "I am saying that it refers to Christ and the church" (Eph. 5:31–32 RSV).

We will devote further study to this profound topic in a later chapter. At this juncture, the important point to be grasped is that we cannot understand the church apart from Christ, *nor can we fully understand Christ apart from the church*! Jesus Christ is serious about his

---

19 Was it Luke who was Paul's amanuensis, or secretary, for the writing of Ephesians? Compare the Greek style of Ephesians with that of Luke-Acts. (Also note Romans 16:22.)

20 See Dale Moody, *Christ and the Church* (Grand Rapids: Eerdmans, 1963).

church. The church, however, serves an even greater reality, namely, the kingdom of God.

Jesus and the Kingdom

As we have already seen, Jesus preached the good news of the kingdom. In fact, it would not be overstating the case to say that Jesus was *obsessed* with the kingdom of God. For Mark, the "beginning of the gospel about Jesus Christ, the Son of God" (Mark 1:1 NIV) included the preparatory ministry of John the Baptist, Jesus' baptism, the wilderness temptations, and—after John's arrest—the start of Jesus' Galilean ministry: "Now after John was arrested, Jesus came into Galilee, preaching the gospel of God, and saying, 'The time is fulfilled, and the kingdom of God is at hand; repent, and believe in the gospel'" (1:14–15 RSV).

> *The kingdom is the* rule *of God; it is a reign rather than a realm.*

Such proclamation could only raise the highest expectations among God's people, the Jews. In fact, Jesus' kingdom message was almost certainly what attracted his band of followers. John had already brought things to a fever pitch with his message of repentance: After four centuries, the voice of prophecy was once again speaking. Many even wondered whether John himself might be the Messiah. Jesus' kingdom language was messianic in flavor. Could he really be the long-awaited Messiah? He avoided that question until he could, at the right time, make crystal clear that he must suffer the cross of Calvary for our sins and rise, triumphant, from the grave. The Suffering Servant of Isaiah and the Messiah were one and the same—something the Jews had never fully considered.

The ministries of Paul and Jesus were similar in one fundamental respect: Both were largely rejected by the Jews. Jesus and his disciples first went to "the lost sheep of the house of Israel" (Matt. 10:6; 15:24). Just as most of the Jewish leaders spurned John's message and ministry, so they resisted Jesus and his disciples. Yet Jesus' outreach to the social outcasts of his day—the tax collectors and "sinners," for example—was considered even more reprehensible. It was within this milieu that Jesus' plans for the church began to emerge (Matt. 16:18).[21]

---

[21] See George Eldon Ladd, *The Gospel of the Kingdom* (Grand Rapids: Eerdmans, 1959), 107–22.

Jesus not only proclaimed the good news of the kingdom, he also performed healings and miracles as signs of the kingdom and taught the meaning and nature of the kingdom, notably through his use of parables. The kingdom is the *rule* of God; it is a reign rather than a realm. Jesus taught his followers to pray for God to rule and save them (Matt. 6:9–13), and the church is viewed from a distinctive perspective in relation to the kingdom.

George Eldon Ladd has succinctly stated the relation between the church and the kingdom: (1) The church is not the kingdom; (2) the kingdom creates the church; (3) the church witnesses to the kingdom; (4) the church is the instrument of the kingdom; (5) the church is the custodian (holds the keys) to the kingdom.[22] At the mention of Jesus Christ and his earthly ministry and message, one should *immediately* think of the kingdom of God. What is often overlooked, however, is the close connection between the kingdom and *the Spirit.*

Jesus and the Spirit

> *Wherever the Spirit of God is present and active,* there *is the kingdom!*

The Pharisees had room in their theology for the miraculous, but they did not have room for Jesus. When Jesus cured a blind and mute demoniac, the crowds were amazed, but the Pharisees were enraged. They claimed that Jesus performed this miracle by the power of the devil. Jesus' reply to them is instructive: "But if it is by the Spirit of God that I cast out demons, then the kingdom of God has come upon you" (Matt. 12:28 RSV). Notice the contiguity of the Spirit and kingdom. Wherever the Spirit of God is present and active, *there* is the kingdom! This helps us to understand why the preaching of the early church put more emphasis on the Spirit, while Jesus' message highlighted the kingdom. From the advent of the Spirit at Pentecost there was a shift in nomenclature, as it were. Mention is still made of the kingdom, but now there is a greater emphasis on the gift of the Holy Spirit.

What is often overlooked in theological circles is the key role of the Spirit in the incarnation of the Son. In this regard, Luke is one of the most helpful of the theologians of the New Testament. For example, the angel Gabriel announces to Mary:

---

[22] George Eldon Ladd, *A Theology of the New Testament* (Grand Rapids: Eerdmans, 1974), 111–19.

> "And now, you will conceive in your womb and bear a son, and you will name him Jesus. He will be great, and will be called the Son of the Most High, and the Lord God will give to him the throne of his ancestor David. He will reign over the house of Jacob forever, and of his kingdom there will be no end." Mary said to the angel, "How can this be, since I am a virgin?" The angel said to her, "The Holy Spirit will come upon you, and the power of the Most High will overshadow you; therefore the child to be born will be holy; he will be called Son of God." (Luke 1:31–35)

These awesome words refer to Jesus' name, greatness, divine sonship, and kingdom and explain the means of the miraculous conception: the Holy Spirit. *It is through the action of the Holy Spirit that the virginal conception will take place and the incarnation will be effected.*

> *Jesus is also our example in the Spirit-led walk.*

In fact, Luke's Gospel contain many references to the work of the Spirit. The angel Gabriel informed Zechariah that John would be filled with the Holy Spirit "even before his birth" (Luke 1:15). When Mary greeted Elizabeth, John leaped in her womb and she was "filled with the Holy Spirit" (v. 41). Later Zechariah was also filled with the Holy Spirit and prophesied (v. 67). The Holy Spirit was active in the life of devout Simeon, leading him into the temple to see the child Jesus (2:25–32). Clearly, the Spirit was much involved in bringing forth the Christ child!

When Jesus was baptized by John "and was praying, the heaven was opened, and the Holy Spirit descended upon him in bodily form like a dove" (Luke 3:21–22). Then "Jesus, full of the Holy Spirit, returned from the Jordan and was led by the Spirit in the wilderness" (4:1). "And Jesus returned in the power of the Spirit into Galilee" (4:14 RSV). In his inaugural sermon in Nazareth, Jesus read from Isaiah 61:1–2 ("The Spirit of the Lord is upon me") and announced, "Today this scripture has been fulfilled in your hearing" (Luke 4:18, 21).

At the joyful return of the seventy, Jesus "rejoiced in the Holy Spirit" (10:21). As he taught on persistent prayer, Jesus promised that the Father would "give the Holy Spirit to those who ask him" (11:13). Luke highlights prayer as the key to the Spirit's power, guidance, and action, both in Jesus' life and in the life of the early church (see also Luke 1:10, 13; 2:37; 3:21; 6:12; 9:18, 28–30; 11:1–13; 22:39–46; 23:34; Acts 1:14; 2:42; 4:23–31; 6:4; 9:11; 10:2, 4, 9, 30, 31; 16:13, 16).

Therefore, not only is Jesus the one who baptizes in the Holy Spirit, sending the Spirit on his disciples (see Matt. 3:11; Mark 1:8; Luke 3:16; John 1:33; 15:26; 16:7), *he is also our example in the Spirit-led walk.* It is precisely this recovery of the biblical picture of the relation between Jesus and the Spirit that is one of the most significant contributions of contemporary theology to the church's understanding of the person of Christ. It is also a key to authentic spirituality.

Historically, the church has focused more, in its Christological formulations, on Jesus' relation to the Father. This dimension is obviously a crucial aspect of the biblical picture of Christ, and we will have more to say below concerning this relationship. Also, the Nicene Creed makes reference to the fact that Jesus "was incarnate by the Holy Spirit of the Virgin Mary, and was made man." But the creed does not develop this truth as it does Jesus' relation to the Father. The Spirit is the key to more fully appreciating Christ's humanity as well as the Trinitarian relationships with respect to the Incarnation.

Jesus Christ not only claimed a unique relationship with God the Father, he also acknowledged his dependence on the Holy Spirit. Jesus had a prayer life. He *grew* in his knowledge of God and of himself. He set *the* example of what humanity should be, of how one should relate to God, of what it means to walk in the fullness of the Holy Spirit. He was much involved with his social and religious context and practiced "a politics of compassion," as Marcus Borg has termed it.[23] John C. Haughey has written that we tend to "pedestalize" Jesus, denying his full humanity and, for all practical purposes, setting him aside in terms of his relevance to our daily walk.[24] This is as dangerous and destructive a heresy as denying Jesus' full divinity. Rejection of Christ's full humanity was the first heresy with which the early church struggled (see 1 Cor. 12:1–3; 1 John 4:1–3).

One volume that provides a unique tonic in this regard (more fully appreciating Jesus' humanity) is Andrew Hodges's *Jesus: An Interview Across Time.* Hodges, a psychiatrist, writes an imaginative interview with

---

[23] See Marcus J. Borg, *Jesus: A New Vision: Spirit, Culture, and the Life of Discipleship* (San Francisco: Harper & Row, 1987). In many respects Borg's Christology in this volume comes the closest to a full explication of the relation between Jesus and the Spirit currently available. See also Max Turner, *Power from on High: The Spirit in Israel's Restoration and Witness in Luke-Acts* (Journal of Pentecostal Theology Supplement Series 9; Sheffield, England: Sheffield Academic Press, 1996).

[24] John C. Haughey, *The Conspiracy of God: The Holy Spirit in Us* (Garden City, N.Y.: Doubleday, 1973), esp. ch. 1, "Jesus of Nazareth and the Spirit of God," 10–37.

Jesus that brings out his humanity in a vivid way. Praised by numerous evangelical scholars of impeccable credentials, Hodges's courageous presentation would nevertheless threaten many modern docetists (those who deny Christ's complete humanity). A good example of Jesus' developing sense of his own identity is seen in Hodges's rendition of Jesus' reflections on the time when he was left in Jerusalem at twelve years of age—an important account of Jesus' boyhood that only Luke provides (Luke 2:41–52):

Jesus' humanity becomes thereby the wellspring of authentic spirituality.

> He was actually my real father. I was His only son. It seemed incredible! And as that thought kept coming back, I became more curious. These men [the scholars at the temple] who had studied my Father—what else did they know about Him? What was He like? What was He trying to do here on this earth? . . . After several more days of questioning, I began to understand what my Father was about—His complexity, the mystery of His plan. He intended to preserve justice eternally and yet simultaneously to save His people who would be destroyed by His justice.[25]

We worship Jesus Christ as our Lord and our God and as the head of the church, but we should also be inspired, instructed, and encouraged by his earthly pilgrimage. His humanity becomes thereby the wellspring of authentic spirituality.[26]

In the final analysis, as far as the New Testament witness is concerned, Jesus in part defines the Spirit, and the Spirit in part defines Jesus. Romans 8:9–11 contains a *locus classicus* illustrative of this principle:

> But you are not in the flesh; you are in the Spirit, since the Spirit of God dwells in you. Anyone who does not have the Spirit of Christ does not belong to him. But if Christ is in you, though the body is dead because of sin, the Spirit is life because of righteousness. If the Spirit of him who raised Jesus from the dead dwells in you, he who raised Christ from the dead will give life to your mortal bodies also through his Spirit that dwells in you.

Notice how the apostle here uses "the Spirit," "the Spirit of God," "the Spirit of Christ," "Christ," and "the Spirit of him who raised Jesus from

---

[25] Andrew G. Hodges, *Jesus: An Interview Across Time: A Psychiatrist Looks at HIS Humanity* (Birmingham, Ala.: Village House, 1986), 25.

[26] Haughey's *The Conspiracy of God* is a good place to begin exploring that spirituality.

the dead." To have the Spirit of Christ is to have Christ in you. Elsewhere the Holy Spirit is referred to as "the Spirit of Jesus" (Acts 16:7) and as "the Spirit of his [God's] Son" (Gal. 4:6). Jesus, as "the life-giving Spirit" (1 Cor. 15:45 GNB; see also 1 John 5:11–12), and the Holy Spirit, as "the Spirit of Christ," are not equated. But because of the unity of the Godhead, it can be said scripturally that Christ indwells us through the Holy Spirit. Jesus and the Spirit define one another.

Our filial relationship with God is based on our having the Spirit: "If a man does not possess the Spirit of Christ, he is no Christian" (Rom. 8:9 NEB). The Holy Spirit is the "Spirit that makes us sons, enabling us to cry 'Abba! Father!'" (8:15 NEB; see also Gal. 4:6). This cry, "Abba! Father!" is crucial to our further understanding of the person of Christ.

Jesus and the Father

One is at the heart of the New Testament revelation of Jesus Christ when exploring his relationship with the Father!

Perhaps no one has helped us to see Jesus' intense filial relation with the Father better than Joachim Jeremias. A number of things marked Jesus off in his uniqueness—his message of the kingdom, his use of parables, the way he used "amen" to preface important statements, and *his use of the name "Abba" to address the Father.*[27] Such intimate address of God was unquestionably revolutionary in his day—even blasphemous! It was in essence a claim to equality with God (see John 5:18). Yet Jesus taught his disciples to address God this way in prayer. (We have already noted how the Holy Spirit imparts a filial relationship to the believer with this same cry of intimacy.) Perhaps "Daddy" is the closest equivalent in our own parlance to the name "Abba." And this address "expresses the heart of Jesus' relationship to God. He spoke to God as a child to its father: confidently and securely, and yet at the same time reverently and obediently."[28] *One is at the heart of the New Testament revelation of Jesus Christ when exploring his relationship with the Father!*

We can only rightly understand God in relation to Jesus Christ, and we can only rightly understand Jesus Christ in terms of his supremely personal and intimate relationship with the Father. Our instinct—and

---

[27] Joachim Jeremias, *New Testament Theology: The Proclamation of Jesus* (New York: Charles Scribner's Sons, 1971), 29–37, 61–68.

[28] Ibid., 67.

correctly so—is to turn to the Fourth Gospel for the most complete picture of this relationship. There is in Matthew (and Luke), however, what can be called "a Johannine bolt out of the blue!"[29] Jesus asserts: "All things have been handed over to me by my Father; and no one knows the Son except the Father, and no one knows the Father except the Son and anyone to whom the Son chooses to reveal him" (Matt. 11:27; cf. Luke 10:22). Then in words of compassion and comfort Jesus issues an invitation to salvation—words that also indicate his self-awareness as the unique Son from the Father:

> Come to me, all you that are weary and are carrying heavy burdens, and I will give you rest. Take my yoke upon you, and learn from me; for I am gentle and humble in heart, and you will find rest for your souls. For my yoke is easy, and my burden is light. (Matt. 11:28–30)

To his own disciples Jesus brought similar words of comfort in his Upper Room discourses just prior to his Passion. As Jesus was preparing his disciples for his departure, Thomas asked him to tell them plainly where he was going and the way to it. To this Jesus replied: "I am the way, and the truth, and the life. No one comes to the Father except through me" (John 14:6). Jesus' ensuing words, which echo our Matthean passage above, are some of the most majestic ever to have been spoken:

> "If you know me, then you will also know my Father. From now on you do know him and have seen him." Philip said to him, "Master, show us the Father, and that will be enough for us." Jesus said to him, "Have I been with you for so long a time and you still do not know me, Philip? Whoever has seen me has seen the Father. How can you say, 'Show us the Father'? Do you not believe that I am in the Father and the Father is in me? The words that I speak to you I do not speak on my own. The Father who dwells in me is doing his works. Believe me that I am in the Father and the Father is in me, or else, believe because of the works themselves. Amen, amen, I say to you, whoever believes in me will do the works that I do, and will do greater ones than these, because I am going to the Father. And whatever you ask in my name, I will do, so that the Father may be glorified in the Son. If you ask anything of me in my name, I will do it. (John 14:7–14 NAB)

---

[29] See Karl von Hase's words, "a thunderbolt fallen from the Johannine sky" (*Die Geschichte Jesus* [Leipzig, 1876]), cited in Thomas A. Smail, *The Forgotten Father* (Grand Rapids: Eerdmans, 1980), 49. If my memory serves me, I have used Dale Moody's words—he was always colorful in the classroom setting!—to describe this Matthean passage.

How could Jesus speak more plainly? And what moving words he spoke!

Then Jesus moves to the first of what are called the Paraclete sayings and personalizes the Trinitarian relations in the life-experience of his disciples.[30] *This is Christology at its best, and it is patently revelatory and experiential!* In the first Paraclete saying (John 14:15–24) Jesus repeatedly emphasizes that love for him is demonstrated by obedience to his commandments (vv. 15, 21, 23, 24; see also 15:7, 10; 1 John 2:3–6; 3:22–24; 5:2–3). He says that he will ask the Father, who will give another Paraclete to be with the disciples forever, "the Spirit of truth" (John 14:15–17). Paraclete, translated as "Advocate" (as a lawyer), "Counselor," "Helper," "Comforter" (lit., "one called alongside to help"), is qualified as *allos,* "another of the same kind," in contrast to *heteros,* "another of a different kind." I have heard Oral Roberts say a hundred times, "The Holy Spirit is just more of Jesus." That is an excellent way to communicate what Jesus is saying here (cf. the phrases "Spirit of Jesus," "Spirit of Christ," and "Spirit of God's Son," which we examined earlier).

Through the indwelling of the Spirit, Jesus and the Father come to make their home with us.

Jesus continues in John 14:18–24 to explain how he will indwell his disciples in the future through the Holy Spirit. He speaks in Trinitarian terms with which every believer should be able to identify: "In that day you will know that I am in my Father, and you in me, and I in you. . . . He who loves me will be loved by my Father, and I will love him and manifest [reveal] myself to him. . . . And we [Jesus and the Father] will come to him and make our home with him" (vv. 20–23 RSV). Through the indwelling of the Spirit, Jesus and the Father come to make their home with us. As noted in an earlier chapter, the presence of the Spirit in us inspires two fundamental utterances in the hearts of all true believers: "Abba! Father!" (Rom. 8:15, 16; Gal. 4:6, 7) and "Jesus is Lord" (1 Cor. 12:3; see also Rom. 10:9). That is truly a Trinitarian experience of God! A cold rationalism will never be able to comprehend the Trinitarian mysteries, but a warm evangelical experience of the gospel opens one up to the glorious realities of the Holy Trinity. It is a mystery of *light* and not of darkness, revealed to us through the Christ-event.

---

30 It is difficult at this juncture not to continue to quote in full these profound, moving, and personally vital words. Summarization takes something away. The reader is encouraged to turn to John 14:15–24; 15:26–27; 16:5–15 for prayerful meditation.

In the New Testament it is John, supremely, who describes God as Father, both of Jesus and of believers. The primary way he speaks of God as Father is in relation to Jesus.[31] God's identity is largely defined in terms of this relationship. And Jesus' life and ministry are also vividly depicted in the light of this profoundly personal and intimate relationship. Excellent examples can be drawn from virtually every chapter of John's Gospel (see, e.g., John 1:1–3, 14, 18; 3:16–17, 34–35; 5:17–47; 6:22–59; 8:12–59; 10:15–39; 11:41, 42; 12:26–30; 14–17; 20:17). Jesus' relationship with the Father, as seen in John's full-orbed presentation, is one of the most powerful portions of Holy Scripture.

The apostle Paul also highlights this relationship. For example, his characteristic greeting, "Grace to you and peace from God our Father and the Lord Jesus Christ" (Rom. 1:7; 1 Cor. 1:3; 2 Cor. 1:2; Gal. 1:3; Eph. 1:2; Phil. 1:2; 2 Thess. 1:2; 1 Tim. 1:2; 2 Tim. 1:2; Titus 1:4; Philem. 3), mentions Father and Son in one breath in almost creedal fashion. And God is defined by Paul as "the God and Father of our Lord Jesus Christ" (Rom. 15:6; 2 Cor. 1:3; 11:31; Eph. 1:3; cf. Eph. 1:17; Col. 1:3). Peter uses the same words in his first letter: "Blessed be the God and Father of our Lord Jesus Christ!" (1 Peter 1:3). The God of Christian worship is the one, true, and living God—known *precisely* and *only* as *the God and Father of our Lord Jesus Christ.*

What is being alluded to repeatedly in these considerations is the immanent, ontological, or essential Trinity. Thomas Smail explains the dynamic involved here:

> What [God] does through his Son on earth reveals what he is like from eternity to eternity. His revelation in the gospel tells us the ultimate truth about God's being and nature.... The love of the Father sending, empowering, guiding, finally vindicating his Son, the love of the Son, coming, obeying, suffering, dying, are particular historical expressions of the love that eternally flows between Father and Son at the heart of the life of God. The complex of relationships between Father, Son and Spirit are not just the *means* by which God communicates with us, they are an essential part of the content of that communication. They are not just *how* he speaks, but part of *what* he says.[32]

---

[31] See Morris, *New Testament Theology*, 248–55; Leon Morris, *Jesus Is the Christ: Studies in the Theology of John* (Grand Rapids: Eerdmans, 1989), 130–35.

[32] Smail, *The Forgotten Father*, 23 (Smail's italics).

The comprehensive unity of the doctrines of biblical revelation constantly comes to mind in such considerations. But, of course, one should expect this: The unity of God implies the unity of divine revelation!

The Deity of Christ

One of the oldest extrabiblical descriptions of the early Christians (c. 112) comes to us from a letter written by Pliny the Younger, newly appointed governor of Bithynia in northern Turkey, to the Emperor Trajan. Pliny had already executed a number of Christians, but he was having second thoughts. He describes their exemplary lifestyles and faults only their refusal to worship images of the emperor or of other gods. Pliny says that "on an appointed day [Sunday] they had been accustomed to meet before daybreak, and to recite a hymn antiphonally to Christ, as to a god."[33]

> *The scandal of Christianity has been and always will be the person and work of Christ*

The scandal of Christianity has been and always will be the person and work of Christ—*that he was God incarnate and that through his death and bodily resurrection he offers the only means of salvation to humankind.* Was Jesus Christ really God? Did he claim to be God? The testimony of the Bible and of millions of Christians through the centuries is that Jesus *is* God—God the Son and the only way to the Father. Faith in him as God and Savior transforms a person's life.

John Sherrill was raised in a Christian home. His father was a well-known scholar and seminary professor, and Sherrill himself had been writing for *Guideposts* magazine for ten years. A recurrence of cancer, however, brought him face-to-face with the fundamental issue that confronts us all. Catherine Marshall invited John and his wife, Elizabeth, to her home rather urgently and surprised John with the direct question: "John, do you believe Jesus was God?" Sherrill in all honesty could not tell her yes.

---

[33] Henry Bettenson, ed., *Documents of the Christian Church,* 2d ed. (New York: Oxford Univ. Press, 1963), 3–4.

They talked for awhile about the meaning of faith, and then the Sherrills left. Catherine Marshall had urged John to take the step of faith that would bring in its wake the understanding Sherrill had sought in vain to achieve through intellect alone. To this day Sherrill can still point out the telephone pole he was driving by when moments later he turned to his wife and said: "What do they call it: 'a leap of faith'? All right, I'm going to make the leap: I believe that Christ was God." That confession of faith led to a profound encounter with Christ and an adventuresome spiritual journey that John chronicles in his classic bestseller, *They Speak with Other Tongues.*[34]

We are not dealing here simply with an intellectual puzzle, of interest only to those theologians who would just as soon debate how many angels can dance on the head of a pin. If Christ is not God, our faith is in vain, and our studies in theology are simply a philosophical pursuit with no ultimate meaning. But if he *is* God, then surely he is the most important historical figure ever to have lived. One's personal encounter with the risen Christ and one's own careful study of the biblical and historical evidences related to Christ both confirm a central fact of Christianity (and, for that matter, of all human knowledge): *Jesus Christ is God.*

But did Jesus actually think of himself as God? Could he be both God and a man at the same time? If so, what does this tell us about the nature of God himself? We naturally wonder about Christ's own beliefs concerning himself. Did Jesus himself have a Christology?

David Wells makes a helpful distinction between *self-consciousness,* which is a psychological concept, and *self-understanding,* which is an interpretation of who we are and the meaning of our lives.[35] We will never fully fathom Jesus' self-consciousness, but there are abundant biblical evidences as to Jesus' self-understanding—his stated and implied interpretation of who he was. We have already looked at a number of these in the previous discussion. It often comes down to whether we are able or willing to *accept* Jesus' claims. Even skeptical scholars such as John Knox admit this difficulty: "I, for one, simply cannot imagine a sane human being, of any historical period or culture, entertaining the thoughts about himself which the Gospels, as they stand, often attribute to

---

[34] John L. Sherrill, *They Speak with Other Tongues* (New York: McGraw-Hill, 1964), 9–16.

[35] David F. Wells, *The Person of Christ: A Biblical and Historical Analysis of the Incarnation* (Westchester, Ill.: Crossway, 1984), 36.

[Jesus]."[36] Scholars of this bent often seek to "get behind" the text by the use of literary and historical methods to find the "real" or "historical" Jesus.

It was impossible to remain neutral toward Jesus when faced with his awesome authority.

For example, some scholars have made use of *Traditionsgeschichte*—"tradition history" or traditio-historical criticism—to determine which statements of Jesus in the Gospels are authentic. However, the working principles of such methods too often beg the question. Consider, for instance, this explanation of R. H. Fuller:

> As regards the sayings of Jesus, traditio-historical criticism eliminates from the authentic sayings of Jesus those which are paralleled in the Jewish tradition on the one hand (apocalyptic and Rabbinic) and those which reflect the faith, practice and situations of the post-Easter church as we know them from outside the gospels.[37]

Fuller's statement is a precise description of traditio-historical criticism. But what an incredible method! One would assume that if Jesus was a first-century Jewish man, raised in the Jewish faith and in part addressing his own people, his sayings would reflect apocalyptic and rabbinic traditions. And if Jesus really was the founder of Christianity, then surely one should expect the faith and practice of the church he founded to reflect what he taught. This is *muddled thinking*, plain and simple.

In actuality, the New Testament documents are historically reliable as they stand. Jesus Christ really did make the implicit and explicit claims to his uniqueness and even to his divinity, as these are recorded in the New Testament.[38] As we have already seen, Jesus said and did many things that implied or demonstrated a unique prerogative reserved only for deity. Even Fuller acknowledges the clear implications of such evidences:

> An examination of Jesus' words—his proclamation of the Reign of God, and his call for decision, his enunciation of God's demand, and his teaching about the nearness of God—and of his conduct—his calling men to follow him and his healings, his eating with publicans and sinners—

[36] John Knox, *The Death of Christ* (New York: Abingdon, 1958), 58; cited in I. Howard Marshall, *The Origins of New Testament Christology* (Downers Grove, Ill.: InterVarsity Press, 1976), 43.

[37] Fuller, *The Foundations of New Testament Christology*, 18; cited in Marshall, *The Origins of New Testament Christology*, 43.

[38] Compare F. F. Bruce, *The New Testament Documents: Are They Reliable?* (Downers Grove, Ill.: InterVarsity Press, 1960).

forces upon us the conclusion that underlying his word and work is an implicit Christology. In Jesus as he understood himself, there is an immediate confrontation with "God's presence and his very self," offering judgment and salvation.[39]

It was impossible to remain neutral toward Jesus when faced with his awesome authority. As we saw in the previous chapter, Jesus always confronted his hearers with a choice, such as those listed in the Sermon on the Mount:

> The so-called six antitheses of the sermon (Matt. 5:17–48) illustrate Jesus' authority over the law of Moses: "You have heard that it was said, . . . But I say to you . . . " (see vv. 21, 27, 31, 33, 38, 43). Only careful study and thoughtful reading of such verses will yield the proper impact that they should have in our own day. From the Jewish perspective, Jesus could not have been more audacious. Jesus did not, in rabbinical fashion, appeal to external authorities, nor did he claim prophetic inspiration. He simply claimed "to know the will of God which lay behind the law," and he "claimed the right to give the authoritative interpretation": "He thus spoke as if he were God."[40]

Mark's "action" Gospel is filled with similar implicit Christology indicative of Jesus' divinity. The opening chapters alone provide numerous examples of his unique authority—an authority appropriate only to God himself. Already the scenes in the prologue (Mark 1:1–13) are of immense Christological import. John the Baptist introduces Jesus as the greater one who baptizes in the Holy Spirit (vv. 1–8). The fullness of the Godhead is manifested at Jesus' baptism (vv. 9–11). During Jesus' temptations "the angels waited on him" (vv. 12–13), and then Jesus announces the arrival of the kingdom of God (vv. 14–15).

Next we see Jesus walking by Lake Galilee and summoning the fishermen, Peter, Andrew, James, and John, to discipleship. His words, "Follow me and I will make you fish for people," still ring clearly in the twentieth century, calling us as well to discipleship (Mark 1:16–20). The people in the Capernaum synagogue "were astounded at his teaching, for he taught them as one having authority, and not as the scribes" (1:21–22). Right there in the synagogue an unclean spirit acknowledged the authority of Jesus, "the Holy One of God"; Jesus silenced the demon

---

[39] Fuller, *The Foundations of New Testament Christology*, 106; cited in Marshall, *The Origins of New Testament Christology*, 51–52.

[40] Marshall, *The Origins of New Testament Christology*, 49–50.

and cast him out with a word. Again, the people were amazed: "A new teaching—with authority! He commands even the unclean spirits, and they obey him" (1:23–28). Then at Peter's house nearby he cures Peter's mother-in-law of a fever, and that evening delivers and heals many others (1:29–34).

Soon we see Jesus choosing to heal someone of the dread disease of leprosy (Mark 1:40–45). Later, back at his home in Capernaum, the crowds have gathered in numbers beyond capacity, and a paralytic is lowered into the room through the roof. Jesus says to him, "Son, your sins are forgiven." The scribes' response is: "It is blasphemy! Who can forgive sins but God alone?" Jesus proves that "the Son of Man has authority on earth to forgive sins" by healing the paralytic: "They were all amazed and glorified God, saying, 'We have never seen anything like this!'" (2:1–12). The whole world, literally, has not "seen anything like this," before or since!

Levi responds immediately to Jesus' "Follow me," and he invites Jesus and his disciples home to have dinner with him and his friends. The scribes of the Pharisees are scandalized that Jesus has table fellowship with "tax collectors and sinners." Jesus announces himself as the "physician" for sinners: He alone is the answer to the most profound need (sin) of all us sinners (Mark 2:13–17). The next two incidents demonstrate that "the Son of Man is lord even of the sabbath" (2:23–28; 3:1–6). The crowds almost crush Jesus as they seek his teaching and healing ministry. "Whenever the unclean spirits saw him, they fell down before him and shouted, 'You are the Son of God!' But he sternly ordered them not to make him known" (3:7–12). Only one conclusion can be drawn from these events: *God, the only Son, was in the midst of humankind!* The kingdom of God was at hand!

A title we notice throughout the Gospels is the enigmatic phrase "Son of Man." Jesus, for example, referred to himself as the Son of Man who had authority to forgive sins (Mark 2:10) and who was also Lord of the Sabbath (2:28). In both of these instances Jesus is *serving* people in need. The exalted Son of Man in Daniel 7:13–14 is also one who comes to us as a humble servant—and one who comes to suffer and die for our sins as well as rise from the dead (Mark 8:31; 9:9, 31; 10:33–34). He is also the one who will one day return in eschatological glory (8:38; 13:26). Matthew and Luke evince these same emphases, and John's Gospel also portrays the Son of Man in similar terms (see, e.g.,

John 3:14–15; 5:26–27; 8:28; 12:31–36). Perhaps Jesus used this title so extensively precisely because of its vagueness. It referred clearly enough to his messianic mission without the dangerous political overtones for which the Jews in particular looked.

Traditionally, Son of Man has been used to refer to Jesus' humanity. However, as we have already seen, the title refers to much more than Jesus' role as a representative man. "The title implies more than just earthly status—it connotes supernatural origin and status as well. Accordingly, it amounts to an implicit claim to deity."[41] When one moves to the title "Son of God," however, implicit Christology gives way to *explicit* Christology.

The Son of God

In one sense, the Gentile question, "Who is this Son of Man?" (John 12:34), is answered most directly by the Roman centurion who observed Jesus' breathing his last at the crucifixion: "Truly this man was the Son of God!" (Mark 15:39 RSV). He was a complete human being ("this man"), but he was also more than a man; he was deity as well ("the Son of God"). Whether the centurion had fully in mind that day what the church later would come to associate with this title is doubtful, but he at the very least was reverently acknowledging Jesus' uniqueness and the awesome dignity of his death.

The church down to the present has highlighted the title Son of God *as its key creedal identity for Christ.*

Through several centuries of correcting heresies and hammering out orthodox doctrinal parameters, the church down to the present has highlighted the title *Son of God* as its key creedal identity for Christ.

> So much so that it is generally taken for granted, axiomatic, part of the basic definition of what Christianity is, that to confess Jesus as "the Son of God" is to confess his deity, and very easily assumed that to say "Jesus is the Son of God" means and always has meant that Jesus is the pre-existent, second person of the Trinity, who "for us men and our salvation became incarnate."[42]

---

[41] Millard J. Erickson, *The Word Became Flesh* (Grand Rapids: Baker, 1991), 19. In my opinion, Erickson's work—"A Contemporary Incarnational Christology" (from the dust cover)—is the most comprehensive and creative Christology from an evangelical (or any other) perspective to appear in recent years.

[42] James D. G. Dunn, *Christology in the Making: A New Testament Inquiry into the Origins of the Doctrine of the Incarnation* (Philadelphia: Westminster, 1980), 12–13. Unfortunately, Dunn himself is

Once again, Mark's Gospel is representative of the New Testament in general of Jesus' sense of divine sonship. Mark's opening words are: "The beginning of the good news of Jesus Christ, the Son of God" (Mark 1:1). Shortly thereafter the Father affirms about Jesus: "You are my Son, the Beloved; with you I am well pleased" (1:11). Mark further informs us, "Whenever the unclean spirits saw him [Jesus], they fell down before him and shouted, 'You are the Son of God!' But he sternly warned them not to make him known" (3:11–12). (The verb tenses in this passage indicate *repeated* action.) At Jesus' transfiguration the Father again affirms about Jesus: "This is my Son, the Beloved; listen to him!" (9:7) The disciples were not to put Jesus on the same level with even Moses or Elijah. In his prayer at Gethsemane Jesus utilizes the revealing address, "Abba, Father" (14:36). And at the close of his ministry the centurion, as we have already noted, acknowledges Jesus' uniqueness (15:39). Mark refers briefly to Jesus' temptations by the devil (1:12–13), but it is Matthew and Luke who inform us that the devil prefaced some of his temptations with the words, "If you are the Son of God" (Matt. 4:3, 6; Luke 4:3, 9).

It was in part because Jesus accepted the title of Son of God that he was condemned to death by the Jewish authorities. Caiaphas the high priest challenged Jesus: "I put you under oath before the living God, tell us if you are the Messiah, the Son of God" (Matt. 26:63). Jesus answered affirmatively and went on to identify himself as the Son of Man (26:64). For all the authorities present, this response warranted the charge that Jesus had spoken blasphemy and deserved death (26:65–66). Caiaphas put Jesus under oath before the living God, oblivious to the fact that he himself was "before" the living God incarnate!

The apostolic witness to Christ's divine sonship is strong. After his dramatic conversion and commission, the apostle Paul immediately "began to proclaim Jesus in the synagogues, saying, 'He is the Son of God'" (Acts 9:20). We have already noted how he describes "the gospel of God" as "the gospel concerning his Son" and "the gospel of his Son," and how Christ "was declared to be Son of God with power," through the Spirit of holiness, "by resurrection from the dead" (Rom. 1:1, 3–6, 9). In fact, the resurrection itself is a key witness to Christ's divinity, as we will soon note.

---

unable to see what is obvious to most other students of the New Testament—that "Son of God" in Scripture is incarnational in connotation and even denotation.

Peter made his confession, "You are the Messiah, the Son of the living God," through revelation from the Father (Matt. 16:16–17). His later exultation, "Blessed be the God and Father of our Lord Jesus Christ!" (1 Peter 1:3), is an implicit statement of Jesus' divine sonship. As the writer of Hebrews says, "in these last days, he [God] has spoken to us by his Son" (Heb. 1:2 NIV).

But it is the apostle John who utilizes the title "Son of God" most forcefully. His stated purpose in writing his Gospel is that we will believe that "Jesus is . . . the Son of God" (John 20:31). John uses this title numerous times. But "even more significant is the absolute use of the Father-Son relationship which permeates the words of Jesus in this gospel."[43] Jesus refers to God as his Father more than a hundred times, and his consciousness of divine sonship is constant in John's narratives. "This indeed is the dominant feature in John's Christology and distinguishes it from that of the synoptic gospels. . . . [It was] an 'absorbing interest' for John."[44] Earlier we noted numerous examples from John's Gospel of this profound and revealing intimacy of relationship between Jesus and the Father.[45]

There are also two distinctive ways in which John guards the uniqueness of Jesus' sonship. First, he never uses the Greek term for "son" (*huios*) to express our filial relationship to God through Christ (as does Paul, for example). Rather, he reserves the use of this term for Jesus alone.[46] The first chapter of his Gospel provides an apt illustration: John notes the poignant fact that Jesus came to his own people and they did not receive or welcome him. "But to all who received him, who believed in his name, he gave power [*exousia*, authority or right] to become children [*tekna*] of God" (John 1:11, 12; cf. 1 John 3:1; 5:2).

The second and more important way that John expresses Christ's uniqueness is in his use of the term *monogenes*. Unfortunately, the translation of this term best known to English readers of Scripture is "only begotten." However, if John had wanted to say "only begotten," he would have used the term *monogennetos*. *Monogenes* is comprised of *monos* ("one, single") and *genos* ("kind"). In other words, the term signifies "one of a

---

[43] Donald Guthrie, *New Testament Theology* (Downers Grove, Ill.: InterVarsity Press, 1981), 312.

[44] Ibid., 312.

[45] See also ibid., 313–16.

[46] See Leon Morris, *Jesus Is the Christ*, 92.

kind," "unique," "only," or, as the NIV renders it, "one and only."[47] The use of this term in other New Testament passages (e.g., Luke 7:12; 8:42; 9:38) makes it clear how one should understand this word. Perhaps Hebrews 11:17 best illustrates its significance. Isaac is referred to as Abraham's only (*monogenes*) son, when we know that Abraham had other sons (see Gen. 16:11; 25:1–6). But Isaac was Abraham's *unique* son, the son of promise.[48]

> *Jesus is the supreme revelation of God; he is literally God incarnate!*

Such key passages as John 1:14, 18; 3:16, 18 communicate authoritatively Christ's unique sonship, his deity. He is (in literal translation) "the unique one from the Father" (1:14), "the only God who is in the bosom of the Father" (1:18). In some of the best-known words ever penned, John gives majestic expression to the essence of the Church's message to the world:

> For God so loved the world that he gave his only Son, so that everyone who believes in him may not perish but may have eternal life.
>
> Indeed, God did not send the Son into the world to condemn the world, but in order that the world might be saved through him. Those who believe in him are not condemned; but those who do not believe are condemned already, because they have not believed in the name of the only Son of God. (3:16–18)

We should notice that God *sent* his Son into the world, an important concept in John's theology that implies Christ's preexistence. This preexistence is made explicit in John's prologue (1:1–18), which not only describes Jesus as the unique one (*monogenes*) but also calls him "the Word" (*logos*).

To both Jew and Greek the *Logos* was both the originator of the universe and the one who gave order to it. John uses this concept to communicate in the most exalted terms imaginable just who Jesus Christ really is. He is the preexistent divine being (both "God" and "with God," John 1:1) through whom the universe was created. He is the supreme revelation of God, and—most amazing of all!—he became flesh and

---

[47] See Dale Moody, "Only Begotten," *The Interpreter's Dictionary of the Bible* (Nashville: Abingdon Press, 1962), 3:604; idem, "God's Only Son: The Translation of John 3:16 in the Revised Standard Version," *JBL* 72 (1953): 213–19.

[48] See Morris, *Jesus Is the Christ*, 92; idem, *New Testament Theology*, 232–33; Guthrie, *New Testament Theology*, 312–13.

"tabernacled," or "pitched his tent," among us. He is literally God incarnate! Space does not permit the delightful task of a full exegesis of this crucial passage,[49] but it is one of the most important biblical attestations to the divinity of Christ. We will look next at a few other such passages.

Direct Biblical Statements of the Deity of Christ

Hebrews 1 is an excellent place to begin. In an earlier chapter we noted the revelatory dynamic of the person of Christ: "He is the reflection of God's glory and the exact imprint of God's very being, and he sustains all things by his powerful word" (Heb. 1:3). These descriptive words also point to the divinity of Christ. But further testimony is added. Christ "made purification for sins" and is now seated in authority "at the right hand of the Majesty on high" (1:3). Next, the writer of Hebrews asserts his superiority to the angels (1:4), utilizing key Old Testament texts, depicts the Father as referring to Christ as his Son, whom all the angels are commanded to worship (1:5–8).

Then the Father, using the words of Psalm 45:6–7, addresses his Son explicity as God:

> But of the Son he says,
>
> "Your throne, O God, is forever and ever,
> and the righteous scepter is the scepter of your kingdom.
> You have loved righteousness and hated wickedness;
> therefore God, your God, [or, therefore, O God, your God (cf. REB)] has anointed you
> with the oil of gladness beyond your companions." (Heb.1:8–9).

At least once, and probably twice, Christ is called God.[50] "In him, as the incarnate Son, the divine and the human meet and the Davidic kingdom becomes truly the kingdom of God."[51]

Next Christ is addressed as "Lord" and described as the eternal Creator of the universe (Heb. 1:10–12), another reference to his divinity. Finally, his authority and his superiority to the angels is again asserted (1:13–14). The thematic parallels to John's prologue are clear. As Oscar

---

[49] See Erickson, *The Word Became Flesh*, 26–27, for a useful theological summary.

[50] See Oscar Cullmann, *The Christology of the New Testament*, trans. Shirley C. Guthrie and Charles A.M. Hall, rev. ed. (Philadelphia: Westminster, 1963), 310.

[51] Philip E. Hughes, *A Commentary on the Epistle to the Hebrews* (Grand Rapids: Eerdmans, 1977), 64.

Cullmann has pointed out, the same paradox is implicit: Christ is both "God" and "with God."[52]

In addition to his prologue, John provides another direct statement of Christ's deity. Thomas exclaims, after seeing the risen Savior, "My Lord and my God!" (John 20:28). And Jesus accepts his words and his worship. Both "Lord" and "God" are ascriptions of deity. Thomas's confession confirms the prologue ("the Word was God," 1:1) and provides a fitting Christological climax similar to the centurion's words in Mark's Gospel (Mark 15:39).[53] As Erickson points out, "the disciple who had been most skeptical [of the resurrection] gives utterance to the most complete expression of conviction of the divine status of Jesus."[54] Authentic Christian faith always entails this confession of Jesus Christ: *My Lord and my God!*

Authentic Christian faith always entails this confession of Jesus Christ: My Lord and my God!

The confession of Jesus as Lord was in effect the earliest Christian creed. The first believers were often faced with a life or death choice. They could either acknowledge Caesar as divine with the confession "Lord Caesar" and thereby compromise their faith, or they could hold fast to the Christian confession—"Lord Jesus" or "Jesus is Lord"—and thereby acknowledge the deity of Christ and their allegiance to him. The latter often cost them their lives.

Paul made it clear to the Romans that salvation comes "if you confess with your mouth, 'Jesus is Lord,' and believe in your heart that God raised him from the dead.... For it is with your heart that you believe and are justified, and it is with your mouth that you confess and are saved" (Rom. 10:9–10 NIV). He made it clear to the Corinthians that this saving confession can only be made genuinely through the power of the Holy Spirit—"no one can say 'Jesus is Lord' except by [or in] the Holy Spirit" (1 Cor. 12:3).

Peter's testimony to the house of Israel was that God had raised Jesus from the dead and that, according to Psalm 110:1, Jesus was even David's Lord: "God has made him both Lord and Messiah, this Jesus whom you crucified" (Acts 2:34–36). Psalm 110:1 was one of the key Old Testament

---

[52] Cullmann, *The Christology of the New Testament*, 310–11.

[53] See F. F. Bruce, *The Gospel of John* (Grand Rapids: Eerdmans, 1983), 394.

[54] Erickson, *The Word Became Flesh*, 461.

texts used by the early believers to communicate the significance of Christ. Jesus himself used it in asking his unanswerable question to his Jewish opponents (Matt. 22:41–46; Mark 12:35–37; Luke 20:41–44).

> *It was Christ's resurrection from the dead that, more than anything else, designated Christ's divine lordship.*

But it is the early Christian hymn found in Philippians 2 that perhaps expresses the full significance of the lordship of Jesus Christ. In the process of exhorting the Philippian believers to have the same humble, servant attitude that Jesus had, the apostle uses a hymn about Christ that is perhaps "the clearest statement of who Jesus was and where he came from" to be found in the New Testament.[55] Paul writes:

> Christ was truly God.
> But he did not try to remain equal with God.
> He gave up everything and became a slave,
> when he became like one of us.
> Christ was humble.
> He obeyed God and even died on a cross.
> Then God gave Christ the highest place
> and honored his name above all others.
> So at the name of Jesus everyone will bow down,
> those in heaven, on earth, and under the earth.
> And to the glory of God the Father
> everyone will openly agree, "Jesus Christ is Lord!" (Phil. 2:6–11 CEV)

The risen Lord is the reigning Lord. He is God with us, for us, and over us. "The confession 'Jesus is Lord' ascribes to him a degree of honor that cannot be surpassed: in saying that, we say all. 'Jesus is Lord' remains the sufficient Christian confession."[56]

For Christians, Paul tells the Corinthians, "there is one God, the Father, from whom are all things and for whom we exist, and one Lord, Jesus Christ, through whom are all things and through whom we exist" (1 Cor. 8:6). To confess the lordship of Christ means also that we live according to the knowledge of his *present* divine sovereignty. Oscar Cullmann expresses this truth in the strongest terms:

> If we are really to grasp the Christology of the New Testament, we must consider the central place in the Church's life occupied by the triumphant

---

[55] Millard J. Erickson, *Does It Matter What I Believe?* (Grand Rapids: Baker, 1992), 89.

[56] Bruce, *Jesus: Lord and Savior,* 204. Bruce adds: "But it carries with it the corollary on which he himself insisted: that those who call him 'Lord' should do what he says (Luke 6:46)" (204–5).

certainty that Christ reigns now. Since his exaltation he is the only Lord and King.[57]

Ethelbert Stauffer sees "Lord" as the richest of all the Christological titles, and for good reason.[58] It is a comprehensive term that not only identifies Christ but also reminds us of his access to and sovereignty over our lives.[59] We must remind ourselves, however, that, historically speaking, it was Christ's resurrection from the dead (an unparalleled event in human history) that, more than anything else, designated Christ's divine lordship.

The Resurrection of Christ

"For to this end," Paul wrote, "Christ died and lived again, so that he might be Lord of both the dead and the living" (Rom. 14:9). Thus tying together Christ's resurrection and Christ's lordship, the apostle further demonstrates the centrality of the resurrection to both his gospel and his Christology. We have already seen how Paul views the resurrection as a declaration of Jesus as the Son of God (1:4). For Paul Christ's death and resurrection must always be held closely together. Those "who believe in him who raised Jesus our Lord from the dead" are reckoned as righteous by God; it was this Jesus "who was handed over to death for our trespasses and was raised for our justification" (4:24–25). We are reconciled to God through his death, and we are saved by his life (5:10). Our new life as believers is tied up with Christ's death and resurrection (chs. 6–8; esp. 6:4–11; 7:4; 8:34).

Paul was precise in his definition of the gospel. It was and is the message of the death, burial, resurrection, and appearances of our Lord (1 Cor. 15:3–8). And for the apostle there was no compromising the resurrection: "If Christ has not been raised, then our proclamation has been in vain and your faith has been in vain" (15:14). Without the resurrection our faith is futile, and we are still in our sins (15:17). There is no gospel and no hope without the resurrection of Christ. "Then those also who have died in Christ have perished. If for this life only we have hoped in Christ, we are of all people most to be pitied" (15:18–19). In

---

57 Cullmann, *The Christology of the New Testament*, 236.

58 Ethelbert Stauffer, *New Testament Theology*, trans. John Marsh (New York: Macmillan, 1955), 114.

59 Space does not permit treatment of numerous other New Testament passages that are (or *may* be) direct statements of Christ's divinity: Matt. 1:23; John 17:3; Rom. 9:5; Col. 2:2; 2 Thess. 1:12; 1 Tim. 1:17; Titus 2:13; James 1:1; 2 Peter 1:1; 1 John 5:20.

Christ's resurrection and in our own resurrection God graciously "gives us the victory through our Lord Jesus Christ" (15:57).

So central was the resurrection in Paul's preaching that the Athenians thought he was introducing two new deities to add to their already long list of gods: the male god, Jesus, and the goddess, *Anastasis* (Acts 17:18). Paul, Luke tells us, preached "Jesus and the resurrection," and the philosophers thought that the term resurrection (*anastasis*) was the name of a new deity!

According to the above biblical testimony and numerous other passages, the resurrection was a *validation* of Jesus' entire life, message, and ministry. It was also a *vindication* of Jesus in his righteous death on our behalf. Finally, it was a glorious *victory* over sin, death, and the devil. The objective fact of the bodily resurrection of Christ is the bedrock of New Testament faith. The tomb was empty. Many had actually seen our resurrected Lord, and his cowardly disciples had been transformed. The church with its radiant good news began to spread rapidly.

> *The resurrection sets Jesus apart from every other religious figure who has ever lived.*

It can be cogently argued, as Wolfhart Pannenberg has done, that the resurrection is the greatest evidence for the deity of Christ.[60] Unlike numerous modern theological skeptics, Pannenberg believes that there "are good and even superior reasons for claiming that the resurrection of Jesus was a historical event, and [that] consequently the risen Lord himself is a living reality."[61] In fact, Christ's resurrection is the clue to just about everything central to Christian belief. As only he can, J. I. Packer gives vivid expression to this fact:

> The Easter event . . . demonstrated Jesus' deity; validated his teaching; attested the completion of his work of atonement for sin; confirms his present cosmic dominion and his coming reappearance as Judge; assures us that his personal pardon, presence, and power in people's lives today is fact; and guarantees each believer's own reembodiment by Resurrection in the world to come. Such is the significance of Jesus' bodily Resurrection in the eyes of Christians.[62]

---

60 See Wolfhart Pannenberg, *Jesus—God and Man* (Philadelphia: Westminster, 1968).

61 Gary R. Habermas and Anthony G. N. Flew, *Did Jesus Rise from the Dead? The Resurrection Debate*, ed. Terry L. Miethe (San Francisco: Harper & Row, 1987), 134–35. (Pannenberg was a respondent to the debate between Habermas and Flew.) Habermas also states that the resurrection is "the best argument for Jesus' deity" (179–80).

62 Habermas and Flew, *Did Jesus Rise from the Dead?* 143. (Packer was also a respondent to this debate.)

The resurrection also sets Jesus apart from every other religious figure (and, for that matter, from every other *person*) who has ever lived. Christianity is unique among the religions of the world in its good news of a gracious God who pursues us to save us. Christianity is unique because its founder is unique in the history of humankind.

There are clearly many good teachings to be found among the religions of the world:

> But world religions do not contain anything which is good and true which cannot be found in Christianity. And none of them but Christianity will tell you about a God who loves you enough to die for you, to rise from the grave as a pledge of your future, and to be willing here and now to come and share your life with you. You will find nothing of that elsewhere. Islam has ninety-nine names for God, but none of them is Father. Hinduism can offer you no power of forgiveness to break the iron grip of *karma.* The Maharishi cannot come and indwell his disciples.[63]

But the risen Christ can and does indwell his disciples through the Holy Spirit. His resurrection permanently sets him apart as *the* unique one of the human race—precisely because he was more than a man.[64]

The Living Christ

In 1933, Alfred H. Ackley was attempting to share his Christian faith with a young Jewish man. The young man startled Ackley when he said, "Why should I worship a dead Jew?" to which Ackley responded immediately and spontaneously, "He lives!" After reflecting on that conversation and rereading the New Testament resurrection accounts, Alfred Ackley wrote both the words and the music to one of the classic hymns of the faith, "He Lives," which ends with these powerful words: "You ask me how I know he lives? He lives within my heart." One of the greatest evidences for the deity of Christ is the Christian experience itself! Millions upon millions of believers in every generation give personal testimony to the reality of the risen Christ in their own lives.

Jesus himself promised us in the Great Commission his continuing personal presence: "And remember, I am with you always, to the end of the age" (Matt. 28:20). Perhaps Paul of all the New Testament writers gives the most complete picture of what it means to know the contemporary

---

[63] Michael Green, *The Empty Cross of Jesus* (Downers Grove, Ill.: InterVarsity Press, 1984), 129.

[64] See Russell F. Aldwinckle, *More Than Man: A Study in Christology* (Grand Rapids: Eerdmans, 1976); see also Erickson, *The Word Became Flesh,* 481–82.

Christ, the Christ of faith, the living Christ who indwells every true believer (Rom. 8:9; 1 Cor. 15:45). Scholars often call this Paul's Christ-mysticism, which is perfectly acceptable if one rightly defines mysticism. Too often, however, what should be considered normal Christian experience is bracketed off as "mysticism," understood as a sort of irrelevant spiritual navel-gazing. Generally, the theological extremes of both the right and the left level this criticism in their imbalanced rationalism. Nevertheless, healthy Christian faith and practice has always evinced a vital blend of heart religion and head religion.

In marked contrast to some contemporary theologians, Paul identified the Jesus of history with the Christ of faith. Prior to his conversion, Paul did "many things against the name of Jesus of Nazareth" (Acts 26:9). But when on the Damascus Road he asked, "Who are you, Lord?" the reply was, "I am Jesus of Nazareth whom you are persecuting" (22:8). Unlike the Twelve, Paul never knew Jesus intimately during his earthly ministry. However, Paul never once indicates that the one with whom he had such a personal walk was anyone other than that same Jesus of Nazareth. He wrote to the Galatians: "I have been crucified with Christ and yet I am alive; yet it is no longer I, but Christ living in me" (Gal. 2:19, 20 NJB).[65] He then adds: "And the life I now live in the flesh I live by faith in the Son of God, who loved me and gave himself for me" (2:20).

How did Paul come to the place where he perceived Jesus, the Son of God, dying personally for him? He did it the same way that we do today! He had a personal encounter with him who is both God and human: Jesus Christ. Here was the apostle's passion: "I want to know Christ and the power of his resurrection and the sharing of his sufferings by becoming like him in his death, if somehow I may attain the resurrection from the dead" (Phil. 3:10–11). He went on to comfort the Philippians with these words: "The Lord is near. Do not worry about anything" (4:5). Paul was also energized for ministry through the indwelling Christ: "For I will not venture to speak of anything except what Christ has accomplished through me to win obedience from the Gentiles, by word and deed, by the power of signs and wonders, by the power of the Spirit of God" (Rom. 15:18–19).[66]

---

[65] This is actually a more literal rendering of the Greek than the more traditional and still excellent translation: "I have been crucified with Christ; and it is no longer I who live, but it is Christ who lives in me."

[66] See Bruce, *Jesus: Lord and Savior,* 147–55.

The first disciples may have encountered the Jesus of history first and then gone on to know the resurrected and ascended Christ of glory (again, one and the same person). But we now first encounter the heavenly Christ as God himself and then learn more about the "days of his flesh" through the New Testament. This fact alone forms the rationale for the methodology we are using, beginning with the deity of Christ and then turning to consider his humanity.

The Humanity of Christ

It is just as crucial to our salvation to believe in the complete humanity of Christ as it is to believe in his divinity. In fact, the first heresy the church had to confront was this very denial of Christ's full humanity (see 1 John 4:1–3; cf. 1 Cor. 12:1–3).[67] Jesus Christ was a first-century Jewish man. He was *a man,* not just "Man." The mystery, miracle, and meaning of the Incarnation is that Jesus was both a complete human being and at the same time the eternal Son of God.

It is just as crucial to our salvation to believe in the complete humanity of Christ as it is to believe in his divinity.

John provides us with a vivid illustration of this truth in one of Jesus' controversies with the Jewish leaders. Jesus declared himself to be "the light of the world" (John 8:12) and goes on repeatedly to refer to his uniqueness and to his unparalleled relation to the Father (8:12, 16, 19, 23, 26, 29, 42, 51). He alludes to his preexistence (8:38) as the one "sent" by the Father (8:16, 26, 29, 42) and even declares his sinlessness (8:46). But the most scandalous thing that Jesus said in this exchange—words that prompted his opponents to pick up stones to execute him on the charge of blasphemy (8:59)—was: "Amen, amen, I say to you, before Abraham came to be, I AM" (8:58 NAB). Jesus was declaring himself to be the Yahweh of Exodus 3:14–15! At the same time, he refers in a matter-of-fact way to his complete humanity as well: "but now you are trying to kill me, a man who has told you the truth that I heard from God" (8:40). In this one dramatic conversation

---

[67] See, e.g., James D. G. Dunn, *Jesus and the Spirit* (London: SCM, 1975), 234–35.

we hear Jesus himself giving explicit testimony to both his divinity and humanity.

Even though John's writings give the most explicit portrayal of Christ's divinity, they also provide strong testimony to his humanity. Christ is the preexistent Word, to be sure (John 1:1–5), but he is also the Word who "became flesh and lived among us" (1:14). The "Word of life," asserts John, is something "which we have heard, which we have seen with our own eyes, which we have watched and touched with our own hands" (1 John 1:1 NJB). This crassly physical description would have scandalized the heretics of John's day, who could not countenance the concept of the enfleshment of the Word of God. But John's Jesus gets tired (John 4:6) and thirsty (4:7; 19:28). He shows great emotion—at Lazarus' tomb, for example (11:33–38). And he dies a real death (19:34). John's Jesus is as far from the gods of Greek mythology as the east is from the west. Jesus' humanity is real and complete; it is no disguise.

Jesus' temptations were real. Nevertheless, he never gave in to temptation

The Jesus of the New Testament was born like any other child. (We will consider his miraculous conception in the virgin Mary's womb later.) He had a lineage as does everyone else (Matt. 1:1–17; Luke 3:23–38; cf. Rom. 1:3). He grew and developed as a child (Luke 2:40, 52). He experienced physical hunger (Matt. 4:2; 21:18). He had an authentic religious life of prayer, worship, and trust. He had limited knowledge as does any human being (Mark 9:21; 13:32). At the same time, through the power of the Holy Spirit—with wisdom, knowledge, and discernment like those gifts distributed by the Holy Spirit to the church (1 Cor. 12:8–10)—Jesus demonstrated amazing knowledge and insight (Luke 6:8; 9:47; John 1:47, 48; 2:25; 4:18, 29).

Unlike us, Jesus never made an error in statement, action, or judgment (2 Cor. 5:21; Heb. 4:15; 1 Peter 2:22). In addition, without original or actual sin, Jesus possessed an exceptional mental, emotional, and physical health. His temptations were real—and even more intense because of his perfection in moral character. Nevertheless, Jesus never gave in to temptation, and because of who he was, it was impossible for him to sin.[68] He was everything anyone would ever hope to be as a per-

[68] Could Jesus have sinned? Because the Incarnation itself is paradoxical, the answer to this question must also, of necessity, be paradoxical. Jesus' temptations were real, and he theoretically

son. He was both glorious deity and perfect humanity. He is both potentate and paradigm. He is totally unlike us, and yet precisely like us in his full humanity. He is the model of our new humanity! He is the incomparable Christ![69]

In hymnic form Paul communicates majestically the meaning of the incarnate Son of God. For

> there is one God
> and one mediator between God and humankind,
> the man Christ Jesus,
> who gave himself a ransom for all. (1 Tim. 2:5, author's trans.)

Paul soars back and forth between earth and heaven to tell the gospel story about Jesus:

> He was manifested in the flesh [earth],
> vindicated in the Spirit [heaven],
> seen by angels [heaven],
> preached among the nations [earth],
> believed on in the world [earth],
> taken up in glory [heaven] (1 Tim. 3:16 RSV).

The appropriate response to such beautiful hymns is the Hebrew term *Hallelujah!*

Affirming the humanity of Christ entails affirming his historicity. Since the Enlightenment, various "quests" for the historical Jesus have emerged with the intent of getting at the Jesus *behind* the Gospels—a portrait based on solid historical investigation. The concept seems noble enough. But, as Robert H. Stein has observed, where we *start* determines where we *end up* in such a quest.[70] Beginning with the assumption that the Gospels are faith documents with questionable historical reliability results in a portrait of Christ quite different from the traditional views based on the Gospels as they stand. In other words, the "Jesus of history" differs significantly from the "Christ of faith" in this approach.

---

could have sinned because he was a human being. At the same time, we must say that he *would not* have ever sinned because he was also God. We must remember that the Incarnation is *God's* act of taking on human nature (Augustine). Also, a question is raised by the *continuing* incarnation in Jesus' (albeit glorified) postexistence. Is he still subject to temptation? Surely he is not.

69 See also Leon Morris, *The Lord from Heaven* (Downers Grove, Ill.: InterVarsity Press, 1974), 42–54; Erickson, *Christian Theology*, 705–22.

70 Robert H. Stein, *Jesus the Messiah: A Survey of the Life of Christ* (Downers Grove, Ill.: InterVarsity Press, 1996), 17.

Timothy Luke Johnson warns us that such quests are generally misguided and unfruitful—that the "real" Jesus is precisely the Christ whom we know by faith and through the Scriptures. Johnson shows us the limits of historical study.[71] N. T. Wright, by contrast, argues strongly that it is imperative to root Jesus Christ solidly in history by means of careful historical investigation precisely because the biblical revelation of Jesus is patently *historical* revelation.[72] Johnson's view (similar to that of Martin Kähler in the nineteenth century) could leave the door wide open to the postmodern gnostic and New Age ideologies of our day, while Wright's approach could make the average believer dependent on the often tentative and contradictory conclusions of the historians and theologians. Careful scholars like Paul Barnett and Darrell L. Bock have bridged this gap, combining full commitment to biblical authority and careful historical research.[73]

Such debate and scholarly endeavor is essential in our times because spurious, yet popular, enterprises such as the Jesus Seminar have largely sought to discredit the Christology of the New Testament with the "assured results" of their research, based on a naturalistic methodology. This gangrenous unsound doctrine needs to be countered by sound doctrine that nourishes Christian faith and life. Further, the Christ of the Gospels must be proclaimed in all his natural and supernatural grandeur to a world hungering for the Bread of Life.[74]

Savior *emerges in the New Testament as perhaps* the *comprehensive title for the person and work of Christ.*

[71] See Timothy Luke Johnson, *The Real Jesus* (San Francisco: HarperSanFrancisco, 1996); idem, *Living Jesus* (San Francisco: HarperSanFrancisco, 1999).

[72] See, e.g., N. T. Wright, *Jesus and the Victory of God* (Minneapolis: Fortress, 1996); idem, *The Challenge of Jesus: Rediscovering Who Jesus Was and Is* (Downers Grove, Ill.: InterVarsity Press,1999).

[73] Paul Barnett, *Jesus and the Rise of Early Christianity* (Downers Grove, Ill.: InterVarsity Press, 1999); Darrell L. Bock, *Jesus according to Scripture: Restoring the Portrait from the Gospels* (Grand Rapids: Baker, 2002).

[74] See Ben Witherington III, *The Jesus Quest: The Third Quest for the Jew of Nazareth*, 2d ed. (Downers Grove, Ill.: InterVarsity Press, 1997); Jeffery L. Sheler, *Is the Bible True?* (San Francisco: HarperSanFrancisco/Zondervan, 1999), 173–92; Hans Schwarz, *Christology* (Grand Rapids: Eerdmans, 1998), 7–71; Veli-Matti Kärkkäinen, *Christology: A Global Introduction* (Grand Rapids: Baker, 2003), 85–108; James D. G. Dunn, *Jesus Remembered* (Christianity in the Making 1; Grand Rapids: Eerdmans, 2003), 11–136; Michael J. Wilkins and J. P. Moreland, *Jesus Under Fire: Modern Scholarship Reinvents the Historical Jesus* (Grand Rapids: Zondervan, 1995).

The Savior of the World

The Samaritans of Sychar said of Jesus, "We have heard for ourselves, and we know that this is truly the Savior of the world" (John 4:42). Similarly, John wrote, "And we have seen and do testify that the Father has sent his Son as the Savior of the world" (1 John 4:14). An angel of the Lord instructed Joseph to name the child Mary had conceived by the power of the Holy Spirit "Jesus, for he will save his people from their sins" (Matt. 1:21). "Jesus" (*Iesous*) is the Greek form of the Hebrew name Joshua, which means "Yahweh saves." An angel of the Lord told the shepherds, "Do not be afraid; for see—I am bringing you good news of great joy for all the people: to you is born this day in the city of David a Savior, who is the Messiah, the Lord" (Luke 2:10–11).

The title "the Savior of the world" helps us to understand the *unity* in our Christology. This title reminds us of two things: (1) the unity of the *person* of Christ in his humanity and his divinity, and (2) the unity of the *person* and the *work* of Christ. To call Jesus *Savior* is to acknowledge who he is (the divine-human Redeemer of humankind) and what he has done (delivered or rescued us from our sinful plight).

The Old Testament Scriptures refer often to God as Savior (see, e.g., Ps. 106:21; Isa. 43:11; 45:2). In the New Testament era the term was often applied to pagan deities and even to rulers. The New Testament itself, drawing from its Old Testament heritage, depicts the unity of God and Jesus in bringing forth salvation for humankind. Both are referred to as Savior—Jesus more often than the Father. And *Savior* emerges in the New Testament as perhaps *the* comprehensive title for the person and work of Christ.

Having grown up in the evangelical tradition, I have noticed that one of our favorite ways of referring to Jesus is as "our Lord and Savior Jesus Christ" (2 Peter 1:11; 2:20; 3:18). This is appropriate for a group that emphasizes the proclamation of the saving message of Jesus Christ. Furthermore, I have noticed that evangelicals refer to Jesus more as "Christ," while charismatics simply say "Jesus"—the former connoting Jesus' exalted state and the latter his "down-to-earth" personal intimacy. Both emphases are important, and this is another way in which Christians can balance out one another.

A number of emphases emerge as we examine the saving work of Christ. First, he is depicted as the Savior of the *world.* John the Baptist declared of him: "Here is the Lamb of God who takes away the sin of the world!" (John 1:29). "Indeed," we are told, "God did not send the Son into the world to condemn the world, but in order that the world might be saved through him" (3:17; cf. v. 16, perhaps the best-known verse of Scripture, beginning "for God so loved the world"). Later Jesus said: "I came not to judge the world, but to save the world" (12:47). Such statements in John's Gospel are all the more remarkable in view of the fact that, in John, the term "world" (*kosmos*) generally refers to the sinful world system set against God and his righteous purposes. In his first letter John assures believers, "But if anyone does sin, we have an advocate with the Father, Jesus Christ the righteous; and he is the atoning sacrifice for our sins, and not for ours only but also for the sins of the whole world" (1 John 2:1–2).

"Here is a saying," writes Paul, "that you can rely on and nobody should doubt: that Christ Jesus came into the world to save sinners" (1 Tim. 1:15 NJB). New Testament scholar Gordon D. Fee has concluded that this was probably a well-known saying that went back to Jesus himself (Luke 19:10; cf. John 12:46; 18:37). In the saying, "two points are made: Incarnation and Redemption, with the emphasis on the latter."[75] Again, Christ's saviorhood encompasses both his person and his work. Jesus himself summed up his ministry in terms of his saving work: "For the Son of Man came to seek out and to save the lost" (Luke 19:10). Paul says that God's grace "has now been revealed through the appearing of our Savior Christ Jesus, who abolished death and brought life and immortality to light through the gospel" (2 Tim. 1:10; cf. 2:10; Titus 1:4; 3:4–8).

If Jesus Christ is less than God or less than human, then he cannot be our Savior.

Jesus Christ is also presented as the Savior of *Israel.* Peter and the apostles testified before the Jewish council in Jerusalem that God had exalted Jesus "at his right hand as Leader and Savior that he might give repentance to Israel and forgiveness of sins" (Acts 5:31). Paul announced to the synagogue at Antioch of Pisidia that of David's posterity "God has brought forth to Israel a Savior, Jesus, as he promised" (13:23). Jesus in his ministry initially focused on the house of Israel, as did Paul—"to the Jew first and also to the Greek" (Rom. 1:16).

[75] Gordon D. Fee, *1 and 2 Timothy* (NIBC; Peabody, Mass.: Hendrickson, 1988), 52–53.

Paul also highlights Jesus' saving relation to the *church*. He asserts that "Christ is the head of the church, the body of which he is the Savior" (Eph. 5:23).

Peter mentions the *kingdom* in relation to Christ's work as Savior: "For in this way, entry into the eternal kingdom of our Lord and Savior Jesus Christ will be richly provided for you" (2 Peter 1:11).

Both the divinity and humanity of Christ are included in his saviorhood. He is the *preexistent* Son sent by the Father to be the Savior of the world (1 John 4:14). He is also the *ascended* and *exalted* Christ, whose return from heaven we await: "We are expecting a Savior, the Lord Jesus Christ" (Phil. 3:20); "we wait for the blessed hope and the manifestation of the glory of our great God and Savior, Jesus Christ" (Titus 2:13). At the same time, he is "Jesus Christ of Nazareth," who was crucified, but "whom God raised from the dead.... There is salvation in no one else, for there is no other name under heaven given among mortals by which we must be saved" (Acts 4:10–12). Christ in the *unity* of his divine/human personhood is our Savior!

If Jesus Christ is less than God or less than human, then he cannot be our Savior. But Jesus is also *one* person. He is either a *miracle* or a *monster*. He is either the divine-human Savior who both entered (virginal conception) and exited (bodily resurrection and ascension) this world in a supernatural manner,[76] or he is a monster who was neither God nor human or was two persons in one body. The Bible portrays him as the supernaturally natural and naturally supernatural God-man, Jesus Christ of Nazareth, the Son of the living God.[77] The Christological debates of the patristic era (the first five centuries of the church's history) reveal how difficult it was for believers to hold faithfully to this admittedly impossible intellectual puzzle: How could Jesus be God and there still be only one God? How could Jesus be completely God and completely a man at the same time? And if so, how could he be one person? The human intellect always wants to dissolve such tensions, but we do so only at the expense of our own spiritual peril.

---

[76] J. I. Packer, *Concise Theology* (Wheaton, Ill.: Tyndale, 1993), 112.

[77] I owe the delightful phrase "supernaturally natural and naturally supernatural" to Oral Roberts, who uses these words to describe God's goal for us as Spirit-filled Christians. God desires for us to be naturally supernatural through the power of the Spirit and, at the same time, supernaturally natural as persons whose humanity is being made whole and complete through the indwelling Spirit of Christ. We are not meant to be "spooks," in some super-spiritual spirituality that is foreign to the New Testament. Neither was Jesus Christ a "spook." Otherwise, how would children have ever been attracted to him?

Let us, then, turn to a brief consideration to the heresies that emerged quite early in the church's history and that find expression today both at the grass roots level and in the often arid heights of modern theology. There are, it turns out, six basic distortions of the biblical picture of the person of Christ that require correction. Logically speaking, they are patently predictable. Our finite, plodding intellects so easily distort God's liberating truth!

Six Heresies

Heresy is not a popular term these days, and the Lord knows we don't need any more heresy hunters in America. Such self-appointed prophets and judges, with their destructive witch-hunts, tar everyone with their "New Age" accusations and tear apart institutions and individuals. Nonetheless, heresy, defined as a departure from the teachings of Scripture and the basic historical consensus of the church (in the creeds and councils), is still a useful concept.

"The history of Christian theology is in large part a history of heresies because Jesus and the claims he made, as well as the claims his disciples made about him, seemed to be incredible."[78] This statement from Harold O. J. Brown's excellent survey of historical theology in relation primarily to Christological heresy, puts the challenge of orthodoxy in its most judicious and constructive light. It would be a fascinating study to explore the drama, pathos, and even humor of the pageant of patristic theological developments, but time does not permit. We will simply note the key disputes, at times bypassing interesting historical developments beyond the purview of this volume. The six heresies we will mention relate to the deity, humanity, unity, and two natures of the person of Christ.

Ebionism

Because the doctrine of the Incarnation is an offense to reason, it is easy to anticipate departures from it. Some of the earliest believers looked back to the Judaism from which most of them had come. Here is an example where conservatism can be as great a danger as a more progressive mentality. Paul was considered a radical by many because of his break with pharisaical legalism. Early on advocates of a Judaistic Christianity that absolutized such things as circumcision as a requirement for

[78] Harold O. J. Brown, *Heresies: The Image of Christ in the Mirror of Heresy and Orthodoxy from the Apostles to the Present* (Garden City, N.Y.: Doubleday, 1984), xxiii.

salvation opposed him. Paul stood his ground in the defense of the gospel, and the Galatians documents this struggle as well as explains the freedom of the gospel. There were even tensions between the apostle and the Jerusalem stalwarts Peter and James (the Lord's brother).[79] Paul almost single-handedly saved Christianity from being a mere sect of Judaism rather than a worldwide faith that has transformed the lives of millions!

These Judaizers were the forerunners of a diversified movement that we know today as *Ebionism.* The origin of the name Ebionism is uncertain, but the heretical tendency of the movement is clear: It is a "low Christology" in which Christ is seen as a mere man whom God "adopted" either at his birth or his baptism. Jesus was the product of the marital union of Mary and Joseph, not a virginal conception. The Christ who descended on Jesus at his baptism (or birth) withdrew from him toward the end of his life. Jesus was an exceptional man of wisdom and righteousness, but he was not deity. The tension between Jewish monotheism and Christian belief in the divinity of Christ was alleviated, but (the church ultimately concluded) at too great a price. Adoptionistic Christologies persist to this day in the church's more liberal traditions.

Docetism

Another heresy, however, became an even greater threat to orthodoxy. *Docetism,* "more a broad cultural trend than a specific movement,"[80] espoused a misleading "high Christology" that denied the humanity of Christ. Attuned to a prevailing worldview that saw the material dimension as innately evil, Docetism (from the Greek *dokeo,* meaning "to seem, appear") rejected the incarnation and sufferings of Christ. We have already seen how Paul and John had to deal with this heretical trend in their churches. In the full-blown Gnostic Christianity that emerged, an alternative message of salvation rivaled the authentic gospel of Jesus Christ.

> *During the first two centuries of the church's life John's Logos Christology set the pattern for orthodoxy.*

Gnosticism as a syncretistic religious movement simply wanted to "add" Jesus into a spurious super-spiritual message of

---

[79] See Gal. 1–2.

[80] Erickson, *The Word Became Flesh,* 47.

redemption through *gnosis*—a knowledge or revelation that provided a final escape from the evil material world. The watchword was *soma sema,* "the body is a tomb." In contrast to the biblical doctrine of a cosmic redemption, which included the resurrection of the body, salvation from the gnostic perspective was an *escape* from the physical body, considered innately evil. From such a perspective, the idea of incarnation was repulsive. Christ was a Savior only in terms of providing the *gnosis* required for liberation from the evil material world.

Docetism can also be found in the teachings of the first great heretic of the church, Marcion, who died around 160. Whereas the gnostic teachers simply spread their heresies among any whom they could attract, Marcion, being a great organizer, founded a rival church that provided stiff competition to orthodoxy. Marcion's false teachings and his collection of a primitive canon of Scripture (comprised of ten of Paul's letters and an edited version of Luke's Gospel—he rejected the Old Testament in total) further drove the church toward developing creedal statements, theological precision, institutional development, and an authoritative canon. The docetic Christology Marcion taught was bizarre. Jesus simply appeared full-grown, teaching in the synagogue in Capernaum. His was an angelic sort of body, since a material body would have entailed both physical and moral corruption. It is important that theological conservatives remember that denial of the full humanity of Christ is just as spiritually and theologically dangerous as rejection of the full divinity of Christ.

Arianism

During the first two centuries of the church's life John's Logos Christology set the pattern for orthodoxy. However, the inevitable question as to the relation between Jesus and the Father was inescapable. This was really a Trinitarian question. If God is one and Jesus is God and Jesus is other than the Father, then how can there actually be one God? One could anticipate that controversy would soon emerge concerning these puzzling implications of Logos Christology. The so-called Alogi or Alogoi were the first to voice opposition. As the name implies, this group rejected Logos Christology. But it was Monarchianism that would present the strongest challenge.

Monarchianism sought to guard the oneness of God in favor of a strict monotheism. One form, Dynamic Monarchianism (Adoptionism), maintained that Jesus was a man endowed with divine power, adopted by God at his birth or baptism to be our Savior. This was Ebionism revisited. The other form, Modalistic Monarchianism, denied that Jesus was other than the Father. Also named Sabellianism, after one Sabellius (a third-century heretic), this teaching depicts God as having three names or roles. Father, Son, and Spirit are really three ways of referring to one person. First God manifested himself in the mode (*prosopon*) of Father, Creator, and Lawgiver. Then he came to us as Son, the Redeemer. Finally, he returned as Spirit, Lifegiver. God is one person manifesting himself in three ways. Both of these approaches eased the intellectual tension of the doctrine of the Trinity, but they also compromised its saving truth.

All these debates formed the backdrop for the heresy that more than any other threatened to destroy the church: *Arianism.* Arius (c. 256–336), a presbyter of the church in Alexandria, developed a nuanced and sophisticated—albeit heretical—theology that threatened to win the day, had it not been for one of the truly heroic theologians in the history of the Christian church: Athanasius (c. 296–373). Arius saw the uniqueness and transcendence of the Father in the starkest terms. Nothing and no one could share his essence and attributes, including the Son, Jesus. God created Jesus first and then through him the rest of the universe. Jesus shared the essence of neither God nor humankind. He was a sort of *tertium quid* ("a third something"), through whom God created and redeemed us.

Because Arius could be persuasive in his appeal to the Scriptures—texts noting the limitations of Christ through the Incarnation and the like—and because he could speak of Jesus in such exalted terms and in such a worshipful tone, still maintaining that Jesus is our Savior, many were tolerant of his view or even embraced it. Athanasius, however, saw the devastating implications of Arius's heresy. Not only did it contradict the scriptural witness to Christ, but it also vitiated the Church's message of salvation. At times Athanasius stood virtually alone in his defense of the faith, but in the end the church—guided by the Holy Spirit, no doubt—held true to the gospel. The Council of Nicea in 325, the first ecumenical council, and later the Council of Constantinople in 381 categorically rejected Arianism.

Arius had said that Christ was of a completely different essence from the Father (*heterousios*). The church fathers maintained that Jesus was "of one substance [*homoousios*] with the Father" (see the Nicene Creed). Perhaps Arius is best known for the heretical statement, "there was a time when he [Christ] was not." The Church officially condemned this doctrine and numerous other related teachings. This was one of the most dramatic periods in the history of the Church, but in the end the truth of God prevailed.

Apollinarianism

The Christological battles were not over, however. The next question raised was with regard to the relation of the divine and human natures of Christ. Nicea had authoritatively established that Jesus was fully God and fully human. For the next several centuries the church debated the precise character of the relation of the divine and human in the person of Christ. As both God and human, how could Jesus Christ still be *one* person? Apollinarius (c. 310–390) was the first church leader to deal decisively with this question. Unfortunately, he took an errant path, which we know as *Apollinarianism* today.

Apollinarius, a presbyter and teacher of the church at Laodicea, was an ardent supporter of Athanasius. Wanting to end Arianism once and for all, Apollinarius devised an explanation of the union of the divine and human in Christ that combined the traditional Greek trichotomy of human nature with the Logos Christology that had served the church so well. In Greek thought a human being was composed of flesh (a physical body), an animal soul (animating or human), and a rational soul (spirit, reason, or mind). According to Apollinarius, Jesus had a human body and soul, but not a human spirit or reason (or mind). Since reason was considered by many as a source of sin in humankind, Apollinarius suggested that the divine Logos replaced Jesus' mind (or spirit). The human and divine were merged in an organic union into one nature.

This schema was an ingenious way of arguing for both the deity of Christ and the unity of his person. Unfortunately, Apollinarius made the same mistake as Arius. Jesus becomes a *tertium quid* with this understanding of his humanity and divinity. Whereas Arianism "made Jesus more than human, but less than fully God, or in other words a demigod,"[81] Apollinarianism made Jesus less than human. The Council of Constantinople (381) rightly condemned both.

Nestorianism

My background as a Southern Baptist helps me more fully to appreciate the story surrounding the emergence of the next heresy: *Nestori-*

---

[81] Erickson, *The Word Became Flesh*, 58.

anism. Like the Southern Baptists in the twentieth century, the church of the fifth century was as much influenced by ecclesiastical politics as it was by doctrinal controversy. Bitter rivalry and political maneuvering were more dominant in the contention surrounding Nestorius (c. 380–451) than any theological precision. Ironically, Nestorius, an ardent heresy hunter in his own right, was condemned—almost certainly unjustly—as a heretic himself.

From a purely theological perspective we are dealing simply with the inability of the finite human intellect to comprehend fully the mysteries and paradoxes of the faith. For example, Western Christianity, as we have already seen, has always had the tendency to begin with the oneness of God and move to his threeness. Eastern Christianity, by contrast, has tended to begin with the threeness of God and move to his oneness. Both approaches are clearly within the parameters of orthodoxy, although the West has often been depicted as modalistic and the East as tritheistic. The same is true in relation to the mystery of the two natures of Christ.

During the late patristic period (the fourth and fifth centuries), two major schools of thought emerged—one centered in Alexandria and the other in Antioch—whose theological approaches sharply differed. Under the influence of Platonic thought, Alexandria was noted for a sharp differentiation between God and creation, allegorical interpretation of Scripture, and a "high Christology" that stressed the deity of Christ in what has been called a Word/flesh concept. In this orientation the human soul of Christ recedes into the background, and the Logos is seen as the primary actor in the Incarnation. The unity of the person of Christ was thus guarded. At the same time, the tendencies of Arianism and Apollinarianism emerged from this conceptualization. Athanasius provided the orthodox expression of the person of Christ from this vantage point.

In contrast, Antioch was known for its grammatical/historical interpretation of Scripture from an Aristotelian perspective and for a stress on the full humanity of Christ. A Word/man Christology typified this school of thought. The importance of the complete human psychological makeup of Christ was highlighted. Theodore of Mopsuestia (c. 350–428; affectionately known as "Teddy the Mop" by many a seminarian!) provided an excellent, though somewhat incomplete, expression of Christology from this perspective.

Nestorius, perhaps one of Theodore's students, got himself into trouble when, as the newly appointed patriarch of Constantinople (in 428), he questioned the unqualified use of the popular description of Mary as *theotokos,* "the God-bearer." Troubled by the obvious connotation of Mary's being God's mother, Nestorius suggested accompanying the term with the additional description *anthropotokos,* "the man-bearer," or even better to refer to Mary as simply *Christokos,* "the Christ-bearer." In addition, Nestorius's Christology put such a stress on the complete humanity, understood as being in "conjunction" with the divine nature, that many thought he was describing "two sons."

Ultimately, Nestorianism—understanding Jesus as two distinct persons, the Son of God indwelling the man, Jesus of Nazareth—was condemned by the Council of Ephesus (431). Nestorius was exiled for espousing a heresy named after him but which he never personally believed. His manner of expression at times seemed to imply two persons in Christ, but there is reason to believe that Nestorius was actually orthodox in his Christology—perhaps more so than his opponent, Cyril of Alexandria, who politically maneuvered him into exile.

Eutychianism

Eutychianism was a heresy named for a person whose precise views are also uncertain. Eutyches (c. 375–454) taught that Jesus had two natures before his incarnation but only one afterward. Whether he made Jesus a hybrid or simply believed that the divine nature "swallowed up" the human nature is uncertain. In any case, the church ultimately recognized that the authentic biblical picture of Christ was being distorted and officially condemned this heresy. Later, Monophysitism continued this one-nature heresy, and Monothelitism, which asserted that Christ had only one will (whereas two natures require two wills—albeit with the human will in complete submission to the divine), would also emerge. Both of these distortions were officially condemned by the church.

These six heresies challenged strongly the church's faithful stand for the gospel and have continued to recur perennially down through history. Ebionism flatly denied the deity of Christ. Docetism jettisoned Christ's humanity. Jesus' deity was incomplete in Arianism. His humanity was incomplete in Apollinarianism. In Nestorianism Jesus was portrayed as two persons; the unity of his one person was compromised.

Jesus' divine and human natures were blended into one in Eutychianism.[82] The touchstone for orthodoxy in relation to Christology in the final analysis became the formula which was developed at the Council of Chalcedon (451).

The Chalcedonian Formula

In the definition of Chalcedon, it turns out, the parameters for Christological orthodoxy were laid out for all subsequent generations of believers. This was more of a statement of guidelines, outside of which one is sure to stray from the biblical picture of Christ, than it was a creative statement. Nevertheless, because of its normative value, majestic tone, and precise wording, it merits full citation here:

> *Jesus is fully God and fully human, one person with two natures. What a wonderful Savior!*

> Therefore, following the holy Fathers, we all with one accord teach men to acknowledge one and the same Son, our Lord Jesus Christ, at once complete in Godhead and complete in manhood, truly God and truly man, consisting also of a reasonable soul and body; of one substance [*homoousios*] with the Father as regards his Godhead, and at the same time of one substance with us as regards his manhood; like us in all respects, apart from sin; as regards his Godhead, begotten of the Father before the ages, but yet as regards his manhood begotten, for us men and for our salvation, of Mary the Virgin, the God-bearer [*theotokos*]; one and the same Christ, Son, Lord, Only-begotten, recognized IN TWO NATURES, WITHOUT CONFUSION, WITHOUT CHANGE, WITHOUT DIVISION, WITHOUT SEPARATION; the distinction of natures being in no way annulled by the union, but rather the characteristics of each nature being preserved and coming together to form one person and subsistence [*hypostasis*], not as parted or separated into two persons, but one and the same Son and Only-begotten God the Word, Lord Jesus Christ; even as the prophets from earliest times spoke of him, and our Lord Jesus Christ himself taught us, and the creed of the Fathers has handed down to us.[83]

---

[82] See Millard J. Erickson, *Introducing Christian Doctrine*, ed. L. Arnold Hustad (Grand Rapids: Baker, 1992), 230, for a helpful schematic presentation of these heresies regarding the person of Christ.

[83] See Bettenson, ed., *Documents of the Christian Church*, 51–52.

Jesus is fully God and fully human, one person with two natures. This is the inescapable conclusion that must be drawn from all the evidence. What a wonderful Savior!

With our limited intellects we will never fully comprehend such a mystery. But it is a mystery of *light* rather than darkness. The heart and mind of the believer delight in contemplating this glorious reality! To be sure, we will always find ourselves correcting one another. Those with an Antiochene bent will often be accused of Nestorianism because of their strong stand for Jesus' complete humanity, when in reality their accusers may be inadvertently guilty of Apollinarianism. Harold O. J. Brown has stated this well:

> Much modern twentieth-century conservative Protestantism is implicitly Apollinarian because while it ringingly confesses the deity of Christ, it finds it hard to think that he was really a man. Firmly to assert the deity of Christ is not the same thing as to confess the New Testament faith in him, for in the New Testament he is definitely a man who is revealed to be the Son of God, with all that that implies—not a divine being who reveals himself in human form.[84]

On the other hand, the Logos/*sarx* (Word/flesh) approach of Alexandria serves as a balance for the Antiochene Logos/*anthropos* (Word/man) orientation by preserving the "unity of subject" in Jesus Christ. Jesus was not a "compound" of God and a human being. He was the Word *made* flesh, not merely a man indwelt by God.[85] Thanks to Athanasius, to the Alexandrians, and to Chalcedon, the *unity* of the person of Christ has been preserved. Both perspectives need to be held together in a dynamic and creative tension in order that we see the full picture of Christ.

The Virgin Mary

As we have seen, it was the issue of the Virgin Mary that initially provoked the Nestorian controversy. To this day the church is divided over Mary. On the one hand, it is difficult to deny the existence of Mariolatry in the church. On the other hand, there has also been a pronounced lack of a full appreciation for Mary and the price she was willing to pay

---

[84] Brown, *Heresies*, 170.

[85] Compare Aloys Grillmeier, *Christ in Christian Tradition*, 2d ed., trans. John Bowden (Atlanta: John Knox, 1975), 1:328.

to be the mother of Jesus. *Theotokos* as a key description of Mary ultimately led to a Mariology in which Mary is viewed as the Mother of all God's creatures, as co-redemptrix, and as the Queen of Heaven with a cosmic intercessory ministry—none of which have a biblical basis. At the same time, we should acknowledge that Mary is one of the most important persons in Scripture in terms of God's redemptive plan: "In freely consenting to enable Christ to be present in the world and in history, Mary is also consenting to cooperate in the salvation of the world."[86] Mary's submission to God's will mirrors our own submission, and the cost of her discipleship was exceedingly high.

> *We must always remember that the* man *Christ Jesus, our Lord and Savior, was "born of a* woman*" (Gal. 4:4).*

It was the Virgin Mary who gave birth to the Savior of the world. Fully aware of the shame and slander the miraculous conception would bring on her, she was still willing to be the Lord's servant (Luke 1:37). In contrast to many of the disciples, Mary was "standing near the cross" (John 19:25) when Jesus breathed his last. She was among those assembled in the Upper Room in prayerful preparation for Pentecost (Acts 1:14). At Elizabeth's house Mary humbly acknowledges, through her song that we today call *The Magnificat,* her need of God as "Savior" (Luke 1:47). Unfortunately, it is Mary's sinlessness that is mistakenly taught to millions of Christians today, when it is our Lord's sinlessness that should be proclaimed.

I have already mentioned both Jesus' virgin birth and his sinlessness. Here we add a few more comments. In actuality, the miraculous conception by the power of the Holy Spirit in the womb of a virgin was not necessary to Jesus' sinlessness. Scripture nowhere indicates that Mary was free from original sin; in fact, as we just saw, it contradicts such a claim. How then could Jesus have been born without sin? It was clearly by God's miraculous power. Based on our knowledge of the infinite power of God, we know that the sinless Son of God could have come into the world *without* the virgin birth. We also know he *did* come into the world in this miraculous way. Why?

---

86 Léon Joseph Cardinal Suenens, *A New Pentecost?* trans. Francis Martin (New York: Seabury, 1974), 203.

There are a number of reasons. As Barth said, Jesus' life was bracketed by a miraculous entrance and exit: his virgin birth and bodily resurrection. The crucial point is that our salvation is all of God and has nothing to do with us.[87] Matthew's account establishes a clear link between the virgin birth and the Incarnation (Matt. 1:18–25). As Isaiah predicted, the virgin would give birth to Immanuel, God with us (1:23). Both Matthew and Luke emphasize the role of the Holy Spirit in the Incarnation (Matt. 1:18, 20; Luke 1:35). Thus, Cardinal Suenens of Belgium characterizes Mary as "the first Christian, the first charismatic."[88] This description is not precisely accurate, but Suenens is correct in highlighting the role of the Holy Spirit as an important ingredient in a full appreciation of the significance of the Virgin Mary.[89]

As we have already seen, the Incarnation was fully a Trinitarian event. Gabriel announced to Mary that the kingdom of this holy child was an eternal one (Luke 1:33). Truly, Jesus' uniqueness is pointed to at every turn. Finally, in our generation it is meaningful to reflect on one other crucial fact related to our Lord: From the beginning of Jesus' earthly life to the end, the role of women is elevated. We must always remember that the *man* Christ Jesus, our Lord and Savior, was "born of a *woman*" (Gal. 4:4, italics added).

Unfortunately, from the standpoint of evangelicals, the doctrine of the virgin birth has become freighted with unscriptural dogmas that detract from our Lord: Mary's immaculate conception (which supposedly freed her from original sin), her perpetual virginity, and bodily assumption. But it is *Jesus'* sinlessness that is crucial (John 8:46; 2 Cor. 5:21; Heb. 4:15; 7:26; 9:14; 1 Peter 2:22; 1 John 3:5). Only thus could he be complete in his humanity (we are subhuman in our sinfulness), and only thus could he be the sin-bearer for the whole world.

Historically, the virgin birth has been important to evangelicals for another essential reason: It is the testimony of our authoritative Scriptures. To reject the miraculous conception of Jesus in the womb of the Virgin Mary is to reject the clear statement of the Bible. Jesus' birth was a normal birth; he did not pass through the wall of the womb as he passed through the wall of the tomb, as has been erroneously taught. But the virginal conception nine months earlier *was* miraculous! As Bernard Ramm stated: "Incarnation, virgin birth, revelation, and inspiration are

---

87 Cf. Erickson, *Introducing Christian Doctrine,* 221: "Not only are humans unable to secure their own salvation, but they could not even introduce the Savior into their society."

88 Seunens, *A New Pentecost?* 197.

89 Ibid., 196–211 (ch. 11).

all one piece."[90] The sinless Son of God, Jesus Christ, was born of a virgin. And the virgin's name was Mary—a name that is precious to Christians of every generation. We should at least revere Mary in the sense that Elizabeth did, for Mary truly was "the mother of our Lord" (cf. Luke 1:43).

Additional Issues and Concepts

The perennial problem of Christology has been the relation of the divine and human natures of Christ. Little has changed since the patristic era in terms of these fundamental issues. Even with the liberal shift away from supernaturalism, the questions remain basically the same. Modern theologians often debate *anhypostasia* versus *enhypostasia* with varying definitions of these concepts. In effect, we are back to the dispute between the Alexandrians and the Antiochenes. If anhypostatic Christology is seeking to avoid the Nestorian heresy by affirming the fundamental unity of the person of Christ, then it serves a useful purpose. If, however, it staunchly defends the "impersonal humanity" of Christ, then it may become Apolliniarian. At this point enhypostatic Christology comes to the rescue!

> *Either/or thinking can hinder us from enjoying a more complete vision of the mystery of the person of Christ.*

Enhypostasia asserts the full humanity of Christ within the unity of his person. The brilliant sixth-century theologian Leontius of Byzantium expounded this concept in his defense of Chalcedonian Christology. Leontius wanted to avoid the mistakes of both the Nestorians and the Eutychians, and his analogy of fire illustrates his argument. Two different realities can be related in three fundamental ways. They can be in a simple conjunction, as, for example, when Christ's divine and human natures are simply juxtaposed, as in Nestorianism. Their union can be such that one reality "consumes" the other or a new reality is formed, and the two original realities disappear or are fundamentally altered: Eutychianism. The third possibility, however, is that both realities persist and yet form a single existence—as when, for example, a flame and a

90 Bernard L. Ramm, *An Evangelical Christology: Ecumenic and Historic* (Nashville: Thomas Nelson, 1985), 65.

fuel unite to form fire. (Push this, or any analogy, too far and it will obviously break down.) The body and soul of the human, Leotius argued, unite in this way. Each has its own nature, yet unite to form one person. So it is with Christ.[91] This is a satisfying statement of Chalcedonian Christology, which can be just as meaningful to a twentieth-century believer as it was centuries ago.

At the same time, it must be admitted that enhypostatic Christology today is often expressed in near-Nestorian (or in adoptionistic) terms. Jesus is at times portrayed as having a virtually independent existence from God. Functional Christologies, which assiduously avoid talk of "natures," "substances," and the like, portray Jesus simply as the man through whom God worked in a unique way. Jesus' personal, spiritual, and moral union with God was unparalleled, but that was all it was; all talk of two natures in one person is so much "theobabble."

But what if this is all a matter of perspective? What if from the human perspective (Christology "from below," functional Christology) it is *true* that Jesus was the most God-conscious person who has ever lived? What if it is true that Jesus enjoyed a loving, personal union with God (as Norman Pittenger has persuasively argued) that virtually defies our understanding? Do these realities necessarily cancel out the heavenly perspective of ontological Christology, which wants to acknowledge the divinely revealed Christology "from above" that sees the eternal Logos at work in this world as Jesus of Nazareth? Either/or thinking can hinder us from enjoying a more complete vision of the mystery of the person of Christ.

The Son of God does not have to surrender his divine powers and attributes to become incarnate, as kenotic Christologies (appealing to Phil. 2:7) have argued. He did come "down from his glory," but he functioned as a unified person in both his divinity and humanity. There has been a rise of interest in recent years in the subject of mythology, and on the theological scene there emerged a few years back an attempt to interpret the Incarnation in mythological terms.[92] A response was quick in forthcoming—asserting the historical *fact* of the Incarnation, in faithfulness to the biblical revelation.[93]

---

[91] See Justo L. González, *A History of Christian Thought* (Nashville: Abingdon, 1971), 2:94–96.

[92] See John Hick, ed., *The Myth of God Incarnate* (Philadelphia: Westminster, 1977).

[93] Michael Green, ed., *The Truth of God Incarnate* (Grand Rapids: Eerdmans, 1977).

The "problem" of the Incarnation is really one of God's relation to his creation. Too often we seek to define humanity apart from God in a deistic or even secularist fashion. A faulty Christological method results as well. Epimenedes may have first said it, but it is a scriptural truth: "In him we live and move and have our being" (Acts 17:28). Our experience of the immanent, personal presence of God in our lives does not destroy or subvert our humanity, but rather actualizes it, fulfills it, completes it. We come to our true selves, our true humanity, only in God. The venerable Southern Baptist theologian, W. T. Conner, expressed this truth well:

> This ought to help us to understand that God could go beyond his general immanence in human nature and his special immanence in Christian experience to a personal Incarnation in a human life; and that he could do this and leave man truly man. Rather it would help us to understand that God's absolute possession of the life of Jesus, instead of perverting his humanity, really made it what it should be. It would help us to understand that his deity is the only and proper basis of his perfect humanity—perfect in the sense of wholeness and completeness—perfect in that it possesses all the powers and capabilities of man, and perfect in its ethical completeness. . . . He is complete man, not in spite of being the embodiment of the divine, but because of that fact.[94]

This is theology at its noblest, profoundest, most practical, and most edifying. It is a thoroughly Chalcedonian, yet modern expression of the person of Christ. Knowing who Jesus is in these terms can only transform one's life. Yet this is only half the story. Now we must explore what Jesus did for us: the work of Christ for sinful humanity.

Humiliation and Exaltation

Whenever the subject of the work of Christ is mentioned, we most often think of the "days of his flesh," his earthly ministry in general, and of his crucifixion and resurrection, his work of atonement in particular. The Bible testifies, however, to a *preincarnate* work of Christ as well as his *present* and *future* work. Since the Reformation, Christ's saving work has been summarized as a humiliation and exaltation and his saving titles as those of prophet, priest, and king.

---

94 Walter Thomas Conner, *Revelation and God: An Introduction to Christian Doctrine* (Nashville: Broadman, 1936), 190–91.

The New Testament provides glimpses of how the early believers communicated the good news about Jesus. To a Jewish audience—people with a historical/eschatological mindset, looking for the fulfillment of time in the coming of Messiah—the message was: (1) Jesus died, (2) he was raised, and (3) he is coming again (see, e.g., 1 Cor. 15:3–28). The emphasis was on the fulfillment of the promises of Scripture. To the Hellenistic world of the first century—people with a cosmological/metaphysical bent—the first Christians announced a Christ who (1) preexisted as God, (2) humbled himself in his incarnation and atoning death, and (3) rose from the dead and ascended to heaven (Phil. 2:6–11; Col. 1:15–23; 1 Tim. 3:16). In other words, the gospel was "translated" into terms best suited for communicating within that culture.[95]

Pannenberg and Moltmann have, in effect, reminded us that the eschatological approach, which looms large in both Old and New Testaments, can still be used effectively in communicating the gospel. The message and full theological implications of the second coming of Jesus Christ have perennial relevance—as Billy Graham has demonstrated by always including at least one sermon on Christ's return in every one of his crusades. It is this ancient Hellenistic approach, however, that has tended to dominate much of modern evangelical theology. It too is biblically based and dramatic in format: humiliation and exaltation! And it too has been the staple preaching of the great evangelists of church history, such as Dr. Graham.

We have already seen how the Incarnation was an event of great humility and humiliation on the part of Christ. In taking on himself human nature, he disregarded his equality with God, took the form of a lowly servant, and "humbled himself and became obedient to the point of death—even death on a cross" (Phil. 2:6–8). In being sent by God, the Son was "born of a woman, born under the law, in order to redeem those who were under the law" (Gal. 4:4, 5). How can we ever comprehend such statements? According to the apostle John, Jesus forever transformed what is meant by the glory of God by his humble life and sacrificial death.

Few have taken notice of John's unique theological contribution at this juncture. He announces: "And the Word became flesh and lived

---

[95] See Michael Green, *Evangelism in the Early Church* (Grand Rapids: Eerdmans, 1970), 78–143, for a helpful analysis of how the early believers evangelized among the Jews and the Gentiles.

among us, and we have seen his glory" (John 1:14). The Incarnation is majestically referred to here as well as the divine glory. One immediately thinks of the Shekinah glory of the tabernacle and the temple and of Christ's divine origin. However, John redefines, or at least amplifies, what is meant by this divine glory throughout the rest of his Gospel. No one better grasps this motif in John than Leon Morris:

The incarnation of the eternal Son of God involved a submission of his divine attributes to the will of the Father and to the control of the Spirit.

> For John glory, real glory, is to be seen when someone who could occupy a majestic and exalted place accepts instead a place of lowly service. Supremely is glory to be seen in the Cross, for there One who had no need to die suffered on behalf of others. So when John says that Jesus was "glorified," he often means that he was crucified (7:39; 12:16, 23; 13:31; cf. 21:19). To understand glory as John did is to see the Cross casting its shadow over the whole of the life of Jesus.[96]

Reading through John's Gospel, alert to this fact, one is continually amazed at how sinful humanity relates to humble divinity. Clearly perceived, this amazing, humble, serving, and supremely *gracious* incarnate love of God is irresistible!

The incarnation of the eternal Son of God involved a submission of his divine attributes to the will of the Father and to the control of the Spirit. In this way he maintained the unity and integrity of his divine and human natures. He thus perfectly revealed the essence of both God and humanity. He showed forth the humble glory of God and the dignity and purpose of humankind. His obedience to the Father led him to the ignominious death of the cross. This event was both the ultimate humiliation of the Son and at the same time, as John would say, it was his greatest glory.

Jesus was mocked and challenged at every point. The Jewish council derided Jesus as prophet: "Prophesy to us, you Messiah! Who is it that struck you?" (Matt. 26:68). The ironic inscription, "The King of the

---

96 Morris, *New Testament Theology*, 271; cf. idem, *Jesus Is the Christ*, 56–57. Morris provides an expanded treatment of this subject in his *Reflections on the Gospel of John* (Grand Rapids: Baker, 1986), 1:17–26.

Jews," above Jesus' head as he hung on the cross and the taunt of the Roman soldiers, "If you are the King of the Jews, save yourself!" ridiculed Christ's kingship (Luke 23:37–38). And the rulers scoffed at his saving priestly role with the words: "He saved others; let him save himself if he is the Messiah of God, his chosen one!" (23:35).[97] The whole world seemed to be saying, "This so-called Messiah is no prophet, priest, or king!" Jesus experienced utter rejection. When he cried out, "My God, my God, why have you forsaken me?" (Mark 15:34), he was dying the God-forsaken death every one of us deserves to die in our sins. This was the ultimate humiliation: Jesus became the sin-bearer for the whole human race.[98]

> *As prophet, Jesus Christ not only proclaims the Word of God, he* is *the Word of God!*

"Therefore," exults the apostle, "God also highly exalted him and gave him the name that is above every name, so that at the name of Jesus every knee should bend . . . and every tongue should confess that Jesus Christ is Lord, to the glory of God the Father" (Phil. 2:9–11). Christ was raised from death, appeared to many, ascended back to the Father, poured out the Holy Spirit, and continues to intercede for the saints. What assurance! "It is Christ Jesus, who died, yes, who was raised, who is at the right hand of God, who indeed intercedes for us" (Rom. 8:34). "Consequently he is able for all time to save those who approach God through him, since he always lives to make intercession for them" (Heb. 7:25). Furthermore, Jesus repeats the promise time and again: "I will come again" (John 14:3). The whole world will then see the Christ depicted so majestically in Revelation.

Prophet, Priest, and King

When John introduces his revelation of Jesus Christ, his greeting to the seven churches contains these programmatic words: "Jesus Christ, the faithful witness [prophet], the firstborn of the dead [priest], and the ruler

---

[97] See Erickson, *Christian Theology*, 772–73.

[98] Some would add a further humiliation in a supposed descent into hell, but the biblical support for such a teaching (e.g., Ps. 16:10; Eph.4:8–9; 1 Tim. 3:16; 1 Peter 3:18) is tenuous. See Erickson, *Christian Theology*, 773–76; Gordon R. Lewis and Bruce A. Demarest, *Integrative Theology* (Grand Rapids: Zondervan, 1990), 2:382, 396–97. But compare Moody, *The Word of Truth*, 387–88. (I have heard some dramatic sermons related to this topic and have read, among charismatic writers, some heretical teachings. Where the Bible does not speak clearly it is better to tread softly rather than to pontificate boldly!)

of the kings of the earth [king]" (Rev. 1:5). John then describes Christ's saving work: "To him who loves us and freed us from our sins by his blood, and made us to be a kingdom, priests serving his God and Father, to him be glory and dominion forever and ever. Amen" (1:5–6). Christ in his threefold office spreads the reign of God (the kingdom), establishes a people of God (the church), and provides redemption (salvation) for the totality of humankind.

As prophet, Jesus Christ not only proclaims the Word of God, he *is* the Word of God! With the arrival of his forerunner, John the Baptist, and with the appearance of Jesus himself, the voice of prophecy, silent for four centuries, now bursts on the scene with profound impact. As the supreme revelation of God, Jesus Christ stands forever as both the core and circumference of the Christian faith. There is nothing more to be said—apart from merely announcing this good news.

As king, Jesus brings us salvation in the eternal, spiritual kingdom of God.

In his discussion of the prophetic/revelatory role of Christ, John Calvin reminds us of this centrality: "All those, then, who, not content with the gospel, patch it with something extraneous to it, detract from Christ's authority." Now Christ's prophetic anointing is "diffused from the Head to the members," who are literally enthralled with their Redeemer: "Outside Christ there is nothing worth knowing, and all who by faith perceive what he is like have grasped the whole immensity of heavenly benefits."[99]

As king, Calvin continues, Jesus brings us salvation in the eternal, spiritual kingdom of God and, as "the eternal protector and defender of his church," perpetuates the people of God throughout all generations.[100] Here Calvin describes how Christ as king gives provision, protection, and victory even though we must all pass through difficult days:

> Thus it is that we may patiently pass through this life with its misery, hunger, cold, contempt, reproaches, and other troubles—content with this one thing: that our King will never leave us destitute, but will provide for our needs until, our warfare ended, we are called to triumph.

---

[99] John Calvin, *Institutes of the Christian Religion*, 2 vols., ed. John T. McNeill, trans. Ford Lewis Battles (Philadelphia: Westminster, 1960), 1:496 (II.xv.2). To be sure, Calvin makes reference in this context to the end of prophecy (which we will later contest), but his main point is still well taken.

[100] Ibid., 1:497 (II.xv.3).

> Such is the nature of his rule, that he shares with us all that he received from the Father. Now he arms and equips us with his power, adorns us with his beauty and magnificence, enriches us with his wealth. These benefits, then, give us the most fruitful occasion to glory, and also provide us with confidence to struggle fearlessly against the devil, sin, and death. Finally, clothed with his righteousness, we can valiantly rise above all the world's reproaches; and just as he himself freely lavishes his gifts upon us, so may we, in return, bring forth fruit to his glory.[101]

Then, as priest, Christ graciously brings reconciliation as well as an ongoing ministry of intercession on behalf of the saints.[102] Few treatments of the threefold office of Christ can match that of John Calvin. For our own time Millard J. Erickson has perhaps given the best contemporary expression of this doctrine.[103]

As priest, Christ brings reconciliation as well as an ongoing ministry of intercession on behalf of the saints.

Jesus' prophetic role loomed large during his earthly ministry. One need only read Luke 1–4 to catch the strong prophetic ethos that surrounded the inception of Christ's earthly ministry—beginning from the virginal conception. Someone of at least the stature of Moses had appeared on the scene (see Deut. 18:15; Acts 3:22; 7:37). Dale Moody is typically to the point: "What Moses was to Old Testament prophecy, Jesus was to New Testament prophecy."[104] And yet, as we will see as we glance at the "past" and "future" work of Christ, the prophetic model is limited in terms of fully expressing the significance of Christ and his work.[105]

Christ's priestly work is the rubric for our discussion of his atoning death, and his kingship is a comprehensive concept for his creative, revelatory, and redeeming activity. It is clearly helpful to think of our Lord as prophet, priest, and king.

> We are enlightened in the knowledge of the truth; we are reconciled unto God by the sacrificial death of his Son; and we are delivered from the power of Satan and introduced into the kingdom of God; all of

---

[101] Ibid., 1:499 (II.xv.4).

[102] Ibid., 1:501–2 (II.xv.6).

[103] See his *Does It Matter What I Believe?* 101–12; *Introducing Christian Doctrine,* 239–41; *Christian Theology,* 762–69.

[104] Moody, *The Word of Truth,* 368.

[105] See Cullmann, *The Christology of the New Testament,* 43–50.

which supposes that our Redeemer is to us at once prophet, priest, and king. This is not, therefore, simply a convenient classification of the contents of his mission and work, but it enters into its very nature, and must be retained in our theology if we would take the truth as it is revealed in the Word of God.[106]

Past, Present, and Future

John is emphatic that it was through Jesus, as the preexistent Logos, that the entire creation came into being (John 1:3). Paul also asserted the creative activity of Christ, adding that even now Christ holds the universe together (Col. 1:15–17). The letter to the Hebrews also gives testimony to the fact that God created the universe through Christ and that it is sustained by Christ's "powerful word" (Heb. 1:2–3). Both Paul (1 Cor. 10:4) and the Lord's brother Jude (Jude 5) saw Christ with Israel in the wilderness.[107] And what are we to make of the apparent preincarnate appearances of Christ in various theophanies of the Old Testament? But there are also present and future dimensions to the work of Christ.

At first Jesus' crucifixion seemed to be the tragic and unjust end to his work. The two disciples on the road to Emmaus described him as "a prophet mighty in deed and word before God and all the people," and that they had "hoped that he was the one to redeem Israel" (Luke 24:19, 21). But Jesus of Nazareth had been condemned as a false prophet and a false Messiah. But Luke, more than any other New Testament writer, tells us about the *continuing* work of Jesus after his resurrection. The first words of Acts refer to "all that Jesus began to do and teach, until the day when he was taken up" (Acts 1:1–2 RSV). Thus, Jesus is now continuing his ministry through his church. In the Great Commission he promised his continuing presence with his followers to the end of the age (Matt. 28:20). And Mark 16:20 reads this way: "And they went out and proclaimed the good news everywhere, while the Lord worked with them and confirmed the message by the signs that accompanied it."

Every believer knows the present work of Christ in his or her heart and life. There is an "abiding in Christ" that empowers our daily living

---

106 Charles Hodge, *Systematic Theology* (London: James Clarke & Co., 1960), 2:461; cited in James Montgomery Boice, *Foundations of the Christian Faith* (Downers Grove, Ill.: InterVarsity Press, 1986), 296.

107 See F. F. Bruce, *What the Bible Teaches About What Jesus Did* (Wheaton, Ill.: Tyndale, 1979), 99–102.

(see John 15:1–17). There is an identification with Christ in his death and resurrection, so that it is no longer we who live but Christ who lives in us and through us (Gal. 2:19–20). Concerning his own ministry, Paul would not "dare to speak of anything except what Christ has accomplished through me" (Rom. 15:18 NAB). We begin our Christian walk through the work of Christ—his work both in history and in our hearts (see Gal. 4:4–7)—and we progress in our lives and ministries only through his continuing work. Christ initiates us into his body, the church, and empowers us for our mission.

> *There is a great future for God's people!*

After appearing to his disciples, Jesus prepared them to be empowered for their mission through baptizing them in the Holy Spirit (Luke 24:49; Acts 1:3–8; cf. the prediction of John the Baptist in Matt. 3:11; Mark 1:7–8; Luke 3:15–16; John 1:29–34). The disciples were "filled with the Holy Spirit" on the day of Pentecost, and Peter later explained to the crowds that it was the risen Lord who had poured out the Holy Spirit on his followers that day (Acts 2:4, 32–36).[108] This activity of baptizing in the Holy Spirit is, as F. F. Bruce has pointed out, "a very important work of Christ."[109] In fact, as we will see, this Spirit baptism metaphor for the work of Christ can be seen as an all-inclusive description of Christ's eschatological redemption of humanity.

The Apostles' Creed emphasizes a decisive work of Christ at the end of the age: "The third day he rose again from the dead; he ascended into heaven and is seated on the right hand of God the Father almighty; from thence he shall come to judge the living and the dead." Jesus Christ, the Son of Man, will one day come in his glory with all the angels. He will sit on his glorious throne and judge the nations (Matt. 25:31–46; see also Rev. 20:11–15). One day "the dead will hear the voice of the Son of God" and come to life. For some it will be "the resurrection of life," and for others it will be "the resurrection of condemnation" (John 5:25–29). "Indeed, just as the Father raises the dead and gives them life, so also the Son gives life to whomever he wishes. The Father judges no one but has given all judgment to the Son, so that all may honor the

---

[108] It is just as important to note the role of the Father in the gift of the Spirit, that the Holy Spirit as the "promise of the Father" also proceeds from him (Luke 24:49; Acts 1:4–5; cf. John 14:16, 26; 15:26).

[109] Bruce, *What the Bible Teaches About What Jesus Did*, 45–46. Much more should and will be said later about this "baptism in the Spirit."

Son just as they honor the Father" (5:21–23). As Peter explained to Cornelius and his household, Jesus is "the one ordained by God as judge of the living and the dead" (Acts 10:42).[110]

The second coming of Christ will culminate God's plan of redemption. Christ will return in triumph, and all sin and evil will be done away with forever (Rev. 19:11–20:15). We will see for the first time the place he has been preparing for us (John 14:1–2). There is a great future for God's people! The Father's intention is to "bring everything together under Christ, as head, everything in the heavens and everything on earth" (Eph. 1:10 NJB). (Irenaeus made this promise the cornerstone of his theology.) Finally, Jesus will hand over the kingdom to the Father, and God will be "all in all" (1 Cor. 15:24–28). *This is the final work of Christ, and it should cause the saints to continually rejoice!* We must never forget, however, the tremendous price that was paid in order that we might have this living hope. This is the subject, the atoning death of Christ, to which we now turn.

> *The cross is the* crux *of Christianity.*

Christ Crucified

World-renowned biblical scholar F. F. Bruce stated: "The death of Christ on the cross is by far his greatest work."[111] That is the clear message of the Scriptures in their totality. In the apostle Paul's memorable words: "For Jews demand signs and Greeks desire wisdom, but we proclaim Christ crucified, a stumbling block to Jews and foolishness to Gentiles, but to those who are the called, both Jews and Greeks, Christ the power of God and the wisdom of God" (1 Cor. 1:22–24). *Christ crucified.* This in a nutshell is the message of Christianity.

At the center of the Christian faith is a scandalous cross. No one better reminds us of this fact than Jürgen Moltmann: "Today the church and theology must turn to the crucified Christ in order to show the world the freedom he offers. This is essential if they wish to become what they assert they are: the church of Christ, and Christian theology."[112] "Christian faith stands and falls with the knowledge of the crucified Christ, that

---

[110] Ibid., 114–28.

[111] Bruce, *What the Bible Teaches About What Jesus Did*, 136.

[112] Jürgen Moltmann, *The Crucified God*, trans. R. A. Wilson and John Bowden (London: SCM, 1974), 1.

> *In his saving death and resurrection, Christ defeated for all eternity our three greatest enemies: sin, death, and the devil.*

is, with the knowledge of God *in* the crucified Christ."[113] Finally, in order to make his conviction crystal clear, Moltmann writes: "The issue is not that of an abstract theology of the cross and of suffering, but of a theology of the crucified Christ."[114]

There is simply no way to overstate how *crucial* the cross is to the Christian faith. The cross is the *crux* of Christianity.[115] Martin Hengel asserts that the most important question we must answer is this:

> How did it come about that the disciples of Jesus could proclaim that cruel, disastrous execution of their master as the saving event *par excellence?* In other words, how did the crucifixion of Jesus come to take its place at the centre of early Christian preaching? How was it that this infamous death could so quickly be interpreted as a representative, atoning, sacrificial death, and in what interpretative framework was such an understanding possible at all?[116]

How does the *death* of Jesus bring us *life*? This is the puzzle that the Christian message evokes in the world's consciousness. And the biblical doctrine of the atonement answers that question. To be sure, there is still a great mystery to the cross, but there is also great meaning, as anyone who has received the gospel can testify.

When Jesus cried on the cross, "My God, my God, why have you forsaken me?" (Matt. 27:46; Mark 15:34; cf. Ps. 22:1), he was asking the central question of the Christian faith. Again, Moltmann is to the point: "All Christian theology and all Christian life is basically an answer to [that question]."[117] What kind of a cry was it? The only adequate answer is that it was literally a cry of dereliction—*abandonment.* Jesus was dying the Godforsaken death every one of us deserves to die. He was dying in

---

[113] Ibid., 65 (Moltmann's italics).

[114] Ibid., 4.

[115] These two sentences are in actuality redundant since, as Leon Morris is fond of pointing out, both words, *crucial* and *crux,* are derived etymologically from the Latin word for *cross.* See Leon Morris, *The Cross of Jesus* (Grand Rapids: Eerdmans, 1988), 1.

[116] Martin Hengel, *The Atonement,* trans. John Bowden (London: SCM, 1981), 1; cited in Morris, *The Cross of Jesus,* 1, fn. 1.

[117] Moltmann, *The Crucified God,* 4.

our place in order to save us. He was doing something for us in space, time, and history that we could never do for ourselves. He took our sin, guilt, and judgment on himself in order that we might be saved from them. In his saving death and resurrection, Christ defeated for all eternity our three greatest enemies: sin, death, and the devil. This is the *objective* significance of the atonement. There is no more important truth to grasp, and it can transform our lives.

We are not dealing here with a *myth,* among many myths, that can give meaning to human life. We are faced rather with a supreme historical *fact.* God acted in human history to save us. The cross was *the* concrete saving event. As Francis Schaeffer often explained, if you had been there that day, you could have run your finger down the cross and gotten a splinter. It does not matter whether we *feel* a certain way. To trust in Christ as our Savior is to receive the full benefits of his *objective, historical,* atoning death. Our eternal forgiveness is full and final. The debt is paid. We are *not guilty, period!* Justification, the Bible calls it. Grace. Apart from any religious works or spiritual achievement, we are objectively *saved.* This is the good news for which Christians down the centuries have been willing, literally, to die.

When D. Martyn Lloyd-Jones, that great prince of evangelical expositors, obtained a firm grasp on this truth of the objective meaning of the atonement, it transformed his life and ministry.[118] Evangelical theology highlights such essential theological terms as substitution, satisfaction, and propitiation in order to most effectively conserve and communicate this central saving message of the atonement. Why did Christ die? In order to save us. How does his death save us? That is the central issue of the doctrine of the *atonement.*

Why Christ Died

When Paul communicated the message of salvation in the Jewish synagogue at Antioch of Pisidia, he referred to a central paradox of the faith:

> Because the residents of Jerusalem and their leaders did not recognize him or understand the words of the prophets that are read every sabbath, they fulfilled those words by condemning him. Even though they found no cause for a sentence of death, they asked Pilate to have him killed. (Acts 13:27–28)

[118] See John R. W. Stott, *The Cross of Christ* (Downers Grove, Ill.: InterVarsity Press, 1986), 9–10.

Here we see events taking place on two levels. There is the normal cause-and-effect progression of historical occurrences and, *at the same time*, the hand of God is at work. It is the perennial puzzle of the relation between divine sovereignty and human freedom. In the crucifixion of Christ we have a classic example of the concurrence of so-called secular history and saving history.

Because Jesus did not meet people's expectations and because he often threatened their privileged positions, he was ultimately rejected and crucified. But much more than these sociological factors were present. Peter pointed this out in his Pentecost sermon: "This Jesus, delivered up according to the definite plan and foreknowledge of God, you crucified and killed by the hands of lawless men" (Acts 2:23 RSV). People were acting on their own misled initiative, while at the same time God was working out his sovereign, saving purposes. Only God could take the worst crime and injustice ever committed—the crucifixion of the sinless Son of God—and turn it into the supreme act of redemption.

Because of who he was as a person and because of what he said and did, Jesus was shunned by Jew and Gentile alike. Jesus was a threat to the legalistic, self-righteous, exclusive Pharisees because he rejected the authority of their oral traditions and often censured them for their hypocrisy and mean-spiritedness. He simply did not match up with their preconceptions of what the Messiah should be like. The Sadducees saw Jesus as a potentially dangerous revolutionary who could easily disturb the fragile status quo that kept them in power. Many common folk finally decided that Jesus was simply not the Messiah-king they had hoped for—especially, of course, after his ignominious death. Pilate knew Jesus was innocent but decided that it was expedient, in order to avoid further trouble, to allow Jesus to be crucified.[119]

Any careful historical investigation would flesh out the details of this scenario. But knowledge of the historical *fact* of the death of Jesus is not enough. We must understand its *meaning*. Here again we see the organic unity of biblical revelation. Every biblical teaching we have studied thus far has led up to the cross, and every doctrine we will explore subsequently is an outworking of this doctrine of the atoning death of Christ. The saving message of the gospel is a historical message. It is, therefore, imperative that we give careful consideration to this doctrine both in its

---

[119] See Bert Dominy, *God's Work of Salvation* (Layman's Library of Christian Doctrine 8; Nashville: Broadman, 1986), 75–78.

organic relation to the other doctrines of Scripture and as a product of divine saving revelation in what has been called "salvation history." Robert H. Culpepper has stated it well:

> The effective communication of the gospel demands an intelligent understanding of the Christian message. Nothing is more central in this message than the good news of God's saving action in Jesus Christ. This message reaches its climax in the story of the death and resurrection of God's Son. This was the center of the *kerygma* (proclamation) of the earliest church as the sermons in Acts, the epistles of Paul, and the passion narrative in the gospels make clear.
>
> The Bible concerns itself with a particular stream of history that reaches its climax in the Christ-event. This stream of history has its root in God's redemption of Israel from bondage in Egypt and his choice of her to be his own people; it has its fruit in God's redemption of the church and his choice of this people to have a servant ministry to the world. Standing between these two as the connecting link and the integrating center is the Christ-event, centering in the incarnation, life, death, and resurrection of the Son of God.
>
> Christian faith dares to affirm that what happened to Jesus of Nazareth in ancient Palestine somewhere between 25 and 32 A.D. "did not happen in a corner," but that this particular stream of history is redemptive history with universal significance for all history. In the New Testament, event and interpretation are inseparably bound together. Interpretation without event would be mythology. Event without interpretation would be "mere history." The two together in indissoluble union constitute salvation-history.[120]

This captivating true story of the crucified and risen Christ is patently good news with universal significance!

Why did Christ come? "Christ Jesus came into the world to save sinners" (1 Tim. 1:15). Why did Christ die? "Christ died for our sins, according to the Scriptures" (1 Cor. 15:3 NIV). "For Christ also died for sins once for all, the righteous for the unrighteous, that he might bring us to God" (1 Peter 3:18 RSV). *The cross of Christ was the supreme revelation of the holy love of God for sinful humanity.*

> *The cross is the greatest revelation of God's love.*

[120] Robert H. Culpepper, *Interpreting the Atonement* (Grand Rapids: Eerdmans, 1966), 7–8 (from the preface).

This simple declaration incorporates every doctrine we have studied thus far: The cross is a central feature of divine *revelation.* It is a revelation of *God* in his holiness and love. This God of holy love steps into his *creation* as a human being in order to redeem *humanity* from its most profound dilemma, *sin.* (As we will see, this is a cosmic redemption, since the entire creation has been impacted by humanity's rebellion against its Creator.) "Christ crucified" is the Bible's terse summary of this divine saving activity: "Christ" (his person); "crucified" (his work). "In the person of Christ there is the revelation of God, and in the death of Christ there is the redemption of man. In his incarnate life he brought God to man, and in his atoning cross he brought man to God."[121]

For God So Loved . . .

The best-known verse in the Bible is an excellent place to begin as we explore the full significance of the atoning death of Christ: "For God so loved the world that he gave his only Son, so that everyone who believes in him may not perish but may have eternal life" (John 3:16). This one verse, understood in its context, expresses every major rubric of the biblical doctrine of the atonement!

One notices first *the love of God.* The cross is the greatest revelation of God's love. Far from pitting a loving Son against an angry Father, the cross shows the *unity* of the Godhead in the supreme saving event of the death of Christ. As Paul wrote, "But God proves his love for us in that while we still were sinners Christ died for us" (Rom. 5:8). God was reaching out to a rebellious people in love; "in Christ God was reconciling the world to himself, not counting their trespasses against them" (2 Cor. 5:19). "Indeed," John adds, "God did not send the Son into the world to condemn the world, but in order that the world might be saved through him" (John 3:17).

But we must note carefully the object of God's love: *the world.* Almost without exception "the world" (*kosmos*) in John's writings refers to the world system set against God and his kingdom purposes. The world is human society deliberately organized to exclude God. We do this quite naturally. God is seen as an intruder. We are innately at enmity with God.

---

[121] H. D. McDonald, *The Atoning Death of Christ* (Grand Rapids: Baker, 1985), 18. It is difficult to conceive of a more comprehensive, theologically rich, and helpful treatment of the doctrine of the atonement than this work.

As Paul reminds us, "While we were enemies, we were reconciled to God through the death of his Son" (Rom. 5:10).

The most profound problem of the human race is *sin.* This is why John tells us early in his Gospel that Jesus is "the Lamb of God who takes away the sin of the world" (John 1:29). Notice that he refers to "sin" in the singular. Our particular sins (plural) are the manifestations of our being in the enduring state of sin (what we called original sin earlier). "And this is the judgment," John explains, "that the light has come into the world, and people loved darkness rather than light because their deeds were evil" (3:19). Our finest spiritual leaders hated, unjustly condemned, and lynched the sinless Son of God. The cross is also, therefore, the greatest revelation of the sinfulness of humanity.

Notice here John's mention of *judgment.* Jesus had already set his declaration of God's love (John 3:16) in this context when he mentioned the wilderness judgment (Num. 21:4–9) of Moses' day: "And just as Moses lifted up the serpent in the wilderness, so must the Son of Man be lifted up, that whoever believes in him may have eternal life" (John 3:14–15). Serpents were sent among the people in judgment, but God instructed Moses to fashion a bronze replica of one of the serpents and raise it up on a pole. Whoever looked at that serpent would be healed of their serpent bite (Num. 21:8–9). Thus, in this particular context the serpent became symbolic of both judgment and salvation. In the same way, Jesus was explaining, his atoning death was at the same time both judgment and salvation. It was God's righteous judgment on our sins, and it was also God's means of saving us from our sins. There is therefore a *penal* or *judgment* dimension to his atoning death. In this way our holy God is both just and the justifier of "the one who has faith in Jesus" (Rom. 3:26).

The forgiveness and salvation offered us in the Bible's greatest promise (John 3:16) is costly. Salvation in Scripture always entails a sacrifice that removes sin's defilement through a righteous judgment, an atoning and reconciling death, and a covenant of blood. Grace is absolutely free, but it is never cheap. God's claims on us are total. It is a costly grace (Bonhoeffer). The death of Jesus was essential to our salvation. He came to make an eternal atonement for our sins. As Morris asserts: "To say that no atoning act is needed is to give us a non-Christian view of salvation." It is on careful reflection truly a "calamitous position."[122]

---

122 Morris, *The Cross of Jesus*, 5.

Jesus felt this "divine necessity" throughout his earthly ministry: "Then he [Jesus] began to teach them that the Son of Man must undergo great suffering, and be rejected by the elders, the chief priests, and the scribes, and be killed, and after three days rise again" (Mark 8:31).[123] In one of Luke's programmatic passages we read: "When the days drew near for him to be taken up, he set his face to go to Jerusalem" (Luke 9:51). Jesus was fiercely intent on going to Jerusalem in order to atone for our sins. When Peter tried to avert him from this task, the disciple received Jesus' most stinging rebuke: "Get behind me, Satan!" (Matt. 16:23). Thus, the "giving" referred to in John 3:16 indicates both God's sending his Son into human history in the Incarnation and his provision of Christ's atoning death for our sins.

Finally, John 3:16 mentions *faith.* God promises eternal life to those who *believe* in Jesus. John's most frequent construction is *pisteuo eis* ("believe in/into") Christ; that is, we enter into a personal union with Christ.[124] This is saving faith according to Scripture. It is much more than mere intellectual assent. It is a life-commitment (the full ramifications of which we will explore in the next chapter).

John sees no contradiction between the wrath of God and the love of God:

> God's love was revealed among us in this way: God sent his only Son into the world so that we might live through him. In this is love, not that we loved God but that he loved us and sent his Son to be the atoning sacrifice for our sins. (1 John 4:9–10)

The English phrase "atoning sacrifice" translates the Greek word *hilasmos,* which can be legitimately rendered "propitiation." John is saying in part that Jesus' atoning death turned away God's righteous anger against our sin. This also is a central significance of the atonement. Leon Morris succinctly spells out the full implications of this majestic passage: "When we see man for what he is, the wrath of God for what it is, and the cross for what it is, then and only then do we see love for what it is."[125] Through Christ's substitutionary death for sinful humanity the God of holy love offers us forgiveness, salvation, reconciliation, and eter-

---

[123] See I. Howard Marshall, *The Work of Christ* (Grand Rapids: Zondervan, 1969), 17–18.

[124] See Morris, *New Testament Theology,* 274–76.

[125] Leon Morris, *Testaments of Love: A Study of Love in the Bible* (Grand Rapids: Eerdmans, 1981), 131.

nal hope. The atoning death of Christ was God's greatest gift to his rebellious creatures.

Advocate, Atonement, and Example

Staying with John's writings a little longer, we should note one further statement on the person and work of Christ:

> My little children, I am writing these things to you so that you may not sin. But if anyone does sin, we have an advocate [*parakletos*] with the Father, Jesus Christ the righteous; and he is the atoning sacrifice [*hilasmos*] for our sins, and not for ours only but also for the sins of the whole world.
>
> Now by this we may be sure that we know him, if we obey his commandments.... By this we may be sure that we are in him: whoever says, "I abide in him," ought to walk just as he walked. (1 John 2:1–6)

In Christ, God himself champions the cause of our redemption!

In the process of addressing a very practical issue (sanctification; see also 1:5–10), John also provides us with a wide-ranging statement concerning Christ.

John first describes Jesus as our "*advocate* [Paraclete] with the Father" (1 John 2;1). Recall that in John's account of Jesus' Upper Room discourses Jesus refers to the Holy Spirit as the Paraclete *with us* (John 14:16, 26; 15:26; 16:7). The Holy Spirit is the one "called alongside" us to help, counsel, teach, guide, and empower us. In 1 John the apostle uses the designation Paraclete in its strictest sense, which always carries a forensic overtone. Gary Burge, a specialist in Johannine studies, states it succinctly: "Jesus stands as a defense counsel before a heavenly court."[126] In Christ, God himself champions the cause of our redemption! The apostle Paul also refers to this intercessory ministry of our Lord: "Who will bring any charge against God's elect? It is God who justifies. Who is to condemn? It is Christ Jesus, who died, yes, who was raised, who is at the right hand of God, who indeed intercedes for us" (Rom. 8:33–34). Note also Jesus' high priestly ministry as described by the writer of Hebrews (see Heb. 7:25; 9:24).[127]

---

126 Gary M. Burge, *The Anointed Community: The Holy Spirit in the Johannine Tradition* (Grand Rapids: Eerdmans, 1987), 7.

127 Ibid., 6; cf. Bruce, *What the Bible Teaches About What Jesus Did*, 132–33.

John also refers to the *atonement.* Jesus is the *hilasmos* for our sins: Some prefer the translation "expiation"—that is, Jesus' death provides cleansing from the defilement of our sins. Others insist on the older rendering "propitiation," the averting of God's wrath through the sacrificed life of Christ. Neither concept excludes the other, and both are essential for a comprehensive understanding of the atonement. God provided the means for the removal of the defilement of our sins. He also absorbed into himself his righteous indignation against our sins.[128] In a just manner—in which both the holiness of God and the dignity of humanity (as created in the divine image) are preserved—God offers us, in Christ, eternal forgiveness!

John's words allude also to Christ as our *example.* Our personal knowledge of Christ and our union with him include, John argues, that we "ought to walk just as he walked" (1 John 2:6). Here the apostle is tying his atonement teaching in with his instruction on discipleship and church life (see 2:7–11). Jesus himself said, "If any want to become my followers, let them deny themselves and take up their cross daily and follow me" (Luke 9:23). The obedient discipleship of our risen Lord is the authenticating sign that he is truly our advocate and atonement.

The Gospel According to Paul

We have been listening primarily to the witness of the apostle John. The other theological giant of the New Testament is, of course, the apostle Paul. There is no better place to turn for a full analysis of the atoning death of Christ—considered within the context of both the gospel message in particular and Christian faith and life in general—than to Paul's letter to the Roman's, sometimes appropriately referred to as "the Gospel according to Paul."

> *Paul had sought a righteousness based on keeping the law, only to discover that such a quest was futile.*

Martin Kähler has called the Gospels passion narratives with extended introductions. While one can find a number of key theologically interpretive passages in the Gospels, their primary accent is on the *fact* of the atoning death of Jesus, presented in a full and moving narrative. Christian history has proven that the Holy Spirit can use the simple retelling of

---

[128] Bruce, *What the Bible Teaches About What Jesus Did,* 133–34.

the story of Jesus' life, death, and resurrection to bring people to salvation. Certainly Mel Gibson's *The Passion of the Christ* has demonstrated this truth in our own day.[129] Paul, however, did not follow Jesus during his earthly ministry. It is therefore understandable that he would accent theological interpretation. In Romans, we have his "systematic theology"—a handbook on the Christian faith and life. Its theme verses are Romans 1:16–17:

> I am not ashamed of the gospel, because it is the power of God for the salvation of everyone who believes: first for the Jew, then for the Gentile. For in the gospel a righteousness from God is revealed, a righteousness that is by faith from first to last, just as it is written: "The righteous will live by faith." (NIV)

As C. K. Barrett has written, these words summarize not only the letter but also "Paul's theology as a whole."[130] Then the words, "For the wrath of God is revealed from heaven against all ungodliness and wickedness," introduce an extended section on the sin problem of humanity, both Jew and Gentile (1:18–3:20; see my previous chapter on sin). Thus, three salient themes emerge early: (1) the righteousness of/from God, (2) faith, and (3) the wrath of God. Paul will develop these themes throughout the rest of the letter, and they loom large in his presentation of the atonement. For our purposes, the key passages to consider are 3:21–26; 5:1–11; and 8:1–4.

As a fervent Pharisee, Paul had sought a righteousness based on keeping the law, only to discover that such a quest was futile. Through the law "every mouth [is] silenced, and the whole world [is] held accountable to God"; "through the law comes the knowledge of sin"; "the law brings wrath" (Rom. 3:19–20; 4:15). Yes, the law itself is "holy and just and good" (7:12), but it is powerless to free us from the downward pull of sin (see all of Rom. 7). Paul's gospel declares that the "law of sin and of death" (8:2; cf. 7:22) that holds us captive can be conquered only through the atoning death of Jesus and through the presence of his Spirit in our lives:

> There is therefore now no condemnation for those who are in Christ Jesus. For the law of the Spirit of life in Christ Jesus has set you free from the law of sin and of death. For what the Law could not do, weak as it was through the flesh, God did. (Rom. 8:1–3 NASB)

---

129 See Lee Strobel and Garry Poole, *Experiencing the Passion of Jesus* (Grand Rapids: Zondervan, 2004).

130 C. K. Barrett, *A Commentary on the Epistle to the Romans* (HNTC; New York: Harper & Row, 1957), 27.

What precisely was it that God did? And what was his ultimate purpose?

> By sending his own Son in the likeness of sinful flesh and for sin [or as an offering for sin], he condemned sin in the flesh, in order that the righteous requirement of the law might be fulfilled in us, who walk not according to the flesh but according to the Spirit (8:3–4 ESV).

In another context, the apostle asserts, "For the love of Christ urges us on, because we are convinced that one has died for all; therefore all have died. And he died for all, so that those who live might live no longer for themselves, but for him who died and was raised for them" (2 Cor. 5:14–15).

I vividly remember a conversation I had as a young seminarian with the renowned New Testament scholar George Beasley-Murray. Referring to the above-quoted Corinthian passage, Beasley-Murray stated that this scripture is one of the most important *objective* expressions of the significance of Christ's atoning death to be found in the entire New Testament. He added that few ever notice this fundamental statement relating to Paul's view of the atonement. James D. G. Dunn is one New Testament scholar who has noticed. Through the representative/substitutionary death of Christ, observes Dunn, God has destroyed sin and has begun a new humanity![131]

Dunn suggests vaccination as a helpful modern analogy:

> In vaccination germs are introduced into a healthy body in order that by destroying these germs the body will build up its strength. So we might say the germ of sin was introduced into Jesus, the only one "healthy"/whole enough to let that sin run its full course. The "vaccination" seemed to fail, because Jesus died. But it did not fail, for he rose again; and his new humanity is "germ-resistant," sin resistant. It is this new humanity in the power of the Spirit which he offers to share with men.[132]

"For our sake," writes Paul, "he [God] made him [Christ] to be sin who knew no sin, so that in him we might become the righteousness of God" (2 Cor. 5:21). "Christ redeemed us from the curse of the law by becoming a curse for us," he explains in Galatians 3:13.

---

[131] James D. G. Dunn, "Paul's Understanding of the Death of Jesus" in *Reconciliation and Hope*, ed. Robert Banks (Grand Rapids: Eerdmans, 1974), 124–41.

[132] Ibid., 139. Unfortunately, Dunn fails to see that Jesus' death was *both* a *destruction* (of sin) and a *judgment* or *punishment*.

Through faith in Christ's atoning death, we who were "weak" (Rom. 5:6), "sinners" (v. 8), and "enemies" (v. 10) have been "justified" (vv. 1, 9) and "reconciled" (vv. 10–11). We no longer face the prospect of God's wrath (vv. 1, 9). Dunn aptly summarizes Paul's gospel:

> For Paul the essence of Christianity is acceptance by God (justification) in an intimate relationship, entered into and lived in by faith on man's side, made possible and empowered by the gift of grace, the gift of the Spirit (see particularly Rom. 3:21–5:21; Gal. 2:16–4:7). This seems to be the core of Paul's kerygma, distinctive both in its central emphases and in its developed expression.[133]

But Now . . .

When we turn to what has been called the "heart" of Paul's letter to the Romans (Rom. 3:21–26), we find the distilled essence of Paul's gospel: "But now a righteousness from God, apart from law, has been made known, to which the Law and the Prophets testify" (3:21 NIV). "Now" (*nuni*) is emphatic in the Greek. A new era has dawned—a new epoch of salvation! Faith replaces law (cf. 4:13–17). The Spirit now liberates us for obedience. "This righteousness from God comes through faith in Jesus Christ to all who believe" (3:22 NIV). For Paul, knowing Christ was everything (Phil. 3:8, 10): "not having a righteousness of my own that comes from the law, but one that comes through faith in Christ, the righteousness from God based on faith" (v. 9).

> *Our incarceration on sin's "death row" is ended! Our slavery to sin is over!*

All human beings, Jew and Gentile alike, have the same problem: sin (Rom. 1:18–20, 23). But God has provided a glorious salvation from sin for humankind! Leon Morris describes Paul's paragraph-long sentence, which reduces his gospel to its essence (3:21–26), in these words:

> In what is possibly the most important single paragraph ever written, Paul brings out something of the grandeur of Christ's saving work. He speaks of the righteousness of God, the sin of man, and the salvation of Christ. He views this salvation in three ways: as justification (imagery

---

[133] James D. G. Dunn, *Unity and Diversity in the New Testament* (Philadelphia: Westminster, 1977), 22–23.

from the law court), as redemption (imagery from the slave market), and as propitiation (imagery from the averting of wrath).[134]

It is imperative, therefore, that we consider this passage carefully. Paul's description runs as follows (Rom. 3:23–24, author's trans.): "BEING JUSTIFIED [declared righteous], AS A GIFT [Gk. *dorean*], BY HIS GRACE [God in his goodness and mercy showing us undeserved favor by acting to save us], THROUGH THE REDEMPTION THAT IS IN CHRIST JESUS [which pays the price of our freedom from sin and death], WHOM GOD PUT FORWARD AS A PROPITIATION [*hilasterion*—atoning sacrifice that averts God's wrath], THROUGH FAITH [trust], IN *HIS* [Christ's; emphatic in the Gk.] BLOOD [which brings the propitiation]." Paul then adds that it was through Christ's atoning death that God showed his own righteousness and was able to justly acquit those who have faith in Jesus (3:25–26).

Our righteousness, our legal acquittal, our acceptance with God, is his gracious gift to us, provided through Christ's atoning death. Our incarceration on sin's "death row" is ended! Our slavery to sin is over! God's wrath is now turned away! We are "not guilty," simply because we trust in Christ and his finished work! This priceless gift came to us at the infinite cost of the blood of Christ himself, the sinless Son of God.

Some (esp. those who are troubled with the concept of God's wrath) resist the rendering "propitiation." But, as Morris expresses it, "unless *hilastērion* means 'propitiation,' Paul has put men under the wrath of God and left them there."[135] The "sub-personal" rendering "expiation" is only a partial translation. "Nothing deals with salvation from the divine wrath other than *hilastērion*, which means 'the averting of wrath.'"[136] Paul wants us to see clearly the Christ "who was handed over to death for our trespasses and was raised for our justification" (Rom. 4:25). He wants to rivet our attention on God's righteous judgment of our sins at Calvary and on the salvation that cost Jesus Christ his life's blood.[137] Literally, only a forensic view of the atonement does it ultimate justice. But note that this perspective takes nothing away from the other crucial dimension of Christ's saving work.

---

[134] Leon Morris, *The Epistle to the Romans* (Grand Rapids: Eerdmans, 1988), 173.

[135] Leon Morris, *The Atonement* (Downers Grove, Ill.: InterVarsity Press, 1983), 169.

[136] Ibid., 169.

[137] See Herman Ridderbos, *Paul: An Outline of His Theology*, trans. John Richard de Witt (Grand Rapids: Eerdmans, 1975), 167–68.

In the person and work of Christ we have what Herman Ridderbos would call the epochal "revelation of the righteousness of God."[138] It is news of supreme importance for all humankind. We find a number of picture words in the Bible that vividly depict this redemptive event: the Christ event.[139]

Sacrifice

When Sadhu Sundar Singh of India was asked what he found in Christianity that he had not found in any of the other world religions, he replied simply, "Jesus Christ!" This is a profound response indeed! It is the supremacy of Jesus Christ that sets Christianity apart among the religions of the world. Jesus was certainly the difference between Judaism and Christianity in the first century, and it is his self-sacrifice on the cross and his bodily resurrection, as the central saving events of the Christian faith, that form the ground of our uniqueness to this day. Paul stressed Christ's supremacy when the Colossians were being tempted toward syncretism. The book of Hebrews emphasizes Christ's superiority to those Jewish believers who were considering a safe return to Judaism.

> *We must approach God* on his terms, *not ours.*

If Paul and John are the two major theologians of the New Testament in general, the writer of Hebrews may be called the major theologian of Jesus' atoning self-sacrifice in particular. Bruce Metzger calls Hebrews "the longest sustained argument of any book in the New Testament."[140] Christ is majestically portrayed in Hebrews as superior to the prophets (Heb. 1:1–3), the angels (1:4–2:18), Moses (3:1–19), and Joshua (4:1–13). His high priesthood, "according to the order of Melchizedek," is superior to that of the Aaronic line (4:14–7:28). And, finally, his "once for all" sacrifice, issuing in a new and better covenant, is superior to all the sacrifices of the Old Covenant (8:1–10:18). Of this final section, Donald Guthrie writes:

> Nowhere else in the New Testament is the sacrificial aspect of the work of Christ brought out so forcefully. Any doctrine of the atonement which

---

[138] Ibid., 159–81.

[139] I owe the concept of "picture words" to Leon Morris: see *The Atonement*, 13; *The Cross of Jesus*, 5–8.

[140] Bruce M. Metzger, *The New Testament: Its Background, Growth, and Content* (Nashville: Abingdon, 1965), 190.

> is based on the New Testament must take full account of the testimony of this epistle on the significance of the blood of Christ.[141]

The concept of an atoning sacrifice may sound foreign to us in the twentieth century. But if we take time to explore its depths, the rewards are many. The reality of sacrifice can touch the innermost reaches of the human heart in *every* generation.

In biblical times sacrifice as a means of atonement was commonplace. The Lord gave Israel blood sacrifices for making atonement for their lives: "It is the blood that makes atonement" (Lev. 17:11). The term most often used in the Old Testament for atonement is *kapar,* which means "to cover." The sacrifice of atonement provided worshipers release from punishment through the covering of sin. Twentieth-century persons may be repulsed by such practices, but the bottom line is that we must approach God *on his terms,* not ours. "Indeed, under the law almost everything is purified with blood, and without the shedding of blood there is no forgiveness of sins" (Heb. 9:22; cf. Rom. 3:23; 5:9). Christ's giving of his own life's blood as atonement (Eph. 1:17; 2:13; Col. 1:20) was "a fragrant offering and sacrifice to God" (Eph. 5:2).

Behind such statements lies the whole sacrificial system practiced for centuries by Israel. One immediately thinks of the Passover lamb, whose blood was put on the doorposts and lintels (Ex. 12). Reflecting on this, Paul wrote: "For our paschal lamb, Christ, has been sacrificed" (1 Cor. 5:7). John the Baptist announced Jesus in similar terms: "Here is the Lamb of God who takes away the sin of the world!" (John 1:29; cf. v. 36). The apostle John, who recorded these words, later made special note of the blood and water that issued from Jesus' side after the soldier pierced him with a spear (19:34).[142]

One also thinks of the burnt, grain, peace, sin, and guilt offerings overseen by the Levitical priesthood (Lev. 1–7). Again, blood played a prominent role. The burnt offering is a good example: (1) The sacrificial animal must be "without blemish." (2) The worshiper lays hands on the animal, thereby confessing sin and transferring guilt. (3) Then the blood of the slaughtered victim is offered in atoning sacrifice (1:3–4). Old Testament prophets spelled out in more explicit terms what for Christians centuries later was an obvious typology—none better than Isaiah.

---

[141] Donald Guthrie, *The Letter to the Hebrews* (TNTC; Grand Rapids: Eerdmans, 1983), 54.

[142] Did John see an often overlooked significance here: (1) blood: "the Lamb of God who takes away the sin of the world" (1:29), and (2) water: "the one who baptizes with the Holy Spirit" (v. 33)?

What separated Jews and Christians early on was the Christians' identification of the Messiah with the Suffering Servant of Isaiah. But Isaiah's fourth servant song (Isa. 52:13–53:12) is one of the most vivid depictions and predictions of Christ's atoning passion to be found in the Old Testament. Gleason Archer describes Isaiah 53 as follows:

> The profoundest remarks upon the meaning of Calvary are not to be found in the New Testament. It is an impressive evidence of divine inspiration of the Scriptures that an Old Testament passage, composed more than eight hundred years before the event, presents the fullest and tenderest interpretation of the Crucifixion to be discovered in the entire Bible. The sufferings of our Saviour for mankind meant so much to the Father that He caused the prophet Isaiah to describe them with heart-searching poignancy centuries before they were endured. So appropriate is every phase of this marvelous chapter that it reads as though it had been composed by some witnessing disciple in the shadow of the Cross.[143]

Christ's superior priesthood and sacrifice have secured for us an eternal salvation!

Each of the five stanzas of this Servant Song (composed of three verses each) brings out an important significance of Christ's saving death. Christ's humiliation and exaltation are described in the first stanza (Isa. 52:13–15; cf. Phil. 2:5–11). The next stanza (Isa. 53:1–3) depicts the Servant as seen by humankind: despised and rejected. From God's perspective, however, he is our Redeemer. Stanza three (53:4–6) contains perhaps the best-known words of the song, words that clearly describe Jesus as our substitute and sin-bearer. From the human standpoint Jesus' death was a tragic failure (stanza four; 53:7–9). But from the divine perspective it was a glorious success (stanza five; 53:10–12). Jesus made his soul or life "an offering for sin" (v. 10); "he bore the sin of many, and made intercession for the transgressors" (v. 12). A separate volume could be written on these verses and their fulfillment in the New Testament![144]

---

143 Gleason L. Archer, Jr., *In the Shadow of the Cross: Insights into the Meaning of Calvary, Drawn from the Hebrew Text of Isaiah 53* (Grand Rapids: Zondervan, 1957), 3.

144 Archer's outline of this chapter, and that of Harold Lindsell, coincide precisely and provide an excellent overview: Archer, *In the Shadow of the Cross,* passim, and Lindsell, *NRSV Harper Study Bible,* ed. Verlyn D. Verbrugge (Grand Rapids: Zondervan, 1991), 1063–64.

The New Testament writer to the Hebrews used this fourth Servant Song centuries later. But the Old Testament image that loomed largest for him was the Day of Atonement, *Yom Kippur* (Lev. 16). Christ, our high priest, has "entered once for all into the Holy Place, not with the blood of goats and calves, but with his own blood, thus obtaining eternal redemption" (Heb. 9:12). If the sacrifices of the Old Covenant brought purification from sins, "how much more will the blood of Christ, who through the eternal Spirit offered himself without blemish to God, purify our conscience from dead works to worship the living God!" (9:14). H. D. McDonald observes: "In the one verse of 9:14 there is packed and particularized for the writer of Hebrews all that went into Christ's saving work."[145] Christ's superior priesthood and sacrifice have secured for us an eternal salvation!

> *Redemption meant* freedom!

Jesus is "the mediator of a new covenant" (Heb. 9:15). "And just as it is appointed for mortals to die once, and after that the judgment, so Christ, having been offered once to bear the sins of many, will appear a second time, not to deal with sin, but to save those who are eagerly waiting for him" (9:27–28). The words "to bear the sins of many" come from Isaiah 53:12 (LXX). Jesus was the sin-bearer. As Peter wrote, "He himself bore our sins in his body on the cross" (1 Peter 2:24). Note again John the Baptist's words: "Here is the Lamb of God who takes away the sin of the world!" (John 1:29). Jesus' eternal sacrifice for our sins is all we need—and our only hope!

Covenant

At his Last Supper, Jesus instituted for the church the sacred meal that has forever memorialized his Passion. He said to his disciples: "I have eagerly desired to eat this Passover with you before I suffer; for I tell you, I will not eat it until it is fulfilled in the kingdom of God" (Luke 22:15–16). The Passover meal commemorates the Exodus event, but it has found its ultimate fulfillment in the Easter event that is reenacted and remembered in the Lord's Supper. Christ's new covenant sacrifice brings the blessings of the kingdom (which include the gift of the Spirit) to the

---

145 McDonald, *The Atoning Death of Christ*, 104.

church. This is the new covenant about which Jeremiah prophesied (Jer. 31:31–34). Without a doubt, the Bible is a covenant book, our God is a covenant God, and the new covenant in the blood of Jesus is God's greatest gift to humankind.

Redemption

Redemption is another picture word for the atonement that we should notice. We have already used this term a number of times. But in order for us to appreciate fully the atoning work of Christ we must look at this metaphor carefully.

The laws of the old covenant covered even the eventuality of one's ox goring one's neighbor to death (Ex. 21:28–32): "If a ransom is imposed on the owner, then the owner shall pay whatever is imposed for the redemption of the victim's life" (21:30). As R. Alan Cole comments, "*Ransom* and *redemption* are important words for the later theology of salvation."[146] A death sentence is averted by a price. In biblical times prisoners of war and slaves could be ransomed for a price. Redemption meant *freedom*!

In one of Jesus' most important statements concerning his mission he announces: "For the Son of Man came not to be served but to serve, and to give his life a ransom for many" (Mark 10:45). Jesus came as a slave to free slaves. The Savior paid the price of release, or ransom (*lytron*), for our sins. He bought us out of the slave market of sin and set us free. We were prisoners of war, and he ransomed us. We were on death row, and he took our death sentence. He literally substituted himself for (*anti*) us. "Christ redeemed us from the curse of the law by becoming a curse for us" (Gal. 3:13). He hung on that tree to bear our condemnation for us *and* to provide the promise of the Spirit, who makes us God's daughters and sons (see Gal. 3:14; 4:4–7). One aspect of our freedom in Christ is a filial relationship with the Father—we are no longer slaves but children and heirs (4:7)!

To be sure, there is a future dimension to this redemption: We still must await "the redemption of our bodies" at the resurrection (Rom. 8:23). But the decisive liberation has occurred, and beyond all question, "there is . . . now no condemnation for those who are in Christ Jesus"

---

146 R. Alan Cole, *Exodus: An Introduction and Commentary* (TOTC; Downers Grove, Ill.: InterVarsity Press, 1973), 170 (Cole's italics).

(8:1)! Additionally, "so great a salvation" (Heb. 2:3) is, as we have already seen, profoundly personal and relational. The *relationship* between God and humankind has been restored—a reality referred to in the Bible by the term *reconciliation.*

Reconciliation

The apostle Paul declared: "In Christ God was reconciling the world to himself, not counting their trespasses against them" (2 Cor. 5:19). This divine initiative brings great assurance to the believer: "For if while we were enemies, we were reconciled to God through the death of his Son, much more surely, having been reconciled, will we be saved by his life" (Rom. 5:10). *We are at the heart of the faith when we consider this reality!* Our God is profoundly personal, and the salvation he offers us in Christ is profoundly personal as well. God offers us *himself* in a personal communion of faith, hope, and love. And he draws us into a *community* of faith, hope, and love: the church. Furthermore, he sends us on mission to the world with a ministry and message of reconciliation (2 Cor. 5:18–21).

The Bible is a love story. It is the *love story of the ages.*

The cause of offense—sin—was removed by the atoning death of Jesus, and "we have peace with God through our Lord Jesus Christ" (Rom. 5:1). Not only are alienation from God and enmity abolished at the cross, but Christ has also brought about reconciliation on the horizontal level. Jew and Gentile join together to form the one body of Christ (Eph. 2:11–22). All ethnic, gender, and socioeconomic barriers have been removed: "There is no longer Jew or Greek, there is no longer slave or free, there is no longer male and female; for all of you are one in Christ Jesus" (Gal. 3:28). It has been said that the ground at the foot of the cross is level. The kingdom ethic is one of peacemaking (Matt. 5:9). Though estranged from God and hostile toward him, humankind has been reconciled to God in Christ's atoning death (Col. 1:21, 22). The waiting Father welcomes us back home (Luke 15:11–32). What a rich and noble term—reconciliation!

Propitiation

Even though we have already dealt with the concept of propitiation, it is helpful to highlight it once again in order to view it in its broader context. The doctrine of atonement forms an organic unity that relates integrally to the rest of the Bible's teachings, and the concept of propitiation provides an excellent example of this unity of biblical revelation.

The Bible is a love story. It is *the* love story of the ages. That we would spurn the holy love of our Creator is incomprehensible. But we did, and we do. Because he is a God of holy love, as we have already seen, the lengths to which he went to save us are the doxological theme of the ages. Because we are dealing with a personal *relationship*, it is reasonable to accept the biblical picture of God's wrath against our sinful rebellion. Propitiation means that God absorbs his righteous anger and judgment against our sin back into himself. It is a *self*-substitution in an atoning death that averts his wrath forever.

Thus we are able, by means of the cross, to view the holiness of God and the gravity of sin with utmost clarity. Could there ever be a greater revelation of the love of God? Propitiation, therefore, integrates the doctrines of God, humanity, and sin, and it further elucidates what Jesus acccomplished in his atoning death at Calvary. Contrary to the notions of the opponents of this doctrine, propitiation is a grace word. It actually enriches and strengthens the biblical depiction of the holy love of our personal, infinite God.

Justification

It is also advantageous to draw further attention to the term justification. A careful study of all the New Testament words derived from the Greek root *dik-* opens up much of what the Scriptures have to say in relation to the saving death and resurrection of Christ. The good news is that even though we have the damning problem of unrighteousness (*adikia*; cf. Rom. 1:18), we can through faith in Christ be justified (*dikaioo*; see 5:1). Righteousness (*dikaiosyne*) is God's gift to us in Christ Jesus our Lord. Through his atoning death, God shows himself both just (*dikaios*) and the justifier (*dikaion*) (3:26). What troubles many theologians, however, is the clearly *legal* connotation of this doctrine.

To allow a penal significance to the death of Christ is for some an odious notion. As with any metaphor or picture word, the courtroom setting can be carried too far. The larger question is, of course, which system of law serves as the paradigm. Do we turn to the legal traditions of the ancient Near East, to medieval law, or to modern jurisprudence as practiced in the United States? To absolutize any of these traditions in an attempt to grasp fully what the Bible means by justification would be a serious mistake. Nevetheless, to jettison the penal concept of the atonement altogether is equally erroneous. *The concept of justice is crucial to this dimension of the saving death of Christ.*

The desire for justice is endemic to human nature (another aspect of the divine image within us). Justification means that, for the believer, his or her status at the end-time judgment of our just God has already been settled. We are at this present moment acquitted! The penalty is paid; the infinite debt is canceled. Grace exercises "dominion through justification leading to eternal life through Jesus Christ our Lord" (Rom. 5:21)!

Timothy George rightly states that "Protestantism was born out of the struggle for the doctrine of justification by faith alone."[147] Martin Luther literally put his life on the line for this truth. Justification lies at the heart of the gospel and must never be compromised. Jesus "was handed over to death for our trespasses and raised for our justification" (Rom. 4:25). This is the saving message of Christianity that must be heralded throughout the earth.

> *What is often overlooked in Christ's decisive victory is the essential role of the Holy Spirit.*

Victory

One final theme related to the atoning work of Christ should be mentioned briefly before turning to the major historical theories of the atonement—the note of *victory* that runs through the New Testament portrayal of Christ's saving work. The apostle Paul continually exulted in the victory of Christ's atoning death:

> The sting of death is sin, and the power of sin is the law. But thanks be to God, who gives us the victory through our Lord Jesus Christ. (1 Cor. 15:56–57)
>
> But thanks be to God, who in Christ always leads us in triumphal procession, and through us spreads in every place the fragrance that comes from knowing him. (2 Cor. 2:14)
>
> No, in all these things we are more than conquerors through him who loved us. (Rom. 8:37)

---

147 Timothy George, *Theology of the Reformers* (Nashville: Broadman, 1988), 62.

In his sinless humanity Jesus, the incarnate Son of God, could do for us what no one else could do. It is paradoxical, mysterious, even contradictory to the natural mind that Christ could conquer sin, death, and the devil through death, but that is precisely what he did. He could do so because he was the sinless, eternal Son. He took on our nature, says the writer of Hebrews, "so that through death he might destroy the one who has the power of death, that is, the devil, and free those who all their lives were held in slavery by the fear of death" (Heb. 2:14).

Perhaps Paul, more than any other New Testament writer, rings loudest this victory bell! In Colossians 2:13–15, with an economy of words, he depicts the total triumph that Christ makes available to us. F. F. Bruce describes this passage as "a striking word-picture of the decisive battle and the overthrow of hostile forces. . . . Nowhere has Paul given us a more dramatic presentation of the work of Christ than this."[148] Christ nailed the bond of our sin-debt to the cross. Further, he "disarmed the rulers and authorities and made a public example of them, triumphing over them in it" (2:15). "Therefore," Gustaf Aulén argued convincingly in his classic *Christus Victor*, "the note of triumph sounds like a trumpet-call through the teaching of the early church."[149]

What is often overlooked in relation to this decisive victory, however, is the essential role of the Holy Spirit. And the *locus classicus* of the New Testament in this regard is Romans 8. The Spirit alone can communicate to us the saving benefits of Christ's death. Our victory comes through the Spirit's application of the Savior's atoning death. In his *Church Dogmatics*, Karl Barth's section "Jesus Is Victor" is followed immediately by the section "The Promise of the Spirit."[150] Indeed, Christ's *entire* work is a victorious saving work as he enters human history, routs the enemy throughout his earthly ministry, dies his atoning death, rises triumphantly from the grave, ascends to the Father, intercedes for us, and returns to earth as "King of kings and Lord of lords" (Rev. 19:16)!

Historical Theories of the Atonement

During its first two centuries the church made little effort to derive a "theory" of the atonement. Using the prophecies and sacrificial images

148 Bruce, *What the Bible Teaches About What Jesus Did*, 66–67.

149 Gustaf Aulén, *Christus Victor*, trans. A. G. Hebert (New York: Macmillan, 1931), 59.

150 Karl Barth, *Church Dogmatics:* Volume IV: *The Doctrine of Reconciliation* (3/1), trans. G. W. Bromiley (Edinburgh: T. & T. Clark, 1961), 165–367.

of the Old Testament and the developing canon of apostolic writings, these early believers were content simply to bear witness to the saving work of Christ without elaborate explanation.[151] But beginning with Irenaeus a *dramatic* view of the atonement began to emerge that would loom large in the theology of the church for centuries. Theological giants such as Origen and Augustine wrote of Christ's atoning death in terms of the great *victory* won for us by Christ.

More often than not, this dramatic theory of the atonement depicted Christ's death as a ransom paid to the devil in order to free humankind. This view is generally called the *ransom theory*. Our bondage to the devil because of sin is broken, and we are freed by Christ from Satan's cruel grasp. Jesus paid the price of our freedom. Gustaf Aulén helped restore this theory to modern theology in his little classic volume, *Christus Victor*. Although Aulén sometimes overstates his case, he is correct in asserting that the concept of the atonement as a cosmic conflict and divine victory is central to the New Testament witness and the faith of the Church.[152] Robert H. Culpepper summarizes Aulén's contribution in these words:

> The idea that Christ through his incarnation, life, death and resurrection wins a decisive victory over all the evil powers which hold man in bondage—sin, death, and the devil—is certainly biblical. And Aulén has made us all indebted to him by revitalizing this biblical theme for our day.[153]

Erickson states that the ransom theory was probably "the standard view in the early history of the church."[154] Certainly in our own day—with the obvious intensification of spiritual warfare in many quarters—this dramatic view of the atonement carries tremendous power.[155] We should note that according to Scripture, no ransom was paid to the devil. Nonetheless, without question, our ancient foe was dealt the fatal blow by our conquering Savior at Calvary!

The second major historical view of the atonement is the *satisfaction theory* of Anselm (1033–1109), Archbishop of Canterbury from 1093

---

[151] See Robert S. Paul, *The Atonement and the Sacraments* (Nashville: Abingdon, 1960), 61.
[152] Aulén, *Christus Victor*, 20–23.
[153] Culpepper, *Interpreting the Atonement*, 77.
[154] Erickson, *Introducing Christian Doctrine*, 243.
[155] See Michael Green, *I Believe in Satan's Downfall* (Grand Rapids: Eerdmans, 1981).

until his death. Anselm's *Cur Deus Homo?* (*Why Did God Become Human?*) is unquestionably a landmark in the history of Christian thought. As Robert S. Paul has observed,

> With this brief treatise Anselm completely destroyed the predominance held by the theory of a ransom paid to the devil and substituted a completely new series of categories in which the doctrine of the Atonement was largely to be cast for the next eight hundred years.[156]

Anselm wanted to provide an evangelistic apologetic, and he wanted to strengthen the faith of the simplest saint. "This attempt to present theology in a form which could be understood by the simple is perhaps not the least important lesson that theologians have to learn from Anselm."[157] He argued powerfully for a full appreciation of the seriousness of sin and for the *necessity* of the Incarnation and the atonement.

Interpreting the death of Christ from the perspective of the medieval feudal system of lords and vassals, Anselm asserted that payment was made to *God,* not the devil, in Christ's atoning death. We have dishonored God by our sinful rebellion, and a satisfaction is thereby required for our redemption. Unfortunately, we face a dilemma. We owe God a debt that is impossible for us to pay, and without such payment we are hopelessly lost. According to the law of Anselm's day, satisfaction entailed *additional* payment. But what can we give to God beyond what we already owe him—full honor and obedience? Only the God-man, Jesus Christ, could pay such a satisfaction—and he did!

As we noted with justification, the law analogy breaks down when absolutized. Feudal law cannot be seen as normative with respect to the relation between God and humankind.[158] Using Anselm's basic model, the Reformers found it necessary to shift from the concept of merit satisfying God's honor to that of a penalty satisfying God's law. In this manner they more accurately communicated the biblical picture of the atonement. But with Anselm we are forced to see the seriousness of sin as well as the centrality of the law in God's working out his righteous, saving purposes. There truly is an *objective* significance

---

[156] Paul, *The Atonement and the Sacraments,* 65.

[157] Ibid., 67.

[158] See F. W. Dillistone, *The Christian Understanding of Atonement* (Philadelphia: Westminster, 1968), 194.

to the atonement. An eternal transaction was effected—a finished work of universal importance.

But exactly why did God go to such lengths to save us? The only adequate answer is that he is a God of infinite love, mercy, and compassion. Both Paul and John place Christ's substitutionary, propitiatory death within this context of God's incomprehensible, gracious love:

> But God proves his love for us in that while we were still sinners Christ died for us. (Rom. 5:8)

> God's love was revealed among us in this way: God sent his only Son into the world so that we might live through him.... He loved us and sent his Son to be the atoning sacrifice for our sins. (1 John 4:9–10)

> For God so loved the world that he gave his only Son, so that everyone who believes in him may not perish but may have eternal life. (John 3:16)

In terms of historical theories, the name associated with this emphasis on the *love* of God as the explanation of the atonement is that of Peter Abelard (1079–1142).

A younger contemporary of Anselm, Abelard reacted to both the dramatic view of the atonement and to Anselm's satisfaction theory. Abelard's name has come to symbolize the *subjective, moral influence*, or *exemplarist* theories of atonement. According to Abelard, it is Christ's *example* of love—expressed supremely at Calvary—that saves us. Modern liberal theology, unhappy with both the dramatic and satisfaction views, has seized on Abelard's categories to express its own concepts of the atonement (e.g., Horace Bushnell and Hastings Rashdall).

> *Amazing love! Perfect holiness! Triumphant grace! All revealed in the sinless Son of God.*

Abelard could not see the justice of an innocent person suffering for the guilty. Would not that sin—that crime, that injustice—require an even greater satisfaction? *We* are the ones with the problem, according to Abelard, not God. He has no problem in forgiving us, but our own attitudes keep us separated from him. Jesus' example of love evokes our repentance, faith, and lifestyle of love.

How should we evaluate Abelard's position? It is important first to acknowledge Abelard's insight: "God *is* love" (1 John 4:8, 16 [italics added]). And: "*We* love because he first loved us" (4:19 [italics added]). If we do not see the cross in the heart of God as the source of the cross on Golgotha's hill, we miss the essence of the gospel. Nevertheless, there is a huge gap in Abelard's thinking. Unless there is an *objective* significance to the death of Christ, precisely how is his death an expression of love? Do I prove that I love you by stepping in front of a fast moving car? Not really. But if that car is headed in your direction and I shove you out of its path at the expense of my own life, then my death is truly an expression of love. The subjective view of the atonement cannot stand alone. This fact accounts for the distortions that result from an attempt to "fit all the eggs into one basket"—a mistake made by Aulén, Anselm, and Abelard alike.

We need the insights of all three schools of thought. The atonement *is* "a victory over evil"; it *is* "the payment of our penalty"; and it *is* "the outpouring of love that inspires us to love in return."[159] P. T. Forsyth aptly refers to the unity of the atonement as a "threefold cord."[160] John Stott provides this helpful summary: "In the 'objective' view God satisfies himself, in the 'subjective' he inspires us, and in the 'classic' he overcomes the devil."[161] All three perspectives are needed to see the atonement in its fullness.

Amazing love! Perfect holiness! Triumphant grace! All revealed in the sinless Son of God, who loved us and gave himself for us (see Gal. 2:20). The person and work of Christ form the central core of the Christian faith—a faith that receives from God "so great a salvation" (Heb. 2:3).

---

[159] Morris, *The Cross of Jesus*, 115.
[160] P. T. Forsyth, *The Work of Christ* (London: Hodder & Stoughton, 1910), 199–235.
[161] Stott, *The Cross of Christ*, 230.

8 Faith
What Is the Nature of the Salvation God Offers Us?

(continued on next page)

The just shall live by faith.

—Romans 1:17 KJV

For through the Spirit, by faith, we eagerly wait for the hope of righteousness. For in Christ Jesus . . . the only thing that counts is faith working through love.

—Galatians 5:5–6

But you will receive power when the Holy Spirit has come upon you; and you will be my witnesses . . . to the ends of the earth.

—Acts 1:8

But if it is by the Spirit of God that I cast out demons, then the kingdom of God has come upon you.

—Matthew 12:28

Faith in Christ and hope for the kingdom are due to the presence of God in the Spirit. . . . [The Church's] fellowship with Christ is founded on the experience of the Spirit. . . . Its fellowship in the kingdom of God is founded on the power of the Spirit.

—Jürgen Moltmann[1]

The church needs another Pentecost. Every revival is a repetition of Pentecost, and it is the greatest need of the Christian church at this present hour.

—Martyn Lloyd-Jones[2]

---

[1] Jürgen Moltmann, *The Church in the Power of the Spirit,* trans. Margaret Kohl (New York: Harper & Row, 1977), 197.

[2] Martyn Lloyd-Jones, *Joy Unspeakable: Power and Renewal in the Holy Spirit,* ed. Christopher Catherwood (Wheaton, Ill.: Harold Shaw, 1984), 280.

THE APOSTLE PAUL ANNOUNCED TO THE CHRISTIANS OF ROME: "For the wages of sin is death, but the free gift of God is eternal life in Christ Jesus our Lord" (Rom. 6:23). The previous two chapters have basically been an elaboration of these words. The concluding three chapters of this volume will, in effect, "unwrap" this marvelous gift of God to which the apostle refers. It is the grace of God that provides this gift of salvation: "For by grace you have been saved through faith, and this is not your own doing; it is the gift of God—not the result of works, so that no one may boast" (Eph. 2:8–9). Jesus described this gift to the Samaritan woman at Jacob's well as "a spring of water gushing up to eternal life" (John 4:10, 14). Paul exulted: "Thanks be to God for his indescribable gift!" (2 Cor. 9:15). The gospel proclaims that we are "justified by his grace as a gift, through the redemption that is in Christ Jesus" (Rom. 3:24).

The writer of the letter to the Hebrews describes Christians as those who have "tasted the heavenly gift, and have shared in the Holy Spirit, and have tasted the goodness of the word of God and the powers of the age to come" (Heb. 6:4–5). He also warns that the gospel of our salvation is not to be taken lightly.

> Therefore we must pay greater attention to what we have heard, so that we do not drift away from it. For if the message declared through angels was valid, and every transgression or disobedience received a just penalty, how can we escape if we neglect so great a salvation? It was declared at first through the Lord, and it was attested to us by those who heard him, while God added his testimony by signs and wonders and various miracles, and by gifts of the Holy Spirit, distributed according to his will. (Heb. 2:1–4)

Notice that God himself attested to the message of salvation through the miraculous workings of the Holy Spirit!

In a similar vein, as the apostle Paul commends the Colossian believers, he portrays the spread of this powerful gospel.

> In our prayers for you we always thank God, the Father of our Lord Jesus Christ, for we have heard of your faith in Christ Jesus and of the love that you have for all the saints, because of the hope laid up for you in heaven. You have heard of this hope before in the word of the truth, the gospel that has come to you. Just as it is bearing fruit and growing in the whole world, so it has been bearing fruit among yourselves from the day you heard it and truly comprehended the grace of God. This

> you learned from Epaphras, our beloved fellow servant. He is a faithful minister of Christ on your behalf, and he has made known to us your love in the Spirit. (Col. 1: 3–8)

The scope of the biblical portrait of our salvation is vast! Some of the terms and descriptions relating to salvation have already been mentioned, some are to come: grace, faith, hope, love, the spirit, the kingdom, the church, acquittal, reconciliation, liberation, healing, deliverance, holiness, new birth, life, growth, glory, new heavens, new earth. It is to these dimensions of salvation we now turn under the rubrics of faith, hope, and love (see 1 Cor. 13:13).

> *The scope of the biblical portrait of our salvation is vast!*

Without question, the best way to approach this task is to look briefly at the next major event in the Bible after the crucifixion, resurrection, and ascension of Christ—Pentecost!

Pentecost

Here we make an important transition to the third major division of Christian theology. We often associate the work of creation with the Father and the work of redemption with the Son (although, of course, these are both Trinitarian realities). Now we will explore the *application* of Christ's redemptive work, portrayed in the Scriptures as the particular domain of the Holy Spirit.

Mention of the Holy Spirit, even among professing Christians in our day, evokes a variety of responses. It seems that sincere saints are moving in opposite directions in this regard. On the one hand, many mainline believers look askance at the very concept of spirit. Catholic theologian Walter Kasper observes, "The loss of the dimension and reality which Western thinking has described by the term 'spirit' is perhaps the most profound crisis of the present time."[3] In surely one of the most brilliant and moving treatments of the subject, John V. Taylor is even more to the point: "The whole of our uneasy debate about the meaning of the word 'God' for modern man cries out, I believe, for a recovery of a significant doctrine of the Holy Spirit."[4]

---

[3] Walter Kasper, *The God of Jesus Christ*, trans. Matthew J. O'Connell (New York: Crossroad, 1984), 198.

[4] John V. Taylor, *The Go-Between God: The Holy Spirit and the Christian Mission* (London: SCM, 1972), 5.

On the other hand, there is a worldwide *explosion* of interest in—more accurately, *experience* of—the Holy Spirit. More than a half billion believers globally now call themselves Pentecostal or charismatic Christians, when before 1900 no one had ever heard of such a description. Along this continuum there are gradations from contemplatives to "charismaniacs." Even mainline theologian Harvey Cox, perhaps best known for his book *Secular City*, has now acknowledged the phenomenal growth of *experiential* (i.e., Pentecostal/charismatic) Christianity in recent decades and has offered a critical yet sympathetic analysis of future prospects.[5]

This new breed of believers views Pentecost not only as a key redemptive event recorded in the Scriptures but also as an experience of empowerment available to contemporary Christians. It is this latter revival experience that has undoubtedly done more to draw the church's attention to the Bible's teachings on the Spirit than any other development. Before looking at the historic event of Pentecost itself, let us consider briefly this modern testimony to Pentecostal experience and empowerment.

A Personal Pentecost

As I type these words, I am seated in my office in the School of Theology and Missions of Oral Roberts University in Tulsa, Oklahoma—a major center of the global Pentecostal/charismatic revival. Earlier on this lovely spring day in the rolling hills of Oklahoma, I sat on the steps of the Learning Resources Center and looked across the campus. I was inundated with symbols, metaphors, and memories. The perennial winds of this region, known as Green Country, stirred the newly budding trees and shrubs. I thought of the mysterious *ruaḥ* of the Old Testament and *pneuma* of the New Testament ("wind, breath, spirit")—key metaphors for the person, power, and presence of the Holy Spirit in the Bible.

A modern-day cross, planted in the very center of the campus—the Prayer Tower—dominated my view. At the center of this structure is a representation of the crown of thorns with which our Lord was afflicted during his Passion. Two flames of fire burn in this section of the campus—one in the midst of a cascading fountain (also reminiscent of the Spirit) at the entrance to the Learning Resources Center, the other atop the

[5] Harvey Cox, *Fire from Heaven* (New York: Addison-Wesley, 1995).

Prayer Tower itself. Neither the flame of the tower nor the prayers of the saints inside have ceased since this building was opened. At the base lie lovely prayer gardens where one can pray and meditate.

Directly behind the Prayer Tower I could barely see the Timko-Barton building, which will always have a personal significance for me. As an eighteen-year-old I sat in an auditorium there, among more than seven hundred other young people attending a youth seminar. We listened with rapt attention as world-renowned healing evangelist Oral Roberts, American Baptist scholar Howard Ervin, budding Christian broadcaster Pat Robertson, and others taught about the mighty move of the Spirit and the power for witness that one could receive through the baptism in the Holy Spirit.

As a serious follower of Jesus Christ, I had had many meaningful experiences with the Lord, and I have had many such experiences since. But what happened to me during that seminar was unique. I can only describe it as a *Pentecost* experience. My life and ministry would never be the same. I was startled at how similar this encounter with Christ was to my conversion as a seven-year-old. Since that time I have seen and experienced similar revival outpourings. I am more convinced than ever that this dimension of the Holy Spirit's work is key to the church's end-time mission. It is a sorely neglected biblical teaching and dynamic, which Pentecostal/charismatic Christians in large measure are helping to restore to the church. Too often theologians have ignored this revival/empowerment dimension of the Spirit. More will be said about this perspective later. But what about the historical event of Pentecost itself? What was its significance?

Preparation

Pentecost was one of three major festivals of worship that all Jewish males were expected to attend. Celebrated fifty days after Passover, it was a harvest festival during which God's people acknowledged God's faithful provision. During such days Jerusalem was jammed with pilgrims from across the Mediterranean world. But the particular festival Luke describes in Acts—one that occurred only fifty days after the resurrection of our Lord—was to become one of the most significant events in the long history of God's saving work on behalf of humankind.

Jesus had prepared his disciples for this occasion. Their instinct after the ascension of Christ might have been to return to Galilee, where so much of Jesus' ministry had transpired. But his specific instructions were for them to remain in Jerusalem. In preparing his disciples for this event, Jesus imparted to them the Great Commission vision that would inform everything they and their progeny would do for the next two millennia.

It was Easter Sunday evening. The disciples had locked their doors "for fear of the Jews" (John 20:19). Their hopes and dreams had been smashed by the ignominious and torturous death of their Lord. Suddenly Jesus appeared to them. "They were startled and terrified, and thought that they were seeing a ghost" (Luke 24:37). Jesus offered them empirical proof of his bodily resurrection by showing them his hands, his feet, and his side, and even by eating a piece of broiled fish (24:39–43; John 20:20). In both Luke's and John's accounts of this appearance Jesus immediately gives what could only be described as a Great Commission:

Both Luke and John link closely commissioning and anointing, the mission and the Spirit.

> Jesus said to them again, "Peace be with you. As the Father has sent me, so I send you." When he had said this, he breathed on them and said to them, "Receive the Holy Spirit. If you forgive the sins of any, they are forgiven them; if you retain the sins of any, they are retained." (John 20:21–23)

Scholars debate this particular passage. Was this John's literary version of Pentecost? Was this encounter with Christ a new birth experience for the ten apostles? Was Jesus merely preparing his disciples for Pentecost?

One thing is clear: Both Luke and John link closely commissioning and anointing, the mission and the Spirit. In Matthew's Great Commission the emphasis is on discipleship expressed through the baptizing and teaching ministries of the church (Matt. 28:18–20). Mark adds a note of condemnation for those who reject the gospel and mentions charismatic "signs" that will accompany the mission (Mark 16:15–18). But John, briefly, and Luke, more extensively, highlight the Spirit's role in the Church's mission.[6]

Jesus' breathing on the disciples is reminiscent of the creation of the man in Genesis 2:7. Jesus had already compared his sending of the

---

[6] See Gary M. Burge, *The Anointed Community: T4he Holy Spirit in the Johannine Tradition* (Grand Rapids: Eerdmans, 1987), 199.

disciples with his own sending (John 17:18, 21). He also refers to the forgiveness of sins (cf. Luke 24:47). This is the primary mission of the church. Lloyd John Ogilvie, chaplain of the United States Senate, writes, "Communicating forgiveness is really the calling of the priesthood of all believers. A sure sign we have experienced the Easter miracle and have been filled with the Spirit is that we are communicators of forgiveness."[7]

But if John reminds us of the priesthood of the believers, it is Luke who portrays the *prophethood* of the believers. To step into the world of Luke-Acts is to be transported back to the charismatic and prophetic work of the Spirit in Old Testament times. Luke, perhaps more than any other New Testament writer, shows us the *continuity* of the Old and New Testaments in relation to the person and work of the Holy Spirit. Jesus himself helped his disciples in this regard that same Easter Sunday evening.

Promise

Jesus first interpreted his entire life and ministry, death and resurrection, through a survey of the Scriptures (Luke 24:44–47). He then commissioned them "that repentance and forgiveness of sins is to be proclaimed in his name to all nations, beginning from Jerusalem" (v. 47). Then Jesus said that he was sending "the promise of my Father" upon his disciples (24:49 RSV). Acts picks up this same theme: "While staying with them, he ordered them not to leave Jerusalem, but to wait there for the promise of the Father" (Acts 1:4). The promise to which Jesus referred was the gift of the Holy Spirit. Near the conclusion of his Pentecost sermon, the apostle Peter says of the risen Christ, "Being therefore exalted at the right hand of God, and having received from the Father the promise of the Holy Spirit, he has poured out this that you both see and hear" (2:33).

Peter's hearers "were cut to the heart" and wanted to know what they should do (Acts 2:37).

> Peter said to them, "Repent, and be baptized every one of you in the name of Jesus Christ so that your sins may be forgiven; and you will receive the gift of the Holy Spirit. For the promise is for you, for your children, and for all who are far away, everyone whom the Lord our God calls to him. (2:38–39)

---

[7] Lloyd John Ogilvie, *Silent Strength for My Life* (Eugene, Ore.: Harvest House, 1990), 107.

When was this promise of the gift of the Holy Spirit given?

The Old Testament prophets predicted an end-time outpouring of the Spirit (see Isa. 32:15; Ezek. 36:27; 39:29; Joel 2:28–32; cf. Jer. 31:31–34; Ezek. 11:19–20). Then we have John the Baptist's proclamation (Matt. 3:1–12; Mark 1:1–8; Luke 3:2–18; John 1:19–34), to which Jesus himself referred (Acts 1:5; cf. 11:15–17). Both John and Jesus predicted a "baptism in the Holy Spirit" that would empower the church's mission. Finally, Jesus taught extensively on the Holy Spirit, the Paraclete, in the Upper Room the night prior to his crucifixion (John 14–16). In these "Paraclete sayings" the role of the Father in relation to the gift of the Spirit looms large.

Earlier Jesus had taught his disciples about the Holy Spirit in his exhortation to pray persistently (Luke 11:5–12). We are to ask, search, and knock—tenaciously! He added, "If you then, who are evil, know how to give good gifts to your children, how much more will the heavenly Father give the Holy Spirit to those who ask him!" (11:13). A closer examination of this passage reveals that Jesus is referring here to an ongoing appropriation of the Spirit in the Christian life.[8] The consistency, effectiveness, and fruitfulness of our Christian walk require our persevering prayer for the fullness of the Holy Spirit. Paul reminds us that this dynamic is entirely the work of God; he enables our prayer and supplies his Spirit solely on the basis of his grace (Gal. 3:1–5; Phil. 2:13).

Purpose

We have already touched on the purpose of the gift of the Holy Spirit. During the days of his resurrection appearances Jesus spoke often about the kingdom of God (see Acts 1:3). When he spoke of Spirit baptism, the disciples asked, "Lord, is this the time when you will restore the kingdom to Israel?" (1:6). Jesus then forcefully identifies the purpose of their imminent Pentecostal empowerment: "But you will receive power when the Holy Spirit has come upon you; and you will be my witnesses in Jerusalem, in all Judea and Samaria, and to the ends of the earth" (1:8). As American Baptist scholar Howard M. Ervin states, "The purpose of Pentecost is unmistakably world evangelism."[9]

---

[8] George T. Montague, *The Holy Spirit: Growth of a Biblical Tradition* (New York: Paulist, 1976), 259–60.

[9] Howard M. Ervin, *Spirit Baptism: A Biblical Investigation* (Peabody, Mass.: Hendrickson, 1987), 38.

Acts goes on to describe the Holy Spirit's direction and enablement of the church's explosive mission in the Roman Empire. As John V. Taylor observes,

> The chief actor in the historic mission of the Christian church is the Holy Spirit. He is the director of the whole enterprise. The mission consists of the things that he is doing in the world. In a special way it consists of the light he is focussing upon Jesus Christ.[10]

Luke's message is clear: The secret to the bold witness and amazing growth of the New Testament church was the person, presence, and power of the Holy Spirit. As helpful as studies in church growth and leadership have been, authentic church growth and vitality are based first and foremost through prayerful dependence on and obedience to the Holy Spirit. Southern Baptist leader Ken Hemphill has written powerfully concerning this important truth:

The secret to the bold witness and amazing growth of the New Testament church was the person, presence, and power of the Holy Spirit.

> Pentecost marks the beginning and the empowering of the New Testament church. It marks a unique transformation in the lives of the members of the early church. After Pentecost we see high-voltage Christianity. If we ourselves and our churches do not have a Pentecost experience, we will never be bold witnesses and never know supernatural church growth.[11]

Another Southern Baptist scholar, Boyd Hunt, has sought to place this insight in its broadest scriptural context—relating the Spirit, the kingdom, the church, and the Christian life:

> *Pentecost was the coming of the Holy Spirit to effect in history the presence and power of God's kingdom purposes in Christ.* The work of the Spirit in the Christian life and the church should be studied in the context of New Testament teaching regarding the kingdom of God. The Christian life and the church are fundamentally kingdom realities, and they must be understood in the light of God's kingdom purpose in Jesus Christ. Pentecost was a kingdom event! It was the inauguration in history of the long-awaited messianic kingdom, the outpouring of spiritual abundance

---

[10] Taylor, *The Go-Between God*, 3.

[11] Ken Hemphill, *The Antioch Effect* (Nashville: Broadman & Holman, 1994), 27–28.

promised throughout the Old Testament for the last days. Yet the inauguration of the kingdom was not its consummation. The kingdom is already present in power, but its consummation awaits the return of Christ.[12]

Prayer

One notes also in Luke's narrative and theology how prayer and the power of the Holy Spirit are inextricably linked. We have already noted how prayer was central in every crucial juncture in the life and ministry of both Jesus and the early church.[13] *This may be one of the most important theological and strategic insights Christians can garner from Luke.* In view of the controversies surrounding the work of the Holy Spirit, we must remember that prayer is an incontrovertible factor in the empowered Christian life and mission. Luke-Acts is a clarion call to Christians of every stripe—mainline, evangelical, Pentecostal, charismatic—to humble, unified, dependent prayer. This is God's kingdom mandate to all of us![14]

Prophecy

Not only was prayer central to the event of Pentecost (Acts 1:14); prophecy also played a major role. Peter pointed to Joel's prophecy of an end-time outpouring of the Spirit (Joel 2:28–32; see Acts 2:16–21) when he explained what had transpired that day. The manner in which Peter rendered Joel's words heightens this emphasis. Whereas Joel said, "Then afterward" (Joel 2:28), Peter says, "In the last days" (Acts 2:17). And to Joel's words predicting an outpouring of the Spirit on even the male and female slaves (Joel 2:29), Peter adds, "and they shall prophesy" (Acts 2:18). "Luke (through Peter) thus identifies the whole Pentecost event as a manifestation of prophecy, very much like the coming of the spirit upon the seventy elders in Numbers 11:27."[15] Characteristically for Luke, this infilling of the Spirit is understood in terms of "tongues as praise and prophetic speech as proclamation."[16]

---

12 Boyd Hunt, *Redeemed! Eschatological Redemption and the Kingdom of God* (Nashville: Broadman & Holman, 1993), 16–17 (Hunt's italics). More precisely, Christ himself inaugurated the kingdom.

13 See 290–291 above.

14 See Stephen S. Smalley, "Spirit, Kingdom and Prayer in Luke-Acts," *Novum Testamentum* 15 (1973): 59–71.

15 Montague, *The Holy Spirit*, 285.

16 Ibid.

Vital Christianity is known for its exuberant praise and bold proclamation, both of which are inspired by the Holy Spirit.

To this day, vital Christianity is known for its exuberant praise and bold proclamation, both of which are inspired by the Holy Spirit. For Luke this is *prophetic* activity. Eduard Schweizer highlights this distinctive Lukan perspective in his study of *pneuma* ("Spirit") in the New Testament. Consider his comments:

(1) "[To prophesy] is for Luke quite central as *the* work of the Spirit.... The eschatological community is for Luke the community of the prophets."
(2) "Luke thus shares with Judaism the view that the Spirit is essentially the Spirit of prophecy."
(3) "The prophets are no longer isolated individuals. All the members of the eschatological community are prophets."
(4) "In the new age of salvation all members of the community rather than special individuals are bearers of the Spirit, and ... the action of the Spirit is almost exclusively taken to be prophetic action."[17]

Thus, to the Protestant paradigm of "the priesthood of all believers" we can add the equally essential Lukan concept of "the prophethood of all believers"![18]

Provocation!

Perhaps God deliberately intended that, by its very nature, the Pentecost experience would *provoke*! He continually works to stir things up, incite interest in kingdom issues, arouse sleepy saints, and stimulate action. Naturally, we prefer the secure, safe, and predictable. The church is always working to be "in control." Yet her greatest need is to

---

[17] Eduard Schweizer, "πνεῦμα, κτλ," *Theological Dictionary of the New Testament*, ed. Gerhard Friedrich, trans. and ed. Geoffrey W. Bromiley (Grand Rapids: Eerdmans, 1968), 6:408–9, 412 (Schweizer's italics).

[18] Roger Stronstad, "Affirming Diversity: God's People as a Community of Prophets" (Presidential Address for The Society for Pentecostal Studies, November 10–12, 1994, Wheaton College, Wheaton, Ill.). See also Roger Stronstad's groundbreaking study, *The Charismatic Theology of St. Luke* (Peabody, Mass.: Hendrickson, 1984). Stronstad's work has strongly influenced my own thinking in relation to the work of the Holy Spirit. Another important study of this Lukan leitmotif is Robert Menzies's *Empowered for Witness: The Spirit in Luke-Acts* (Journal of Pentecostal Theology Supplement Series 6; Sheffield, England: Sheffield Academic Press, 1991).

be controlled by her Lord and Savior. Too often we fail to pursue God's power. Rather, we attempt to substitute our own abilities, resisting and even resenting God's intrusions!

William H. Willimon, dean of the chapel at Duke University, in his own provocative style observes:

> All evidence to the contrary, we continue to sin against Pentecost, continue to attempt to explain away the disruptive descent of the Spirit. And you know why. The Acts 2 threat that one Sunday we might all gather here in our bolted down pews, with our smug reasonableness, our bourgeois respectability, only to be grabbed by our collective collar, shaken up, thrown into confusion, intoxicated, is not a suggestion we welcome. Most of us come in here to be confirmed in what we think we already know; not to be dislodged, led by the Spirit into *terra incognita* we do not know. But be careful. As you come to the table today, with hands open, maybe even minds open, be careful. The wind blows where it will (John 3), God's Spirit will not be housebroken by us, and your soul might catch fire, even yet, even here.
>
> I would hate to see nice, respectable people like you with mortgages go out of here *drunk*.
>
> No I wouldn't.[19]

Willimon's delightful, yet disconcerting, diagnosis is disturbingly accurate.

The Spirit does much more, however, than stimulate us to action. The portrayal of his mighty works spans the Scriptures from Genesis to Revelation.

Wind

Pentecost was a sudden, sovereign action of God right out of heaven! "And suddenly from heaven there came a sound like the rush of a violent wind, and it filled the entire house where they were sitting" (Acts 2:2). In Scripture the metaphor of wind serves as a fundamental model of the Spirit.

Perhaps because of my roots in West Texas, I have always been fascinated by the wind. The wind is almost incessant in that part of the country. Many an afternoon as I shot baskets at my outdoor goal, I would rebuke the wind for blowing my shots off course. Even more dramatic

---

19 William H. Willimon, "They're Drunk," Pentecost Sermon, Duke University Chapel, May 22, 1994 (transcipt), 3–4. (Willimon's italics).

were the sandstorms. Just thirty miles south of my hometown is the Monahans Sandhills State Park, with Sahara-like dunes stretching for miles. When the winds pick up tons of that sand and move it across the plains in dark swirling clouds, they can turn midday to midnight and signal a virtual apocalypse.

Residing now in Oklahoma, where the wind comes sweeping down the plain, my fascination continues. *Ruaḥ* in Hebrew and *pneuma* in Greek both point to the mysterious presence and power of the Spirit of God as wind, breath, or spirit. Explaining the work of the Spirit to Nicodemus, Jesus said: "The wind blows where it chooses, and you hear the sound of it, but you do not know where it comes from or where it goes. So it is with everyone who is born of the Spirit" (John 3:8). The words "wind" and "Spirit" both translate the same Greek term (*pneuma*).

> *Pentecost was a sudden, sovereign action of God right out of heaven!*

In identifying the outpouring of the Holy Spirit at Pentecost as the fulfillment of Joel's prophecy (Acts 2:16–21; see Joel 2:28–32), Peter uses an important hermeneutical tool, that of interpreting Scripture with Scripture—or a canonical approach to the text. While the Old Testament writers did not possess a Trinitarian understanding of God, with the New Testament application of this key Old Testament passage we see the Pentecost event and the Holy Spirit as the Spirit of God portrayed so majestically and mysteriously in numerous Old Testament passages.[20] The metaphor of the Spirit as wind takes us back to the opening words of Genesis.

Creation

The Scriptures begin with a majestic announcement and poetic description of the Creator God and his awesome creation.

> In the beginning God created the heavens and the earth. The earth was without form and void, and darkness was upon the face of the deep; and the Spirit of God was moving over the face of the waters. (Gen. 1:1–2 RSV)

A "mighty wind swept over the waters" (1:2 NAB). In our mind's eye we see a violent wind sweeping across endless, dark, tumultuous waters. One is reminded of the wind God made to blow over the earth after

---

[20] See Millard J. Erickson, *Christian Theology* (Grand Rapids: Baker, 1985), 866.

Noah's flood (8:1). And at the Exodus it was a strong east wind that blew all night and "turned the sea into dry land" (Ex. 14:21).

It is this powerful, mysterious, creative Spirit of God whom helpless humankind must seek and surrender to. Michael Green makes this classic statement:

> We are in danger of forgetting that it is God we are talking about: the God who created us, the God who sustains us and has sovereign rights over us. This God can and does break in to human life, and sometimes he does it through the violent, the unexpected, the alien.... Perhaps this surrender to the invading power of God's Spirit, this willingness for him to take us and break us and use us, is one of the prime lessons which the charismatic movement throughout the Churches is teaching us at the present.[21]

The twentieth century church needs again to hear "a sound like the rush of a violent wind" (Acts 2:2)!

The same Holy Spirit who, with the Father and the Son, brought forth the creation also sustains it:

> When you send your Spirit, they are created, and you renew the face of the earth. (Ps. 104:30 NIV)

> The Spirit of God has made me; and the breath of the Almighty gives me life. (Job 33:4 NIV)

> If he should take back his spirit to himself, and gather to himself his breath, all flesh would perish together, and all mortals return to dust. (Job 34:14–15)

In Job 34, Elihu refers first to God's Spirit (*ruaḥ*) and then to his breath (*nešamah*). These two terms are closely related in the Hebrew Scriptures. God *breathed* the breath (*nešamah*) of life into the man at the creation (Gen. 2:7). Through the breath of God we have the Scriptures themselves: "All Scripture is God-breathed [*theopneustos*]" (2 Tim. 3:16 NIV). But the breath of God can also bring judgment. The "blast of the breath" of God's nostrils can reveal the very "channels of the sea" and "foundations of the world" (2 Sam. 22:16; Ps. 18:15). Isaiah predicted that "the breath of the LORD, like a stream of sulfur" would bring the

---

21 Michael Green, *I Believe in the Holy Spirit* (Grand Rapids: Eerdmans, 1975), 20–21. Green illustrates his point by relating two accounts of contemporary charismatic miracles that changed the lives of the recipients.

flame of God's judgment against Assyria (Isa. 30:33).[22] It is to this metaphor of God's Spirit as *fire* to which we now turn.

Fire

Along with the sound of the violent wind at Pentecost came tongues "as of fire" (Acts 2:3). Paul exhorted the Thessalonians, "Do not quench the Spirit" (1 Thess. 5:19). He encouraged young Timothy's faith with these words: "That is why I am reminding you now to fan into a flame the gift of God that you possess through the laying on of my hands" (2 Tim. 1:6 NJB). And the apostle urged the Christians of Rome to never "flag in zeal, [but to] be aglow with the Spirit, [and] serve the Lord" (Rom. 12:11 RSV). A church ablaze with God's Spirit will have the attention of the world!

A church ablaze with God's Spirit will have the attention of the world!

Dove

The symbol of the dove has become *the* metaphor for the Holy Spirit in our own day. One can even trace this bird-metaphor back to the creation account itself: "and the Spirit of God was hovering over the waters" (Gen. 1:2 NIV). Here we have the image of a great bird brooding over the creation, protecting and providing for its own.[23]

A New Testament reference, of course, is the account of Jesus' baptism, when the Holy Spirit descended on him. "When Jesus had been baptized, just as he came up from the water, suddenly the heavens were opened to him and he saw the Spirit of God descending like a dove and alighting on him" (Matt. 3:16). Mark says that Jesus "saw the heavens torn apart and the Spirit descending like a dove on him" (Mark 1:10). Typically, Luke is even more thorough and precise, adding that it was while Jesus "was praying" that "the heaven was opened, and the Holy Spirit descended upon him in bodily form like a dove" (Luke 3:21–22). Notice Luke's specific "in bodily form." John notes that John the Baptist also saw the Spirit's descent:

---

[22] See Dale Moody, *Spirit of the Living God* (Philadelphia: Westminster, 1968), 12.

[23] The wind metaphor seems to be the more obvious interpretation of this passage. Nevertheless, neither view should be quickly dismissed.

> And John testified, "I saw the Spirit descending from heaven like a dove, and it remained on him. I myself did not know him, but the one who sent me to baptize with water said to me, 'He on whom you see the Spirit descend and remain is the one who baptizes with the Holy Spirit.' And I myself have seen and have testified that this is the Son of God." (John 1:32–34)

Jesus began his inaugural sermon by reading from Isaiah's messianic prophecy: "The Spirit of the Lord is upon me, because he has anointed me" (Luke 4:18; see Isa. 61:1).

Tertullian of Carthage (ca. 160–ca. 225) fought for both the preservation of the doctrine of the Trinity and the charismatic dimension of the Holy Spirit, specifically the place and importance of the gift of prophecy. He had joined ranks with the charismatic renewal movement of his day known as Montanism. One of his opponents was a certain Praxeas, who espoused a Unitarian teaching in Rome known as Monarchianism. Tertullian, one of my favorites among the early fathers,[24] wrote in response to Praxeas' heretical teachings: "Thus Praxeas at Rome managed two pieces of the devil's business: he drove out prophecy and introduced heresy; he put to flight the Paraclete and crucified the Father" (*Against Praxeas* 1).[25] Perhaps every new generation of the church needs a charismatic movement to keep her honest in relation to the work of the Holy Spirit.

In fact, the doctrine of the Holy Spirit has often been neglected in the teaching of the Church—but no more! Alister McGrath writes:

> The Holy Spirit has long been the Cinderella of the Trinity. The other two sisters may have gone to the theological ball; the Holy Spirit got left behind every time. But not now. The rise of the charismatic movement within virtually every mainstream church has ensured that the Holy Spirit figures prominently on the theological agenda. A new experience of the reality and power of the Spirit has had a major impact upon the theological discussion of the person and work of the Holy Spirit.[26]

Too often in our day Enlightenment rationalism, New Age paganism, and even dead orthodoxy have put the dove of the Spirit to flight. But

---

[24] Perhaps this is so because he reminds me so much of my mentor, Dale Moody, who also was a bold battler for biblical truth, including the charismatic dimension of the work of the Spirit!

[25] Cited in Dale Moody, *The Word of Truth* (Grand Rapids: Eerdmans, 1981), 122. See the standard edition by Ernest Evans, *Tertullian's Treatise Against Praxeas* (London: SPCK, 1948).

[26] Alister E. McGrath, *Christian Theology: An Introduction* (Cambridge, Mass.: Blackwell, 1994), 240.

recent outpourings of the Spirit seem to be ensuring us against the persistence of this heretical tendency.

Water

The Spirit was *poured out* on the day of Pentecost (Acts 2:17; see Joel 2:28; Acts 2:33). The metaphor of water looms large in the Scriptures. Isaiah writes of Israel's ultimate salvation, "Until the Spirit is poured out upon us from on high, and the wilderness becomes a fertile field" (Isa. 32:15 NASB); "for I will pour water on the thirsty land, and streams on the dry ground; I will pour my Spirit upon your descendants, and my blessing on your offspring. They shall spring up like grass amid waters, like willows by flowing streams" (Isa. 44:3, 4 RSV). Ezekiel adds, "I will not hide my face any more from them, when I pour out my Spirit upon the house of Israel, says the Lord God" (Ezek. 39:29 RSV). Could there be a more beautiful picture of salvation? Jesus himself spoke of this saving water (John 4:7–15; 7:37–39). At the same time, he made it crystal clear that this same Holy Spirit, symbolized by water, is a *person* (cf., e.g., 14:16–17, 26; 15:26; 16:7–15).

The *Personal* Spirit

Metaphors serve an important function in communication, but the literally minded often misconstrue the truth. This has been especially so in relation to the Holy Spirit. How often do we hear someone refer to the Holy Spirit as "it"? We have already looked at the symbols of wind, fire, dove, and water. But the Bible's testimony is unmistakable: The Holy Spirit is *personal*! J. I. Packer, in his concise yet comprehensive style, provides an apt summary of this doctrinal truth:

> Paraclete ministry, by its very nature, is personal, relational ministry, implying the full personhood of the one who fulfills it. Though the Old Testament said much about the Spirit's activity in Creation (e.g., Gen. 1:2; Ps. 33:6), revelation (e.g., Isa. 61:1–6; Mic. 3:8), enabling for service (e.g., Exod. 31:2–6; Judg. 6:34; 15:14–15; Isa. 11:2), and inward renewal (e.g., Ps. 51:10–12; Ezek. 36:25–27), it did not make clear that the Spirit is a distinct divine Person. In the New Testament, however, it becomes clear that the Spirit is as truly a Person distinct from the Father as the Son is. This is apparent not only from Jesus' promise of "another

Counselor," but also from the fact that the Spirit, among other things, speaks (Acts 1:16; 8:29; 10:19; 11:12; 13:2; 28:25), teaches (John 14:26), witnesses (John 15:26), searches (1 Cor. 2:11), determines (1 Cor. 12:11), intercedes (Rom. 8:26–27), is lied to (Acts 5:3), and can be grieved (Eph. 4:30). Only of a personal being can such things be said.[27]

The Holy Spirit is profoundly personal, even *inter*personal. He relates personally, and he promotes personal relationships—between God and us, and among ourselves. Furthermore, he may rightly be considered the unity of the Godhead: Taylor's "Go-Between God," Macquarrie's "unitive" Being, who also unites the creation back to the Creator,[28] and Augustine's God of love.[29]

The *Divine* Spirit

From what has already been said, it is abundantly clear that the Spirit is divine. To speak of the Spirit is to speak of deity. He is the Creator Spirit. He is also "the eternal Spirit" (Heb. 9:14). He gave us the Scriptures (2 Tim. 3:16; 2 Peter 1:21). To lie to the Holy Spirit is to lie to God (Acts 5:3, 4). We baptize "in the name [singular] of the Father and of the Son and of the Holy Spirit" (Matt. 28:19), and we confess the Spirit as one with the Godhead (2 Cor. 13:14).

Our salvation is truly a Trinitarian reality. We "have been chosen according to the foreknowledge of God the Father, through the sanctifying work of the Spirit, for obedience to Jesus Christ and sprinkling by his blood" (1 Peter 1:2 NIV).[30] That is, "God planned long ago to choose you by making you his holy people, which is the Spirit's work. God wanted you to obey him and to be made clean by the blood of the death of Jesus Christ" (1 Pet. 1:2 NCV). The work of the personal, divine Spirit of God is to *apply* the saving work of Christ to each of us.

---

[27] J. I. Packer, *Concise Theology* (Wheaton, Ill.: Tyndale, 1993), 143–44.

[28] John Macquarrie, *Principles of Christian Theology* (New York: Charles Scribner's Sons, 1966), 182–93.

[29] See Alister McGrath's presentation of Augustine's doctrine of the Trinity, in which the Holy Spirit is portrayed as unifying love, both among God's people and within the Trinity: *Christian Theology*, 257–60.

[30] See Erickson, *Christian Theology*, 859.

The One Work of the Holy Spirit

Because God is one, his revelation, as we have already seen, is one. And because there is "one Spirit" (Eph. 4:4), there is also a unity to the work of the Spirit. There is *one work* of the Holy Spirit, and there are *three fundamental dimensions* to that one work. It is vitally important to notice the three dimensions of the Spirit's work; it is just as essential to guard the unity of his work. All sorts of distortions and misunderstandings can be avoided or alleviated by remaining faithful to these two fundamental biblical truths.

I find it helpful to display the work of the Spirit in the following manner:

Paschal	*Purifying*	*Pentecostal*
Salvation	Sanctification	Service
Conversion	Consecration	Charisma
How to . . . Get Started	Get Straight	Get Strong
John	Paul	Luke

Paschal refers to the Holy Spirit's direct application of Christ's saving work at Calvary. It is his initiating work. It is the manner in which he imparts to us eternal life. Paul refers to Christ as "our paschal lamb" (1 Cor. 5:7), but John focuses on this paschal dimension more perhaps than any other New Testament theologian.[31] *Purifying* denotes the sanctifying dimension of the work of the Spirit; Paul's letters provide us with the most profound explication of this subject. Finally, *Pentecostal* points to the empowering dimension of the Spirit's work (esp. seen in Luke).

The Paschal Work of the Holy Spirit[32]

The apostle John mentions an important detail related to Jesus' death. When one of the Roman soldiers pierced Jesus' side with a spear, "at once blood and water came out" (John 19:34). John emphasizes that he is relating an eyewitness account, and he implies that this fact is important to a full understanding of Jesus' death. First, the *actuality* of Jesus' death is probably being indicated. Jesus was indeed dead. But John may see a further significance—a spiritual and theological insight

[31] Each of these dimensions can be found throughout the New Testament. But John, Paul, and Luke have distinctive emphases.

[32] I will refer to "the paschal work," "the purifying work," and "the Pentecostal work" for the sake of brevity. However, the reader should never lose sight of the unity of the work of the Spirit.

that will necessitate our reviewing the beginning of his Gospel to fully appreciate what was being symbolized here.

At the outset of John's Gospel John the Baptist bears a threefold witness to Jesus: (1) "Behold, the Lamb of God, who takes away the sin of the world!" (John 1:29 RSV; cf. 1:36); (2) "this is [the one] who baptizes with the Holy Spirit" (1:33, God's message to John the Baptist); (3) "this is the Son of God" (1:34). The phrase "Son of God" is a key Christological title in the Johannine literature, and it serves here as the culmination of the Baptizer's testimony. But the first two elements comprise a programmatic framework for interpreting the life and ministry of our Lord.

> *There is* one work *of the Holy Spirit, and there are* three fundamental dimensions *to that one work.*

Notice how John frames his Gospel: "At once came out blood and water." *Blood:* "Behold, the Lamb of God, who takes away the sin of the world!" *Water:* "This is the one who baptizes with the Holy Spirit." Jesus is the one who lays down his life and sheds his blood for the forgiveness of our sins. He is also the source of the rivers of living water, the Holy Spirit, who mediates eternal life to us.[33]

Jesus told the Samaritan woman about "living water" (John 4:10): "The water that I will give will become in them a spring of water gushing up to eternal life" (4:14). Previously, he had told Nicodemus about the necessity of "being born of water and Spirit" (3:5). Then John relates the dramatic event of Jesus' declaration during the Feast of Tabernacles, or "festival of Booths":

> On the last day of the festival, the great day, while Jesus was standing there, he cried out, "Let anyone who is thirsty come to me, and let the one who believes in me drink. As the scripture has said, 'Out of the believer's heart [lit. out of his belly] shall flow rivers of living water.'" Now he said this about the Spirit, which believers in him were to receive; for as yet there was no Spirit [or, the Spirit had not yet been given], because Jesus was not yet glorified. (John 7:37–39)

---

[33] Cf. 1 John 5:6–8 CEV: "Water and blood came out from the side of Jesus Christ. It wasn't just water, but water and blood. The Spirit tells about this, because the Spirit is truthful. In fact, there are three who tell about it. They are the Spirit, the water, and the blood, and they all agree." See also the note on verse 6 in the CEV.

These words, combined with the Paraclete sayings of John 14–16, portray dramatically the work of the Holy Spirit mediating eternal life. Throughout these narratives one perceives the close connection of the Spirit with Jesus himself, his person and his work.

The paschal work of the Spirit brings salvation, conversion, and a new start (a new birth, a birth from above; John 3:3–8). This is how one gets started in the Christian life. I will say more about this regenerating work of the Holy Spirit later. But it is important at this juncture to go on to the *purifying* work of the Spirit. He not only gives us new life; he also conforms us and transforms us into the image of Jesus Christ.

The Purifying Work of the Holy Spirit

The apostle Paul, in poignant terms, reminded the believers at Corinth of the kingdom mandate of holiness that accompanies our salvation.

> Do you not know that wrongdoers will not inherit the kingdom of God? Do not be deceived! Fornicators, idolaters, adulterers, male prostitutes, sodomites, thieves, the greedy, drunkards, revilers, robbers—none of these will inherit the kingdom of God. And this is what some of you used to be. But you were washed, you were sanctified, you were justified in the name of the Lord Jesus Christ and in the Spirit of our God. (1 Cor. 6:9–11)

When Paul writes "you were sanctified . . . in the Spirit of our God," he is referring to the sanctifying work of the Holy Spirit that takes place at the beginning of the Christian life. At the same time, he is exhorting the Corinthians to holy living *in the present*!

This concern for holiness characterizes Paul's writings. In one of his earliest letters, Paul reminds his hearers that "this is the will of God for you, your sanctification" (1 Thess. 4:3). "For God did not call us to impurity but in holiness. Therefore whoever rejects this rejects not human authority but God, who also gives his Holy Spirit to you" (4:7–8). The clenching argument for holiness, according to Paul, is that the God who called us to sanctification/holiness (*hagiasmos*)[34] has given us his *Holy* (*hagios*, v. 8) Spirit. But it is when Paul presents (Romans) and defends (Galatians) his gospel that he provides us with the most complete explication of the dynamics of holiness—a sanctification that, in the final analysis, is effected by the Holy Spirit.

---

[34] This Greek term is translated either as "sanctification" or as "holiness."

Paul thought in Old Testament categories. It is beautiful to see how he ties the Scriptures together while providing his systematic presentation of the gospel in his letter to "all God's beloved in Rome" (Rom. 1:7). He evokes the names of great Old Testament saints such as Abraham and David (ch. 4). But the ancient figure who looms the largest in the first eight chapters, which expound the good news in concise, yet comprehensive, terms, is *Adam*—Adam as primordial and representative man.

Following his introductory words (Rom. 1:1–17), the apostle launches into an exhaustive presentation of the fundamental problem of humankind: sin (1:18–3:31). His description of our dilemma draws extensively on

> the Genesis account of Adam's fall—man's refusal to acknowledge God as God, to recognize his own creatureliness, resulting in the diminution of his humanity, his fitness to be a companion of God, a plight embracing not only Gentile idolatry and immorality, but also Jewish presumption of a favoured status before God.[35]

This devastating depiction of our universal guilt (3:9–20) is alleviated by Paul's summary of the gospel in 3:21–26. His presentation of the good news of God's gracious gift of righteousness (justification) culminates with the great Adam/Christ typology of 5:12–21.

Paul provides a virtual psychology of sin in Romans 7, and, again, the story of the Fall hovers like a specter in the background. Sin, like Satan, seizing the opportunity of God's commandment, deceives us and kills us (Rom. 7:7–12; cf. Gen. 3:1–13). Consequently, all people are "sold into slavery under sin" (Rom. 7:14). The apostle acknowledges—autobiographically and undoubtedly in a representative fashion—a sort of spiritual schizophrenia (7:14–21). Even as religious people—both Jews and Christians—we may delight in God's law mentally and spiritually. But the law of sin and death, which has its camp in our physical members, our bodies, prevents us from fulfilling that law (7:22–25). Is there a remedy for such helplessness and hopelessness? God provides a twofold remedy with both an objective pole and a subjective pole: (1) the cross of Christ and (2) the Spirit of Christ.

---

[35] James D. G. Dunn, "Salvation Proclaimed: Part VI: Romans 6:1–11: Dead and Alive," *Expository Times* (June, 1982): 259.

Dying and Rising with Christ

Beginning with Romans 6, Paul shows how justification and sanctification are inextricably bound together in God's saving gospel. The church of the twentieth century is weakened in large measure because she has attempted to divide what God has joined. Justification without sanctification is cheap grace. Sanctification apart from justification is legalism. The gospel is both gift and demand. It is a divine call to both forgiveness and discipleship. It invites us both to "come and dine" and to "come and die." The gospel means *transformation* through regeneration and sanctification. We must be willing to change, convert, repent, and believe.

Today we have too many "celebrity saints"—not to mention myriad nominal "Christians"—who show no evidence of this kind of change. "They make a pretense of religion but deny its power" (2 Tim. 3:5 NAB). These words are not meant to discourage immature saints. But they *are* intended to encourage the proclamation of God's good news. J. I. Packer warns us,

> God has joined faith and repentance as the two facets of response to the Savior, and made it clear that turning to Christ means turning from sin and letting ungodliness go. Biblical teaching on faith joins credence with commitment and communion; it exhibits Christian believing as not only knowing facts about Christ, but also coming to him in personal trust to worship, love, and serve him. If we fail to keep together these things that God has joined together, our Christianity will be distorted.
>
> ... Bare assent to the gospel, divorced from a transforming commitment to the living Christ, is by biblical standards less than faith, and less than saving, and to elicit only assent of this kind would be to secure only false conversions.[36]

The apostle Paul made clear time and again that it is only through the power of the Holy Spirit that we can rightly proclaim, savingly appropriate, and effectively live out the gospel.[37] His gospel, which he described as "the power of God for salvation to everyone who has faith," is a liberating message of *both* the grace of God's forgiveness *and* the power we need to live holy lives. The good news to those who receive

---

[36] J. I. Packer, Foreword to: John F. MacArthur Jr., *The Gospel According to Jesus* (Grand Rapids: Zondervan, 1988), ix.

[37] See also the masterful treatment of Paul's doctrine of the Holy Spirit by Gordon D. Fee: *God's Empowering Presence: The Holy Spirit in the Letters of Paul* (Peabody, Mass.: Hendrickson, 1994).

Christ is this: No condemnation! How? Through Christ's cross and through his indwelling Spirit.

Our identity with Christ's death and resurrection frees us from slavery to sin (see Rom. 6). Paul gives expression and application to a fourfold understanding of Christ's death and its meaning for the Christian life. In one of his most profound and programmatic statements about the cross, he states that "one has died for all; therefore all have died" (2 Cor. 5:14). Thus, the Christian experiences the death of Christ in four ways. (1) By God's gracious decision, when Christ died, we all died. God was starting over. He was beginning a whole new humanity in the person of his resurrected Son (see Col. 3:1–4). C. E. B. Cranfield calls this the *juridical* sense.[38]

> *Justification without sanctification is cheap grace. Sanctification apart from justification is legalism.*

(2) Then we died with Christ and were raised with him at our conversion (Col. 2:12). Paul clearly refers to this event in Romans 6:1–4. Cranfield calls this the *baptismal* sense.

(3) But there are also present and future dimensions to our death with Christ. There is a sense in which we experience Christ's death on a daily basis. Paul experienced this reality in the literal sense of physical peril and suffering for the sake of the gospel (1 Cor. 15:31: "I die every day!"; 2 Cor. 4:11; 1:9). A whole theology of suffering derives from these experiences! Christians are called to put to death daily the evil deeds of the body "by the Spirit" (Rom. 8:13). Just as our Lord was mercilessly crucified, so we must mercilessly crucify our sins daily. We must allow the Spirit to apply Christ's death to our sins and liberate us to holy living (ch. 6) on a daily basis. Repentance, in the final analysis, is dying the death of Christ to our sins. This is the *moral* sense in Cranfield's presentation.

(4) Finally, when we die *physically,* we do so in union with Christ's death—and our struggle with sin is ended. At present, however, we "groan inwardly while we wait for adoption, the redemption of our bodies" (Rom. 8:23). As long as we are in these mortal bodies, we will struggle against

[38] C. E. B. Cranfield, *The Epistle to Romans,* vol. 2 (ICC; Edinburgh: T. & T. Clark, 1979), 831. The following comments on the four ways in which Christians die with Christ are an adaptation of Cranfield's helpful summary in Essay 2 of this second volume of his masterful commentary on Romans.

sin, sickness, sorrow, and death. But when "Christ Jesus our hope" (1 Tim. 1:1) appears, the battle is over and victory is fully won!

But what about the battle at present? Can we hope for victory in our *present* struggle against sin? Paul's answer is a resounding Yes! Through the power of the indwelling Spirit of Christ we can have power to live holy lives.

The Law of the Spirit of Life in Christ Jesus

In Romans 8, which completes the first major division of the letter, Paul highlights the role of the Holy Spirit in making possible a holy Christian life. He mentions three "laws," or working principles, of the Christian life in the opening verses:

> There is therefore now no condemnation for those who are in Christ Jesus. For the law of the Spirit of life in Christ Jesus has set you free from the law of sin and death. For what the Law could not do, weak as it was through the flesh, God did: sending His own Son in the likeness of sinful flesh and as an offering for sin, He condemned sin in the flesh, in order that the requirement of the Law might be fulfilled in us, who do not walk according to the flesh, but according to the Spirit. (Rom. 8:1–4 NASB)

The *law of sin and death* has its camp in our physical members (cf. Rom. 7:23–25).[39] It is like the law of gravity, which continually pulls us down. The *Law* of Moses is holy, just, good, and spiritual (7:11–16), but it is powerless to free us from the downward pull of sin. It is "weakened by the flesh" (8:3). But the *law of the Spirit of life in Christ Jesus* liberates us from the law of sin and death. It is like the law of aerodynamics, which can literally supersede the law of gravity!

"For God has done what the law . . . could not do" (Rom. 8:3). First, by "sending His own Son in the likeness of sinful flesh and as an offering for sin, He condemned ['pronounced the death penalty upon'; cf. the noun form of this word ('condemnation') in v. 1] sin in the flesh" (v. 3 NASB). Through Christ's atoning death God pronounced the death penalty on sin. *And his ultimate purpose was that through the "law of the Spirit of life in Christ Jesus," through our walking "according to the Spirit," we might fulfill the righteous requirement of the law* (8:2, 4). Paul goes on to talk about

---

[39] Perhaps this is why Paul risks referring to our fallen nature in its totality (spiritual and physical) as "flesh." It is not that the body itself is evil. It is rather that the law of sin has found an inroad there, so that it really is a "body of death" (Rom. 7:24; see also 8:10).

the mindset (*phronema*) of the Spirit (8:5–8) and about putting to death the evil deeds of the body "by the Spirit" (8:13). These are the principles by which we can live Spirit-empowered holy lives!

Paul makes the same point while defending his gospel against the Judaizers who sought to infiltrate the churches of Galatia. The apostle knew that to require circumcision for salvation was to compromise the grace and freedom of the gospel. "O foolish Galatians!" he writes. "Who has bewitched you, before whose eyes Jesus Christ was publicly portrayed as crucified?" (Gal. 3:1 RSV). Typically, Paul takes his readers back to the cross. He reminds the Galatians of the basis on which they initially received the Spirit: "Did you receive the Spirit by the works of the law, or by the hearing of faith?" (3:2 NKJV). The phrase "hearing of faith" is both intriguing and important. It is accurately rendered by The Good News Bible as "hearing the gospel and believing it." The gospel brings the gift. The basis for receiving the gift of the Holy Spirit is solely our response to the gospel—the hearing of faith.

The basis for receiving the gift of the Holy Spirit is solely our response to the gospel—the hearing of faith.

The apostle warns the Galatian Christians of the stupidity of reverting back to "the works of the law." "Are you so foolish? Having started with the Spirit, are you now ending with the flesh?" (Gal. 3:3). The CEV is excellent here: "How can you be so stupid? Do you think that by yourself you can complete what God's Spirit started in you?" The Christian life *in its totality* is completely the Spirit's work.

Paul adds that the charismatic dimension of the work of the Holy Spirit is also based on grace. "Well then, does God supply you with the Spirit and work miracles among you by your doing the works of the law, or by your believing what you heard [again, lit., 'the hearing of faith']?" (Gal. 3:5). It was the gospel of the crucified Christ that brought the miraculous power of the Spirit into the lives of the Galatian believers. The warning is clear:

> You who want to be justified by the law have cut yourselves off from Christ; you have fallen from grace. For through the Spirit, by faith, we eagerly wait for the hope of righteousness. For in Christ Jesus neither circumcision nor uncircumcision counts for anything; the only thing that counts is faith working through love. (Gal. 5:4–6)

Salvation is thus described in the following terms: justified, Christ, grace, the Spirit, faith, hope, righteousness, love. To these we add the quintessential Pauline term—*freedom* (Gal. 5:1, 13). F. F. Bruce called Paul "the Apostle of the Free Spirit."

For Paul this is not a freedom of self-indulgence but a freedom to love and thus fulfill the whole of the law (Gal. 5:13–14). The faith-walk in the Spirit is a holy walk. "But I say, walk by the Spirit, and you will not carry out the desire of the flesh" (5:16 NASB). Led by the Spirit, we are no longer under the law (5:18). In addition, our lives are no longer characterized by "works of the flesh," such as fornication, strife, envy, drunkenness, and the like; "those who do such things will not inherit the kingdom of God," Paul warns (5:19–21). "By contrast, the fruit of the Spirit is love, joy, peace, patience, kindness, generosity, faithfulness, gentleness, and self-control. There is no law against such things" (5:22–23).

Paul then takes us back to the cross one more time: "Those who belong to Christ Jesus have crucified the sinful nature ['the flesh'] with its passions and desires. Since we live by the Spirit, let us keep in step with the Spirit" (Gal. 5:24, 25 NIV). The Greek word translated here as "keep in step" (usually rendered "walk") is a military term, *stoikeo.* The NIV helpfully brings out this nuance. In other words, the apostle argues, if we receive our very life by the Spirit, then we should keep in step with him—allow him to bring forth his fruit and make us like Jesus.

If the charismatic movement had taught the power of the Spirit for holy living with the same diligence with which it taught the power of the Spirit for signs and wonders, it probably would not find itself on some of the shoals in which it is presently floundering.[40] The purifying work of the Spirit is just as essential as the paschal and Pentecostal work. The Spirit has come to enable sanctification, consecration, full commitment, and dedication to Christ. He wants to help us "get straight." But—as Pentecostal and charismatic saints faithfully remind us—the Spirit has also come to empower us to do the same kingdom work our Lord did in his earthly ministry. And that work was in major part a *charismatic* work.

The Pentecostal Work of the Holy Spirit

Any concept of the work of the Spirit that is not cross-centered will ultimately become a shallow triumphalism (such as Paul combated in

---

[40] See J. Lee Grady, *What Happened to the Fire? Rekindling the Blaze of Charismatic Renewal* (Grand Rapids: Chosen, 1994).

the Corinthian church). Calvary and Pentecost are inseparable. What is desperately needed in our day is an *integration* of the Calvary and Pentecost "dialects" in which we communicate. Evangelicals emphasize the cross and the call to conversion and character. Charismatics stress the Spirit and the need for supernatural capabilities and charisms—signs and wonders. Both perspectives are essential. It is the biblical *unity* of these two emphases to which we should be aspiring. Years ago, Timothy L. Smith addressed this need in his article, "The Cross Demands, the Spirit Enables."[41] The Holy Spirit exalts Christ, enables holy living, and empowers Christian ministry. The New Testament theologian who highlights the empowering work of the Holy Spirit is Luke.

We have already glimpsed Luke's vision of the Holy Spirit. His is truly a Pentecostal or charismatic theology. In terms of the work of the Holy Spirit, Luke focuses almost solely on the "external" dimension—the Spirit's charismatic activity in the ministry of Jesus and the church. Roger Stronstad has shown that Luke was heavily influenced by the terminology of the Septuagint (the Greek translation of the Hebrew Scriptures) in its depiction of the charismatic, enabling work of the Spirit throughout the Old Testament narratives.[42] One can trace this charismatic activity of the Spirit all the way back to the founding days of the nation of Israel.

Moses' generation witnessed a great deal of the charismatic activity of the Spirit, but four centuries before Moses, Joseph evidenced this same sort of enabling power of the Spirit in his God-given ability to interpret dreams. Pharaoh said it all: "Can we find such a man as this, in whom is the Spirit of God?" (Gen. 41:38 RSV). Joseph's Spirit-inspired wisdom and administrative ability resulted in his being placed over all the house of Pharaoh. This sort of phenomenon was rare in those days, but with the formation of the nation of Israel in the wilderness there came a flurry of such spiritual activity.

Bezalel was "filled . . . with the Spirit of God, with ability and intelligence, with knowledge and all craftsmanship, to devise artistic designs, to work in gold, silver, and bronze, in cutting stones for setting, and in

---

[41] See this article in *Christianity Today* (February 16, 1979), 22–26.

[42] Cf., e.g., Stronstad, *The Charismatic Theology of St. Luke,* 17–22. Again, I find Stronstad's thesis persuasive, and the presentation that follows has definitely been informed by his work. Max Turner provides a comprehensive treatment of Luke's "Pentecostal" pneumatology in his *Power from on High: The Spirit in Israel's Restoration and Witness in Luke-Acts* (Journal of Pentecostal Theology Supplement Series 9; Sheffield, England: Sheffield Academic Press, 1996).

carving wood, for work in every craft" (Ex. 31:3–5 RSV; cf. 35:31–35). In addition, the Lord inspired both Bezalel and Oholiab to teach. Others were also given ability and intelligence by the Lord to make the vestments and the sanctuary (28:3; 35:35–36:2). The New Testament does not indicate anywhere that the various lists of spiritual gifts are intended to be exhaustive. Could it be that we are blinded to the myriad ways the Holy Spirit has endowed people for service in the church because of our false assumption of a very limited range of the Spirit's activity? These Old Testament examples should serve to remind us that the Spirit works through both miraculous signs *and* practical service.

When Moses cried out to the Lord about the intolerable burden of the Israelitest, the Lord instructed him to assemble the seventy elders at the Tent of Meeting. "I will take of the Spirit that is on you and put the Spirit on them" (Num. 11:17 NIV). The result was that "when the Spirit rested on them, they prophesied, but they did not do so again" (11:25 NIV). Eldad and Medad "had remained in the camp." "Yet the Spirit also rested on them, and they prophesied in the camp" (11:26 NIV). Moses was informed of this, and Joshua, who was one of those who had experienced the Spirit that day at the Tent of Meeting, said, "Moses, my lord, stop them!" (11:28 NIV). "But Moses replied, 'Are you jealous for my sake? I wish that all the LORD's people were prophets and that the Lord would put his Spirit on them!'" (11:29 NIV). Moses' wish was fulfilled at Pentecost!

Joshua, "a man in whom is the Spirit" (Num. 27:18 NASB), was chosen by the Lord as Moses' successor. Joshua was "filled with the spirit of wisdom, for Moses had laid his hands on him" (Deut. 34:9 NASB). Similar transferences of spiritual power is also seen in the New Testament.

> *The Spirit works through both miraculous signs* and *practical service.*

Finally, during this period we see even the Mesopotamian Balaam, whose character and teaching are certainly not to be emulated (2 Peter 2:15; Jude 11; Rev. 2:14), experiencing the charismatic dimension of the work of the Spirit. The Lord "put a word" in his mouth, and "the Spirit of God came upon him" (Num. 23:5; 24:2 RSV). The point of the Balaam stories is that God's providence is infinitely more powerful than pagan magic. Moreover, we learn, as Paul later warned the Corinthians, that charisma and character are not always linked—although ideally they should be. Giftedness and spiritual power do not always indicate godliness and spirituality.

During the fourteenth through the eleventh centuries B.C., dismal years of repeated apostasy and judgment, the Lord raised up mighty military leaders, judges (*šopetim*), to bring deliverance to his people. Many of these warrior leaders experienced the charismatic power of the Spirit that enabled their leadership and even provided (in Samson's case) miraculous physical strength. "The Spirit of the LORD came upon [Othniel], and he judged Israel; he went out to war, and the Lord gave [military victory]" (Judg. 3:10 RSV). The "Spirit of the LORD took possession of Gideon" (lit., "clothed himself with Gideon"; 6:34 RSV). The word in the LXX is *endyo*, used later of Amasai (1 Chron. 12:18) and Zechariah (2 Chron. 24:20) and found also in the New Testament, where Jesus prepared the disciples for Pentecost by instructing them to stay in Jerusalem until they had been "clothed with power from on high" (Luke 24:49).

Jephthah was another judge who experienced the charismatic activity of the Spirit. "Now Jephthah the Gileadite, the son of a prostitute, was a mighty warrior" (Judg. 11:1). Driven out by his father's legitimate sons, he collected a band of outlaws around him and "went raiding" (11:2–3). The "Spirit of the LORD came upon Jephthah" (11:29) also, and he defeated the Ammonites. Dale Moody, in typically colorful fashion, called Jephthah "the Robin Hood of the Old Testament"![43]

But it was Samson who perhaps exemplified more than anyone else this primitive, ecstatic, frenzied seizure by the Spirit of God—a charismatic experience that, in the instances recorded for us, seemed primarily to bring miraculous physical strength to Samson. "This hero of the tribe of Dan was conceived and born in wonder and lived the ascetic life of a Nazirite. The *ruaḥ* of the LORD 'began to stir him in Mahaneh-dan'" (Judg. 13:25).[44] When the Spirit of the Lord "came mightily upon him" (RSV; lit. "rushed on him"; cf. NRSV), Samson could tear a lion apart barehanded (14:6), kill thirty men at Ashkelon (14:19), break new ropes from his arms and bonds from his hands, and slaughter a thousand Philistines with the jawbone of a donkey (15:14–15).

Alasdair Heron summarizes the spiritual phenomena encountered:

> This is something very different from unusual gifts, skills, or wisdom. It is a violent and temporary possession of a person by a force rushing upon him from without, manifested in an ecstatic form comparable with that associated with some kinds of prophecy. The case of Saul in fact

---

[43] Moody, *Spirit of the Living God*, 15.

[44] Ibid.

supplies a remarkable connection between the military and prophetic forms.[45]

The Lord had chosen Samuel—judge, priest, and prophet—as the transitional figure between the period of the judges and the united kingdom. When led to anoint Saul as king, Samuel gave Saul a series of signs, one of which was that Saul would encounter "a band of prophets coming down from the shrine with harp, tambourine, flute, and lyre playing in front of them; they will be in a prophetic frenzy" (1 Sam. 10:5). The Spirit of the Lord would come mightily on Saul (lit., "rush on him" in the LXX; cf. Judg. 14:6, 19), Samuel predicted, "and you will be in a prophetic frenzy along with them and be turned into a different person" (1 Sam. 10:6).

"Now when these signs meet you," Samuel continued, "do whatever you see fit to do, for God is with you" (1 Sam. 10:7). When Saul turned to leave, "God gave him another heart" (10:9). Saul did prophesy, just as Samuel had said (10:9–13). When all the people saw him prophesying among the prophets, the proverb emerged, "Is Saul also among the prophets?" (10:11). When Samuel presented Saul to the people as their king, they shouted, "Long live the king!" (10:24). Saul returned "to his home at Gibeah, and with him went warriors whose hearts God had touched" (10:26). Evidently, the warriors had had a similar experience of the Spirit.

Through the power of the Spirit Saul was able to lead God's people in victory over the Ammonites (1 Sam. 11; esp. v. 6). Later both Saul and his messengers fell into a prophetic frenzy while among the prophets under Samuel's charge (19:20–24): Saul "too stripped off his clothes, and he too fell into a frenzy before Samuel. He lay naked all that day and all that night. Therefore it is said, 'Is Saul also among the prophets?'" (19:24). Tragically, this happened while Saul was in pursuit of David to kill him. Right after Samuel anointed David king, the Spirit of the Lord "came mightily upon David from that day forward" (16:13), and the Spirit "departed from Saul, and an evil spirit from the LORD tormented him" (16:14). The nadir of Saul's career came when he resorted to consulting the medium at Endor (ch. 28). Saul truly was "the Hamlet of the Old Testament."[46]

---

[45] Alasdair I. C. Heron, *The Holy Spirit* (Philadelphia: Westminster, 1983), 13.
[46] Moody, *Spirit of the Living God*, 17.

During the period of the divided kingdom, Elijah the Tishbite appears on the scene as a great charismatic prophet (*nabî*), calling apostate Israel back to the Lord. A mighty man of God, Elijah was even transported geographically from one place to another by the Spirit (1 Kings 18:12; see also 2 Kings 2:16). No wonder Elisha wanted a double portion of Elijah's spirit (2 Kings 2:9)! The same kind of rapture by the Spirit happened to Philip when he disappeared from the Ethiopian eunuch (Acts 8:39).

While brief reference has already been made to the exilic and post-exilic periods (see Amasai and Zechariah above), Stronstad provides a helpful summary of the Spirit's work during these times.

> Finally, the Babylonian exile and subsequent restoration is also a time of charismatic activity. Of all the classical prophets, Ezekiel is most conscious of the power of the Spirit of the Lord in his life (Ezekiel 2:2; 3:12, 14, 24; 8:3; 11:1, 5, 24; 37:1; 43:5). Moreover, the post-exilic Chronicler consistently associates the gift of the Spirit with inspired speech, with particular emphasis on prophets and priests. This identification is made for the gift of the Spirit to Amasai (1 Chronicles 12:18), Jahaziel a Levite (2 Chronicles 20:14), and Zechariah the son of Jehoiada the priest (2 Chronicles 24:20). In retrospect, it was recognized that the Spirit had also been given to Israel to instruct them (Nehemiah 9:20) and to witness to them (Nehemiah 9:30).[47]

Thus, the charismatic dimension of the Holy Spirit's work can be traced throughout Israel's history.

What one immediately notices, however, is that such activity of the Spirit is sporadic—just as the history of the church has witnessed only occasional activity of this nature. The present-day Pentecostal/charismatic phenomenon is unparalleled in church history. Nevertheless, it has usually been at critical junctures in the pilgrimage of God's people that the charismatic activity of the Spirit has been most prominent, both before Christ and up to the present. Moreover, the implication is that this dimension is always present, but only occasionally highlighted dramatically in the records of God's people.[48] But Luke's historical, missiological, and theological perspectives provide us with an important insight in relation to the church's kingdom mandate: *the constant need for revival*!

---

[47] Stronstad, *The Charismatic Theology of St. Luke*, 16.

[48] See ibid., 14–17.

Revival

The book of Acts is a problem for many theologians, if not for many Bible-believing Christians. Why is the Christian experience we read about there so different from what we experience today? How do we evaluate the charismatic phenomena? Can the idea of a completed New Testament canon adequately substitute for the supernatural signs and wonders that launched the church on her mission? How does this book fit into the canon?

Theologians often argue as to how we should use this book in formulating our doctrines. Comprised primarily of historical narrative, does it also teach us doctrinal truth? What are the *practical* applications of this book to our lives? Recent New Testament scholarship has come to appreciate Luke as a theologian as well as a historian, and we have had opportunity to explore his theological perspective in this volume. Furthermore, Paul's letters and other New Testament books also refer to the supernatural workings of the Holy Spirit. Because God has exhibited these same kinds of charismatic manifestations of his Spirit in our own times, we have begun to read such materials in the New Testament with new eyes. Perhaps most important in our study of Luke-Acts is the inspiration toward *revival.*

Acts is a portrait of God's people in revival!

Acts is a portrait of God's people in revival! Every authentic revival is in reality a repetition of Pentecost. It is a sovereign outpouring of God's Spirit on his people. No one, in my opinion, has brought this truth home more poignantly than the late Martyn Lloyd-Jones. His messages on revival, given in 1959, are classic.[49] He points out that because theologians and other Christians no longer believe in the *experience* of Pentecost—of the baptism in the Holy Spirit as an outpouring of God's Spirit on God's people to empower them to evangelize, disciple, and impact their world for good—teaching on revival and spiritual empowerment as a present as well as historical reality is hard to find. One must return to the older works of the last century for this kind of teaching.[50]

Fortunately, Lloyd-Jones himself has provided just what has been needed in his own inimitable expositional style:

---

[49] Martyn Lloyd-Jones, *Revival* (Wheaton, Ill.: Crossway, 1987).
[50] Ibid., 53–54.

> Even Evangelical writers do not mention revival. They do not even think of it. And surely this is to quench the Holy Spirit of God because the Holy Spirit not only has what we may call his ordinary work, he has his extraordinary work, and that is revival. Of course, we must evangelise, of course we must preach about being filled with the Spirit, yes, but over and above that we must cry unto God to pour out his Spirit upon the Church. And that is revival, the descent, the outpouring of the Spirit over and above his usual, ordinary work; this amazing, unusual, extraordinary thing, which God in his sovereignty and infinite grace has done to the Church from time to time during the long centuries of her history.
>
> Examine again your doctrine of the Holy Spirit, and in the name of God, be careful lest, in your neat and trimmed doctrine, you are excluding and putting out this most remarkable thing which God does periodically through the Holy Spirit, in sending him upon us, in visiting, in baptising us, in reviving the whole Church in a miraculous and astonishing manner.[51]
>
> Do you believe in revival, my friend? Are you praying for revival? What are you trusting? Are you trusting the organizing power of the church? Or are you trusting in the power of God to pour out his Spirit upon us again, to revive us, to baptize us anew and afresh with his most blessed Holy Spirit? The church needs another Pentecost. Every revival is a repetition of Pentecost, and it is the greatest need of the Christian church at this present hour. Oh may God open the eyes of our understanding on this vital matter, that we may look to him and wait upon him until in his infinite mercy and compassion he once more sends down from on high the power of the Holy Spirit upon us.[52]

What powerful and relevant words! But precisely what does it mean to be "baptized in the Holy Spirit"? Opinions have differed widely.

Spirit Baptism

Traditionally, Spirit baptism has been understood in the initiatory sense of 1 Corinthians 12:13: "For in one Spirit we were all baptized into one body—Jews or Greeks, slaves or free—and all were made to drink of one Spirit" (ESV). Every true believer is baptized in the Holy Spirit at the

---

[51] Ibid., 54.

[52] Lloyd-Jones, *Joy Unspeakable*, 280.

new birth and indwelling of the Spirit. It is what constitutes one as a Christian.

Pentecostals, keying primarily on Luke's theology, have understood Spirit baptism in the empowering sense, seeing Acts 2, 8, 9, 10, and 19 as establishing a second-blessing empowerment *subsequent* to conversion and signified by speaking in tongues. Charismatics in other ecclesial traditions generally shy away from a "law of tongues" and interpret Spirit baptism in an "organic" or sacramental sense. Charismatic renewal, then, is seen simply as an *appropriation* of a power and giftedness already present within the believer. Wesleyan and Holiness advocates tend to see Spirit baptism in terms of the sanctifying work of the Spirit. Perhaps the doctrinal impasse is the result of too narrow a conception of Spirit baptism.

> *We have* all *been baptized in the Holy Spirit in the Pauline initiatory sense, and we can* all *be empowered for ministry in the Lukan sense!*

John the Baptist, who first broached the subject, seemed to use this metaphor in the broadest sense as descriptive of Jesus' saving work. He referred to (1) Jesus' total eschatological redemptive work, (2) Christian initiation, (3) the Christian life, and (4) empowerment for Christian mission and ministry. Thus, utilizing the *dimensional* approach to the work of the Holy Spirit outlined above, a theological bridge can be built between warring factions. The evangelicals and the Pentecostals/charismatics are both right. We have *all* been baptized in the Holy Spirit in the Pauline initiatory sense, and we can *all* be empowered for ministry in the Lukan sense! Craig S. Keener has given this perspective eloquent, irenic, and practical expression—based on careful biblical analysis—in his *Gift and Giver: The Holy Spirit for Today*.[53] But it all begins with repentance, the subject to which we now turn.

Repentance

The launching of Jesus' earthly ministry was characterized by the clarion call to repentance: "In those days came John the Baptist, preaching in the wilderness of Judea, 'Repent, for the kingdom of heaven is at hand'" (Matt. 3:1–2 RSV). And the people came, "confessing their sins"

---

[53] Craig S. Keener, *Gift and Giver: The Holy Spirit for Today* (Grand Rapids: Baker, 2001).

(3:6). John proclaimed "a baptism of repentance for the forgiveness of sins" (Mark 1:4), and he demanded that the people bear "fruits worthy of repentance" (Luke 3:8).

What happened next always happens when people are being dealt with by God: "And the crowds asked him, 'What then should we do?'" (Luke 3:10). "In reply [John] said to them, 'Whoever has two coats must share with anyone who has none; and whoever has food must do likewise'" (3:11). Tax collectors and soldiers were also given specific ethical instruction (3:12–14.). People change and society changes when true repentance occurs! Finally, John pointed the crowds to "the Lamb of God who takes away the sin of the world" (John 1:29; see also v. 36), "the one who baptizes with the Holy Spirit" (v. 33), "the Son of God" (v. 34). This was the "beginning of the gospel of Jesus Christ, the Son of God" (Mark 1:1 RSV).

After John's arrest, "Jesus came into Galilee, preaching the gospel of God, and saying, 'The time is fulfilled, and the kingdom of God is at hand; repent, and believe in the gospel'" (Mark 1:14–15 RSV). Then immediately we see Jesus by Lake Galilee calling out to Simon and Andrew, who were casting their fishing net into the lake: "Follow me and I will make you fish for people" (1:16–17). Repentance entails a change of direction—following Jesus on a new path of life.

When Peter proclaimed Christ on the day of Pentecost, the people were "cut to the heart and said to Peter and to the other apostles, 'Brothers, what should we do?'" (Acts 2:37). The people are asking what concretely they should *do*. "Peter said to them, 'Repent, and be baptized every one of you in the name of Jesus Christ so that your sins may be forgiven; and you will receive the gift of the Holy Spirit'" (2:38).

> *People change and society changes when true repentance occurs!*

Through the words of John the Baptist, Jesus, and Peter, we see the nature of repentance. It involves a call, contrition, and change. It deals with sin, brings confession and forgiveness of sins, and produces a changed life. We catch a glimpse of God's grandeur, his kingdom majesty, his gracious and powerful Spirit. We see sin from God's perspective ... *and we repent!*

The Old Testament picture of repentance informs that of the New Testament. To repent means to turn *from* sin and to turn (or return) *to* God. It involves a change in the direction of one's life. The most common

Hebrew word for repentance is *šub.* King Josiah was able to lead God's people in revival in part because he was quick to repent. "Before him there was no king like him, who turned to the LORD with all his heart, with all his soul, and with all his might, according to all the law of Moses; nor did any like him arise after him" (2 Kings 23:25). God's promise to Solomon applies to every generation: "If my people who are called by my name humble themselves, pray, seek my face, and turn from their wicked ways, then I will hear from heaven, and will forgive their sin and heal their land" (2 Chron. 7:14). In Isaiah's day God's gracious offer of the waters of salvation was predicated on his people's seeking the Lord, forsaking their sins, and returning to the Lord (Isa. 55:1–9).

If God's people are willing to change—to turn from their sins and return to God—God will change his judgment into blessing (Jer. 18:8; Joel 2:12–14; Jonah 3:10). The prophets called for genuine contrition and a repudiation of sinful rebellion. The other Hebrew term for repentance, *naḥam,* implies this sense of remorse or regret. Interestingly enough, this term is used most often in relation to God himself. During Noah's day "the LORD was sorry that he had made humankind on the earth, and it grieved him to his heart" (Gen. 6:6; cf. Ex. 32:11–14; 1 Sam. 15:11, 29, 35).

In the New Testament the verb for this kind of grieving or sorrowing is *metamelomai.* It may refer to a defective remorse or to genuine contrition leading to a changed life. For example, in the parable of the two sons (Matt. 21:28–32) Jesus contrasts the chief priests and elders, who were challenging his authority (21:23–27), with the tax collectors and prostitutes, who received John's preaching and repented (21:31–32). One son said he would go into the vineyard and work, but did not. The other said no to his father, but "he afterward regretted it and went" (21:30 NASB). Even when they saw the tax collectors and prostitutes repenting and believing, Jesus told the religious leaders, "you ... did not even feel remorse afterward so as to believe him" (21:32 NASB; the KJV rendering is "repented" in both verses). Notice how Jesus links true repentance and faith. Jesus told his opponents, "Truly I tell you, the tax collectors and the prostitutes are going into the kingdom of God ahead of you" (21:31).

However, in this same Gospel we see Judas sorrowing for his betrayal of Jesus, yet committing suicide rather than returning to Jesus (Matt.

27:3–5). Contrast this with Peter, who also grieved for having denied Christ (Matt. 26:75) but who repented and became one of the great leaders of the church.

Paul later explained to the Corinthians: "Godly sorrow produces repentance [*metanoia*] leading to salvation, not to be regretted [cf. *metamelomai*]" (2 Cor. 7:10 NKJV), while "worldly sorrow brings death" (7:10 NIV). We have here a biblical psychology of repentance. As we have already seen, true repentance entails *change*: a change of mind (verb: *metanoeo*; noun: *metanoia*) and a change of direction in life (*šub*). If we regret our sins only because of their destructive effects or because of our embarrassment at having been "caught," then we are only experiencing "worldly sorrow." But "godly sorrow," which sees sin from God's perspective, produces authentic change. This God-given contrition brings with it *conversion*, which we will examine later.

> *True repentance entails* change: *a change of mind and a change of direction in life.*

Then comes the joy! According to Jesus' parables of the lost sheep, the lost coin, and the lost son, there is heavenly joy when sinners repent and the lost are found (Luke 15). Philip preached Christ in the city of Samaria, and "there was great joy in that city" (Acts 8:8). "Happy are those who mourn; God will comfort them," Jesus taught in the Sermon on the Mount (Matt. 5:4 GNB). Examples abound in the New Testament of this kingdom joy. "For the kingdom of God is not food and drink but righteousness and peace and joy in the Holy Spirit" (Rom. 14:17).[54] But before the joy and rejoicing come the call, the contrition, the change, and the condonation (forgiveness).

In large measure, the church today has lost sight of the imperative of repentance. Cheap grace, Bonhoeffer warned us, preaches "forgiveness without requiring repentance." It is a crossless, spurious Christianity. Costly grace, on the other hand, is "the kingly rule of Christ ... it is the call of Jesus Christ at which the disciple leaves his nets and follows him."[55] It is this *call* that we now must examine, for it is the gateway to our salvation.

---

[54] See William G. Morrice, *Joy in the New Testament* (Greenwood, S.C.: Attic, 1984).
[55] Dietrich Bonhoeffer, *The Cost of Discipleship* (New York: Macmillan, 1963), 47.

The Call

On the day of Pentecost, Peter issued the gospel invitation: "Repent, and be baptized every one of you in the name of Jesus Christ so that your sins may be forgiven; and you will receive the gift of the Holy Spirit. For the promise is for you, for your children, and for all who are far away, everyone whom the Lord our God calls to him" (Acts 2:38–39). We have already looked at the promise; now we must look at the call. The Lord's call is to "all," to "everyone." And he calls us through the gospel.

In one of his earliest letters, Paul refers to this gospel call: "But we must always give thanks to God for you, brothers and sisters beloved by the Lord, because God chose you as the first fruits for salvation" (2 Thess. 2:13). God takes the initiative in our salvation. The biblical doctrine of election, God's "choosing" of us—closely related to the call and examined below—reminds us of this fact. Paul describes this salvation as coming to us "through sanctification by the Spirit and faith in the truth" (2:13 NASB). Our salvation is the work of the Spirit, who brings spiritual transformation and enables faith. "To this he called you through our gospel, so that you may obtain the glory of our Lord Jesus Christ" (2:14 RSV). The divine call to salvation in its most fundamental sense comes through the gospel and ultimately brings us into "the glory of our Lord Jesus Christ."

Jesus issued this universal gospel invitation in these timeless words:

> Come to me, all you that are weary and are carrying heavy burdens, and I will give you rest. Take my yoke upon you, and learn from me; for I am gentle and humble in heart, and you will find rest for your souls. For my yoke is easy, and my burden is light. (Matt. 11:28–30)

This was a call to salvation, discipleship (including sanctification), and service.[56] Jesus instructed his disciples to issue this same gospel invitation across the globe (24:14; 28:18–20).

Jesus also explained that not everyone will respond to this gracious good news. "For many are called, but few are chosen," he said (Matt. 22:14). These intriguing words culminate a kingdom parable (22:1–13) in which Jesus depicts the indifferent (v. 5), the rebellious (v. 6), and the self-righteous (v. 12) who decline the king's invitation to the wed-

---

[56] See Charles Caldwell Ryrie, *Ryrie Study Bible: Expanded Edition* [NASB 1995 Update] (Chicago: Moody Press, 1995), 1,532 (note on Matt. 11:28–30).

ding banquet.[57] But what do we make of Jesus' differentiation between the "called" and the "chosen"? The chosen are those who have accepted the call. And what are the fuller implications of Jesus' parable? Perhaps Paul's rich theology of the call will amplify our understanding.

Paul's whole apostolic/missionary ministry was a result of divine calling. His own personal confession was that he was "called to be an apostle" (Rom. 1:1; 1 Cor. 1:1), which was "the will of God" for him (1 Cor. 1:1; 2 Cor. 1:1; Eph. 1:1; Col. 1:1; 1 Tim. 1:1). His was no "human commission" (Gal. 1:1); rather, he was commissioned "by the command of God our Savior and of Christ Jesus our hope" (1 Tim. 1:1). The apostle saw himself as "set apart for the gospel of God" (Rom. 1:1). His first missionary journey was initiated by divine calling: "While they [the Antiochene prophets and teachers] were worshiping the Lord and fasting, the Holy Spirit said, 'Set apart for me Barnabas and Saul for the work to which I have called them'" (Acts 13:2). During his second missionary journey, a vision of "a man of Macedonia" took Paul, Silas, Timothy, and Luke there, "being convinced that God had called us to proclaim the good news to them" (16:9–10).

This sense of divine calling corresponds to that of the prophets and other servants of God in the Old Testament. Isaiah's heavenly vision brought conviction, cleansing, and commission—a calling to "go and say to this people . . . " (Isa. 6:1–9). God calls his servants by name (Ex. 3:4; 1 Sam. 3:4). This same personal calling sets apart persons for the gospel ministry today.

This same personal calling sets apart persons for the gospel ministry today.

The calling to preach and teach God's Word has virtually dominated my life from my earliest years. During my junior year in college I came to a full acknowledgment of and surrender to that calling. Later, in seminary, I was asked to write out an account of my understanding of God's call upon my life. But it was an intensive study of the call in the Scriptures (during that junior year in college)—a time of struggle and searching that preceded my full acknowledgment of the call—that afforded me the equally important insight that *all* of God's people are called.

Oral Roberts's ministry of healing evangelism has always been solidly rooted in this biblical concept of divine calling.

---

[57] Ibid., 1,555 (note on Matt. 22:14).

> To embark on a life of ministry is no easy task, I have found—particularly having a healing ministry and building a university. So why did I do it? Simply because God told me to do it.
>
> If there's a major conviction in my life that sums up how I've accomplished what I have, it is this: God speaks to those who will listen, and when we hear and obey His voice, He in effect becomes the Head Partner with us in the endeavor.
>
> I have also discovered that when someone believes that God does speak to people, and then makes a decision not only to listen but also to obey His voice, some type of divine calling inevitably comes with that commitment.[58]

The apostle Paul would enthusiastically endorse these words.

Foundational to Paul's concept of God's people, the church, is this experience of divine calling. We are "called to belong to Jesus Christ" (Rom. 1:6; lit., "called *of* Jesus Christ"). We are (lit.) "called to be saints" (Rom. 1:7; 1 Cor. 1:2). Further, we "know that all things work together for good for those who love God, who are called according to his purpose" (Rom. 8:28). The message of the cross may be scandalous and foolish to others, but to us, "the called," Christ is "the power of God and the wisdom of God" (1 Cor. 1:23–24). This is Paul's concept of the call in its essence. The calling and election of God's people is to *both* salvation and service, and it is *both* corporate and personal.

We should also remember that it is through *preaching*—the preaching of the gospel—that God issues his call to us. As the apostle reminded the Thessalonians, salvation, "through sanctification by the Spirit and through belief in the truth," is something to which God has "called you through our proclamation of the good news" (2 Thess. 2:13–14). God, "who never lies," promised us eternal life (Titus 1:2). And, as Paul explains to Titus, "at the right time God let the world know about that life through preaching. He trusted me with that work, and I preached by the command of God our Savior" (1:3 NCV).

People need to hear the gospel story of Jesus. "And how are they to hear without a preacher?" (Rom. 10:14 RSV). The doctrines of the church and of election and predestination are closely tied to the doctrine of the call. More will be said about these essential truths later, but it is our response of *faith* that is the crucial element in this divine saving call. It is "by hearing about Christ and having faith in him" (Gal. 3:2 CEV) that we

---

[58] Oral Roberts, *Expect a Miracle: My Life and Ministry* (Nashville: Nelson, 1995), v. Consider the title of Roberts' earlier autobiography: *The Call* (New York: Doubleday, 1976).

are saved. "No one can have faith without hearing the message about Christ" (Rom. 10:17 CEV). Thus, we now turn to examine saving faith.

Faith

In midnight darkness Paul and Silas announced to the Philippian jailer: "Believe on the Lord Jesus Christ, and you will be saved, you and your household" (Acts 16:31 NKJV). It is through faith alone—faith plus nothing—that we are saved. To be sure, this is a Spirit-enabled faith, as well as a faith conjoined with a Spirit-enabled repentance. It is also (as we will see later) a faith that sanctifies—a "live" faith inevitably accompanied by good works. But it is nevertheless faith alone that brings salvation. The church owes a great debt to Martin Luther for putting his life on the line in order to preserve the doctrine of "justification by faith alone." More accurately, Luther taught "justification *by* grace *through* faith" and thereby avoided making faith a human "work," as it were. But the great reformer was convinced that many do not fully comprehend what faith really is.

"The reason why some people do not understand why faith alone justifies," said Luther, "is that they do not know what faith is." Faith as described in Scripture, he pointed out, is *not* merely giving credence to the historical *facts* of the gospel story. It is believing that Christ came to save us personally. It is *trust* (*fudicia*) in Christ. It is *acting* on his promises, *relying* on him to save us—just as we might rely on a ship to transport us across the ocean. We do not really believe in that boat until we actually board it and join the great adventure. Finally, true faith brings us into personal *union* with Christ. It is not merely a set of beliefs about Christ. We *join* Christ, and everything he has is ours—including justification, grace, life, salvation, and hope.[59] He takes our sin and we take his salvation: the Great Exchange—Hallelujah!

> *The Bible's portrayal of saving faith is a personal trust that brings one into union with Christ.*

In this analysis, Luther went to the heart of the Bible's portrayal of saving faith. It is a personal trust that brings one into union with Christ.

---

[59] I owe the Luther quote and this brief summary of Luther's concept of saving faith to Alister McGrath, *Christian Doctrine*, 127–29, 383–85.

It is this trust in our saving God that characterizes faith in both the Old and New Testaments.

Trust is one of the key nuances of faith that the Old Testament highlights. David's wisdom psalm (Ps. 37) is a classic passage that describes the full significance of this saving trust. In contrasting the righteous with the wicked, he exhorts God's people not to fret or be envious of the wicked who may be prospering now but face a bleak final state. He uses many important Old Testament terms related to faith, while encouraging the trust that brings the blessings of God's faithful, saving love.

"Trust [*bataḥ*] in the LORD, and do good," David writes (Ps. 37:3). Already we see that faith is both *attitude* and *action.* We place our faith and confidence in the Lord (attitude), and we "do good" (action; cf. James 2:14–26). Authentic faith is both dependence or reliance (passive) and obedience (active; cf. Paul's phrase, "the obedience of faith," in Rom. 1:5; 16:26). Then, "Dwell in the land and cultivate faithfulness" (Ps. 37:3 NASB). We are to pursue faithfulness (*ʾemunah*), another important dimension of biblical faith. Saving faith is fidelity, a covenant loyalty to God our Savior, whose own faithfulness undergirds and enables our faith.

"Delight yourself in the LORD and he will give you the desires of your heart," the psalmist continues (Ps. 37:4 NIV). There is great pleasure and fulfillment in the life of faith. As we take our ultimate joy and delight in God, he conforms our inmost desires to his holy will and our God-given dreams are realized. One is reminded of Paul's exhortation to the Philippians to "work out your own salvation with fear and trembling; for it is God who is at work in you, enabling you both to will and to work for his good pleasure" (Phil. 2:12–13). The New American Bible renders verse 13: "For God is the one who, for his good purpose, works in you both to *desire* and to work" (italics added). Eugene Peterson's paraphrase of these two verses captures the subtleties of the Greek as well as Paul's passion and purpose:

> What I'm getting at, friends, is that you should simply keep on doing what you've done from the beginning. When I was living among you, you lived in responsive obedience. Now that I'm separated from you, keep it up. Better yet, redouble your efforts. Be energetic in your life of salvation, reverent and sensitive before God. That energy is *God's* energy, an energy deep within you, God himself willing and working at what will give him the most pleasure.[60]

---

[60] Eugene H. Peterson, *The Message: The New Testament in Contemporary Language, with Psalms and Proverbs* (Colorado Springs, Colo.: NavPress, 1993), 491 (Peterson's italics).

Our life of salvation through faith is God's work from start to finish. It is "from faith to faith" (Rom. 1:17 NASB). "*Sola fide!*" the Reformers cried as they restored the gospel to the church. And Jesus is "the pioneer and perfecter [the author and finisher (KJV)] of our faith" (Heb. 12:2). (Earlier, the author of Hebrews referred to Jesus as the pioneer or author of our *salvation* [2:10].) What could bring greater assurance of God's finishing what he starts (cf. Phil. 1:6)?

The psalmist then says: "Commit your way to the LORD; trust in him, and he will act" (Ps. 37:5). Notice the word "trust" (*bataḥ*) again. And "commit" (*galal*) is a vivid term that connotes *rolling* our burden onto the Lord (see Prov. 16:3, esp. in the Amplified Bible). Those who commit and trust receive the fullness of their salvation (Ps. 37:6).

Finally, note the call to a serenity of faith. "Be still before the LORD, and wait patiently for him" (Ps. 37:7)—"Rest in the LORD" (NASB); "Wait quietly before the LORD" (REB). *Damam,* the Hebrew verb here, means "to be silent, be still" ("quiet down," as Peterson phrases it).[61]

> *People of faith refuse to rely on their own wisdom and insight. Instead, they choose to trust God wholeheartedly.*

Solomon's wisdom corroborates that of David: "Trust [*bataḥ*] in the LORD with all your heart and lean not on your own understanding; in all your ways acknowledge him, and he will make your paths straight" (Prov. 3:5–6 NIV). People of faith refuse to rely on their own wisdom and insight. Instead, they choose to trust God wholeheartedly. In all their ways they seek to know him, and he clears their path. Furthermore, they know that this personal trust entails fearing the Lord and turning away from evil, rather than being wise in their own eyes (v. 7). The Lord himself says: "Cursed are those who trust [*bataḥ*] in mere mortals and make mere flesh their strength" (Jer. 17:5). Isaiah echoes this theme: "Stop trusting in man [lit., 'cease from man,' or 'give up on man'], who has but a breath in his nostrils. Of what account is he?" (Isa. 2:22 NIV).[62] And the Lord promises, "Blessed are those who trust [*bataḥ*] in the LORD, whose trust is the LORD" (Jer. 17:7). Theirs is the consistently fruitful life, no matter what the circumstances (17:8).

---

[61] Ibid., 699.

[62] *The NIV Study Bible* (gen. ed. Kenneth Barker [Grand Rapids: Zondervan, 1985], 1,021) notes the shared terminology with Isa. 53:3: Sinful humankind rejects the Savior, refuses to esteem him, and chooses rather to revere mere mortals and to look to them for help and salvation.

Our Father Abraham

With the life of Abraham the Scriptures teach us how salvation under both the old and new covenants has always been God's gracious gift *received through faith.* The Judaism of Jesus' day—especially among his opponents—had, in the main, apostatized. Later Saul, the zealous Pharisee, would, through his shattering encounter with the risen Christ, come to realize this fact. In seeking faithfully to uphold the law, he found himself at enmity with God in his persecution of the Christians. The apostle Paul saw in Abraham's example of faith the paradigm of saving faith. Rabbinic Judaism held forth Abraham's life as documentation of righteousness through the works of the law. Therefore, Paul must have seen it as even more imperative to highlight the true nature of Abraham's saving faith, based on the promise of grace.

"Understand, then, that those who believe are children of Abraham," wrote Paul to the Galatians (Gal. 3:7 NIV). Or as he noted in Romans, Abraham is "the father of all who believe without being circumcised and who thus have righteousness reckoned to them, and likewise the father of the circumcised who are not merely circumcised but also follow the example of the faith which our father Abraham had before he was circumcised" (Rom. 4:11–12 RSV). In both these passages Paul was appealing to one of the key Old Testament passages on saving faith: "And he [Abraham, called Abram at that time] believed [ʾ*aman*] the LORD; and the LORD reckoned it to him as righteousness" (Gen. 15:6; see Rom. 4:3; Gal. 3:6).

The apostle based his argument on the classic text that became the Reformers' rallying cry: "The righteous live by their faith [ʾ*emunah*]" (Hab. 2:4; Rom. 1:17; Gal. 3:11). The writer to the Hebrews quotes this verse to encourage persevering faith and then launches into an extended discussion of faith, using Abraham as one of his prime examples (Heb. 10:38–11:40). Clearly, the Old Testament provides the foundation for the New Testament's teaching on saving faith.

"Let Us Now Praise Famous Men . . ."

The Academy Award-winning *Chariots of Fire* begins with these words, spoken at a memorial service at St. Mary's Church in London in 1978—a service in honor of Britain's legendary Harold Abrahams. The movie enshrines the exemplary lives of Abrahams, a Jew, and Eric Liddell, a Christian, both heroes of the 1924 Olympics. The words themselves are from a classic passage in the Apocrypha (Sirach 44:1–50:22) and, as such, represent a genre of literature that praises past heroes for their noteworthy achievements.

The writer to the Hebrews provides a similar list in the epic chapter 11, popularly known as "the faith chapter." In contrast to other such lists of greats of the past, however, Hebrews notes only one virtue that sets these people apart: faith.[63] We find, in the opening words of the chapter the closest thing to a formal definition of faith in the New Testament: "Now faith is the assurance of things hoped for, the conviction of things not seen" (Heb. 11:1). This definition places faith in the broadest biblical perspective, an *eschatological* point of view that looks to the future and is rooted in hope. This *kingdom* perspective carries with it an already/not yet tension as well as the unconquerable optimism that characterizes God's people. Furthermore, the context is *corporate*; this definition of faith occurs within a broader passage exhorting God's people, the church, to the endurance of faith (10:19–12:29; see esp. 10:19–25).

The writer does not give us an exhaustive definition of faith. Even the immediate context indicates this fact. Faith entails being "enlightened" (Heb. 10:32), having "confidence" (v. 35), evincing "endurance" (v. 36), and *doing* "the will of God" (v. 36).

Nevertheless, we penetrate here to the essence of saving faith. The writer to the Hebrews expounds the very faith principle that Paul addresses in Galatians and Romans: "but my righteous one will live by faith" (Heb. 10:38; cf. Hab. 2:4; Rom. 1:17; Gal. 3:11). Always the encourager (is the author Barnabas, "son of encouragement" [Acts 4:36]?),[64] the writer concludes, "But we are not among those who shrink back and so are lost, but among those who have faith and so are saved" (Heb. 10:39). Just as "our ancestors received approval" by faith, so do we (11:2), and with this faith comes an *understanding* that only people of faith can have.

"By faith we understand that the universe was formed by God's command [the word of God], so that the visible came forth from the invisible" (Heb. 11:3 REB). In this verse we are provided two foundational principles of Christian faith. First, "by faith we understand." Faith always precedes full understanding. Anselm set the pattern with his memorable words, "I believe in order that I may understand" (*Proslogion* 1; originally

---

[63] See Leon Morris, *New Testament Theology* (Grand Rapids: Zondervan, 1986), 309.

[64] I owe this convincing suggestion as to the authorship of Hebrews to Dale Moody.

called *Faith Seeking Understanding*). Second, faith brings understanding of both the "visible" and the "invisible" ("things not seen," 11:1). The Christian worldview contradicts the prevailing Enlightenment mindset that denies transcendence. Unfortunately, even conservative, Bible-believing Christians can be brainwashed by their surrounding culture into believing that God only acted and spoke "once upon a time."[65]

In addition, it is important to note that faith always has *content.* Anyone who comes to God "must believe that he exists and that he rewards those who seek him" (Heb. 11:6). Not only is the priority of faith asserted here but also its content. "[We] must believe *that*. . . ." John wrote his Gospel "that you may believe that Jesus is the Christ, the Son of God, and that believing you may have life in his name" (John 20:31 RSV). In other words, Christian faith is rooted in eternal truth, not fanciful, albeit well-intentioned, wishes. A drug-induced confidence that one can fly is quickly proven illusory after a fateful leap from the precipice.

The Christian worldview contradicts the prevailing Enlightenment mindset that denies transcendence.

Notice how often the writer to the Hebrews uses the phrase "by faith" (Heb. 11:3, 4, 5, 7, 8, 11, 17, 20, 21, 22, 23, 24, 27, 28, 29, 30, 31). His intention is unmistakable: "Without faith it is impossible to please God" (11:6). All the "famous men" (and women) he mentions were approved by God because of their *faith*! Further, these stalwart saints were willing to accept the *paradox* that often accompanies faith. As John Calvin discovered, walking "by faith, not by sight" (2 Cor. 5:7) always entails placing the greater value on "what cannot be seen" (4:18).

> These two things apparently contradict each other, but yet they agree perfectly when we are concerned with faith. The Spirit of God shows us hidden things, the knowledge of which cannot reach our senses. Eternal life is promised to us, but it is promised to the dead; we are told of the resurrection of the blessed, but meantime we are involved in corruption; we are declared to be just, and sin dwells within us; we hear that we are promised an abundance of all good things, but we are often hungry and thirsty; God proclaims that he will come to us immediately, but seems to be deaf to our cries. What would happen to us if we did not rely on our hope, and if our minds did not emerge above the world out

---

[65] See Charles Kraft, *Christianity with Power* (Ann Arbor: Vine, 1989), and Zeb Bradford Long and Douglas McMurry, *The Collapse of the Brass Heaven* (Grand Rapids: Chosen, 1994).

> of the midst of darkness through the shining Word of God and his Spirit? Faith is therefore rightly called the substance of things that are still the objects of hope and the evidence of things not seen.[66]

Notwithstanding the agony and ecstasy of such an eschatological faith, the Christian pilgrimage is a truly glorious journey!

The Cruciality of Faith

Clearly then, faith (*pistis*), the noun, and believing (*pisteuo*), the verb, are central to the biblical doctrine of salvation. Thomas Oden offers this summary: (1) "Faith (*pistis*) is the means by which salvation is appropriated through personal trust in the Son as Savior"; (2) "the benefits of Christ's mediatorial work are applied by the Spirit and appropriated by the believer *through faith*"; (3) "faith is the reception of grace."[67] "For by grace you have been saved through faith, and this is not your own doing; it is the gift of God—not the result of works, so that no one may boast" (Eph. 2:8–9).

I refer specifically to the *cruciality* of faith because the English words "cruciality," "crucial," and "crux" all derive from the Latin *crux*, meaning *cross*. Atonement. Justification. Reconciliation. Propitiation (averting God's wrath). Expiation (cleansing from the defilement of sin). Redemption (liberation, freedom). All these and more come to us as God's gracious gifts through Christ's cross, Christ's blood—and all are received *through faith* (Rom. 3:21–26). The cross is the crux (central feature) of saving faith! Faith is crucial (essential, decisive) to our salvation!

Even as early as the New Testament era, faith became the summary term for the saving message of the church. The phrase "the faith" was used to refer to the basic body of truths promulgated by the church, the gospel and all its implications. Luke epitomizes the opening years of the church's missionary movement with these words: "The word of God continued to spread; the number of the disciples increased greatly in Jerusalem, and a great many of the priests became obedient to the faith" (Acts 6:7; cf. 13:8). On their first missionary journey, Paul and Barnabas returned through Lystra and Iconium to Pisidian Antioch "strengthening

---

66 Cited in Philip E. Hughes' masterful work, *A Commentary on the Epistle to the Hebrews* (Grand Rapids: Eerdmans, 1977), 441.

67 Thomas C. Oden, *Life in the Spirit* (San Francisco: HarperSanFrancisco, 1992), 128–29 (Oden's italics). (I have excerpted and enumerated these statements out of sequence in terms of their appearance on these two pages.)

the souls of the disciples, encouraging them to continue in the faith, and saying, 'Through many tribulations we must enter the kingdom of God'" (14:22 NASB). Luke characterizes the consolidating work of Paul's second missionary journey with these words: "So the churches were strengthened in the faith and increased in numbers daily" (16:5). O that those words might be descriptive of the churches of our own day—"strengthened in the faith and [increasing] in numbers *daily*"!

During Paul's earlier years, the churches of Judea "kept hearing that 'the one who once was persecuting us is now preaching the faith he once tried to destroy.'" (Gal. 1:23 NAB). The apostle's choice of words in this early letter is revealing. He had tried to destroy "the faith"; now he was preaching it. The verb used here for preaching (*euangelizo*) gives us our English term *evangelize*; containing the word for "the gospel" (*euangelion*), it can literally be rendered "gospelize"! Thus, early on we see the close connection between "the faith" and the gospel.

Karl Barth once defined theology in these terms: "Christian doctrine is the attempt, undertaken as a responsibility of the church, to summarize the gospel of Jesus Christ as the content of the church's preaching."[68] It is a proven historical fact that churches that focus on the task of world evangelism generally remain more faithful to sound, orthodox doctrine—"the faith." My own mother church, the Southern Baptist Convention, is a prime example. The Scriptures urge us "to contend for the faith which was once for all delivered to the saints" (Jude 3 RSV).

Those words come to us from Jude, one of Jesus' four brothers (see Mark 6:3, where it is translated "Judas"). Their context is quite revealing:

> Beloved, while eagerly preparing to write to you about the salvation we share, I find it necessary to write and appeal to you to contend for the faith that was once for all entrusted to the saints. For certain intruders have stolen in among you, people who long ago were designated for this condemnation as ungodly, who pervert the grace of our God into licentiousness and deny our only Master and Lord, Jesus Christ. (Jude 3–4)

"The faith" concerns "our common salvation" (Jude 3 RSV), "the grace of our God" (v. 4), and "our only Master and Lord, Jesus Christ" (v. 4). It was once for all authoritatively delivered (*paradidomi*; cf. 1 Cor. 15:3–8, where Paul defines the apostolic gospel message he handed on to the Corinthians) to the saints, the church. It is a kingdom message (Acts

[68] Karl Barth, *Learning Jesus Christ through the Heidelberg Catechism*, trans. Shirley C. Guthrie Jr. (Grand Rapids: Eerdmans, 1964), 17.

14:22). And it is the gospel message (Phil. 1:27, which refers to "the faith of the gospel").

Furthermore, Jude expects us to "contend" for this message, to earnestly agonize (*epagonizomai*) for it. We are to live our lives "in a manner worthy of the gospel of Christ . . . standing firm in one spirit, striving side by side with one mind for the faith of the gospel" (Phil. 1:27). As Paul wrote Timothy, we are to

> pursue righteousness, godliness, faith, love, endurance, gentleness. Fight [*agonizomai*] the good fight of the faith; take hold of the eternal life, to which you were called and for which you made the good confession in the presence of many witnesses. (1 Tim. 6:11–12)

Earlier in this letter Paul had reminded Timothy, "If you put these instructions before the brethren, you will be a good minister of Christ Jesus, nourished on the words of the faith and of the good doctrine which you have followed" (1 Tim. 4:6 RSV). Paul addresses Titus in Titus 1:4 as "my loyal child in the faith we share" (or "my true child in a common faith," RSV). The church is "the household [or the family] of the faith" (Gal. 6:10 NASB). *The Faith* would be an apt title for this entire book!

> *Being "in the faith" is all-important.*

Among Jude's concluding exhortations we find these powerful words:

> But you, beloved, building yourselves up on your most holy faith, praying in the Holy Spirit, keep yourselves in the love of God, waiting anxiously for the mercy of our Lord Jesus Christ to eternal life. (Jude 20–21 NASB)

The foundation of our lives is our "most holy faith." If we keep ourselves in the love of God and build ourselves up on the foundation of the faith, "praying in the Holy Spirit"—eagerly awaiting our Lord's return and the culmination of our salvation—we will find that God is "able to keep [us] from falling, and to make [us] stand without blemish in the presence of his glory with rejoicing" (Jude 24).

Nevertheless, the warnings of Jude are relevant as well. As Paul cautioned Timothy, "Now the Spirit expressly says that in later [or the last] times some will renounce the faith by paying attention to deceitful spirits and teachings [or doctrines] of demons" (1 Tim. 4:1). He also exhorted the Corinthians, "Examine yourselves to see whether you are living in the faith. Test yourselves. Do you not realize that Jesus Christ is in you?—unless, indeed, you fail to meet the test!" (2 Cor. 13:5). Being "in the faith" is all-important. The Reformers reminded us that this saving faith entails (1) knowledge of the truth (*notitia*), (2) intellectual assent to that saving truth (*assensus*), and (3) personal trust in our saving God (*fiducia*)—*all three* taken together!

Jesus, the Faith Teacher

It may shock some to refer to Jesus as a "faith teacher." To these persons "faith teaching," "faith teachers," and the like connote a superficial triumphalism—a "prosperity gospel" that allows no room for mystery or divine sovereignty. To be sure, such a "formula" approach to faith does exist. But the church also owes a debt to the "faith" emphasis of the charismatic movement for calling our attention to Jesus' own teaching on faith.[69]

Living by faith entails relating *all* of life to Christ. The Sermon on the Mount makes this crystal clear. Our "Father knows what [we] need before [we] ask him" (Matt. 6:8). Jesus encourages us to pray for "our daily bread" (6:11). He instructs us to look to the Father for the basic necessities of life and never to be anxious about these matters. "But if God so clothes the grass of the field, which is alive today and tomorrow is thrown into the oven, will he not much more clothe you—you of little faith?" (6:30). Everyone strives for such things, "and indeed your heavenly Father knows that you need all these things. But strive first for the kingdom of God and his righteousness, and all these things will be given to you as well" (6:32–33). His entire teaching in this immediate context (6:25–34) suggests we live either in anxiety ("you of little faith") or we learn to trust *him* for even these matters. Yet how many Christians actually live out their faith in these areas?

Jesus instructs us to keep on asking, seeking, and knocking, fully assured that our heavenly Father is even more generous and eager to give us good things than we are as parents to give things to our own chil-

---

69 For a fair and constructive analysis of the issues raised by the faith movement, see Bruce Barron, *The Health and Wealth Gospel* (Downers Grove, Ill.: InterVarsity Press, 1987). See also William DeArteaga's thorough defense of charismatic beliefs and practices: *Quenching the Spirit* (Orlando: Creation House, 1996). Much can be learned from each of these perspectives.

dren (Matt. 7:7–11). Yet how often do we even think of pausing and praying with expectant faith for healing before calling our doctor? If we pursue healing through medical science, then why not seek it through prayer as well? Does not Jesus' authority extend to these areas, or does he deal only with so-called "spiritual" matters?

As if to hammer this truth home to us, Matthew, in the ensuing narrative section (Matt. 8–9), relates a string of ten miracles in which we see the King of the kingdom acting with authority. Jesus was amazed at the centurion's acknowledgment of Jesus' authority: "Truly I tell you, in no one in Israel have I found such faith" (8:10). "And to the centurion Jesus said, 'Go; let it be done for you according to your faith.' And the servant was healed in that hour" (8:13). Our Lord clearly connected the miracle with the centurion's faith. Yet we are so used to living as practical atheists that we are often uncomfortable with this fact. The biblical *fact* that faith does not always bring deliverance (see, e.g., Heb. 11:35–40) should not discourage us from exercising this dimension of our faith. The disciples were understandably afraid as their boat was deluged by the wind-swept waves. But Jesus asked them: "Why are you afraid, you of little faith?" (Matt. 8:26). In the storms of life our faith is "stretched"—and we discover afresh Christ's authority (8:26–27)!

Salvation is much more holistic in Scripture than many church folk are willing to acknowledge.

"When Jesus saw their faith" (the people carrying the paralyzed man, Matt. 9:2), he forgave and healed the man. "When the crowds saw it, they were filled with awe, and they glorified God, who had given such authority to human beings" (9:8). Touching the fringe of Jesus' garment, a woman suffering from hemorrhaging said to herself, "If only I can touch his cloak I shall be saved" (9:21 NJB). "Jesus turned round and saw her; and he said to her, 'Courage, my daughter, your faith has saved you.' And from that moment the woman was saved" (9:22 NJB). Notice in this story the three references to *salvation.* Salvation is much more holistic in Scripture than many church folk are willing to acknowledge.

Not only did the Master deal with physical needs in these recorded miracles; he also dealt with social and religious issues. He touched and affirmed social outcasts, the blind, the dumb, women, even a woman whom the rabbis considered unclean because of her menstrual flow.[70]

[70] See Michael Green, *Matthew for Today* (Dallas: Word, 1988), 106.

The salvation Jesus came to bring changes society as well as the individual. Ultimately, it brings even a new heaven and a new earth. Jesus came to save the whole person and the whole world. Forgiveness of sins is always the greatest miracle, but Jesus also came to reverse the effects of the entrance of sin into the human race, even though his completed program awaits his second coming!

Frederick Dale Bruner entitles in part his treatment of Matthew 8–9 "Introduction to the Doctrine of Salvation."[71] He hits the target dead center! Jesus communicates *grace* in these miracles—even in his statements concerning faith. "In this Gospel though Jesus always praises big faith, he never requires big faith before he will help.... Legalistic preaching requires big faith on our part before God will deliver big help on his."[72] Furthermore, when Jesus sends out the Twelve (Matt. 10), he does not tell them to go out and teach people how to achieve miracle-working faith. He simply sends them out to work the miracles—to heal the sick, cast out demons, and so forth. I personally get impatient and even angry with those who burden the sick by "laying a teaching or formula" on them rather than simply healing them. A delayed cure is laid at the feet of the suffering ones as the supposed result of their incomplete faith or unconfessed sin. How unlike Jesus!

At the same time, Jesus *expects* us to take courageous steps of faith in order to bear fruit for the kingdom. When Peter stepped out on the sea, he became frightened and began to sink. Jesus said to him, "You of little faith, why did you doubt?" (Matt. 14:31). Nevertheless, Jesus *did* save him. Later Jesus told his disciples that they were unable to cure the epileptic boy because of their "little faith." But he also added: "For truly I tell you, if you have faith the size of a mustard seed, you will say to this mountain, 'Move from here to there,' and it will move; and nothing will be impossible for you" (17:20).

After cursing the fig tree, Jesus again taught about a mountain-moving faith, concluding with these words: "And all things you ask in prayer, believing, you will receive" (Matt. 21:22 NASB). Jesus exhorted his disciples to be expectant and persistent in their prayers. Luke's twin parables about the importunate friend (Luke 11:5–8) and the widow and the unjust judge (18:1–8) illustrate this teaching. In *Jesus the Jewish Theologian*, Brad Young provides a helpful analysis of these parables in his chapter

[71] Frederick Dale Bruner, *The Christbook: A Historical/Theological Commentary: Matthew 1—12* (Dallas: Word, 1987), 298.

[72] Ibid., 325.

entitled "Faith as *Chutzpah!*"[73] Christians could learn a lot about this kind of tenacious faith by studying the Hebrew word *chutzpah*!

When the apostles requested of the Lord, "Increase our faith!" he told them that faith "the size of a mustard seed" would get the job done (Luke 17:5–6). All we need to do is utilize the seed of faith we have. Where are the leaders of faith in our generation? To be sure, we have inspiring stories of leaders such as Francis and Edith Schaeffer, Pat Robertson, Oral Roberts, and others, who have blazed trails of faith resulting in far-reaching and fruitful ministry.[74] But far too many of us are timid and even lazy when it comes to taking the steps of faith that the Lord, whom we profess to be following, asks us to take.

Simple *unbelief* may be the besetting sin of this generation. Learning to trust God when life is painfully mystifying and difficult,[75] courageously taking obedient steps of faith to fulfill our callings in life, and simply committing to God the pressing daily needs of life—all these require a faith for living the Christian life that far too seldom is taught in Christian theology. No wonder some fail to see the relevance and necessity of theology when such vital dimensions of the faith are deleted!

Finally, we simply miss out on a lot of the joy, adventure, and fulfillment of the Christian life when we ignore Jesus' teachings on faith. "If you then, who are evil," Jesus said, "know how to give good gifts to your children, how much more will your Father in heaven give good things to those who ask him!" (Matt. 7:11). And in his Upper Room discourse Jesus exhorted: "Until now you have not asked for anything in my name. Ask and you will receive, so that your joy may be complete" (John 16:24). In a seminary chapel service I heard one particular sermon that I will never forget. Carl Bates, former president of the Southern Baptist Convention, told us that he was convinced that when we get to heaven, one of the first things our Lord is going to ask us is, "Why didn't you let me bless you more?" Here, I think, he caught the spirit of Jesus' teachings on faith!

---

[73] Brad H. Young, *Jesus the Jewish Theologian* (Peabody, Mass.: Hendrickson, 1995), 171–80.

[74] See Edith Schaeffer, *L'Abri* (Wheaton, Ill.: Tyndale, 1969); idem, *The Tapestry: The Life and Times of Francis and Edith Schaeffer* (Dallas: Word, 1981); Pat Robertson, *Shout It from the Housetops*, with Jamie Buckingham, CBN 25th Anniversary Edition 1961–1986 (Virginia Beach, Va.: Christian Broadcasting Network, 1986); Oral Roberts, *Expect a Miracle: My Life and Ministry: An Autobiography* (Nashville: Thomas Nelson, 1995).

[75] As Jerry Bridges so helpfully teaches us to do in his classic, *Trusting God* (Colorado Springs, Colo.: NavPress, 1988).

Faith Alone

Every new generation of Christian believers needs to discover afresh Paul's Magna Carta of Christian liberty, the book of Galatians. In this powerful letter the apostle passionately defends the central Christian tenet of justification by faith apart from works of the law: "A person is justified not by the works of the law but through faith in Jesus Christ" (Gal. 2:16). *Faith alone.* This saving faith is a "live" faith that brings us into a personal union with Christ (2:20). It is a faith wrought by the Spirit through the gospel (3:1–5). "For through the Spirit, by faith, we eagerly wait for the hope of righteousness. For in Christ Jesus . . . the only thing that counts is faith working through love" (5:5–6). There is no better depiction of what the New Testament means by saving faith.

The Heidelberg Catechism (1563) captured the essence of *sola fide,* couched in the confessional teaching form of question and answer.

> Q: How are you right with God?
> A: Only by true faith in Jesus Christ.
> Even though my conscience accuses me
>   of having grievously sinned against all God's commandments
>   and of never having kept any of them,
> and even though I am still inclined toward all evil,
> nevertheless,
>   without my deserving it at all,
>   out of sheer grace,
> God grants and credits to me
> the perfect satisfaction, righteousness, and holiness of Christ
>   as if I had never sinned nor been a sinner,
>   as if I had been as perfectly obedient
>   as Christ was obedient for me.
> All I need to do
> is to accept this gift of God with a believing heart.[76]

How better could our gracious gospel be expressed!

R. C. Sproul has provided a thorough historical/theological presentation of this doctrine of grace in his *Faith Alone,* and Jerry Bridges has effectively explained the practical living-out of this doctrine in his *Transforming Grace.*[77] It is the only gospel there is! It is the essence of the

---

[76] *The Heidelberg Catechism* (Grand Rapids: Board of Publications of the Christian Reformed Church, 1975), 8.

[77] R. C. Sproul, *Faith Alone: The Evangelical Doctrine of Justification* (Grand Rapids: Baker, 1995); Jerry Bridges, *Transforming Grace: Living Confidently in God's Unfailing Love* (Colorado Springs, Colo.: NavPress, 1991).

Christian faith. This justifying faith ushers us into a Spirit-empowered walk of obedience, the salient characteristic of which is love (Gal. 5).

To walk by faith is to "sow to the Spirit," to do "what is right," and to "reap at harvest time" (Gal. 6:8–9). As Paul explained to the Philippians, we "work out [our] own salvation with fear and trembling; for it is God who is at work in [us], enabling [us] both to will and to work for his good pleasure" (Phil. 2:12–13). James expresses the same thing when he argues that "faith by itself, if it has no works, is dead" (James 2:17). Paul's words "faith working through love" (Gal. 5:6) say it all! To enter into such a life of faith through the Spirit brings transformation to our lives.

> *Justifying faith ushers us into a Spirit-empowered walk of obedience.*

Change

In the kaleidoscopic world in which we live, "change or die" has become the watchword of both the business community and the church. In effect, this was also the watchword of Jesus. "Truly I tell you, unless you change and become like children, you will never enter the kingdom of heaven" (Matt. 18:3). This change to which Jesus refers is what theologians call conversion. In actuality, we have already been studying this reality. God *calls* us through the gospel of Christ to salvation. We *repent* of our sins, and by *faith* we receive Christ and his forgiveness and so are *justified.* We enter into a personal, life-transforming *union* with Christ. God becomes our Father in that unique, saving sense that only believers in Christ can claim.

Jesus said, "Unless you change...." The word translated "change" (*strepho*) is also rendered as "turn" (cf. RSV) or "convert" (see KJV, NKJV, NASB). It points to the radical reorientation entailed in becoming a Christian. Notice: no conversion, no entrance into the kingdom! The whole context of this passage (Matt. 18) is a kingdom/church reality. Sadly, millions of church members today have never truly been converted. To become a Christian is to convert, to turn (*strepho*: John 12:40; Acts 7:39, 42; *epistrepho*: Matt. 13:15; Luke 1:17; 17:4; Acts 9:35; 11:21; 14:15; 28:27). This change may be instantaneous and dramatic or it may be a quiet and gradual process—but change there must be!

Further, Jesus said, "Unless you change and become like children, you will never enter the kingdom of heaven." (Matt. 18:3). Earlier Jesus had prayed: "I praise you, Father, Lord of heaven and earth, because you have hidden these things from the wise and learned, and revealed them to little children. Yes, Father, for this was your good pleasure" (Matt. 11:25 NIV). Then follows his gracious gospel invitation to find rest for our souls (11:28–30). Jesus' *Abba*-teaching was revolutionary in his generation. It still is. Through faith in Jesus we can actually call God our Father (Daddy)! We are called to a childlike trust and a filial relationship. It is here—in what can be called the biblical doctrine of *adoption*—that the unity of the work of Christ and the Spirit is most evident.

Returning to Galatians, we read:

> But when the fullness of time had come, God sent his Son, born of a woman, born under the law, in order to redeem those who were under the law, so that we might receive adoption as children. And because you are children, God has sent the Spirit of his Son into our hearts, crying, "Abba! Father!" So you are no longer a slave but a child, and if a child then also an heir, through God. (Gal. 4:4–7)

Paul refers to two stages here. First, "God sent his Son . . . so that we might receive adoption as children" (4:4–5); God sent his Son into history. Then he sent "the Spirit of his Son into our hearts, crying, 'Abba! Father!'" (4:6).

As I write these words, it is the Christmas season, and the words and tunes of favorite carols and hymns echo in my mind. I recall that Dale Moody loved to preach a sermon this time of year that he entitled "The Two Births of Christ." This Galatians 4 passage served as his text. He coupled this text with Phillips Brooks' immortal hymn *O Little Town of Bethlehem.* It was to the last verse of the hymn that Moody drew attention, but I would like to highlight the third verse as well. Neither of these is as familiar to most people as the first two verses.

> How silently, how silently
> The wondrous gift is giv'n!
> So God imparts to human hearts
> The blessings of His heav'n.
> No ear may hear His coming,
> But in this world of sin,
> Where meek souls will receive Him still
> The dear Christ enters in.

O holy Child of Bethlehem!
Descend to us, we pray;
Cast out our sin, and enter in;
Be born in us today.
We hear the Christmas angels
The great glad tidings tell;
O come to us, abide with us,
Our Lord Emmanuel. (Phillips Brooks, 1868)

The first birth of Christ took place, of course, in *history*—in the little town of Bethlehem. But Brooks reminds us of the essential second "birth" of Christ—in our *hearts*: "Be born in us today"! Paul depicts both in Galatians 4:4–7.

Paul reminded the Roman believers that to be a Christian is to be "in the Spirit," to have "the Spirit of God" dwelling in you, to "have the Spirit of Christ," to have "Christ in you" (Rom. 8:9–11). "For all who are led by the Spirit of God are children of God" (8:14). To become a Christian is to receive "the Spirit of adoption, enabling us to cry out, '*Abba*, Father!' The Spirit himself joins with our spirit to bear witness that we are children of God" (8:15–16 NJB). God sends "the Spirit of his Son into our hearts" (Gal. 4:6). He is "the Spirit of adoption" (Rom. 8:15 NJB). God's Son and the Spirit of God's Son, the Holy Spirit, make possible our adoption (lit., our *sonship*). "The Spirit you have received is not a spirit of slavery leading you back into a life of fear, but a Spirit that makes us sons, enabling us to cry 'Abba! Father!'" (8:15 NEB). Our sonship is possible because the Father sent his Son into history and the Spirit of his Son into our hearts.

> *The first birth of Christ took place in* history; *the essential second "birth" of Christ takes place in our* hearts.

J. I. Packer explains:

> In Paul's world, adoption was ordinarily of young adult males of good character to become heirs and maintain the family name of the childless rich. Paul, however, proclaims God's gracious adoption of persons of bad character to become "heirs of God and co-heirs with Christ" (Rom. 8:17).[78]

[78] Packer, *Concise Theology*, 167.

Why would Holy God want us as his daughters and sons? That is the glorious mystery of grace!

Conversion initiates us into union with Christ and adoption into God's family. It is a *single* turning—a turning *from* our sin and at the same time a turning *to* God. It is the two-sided coin of repentance and faith. "As repentance turns away from the past, the old Adam, the failed era of despairing freedom, so faith turns toward God's future, the new Adam, the emerging era of freedom amid the governance of God made known in Christ (Rom. 5:12–17)."[79] Fallen humanity must change, be transformed, before a saving entrance into the kingdom of God is possible. Paul reminded the Corinthians of this kingdom standard:

Conversion initiates us into union with Christ and adoption into God's family.

> Do you not know that wrongdoers will not inherit the kingdom of God? Do not be deceived! Fornicators, idolaters, adulterers, male prostitutes, sodomites, thieves, the greedy, drunkards, revilers, robbers—none of these will inherit the kingdom of God. And this is what some of you used to be. But you were washed, you were sanctified, you were justified in the name of the Lord Jesus Christ and in the Spirit of our God. (1 Cor. 6:9–11)

Here the apostle adds regeneration and sanctification to the terms we have already studied. More will be said about these later. What should be noted here is the decisive, fundamental change that provides entrance into God's kingdom.

Thomas C. Oden provides a theological summary of all that we have considered thus far:

> There is an intimate inner correlation between each of the major phases of the order of salvation, whose topics include call, repentance, justification, faith, regeneration, adoption, sanctification, and union with Christ. To lack any of these exegetical motifs would be to leave something deficient in the teaching of salvation. Though distinguishable, they cannot artificially be separated and are united in the one Spirit.[80]

Only God's miraculous grace can make all these blessings possible. He offers us a brand new beginning!

---

[79] Oden, *Life in the Spirit*, 128.
[80] Ibid., 129.

"Behold, I Make All Things New"[81]

There is something irresistibly appealing about *newness*—a new car, a new home, a new year (with the hope of a new beginning and a clean slate). The Bible speaks of our salvation in terms of newness as well. John saw "a new heaven and a new earth," and he saw "the holy city, the new Jerusalem, coming down out of heaven from God, prepared as a bride adorned for her husband" (Rev. 21:1–2). A loud voice from the throne announces that there will be no more death, grief, tears, or pain (21:3–4). "And the one who was seated on the throne said, 'See, I am making all things new'" (21:5).

Many Christians do not realize that John is describing *regeneration* here. Jesus pointed to this same consummation of the kingdom when he referred to "the regeneration when the Son of Man will sit on His glorious throne" (Matt. 19:28 NASB). The specific word "regeneration" (*palingenesia*) is used in the New Testament only here and in Titus 3:5, where it refers to the believer's new birth. Thus, regeneration is both cosmic and personal. The various translations of *palingenesia* in its cosmic sense, as used by Jesus in Matthew 19:28, are revealing: "the renewal of all things" (NRSV, NIV), "the new world" (RSV), "when everything is made new again" (NJB), and even "the New Age" (GNB).

> *Regeneration is both cosmic and personal.*

Peter refers to this same eschatological reality in his second sermon in Jerusalem. He explains that Jesus will "remain in heaven until the time of universal restoration [*apokatastasis*] that God announced long ago through his holy prophets" (Acts 3:21). One day, Paul explained, the groaning creation itself "will be set free from its bondage to decay and will obtain the freedom of the glory of the children of God" (Rom. 8:21). Peter also exhorted his readers to holy living in view of "the coming of the day of God," which brings a great end-time conflagration in which "the elements will melt with fire" (2 Peter 3:10–12). "But according to his promise we wait for new heavens and a new earth in which righteousness dwells" (3:13 RSV). Our salvation will be complete at the great cosmic regeneration!

But what will be true of the whole universe, after the last judgment and the removal of all evil, is true spiritually of the believer even now: "So if anyone is in Christ, there is a new creation [*kaine ktisis*]: everything

[81] Revelation 21:5 RSV.

old has passed away; see, everything has become new!" (2 Cor. 5:17). Paul likewise speaks of a new humanity. Christ came in part "that he might create [*ktizo*] in himself one new humanity [*kainos anthropos*] in place of the two [Jew and Gentile]" (Eph. 2:15). Here our new life in Christ is spoken of in *corporate* terms. Christ came not only to save us individually but also to form us into a body. In both instances, the larger context is one of *reconciliation* (2 Cor. 5:18–21; Eph. 2:11–22), about which we will say more later.

Paul mentions the new humanity again in Ephesians, in the practical portion of the letter, as he exhorts the believers to "give up living as pagans do" (Eph. 4:17 REB). He reminds them that they were taught in Jesus "to put aside your old self [the old man, the old humanity], which belongs to your old way of life and is corrupted by following illusory desires" (4:20–22 NJB). Instead, they are to be renewed spiritually and mentally, and to "put on the New Man [the new humanity, the new self]" (4:23–24 NJB). This new humanity is "created [*ktizo*] according to the likeness of God in true righteousness and holiness" (4:24). John R. W. Stott comments on these verses:

> What had they been taught, then? They had been taught that becoming a Christian involves a radical change, namely "conversion" (as the human side of the experience is usually called) and "re-creation" (the divine side). It involves the repudiation of our former self, our fallen humanity, and the assumption of a new self or re-created humanity.[82]

To become a Christian, according to Ephesians, is to enter into a transforming union with both the *person* of Christ and the *body* of Christ, the church. The New Testament simply does not allow for a "Lone Ranger" Christianity, a churchless Christianity. This, in large measure, is the problem with American individualism. Though we individually become a new creation in Christ, we also become a part of the new humanity created in him.

Paul used earlier another powerful expression to describe the change involved in becoming a Christian. We were in a desperately lost condition (Eph. 2:1–2). "But God, who is rich in mercy, out of the great love with which he loved us even when we were dead through our trespasses, made us alive together with Christ—by grace you have been saved—and raised us up with him and seated us with him in the heav-

---

[82] John R. W. Stott, *God's New Humanity: The Message of Ephesians* (BST; Downers Grove, Ill.: InterVarsity Press, 1979), 181.

enly places in Christ Jesus" (2:4–6; see also Col. 2:13). The picture here is of a resurrection. Perhaps we have part of a baptismal hymn, sung by the congregation at a new believer's baptism, in Ephesians 5:14:

> Awake, O sleeper,
> and arise from the dead.
> and Christ will give you light. (NAB)

Again, we are told that believers have experienced a spiritual resurrection.

What follows this initial transformation is a continual mental and spiritual *renewal* (verb: *anakainoo*; noun: *anakainosis*). "Even though our outer nature is wasting away, our inner nature is being renewed day by day" (2 Cor. 4:16). The new humanity with which we have clothed ourselves "is being renewed in knowledge according to the image of its creator" (Col. 3:10). God saved us through the washing of regeneration and "renewal by the Holy Spirit" (Titus 3:5). We are called to full commitment and continual renewal.

> I appeal to you therefore, brothers and sisters, by the mercies of God, to present your bodies as a living sacrifice, holy and acceptable to God, which is your spiritual worship. Do not be conformed to this world, but be transformed [*metamorphoo*; cf. our "metamorphosis"] by the renewing of your minds, so that you may discern what is the will of God—what is good and acceptable and perfect. (Rom. 12:1–2)

All of this is possible because God has regenerated us, caused us to be born again.

Born Again!

Evangelical Christianity is often known as "born again" religion. This phrase, referring to a spiritual rebirth, came to national prominence when Jimmy Carter acknowledged—in good Southern Baptist style!—that he was "born again." About the same time, Chuck Colson's book *Born Again* was becoming a national bestseller.[83] This was a novel idea for the media and much of the American public, but "old hat" to conservative believers. Most evangelicals knew precisely what it meant to "get saved," to "be born again." And they knew precisely where one might turn in the Scriptures to read about it: John 3.

In this famous chapter, Jesus informs Nicodemus that before he can ever gain entrance into God's kingdom he must be "born [*gennao*] again

---

83 Charles W. Colson, *Born Again* (Old Tappan, N.J.: Revell, 1976).

[*anothen*]" (John 3:3, 7). *Gennao* is actually used of the male parent in much the same way as the old expressions "begotten" or "begat," as with a father begetting a child. In this way John may be highlighting the heavenly Father's role in our regeneration. *Anothen* means "again," "anew," and "from above." In 3:31 Jesus is described as the "one who comes from above [*anothen*]." Therefore, Jesus is referring to a rebirth that comes to us from above—from heaven, from the Father, and by the Spirit.

Nicodemus confused physical birth with spiritual birth, asking, "How can a grown man ever be born a second time?" Jesus replied:

> I tell you for certain that before you can get into God's kingdom, you must be born not only by water, but by the Spirit.[84] Humans give life to their children. Yet only God's Spirit can change you into a child of God. Don't be surprised when I say that you must be born from above. Only God's Spirit gives new life. The Spirit is like the wind that blows wherever it wants to. You can hear the wind, but you don't know where it comes from or where it is going. (John 3:5–8 CEV)

This is a spiritual, supernatural birth, and it is mysterious!

In the opening prologue to his Gospel, John had already referred to the new birth. The world was made through the Word, but it did not know or recognize him when he came in the Incarnation. Even more tragic, he went home to his own people, the Jews, and they did not receive or accept him (John 1:10–11). "But to all who did accept him, to those who put their trust in him, he gave the right [or authority; *exousia*] to become children of God, born [*gennao*] not of human stock, by the physical desire of a human father, but of God" (1:12–13 REB). When we welcome Jesus Christ into our lives as our Lord and Savior, we are given the authority to become God's children and are begotten of God. The apostle Peter praises God for this great miracle:

> Blessed be the God and Father of our Lord Jesus Christ, who according to His great mercy has caused us to be born again [*anagennao*] to a living hope through the resurrection of Jesus Christ from the dead. (1 Peter 1:3 NASB)

---

[84] Perhaps by a "water-and-Spirit" birth Jesus is simply referring to a birth by "spiritual seed," that is, a birth provided by the Holy Spirit: Leon Morris, *Reflections on the Gospel of John:* Vol. 1: *The Word Was Made Flesh: John 1–5* (Grand Rapids: Baker, 1986), 90–91. Craig Keener's rendering of this phrase as the "water of the Spirit" (Greek: one preposition governing two nouns) is probably the best translation, however, in view of John's prevalent use of the water-metaphor with reference to the Spirit: *Gift and Giver*, 139–40.

Finally, both Peter and James tell us that this rebirth comes through the implanted seed of the Word of God, that is, the gospel (1 Peter 1:23; James 1:18, 21).

The Cross That Reconciles

No one in the history of the church has preached this "born again" evangel to more people than Billy Graham. Graham's proclamation has always centered on the cross, where God and humankind are brought together. It is not surprising, therefore, that Graham's first book carried a title pointing to this reconciling work of Christ: *Peace with God.*

> Peace can be experienced only when you have received divine pardon—when you have been reconciled to God and when you have harmony within, with your fellow man and especially with God.[85]

Our salvation includes a divine/human *reconciliation* brought about by the saving death of Christ.

The doctrine of reconciliation is at the heart of the gospel. It speaks of a God of infinite love, who simply will not settle for the universal alienation and destruction of the human race. Rather, as Paul especially emphasized, God chose to take the initiative in restoring our relationship with himself. Paul's "gospel," Romans, is a good place to begin.

> *Our salvation includes a divine/human* reconciliation *brought about by the saving death of Christ.*

Romans 5:1–11 is a *locus classicus* for the doctrine of reconciliation. "Therefore having been justified by faith, we have peace with God through our Lord Jesus Christ" (Rom. 5:1 NASB). Through Christ we have access by faith "to this grace in which we stand" (5:2). We have a sure and certain hope "because the love of God has been poured out within our hearts through the Holy Spirit who was given to us" (5:5 NASB). It was "while we were still helpless" that Christ died for us, "the ungodly" (5:6 NASB). We *might* dare to die for a good person: "But God proves his love for us in that while we still were sinners Christ died for us" (5:7–8). If we are "justified by his blood" in the present, we can

[85] Billy Graham, *Peace with God* (Old Tappan, N.J.: Revell/Spire, 1953), 205 (first published by Doubleday).

be certain that we will be saved from "the wrath of God" in the future (5:9). "For if while we were enemies, we were reconciled to God through the death of his Son, much more surely, having been reconciled, will we be saved by his life" (5:10). The apostle then culminates his statement with the words, "But more than that, we even boast in God through our Lord Jesus Christ, through whom we have now received reconciliation" (5:11).

Justification by faith, peace with God, grace, the love of God, deliverance from divine wrath, reconciliation, salvation—all of these were made available to us while we were still helpless, sinners, and enemies. All of these come to us through the death of Christ and through his indwelling life. And the cross of Christ is continually brought to the fore in Paul's presentation and defense of the gospel.

Syncretism threatened the Colossians' faithfulness to the gospel, making it necessary for Paul to call them back to the supremacy of Christ and to the centrality of Christ's cross.

> For in him [Christ] all the fullness of God was pleased to dwell, and through him God was pleased to reconcile to himself all things, whether on earth or in heaven, by making peace through the blood of his cross.
>
> And you who were once estranged and hostile in mind, doing evil deeds, he has now reconciled in his fleshly body through death, so as to present you holy and blameless and irreproachable before him. (Col. 1:19–22)

Paul thus calls the believers to remain constant in the faith and hope of the gospel (1:23).

In vindicating his ministry to the Corinthians, Paul revealed both the fundamental motivation of his apostolic work and the essence of his message. It was reverential fear of the Lord and Christ's love that kept Paul going. "Therefore, knowing the fear of the Lord, we try to persuade others.... For the love of Christ urges us on, because we are convinced that one has died for all; therefore all have died. And he died for all, so that those who live might live no longer for themselves, but for him who died and was raised for them" (2 Cor. 5:11–15). It is easy to judge others—even Christ—from humans standards, Paul continues, but it is being a new creation in Christ that matters (5:16–17).

Then Paul points to God as the initiator of reconciliation. "All this is from God, who reconciled us to himself through Christ, and has given us the ministry of reconciliation" (2 Cor. 5:18), "namely, that God was in Christ reconciling the world to Himself, not counting their trespasses against them" (5:19 NASB). God came to us in Christ to bring us back to himself. "For our sake he made him to be sin who knew no sin, so that in him we might become the righteousness of God" (5:21). God places our sin and judgment on Christ and gives us his righteousness! And he does one additional thing: He *entrusts* us with "the message of reconciliation" (5:19). "We are therefore Christ's ambassadors. It is as if God were appealing to you through us; we implore you in Christ's name, be reconciled to God!" (5:20 REB). The essence of the church's message and ministry is that of reconciliation.

> *Biblical reconciliation has a* horizontal *dimension in addition to a vertical one.*

Biblical reconciliation has a *horizontal* dimension in addition to a vertical one. In Paul's day a fundamental social division with which the church wrestled was the Jew/Gentile divide. Paul directs our attention to the cross:

> For he is our peace; in his flesh he has made both groups into one and has broken down the dividing wall, that is, the hostility between us. He has abolished the law with its commandments and ordinances, that he might create in himself one new humanity in place of the two, thus making peace, and might reconcile both groups to God in one body through the cross, thus putting to death that hostility through it. (Eph. 2:14–16)

In other words, the church is to model before the world how the gospel can explode every kind of social division. Paul reminded the Galatians, "There is no longer Jew or Greek, there is no longer slave or free, there is no longer male and female; for all of you are one in Christ Jesus" (Gal. 3:28). How often do we sin against this principle today? Sexual chauvinism. Ethnic or denominational pride that promotes divisions among Christians. Class distinctions. Tongues that both bless God and curse others. As James, our Lord's brother, wrote, "My brothers and sisters, this ought not to be so" (James 3:10; cf. 3:9). The testimony of the New Testament is that the faith that brings justification is also the faith that produces righteous living—right relationships with both God and one another.

The Faith That Sanctifies

Faith-union with Christ brings continual change in both the inward and outward dimensions of living. This dynamic of transformation is called sanctification, and we have already studied the Holy Spirit's role in this process. Further comment needs to be made, however, on how faith factors into this reality.

Robert L. Dabney, a leading Presbyterian theologian of the nineteenth century, described the sanctifying power of faith.

> Is it by the instrumentality of faith we receive Christ as our justification, without the merit of any of our works? Well. But this same faith, if vital enough to embrace Christ, is also vital enough to "work by love," "to purify our hearts." This then is the virtue of the free gospel, as a ministry of sanctification, that the very faith which embraces the gift becomes an inevitable and a divinely powerful principle of obedience.[86]

If anyone strongly resisted the legalistic approach to righteousness—that is, a righteousness based on observing the law—it was the apostle Paul. Yet this same apostle referred to our salvation as "the obedience of faith" (Rom. 1:5; 16:26). We are righteous "apart from law ... through faith," he argues (3:21–25), but then he adds these words: "Do we then overthrow the law by this faith? By no means! On the contrary, we uphold the law" (3:31). Later he adds that God sent his Son "to deal with sin" and "so that the just requirement of the law might be fulfilled in us, who walk not according to the flesh but according to the Spirit" (8:3–4). Further, as we walk in love, we fulfill the law (13:8–10).

Jesus, in his own inimitable way, communicates this same gospel truth. For example, in the Sermon on the Mount he begins by explaining the liberating effects of grace, by his use of what we call the Beatitudes (Matt. 5:3–11). He then depicts the righteousness required in his kingdom. "Do not think that I have come to abolish the law or the prophets; I have come not to abolish but to fulfill.... For I tell you, unless your righteousness exceeds that of the scribes and the Pharisees, you will never enter the kingdom of heaven" (5:17, 20). He culminates what are often called "the six antitheses" (5:21–48) with these rather disconcerting words: "Be perfect, therefore, as your heavenly Father is perfect" (5:48).

If this was a moral perfection to which Jesus was referring, as many in the perfectionism camp aver, then he has contradicted himself in this

---

[86] Cited in John Piper, *Future Grace* (Sisters, Ore.: Multnomah, 1995), 21.

sermon—he forgot his first four beatitudes and wrongly instructed us to pray daily for forgiveness (Matt. 5:3–6; 6:12)! To be sure, we are given an unattainable ideal here, but it is an ideal to be pursued. More precisely, it is an *example* that we are to follow, the loving example of our heavenly Father. Paul later expressed the Christian ideal in these words: "Therefore be imitators of God, as beloved children, and live [lit. walk] in love, as Christ loved us and gave himself up for us, a fragrant offering and sacrifice to God" (Eph. 5:1). The apostle John does precisely the same thing as Jesus when he argues for an authentic faith-life of obedience (1 John 2:29–3:10; 5:18), on the one hand, while acknowledging an ongoing battle with sin and a need for continual forgiveness and cleansing (1:5–2:2), on the other.

The error of perfectionism is that of thinking primarily in terms of *externals*—a besetting sin of virtually all renewal movements. Jesus confronted this error head-on with the scribes and the Pharisees: "They tie up heavy burdens, hard to bear, and lay them on the shoulders of others; but they themselves are unwilling to lift a finger to move them. They do all their deeds to be seen by others" (Matt. 23:4–5). Authentic spirituality is perverted into prideful law-keeping. We do it today in the areas of social mores ("I personally never attend movies"), spiritual disciplines ("Have *you* read your nine Bible chapters today?"), and spiritual gifts ("I pray in tongues at least two hours each day"), to name but a few.

Only Christ can change such a heart, and this entails a lifelong process.

Paradoxically, one of the most liberating truths to acquire in living out our faith is that *every* human heart is wicked. "The heart is deceitful above all things, and desperately corrupt; who can understand it?" (Jer. 17:9 RSV). Only Christ can change such a heart, and this entails a lifelong process. We are "predestined to be conformed to the image of his [God's] Son" (Rom. 8:29).

As Christ changes us, we become "doers of the word" (James 1:22). We "care for orphans and widows in their distress" and keep ourselves "unstained by the world" (1:27). We avoid favoritism (2:1–7), live the love command (2:8–13), and, in general, by our *works* show our faith (2:14–26). As Paul phrased it, God gives eternal life "to those who by patiently doing good seek for glory and honor and immortality" (Rom. 2:7).

In other words, the Christian life is an *active, growing* reality. It looks back in gratitude, but it also looks up in humble dependence in the present and forward, in hope, to the future, knowing that " 'Tis grace hath brought me safe thus far, and grace will lead me home" (From "Amazing Grace" by John Newton). This sanctifying power of faith has been given classic expression and explication in John Piper's *Future Grace.*[87] It is to the future-orientedness of faith that Piper draws attention, to what theologians call the eschatological dimension. By faith we live our lives on the basis of the sure promises of God, two of which are his continual companionship and his providential care!

Spiritual Disciplines—the Means of Sanctification

Becoming a disciple of Jesus means entering the discipline of learning. Our teacher is the Holy Spirit (cf. John 14:25, 26; 16:12–15). Our total life experience is his classroom. His one required text is the Bible. Like a skilled coach, he teaches us to learn from both our successes and our failures. He never wastes an adversity but always works good out of it in some way (Rom. 8:28). "Endure hardship as discipline," we are told (Heb. 12:7 NIV); our Father "disciplines us for our good, in order that we may share his holiness" (12:10). We are to *pursue* "the holiness without which no one will see the Lord" (12:14).

Sanctification is *God's* work in our lives, but we are enjoined to cooperate actively with him in this process (Phil. 2:12–13). No one could have said it better than that most colorful and fallible of Jesus' disciples, the apostle Peter:

> His divine power has given us everything needed for life and godliness, through the knowledge of him who called us by his own glory and goodness. Thus he has given us, through these things, his precious and very great promises, so that through them you may escape from the corruption that is in the world because of lust, and may become participants of the divine nature. For this very reason, you must make every effort to support your faith with goodness, and goodness with knowledge, and knowledge with self-control, and self-control with endurance, and endurance with godliness, and godliness with mutual affection, and mutual affection with love. For if these things are yours and are increasing among you, they keep you from being ineffective and unfruitful in the knowledge of our Lord Jesus Christ. For anyone who lacks these things is nearsighted and blind, and is forgetful of the cleansing of past

[87] Ibid.

> sins. Therefore, brothers and sisters, be all the more eager to confirm your call and election, for if you do this, you will never stumble. For in this way, entry into the eternal kingdom of our Lord and Savior Jesus Christ will be richly provided for you. (2 Peter 1:3–11)

We should notice that both the tenor and context of Peter's profound summary of sanctification is *corporate.* The solitary pursuit of true spirituality is foreign to the New Testament. We desperately need each other, as the church, in order to grow up (Eph. 4:14–16). At the same time, each "saint," as we are called in the New Testament, is required to follow Christ personally. He relates to us individually as well.

The Puritan pursuit of piety is a paradigm of the Christian life. "Puritan" is a helpful term because these stalwart believers, often maligned and misrepresented by historians, provide perhaps the best theology and example of what Christian living is all about. All of life, both public and private, is to be related to God. Christ is seen as Lord of culture, preventing any kind of retreat into a privatized faith. Holiness (*piety*) is something the Christian must actively *pursue.* Personal sanctity and social ethics are not seen as antithetical but as complementary. How far we American Christians have drifted from our roots.

We are learning again to appreciate the "means" of sanctification—the spiritual disciplines: worship, prayer, fasting, study, service, evangelism, and the like.

Finally, perhaps out of sheer desperation, we are learning again to appreciate the "means" of sanctification—the spiritual disciplines: worship, prayer, fasting, study, service, evangelism, and the like.[88] A separate

---

88 I find the following works especially helpful in this regard (given in chronological order): J. C. Ryle, *Holiness: Its Nature, Hindrances, Difficulties, and Roots* (Welwyn, Eng.: Evangelical Press, 1979 [Centenary Edition]); Richard F. Lovelace, *Dynamics of Spiritual Life: An Evangelical Theology of Renewal* (Downers Grove, Ill.: InterVarsity Press, 1979); Dallas Willard, *The Spirit of the Disciplines: Understanding How God Changes Lives* (San Francisco: Harper & Row, 1988); Donald Alexander, ed., *Christian Spirituality: Five Views of Sanctification* (Downers Grove, Ill.: InterVarsity Press, 1988); Richard J. Foster, *Celebration of Discipline: The Path to Spiritual Growth,* rev. ed. (San Francisco: HarperSanFrancisco, 1988); Donald S. Whitney, *Spiritual Disciplines for the Christian Life* (Colorado Springs, Colo.: NavPress, 1991); Jerry Bridges, *The Discipline of Grace: God's Role and Our Role in the Pursuit of Holiness* (Colorado Springs, Colo.: NavPress, 1994); Dallas Willard, *The Divine Conspiracy: Rediscovering Our Hidden Life in God* (San Francisco: HarperSanFrancisco, 1998); Richard J. Foster, *Streams of Living Water: Celebrating the Great Traditions of Christianity* (San Francisco: HarperSanFrancisco, 1998); Simon Chan, *Spiritual Theology: A Systematic Study of the Christian Life* (Downers Grove, Ill.: InterVarsity Press, 1998). Rick Warren's *The Purpose-Driven Life* (Grand Rapids: Zondervan, 2002) is already a classic.

volume could easily be devoted to this subject alone. Observing what often is portrayed as "salvation" in some conservative circles, one gets the impression that it entails a *mandatory* instantaneous experience with Christ and then an *optional* following-through with that initial commitment in terms of church affiliation, personal discipleship, holy living, and spiritual growth. This can only be seen as a blatant denial of the New Testament testimony. No one has more effectively addressed this issue, in my opinion, than Dallas Willard:

> Why is it that we look upon our salvation as a moment that began our religious life instead of the daily life we receive from God? We're encouraged somehow today to remove the essence of faith from the particulars of daily human life and to relocate it in special times, places, and states of mind.[89]

As Willard also argues, our salvation is worked out in terms of our *bodily* lives and can only be worked out in that arena. A rather "gnostic" conception of sanctification predominates in even many conservative quarters of the church.

Paul's letter to Titus contains a succinct summary of salvation.

> For the grace of God has appeared, bringing salvation to all, training us to renounce impiety and worldly passions, and in the present age to live lives that are self-controlled, upright, and godly, while we wait for the blessed hope and the manifestation of the glory of our great God and Savior, Jesus Christ. He it is who gave himself for us that he might redeem us from all iniquity and purify for himself a people of his own who are zealous for good deeds. (Titus 2:11–14)

Can we say, then, that we are truly Christ's disciples if there has been no fundamental change in our lifestyles?[90]

To be truly Christian is to be "washed" and "sanctified" as well as "justified" (1 Cor. 6:11). As we have already seen, this initial regeneration is inevitably followed by a lifelong experience of sanctification. Following this line of reasoning, can we claim to be his disciples if our lives are devoid of the spiritual disciplines? If we divorce sanctification from justification, we preach and practice a "cheap grace" foreign to the New Testament and debilitating to the life of the church.

---

[89] Willard, *The Spirit of the Disciplines,* 29. The title of the chapter from which this quotation was taken is "Salvation Is a Life."

[90] See Bill Hull, *Choose the Life: Exploring a Faith That Embraces Discipleship* (Grand Rapids: Baker, 2004).

At the same time, our continual focus should be on Christ and his gospel and not on our performance. Our acceptance and fellowship with God is based on Christ's finished work and not on our inevitably inadequate discipleship. God is the one who is saving us; we are not saving ourselves.

> By God's act you are in Christ Jesus; God has made him our wisdom, and in him we have our righteousness, our holiness [sanctification], our liberation [redemption]. Therefore, in the words of scripture, "If anyone must boast, let him boast of the Lord." (1 Cor. 1:30–31 REB)

The road of discipleship is narrow and difficult (Matt. 7:14). And yet Christ's "yoke is easy" and his "burden is light," and we find "rest" from the wearisome burdens that life often foists upon us (11:28–30).

As is most often the case with life in general, discipline brings freedom. The skilled musician or athlete appears so free and spontaneous in his performance only because of the hours of disciplined practice that preceded it. So it is with Christ. He did not come, nor does he send us, to put religious, legalistic burdens on people. The gospel joyously announces that we have been set free! Again, Paul's "Freedom Letter," Galatians, expresses it well:

> For freedom Christ has set us free. Stand firm, therefore, and do not submit again to a yoke of slavery. . . . For through the Spirit, by faith, we eagerly wait for the hope of righteousness. For in Christ Jesus . . . the only thing that counts is faith working through love. (Gal. 5:1, 5–6)

We can lose our freedom in a "works" righteousness, against which Paul warned the Galatians, or in submission again to the dominion of sin, which, as Paul explained to the Romans, simply does not have to happen because of our identification with Christ's death and resurrection (Rom. 6). Only the freedom of the gospel can liberate us from the slavery of both legalism and antinomianism. It is to this "disciplined freedom" that our Savior calls us.

The Mercies of God—Grace!

For the apostle Paul, literally everything related to salvation and the Christian life can be subsumed under the category of *grace*. In relation to Christian consecration and sanctification there is no better example of this than the familiar exhortation that initiates the practical section in Paul's letter to the Romans:

> I appeal to you therefore, brothers and sisters, by the mercies of God, to present your bodies as a living sacrifice, holy and acceptable to God, which is your spiritual worship. Do not be conformed to this world, but be transformed by the renewing of your minds, so that you may discern what is the will of God—what is good and acceptable and perfect. (Rom. 12:1–2)

Everything related to salvation and the Christian life can be subsumed under the category of grace.

The phrase "the mercies of God" is key. It sums up everything Paul has said thus far in his letter.[91] "Mercy" is also, as we will see shortly, the key word for rightly interpreting the preceding three chapters (Rom. 9–11), which have always attracted a whirlwind of controversy. But it should not go unnoticed that the apostle calls for a consecration of our *bodies,* echoing what was just said in the previous section. Leon Morris's comment on these words is cogent: "Grace affects the whole of life and is not some remote, ethereal affair."[92]

But it is not at all inappropriate to summarize under the rubric of grace the remaining topics related to salvation. In fact, to examine such doctrines as predestination, election, assurance, apostasy, and glorification apart from their moorings in grace is to distort these biblical teachings. The heart of Paul's grace-gospel comes to expression in Romans 8. The familiar words of verses 28–30 provide a launching pad for our exploration of these subjects:

> We know that all things work together for good for those who love God, who are called according to his purpose. For those whom he foreknew he also predestined to be conformed to the image of his Son, in order that he might be the firstborn within a large family [lit., among many brothers]. And those whom he predestined he also called; and those whom he called he also justified; and those whom he justified he also glorified.

This divine promise has brought great comfort and encouragement to believers of every generation—*all things working together for our good.* What a merciful God! Furthermore, we are told that *nothing* can ever separate us from God's love (8:37, 39). There are no stronger words of assurance of God's finishing what he has started in our lives.

---

[91] C. K. Barrett, *The Epistle to the Romans* (HNTC; New York: Harper & Row, 1957), 230–31.
[92] Leon Morris, *The Epistle to the Romans* (Grand Rapids: Eerdmans, 1988), 434.

At the same time, Paul's statements here have also provoked great controversy in that he introduces the idea of predestination and then expands on the concept (in terms of "election") in the ensuing three chapters. What did the apostle mean by the words "those whom he foreknew he also predestined" (Rom. 8:29)? One thing is sure: However we may interpret these words, it is clear that God's goal for us is "to be conformed to the image of his Son" (sanctification), to be a part of "a large family" (the church), and to be "glorified" (resurrection; 8:29–30). These divine purposes work themselves out both in this life, in terms of sanctification and the church, and in the life to come, with our resurrected and glorified bodies. The mercy of God becomes our key interpretive concept as Paul elucidates assurance of faith, even in the face of Jewish rejection of the gospel.

Clearly, for Paul, predestination expresses the Christian's experience of the grace and mercy of God. It also highlights the divine initiative and faithfulness in our salvation. It is not an abstract rational principle that the apostle derived from a concept of some kind of sovereign deity who must *cause* everything to happen in order to remain in control.

James D. G. Dunn highlights the *experiential* taproot of Paul's theology:

> Perhaps the classic example of the failure to appreciate the extent to which Paul's theology is the expression of his experience is the *doctrine* of predestination. So far as Paul is concerned the idea of election speaks neither of an immutable law of God nor of an implacable law of nature, but is simply, in Otto's words, "an immediate and pure expression of the actual religious experience of grace." This continuing "experience of grace" is so much the heart and foundation of Paul's theology and religion that we will never understand him unless we give full weight to its contribution.[93]

Rudolf Otto's classic study further states:

> The recipient of divine grace feels and knows ever more and more surely, as he looks back on his past, that he has not grown into his present self through any achievement or effort of his own, and that, apart from his own will or power, grace was imparted to him, grasped him, impelled, and led him. And even the resolves and decisions that were most his own and most free become to him, without losing the element of freedom, something that he *experienced* rather than *did*.[94]

---

[93] James D. G. Dunn, *Jesus and the Spirit* (London: SCM, 1975), 200 (Dunn's italics); he cites Rudolf Otto, *The Idea of the Holy*, trans. John W. Harvey (London: Oxford Univ. Press, 1923), 91.

[94] Otto, *The Idea of the Holy*, 91 (Otto's italics); cited by Dunn, *Jesus and the Spirit*, 408–9, fn. 3.

Dunn then summarizes Paul's experience and teaching well. "It follows that in a very real sense *the whole of life is for Paul an expression of grace: all is of grace, and grace is all.*[95]

Concerning his apostleship, for example, Paul writes to the Corinthians,

> For I am the least of the apostles, unfit to be called an apostle, because I persecuted the church of God. But by the grace of God I am what I am, and his grace toward me has not been in vain. On the contrary, I worked harder than any of them—though it was not I, but the grace of God that is with me. (1 Cor. 15:9–10)

Dunn helpfully points out the close relation between *grace* and *Spirit* in Paul.[96] One can almost interchange these terms in a given passage in Paul's letters without altering the meaning. This is because grace is a dynamic term for Paul, depicting divine saving *action* on our behalf by the Spirit. It is only by the initiative of the Spirit that we are able to turn to God in repentance and faith and to enter the Spirit-led walk. Our salvation is the work of God's grace and mercy from start to finish. This, in part, is what predestination and election are about—but not all. The apostle was a very *Christ-centered* theologian. In Paul's thought, everything in some way relates to Christ. This is especially true of predestination and election.

"He Chose Us in Christ"[97]

Nothing can better introduce the concepts of our election and predestination than the opening stanza of the Trinitarian hymn with which the Ephesian letter begins (Eph. 1:3–14):

> Blessed be the God and Father of our Lord Jesus Christ,
> who has blessed us
> with every spiritual blessing in the heavenlies
> in Christ Jesus,
> even as he chose us in him
> before the foundation of the world,
> in order that we would be holy and blameless before him
> in love,
> having predestined us for adoption as children unto himself
> through Jesus Christ,
> according to the good pleasure of his will,

---

[95] Dunn, *Jesus and the Spirit*, 204–5 (Dunn's italics).
[96] Ibid., 201–5.
[97] Ephesians 1:4.

> to the praise of the glory of his grace,
> which he graciously gave us
> in the Beloved. (Eph. 1:3–6, author's rendering)

We should first note that *the Father* is the subject of this entire hymn. He is the One who has blessed us (Eph. 1:3), redeemed us (1:7), and sealed us (1:13).

Second, and equally important, all these saving blessings come to us *in Christ,* a phrase used some eleven times in this hymn alone. As Colossians, the twin letter of Ephesians, also indicates, everything God does, both in creation and redemption, he does in and through Christ (Col. 1:15–20; 2:9–10). Thus, the first thing we should notice is that God "chose us in Christ," and he "destined us for adoption as his children through Jesus Christ" (Eph. 1:4–5). Karl Barth, more than any other theologian in the history of the Church, hammered home this biblical truth.

Everything God does, both in creation and redemption, he does in and through Christ.

If there is one book in the Bible that represents best Barth's theology, in my opinion that book is Paul's letter to the Ephesians. The title of Dale Moody's commentary on this letter serves well as a title for the letter itself: *Christ and the Church.*[98] One need only read through Ephesians, marking every reference to Christ and the church—which leaves scantly a verse unmarked—to verify this assertion. With reference to this opening hymn, all the ingredients are there for a full-orbed theology of our saving God: The Father does it all; he does it all in and through his Son; and he does it for the church. Barth elaborates these and other related points in the *more than five hundred pages* that he devotes to the doctrine of election![99]

First, Barth argues, we must acknowledge that we only know God through Jesus Christ:

> That we know God and have God only in Jesus Christ means that we can know Him and have Him only with the man Jesus of Nazareth and with the people which He represents. Apart from this man and apart from this people God would be a different, an alien God. According to the Christian perception He would not be God at all.[100]

---

[98] Dale Moody, *Christ and the Church: An Exposition of Ephesians with Special Application to Some Present Issues* (Grand Rapids: Eerdmans, 1963).

[99] Karl Barth, *Church Dogmatics,* II/2 (Edinburgh: T. & T. Clark, 1957), 1–506.

[100] Ibid., 7.

Further, as the Father of Christ and the church, this God is "the Subject of everything that is to be received and proclaimed in the Christian Church. All His work takes place according to this plan and under this sign" (i.e., through Christ and the church).

Election, as a biblical doctrine, explains and summarizes all that is meant by the word "grace."[101] Predestination, the most commonly used term for this doctrine in the history of Christian dogma, "is first and last and in all circumstances the sum of the Gospel.... It is itself evangel: glad tidings; news which uplifts and comforts and sustains." It is "a proclamation of joy." "It is not a mixed message of joy and terror, salvation and damnation.... It does not proclaim in the same breath both good and evil, both help and destruction, both life and death.... It is light and not darkness."[102]

Finally, Barth boldly asserts:

> The election of grace is the sum of the Gospel—we must put it as pointedly as that. But more, the election of grace is the whole of the Gospel, the Gospel *in nuce.* It is the very essence of all good news. It is as such that it must be understood and evaluated in the Christian Church.[103]

In relation to this Ephesian hymn (esp. Eph. 1:4), Barth reminds us that election "in Christ" means that we must recognize in Christ "not only the electing God but also the elected man."[104]

The progression of Barth's thought on this subject is (1) the election of Jesus Christ, (2) the election of the community, and (3) the election of the individual. These are precisely, in my opinion, the ingredients of the New Testament doctrine. And they are a far cry from the impersonal, rationalistic, speculative, deterministic, fatalistic, and sometimes even repulsive conceptions of predestination and election that have at times been foisted on the church.[105] Jesus Christ is the Elect One (Isa. 42:1; Matt. 12:18; Luke 9:35), and the church is elect in him, as the opening hymn in Ephesians so beautifully expresses it!

---

101 Ibid., 10.

102 Ibid.,12–13.

103 Ibid., 13–14.

104 Ibid., 117.

105 It would be remiss not to mention that Barth's greatest theological weakness—his apparent tendency toward universalism—is also intimated in his treatment of election. But Barth was always elusive on the subject. Dale Moody loved to tell his students about a conversation he had with Barth in which he tried to corner him on this question. Moody asked, "Dr. Barth, do you believe God is going to save everybody?" Barth replied with a wink, "You wouldn't get mad if he did, would you?" The New Testament answer, of course, is that, because God refuses to coerce us, he will *not* save everyone.

"Those Whom He Foreknew"[106]

How does this divine plan work itself out in the life of the believer? Romans 8:29–30 (quoted above) provides us with the heavenly perspective: "For those whom he foreknew he also predestined. . . . And those whom he predestined he also called; and those whom he called he also justified; and those whom he justified he also glorified." Foreknowledge precedes predestination. God foreknows our acceptance or rejection of his saving offer in Christ, and on this basis predestines for glory those who receive Christ! As Moody was fond of explaining, to be on the right plane is to arrive at the right destination. To be in Christ is to be destined for glory!

> *To be on the right plane is to arrive at the right destination. To be in Christ is to be destined for glory!*

Strict Calvinism rejects this interpretation outright. Foreknowledge here is seen totally in personalistic terms, without reference to any divine basis for choosing us for salvation such as prior knowledge of our decisions. Predestination itself is the organizing rational principle for this school of thought. And a certain mnemonic device (TULIP) summarizes the logic of this line of thinking:

- *T* *total depravity* of humankind in sin
- *U* *unconditional election* as predestination apart from foreseen merit
- *L* *limited atonement* in which Christ dies only for the elect
- *I* *irresistible grace* which guarantees the salvation of the elect
- *P* *perseverance of the saints* which expresses their continuing in faith to the end

In the Calvinist's view foreseen faith is tantamount to foreseen merit, which would be, of course, a denial of the gospel of grace itself.

But is faith a merit? Is it not rather to be seen as the empty hands of a beggar accepting a gift? This line of thinking has come to be known as Arminianism, named after Jacob Arminius (1560–1609), who challenged such Calvinistic tenets as limited atonement. According to Arminianism, election is conditioned on divine foreknowledge of our faith, Christ dies for everyone, and grace is viewed as resistible. Also, the terrifying possibility of apostasy, departing from the faith, is accepted.

---

106 Romans 8:29.

The particular brand of Southern Baptist theology in which I was reared held all these views except for the last tenet, which referred to losing one's salvation. In my humble opinion, I was taught the best of both traditions (Calvinism and Arminianism): Christ died for everyone; salvation is offered to everyone; God gives us the choice; our salvation is assured—in general, God does the saving from start to finish but refuses to coerce us to accept his gift of salvation in Christ.

Calvin himself might be somewhat disconcerted at the *Calvinism* one encounters in some quarters today. For Calvin, predestination was simply one of a number of biblical themes to be included in his summary of Christian doctrine we know now as the *Institutes.* His successor, however, Theodore Beza (1519–1605), made predestination the rational principle for a systematic theology that has persisted to the present. Predestination—often expounded under the banner of "sovereign grace"—has become the salient feature of this major brand of Reformed theology. It is true that Calvin taught a strongly deterministic concept of predestination. He did not, however, make this teaching the central motif of his thought.

Calvin's teaching on predestination was not unique. That giant of Western Christendom, Augustine of Hippo (354–430), perhaps the greatest mind in the history of the church, taught a similar doctrine. Augustine tended to emphasize the positive side of the doctrine, however. Out of the totality of sinful humankind, "the mass of perdition," God graciously chose to save some. Calvin went the next logical step, asserting that God also actively chose to condemn others by withholding the offer of salvation. He was straightforward about this: "God adopts some to hope of life, and sentences others to eternal death.... Eternal life is foreordained for some, eternal damnation for others."[107] His summary statement is well-known:

> As Scripture, then, clearly shows, we say that God once established by his eternal and unchangeable plan those whom he long before determined once for all to receive into salvation, and those whom, on the other hand, he would devote to destruction. We assert that, with respect to the elect, this plan was founded upon his freely given mercy, without regard to human worth; but by his just and irreprehensible but incomprehensible judgment he has barred the door of life to those whom he has given over to damnation.[108]

---

[107] John Calvin, *Institutes of the Christian Religion,* 2 vols., ed. John T. McNeill, trans. Ford Lewis Battles (Philadelphia: Westminster, 1960), 2:926 (III.xxi.5).

[108] Ibid., 2:931 (III.xxi.7).

Not surprisingly, Calvin appealed in part to Romans 9–11 as the scriptural basis for his position.[109]

One can only respect Calvin's courage in standing up for what could only be expected to be an unpopular teaching, simply because he saw it to be scriptural. Paul does make statements in Romans 9 (see, e.g., vv. 11–24) that can easily be interpreted as arguing for a double-edged predestinarianism. A consideration of the broader context, however, suggests a different intent on the part of the apostle.

In Romans 8 Paul had just written some of the strongest words of assurance of salvation found in the Bible. But how can we be confident in our hope in the face of the sad fact of the Jewish rejection of the gospel? Why did God's saving purposes seemingly fail in relation to his people Israel? And how can we be confident that he will succeed with us? How precisely do Jew and Gentile fit into God's saving plan? It takes the apostle three substantial chapters to answer these questions, and his key word is *mercy*![110]

Paul had addressed the Jewish question only tangentially in his opening chapters. Now he speaks directly to the issue. The Jews as God's elect had rejected the Messiah. What does that say about God's ability to carry out his saving purposes? Paul's comprehensive response is magisterial! Even the Jewish rejection of Jesus had been factored into God's sovereign plan: It would make way for the great Gentile mission and would one day *give way* to a great harvest among the Jews themselves. God truly does work in mysterious—and wise and merciful—ways, as the apostle concludes in his well-known doxology (Rom. 11:33–36). Morris entitles this section, "The Mercy of God,"[111] and Cranfield refers to the

> joyful confidence that the deep mystery which surrounds us is neither a nightmare mystery of meaninglessness nor a dark mystery of arbitrary omnipotence but the mystery which will never turn out to be anything other than the mystery of the altogether good and merciful and faithful God.[112]

Thus, God's merciful plan of redemption includes both Jew and Gentile. The church can never boast of replacing Israel (11:17–24), but can only think of herself as "a wild olive tree" grafted into "a cultivated olive tree" (11:24).

---

109 Ibid., 2:936–37 (III.xxii.4).

110 See Cranfield, *Romans*, 2:448; Morris, *Romans*, 345.

111 Morris, *Romans*, 427.

112 Cranfield, *Romans*, 2:592.

God chose both Israel and the church for his divine saving purposes. It was an election involving *both* salvation and service. To the Israelites "belong the adoption, the glory, the covenants, the giving of the law, the worship, and the promises; to them belong the patriarchs, and from them, according to the flesh, comes the Messiah, who is over all, God blessed forever. Amen" (Rom. 9:4–5). The church is sent to proclaim the good news of Jesus Christ across the globe (10:14–17). Only those Jews and Gentiles, foreknown of God, who turn from their sins and put their trust in Christ will be saved—only these are in the ultimate sense "the elect." As it is, one finds unbelief rampant among them all. "For God has imprisoned all in disobedience so that he may be merciful to all" (11:32). The issue for both is faith versus unbelief (11:17–24).

> *God chose both Israel and the church for his divine saving purposes. It was an election involving* both *salvation and service.*

Thomas Oden summarizes well what these crucial chapters are all about:

> Paul was not sorrowful because God had from eternity by an inflexible decree of reprobation damned some to death. Rather, he was sorrowful because *so many of God's own called people were willfully rejecting God's own coming.* Nor was Paul anguished because God had failed to keep promises to the descendants of Abraham, but because they were failing to respond freely to God's promise-keeping. Yet they remained the people of promise, recipients of covenant, of election, Torah, and temple. "It is not as though God's word had failed. For not all who are descended from Israel are Israel" (Rom. 9:6).... The subject of the discourse in Romans 9–11 was not the eternal election or reprobation of particular individual persons to eternal life or death, as individualistic exegesis has sometimes argued, but rather the election of the Gentiles to be recipients of the promise equally with the descendants of Abraham, based on faith's response to grace.[113]

Further, the nature of God's sovereignty is at issue, but not in precisely the same way as it is today.

Calvinists today are often seen as the ardent defenders of God's sovereignty. Ironically, their distinctive portrayal of divine sovereignty in actuality *diminishes* God. Only a finite deity would need to *cause* every

---

[113] Thomas C. Oden, *The Transforming Power of Grace* (Nashville: Abingdon, 1993), 142–43 (Oden's italics).

event and decision in order to be in control of them. Wolfhart Pannenberg states it well:

> Some views of divine predestination and providence lead to a perverted concept of God's rule over world occurrence as a tyranny because they see God after the pattern of a finite subject. The world rule of a finite subject would always be tyranny because it would involve total control over the course of events.[114]

The Calvinistic rejection of foreknowledge is also artificial for similar reasons.

Thomas Oden is perhaps the "dean" of the new breed of theologians today who seek to go beyond the Calvinistic/Arminian debate in recovering the classical consensus of the patristic fathers (first five centuries) and beyond. He documents that the position I have sketched out here reflects such a consensus, and that the Augustinian/Calvinistic departure has been misleading in some ways.[115] Calvin himself acknowledged that many of the early fathers such as Ambrose, Origin, and Jerome accepted the view of foreknowledge defended here, but suggested that we "imagine that these fathers are silent."[116]

To follow Paul carefully, grace and faith must be put on the one side, and works, merit, and the like on the other (cf. Eph. 2:8–9 alone!). Faith does not equal merit. God's foreknowing our faith and predestining us for salvation is categorically different from his foreknowing our supposed merit, good works, or righteousness and thus electing us. "Sovereign grace," if one chooses to hold to this phrase, should mean that God initiates the conditions for salvation from the outset and, because of his omniscience, foreknows our response and elects us accordingly.[117] Two other key issues that deserve further attention have surfaced in this discussion.

Assurance and Apostasy

Romans 8 is the great assurance chapter in the Bible. Ironically, it is followed by a rather chilling account of Israel's apostasy (chs. 9–11) that

---

[114] Wolfhart Pannenberg, *Systematic Theology*, vol. 1, trans. Geoffrey W. Bromiley (Grand Rapids: Eerdmans, 1991), 388.

[115] Oden's *The Transforming Power of Grace* deserves a wide reading in this regard.

[116] Calvin, *Institutes*, 2:941–42 (III.xxii.8).

[117] No one has better ferreted out the issues and written more helpfully on this subject, in my opinion, than Jack Cottrell; see, for example, Ch. 9 "Predestination," 331–352 in *What the Bible Says About God the Ruler* (Joplin, Mo.: College Press, 1984).

contains solemn warnings that unbelief even in the church could result in one's being "cut off" (11:22). How can these be reconciled?

Earlier Paul had made the distinction between the outward Jew and the true, inward Jew (Rom. 2:28–29). Here he states, "For not all Israelites truly belong to Israel" (9:6). Similarly, evangelicals today often differentiate between the institutional churches and the "true church" composed of all true believers. There are Christians and then there are Christians! Only a "remnant" of Israel will be saved (9:27; 11:5), but "even those of Israel, if they do not persist in unbelief, will be grafted in, for God has the power to graft them in again" (11:23). The analogies "cut off" and "grafted in" raise the issue of the nature of apostasy in the Bible, particularly as it relates to the greater emphasis in Scripture concerning the assurance of faith.

Jesus himself dealt with the problem of the Jewish rejection of the gospel. The parable of the wedding banquet (Matt. 22:1–14; cf. Luke 14:15–24, where we have a similar story in a different setting) poignantly depicts how God's chosen people reject his invitation and how God broadens his appeal to all types of people. Jesus' culminating words are profound: "For many are called, but few are chosen" (Matt. 22:14).

Gilbert Bilezikian has captured the essence and significance of these words. First, he points out that the "king had not predetermined the decisions of those who turned down the invitation or of those who accepted it. Becoming part of the 'chosen' had been their choice all along."[118] Then, echoing the vision (that people matter to God) of Willow Creek Community Church, of which he has been a significant part, he concludes that "although all humans matter to God, not all will be saved. God had decided even before the beginning of time that only people of faith would enter eternal life."[119] Thus, this one parable of our Lord alone explodes the deterministic approach to election, while at the same time providing a clear and practicable model as to how election actually works in the divine scheme of redemption.

The question remains, however, as to why people who are a part of the community of faith fall away. Perhaps another of our Lord's parables provides the best help here: the familiar parable of the soils (Matt. 13:1–23; Mark 4:1–20; Luke 8:4–15). Sitting on a boat beside Lake Galilee, Jesus told this story to a great crowd of people standing on the shore.

---

[118] Gilbert Bilezikian, *Christianity 101* (Grand Rapids: Zondervan, 1993), 151.

[119] Ibid., 153. Bilezikian's entire presentation in this area is helpful (148–56).

Later he interpreted it to his disciples. Jesus depicts four types of soil that are analogous to four kinds of people. First, there were the seeds on the path that the birds ate. Jesus says that the "seed is the word of God" (Luke 8:11), "the word of the kingdom" (Matt. 13:19). The people represented by this soil hear the Word but do not understand it, and the devil (represented by the birds) comes and steals the Word that has been sown in their hearts "so that they may not believe and be saved" (Luke 8:12).[120]

The rocky soil indicates a shallow faith—people who hear and joyfully receive the Word but have no depth. In times of trouble, persecution, or temptation they fall away. The seeds that fell among the thorns point to those who allow "the cares and riches and pleasures of life" (Luke 8:14) to choke the Word. This is an astonishing description with alarming parallels in American Christianity. But then there is the good soil—those who hear, understand, and accept the Word, who "hold it fast in an honest and good heart, and bear fruit with patient endurance" (Luke 8:15).

> *God is incredibly patient with us, "not wanting any to perish, but all to come to repentance."*

One need only participate in church life a short time to note examples of all four kinds of soil. But certain questions still haunt us: Why are there the first three kinds of soil? What is the nature of their faith—especially the rocky ground and the thorny ground? Also, one notices that the Word of God is sown *on all four kinds of soil*! Again, many are called, but few are chosen. To address these issues in reverse order, we note first of all that the call to salvation is *universal*.

God is incredibly patient with us, "not wanting any to perish, but all to come to repentance" (2 Peter 3:9). He desires "everyone to be saved and to come to the knowledge of the truth" (1 Tim. 2:4). Christ, the "one mediator . . . gave himself a ransom for all" (2:5–6). God loved the world so much that he gave his only Son, "that *whosoever* believeth in him should not perish, but have everlasting life" (John 3:16 KJV, italics added). "For *whosoever* shall call upon the name of the Lord shall be saved" (Rom. 10:13 KJV, italics added). As the famed Baptist musical evangelist J. Edwin McConnell wrote when he was only eighteen years

[120] I am combining the Synoptic accounts. It is interesting to study this parable redactionally (i.e., to see how each Gospel writer edits the material, and each one's unique emphases and insights).

old, "'Whosoever,' surely meaneth me."[121] God called Israel in ancient times, and the church since the coming of Christ, to announce his saving call to the nations. Ironically, many who have identified themselves with God's people will not be saved. But all who truly believe will be saved.

The clear testimony of Scripture is that we may *know* that we have eternal life (1 John 5:11–12). We have already seen how strong this assurance is in Paul's writings. John bears the same witness. Jesus, the Good Shepherd, gives his sheep "eternal life, and they will never perish" (John 10:28). No one can snatch them out of his hand (10:28–30). And what about those who depart from the church? "They went out from us, but they did not belong to us; for if they had belonged to us, they would have remained with us. But by going out they made it plain that none of them belongs to us" (1 John 2:19).

Paul said, "I know the one in whom I have put my trust, and I am sure that he is able to guard until that day what I have entrusted to him" (2 Tim. 1:12). He assured the Philippians that God always finishes what he starts (Phil. 1:6). We "are being protected [kept or guarded] by the power of God through faith for a salvation ready to be revealed in the last time" (1 Peter 1:5). God "is able to keep [us] from falling, and to make [us] stand without blemish in the presence of his glory with rejoicing" (Jude 24). Furthermore, we have the internal witness of the Spirit that we are God's children (Rom. 8:16; Gal. 4:6; 1 John 4:13; 5:10). What, then, do we make of the *warnings* against apostasy?

The book of Hebrews is a classic case in point. Five poignant warnings are issued: Hebrews 2:1–4; 3:7–4:13; 5:11–6:20; 10:19–39; 12:1–29. At the same time, this letter was intended as a "message of encouragement," albeit one the readers had to "bear with" (13:22 NAB). The warnings are also accompanied by words of optimism. Hebrews 6 provides perhaps the best example of these dynamics. The writer speaks of "those who have once been enlightened, and have tasted the heavenly gift, and have shared in the Holy Spirit, and have tasted the goodness of the word of God and the powers of the age to come, and then have fallen away" (6:4–6). This is no "bluff." The danger warned against here is real, not hypothetical or imaginary, and yet encouragement follows:

---

[121] J. Edwin McConnell, "'Whosoever' Meaneth Me" (1910), copyright 1914. See William J. Reynolds, *Hymns of Our Faith* (Nashville: Broadman, 1964), 73–74, 352. Quotation from *Baptist Hymnal*, 1975 edition (Nashville: Convention Press), #169.

> Even though we speak in this way, beloved, we are confident of better things in your case, things that belong to salvation. For God is not unjust; he will not overlook your work and the love that you showed for his sake in serving the saints, as you still do. And we want each one of you to show the same diligence so as to realize the full assurance of hope to the very end, so that you may not become sluggish, but imitators of those who through faith and patience inherit the promises. (Heb. 6:9–12)

We are immediately reminded of Peter's exhortation to "give diligence to make your calling and election sure: for if ye do these things ye shall never fall" (2 Peter 1:10 KJV). Nevertheless, is the writer of Hebrews telling his readers that even though they are true believers, they can still be eternally lost?

The widely respected Methodist New Testament scholar I. Howard Marshall would say yes. He espouses the "saved and lost" theory that states that "a Christian may be saved and then lost through deliberate apostasy."[122] Although the Calvinist New Testament scholar Philip Edgcumbe Hughes takes with utmost seriousness the ominous nature of the warnings, he nevertheless concludes that

> what he [the writer of Hebrews] has reason to fear is that some among them who have professed Christian faith, enjoyed Christian fellowship, and engaged in Christian witness may prove to be hypocrites and enemies of Christ and, by turning away from the light they have known, show that they do not belong to God's people at all.[123]

The Calvinist/Arminian impasse emerges again. Ironically, Wesley and Calvin were much closer on the issue of assurance than the Wesleyanism (Arminianism) and Calvinism that followed them. Wesley once wrote that the "truth of the Gospel is within a hairsbreadth of Calvinism."[124]

Both extreme Calvinism and extreme Arminianism lack assurance of faith. Arminians, saved one day and lost the next, are never really sure they will make it to heaven. Calvinists may doubt whether they are of the elect (thus, the Puritan teaching on the experience of "owning the covenant" in which the Holy Spirit gives assurance to the believer of election). How can we know whether we will persevere and thus prove our election? To what precisely do the New Testament warnings against apostasy refer?

---

122 I. Howard Marshall, *Kept by the Power of God: A Study of Perseverance and Falling Away* (Minneapolis: Bethany, 1969), 145.

123 Hughes, *Hebrews*, 222.

124 Cited in Marshall, *Kept by the Power of God*, back cover.

Perhaps the Southern Baptist patriarch E. Y. Mullins best addresses these questions. First, he notes that extreme Calvinism tends toward a pantheism in which human responsibility is ignored. Predestination and election are pressed as a logical argument in which a God of absolute power accomplishes his sovereign purposes and saves whomever he wills. The New Testament, however, is virtually devoid of such a logical argument, emphasizing rather both God's *moral* and *spiritual* suasion and our response, effort, and perseverance. But extreme Arminianism appears deistic in that God is seemingly placed above and beyond the fray, and we virtually determine our own destiny based on whether we choose to persevere in our faith.[125]

The Christian can enjoy a certainty of faith—not based on performance but knowing that it is God *who is doing the saving.*

Paul exhorted the Philippians to "work out your own salvation with fear and trembling; for it is God who is at work in you, enabling you both to will and to work for his good pleasure" (Phil. 2:12, 13). He thereby *combined* what too often we have put asunder! The Christian can enjoy a certainty of faith—not based on performance but knowing that it is *God* who is doing the saving. Mullins summarizes it well:

> [God] does not preserve us by irresistible grace as by something which overrides our will; but by constraining grace which enlists our will. He does not preserve us in spite of transgressions and backsliding, but by renewing us unto repentance for sins and return from backslidings. His method is not that of the pantheistic view in which God's will is everything and man's nothing. Nor is it the method of the deistic view which exalts the human will to the chief place and reduces that of God to the minimum.[126]

This perspective integrates both the assurances and the warnings of Scripture.

Apostasy may be seen either as a temporary backsliding that is followed by a return to God or, in its fullest sense, as the result of a spurious faith. Authentic faith is thereby a persevering faith, not an insincere "faith" that presumes upon God's grace and ignores moral imperatives.

---

[125] E. Y. Mullins, *The Christian Religion in Its Doctrinal Expression* (Nashville: Broadman, 1917), 432–438.

[126] Ibid., 437.

Both God's gracious initiative and our essential responsibility are kept clearly in view in this perspective.[127]

Nonetheless, because we are dealing here with the deeply mysterious interrelation between an infinite God and a finite humanity, differences of opinion will inevitably persist. A humble tolerance of diversity of perspectives is definitely in order. The key issue, in my own perspective, is that of *assurance.* The overriding emphasis of Scripture is one of assurance—of knowing that we have eternal life, that we are being kept by the power of God, that God is at work within us, and that he finishes what he starts. The warnings concerning apostasy are there as well and must be taken with utmost seriousness. But the triumph of grace is the salient theme of the New Testament doctrine of salvation.

In the practical outworkings of daily church life the results are about the same in a balanced Arminian setting as in a balanced Calvinistic setting. John Piper, a Calvinist, once told a professing Christian that if he continued to live in adultery and refused to fight against this sin, he would go to hell. Of course, Piper believes that no true believer will ever be lost. But he also knows that in the Bible the same authentic faith that brings justification also brings sanctification.[128] But how different is his warning from that of the Arminian who would say precisely the same thing to an errant church member?

> *Authentic faith is a persevering faith.*

We look at a person who once professed Christ but is now living in the world with no profession or apparent possession of faith. The Calvinist would say that his or her initial "faith" was spurious. The Arminian would say that this person may well have had authentic faith at one time but is now apostate. *In either case,* should we not pursue this person, warn this person, and reach out to this person with genuine concern for his or her eternal destiny? In the final analysis, whatever perspective we adopt in relation to these issues—predestination, election, apostasy, and the like—we should always aspire toward *consolidating* people in the faith.

---

127 Ibid., 438. A similar integration of divine sovereignty and human freedom can be found in the work of Herschel H. Hobbs; see ch. 4 "The Priesthood of the Believer and Salvation," in *You Are Chosen: The Priesthood of All Believers* (San Francisco: Harper & Row, 1990), 29–42.

128 Piper, *Future Grace,* 331. For a full-orbed theological argument for this perspective, see Thomas R. Schreiner and Ardel B. Caneday, *The Race Set Before Us: A Biblical Theology of Perseverance & Assurance* (Downers Grove, Ill.: InterVarsity Press, 2001). Schreiner and Caneday thoroughly and fairly present the major competing viewpoints in this discussion. See also Gregory A. Boyd and Paul R. Eddy, *Across the Spectrum: Understanding Issues in Evangelical Theology* (Grand Rapids: Baker, 2002), 165–77.

Thomas Oden highlights this concern in *The Transforming Power of Grace.* Citing two Reformed confessions and one Lutheran confession, he provides the balanced theological and pastoral perspective so needed in our day.

> The doctrine of this high mystery of predestination is to be handled with special prudence and care, that men attending the will of God revealed in his Word, and yielding obedience thereunto, may, from the certainty of their effectual vocation, be assured of their eternal election. [The Westminster Confession (1646)]
>
> If anybody teaches the doctrine of the gracious election of God to eternal life in such a way that disconsolate Christians can find no comfort in this doctrine but are driven to doubt and despair, or in such a way that the impenitent are strengthened in their self-will, he is not teaching the doctrine according to the Word. [The Formula of Concord (1577)]
>
> Let Christ, therefore, be our looking-glass, in whom we may behold our predestination. [The Second Helvetic Confession (1566)][129]

These statements point to a wise and workable theological and pastoral consensus.

We began this discussion with Paul's letter to the Romans. Romans 8:28–30 became, in many ways, the centerpiece of our discussion. What is often overlooked in this passage is the divine *goal* indicated: that we be *glorified*! All "have sinned and fall short of the glory of God" (Rom. 3:23). But we Christians "rejoice in our hope of sharing the glory of God" (5:2 RSV). Because we share in Christ's sufferings, we will also share in his glory (8:17). We "consider that the sufferings of this present time are not worth comparing with the glory about to be revealed to us" (8:18). A glorious freedom awaits us at the redemption of our bodies (8:21, 23).

The context of these verses from Romans indicates that not only will we be perfected but the entire creation will too. One day our sanctification will be completed (either at our death or at our Lord's return). One day our mortal bodies will be raised immortal and God's kingdom rule will be consummated. One day all sin, sickness, sorrow, and death

---

[129] Oden, *The Transforming Power of Grace,* 159. I have found the relevant sections of the Lutheran document, The Formula of Concord, to be particularly helpful in this overall discussion; see *The Book of Concord: The Confessions of the Evangelical Lutheran Church,* trans. and ed. Theodore G. Tappert (Philadelphia: Fortress, 1959), 494–97, 616–32.

will end. We live *daily* in this exhilarating hope. Our salvation is infinitely more than liberation from social or political oppression (as in the various liberation theologies). We have a hope not only for this life but also for that which is to come (see 1 Cor. 15:19)!

In its essence the biblical doctrine of salvation can be summarized in the simplest of terms. There is *one way* of salvation: Christ and his church (John 14:6; Acts 4:12; 9:2; 19:9, 23; 24:14, 22; cf. 16:17; 18:26). There are *two sides* of salvation: God's grace (Rom. 5:12–21; Eph. 2:1–10) and our faith (Rom. 10:8–13). And there are *three stages* of salvation: past (Luke 7:50; Rom. 8:24; Eph. 2:5, 8; Titus 3:5), present (1 Cor. 1:18; Phil. 2:12), and future (Rom. 13:11; 1 Peter 1:5).[130] We know that "the night is far gone, the day is near" (Rom. 13:12). And we "wait for the blessed hope and the manifestation of the glory of our great God and Savior, Jesus Christ" (Titus 2:13). It is to a more detailed consideration of this great Christian hope that we now turn.

---

[130] See Moody, *The Word of Truth*, 308–11.

9 | Hope
What Is Christian Hope?

- Hope for a Despairing World
  - Harbingers of Hope
  - Eschatology
  - Hope and History
  - Hope and Mission
  - Hope and Assurance
  - Hope and Joy
- Death and the Life After
  - Absent from the Body, Present with the Lord
  - She Is Not Dead But Sleeping
  - Paradise!
  - Hades
  - Competing Conceptions of the Afterlife
- The Second Coming of Jesus Christ
  - The Signs of the Times
  - The Fullness of the Gentiles and the Fullness of Israel
  - Parousia, Apocalypse, Epiphany
  - "Then I Saw Heaven Opened . . ."
  - The Devil, the Beast, and the False Prophet
- Pre-, Post-, A-, and . . . Pan-!
  - Premillennialism
  - Postmillennialism
  - Amillennialism
- Resurrection
- The Great White Throne Judgment
- Hell
- A Good God and an Eternal Hell—Reconcilable?
- Heaven

Blessed be the God and Father of our Lord Jesus Christ, who according to His great mercy has caused us to be born again to a living hope through the resurrection of Jesus Christ from the dead.

—1 Peter 1:3 NASB

For in hope we were saved. Now hope that is seen is not hope. For who hopes for what is seen? But if we hope for what we do not see, we wait for it with patience.

—Romans 8:24-25

Yes, I know what plans I have in mind for you, Yahweh declares, plans for peace, not for disaster, to give you a future and a hope.

—Jeremiah 29:11 NJB

What oxygen is for the lungs, such is hope for the meaning of human life.

—Emil Brunner[1]

[Christ] has forced open a door that has been locked since the death of the first man. He has met, fought, and beaten the King of Death. Everything is different because He has done so.

—C. S. Lewis[2]

"Surely I am coming soon."
Amen. Come, Lord Jesus!

—Revelation 22:20

It was the best of times, it was the worst of times, it was the age of wisdom, it was the age of foolishness, it was the epoch of belief, it was the epoch of incredulity, it was the season of Light, it was the season of Darkness, it was the spring of hope, it was the winter of despair, we had everything before us, we had nothing before us, we were all going direct to Heaven, we were all going direct the other way.

—Charles Dickens[3]

---

[1] Emil Brunner, *Eternal Hope*, trans. Harold Knight (Philadelphia: Westminster, 1954), 7.
[2] C. S. Lewis, *Miracles: A Preliminary Study* (New York: Macmillan, 1947), 150.
[3] Charles Dickens, *A Tale of Two Cities* (New York: Oxford Univ. Press, 1859), 1.

CHARLES DICKENS'S MEMORABLE DESCRIPTION of the Reign of Terror during the French Revolution could easily, and quite accurately, describe our own day! Things are getting better and worse at the same time. It is as if two completely different plays are being performed at the same time—one, the worst of all tragedies, the other, the most glorious story ever told. The world is growing darker. The church is shining brighter and brighter! The kingdom inaugurated during the first coming of Christ is to be consummated at his second coming!

Immanuel Kant, in his *Critique of Pure Reason*, stated: "All the interests of my reason, speculative as well as practical, combine in the three following questions: 1. What can I know? 2. What ought I to do? 3. What may I hope?"[4] These three questions correspond to the three eternal realities: faith, hope, and love. Faith in God's Word provides the answer to the question, "What can I know?" Loving God with our whole being and our neighbor as ourselves is Jesus' response to "What ought I to do?" And the kingdom hope of the church is the best answer to Kant's third query, "What may I hope?"[5] The purpose of this chapter is to provide the full Christian answer to Kant's third question.

Hope for a Despairing World

In 1954 the young American evangelist Billy Graham had the privilege of a visit with Sir Winston Churchill, prime minister of Great Britain and without doubt one of the world's leading figures. Churchill asked Graham, "Do you have any hope? What hope do have for the world?" A number of times the prime minister mentioned that he was "an old man." Further, he was appalled by the myriad reports of murder, rape, and hatred in the papers and troubled by the growing peril of communism. Several times Churchill said he was "without hope for the world."

In typical Graham fashion, the evangelist removed his New Testament from his pocket and responded, "Mr. Prime Minister, I am filled with hope." He proceeded to recount the salient events of the gospel, including the bodily return of Jesus Christ to the earth. The young evangelist was telling "Mr. History" of both the new birth that God has made

---

[4] Immanuel Kant, *Critique of Pure Reason*, trans. Norman Kemp Smith (New York: Macmillan, [1781, 1787] 1958), 635.

[5] Peter J. Kreeft, *Heaven: The Heart's Deepest Longing* (New York: Harper & Row, 1980), 1. I also obtained the quotation from Kant from Kreeft's excellent volume (139, fn. 1).

available to every person and the glorious denouement of history at our Lord's return. Graham was communicating the Christian hope.[6]

On April 16, 1963, Dr. Martin Luther King Jr., president of the Southern Christian Leadership Conference and modern-day prophet of hope, issued his now famous "Letter from Birmingham Jail." King was responding to a previous open letter from a group of eight white Birmingham clergymen who criticized both King and his movement of nonviolent resistance. Again and again, Dr. King expressed how he had hoped that white moderates would be able to appreciate and support his efforts for racial equality, only to be continually disappointed. His closing words reveal the spirit of this great leader and the historical hope to which he held tenaciously:

> *I hope this letter finds you strong in the faith. I also hope that circumstances will soon make it possible for me to meet each of you, not as an integrationist or a civil rights leader, but as a fellow clergyman and a Christian brother. Let us all hope that the dark clouds of racial prejudice will soon pass away and the deep fog of misunderstanding will be lifted from our fear-drenched communities and in some not too distant tomorrow the radiant stars of love and brotherhood will shine over our great nation with all of their scintillating beauty.*
>
> *Yours for the cause of Peace and Brotherhood,*
>
> *Martin Luther King, Jr.*[7]

Four months later the entire nation heard Dr. King's classic enunciation of this hope—rooted in the great Christian hope of the Scriptures—in his famous address, "I Have a Dream." Standing in front of the Lincoln Memorial on August 28, 1963, King delivered the keynote address of the March on Washington, D.C., for Civil Rights. The dream Dr. King so eloquently portrayed that historic day resounded with Old Testament prophetic passion and imagery. Mrs. Correta King later commented that at "that moment it seemed as if the Kingdom of God appeared. But only for a moment." As often occurs at such *kairos* occasions, time seemed to stand still. Just prior to his unforgettable concluding words ("Let freedom ring" and "Free at last"), King said: "This

---

[6] John Pollock, *Billy Graham: The Authorized Biography* (New York: McGraw-Hill, 1996), 131–33; see also William Martin, *A Prophet with Honor: The Billy Graham Story* (New York: William Morrow, 1991), 182–83.

[7] James Melvin Washington, ed., *A Testament of Hope: The Essential Writings of Martin Luther King, Jr.* (San Francisco: Harper & Row, 1986), 302.

is our hope. This is the faith that I go back to the South with. With this faith we will be able to [hew] out of the mountain of despair a stone of hope."[8]

On April 3, 1968, the day before his assassination, Dr. King delivered his last address—a sermon at Mason Temple in Memphis, Tennessee, the headquarters of the Church of God in Christ, the great African-American Pentecostal denomination. As if sensing his impending death, he spoke of having "been to the mountaintop," of having "seen the promised land."

> I may not get there with you. But I want you to know tonight, that we, as a people will get to the promised land. And I'm happy tonight. I'm not worried about anything. I'm not fearing any man. Mine eyes have seen the glory of the coming of the Lord.[9]

Martin Luther King Jr. had a historic hope of "liberty and justice for all," rooted in the great Christian hope of the "coming of the Lord."

Jürgen Moltmann was a young German prisoner of war in 1945 when an American chaplain gave him a copy of the New Testament with the Psalms. With the rest of the prisoners, Moltmann felt the despair and hopelessness that came with the knowledge that many of the great German cities lay in ruins—along with the cherished dreams of the German people, now humiliated by the revelations of the Nazi atrocities. In the Psalms the German teenager saw that the Bible dealt with similar pain, humiliation, and despair, yet with an unconquerable spirit of hope. This experience drew him to a wide reading of the Scriptures and ultimately to the study of Christian theology. His groundbreaking volume, *Theology of Hope*, written when he was thirty-nine, has in large measure set the agenda for modern theology in the second half of the twentieth century and beyond.[10]

Harbingers of Hope

The *theology* of hope may have had its origins in Germany. But the real harbingers of hope for the twentieth and twenty-first centuries are surely the African-American Pentecostals, who launched a worldwide revival movement that has given the greatest hope to Christians longing to see

8 Ibid., 217–20.

9 Ibid., 286.

10 A. J. Conyers, *Eclipse of Heaven: Rediscovering the Hope of a World Beyond* (Downers Grove, Ill.: InterVarsity Press, 1992), 59.

the "Church Hesitant" become the "Church Triumphant"—even in the midst of growing opposition and persecution. As Harvey Cox has pointed out, the Pentecostals rightly see both a present and future dimension to the kingdom. Steven J. Land rightly depicts their spirituality as "a passion for the kingdom."[11] From its inception, American Pentecostalism has been eschatological to the core![12] In addition, they have been the most forthright in keeping the vision of people of all colors united in Christian faith, hope, and love to evangelize the world.[13]

From its inception, American Pentecostalism has been eschatological to the core!

Cox's depiction of William J. Seymour, the leader of the Azusa Street revival in Los Angeles that launched the Pentecostal movement, aptly communicates the far-reaching influence of the Pentecostal hope that Seymour and his followers espoused:

> Pentecostalism has become a global vehicle for the restoration of primal hope. The movement started from the bottom. A partially blind, poor, black man with little or no book learning outside of the Bible heard a call. Seymour was anything but a Paul of Tarsus, trained by the leading religious scholars, or an Augustine of Hippo, schooled by the most polished Roman rhetoricians, or a Calvin or Luther educated in the original languages of scripture. He was a son of former slaves who had to listen to sermons through a window and who undoubtedly traveled to Los Angeles in the segregated section of the train. Yet under Seymour's guidance, a movement arose whose impact on Christianity, less than a century after his arrival in Los Angeles, has been compared to the Protestant Reformation.[14]

This development should not surprise us. The Pentecostal vision of the church united and empowered in love by the Spirit of God was precisely that of the apostle Paul, who wrote that "hope does not disappoint,

---

[11] Steven J. Land, *Pentecostal Spirituality: A Passion for the Kingdom* (Journal of Pentecostal Theology Supplement Series 1; Sheffield: Sheffield Academic Press, [1995] 1997).

[12] Perhaps D. William Faupel has given the most thorough explication of this leitmotif of Pentecostal experience and theology: *The Everlasting Gospel: The Significance of Eschatology in the Development of Pentecostal Thought* (Journal of Pentecostal Theology Supplement Series 10; Sheffield: Sheffield Academic Press, 1996).

[13] Harvey Cox, *Fire from Heaven* (New York: Addison-Wesley, 1995), ch. 6 ("The Future Present: The Recovery of Primal Hope," 111–22).

[14] Ibid., 119.

because the love of God has been poured out within our hearts through the Holy Spirit who was given to us" (Rom. 5:5 NASB).

In addition, the Pentecostal "signs and wonders" that witness to the presence of the kingdom in our midst also recall the prophetic prediction of a last-day outpouring of the Holy Spirit "on all flesh," as Joel would express it (Joel 2:28). Revival outpourings have always engendered intense eschatological expectations, and it is these expectations that are in large measure our area of concern when studying Christian hope. But what precisely is meant by "eschatological expectations"?

> *The Pentecostal vision of the church united and empowered in love by the Spirit of God was precisely that of the apostle Paul.*

Eschatology

The word *eschatology* refers to the study (*logia*) of the last things (*eschata*). As such it is a useful shorthand in theological discussion. At the same time, it is a misleading term because Christian eschatology, from the biblical perspective, is all-encompassing. In actuality, the biblical term "hope" is our best choice of terms, since the rather sterile "eschatology" can be taken to mean the study of last things *alone*. Jürgen Moltmann writes:

> From first to last, and not merely in the epilogue, Christianity is eschatology, is hope, forward looking and forward moving, and therefore also revolutionizing and transforming the present. The eschatological is not one element *of* Christianity, but it is the medium of Christian faith as such, the key in which everything in it is set, the glow that suffuses everything here in the dawn of an expected day. For Christian faith lives from the raising of the crucified Christ, and strains after the promises of the universal future of Christ. Eschatology is the passionate suffering and passionate longing kindled by the Messiah. Hence eschatology cannot really be only a part of Christian doctrine. Rather, the eschatological outlook is characteristic of all Christian proclamation, of every Christian existence and of the whole Church.[15]

A careful study of both Old Testament and New Testament theology reveals that Moltmann is correct. The church owes a great deal to the "hope theologians" for fully restoring to us this biblical perspective.

---

[15] Jürgen Moltmann, *Theology of Hope: On the Ground and the Implications of a Christian Eschatology*, trans. James W. Leitch (London: SCM, 1967), 16.

Eschatology, understood biblically, should be seen as referring both to "first things" and "last things."[16] For example, in New Testament times apocalyptists saw the presence of God and his kingdom as an entirely future reality. The present was viewed as totally dominated by evil. Gnostics, by contrast, lost sight of the future, understanding salvation as a completed reality—the kingdom had been consummated. Authentic Christianity, however, maintained the "already/not yet" tension so easily noted in the biblical perspective.

The kingdom is both present and future. Therefore, our hope, based on the knowledge of past saving events as recorded in Scripture, is both present and future.

We are the ones "on whom ends of the ages have come" (1 Cor. 10:11). Jesus Christ has inaugurated the new age, and the church is a part of that end-time reality *now.* "So if anyone is in Christ, there is a new creation: everything old has passed away; see, everything has become new!" (2 Cor. 5:17). The kingdom is both present and future. Therefore, our hope, based on the knowledge of past saving events as recorded in Scripture, is both present and future. Commenting on Paul's words in 1 Corinthians 10:11, Gordon Fee remarks that "there is little question about Paul's point":

> Through his death and resurrection Jesus Christ marks the turning of the ages; the old is on its way out, the new has begun (2 Cor. 5:17). He has set the future irresistibly in motion; and the new people of God, whether Jew or Gentile, bond or free, male or female, who are his by grace alone, are the people of the End, "upon whom the ends of the ages have come" and "toward whom all history has had its goal."[17]

This mind-boggling biblical perspective—too seldom grasped by the average believer—points to the specifically *historical* nature of hope.

Hope and History

A sense of history has always been central to the Judeo-Christian tradition. Jews and Christians believe that God has revealed himself redemptively *in history.* History is not a meaningless cycle of finite events doomed to repeat themselves. Rather, it is *linear.* There was a definite

---

[16] Leon Morris, *New Testament Theology* (Grand Rapids: Zondervan, 1986), 86.

[17] Gordon D. Fee, *The First Epistle to the Corinthians* (NICNT; Grand Rapids: Eerdmans, 1987), 459.

beginning, and there will be a definite end. In between these terminal points lie a series of meaningful events ordered by God for the ultimate good of humankind.

In Deuteronomy, "The Gospel According to Moses," we find a typical confession of the faith of Israel—related as a story, as redemptive history, and as a shared experience of the community of faith:

> A wandering Aramean was my ancestor; he went down into Egypt and lived there as an alien, few in number, and there he became a great nation, mighty and populous. When the Egyptians treated us harshly and afflicted us, by imposing hard labor on us, we cried to the LORD, the God of our ancestors; the LORD heard our voice and saw our affliction, our toil, and our oppression. The LORD brought us out of Egypt with a mighty hand and an outstretched arm, with a terrifying display of power, and with signs and wonders; and he brought us into this place and gave us this land, a land flowing with milk and honey. (Deut. 26:5–9)

The key events of Israel's redemptive history are recited in such liturgies. They formed the central thrust of the total sweep of the Old Testament Scriptures, moving from creation to the fall of humankind to the call of the patriarchs, the Exodus, Sinai, the conquest of Canaan, and the Davidic monarchy—all space/time events of eternal significance.

Furthermore, Israel's faith was always a *forward-looking* reality. God's people looked for a coming Redeemer, the culmination of God's kingly rule *on earth*, a new covenant, a restoration of Israel as God's covenant people, an end-time outpouring of God's Spirit on all flesh, a final judgment (the Day of the Lord), and ultimately a new heaven and new earth.[18] From the Christian perspective, Jesus was the fulfillment of most of these expectations, and his second coming will be the culmination of these hopes in their entirety.

With the arrival of Jesus Christ we have the ultimate eschatological event. He himself announced it: "The time is fulfilled, and the kingdom of God is at hand; repent, and believe in the gospel" (Mark 1:15 RSV). This hope of the gospel pervades the New Testament. "The Gospel According to Paul" (Romans) exemplifies well this dynamic, as we have already seen:

- "[The gospel is] the power of God for salvation to everyone who believes." (Rom. 1:16 NASB)

---

[18] See Anthony A. Hoekema's excellent summary of these salient themes in his treatment of biblical eschatology: *The Bible and the Future* (Grand Rapids: Eerdmans, 1979), 3–12.

- "[We] rejoice in the hope of the glory of God." (5:2 NKJV)
- "[This] hope does not disappoint, because the love of God has been poured out within our hearts through the Holy Spirit who was given to us." (5:5 NASB)
- "Rejoice in hope." (12:12)
- "For salvation is nearer to us now than when we first believed." (13:11 RSV)
- "For whatever was written in former days was written for our instruction, so that by steadfastness and by the encouragement of the scriptures we might have hope." (15:4)
- "May the God of hope fill you with all joy and peace in believing, so that you may abound in hope by the power of the Holy Spirit." (15:13)

Wolfhart Pannenberg, another theologian of hope, summarizes this Christian eschatological perspective:

> The power that fills the gospel is thus connected with the presence of the future of God in the coming of Jesus, and also with the imparting of this presence of eschatological salvation by the Spirit, who through the gospel leads to knowledge of the Son in the human history of Jesus.[19]

Christ Jesus is "our hope" (1 Tim. 1:1). In our faith we are "sure of what we hope for and certain of what we do not see" (Heb. 11:1 NIV). We are "strongly encouraged to seize the hope set before us"; it is a "sure and steadfast anchor of the soul" (6:18–19). We "set all [our] hope on the grace that Jesus Christ will bring [us] when he is revealed" (1 Peter 1:13). Our hope in Christ enables us to persevere, to endure (1 Thess. 1:3). To have this hope is to purify ourselves, just as he himself is pure (1 John 3:3).

Christ Jesus is "our hope" (1 Tim. 1:1).

This historical hope marked indelibly the faith of our Puritan fathers. Theirs was a faith strongly rooted in the hope of heaven. At the same time, their hope inspired in them an optimistic vision of the transformation and evangelization of the world. Iain Murray summarizes well their theological perspective:

> There was an attitude to history and to the world which distinguished them as men of hope. In their own day, this hope came to expression in

[19] Wolfhart Pannenberg, *Systematic Theology*, trans. Geoffrey W. Bromiley (Grand Rapids: Eerdmans, 1994), 2:459.

> pulpits and in books, in Parliaments and upon battlefields, but it did not end there. The outlook they had done so much to inspire went on for nearly two hundred years after their own age and its results were manifold. It coloured the spiritual thought of the American colonies; it taught men to expect great outpourings of the Holy Spirit; it prepared the way to the new age of world-missions; and it contributed largely to that sense of destiny which came to characterize the English-speaking Protestant nations.[20]

This stimulating vision of evangelizing the world reflects the end-time ethos of the New Testament church.

Hope and Mission

One day during the last week of Jesus' earthly ministry, his disciples came to him as he left the temple and called attention to the beautiful buildings. He promptly replied, "Truly I tell you, not one stone will be left here upon another; all will be thrown down" (Matt. 24:2). Later, as they sat opposite the temple on the Mount of Olives, the disciples asked him, "Tell us, when will this be, and what will be the sign of your coming and of the end of the age?" (24:3). Jesus' answer that day has come to be known as the Olivet Discourse (Matt. 24; Mark 13; Luke 21).

Jesus spoke about the fall of Jerusalem (which took place in A.D. 70) as well as about events leading up to his second coming. Then he said, "And this gospel of the kingdom will be preached throughout the whole world, as a testimony to all nations; and then the end will come" (Matt. 24:14 RSV). This passage parallels the words of Jesus known as the Great Commission, which also speak of an evangelization of the world leading up to the end of the age (28:18–20). George Eldon Ladd suggested that Matthew 24:14 is perhaps "the most important single verse in the Word of God for God's people today."[21]

What a motive and meaning for living! "The ultimate meaning of history between the Ascension of our Lord and His return in glory is found in the extension and working of the Gospel in the world."[22] We

---

[20] Iain H. Murray, *The Puritan Hope: A Study in Revival and the Interpretation of Prophecy* (Carlisle, Penn.: Banner of Truth Trust, 1971), xxi–xxii. I was first made aware of this important work, and read this particular quotation from it, in the excellent treatment of hope by David Aikman: *Hope: The Heart's Great Quest* (Ann Arbor: Servant, 1995). Aikman's chapter on the Puritans is truly edifying ("The Puritans: Hope and History," 151–66).

[21] George Eldon Ladd, *The Gospel of the Kingdom* (Grand Rapids: Eerdmans, 1959), 123.

[22] Ibid., 133. Ladd's moving sermon, "When Will the Kingdom Come?" (123–40), needs to be heard again in our own day!

may speculate at length about precisely how and when many of the things Jesus mentions in the Olivet Discourse are fulfilled. But, as Ladd asserted, there is "no verse which speaks as concisely and distinctly as this verse about the time when the Kingdom will come."[23] Moreover, this eschatological teaching gives us *something to do,* not merely something to speculate about, as we eagerly await our Lord's return!

One world Christian leader captivated by this vision is Pat Robertson. Inscribed on a bronze plaque over the main door to the CBN (Christian Broadcasting Network) Headquarters are Jesus' words found in Matthew 24:14. Anyone even vaguely familiar with the astounding worldwide outreach of this powerful ministry cannot but acknowledge what an incredible impact such a hope-based mission can have. If only the church universal could be caught up in this vision. But then, is this not precisely what our Lord Jesus predicted would happen? No matter how dark the days may become, Christians should be the most optimistic people on earth! This "radiant optimism which began with the coming of Christ and which fills the pages of the New Testament"[24] includes a joyful assurance of personal salvation as well.

No matter how dark the days may become, Christians should be the most optimistic people on earth!

Hope and Assurance

As we have already seen, the New Testament is filled with assurances to believers of their security in God's love. We are meant to have a firm conviction that *God* is the One who is saving us and that our sure hope of salvation—past, present, and future—is in him. "I am confident of this," Paul wrote the Philippians, "that the one who began a good work among you will bring it to completion by the day of Jesus Christ" (Phil. 1:6). The apostle was "confident." He knew that God would *complete* his "good work." Notice that this promise is couched in *corporate* terms, referring to the church comprised of all true believers. Finally, observe the reference to "the day of Jesus Christ." Paul was depicting an *eschatological* assurance of salvation, rooted in the hope of the return of Jesus Christ to consummate the kingdom he inaugurated in his first coming.

[23] Ibid., 124.

[24] A. M. Hunter, "Foreword" to William G. Morrice, *Joy in the New Testament* (Greenwood, S.C.: Attic, 1984), 7.

Romans 5–8 vibrate with this assurance and hope. Through Jesus Christ we stand secure in the grace of God, and we boast, we jubilate, we "rejoice in the hope of the glory of God" (Rom. 5:2 NIV). "Hope does not disappoint us" (5:5). Christ's death for us "while we were still weak," "while we still were sinners," and "while we were enemies" enables us to say "much more surely" that we will be saved "from the wrath of God," "saved through his [Christ's] life" (5:6–11). "For in hope we were saved" (8:24). We are *predestined* (8:28–30)! "If God is for us, who can be against us?" (v. 31 NIV). *Nothing* can "separate us from the love of God that is in Christ Jesus our Lord" (v. 39)! Let us be quick to note that this sure hope, as a personal experience, is totally the work of the Holy Spirit.

Our "hope does not disappoint, because the love of God has been poured out within our hearts through the Holy Spirit who was given to us" (Rom. 5:5 NASB). "For through the Spirit, by faith, we wait for the hope of righteousness" (Gal. 5:5 RSV). We were once hopelessly lost. "But when the goodness and loving kindness of God our Savior appeared, he saved us" (Titus 3:4–5 NRSV). How? "By the washing of regeneration and renewal in the Holy Spirit" (3:5 RSV). "This Spirit he poured out on us richly through Jesus Christ our Savior, so that, having been justified by his grace, we might become heirs according to the hope of eternal life" (3:6–7).

Jesus himself gives strong witness to the sure hope of eternal life that we have in him. In John's Gospel we read his words: "My sheep hear my voice. I know them, and they follow me. I give them eternal life, and they will never perish. No one will snatch them out of my hand" (John 10:27–28). He further adds: "My Father, who has given them to Me, is greater than all; and no one is able to snatch them out of the Father's hand. I and the Father are one" (10:29–30 NASB).

The letter to the Hebrews, long a battlefield of debate between Calvinists and Arminians concerning its warnings against apostasy, was actually intended as a "message of encouragement" (Heb. 13:22 NAB). Its message is forward-looking, hope-filled. Early on, we are exhorted to "hold firm the confidence and the pride that belong to hope" (Heb. 3:6). And we can only have pride, or jubilant boasting (*kauchema*), in that of which we are supremely certain!

The stinging warning of Hebrews 6:1–8 is balanced with these encouraging words: "Even though we speak in this way, beloved, we are confident of better things in your case, things that belong to salvation" (Heb. 6:9). Then follows the exhortation, "to realize the full assurance of hope to the very end" (6:11). It is "through faith and patience," we are told, that we "inherit the promises" (6:12). God's covenant promises are based on his character and his word "so that through two unchangeable things . . . we who have taken refuge might be strongly encouraged to seize the hope set before us" (6:18). Donald Guthrie writes:

> This is the sheer anchor of the Christian's conviction. He knows his assurance depends not on the stability or strength of his own faith, but on the absolute trustworthiness of God's word.[25]

Our hope is "a sure and steadfast anchor of the soul, a hope that enters the inner shrine behind the curtain" (6:19). Hope gives us a *stability* and *intimacy*.

This metaphor of the "anchor of hope" is unique to the writer to the Hebrews. It subsequently became a widely used symbol among future generations of believers: Amid the storms of life and of civilizations, hope holds us safe and steady. Further, our confidence and assurance is based on the work of our high priest Jesus himself, who is the "forerunner on our behalf" (Heb. 6:20). In the ultimate sense, *Jesus* is our hope—our living Lord who died and rose for us and who now intercedes for us. Ours is "the new and living way" (10:19). We can have "full assurance of faith" (10:22) as we "hold fast the confession of our hope without wavering, for he who promised is faithful" (10:23). We are "not among those who shrink back and so are lost, but among those who have faith and so are saved" (10:39). This saving faith is "the assurance of things hoped for, the conviction of things not seen" (11:1). Thus, the writer of Hebrews evinces the same hopeful confidence and assurance that we saw in Paul's letters.

Amid the storms of life and of civilizations, hope holds us safe and steady.

We look to Jesus, "the pioneer and perfecter of our faith, who for the sake of the joy that was set before him endured the cross, disregarding its shame, and has taken his seat at the right hand of the throne of God" (Heb. 12:2). Hope and joy, according to the New Testament witness, are inseparably joined.

---

[25] Donald Guthrie, *The Letter to the Hebrews,* Tyndale New Testament Commentaries (Grand Rapids: Eerdmans, 1983), 152.

Hope and Joy

On that dark night before his crucifixion, Jesus prepared his disciples for the trauma to come with the hope-filled promise of his resurrection.

> Very truly, I tell you, you will weep and mourn, but the world will rejoice; you will have pain, but your pain will turn to joy. When a woman is in labor, she has pain, because her hour has come. But when her child is born, she no longer remembers the anguish because of the joy of having brought a human being into the world. So you have pain now; but I will see you again, and your hearts will rejoice, and no one will take your joy from you. On that day you will ask nothing of me. Very truly, I tell you, if you ask anything of the Father in my name, he will give it to you. Until now you have not asked for anything in my name. Ask and you will receive, so that your joy may be complete. (John 16:20–24)

Jesus Christ came to give hope and life to humankind. He came to give us joy in place of our sorrows. He came that we "may have life, and have it abundantly" (10:10).

God has "given us a new birth into a living hope through the resurrection of Jesus Christ from the dead" (1 Peter 1:3), and in this we "rejoice" (1:6). Even though we have not seen him, we love him and "believe in him and rejoice with an indescribable and glorious joy" (1:8). We "set all [our] hope on the grace that Jesus Christ will bring [us] when he is revealed" (1:13).

"Rejoice in hope," Paul wrote the Roman Christians (Rom. 12:12). "For the kingdom of God is not food and drink but righteousness and peace and joy in the Holy Spirit" (14:17). One of the apostle's benedictions toward the end of his letter says it best: "May the God of hope fill you with all joy and peace in believing, so that you may abound in hope by the power of the Holy Spirit" (15:13).

In the revival fires of recent years, the Lord seems to be *restoring* this joy to his people, "for the joy of the Lord is your strength" (Neh. 8:10). This should not surprise us for, as Martyn Lloyd-Jones reminds us, this recovery of joy-filled hope is the church's greatest need.

> The world is not going to pay much attention to all the organized efforts of the Christian church. The one thing she will pay attention to is a body of people filled with a spirit of rejoicing. . . . When the Holy Spirit is operating, this is the inevitable result—a joy which is unspeakable and full of glory.[26]

---

[26] Martyn Lloyd-Jones, *Joy Unspeakable: Power and Renewal in the Holy Spirit* (Wheaton, Ill.: Harold Shaw, 1984), back cover; see 102, 108.

Is this not precisely what has drawn the world's attention to the "Toronto Blessing" and other recent outpourings? It is the God of hope filling us with all joy and peace in believing, so that through the power of the Holy Spirit we might abound in hope (Rom. 15:13)!

The world is hopeless. It tries to substitute a giddy quest for pleasure for genuine joy, but such joy inevitably ends in despair. Yet even some Christians seem to have lost their joy and forgotten their hope. There is, of course, duty and discipline in the Christian walk. But we must never forget that there is also joy and jubilation! Even the medical field has acknowledged the truth found in God's Word: "A joyful heart is good medicine" (Prov. 17:22 NASB). In the final analysis, authentic joy must be rooted in the transcendent hope of the resurrection. "If for this life only we have hoped in Christ, we are of all people most to be pitied," Paul told the Corinthians (1 Cor. 15:19). In other words, the good news of the gospel is that we can look square in the face that old nemesis death—which apart from the risen Christ smashes all joy and hope—and challenge it: "Where, O death, is your victory? Where, O death, is your sting?" (15:55).

Authentic joy must be rooted in the transcendent hope of the resurrection.

Death and Life After

If the Christian faith has no answers for death, then it has no answers at all. But the Scriptures face death squarely. It is appointed for us "to die once, and after that the judgment" (Heb. 9:27). George Bernard Shaw observed that "the statistics on death are quite impressive. One out of one people die." And C. S. Lewis remarked during World War II that war does not increase death; it is *total* in every generation.[27] Billy Graham often reminds the vast crowds in his crusades that in fifty years almost everyone in the stadium will be dead.

The thrust of existentialism is to influence people to face honestly their mortality. We are not ready to live until we are ready to die. Jesus Christ is our greatest example. "The cross is the lectern from which the world's greatest teacher gave us lessons in how to take the final and most

[27] Shaw and Lewis are cited in Billy Graham, *Facing Death and the Life After* (Dallas: Word, 1987), 17.

difficult step of our physical lives," Calvin Miller reminds us.[28] Psalm 90 puts God's eternity and our mortality side-by-side and offers the prayer, "So teach us to number our days that we may get a heart of wisdom" (Ps. 90:12 RSV).

Job asked the ultimate question: "If a man die, shall he live again?" (Job 14:14 RSV). Even in the face of excruciating and unjust suffering, Job made this great confession of faith:

> I know that my Redeemer lives,
> and that in the end he will stand upon the earth.
> And after my skin has been destroyed,
> yet in my flesh I will see God;
> I myself will see him
> with my own eyes—I, and not another.
> How my heart yearns within me! (Job 19:25–27 NIV)

Paul spells out this hope in detail in his letters. He was a realist, poignantly aware that there is a "law of sin and of death" constantly pulling us down like gravity (Rom. 8:2). But he could also exult: "I consider that the sufferings of this present time are not worth comparing with the glory about to be revealed to us" (8:18). Even the entire universe itself has been "subjected to futility," he acknowledges (8:19–20), but God has done this "in hope" (8:20). Creation's groaning and our groaning will cease at the "redemption of our bodies," the culmination of our freedom and glory (8:18–25). Meanwhile, it must be said of us that "though the body is dead because of sin, the Spirit is life because of righteousness" (8:10). Then he adds this mind-boggling conclusion: "If the Spirit of him who raised Jesus from the dead dwells in you, he who raised Christ from the dead will give life to your mortal bodies also through his Spirit that dwells in you" (8:11).

Paul uses an Adam/Christ typology to interpret both our present state as a race and our future hope as a new humanity. Throughout his explanation, both explicitly and implicitly, there is the strong connection between sin and death. The Lord warned Adam not to eat of the tree of the knowledge of good and evil, "for in the day that you eat of it you shall die" (Gen. 2:17). Both the man and the woman ate of the forbidden fruit—and they died. *Spiritual death* ensued immediately in an estrangement from the Lord God and even between themselves (3:1–10). *Physical death* came many years later (see 5:5). *Eternal death* would also have

[28] Calvin Miller, *Once upon a Tree* (Grand Rapids: Baker, 1991), 123–24.

resulted had not the Lord God graciously blocked access to the tree of life (3:22–24). As we have already studied, this sin and death were handed on to subsequent generations of humankind: "Therefore, just as sin came into the world through one man, and death came through sin, and so death spread to all because all have sinned" (Rom. 5:12).

For the apostle, the gospel gives one and only one answer to the reality of our death in sin: the resurrection. "For since death came through a human being, the resurrection of the dead has also come through a human being; for as all die in Adam, so all will be made alive in Christ" (1 Cor. 15:21–22). But because it is literally a death *in sin* (through "trespasses and sins" [Eph. 2:1])—a spiritual death as well as a physical one, resulting, apart from Christ, in an eternal death—we must say that it is both the death and resurrection of Christ that are the answer to this fatal state.

Through the death and resurrection of Jesus Christ, God did away with the old humanity and began a new humanity. "One has died for all; therefore all have died" (2 Cor. 5:14). Christ made atonement in part "that he might create in himself one new humanity" (Eph. 2:15). Jesus was both "the last Adam" and "the second man" (1 Cor. 15:45, 47). Because of his atoning death on our behalf and because of his indwelling presence as a "life-giving Spirit" (15:45 NLT), we have *victory* over sin and death. "The sting of death is sin, and the power of sin is the law. But thanks be to God, who gives us the victory through our Lord Jesus Christ" (15:56–57). In the meantime, however, millions are dying in their sins apart from Christ, and even those of us in Christ die physically. What happens to us when we die before the resurrection?

The answer to this question lies in one's personal response to the gospel. In what has come to be known as the Resurrection Chapter (1 Cor. 15), Paul sums up the gospel as follows: "that Christ died for our sins in accordance with the scriptures, and that he was buried, and that he was raised on the third day in accordance with the scriptures, and that he appeared to . . ." (15:3–5). He then proceeds to emphasize the necessity of the resurrection of Christ without which our faith is in vain and we are still in our sins (15:17). It is important to note the *order* of his presentation. First, Paul emphasizes that "Christ died for our sins" (15:3). Then he proceeds with a detailed depiction and defense of the resurrection, both Christ's and ours. The culmination of events is the final defeat of death itself. "The last enemy to be destroyed is death" (15:26). W. T. Connor states succinctly the achievement of Christ: "In conquering sin he conquered death, for sin and death are inseparable."[29] Thus, Paul ended this central New Testament chapter with words of triumph, referring to Christ's victory over sin and death, and then exhorted the saints to faithful service (15:58).

If we die like dogs and go back into nothingness, then Jean-Paul Sartre was right when he asserted that death "removes all meaning to life."[30] But life is rife with meaning, for history is "his story," and our eternal destiny is determined by how we relate to him in his death and resurrection. Paul exemplifies what the Christian view of death should be in Philippians 1. His basic desire is that "Christ will be exalted now as always in my body, whether by life or by death" (Phil. 1:20). "For to me to live is Christ, and to die is gain," he continues (1:21 RSV). Paul is torn between the need to remain here in "fruitful labor" and the desire "to depart and be with Christ, for that is far better" (1:22–23).

Later in this letter Paul reveals the heartbeat of his life and ministry: "I want to know Christ and the power of his resurrection and the sharing of his sufferings by becoming like him in his death, if somehow I may attain the resurrection from the dead" (3:10–11). Finally, Paul affirms that "our citizenship is in heaven, and it is from there that we are expecting a Savior, the Lord Jesus Christ" (3:20). He "will change our lowly body to be like his glorious body, by the power which enables him even to subject all things to himself" (3:21 RSV). Unfortunately, few Christians *live* these words. The world too often sees how materialistic and this-worldly our hopes and dreams are. Perhaps we are better at applying the comfort of our hope when we inevitably confront the reality of death itself.

Absent from the Body, Present with the Lord[31]

Perhaps the vast majority of humankind has always believed in an afterlife of some kind. Although much mystery remains, the Christian conception of life beyond death is much more concrete and rooted in the larger historical account of

> *The Christian conception of life beyond death is rooted in revelation and redemption.*

[29] Walter T. Connor, *The Gospel of Redemption* (Nashville: Broadman, 1945), 305.

[30] Jean-Paul Sartre, *Being and Nothingness*, trans. Hazel E. Barnes (New York: Philosophical Library, 1956), 539; cited in Dale Moody, *The Word of Truth* (Grand Rapids: Eerdmans, 1981), 491.

[31] See 2 Cor. 5:8 (KJV, NKJV).

revelation and redemption. In simplest terms, most Christians comfort themselves concerning loved ones who have gone on before them with the basic tenet, "to be absent from the body is to be present with the Lord."

The Hebrew Scriptures speak of *Sheol* as the state of death or the realm of the dead. At the very least, there is an ambiguity concerning this state; generally speaking, it is not a desirable state. Death was stark and simple: All people die, and their "shades" (*repa'im*) go to Sheol. It is a place of silence, darkness, weakness—an escapable underworld "imprisonment."

> Who can live and never see death?
>   Who can escape the power of Sheol? (Ps. 89:48)
>
> Do the shades rise up to praise you? (Ps. 88:10)
>
> Are not the days of my life few?
>   Let me alone, that I may find a little comfort
> before I go, never to return,
>   to the land of gloom and deep darkness,
> the land of gloom and chaos,
>   where light is like darkness. (Job 10:20–22)
>
> The dead do not praise the LORD,
>   nor do any that go down into silence. (Ps. 115:17)

Predictably, Job is the most graphic:

> My days are past, my plans are broken off,
>   the desires of my heart.
> They make night into day;
>   "The light," they say, "is near to the darkness."
> If I look for Sheol as my house,
>   if I spread my couch in darkness,
> if I say to the Pit, "You are my father,"
>   and to the worm, "My mother," or "My sister,"
> where then is my hope?
>   Who will see my hope?
> Will it go down to the bars of Sheol?
>   Shall we descend together into the dust? (Job 17:11–16)

Thus, redemption is seen in part as a *liberation* from such an undesirable place.

Believers have a different ultimate destiny from the wicked. The foolhardy "are appointed for Sheol . . . straight to the grave they descend, and their form shall waste away; Sheol shall be their home. But God will ransom my soul from the power of Sheol, for he will receive me" (Ps. 49:14–15). David confessed a resurrection hope:

> Therefore my heart is glad, and my soul rejoices;
> my body also rests secure.
> For you do not give me up to Sheol,
> or let your faithful one see the Pit.
> You show me the path of life.
> In your presence there is fullness of joy;
> in your right hand are pleasures forevermore. (Ps. 16:9–11)

"Great is your steadfast love toward me," David exulted; "you have delivered my soul from the depths of Sheol" (Ps. 86:13). And Solomon's wisdom pointed out the way of salvation: "For the wise the path of life leads upward, in order to avoid Sheol below" (Prov. 15:24).

Perhaps the two best words to portray death for the Christian are *destruction* (*katalysis*) and *departure* (*analysis*).[32] (1) The tragedy of death is not smoothed over in either testament. Death is indeed *destruction.* "Sheol is naked before God, and Abaddon [meaning 'destruction'] has no covering" (Job 26:6). This destiny of humankind is inexorable, voracious: "Sheol and Abaddon are never satisfied" (Prov. 27:20; cf. Hab. 2:5). Our bodily existence is fragile, fleeting, perilous, and temporary.

> *The two best words to portray death for the Christian are* destruction *and* departure.

Paul describes life as living in a tent. In the process of defending his ministry before the Corinthians, Paul described the Christian life and hope as it really is. His words deserve quoting at length:

> For we know that if the earthly tent we live in is destroyed, we have a building from God, a house not made with hands, eternal in the heavens. For in this tent we groan, longing to be clothed with our heavenly dwelling—if indeed, when we have taken it off we will not be found naked. For while we are still in this tent, we groan under our burden, because we wish not to be unclothed but to be further clothed, so that

---

[32] I owe these categories to Dale Moody: "The Double Face of Death," *Review and Expositor* 58 (July 1961): 348–66; *The Hope of Glory* (Grand Rapids: Eerdmans, 1964), 55–77; *The Word of Truth,* 491–502.

> what is mortal may be swallowed up by life. He who has prepared us for this very thing is God, who has given us the Spirit as a guarantee.
>
> So we are always confident; even though we know that while we are at home in the body we are away from the Lord—for we walk by faith, not by sight. Yes, we do have confidence, and we would rather be away from the body and at home with the Lord. So whether we are at home or away, we make it our aim to please him. For all of us must appear before the judgment seat of Christ, so that each may receive recompense for what has been done in the body, whether good or evil. (2 Cor. 5:1–10)

Our mortal body, that temporary "earthly tent," will one day be "destroyed." We "groan under our burden" and long "to be clothed with our heavenly dwelling," "a house not made with hands, eternal in the heavens." The indwelling Spirit is our guarantee that our mortality will one day "be swallowed up by life." We are confident of our destiny, but fully realize that "we walk by faith, not by sight." We sense the eschatological tension of being both at home and yet at the same time on a pilgrimage far from home. To be at home (*endemeo*) in the body is to be away from (*ekdemeo*) the Lord. "We would rather be away from the body and at home with the Lord." In any event, we want to please our Lord, knowing that one day we will be judged by him for how we have lived out our bodily lives. Thus, "the fear of the Lord" (2 Cor. 5:11) and "the love of Christ" (5:14) become the motivating forces of our lives. We no longer live for ourselves, "but for him who died and was raised for [us]" (5:15). We have been entrusted with a message and ministry of reconciliation (5:16–21).

(2) Death for the Christian is, more importantly, a *departure.* In his last will and testament to Timothy, Paul concluded by saying: "The time of my departure has come" (2 Tim. 4:6). Previously, he had written the Philippians, "My desire is to depart and be with Christ, for that is far better" (Phil. 1:23). To die, for a Christian, is to depart on another great adventure! Again, to be absent from the body is to be present with the Lord. The Son of God became incarnate "so that through death he might destroy the one who has the power of death, that is, the devil, and free those who all their lives were held in slavery by the fear of death" (Heb. 2:14–15). He tasted death for everyone (2:9). For the believer, death has no victory, no sting (1 Cor. 15:55). It is a transition to another dimension—from time to eternity. It is like falling asleep and waking up in another world.

"She Is Not Dead But Sleeping"[33]

They were all "weeping and wailing" at Jairus's house for his daughter who died. But Jesus said, "Do not weep; for she is not dead but sleeping" (Luke 8:52). Knowing that she was dead, they laughed at him. But Jesus simply said, "Child, get up!" And her "spirit returned, and she got up at once" (8:53–55). Some time later, Jesus and his disciples were on their way to Lazarus's home, and Jesus said, "Our friend Lazarus has fallen asleep, but I am going there to awaken him" (John 11:11). The disciples remarked that if he had only fallen asleep he would be all right (11:12). "Then Jesus told them plainly, 'Lazarus is dead'" (11:14).

A common euphemism for death in Bible times was that of sleeping, and both Jesus and the early church seized the metaphor in order to communicate the nature of death in the light of the resurrection. According to the New Testament, believers never die—they only fall asleep! Jesus' words to Martha should be inscribed on every church door in the world: "I am the resurrection and the life. Those who believe in me, even though they die, will live, and everyone who lives and believes in me will never die. Do you believe this?" (John 11:25–26). Paul explained to the Thessalonians that they should not grieve for those who had "fallen asleep," as those grieve "who have no hope" (1 Thess. 4:13 RSV). He then went on to describe the glorious second coming of our Lord Jesus Christ (4:16–18).

Leon Morris has summarized well the revolutionary ethos set loose upon the world through the followers of Christ:

> This is an important distinctive of New Testament Christianity. For the ancient world, death was a horror, the end of everything. People might have the thought of the existence of the "shades" in Hades [the Greek translation of *Sheol*], but this was no full-blooded form of life, but a dreary and shadowy affair, the end of all living worth the name. The inscriptions on the tombs of antiquity may be impressive in their use of costly materials, but, rich as they are, they are full of hopelessness. By contrast, the roughly scratched inscriptions in the catacombs where Christians were buried abound in hope, the sure and certain hope of resurrection in Christ. The New Testament does not speak of the followers of Jesus as dying; they simply fall asleep. In contrast, Jesus' death is not called sleep. He underwent the full horror that is death and in doing so transformed death, so that for his followers it is no more than sleep.[34]

---

[33] Luke 8:52.

[34] Leon Morris, *Reflections on the Gospel of John:* Volume 3: *The True Vine: John 11–16* (Grand Rapids: Baker, 1988), 407.

Not only did the early believers exult in the future bodily resurrection. They also took comfort in the intermediate state of the departed awaiting the resurrection. Jesus called it Paradise.

Paradise!

Whenever we experience an event or place of delight or bliss, we often say, "This is paradise!" My family and I often journey on vacation to Orlando, Florida, to Walt Disney World. In so many ways this delightful resort conglomerate is an earthly paradise. My favorite theme park there is Epcot, where one not only encounters the typical Disney garden delights, but also learns much about the past, present, and potential future of humankind and the diversity and dignity of the cultures of the world. My wife's and my favorite place to relax and recharge is Typhoon Lagoon, a water park set in the theme of a tropical paradise of lush flowers and greenery. I have often joked with my family about how I would like to be the chaplain of Disney World.

But as delightful as Walt Disney World is, it is a slum in comparison with what God originally designed for the first couple—as well as what he has in store for his people at the end of the age! Furthermore, according to Scripture, when we die in Christ, we also enter into a paradisial state in the presence of the Lord.

Jesus made reference to this state as he hung on the cross. One of the two criminals who were crucified with Jesus derided him, but the other criminal defended Jesus to the first and said to the Savior, "Jesus, remember me when you come into your kingdom." Jesus replied, "Truly I tell you, today you will be with me in Paradise" (Luke 23:39–43). Later, the apostle Paul would be "caught up to the third heaven" and be given a glimpse of this same "Paradise," where he also "heard things that are not to be told, that no mortal is permitted to repeat" (2 Cor. 12:1–4).

> *In the messianic age the redeemed will live in a park of delight, the likes of which we have never seen.*

And Jesus' message to the church in Ephesus, given through the apostle John, was, "To him who overcomes, I will grant to eat of the tree of life, which is in the Paradise of God" (Rev. 2:7 NASB). Here Jesus was referring to that final state of blessedness in the new Jerusalem, in which God comes to dwell with us in "a new heaven and a new earth" (Rev. 21–22). But behind all these statements lies the primordial paradise of God's communion with humankind, to which the Old Testament Scriptures often referred.

The Puritan poet John Milton (1608–1674) wrote what most consider to be the last great epic of English literature, the masterpiece *Paradise Lost* (1667), which recounts the sinister seductions of Satan and the tragic fall of Adam and Eve. In *Paradise Regained* (1671) Milton relates how Christ reverses the curse of humankind through maintaining the integrity that the first couple surrendered. This blind Puritan prophet captured the very essence of the drama of biblical revelation. The Bible starts in Paradise and ends in Paradise.

The Lord God "planted a garden in Eden" and placed the man there (Gen. 2:8). He "put him in the garden of Eden to till it and keep it" (2:15). The name "Eden" means "delight," and the Septuagint, the Greek translation of the Old Testament, translated "the garden of Eden" as "the garden [or paradise, *paradeisos*] of delight." In Eden was a garden, or park, the beauty and perfection of which no one has seen since. It became a rich symbol in prophetic revelation (Ezek. 28:13; 31:9, 16, 18; Joel 2:3). Isaiah's message of hope to Judah and Jerusalem was that one day God the Creator would deliver his people and reign on the earth.

> For the LORD will comfort Zion;
> he will comfort all her waste places,
> and will make her wilderness like Eden,
> her desert like the garden of the LORD;
> joy and gladness will be found in her,
> thanksgiving and the voice of song. (Isa. 51:3)

In other words, in the messianic age the redeemed will live in a park of delight, the likes of which we have never seen. It will truly be a paradise because true paradise ultimately entails God and humankind in intimate relationship—something our humanistic utopias have never conceived or achieved. The late John Lennon's vision of a peaceful planet with no God, heaven, or hell (in his song "Imagine"), was in actuality the *antichrist* program from the pits of hell. Even Disney's secular affirmation of humanity in general, and the family in particular, pales in comparison with the Bible's vision of the future for God's people!

Unfortunately, humankind must face the fact that Paradise is not the only reality beyond death. There is also an intermediate realm of suffering, where the lost are sent—a place referred to in the New Testament as Hades.

Hades

The term *Hades* was used in the Septuagint to translate *Sheol*, a general reference to the underworld of the dead. During the intertestamental period, however, the idea developed that the righteous and the wicked were assigned different compartments in Hades. By the time of Jesus, this dual conception was commonplace, and Jesus himself used it—albeit in a unique and precise manner. Jesus referred to an intermediate state of the wicked called *Hades* and an ultimate state that he called *Gehenna.* Unfortunately, the KJV translates both terms as "hell," which has caused confusion as to what Jesus had to say about the subject.

Unlike most preachers and teachers of our day, Jesus was not reticent to speak about hell. He was the most caring and compassionate person who has ever lived, yet he refused to be silent about the realities of death and judgment, heaven and hell. Precisely *because* he was so compassionate, he chose to deal realistically with these issues and to warn of the dangers of hell. Can we really say we love people and not seek to avert their going to hell? Or do we actually believe in such a reality? Jesus' parable of the rich man and Lazarus is an important instance of Jesus' teaching on this subject.

> *Jesus was the most caring and compassionate person who has ever lived, yet he refused to be silent about heaven and hell.*

Jesus often warned about the *dangers* of riches, something that American Christianity seems reluctant to acknowledge. In this case, Jesus tells a story about a poor man, Lazarus, who died and "was carried by the angels to Abraham's bosom" (Luke 16:22 RSV) and a rich man who ended up in Hades, "where he was being tormented" (16:23). It is a haunting, terrifying story of an irrevocable destiny beyond death, an uncrossable chasm, and horrifying agony. Jesus' major point was that of listening to the testimony of "Moses and the prophets" (16:31), but surely he was also alluding to the danger of allowing the comforts that riches afford to blind us to our need of salvation. To be with Abraham was to be with the righteous in Paradise. To be in Hades was to be in a place of agony of suffering.

In his revelation to John, Jesus announces that he has "the keys of Death and of Hades" (Rev. 1:18), meaning that he has the ultimate authority over these realities. That Hades is understood as an intermediate state is confirmed in the description of the last judgment and the lake of fire in Revelation 20:13–14. Jesus was unequivocal on the matter: There is a hell to shun and a heaven to gain. At death we either go immediately into Paradise, into the presence of the Lord, or we go to Hades, separated from the Lord. Paradise is a place of rest and comfort; Hades is a place of suffering and torment. We will leave a discussion of the final states of humankind (at Christ's return) for later. This is the testimony of the New Testament. What alternative conceptions of the afterlife do we encounter? How do they fare in relation to the biblical portrait?

Competing Conceptions of the Afterlife

"Life after life" studies seldom mention the realities of judgment and hell. New Age teachings offer a false hope of continued existence, learning, and personal growth beyond the grave, with no awareness of accountability to God. Even in Christian circles, unusual concepts have emerged.

The idea of "soul sleep" is the most understandable alternative to what has been presented here, in view of the biblical metaphor of sleep with reference to death. Martin Luther himself seems to have accepted this teaching. In this view, people are simply unconscious between death and resurrection. But the biblical materials already dealt with seem to fly in the face of this teaching.

An even more appealing alternative is that of universalism. In a personal conversation, Dale Moody tried to corner Karl Barth on the subject. Moody carefully phrased his question something like this: "Dr. Barth, do you believe God is going to save everybody?" Barth smiled and winked at Moody and replied, "You wouldn't get mad if he did, would you?" And who *would* be against such an idea, assuming justice is appropriately served before, say, a Hitler is "saved"? But such a concept is rightly seen as absurd in the light of the divine respect for human choice. More important, the Scriptures in general and Jesus in particular teach against this idea, as we have already seen.

More pressing to this discussion is the Catholic/Protestant divide over the issue of purgatory. Purgatory in Catholic thought is conceived of as a temporary punishment for, purgation (cleansing) from, and atonement for venial (pardonable) sin. In all likelihood, it grew out of the idea of the intermediate state of Hades. Christians not ready to enter directly into God's presence because of a lack of sanctification (most of us?) enter this state after death. Babies who die, not having been cleansed from original sin through baptism, go to a similar preparatory realm (limbo, *limbus infantium*). We can shorten the stay of loved ones in purgatory through mass, prayers, and good works.

Little in Scripture supports this doctrine. Appeal is often made to 2 Maccabees 12:43–45 (in the Apocrypha) and to Matthew 12:32. Primary weight is put on church tradition. Larger issues, therefore, separate Catholics and Protestants on this subject. Since Protestants generally elevate Scripture above church tradition and exclude the Apocrypha from the canon, the Catholic argument seems weak.

Also, the gospel issue of justification by faith looms large here. Purgatory finds its basis in a theology of merit or works that, in effect, is a denial of the gospel of grace, according to Protestants. Contemporary Catholic scholars often acknowledge this difference of approach to the doctrine of grace.[35] Moreover, the biblical evidence we have already examined clearly indicates that at death we enter directly into the presence of the Lord.

The primary focus of the Scriptures, however, is on the *corporate* dimension of Christian hope. The Bible emphasizes the culmination of history in the consummation of the kingdom of God at Christ's return. In this great event the church is perfected, the dead are raised, the judgment of the world transpires, and our salvation is completed.

The Second Coming of Jesus Christ

Jesus Christ is coming again! How many Christians actually *live* as if they believed this fact? Indeed, many liberal theologians over the years have "spiritualized" this belief, denying any literal significance to Jesus' own promise of his return. While Scripture itself indicates "that in the last days scoffers will come ... saying, 'Where is the promise of his coming?'" (2 Peter 3:3–4)—an attitude characteristic of many in every gen-

---

[35] See Zachary J. Hayes, "The Purgatorial View," in *Four Views on Hell*, ed. William Crockett (Grand Rapids: Zondervan, 1992), 107. Hayes's article is even-handed, constructive, and informed. Clark Pinnock, in his response to Hayes, concedes that perhaps even evangelicals should develop their own doctrine of purgatory in terms of a preparatory growth in sanctification (130). But could we, as evangelicals, actually achieve a convincing *biblical* argument for such a reality, however persuasive we might be logically? And would we not also be arguing ultimately against the biblical doctrines of justification and sanctification themselves?

eration since Christ came—in our own day it is the *secularists* who have most often spoken in apocalyptic terms. The impending arrival of the new millennium evoked such thinking. The rampant march of evil in these perilous times, with technology now seemingly out of control, also conjures frightening apocalyptic scenarios. Russell Chandler's *Doomsday: The End of the World—a View through Time*[36] masterfully documents this end-time fever through history. But this phenomenon is more of a religious instinct, whereas the secular world is looking at things in a more pragmatic fashion.

> *Jesus Christ is coming again! How many Christians actually* live *as if they believed this fact?*

There is a virtual consensus in general culture that we are at least approaching the end of *an* age, if not *the* age. The fall of the former Soviet Union has served to usher in the even more perilous era that could easily see the use of nuclear weapons by out-of-control radical groups. The moral crisis is equally as ominous. With crime rates soaring and valued institutions teetering, society as a whole seems out of control. Aleksandr Solzhenitsyn summarized the views of many students of human civilization—while at the same time speaking in the fashion of the prophets of old—when he made the following observations delivered over the BBC on March 24, 1976:

> We are all [East and West], each in his own way, bound together by a common fate, by the same bands of iron. And all of us are standing on the brink of a great historical cataclysm, a flood that swallows up civilization and changes whole epochs. The present world situation is complicated still more by the fact that several hours have struck simultaneously on the clock of history. We all must face up to a crisis—not just a social crisis, not just a political crisis, not just a military crisis—face up to it, but also stand firm in this great upheaval similar to that which marked the transition from the Middle Ages to the Renaissance. Just as mankind once became aware of the intolerable and mistaken deviation of the late Middle Ages and recoiled in horror from it, so too must we take account of the disastrous deviation of the late Enlightenment. We have become hopelessly enmeshed in our slavish worship of all that is pleasant, all that is comfortable, all that is material—we worship things, we worship products.

[36] Russell Chandler, *Doomsday: The End of the World—a View through Time* (Ann Arbor: Servant, 1993).

> Will we ever succeed in shaking off this burden, in giving free rein to the spirit that was breathed into us at birth, that spirit which distinguishes us from the animal world?[37]

Unfortunately, even though many increasingly acknowledge the spiritual and moral issues of our day, the chaos of responses—not the least of which is the New Age explosion—has only served to exacerbate the situation.

The nuclear threat, the dramatic growth of the telecommunications industry, the increased awareness of the global economy, the renewed interest in global management of resources in a New World Order, the misery of myriad military conflicts around the world, the seeming increase of natural catastrophes—famines, earthquakes, and widespread diseases—the emergence of numerous false messiahs and cult leaders who often bring great suffering and destruction in their wake, and the crucial role of the Middle East in world economy and stability—all of these and more point to the uniqueness of our times. The Bible's many prophetic and apocalyptic depictions of the end times could easily dovetail into present realities.[38] Yet many Christians hesitate to speak up. Is there a voice of sanity amid the cacophony of sensationalist, date-setting voices that too often discredit and distract from authentic biblical reflection on our times?

September 11, 2001 now serves as the ultimate apocalyptic symbol. When the majestic towers of the World Trade Center in New York City were turned into towering infernos, blazing at 2,200 degrees Fahrenheit and then collapsing, everyone immediately sensed that the world would never be the same again. History had shifted, and a seemingly unending worldwide battle with the capricious forces of terror was begun. How should Christians interpret such times? What are the signs we should be noting? *Is* the Messiah coming soon, as many maintain?

Once the Pharisees and Sadducees demanded of Jesus "a sign from heaven" to prove his messiahship. He offered them only "the sign of Jonah" and rebuked their spiritual blindness (Matt. 16:1–4). As D. A. Carson comments, "The proof that they cannot discern the 'signs' is that they ask for a sign (v. 1)!"[39] Jesus' words to these Jewish leaders have

---

[37] Aleksandr Solzhenitsyn, *Warning to the West* (New York: Farar, Straus & Giroux, 1976), 145–46. I was first made aware of these words by Harold Lindell's *The Gathering Storm: World Events and the Return of Christ* (Wheaton, Ill.: Tyndale, 1980), 28–30.

[38] See William Sanford LaSor, *The Truth About Armageddon: What the Bible Says About the End Times* (New York: Harper & Row, 1982), esp. the section, "First-Time-Ever Signs," 1–3.

[39] D. A. Carson, "Matthew," in *The Expositor's Bible Commentary*, ed. Frank E. Gaebelein (Grand Rapids: Zondervan, 1984), 361.

equal relevance today. We have become exceedingly skillful at predicting the weather (16:2–3), yet seemingly less able to discern "the signs of the times" (16:3)!

In many respects, Jesus' Olivet Discourse (Matt. 24–25; Mark 13; Luke 21) sets the agenda for a full-orbed exploration of end-time scenarios. For our present purposes we will focus on Matthew's account. Besides predicting the fall of Jerusalem and addressing in general the "sign of [his] coming and of the end of the age" (Matt. 24:3), Jesus also highlights two other major considerations. First, Jesus intends *not* merely to satisfy his disciples' (and subsequently our) curiosity about the end of the age but rather to exhort us to endurance, preparedness, and faithfulness in spreading the gospel. Second, he states categorically that *no one* knows the "day and hour" when he will return (24:36). It is impossible to count how many times overly zealous prophecy "experts" have ignored these dominical words. When Jesus said *no one,* he meant *no one.* But permeating his entire discourse is the Great Commission vision, which is the motivating force of the church. Jesus' end-time statements in Matthew 16, 24, and 25 find their natural fulfillment in the Galilean commission of 28:18–20.

Permeating Jesus' Olivet discourse is the Great Commission vision, which is the motivating force of the church.

Later, in his Upper Room discourse the evening before his crucifixion, Jesus again addressed the issue of his second coming. The disciples were obviously troubled by the announcement of his departure with the words, "Where I am going, you cannot come" (John 13:33). Thus, he quickly added encouraging words that have also brought great comfort to myriad saints since that night: "Let not your heart be troubled; believe in God, believe also in Me. In My Father's house are many dwelling places; if it were not so, I would have told you; for I go to prepare a place for you" (14:1–2 NASB). The phrase "dwelling places" translates a Greek term (*mone*), found elsewhere in the New Testament only in 14:23, where Jesus says the Father and he will make their "home" with the one who keeps his word (14:23—through the Paraclete, the Holy Spirit; cf. 14:16). Jesus adds: "And if I go and prepare a place for you, I will come again [lit. 'I am coming again,' *palin erchomai*] and will take you to myself, so that where I am, there you may be also" (14:3).

Later Jesus uses these exact words to refer to his own indwelling of his disciples through the Holy Spirit. "I will not leave you orphaned; I am coming [*erchomai*] to you" (John 14:18). Finally, Jesus refers to his statement, "I am going away, and I am coming [*erchomai*] to you," while exhorting his disciples to rejoice at his ultimate return to the Father (14:28). Thus, Jesus roots Christian comfort in *both* the promise of his future return *and* in the present experience of the Spirit.[40] Further, as did Matthew, John also relates the *missionary context* of Jesus' words, referring to the disciples' witness (15:26–27) and to their being "sent," when "he breathed on them and said to them, 'Receive the Holy Spirit'" (20:21–22).

Jesus' words "I will come again" (John 14:3, 18, 28) are in the futuristic present, which "denotes an event which has not yet occurred, but which is regarded as so certain that in thought it may be contemplated as already coming to pass."[41] Any attempt to dilute his words can only be considered a denial of our Lord's sure promise: He *is* coming again! Rejoice, Christian!

Luke alone among the evangelists narrates Jesus' ascension (Luke 24:50–53; Acts 1:6–11). Similar to both Matthew and John, the announcement of Christ's return is couched in the Great Commission context. Also, with John, Luke highlights the superintending role of the Holy Spirit. In his Gospel account, Luke has Jesus instructing and commissioning his disciples and commanding them to remain in Jerusalem until he sends the promise of the Father (the Holy Spirit) on them and they are "clothed with power from on high" (Luke 24:44–49). In Acts, Jesus, before "the day when he was taken up to heaven," gives "instructions through the Holy Spirit," appearing over a forty-day period and "speaking about the kingdom of God." He tells the disciples to wait in Jerusalem for "the promise of the Father," that is, to be "baptized with the Holy Spirit" (Acts 1:1–5).

The disciples, still thinking in political terms, ask, "Lord, is this the time you will restore the kingdom to Israel?" (Acts 1:6). Jesus' response is instructive. First he tells them, "It is not for you to know the times or dates the Father has set by his own authority" (1:7 NIV). Date-setters, take

---

[40] See Gary M. Burge, "John" in *Evangelical Commentary on the Bible*, ed. Walter A. Elwell (Grand Rapids: Baker, 1989), 868–69; see also idem, *The Anointed Community: The Holy Spirit in the Johannine Tradition* (Grand Rapids: Eerdmans, 1987), 143–47.

[41] H. E. Dana and Julius R. Mantey, *A Manual Grammar of the Greek New Testament* (New York: Macmillan, 1955), 185.

note! Then Jesus immediately adds: "But you will receive power when the Holy Spirit has come upon you; and you will be my witnesses in Jerusalem, in all Judea and Samaria, and to the ends of the earth" (1:8). Then after Jesus' return to the Father, heavenly messengers ask the disciples, "Men of Galilee, why do you stand looking up toward heaven? This Jesus, who has been taken up from you into heaven, will come in the same way as you saw him go into heaven" (1:11). Thus, the church was being prepared for her launch into worldwide mission by the promise of both her Lord's return in the clouds of glory and in empowerment by the Holy Spirit.

The second coming of Jesus Christ to this earth will be a definite event. The numerous references to it in the Bible (e.g., 1 Thess. 4:15–17; Phil. 3:20–21; Heb. 9:28; James 5:7–8 [and others already mentioned or treated below]) clearly indicate the "eventness" of Christ's return. It is not a symbolic or hidden reality, but a cataclysmic, public culmination of human history and the full realization of God's kingdom. Because the liberal tradition has tended to spiritualize Christ's return, conservatives often use such terms as "personal," "visible," and "bodily" to characterize the Second Coming. This is a valid instinct, and it appropriately summarizes the nature of Jesus' return.

> *People hunger to know the truth about the end of the age. They want to know if there really is hope for the human race.*

One of the most dramatic instances of the New Testament depiction of the definiteness of this event is the way Jesus himself spoke of it during his trial before the Sanhedrin. Caiaphas, the high priest, had grown impatient with Jesus' silence before his accusers and challenged him: "I put you under oath before the living God, tell us if you are the Messiah, the Son of God" (Matt. 26:63). Jesus' response to the high priest's juridical demand still rings down the corridors of time: "Yes, it is as you say. . . . But I say to all of you: In the future you will see the Son of Man sitting at the right hand of the Mighty One and coming on the clouds of heaven" (26:64 NIV). This was all Caiaphas needed. He "tore his clothes and said, 'He has blasphemed!'" (26:65). Christ could not have spoken of himself in more exalted terms. He may not have been the messiah the Jews expected or desired. But he was truly who he claimed to be: the Messiah, the Son of the living God.

The church of the Lord Jesus Christ needs to sound the same clarion call in our own day. Billy Graham has made it a pattern for years to preach at least one message on the second coming of Christ in each of his crusades. The response is always dramatic. People hunger to know the truth about the end of the age. They want to know if there really is hope for the human race. Now is the time for Christians to speak clearly and confidently about our Lord's return. My own church's confession of faith, *The Baptist Faith and Message*, gives an excellent summary of what Christians should proclaim across the globe.

> God, in His own time and in His own way, will bring the world to its appropriate end. According to His promise, Jesus Christ will return personally and visibly in glory to earth; the dead will be raised; and Christ will judge all men in righteousness. The unrighteous will be consigned to Hell, the place of everlasting punishment. The righteous in their resurrected and glorified bodies will receive their reward and will dwell forever in Heaven with the Lord.[42]

Each successive generation of believers must faithfully embrace and announce this hope.

The Signs of the Times

It is especially appropriate for contemporary Christians to ask themselves, "Is Christ coming soon? Are we adequately discerning the signs of our own times? Are we ready?" Jesus' Olivet Discourse is our best reference point for addressing these concerns.

As Jesus and the disciples exited the temple in Jerusalem during Jesus' last week, the disciples pointed out the magnificent buildings Herod the Great had built. Not fully completed, yet shining brilliantly in the Judean sun, the marbled worship center was a wonder to behold. The disciples were duly impressed. Jesus' response shocked them: "You see all these, do you not? Truly I tell you, not one stone will be left here upon another; all will be thrown down" (Matt. 24:2). We still puzzle to this day as to how, precisely, those multi-ton stones were ever put into place. Herod's temple can be considered one of the wonders of the ancient world, alongside the pyramids. Yet Jesus was predicting that the temple would be razed to the ground, and his prediction was fulfilled in the fall of Jerusalem to the Roman army under Titus in A.D. 70.

---

[42] *The Baptist Faith and Message* (2000): Leadership and Adult Publishing, LifeWay Church Resources, One LifeWay Plaza, Nashville, TN 37234–0175.

Later, on the Mount of Olives, the disciples asked Jesus, "Tell us, when will this be, and what will be the sign of your coming and of the end of the age?" (Matt. 24:3). For them, this constituted *one* question, because to their way of thinking such a cataclysmic fall of the temple could only signify the end of the age. In his response, however, Jesus kept the two issues separate: the fall of Jerusalem and the end of the age. To this day followers of Christ have on many occasions misapprehended his teaching, failing to recognize this distinction. A quick overview of Matthew's account of Jesus' end-time discourse yields substantive insight into our own era.

Jesus warns of false (but persuasive) messiahs (Matt. 24:5) and of "wars and rumors of wars"; but, he quickly adds, "the end is not yet" (24:6). In addition to the collision of nations and kingdoms "there will be famines and earthquakes in various places" (24:7). But we are not to be thrown off by these tumultuous events. "All these things are the first birth-pangs of the new age" (24:8 REB). Believers will face torture, hatred, and martyrdom (24:9). Even among church folk there will be betrayal and hatred and a great falling away (24:10). Numerous false prophets will "lead many astray" (24:11). Lawlessness will increase and consequently "the love of many will grow cold" (24:12). "But the one who endures to the end will be saved" (24:13).

Then Jesus adds an all-important culminating description of the church age. "And this gospel of the kingdom will be preached throughout the whole world, as a testimony to all nations; and then the end will come" (Matt. 24:14 RSV). These words tie in with the concluding event of Matthew's Gospel, Jesus' Galilean appearance and the Great Commission (28:16–20). This orientation toward world mission is clearly the most important emphasis of Jesus' teaching on the end of the age. *We are to be preoccupied, not with speculation on the date of our Lord's return, but with spreading the gospel of the kingdom across the globe.* Thus, the opening verses of the Olivet Discourse are descriptive of the church of *every* generation prior to Christ's return.

We are to be preoccupied, not with speculation on the date of our Lord's return, but with spreading the gospel of the kingdom across the globe.

At the same time, even though we are *already* living in the new age, in that the kingdom was inaugurated by Jesus himself at his first coming, we still await the consummation of that kingdom at his second coming. Could there not, therefore, be a further application of these verses as especially descriptive of the period *immediately prior* to Christ's appearing? Many students of Scripture hesitate to acknowledge this possibility on hermeneutical grounds. Perhaps we should reexamine our hermeneutics and allow for a more pneumatic approach. What *is* the Spirit saying to churches? Could it be that the apparent dramatic increase in natural catastrophies, international bloodshed, false religions and religious leaders, lawlessness in society, apostasy in the church, and persecution of believers is a precursor of the soon return of Christ? I raise this question, not for the purpose of *speculation,* but for *motivation.* As with all apocalyptic literature, interpretation is often difficult, and there will frequently be differences of opinion. Our ultimate goal in wrestling with such texts, therefore, should always be the edification and mobilization of the church, not entertainment and sensational speculation—however many book sales these might generate.

The ensuing verses (Matt. 24:15–28) refer to a great tribulation through which the church must pass on her way to the Heavenly City. In his Upper Room discourse, Jesus promised his peace to his disciples, but he also confirmed a fact of life to them that we have also inherited. "In the world you have tribulation [*thlipsis*], but take courage; I have overcome the world" (John 16:33 NASB). Here in the Olivet Discourse, Jesus again refers to this same reality: "For then there will be a great tribulation [*thlipsis*], such as has not occurred since the beginning of the world until now, nor ever shall" (Matt. 24:21 NASB). Jesus is likely referring to two realities: (1) the ongoing opposition to the church and the gospel in this present evil age and (2) the culminating years of history when evil makes its final push across the planet but is defeated by the return of Christ himself.

This portion of Jesus' discourse begins, however, with words that apparently have a triple reference. "Therefore when you see the abomination of desolation which was spoken of through Daniel the prophet, standing in the holy place (let the reader understand), then let those who are in Judea flee to the mountains" (Matt. 24:15–16 NASB). The key phrase here is "the abomination of desolation," and the first reference alluded to is that which Daniel predicted (Dan. 9:27; 11:31; 12:11)—the horror of the desecration of the temple by Antiochus Epiphanes in 168 B.C., when he built an altar to Zeus and offered a pig as a sacrifice, profaning the Most Holy Place. Jesus was preparing his disciples for a similar tragedy when Jerusalem, over which Jesus had already lamented (Matt. 23:37–39), would fall to the Romans (A.D. 70) and the temple would again be desecrated.

But there is likely a third reference as well. Our Lord seems to be describing here a period of unprecedented persecution and tribulation, a time of "great suffering, such has not been from the beginning of the world until now, no, and never will be" (Matt. 24:21)—a definitive end time event. In all probability, the person Jesus is referring to in 24:15 is the same Antichrist that the apostle Paul describes to the Thessalonians:

> Let no one deceive you in any way; for that day will not come, unless the rebellion [or apostasy, *apostasia*] comes first, and the man of lawlessness [some manuscripts read "sin"] is revealed, the son of perdition [destruction], who opposes and exalts himself against every so-called god or object of worship, so that he takes his seat in the temple of God, proclaiming himself to be God. (2 Thess. 2:3–4 RSV)

Paul goes on to describe Christ's destruction of this false miracle worker, who does "signs" and "wonders" by the power of Satan himself. Jesus' second coming *ends* the reign of evil decisively (2:8–10).

In our day it is well to take note of Jesus' words. Production of "great signs and omens" does not necessarily indicate a Spirit-filled ministry, but they could also be the work of "false messiahs and false prophets" (Matt. 24:24). In the Sermon on the Mount, Jesus warned that in the last day he will have to say even to some who have prophesied, cast out demons, and done great miracles in his name, "I never knew you; go away from me, you evildoers" (7:22–23). In my opinion, Pentecostal and charismatic Christians, a dominant force in world Christendom, have *demonstrated* the rightful place for signs and wonders in the spread of the gospel. At the same time, it alarms me at times to hear saints accept the questionable teaching of someone simply because that person can produce miraculous signs. This mentality is a *set-up* for the Antichrist in the last days!

The next section of Jesus' Matthew 24 discourse describes the actual visible, personal return of our Lord "with power and great glory" (Matt. 24:29–31). It will be marked by cosmic events that the entire planet will be able to observe. His angels "will gather his elect from the four winds, from one end of heaven to the other" (24:31). The rest of the discourse deals with the readiness and faithfulness of God's people in view of coming events.

The parable of the fig tree alerted the Jews to the impending destruction of the temple. It warns us of how near Christ's return could be as we seek to discern the signs of the times (Matt. 24:32–35). It takes only one generation to complete all the prophetic predictions. Then 24:36 should be highlighted, as it points out a key principle for interpreting prophetic events—no one knows the precise time of our Lord's return—and also forms a transition to the culminating teachings and parables of this discourse. The days of Noah are instructive for our own day (24:37–41; cf. Luke 17:26–27). Just as Noah's contemporaries were surprised by the judgment flood, so many, if not most, will be caught by surprise when Christ returns. "Keep awake therefore, for you do not know on what day your Lord is coming" (Matt. 24:42). Christ will come unexpectedly, "like a thief in the night" (1 Thess. 5:2), so we must "be ready, for the Son of Man is coming at an unexpected hour" (Matt. 24:43–44).

No matter how much our Lord seems to be delaying his coming, we must continue to be expectant and diligent.

The parables of the faithful and unfaithful slaves (Matt. 24:45–51), the ten bridesmaids (25:1–13), and the talents (25:14–30) share the common thread of readiness and faithfulness. No matter how much our Lord seems to be delaying his coming, we must continue to be expectant and diligent. The discourse climaxes with the well-known parable of the final judgment (25:31–46).[43] As we will study later, one day we will all stand before God to give account for how we have lived our lives. In view of his second coming, Jesus makes it crystal clear what he expects of his followers.

First, we need to be *watching*. Since we do not know when our Lord will return and since his return will be unexpected (Matt. 24:42–44), we need to be watchful, unlike the wicked slave, who thought his master's return would be delayed and behaved inappropriately (24:45–51). Second, we need to be *waiting*. The five foolish virgins, or bridesmaids, did not plan for the bridegroom's delay. Instead, they were unprepared when the bridegroom arrived (25:1–13). We should be watchful and not assume that our Lord's return is a long time off; at the same time, we should be waiting and not assume that his coming will be immediate.

---

[43] For a helpful overview of these materials in Matthew see Craig Blomberg's notes in: David S. Dockery, ed., *Holman Bible Handbook* (Nashville: Holman, 1992), 562.

Finally, we need to be *working*. Jesus' parable of the talents (25:14–30) makes it clear that we are to be good stewards of the time and resources he has given us. Unlike the "wicked and lazy slave" (25:26), we must be watchful, waiting, and laboring in the kingdom.[44] Rightfully discerning the signs of the times entails diligent service to our Lord and Master until he comes.

Although there are doubtless myriad ways one might summarize and categorize the "signs of the times" we have just noted, Anthony Hoekema provides a useful outline. He displays the signs under three rubrics as follows:

1. *Signs evidencing the grace of God:*
   a. The proclamation of the gospel to all nations
   b. The salvation of the fullness of Israel
2. *Signs indicating opposition to God:*
   a. Tribulation
   b. Apostasy
   c. Antichrist
3. *Signs indicating divine judgment:*
   a. Wars
   b. Earthquakes
   c. Famines[45]

Of these signs, the only one not yet mentioned is the "salvation of the fullness of Israel." To this we now turn.

The Fullness of the Gentiles and the Fullness of Israel

Paul agonized for his people, Israel. "I have great sorrow and unceasing anguish in my heart" (Rom. 9:2). They had in large measure rejected the gospel, while the Gentile mission had flourished. What was the significance of these developments? Had God's divine purposes failed? Had God rejected Israel because Israel had rejected his Son? Are Christian believers superior to the Jews for having accepted the Messiah? What precisely is Israel's role in God's plan of redemption? Paul addresses these concerns in Romans 9–11. The key concept in these chapters, as noted in an earlier discussion, is *mercy*. The entire success

---

[44] I owe this (very preachable!) outline—watching, waiting, working—to Millard J. Erickson: "Second Coming of Christ," in Walter A. Elwell, ed., *Evangelical Dictionary of Theology* (Grand Rapids: Baker, 1984), 993–94.

[45] Hoekema, *The Bible and the Future*, 137 (Hoekema's italics). Hoekema's full treatment of this subject is sane, thorough, balanced, and insightful (129–63).

of the Christian mission is based on the inseparable relation between the fullness of the Gentiles and the fullness of Israel.

Rather than feeling superior, Gentile believers should see themselves as "a wild olive shoot," grafted onto "the rich root of the olive tree" ([Israel]; Rom. 11:17). God has allowed a "hardening" to come on Israel "until the fullness [*pleroma*] of the Gentiles has come in" (11:25 NASB). God's ultimate purpose is mercy for *everyone* (11:30–32)! Earlier, 11:12 captures the hope that is entailed in this divine strategy, conveyed beautifully by Dale Moody's translation. *"Now if their fall (*paraptōma*) means riches for the world, and their failure (*hēttēma*) means riches for the Gentiles, how much more will their fullness (*plērōma*) mean!"*[46] Paul was amazed by the wisdom of God in this mysterious strategy (11:33–36!)

Eugene H. Peterson's paraphrase of Romans 11:25–26 communicates well the spirit of Paul's words:

> I want to lay all this out on the table as clearly as I can, friends. This is complicated. It would be easy to misinterpret what's going on and arrogantly assume that you're royalty and they're just rabble, out on their ears for good. But that's not it at all. This hardness on the part of insider Israel toward God is temporary. Its effect is to open things up to all the outsiders so that we end up with a full house. Before it's all over, there will be a complete Israel.[47]

Three key New Testament terms define the second coming of Christ that brings this "fullness" to which the apostle refers.

Parousia, Apocalypse, Epiphany

Of the three biblical terms, (1) *parousia* (now often used as an anglicized transliteration of the Greek word, much as the term "baptism"), (2) *apokalypsis* (apocalypse), and (3) *epiphaneia* (epiphany), the last two are by far the most familiar to the general Christian community. Scholars and more sophisticated students of Scripture are more likely to be familiar with the first term. "Epiphany" and the Sundays following it, of course, have become a meaningful celebration during the liturgical year of those events in our Lord's earthly life and ministry most revelatory

---

[46] Dale Moody, *The Word of Truth* (Grand Rapids: Eerdmans, 1981), 536 (Moody's italics). Moody, in typical Baptist fashion, was always strong at alliteration! A recent contemporary rendering follows Moody's pattern: "If their false step means the enrichment of the world, if their falling short means the enrichment of the Gentiles, how much more will their coming to full strength mean!" (REB).

[47] *The Message* (Colorado Springs, Colo.: NavPress, 1995), 387.

of his identity as the Christ, the Messiah. "Apocalypse" is familiar even to general culture with numerous movies, books, and the like bearing this term in their titles or as a prominent element of their content—all pointing to a cataclysmic end to civilization as we know it. All three terms, however, are central to the biblical portrayal of our Lord's return.

"Parousia" (*parousia*) can appropriately be translated "advent" (another key liturgical season). It further denotes "presence, coming, arrival." It was used in biblical times to indicate the official visit to a province of a person of high ranking, such as a king or an emperor.[48] What an appropriate term, therefore, with which to refer to our Lord's return.

"Apocalypse" (*apokalypsis*), meaning "revelation," is more self-explanatory. Apocalyptic literature, albeit in often highly symbolic language, purports to disclose, or unveil, both the significance of present circumstances, generally for the purpose of encouragement, and future events as well. Both the Old and New Testaments have significant blocks of apocalyptic materials, even entire books (e.g., Daniel and Revelation). Apocalyptic literature always seems to emerge during momentous epochs of human history, which at least in part explains the present intensity of interest in biblical apocalyptic literature.

Finally, "epiphany" (*epiphaneia*), meaning "manifestation, appearing, appearance," is also used in the New Testament with reference to Christ's second coming. This term is singularly appropriate to the subject as well. Decisive events that will complete our salvation are associated with the return of Christ as indicated by this word.[49] A brief perusal of key New Testament passages that utilize these words provides a comprehensive survey of the major eschatological themes of Scripture.

First Thessalonians is perhaps the earliest written letter of the New Testament (unless Galatians is dated before A.D. 51). The Pauline churches are preoccupied with the questions we have been addressing in this chapter. Opposition and persecution, along with a general discrediting of Paul's apostolic authority, mark the beginning days of this fledgling congregation. But they are also concerned about ultimate issues related to death, resurrection, and the second coming.

A further main theme of 1 Thessalonians is a response to questions about eschatology that were troubling the church, that is, questions

---

48 Walter Bauer, rev. and ed. Frederick W. Danker, *A Greek-English Lexicon of the New Testament and Other Early Christian Literature,* 3d ed. (Chicago: Univ. of Chicago Press, 2000), 781.

49 For a succinct overview of all three terms, see Erickson, "Second Coming of Christ," 993.

about the end times. Some of the Thessalonians were perplexed by the deaths of believers and wondered whether those who had died would be excluded from the life of the resurrection. Paul replies with an apocalyptic narrative, a story of the events of the end time, which makes clear that it will not be an advantage to be living when Christ returns; all believers "will be with the Lord forever" (1 Thess. 4:13–18). This section shows that both Paul and his readers expected the end very soon. But Paul follows with another statement, also expressed in traditional apocalyptic language, that emphasizes one cannot predict the time of the end (5:1–11).[50]

It will not be an advantage to be living when Christ returns; all believers "will be with the Lord forever."

The apostle uses emphatic language in order to reassure his readers: "For this we declare to you by the word of the Lord, that we who are alive, who are left until the coming [*parousia*] of the Lord, will by no means [an emphatic negative: *ou me*] precede those who have died" (1 Thess. 4:15). He then provides a brief apocalyptic depiction of Christ's glorious return (4:16–17).

One gains the impression that both Paul and the Thessalonians felt that the Second Coming could be soon. Nevertheless, Paul, echoing Jesus' words in the Little Apocalypse (Matt. 24:43–44), emphasizes that there will always be the element of surprise: "The day of the Lord will come like a thief in the night" (1 thess. 5:2). In addition, the apostle instructs the believers as to how they should *live* in the light of the end time (5:4–22). His earlier benediction expressed this same concern: "And may he [the Lord] so strengthen your hearts in holiness that you may be blameless before our God and Father at the coming [*parousia*] of our Lord Jesus with all his saints" (3:13).

Paul's second letter to the Thessalonians, a few months later, continues the apocalyptic theme. Prior to the second coming of Jesus there will be a great final conflict between good and evil, a period of possible delay that must also be factored into our eschatological perspective (2 Thess. 2:1–12).[51] "As to the coming [*parousia*] of our Lord Jesus Christ and our being gathered together to him . . ." Paul begins. He then warns his readers of those who would mislead "either by spirit [prophetic utterance]

[50] Bruce M. Metzger and Roland E. Murphy, eds., *The New Oxford Annotated Bible* (New York: Oxford Univ. Press, 1991), 291 (NT).

[51] Ibid., 296.

or by word [false report] or by letter [supposedly from Paul]" (2:1–2). This same dynamic is present in modern times. I cannot count the number of times in the 1970s that I heard the report of charismatic prophecies to the effect that Florida was going to fall into the sea. Similar doomsday prophetic warnings were given to residents of Southern California—albeit with more scientific evidence to back them up.

The Thessalonians were being told that "the day of the Lord is already here" (2 Thess. 2:2). One resident in my hometown, Odessa, Texas, announced this exact message in sprawling letters across the side of his or her house for all the city to read. I wondered whether this person had ever read 2 Thessalonians. Paul's rejoinder was unequivocal: Not so! For "that day will not come unless the rebellion [*apostasia*] comes first and the lawless one [lit., man of lawlessness] is revealed, the one destined for destruction [lit., the son of perdition or destruction]" (2:3). This antichrist figure, called by many believers simply "the Antichrist," "the Lord Jesus will destroy with the breath of his mouth, annihilating him by the manifestation [*epiphaneia*] of his coming [*parousia*]" (2:8).

Interestingly, Paul uses the term *parousia* to refer to the appearance of the Antichrist as well, speaking of "the coming [*parousia*] of the lawless one" (2 Thess. 2:9). The warning bears repeating in view of those today who follow after signs and wonders (instead of signs and wonders following them [cf. Mark 16:17–18]): "The coming of the lawless one will be in accordance with the work of Satan displayed in all kinds of counterfeit miracles, signs and wonders" (2 Thess. 2:9 NIV).

Earlier in this same letter the apostle reminded the Thessalonians that even though this present age is marked by persecution, affliction, and suffering, the second coming of Christ will bring relief and rest as well as vindication and vengeance to the saints (2 Thess. 1:3–10). All this would happen "at the revelation [*apokalypsis*] of the Lord Jesus from heaven with his mighty angels, in blazing fire" (1:7–8 NAB). We see here the vantage point for Paul's "theology of suffering" (something too often lacking in charismatic circles). In commending the Thessalonians' faith and endurance during all their persecutions and afflictions, Paul informs them that God's "righteous judgment" is at work and that God is making them "worthy of the kingdom of God, for which [they] are also suffering" (1:5). Believers can endure in faith and love—no matter what their circumstances—because of their certain *hope* in Christ. We know that "the sufferings of this present time are not worth comparing with the glory about to be revealed to us" (Rom. 8:18).

Paul refers to Christ's return as "that day" (2 Thess. 1:10). The final day brings both judgment and glory. Unbelievers "will suffer the punishment of eternal destruction, separated from the presence of the Lord and from the glory of his might," while the saints will glorify the Lord and marvel at his glory (2 Thess. 1:9–10). Toward the end of his life the apostle also related how he had viewed his sufferings for the gospel in the light of Christ's return. "For this gospel I was appointed a herald and an apostle and a teacher, and for this reason I suffer as I do. But I am not ashamed, for I know the one in whom I have put my trust, and I am sure that he is able to guard until that day what I have entrusted to him" (2 Tim. 1:11–12). Paul assured the Corinthians in similar terms:

> I give thanks to my God always for you because of the grace of God that has been given you in Christ Jesus, for in every way you have been enriched in him, in speech and knowledge of every kind—just as the testimony of Christ has been strengthened among you—so that you are not lacking in any spiritual gift as you wait for the revealing [*apokalypsis*] of our Lord Jesus Christ. He will also strengthen you to the end, so that you may be blameless on the day of our Lord Jesus Christ. God is faithful; by him you were called into the fellowship of his Son, Jesus Christ our Lord. (1 Cor. 1:4–9)

Even though Paul had his stormiest relationship with these saints in Corinth, he was confident of their future.[52] God's end-time apocalypse would find them "blameless on the day of our Lord Jesus Christ" (1:8).

It is amazing how Peter's teaching on church life and spiritual gifts parallels that of Paul. Yes, the "end of all things is near" (1 Peter 4:7). Therefore, the manner in which we live and relate to one another is all the more crucial, including our stewardship of spiritual gifts (4:7–11). In addition, our perspective on present sufferings should be informed by our glorious hope:

> Beloved, do not be surprised at the fiery ordeal among you, which comes upon you for your testing, as though some strange thing were happening to you; but to the degree that you share the sufferings of Christ, keep on rejoicing, so that also at the revelation [*apokalypsis*] of His glory, you may rejoice with exultation. (1 Peter 4:12–13 NASB)

---

[52] Further, he commended them for their richness in spiritual gifts, never intending for them to "exterminate" such controversial gifts as tongues and prophecy, for example, but only to regulate them in love. Evangelicals too often have missed this opening commendation and have misinterpreted Paul's counsel on spiritual gifts in 1 Cor. 12–14.

As Paul would tell Timothy and Titus, we are to live godly lives as we long for the appearing (*epiphaneia*) of our Lord in all his glory (1 Tim. 6:14; 2 Tim. 4:8; Titus 2:11–14).

But what precisely should we expect in terms of the sequence of end-time events? There is perhaps no better place to turn for help in this regard than to that final apocalypse of the Scriptures, Revelation 20.

"Then I Saw Heaven Opened . . ."[53]

Although the Revelation to John has been variously interpreted, its central thrust is clear. "The focus of the Book of Revelation is the Second Coming of the Lord Jesus Christ and the definitive establishment of God's kingdom at the end of time."[54] In addition, three prominent millennial views—postmillennialism, amillennialism, and premillennialism—have developed around Revelation 20. "The central truth of all three is the clear and direct affirmation: Christ will return, as he had promised (John 14:3), and will destroy the forces of evil and establish God's eternal kingdom."[55] This is the forest we *must* see before we attempt to apprehend the individual trees.

Furthermore, we must consciously acknowledge that apocalyptic literature like this engages our *imagination* with strong symbolism that demands careful interpretation. Literalism in this domain can definitely mislead us at points.[56] For example, after the praise-filled depiction of the end-time wedding banquet in which Christ and his church are once and for all united (the Marriage Supper of the Lamb, Rev. 19:1–10), John reports seven (his favorite number) visions, each introduced with the words, "Then I saw" (19:11, 17, 19; 20:1, 4, 11; 21:1).[57] The imagery of these apocalyptic reports is vivid, even grotesque, at points. But the message is clear: Christ is victorious!

Christ will return, as he had promised (John 14:3), and will destroy the forces of evil and establish God's eternal kingdom.

---

[53] See Rev. 19:11.

[54] Bruce M. Metzger, *Breaking the Code: Understanding the Book of Revelation* (Nashville: Abingdon, 1993), 18.

[55] Ibid., 95.

[56] Ibid., 11.

[57] Bruce Metzger first drew my attention to these seven visions: ibid., 90.

Regarding vision one (19:11–16), at Christ's return, will we see him riding on a literal white horse and will we see a literal sword protruding out of his mouth, or are these symbolic portrayals of the Parousia? We are probably dealing here with vivid, moving, and appropriate symbolism. At the same time, this first of the seven last visions of John provides us with perhaps the most stirring account of the literal, visible, bodily return of our Lord to be found in all the Scriptures!

> Then I saw heaven opened, and there was a white horse! Its rider is called Faithful and True, and in righteousness he judges and makes war. His eyes are like a flame of fire, and on his head are many diadems; and he has a name inscribed that no one knows but himself. He is clothed in a robe dipped in blood, and his name is called The Word of God. And the armies of heaven, wearing fine linen, white and pure, were following him on white horses. From his mouth comes a sharp sword with which to strike down the nations, and he will rule them with a rod of iron; he will tread the winepress of the fury of the wrath of God the Almighty. On his robe and on his thigh he has a name inscribed, "King of kings and Lord of lords." (Rev. 19:11–16)

What continues from this point is, from this interpreter's point of view, an enumeration of sequential end-time events.

The Devil, the Beast, and the False Prophet

Upon the visible, bodily return of Christ, the three enemies of God and humankind—that unholy trinity most often referred to as the devil, the beast, and the false prophet—will be summarily defeated. We have already been introduced to these formidable foes earlier in John's Apocalypse (chs. 12–13). The background to the apocalyptic images here is Daniel 7:1–8. Beastly images are singularly appropriate to the subject matter. Jesus himself alluded to the Antichrist's activity, as we have already seen (Matt. 24:15). And the apostle Paul provides us with a rather complete narrative of these events as well, as we saw in 2 Thessalonians 2:1–12. John's culminating visions give a dramatic rendering of our Lord's final conquest of evil.

In vision two (Rev. 19:17–18) our conquering King decisively defeats his enemies, "both small and great." The victory is termed "the great supper of God," in stark contrast to his previous depiction of the glorious "marriage supper of the Lamb" (19:9), in which Christ and his bride, the church, are finally and fully united (19:1–10).

Vision three (19:19–21) vividly describes the destruction of the Antichrist ("the beast") and the false prophet. The title "Antichrist" actually is the traditional nomenclature for the one whom the Bible simply refers to as "the beast" (Rev. 13; 19; 20) or "the man of lawlessness," "the son of destruction" (cf. 2 Thess. 2:1–12). In John's letters we learn that the antichrist spirit was already in the world and at work, opposing the message of the Incarnation (1 John 2:18–23; 4:3). The "last hour" is upon us (2:18). Indeed, "many deceivers have gone out into the world, those who do not confess that Jesus Christ has come in the flesh; any such person is the deceiver and the antichrist!" (2 John 7). But at the literal end of the age, the beast and false prophet will emerge to deceive and dominate the entire world—only to be smashed into oblivion by our Lord!

John's fourth culminating vision (Rev. 20:1–3) describes the binding of Satan. At this point interpreters part company in terms of whether the thousand years referred to here and in the subsequent vision (20:4–10) are symbolic or literal. Assuming a literal significance for present purposes, the succession of events depicted in these visions is breathtaking! The "dragon, that ancient serpent, who is the Devil and Satan," is locked up for a thousand years, unable to continue deceiving the nations (20:1–3). Then comes the first resurrection (the saints).

Christians, of all people, should be the most optimistic.

In the fifth visions, the millennial reign of Christ (with the saints) ensues, followed by the release of Satan to once more deceive the nations. The result is what is often called the battle of Gog and Magog (20:4–10). Then "the devil who had deceived them [the nations] [is] thrown into the lake of fire and sulfur, where the beast and the false prophet [are], and they will be tormented day and night forever and ever" (20:10).

Vision six (Rev. 20:11–15) is "one of the most impressive descriptions of the Last Judgment ever written."[58]

Vision seven (21:1–4) is the unforgettable portrait of the new heaven and new earth and the new Jerusalem, the culmination of the Bible's grand story of redemption and the ultimate home of the saints in glory!

God's message comes through loud and clear in these visions. Christians, of all people, should be the most optimistic. As R. H. Charles,

[58] Ibid., 97.

perhaps the greatest scholar of apocalyptic literature, commented, John's purpose was to communicate this optimism, this hope: God's kingdom *will* come. Good *will* triumph over evil. No matter how strong and pervasive evil seems at times, God's people should remain steady and certain: God *will* have the final say![59]

Still, more investigation is necessary. Topics such as the Millennium, the resurrection(s), and the final judgment have been broached in John's visions, and various interpretations of these theological issues deserve to be presented. Certainly, the most controversial of these subjects is that of the Millennium and the related views of the "rapture" of the church.

Pre-, Post-, A-, and . . . Pan-!

Most people who have been in the church any length of time have heard of the three major millennial views, even though they may be uncertain as to what precisely is meant by the terms premillennialism, postmillennialism, and amillennialism. These distinctive positions have often been shortened to their prefixes: pre-, post-, and a-. And the standard joke is that some are premillennialists, some postmillennialists, some amillennialists, and some *pan*millennialists—that is, they simply believe that "it will all *pan out* in the end"!

To complicate things further, there are two major camps among the premillennialists: historic or classic premillennialism, and dispensational premillennialism. An additional controversy among these folk centers on whether Christ comes for the church before the period of the Great Tribulation, in the middle of this period, or at the end of it. A lot of ink (and blood!) has been spilled over these issues, far out of proportion to their importance. Christians will part fellowship with one another over these questions, *oblivious to the hope that is held in common by all!*

A simple lesson of history should serve as a warning for all of us and prompt a little more humility and tolerance on everyone's part: *God's*

---

[59] R. H. Charles, *The Revelation of St. John* (ICC; Edinburgh: T. & T. Clark, 1920), ciii–iv. George R. Beasley-Murray cites Charles in the helpful popular introduction to Revelation, *Highlights of the Book of Revelation* (Nashville: Broadman, 1972), 80. See also Beasley-Murray's excellent commentary: *The Book of Revelation* (NCB; Greenwood, S.C.: Attic, 1974). George Eldon Ladd's *A Commentary on the Revelation of John* (Grand Rapids: Eerdmans, 1972) is another definitive commentary on Revelation that develops the viewpoint presented here.

people thought they had it all figured out scripturally and theologically the first time Jesus came, and they all missed it! They went even further: They lynched the very Messiah they had been awaiting for centuries. It was "church folk" who engineered Jesus' death! Surely there will be surprises for all when it all "pans out"!

Nevertheless, this assurance does not mean that exploring these issues is a worthless endeavor. If for no other reason than the fact that we take what the Bible teaches with utmost seriousness, we should continue to examine these questions. In an insightful overview of the millennial views, Stanley J. Grenz comments on the importance of the topic:

> The anticipation of a climax to human history—a corporate eschatology—and the resultant question concerning the millennium as a specific stage in that climax cannot be relegated to the fringes of the biblical proclamation. On the contrary, it belongs to the heart of what the Bible intends to teach.[60]

Again, we must never lose sight of the hope on which all Bible-believing Christians agree: Jesus Christ is coming again to conquer evil and complete our salvation! A "new heaven and a new earth"—a new creation—is on the way (Rev. 21:1–8). Looking back at the end-time visions of John, we observe that there is a diversity of interpretations of chapters 19–20, but a general consensus on chapters 21–22. It is the Millennium of chapter 20 that is the bone of contention.

> *Jesus Christ is coming again to conquer evil and complete our salvation!*

The Latin term *millenium* means one thousand years. Thus, *premillennialism* refers to the belief that Christ will return *prior to* the Millennium. *Postmillennialism* sees his return as *after* the Millennium, and *amillennialism* interprets the millennial references as *symbolic,* that is, there is no literal thousand-year reign as such (*a*=no). Each of these positions deserves further examination.

Premillennialism

Premillennialists understand John's seven culminating visions (Rev. 19:11–21:8) as providing a virtual chronological narrative of end-time events. The reference to the millennium is literal rather

60 Stanley J. Grenz, *The Millennial Maze: Sorting Out Evangelical Options* (Downers Grove, Ill.: InterVarsity Press, 1992), 27.

than symbolic. George Beasley-Murray summarizes the premillennial interpretation:

> The essential element in the idea of the millennium is the appearing of the kingdom of the Messiah in history, prior to the revelation of the kingdom of God in the eternal and transcendent realm of the new creation.[61]

History is the arena of God's revelatory and saving activity, and the thousand-year reign of Christ is the fitting denouement to that activity. Then, appropriately, the new creation is introduced.

Visions four and five (Rev. 20:1–10) provide John's portrayal of the Millennium. In fact, six times in 20:2–7 (once in each verse) reference is made to a "thousand years" (*chilia ete*). Thus, belief in a literal thousand-year reign of Christ on this earth is often referred to (perhaps derisively at times) as "chiliasm" by its opponents, even though it was the dominant view during the first three centuries of the church (see, e.g., Papias, Justin Martyr, Irenaeus, and Tertullian).

Another distinctive of premillennialism is its interpretation of 20:4–5. Two resurrections are referred to in these verses: "They [the saints] came to life [*ezesan*] and reigned with Christ a thousand years. (The rest of the dead did not come to life [*ezesan*] until the thousand years were ended.) This is the first resurrection." This is the most difficult passage for the amillennial position. Amillennialists usually will assert that the first resurrection mentioned here refers to the new birth. But the use of the same verb in both verses makes this interpretation seem artificial. Also, verse 5 is difficult to get around chronologically. It is the "rest of the dead" who are described as being resurrected *after* the Millennium.

Three key events are portrayed in these two visions: (1) the binding of Satan (Rev. 20:1–3); (2) the millennial reign of Christ (20:4–6); and (3) the temporary releasing of Satan (20:7–10). First, Satan is bound and thrown into the bottomless pit, the Abyss, locked up there for a thousand years and unable to deceive the nations any further. Then comes the resurrection of the righteous and the millennial reign of Christ. Two groups of saints are evidently highlighted as having experienced this "first resurrection": those seated on thrones with "authority to judge"—apparently a description of all believers (cf. Matt. 19:28; Luke 22:30; 1 Cor. 6:3; cf. Dan. 7:22)—and then, among these, the mar-

---

[61] Beasley-Murray, *The Book of Revelation*, 287.

tyrs of the Great Tribulation as worthy of special mention (Rev. 20:4). Over all of these "the second death has no power" (20:6); that is, they will never face the final judgment of the "lake of fire" (cf. 20:14). Thus, the popular saying proves true: "If we're born twice, we only die once; if we're born only once, we die twice." Everyone experiences physical birth, but those not born again face the "second death" of eternal damnation. As we have already seen, the New Testament never describes the physical death of the believer as dying, but rather as falling asleep.

Then, mysteriously, Satan is released and allowed to deceive the nations once more. A final rebellion is quashed in a fiery judgment from heaven, and the devil is thrown into the lake of fire and sulfur, where the beast, the false prophet, and he will be tormented forever (Rev. 20:7–10). Evidently, God allows this final rebellion as evidence of unregenerate humankind's recalcitrance, even in the face of Christ's visible, glorious earthly reign! The resurrection and judgment of the unrighteous follows (20:11–15), about which more will be said later.

Premillennialism is often seen as more pessimistic than the other viewpoints. In view of its portrayal of world events prior to Christ's return, this is not an unfair description. But it can also be depicted as more realistic, in that it sees Scripture as pointing to a necessary divine intervention to put a final end to evil. Historic premillennialism could be seen as perhaps more pessimistic, since, unlike dispensational premillennialism, it does not allow for a secret rapture of the church prior to the Great Tribulation. Even so, historic premillennialism has gained increasing recognition in the last few decades. The numerous writings of George Eldon Ladd have been especially influential in gaining serious consideration of this viewpoint. Also, a number of well-known Christians have publicly endorsed this position, often to the surprise of their admirers.

Corrie ten Boom, having experienced firsthand the tribulation of the death camps during World War II, saw those who taught a pretribulation rapture as false prophets. She noted that much of the church today is already experiencing tremendous suffering and persecution. Pat Robertson, certainly one of the "major religious figures of the twentieth century" and a leading evangelical voice,[62] also espouses historic premillennialism, as evidenced in his powerful novel depicting *The End of the Age*.[63] In many

[62] See Tim Stafford's excellent portrayal of Robertson in these terms in: "Robertson R Us," *Christianity Today* (August 12, 1996), 26–33.

[63] Pat Robertson, *The End of the Age* (Dallas: Word, 1995).

conservative quarters, dispensational premillennialism—with its seven dispensations, eight covenants, and pretribulation rapture teachings—was assumed to be the "authorized" position. But the "minority opinion" of historic premillennialism is gaining ground.

Dispensationalism sees itself more as an approach to the interpretation of the Bible than anything else.[64] It has had a wide influence, in no small measure because of the publication of the *Scofield Reference Bible* in 1909. C. I. Scofield, a former lawyer, popularized the dispensational teachings of J. N. Darby in this excellent study Bible filled with succinct interpretative annotations. Many people are aware of only *one* brand of premillennial teaching—this one. And perhaps no one has popularized this approach more than Hal Lindsey in his *The Late Great Planet Earth*,[65] a milestone in religious publishing, resulting in thousands professing faith in Jesus Christ as Savior and Lord. Literally dozens of titles expounding this viewpoint can be found on religious publication lists at any given time, and a comprehensive bibliography would contain hundreds of volumes. More recently, the mammoth publishing coup of the *Left Behind* series has raised public awareness of the dispensational view. There is nothing like a rousing, captivating tale to rivet attention while disseminating doctrine—Jesus even used this technique!

The distinctives of dispensational eschatology include a highlighting of the role of Israel in end-time scenarios and a pretribulation rapture of the church prior to the seven years of the Great Tribulation. The Millennium from this perspective primarily concerns the fulfillment of God's promises to Israel. Understanding the Great Tribulation to be a precise seven-year period (Daniel's seventieth week: Dan. 9:27), dispensationalists believe that the church will be raptured prior to these end-time woes (see 1 Thess. 4:13–18). A mediating position between the pre- and posttribulational views place the Rapture in the *middle* of the Great Tribulation, just prior to the catastrophic last three-and-a-half years.[66] Then there are partial-rapture theories in which the Lord catches up his saints in stages according to their readiness.[67]

---

[64] Compare Charles Caldwell Ryrie, *Dispensationalism Today* (Chicago: Moody Press, 1965), 9–21.

[65] Hal Lindsey (with C. C. Carlson), *The Late Great Planet Earth* (Grand Rapids: Zondervan, 1970).

[66] For a helpful comparison and interaction among these positions see: *The Rapture: Pre-, Mid-, or Post-Tribulational?* (Grand Rapids: Zondervan, 1984), in which the various viewpoints are presented, advocated, and critiqued by Richard R. Reiter, Paul D. Feinberg, Gleason L. Archer Jr., and Douglas J. Moo.

[67] See Millard J. Erickson, *Contemporary Options in Eschatology* (Grand Rapids: Baker, 1977), 109–81.

My wife epouses the pretribulational position, and I am more convinced by the posttribulational arguments. I once asked her, "What if the Lord raptures us according to our beliefs, taking the pre-folks prior to the Great Tribulation, mid- in the middle, and post- at the end? Would you be willing to wait around for me?" She replied, "No sir, I will be going up!" And I added, "And I will be holding on to your feet!" Perhaps a little humor and tolerance *is* in order as we explore these issues![68]

Postmillennialism

Because premillennialism, especially dispensational premillennialism, has been so predominant in conservative circles in the twentieth century, many are shocked to learn that the postmillennial position was the prevalent perspective of the conservatives of the late eighteenth century and throughout most of the nineteenth century.[69] Behind this mindset lay the great Puritan heritage that brought believers to America's shores in search of religious freedom and opportunity.[70] Jonathan Edwards, perhaps the greatest mind America has produced and a key leader of the First Great Awakening, was a postmillennialist. The impressive list of stalwart exponents of this view includes Daniel Whitby, John Wesley, John Gill, Matthew Henry, Adam Clarke, John Owen, Charles Hodge, B. B. Warfield, Robert L. Dabney, A. H. Strong, B. H. Carroll, and, in our own day, Loraine Boettner, J. Marcellus Kik, and John Jefferson Davis.[71]

It is helpful to point out what this brand of eschatological teaching is *not*. It is not a version of the perennial secular quest for utopia. This is no Darwinian social optimism, liberal social gospel, universalism, or belief in the Manifest Destiny of America.[72] At the same time, the long shadow of Puritanism is clearly evident in conservative American

---

68 On the pre- and posttribulational debate it is helpful to compare John F. Walvoord, *The Rapture Question* (Grand Rapids: Zondervan, 1957), and George E. Ladd, *The Blessed Hope* (Grand Rapids: Eerdmans, 1956). Ladd's *The Last Things: An Eschatology for Laymen* (Grand Rapids: Eerdmans, 1978) is a convenient summary of the eschatological teachings of Scripture. Dave MacPherson's *The Incredible Cover-Up: The True Story on the Pre-Trib Rapture* (Plainfield, N.J.: Logos International, 1975) is a fascinating "detective story" on the origins of the pretribulational teaching.

69 Grenz, *The Millennial Maze*, 66.

70 See Murray, *The Puritan Hope*.

71 Compare Moody, *The Word of Truth*, 553–55; John Jefferson Davis, *Christ's Victorious Kingdom: Postmillennialism Reconsidered* (Grand Rapids: Baker, 1986), 7–22.

72 Davis, *Christ's Victorious Gospel*, 12–16.

Christianity, and many have held strongly to the belief that divine providence has designated America as a gospel lighthouse for the planet.

More recent and controversial forms of postmillennialism can be found in the Reconstructionism of Rousas J. Rushdoony, Gary North, Greg Bausen, David Chilton, and Gary DeMar, as well as the "Kingdom Now" teachings of charismatics such as Earl Paulk and Bill Hamon (influenced by the earlier "Latter Rain" movement). The "constitutionalism" of Herb Titus and Gary Amos, especially associated with the earlier years of Regent University (then known as CBN University), is also a "kissing cousin" of these "dominion" theologies. And the larger context of these movements is the resurgent political activism of the Christian Right during the 1980s.[73]

The strength and attractiveness of postmillennialism, in its traditional conservative Christian form, is its optimism, its scriptural belief in the *present* dimension of the kingdom, and its confidence in the power of the gospel and in the power of the Holy Spirit to transform this world through the work and witness of the church. John Jefferson Davis has shown just how appealing the postmillennial perspective can be in his *Christ's Victorious Kingdom.* He provides an apt summary of this position as follows:

> 1. Through the preaching of the gospel and dramatic outpourings of the Holy Spirit Christian missions and evangelism will attain remarkable success, and the church will enjoy an unprecedented period of numerical expansion and spiritual vitality.
>
> 2. This period of spiritual prosperity, the millennium, understood as a long period of time, is to be characterized by conditions of increasing peace and economic well-being in the world as a result of the growing influence of Christian truth.
>
> 3. The millennium will also be characterized by the conversion of large numbers of ethnic Jews to the Christian faith (Rom. 11:25–26).
>
> 4. At the end of the millennial period there will be a brief period of apostasy and sharp conflict between Christian and evil forces (Rev. 20:7–10).
>
> 5. Finally and simultaneously there will occur the visible return of Christ, the resurrection of the righteous and the wicked, the final judgment, and the revelation of the new heavens and the new earth.[74]

---

[73] Bruce Barron has provided excellent access to and analysis of these developments in *Heaven on Earth? The Social and Political Agendas of Dominion Theology* (Grand Rapids: Zondervan, 1992).

[74] Davis, *Christ's Victorious Kingdom,* 10–11, citing Clarence Augustine Beckwith, "The Millennium," *The New Schaff-Herzog Encyclopedia of Religious Knowledge,* ed. Samuel Macauley Jackson, 13 vols. (New York: Funk and Wagnalls, 1910), 7:377.

Obviously, there is little to offend in this scenario! The question is, is it an accurate biblical portrayal of end-time events, and is its optimism fully grounded? The preceding analysis of Jesus' eschatological teachings and of premillennialism would suggest not.

However, the strong confidence in the King and his present kingdom is a welcome antidote to some of the depression and fatalism one encounters at times among premillennialists. If premillennalists are sometimes alarmist, and amillennialists sometimes apathetic, the voice of postmillennialism will at the very least sound the call to optimistic *action*, no matter how much evil seems to be mounting in the world.

At the same time, it must be acknowledged that the "post-" position is a minority one—and understandably so in view of the two world wars, the proliferation of warfare globally, the rise of terrorism, the economic uncertainties, and the moral collapse of Western civilization. The postmillennialist would simply remind us that such developments could be seen as mere temporary setbacks. But both premillennialists and amillennialists are more inclined to see them as "signs of the times." Historically, as postmillennialism declined in previous generations, amillennialism grew, since the two positions had much in common.

Amillennialism

Because the teachings of postmillennialism and amillennialism are so similar, great saints of the past, such as Augustine and Calvin, have been claimed by both groups. Both see the Millennium as symbolic and the book of Revelation as a whole as descriptive of the church age rather than as a chronological account of end-time events. But whereas postmillennialism believes in an extended literal reign of Christ on this planet (albeit through the church), amillennialists jettison all literal conceptions of a Millennium in favor of the simpler scenario of a second coming followed immediately by the last judgment and the new heavens and earth.

Historically, there has been a decided advantage to this simplicity. Postmillennialism can be parochial at times, with groups as diverse as Southern Baptists (remember B. H. Carroll) and Reconstructionists "bringing in the kingdom." Premillennialists are prone to flights of fancy as they read with the Bible in one hand and the newspaper in the other: "The Pope is the Antichrist. No, it's Kennedy, Kissinger, Gorbachev, or Saddam Hussein!" Confident assertions are made about every beast's horn and angel's trumpet. Certainly, we premills have been shown to have "feet of clay" (see Dan. 2)! At the same time, there is a vigilance among premillennialists that amillennialists could borrow at times.

Whatever our millennial view, we should remain centered on Christ himself and strong in our optimistic and certain hope of his return.

Generally speaking, amillennialists have shown themselves to be sane, sensible, and scholarly exegetes of Scripture. Even though I embrace the premill position, some of my favorite books on eschatology have been written by amillennialists. Anthony Hoekema's *The Bible and the Future* is a capable and serviceable overview of the biblical doctrine of eschatology. Stanley Grenz provides perhaps the best guide through *The Millennial Maze.* My one problem with these brothers and sisters is their handling of Revelation in general and the two resurrections of chapter 20 in particular.[75]

Whatever our millennial view, we should remain centered on Christ himself and strong in our optimistic and certain hope of his return. After all, the clear overriding purpose of Revelation is to provide us with a transforming glimpse of the grandeur of our conquering Savior, whose return we all eagerly await. As is often the case, Baptist patriarch E. Y. Mullins offers sage, practical advice in this area:

> We should ever be as men who look for their Lord, because he commanded it, and because we love him and trust him, and because all the future would be blank without him. He is the key which unlocks for us the hidden things of the coming ages. But we should not become absorbed in apocalyptic calculations and speculations. We should not be so assured of the program of the unrevealed future that we "begin to beat our fellow servants" because they do not accept our particular interpretation (Matt. 24:49). We should not attempt to fix dates or insist too greatly upon detailed programs. We should be faithful in every detail of

---

[75] The following additional resources are indispensable to this discussion: Robert G. Clouse, ed., *The Meaning of the Millennium: Four Views* (Downers Grove, Ill.: InterVarsity Press, 1977), with presentations and interactions by George Eldon Ladd (historic premillennialism), Herman A. Hoyt (dispensational premillennialism), Loraine Boettner (postmillennialism), and Anthony A. Hoekema (amillennialism); and Millard J. Erickson, *Contemporary Options in Eschatology: A Study of the Millennium* (Grand Rapids: Baker, 1977). *The Millennial Maze* by Stanley Grenz examines each position in its most favorable light, showing the contribution of each, and is, in my opinion, the most up-to-date and constructive analysis available at the time of this writing. (Grenz himself takes a nuanced amillennial stance.)

> duty. We should ever watch against temptation and pray for divine strength. We should cultivate a passion for righteousness, individual and social. We should work while it is day, knowing that the night cometh when no man can work. We should be so eager for the coming of our Lord, that if he should come tomorrow we would not be taken by surprise. We should so hold ourselves in restraint, that if his return should be delayed a thousand or ten thousand years, we would not be disappointed. And our hearts should be ever filled with joy at the prospect of his coming and the certain triumph of his kingdom.[76]

Ultimately, all who accept the full authority of Scripture are agreed that the end of the age entails the resurrection of the dead, the final judgment, and the new heavens and new earth. As we culminate our consideration of Christian hope, we will briefly explore each of these subjects.

Resurrection

The centrality of the resurrection to Christian faith has already been emphasized in our study of the person and work of Christ as well as in our mention of the future glorification of the saints. Indeed, even the doctrine of creation contains this ingredient in terms of the final liberation of the universe from decay. Continually in biblical religion our vision is being directed toward the *eschaton*—the ultimate victory of our Lord at his second coming, the judgment, and the culmination of the new creation. Our present new life in Christ is literally a "foretaste of glory divine": Resurrection life begins at the new birth!

Spiritually speaking, we have *already* been raised with Christ (Col. 2:12–13; 3:1) and our lives are "hidden with Christ in God" (3:3). "When Christ who is [our] life is revealed, then [we] also will be revealed with him in glory" (3:4). God has "made us alive together with Christ" and "raised us up with him and seated us with him in the heavenly places in Christ" (Eph. 2:5–6). Our baptism vividly depicts our identification with Christ in his death and resurrection. It marks the beginning of a whole new life. "Therefore we have been buried with him by baptism into death, so that, just as Christ was raised from the dead by the glory of the Father, so we too might walk in newness of life" (Rom. 6:4). Paul adds

[76] Edgar Young Mullins, *The Christian Religion in Its Doctrinal Expression* (Nashville: Broadman, 1917), 471–72; cf. Grenz, *The Millennial Maze*, 214–15.

that our identification with Christ's death guarantees our being "united with him in a resurrection like his" (6:5). The "Spirit is life" in us *right now,* and this also means that our mortal bodies will be made alive in the future (8:10–11). Our covenant-keeping God, who has already given us new life, will complete our salvation at the resurrection.

This was precisely the point Jesus made to his opponents, the Sadducees, during Passion Week. There have always been rationalistic religious opponents of the supernatural. Attempting to trick Jesus with a hypocritical challenge concerning the resurrection (Matt. 22:23–33; Mark 12:18–27; Luke 20:27–40), the Sadducees, a prime example of such "spiritual skepticism," found themselves soundly rebuked by our Lord: "You are wrong, because you know neither the scriptures nor the power of God" (Matt. 22:29). This prescription applies to the contemporary scene as well. Failure to acknowledge the *totality* of the Scriptures, of which the Sadducees were guilty in Jesus' day and liberal scholarship is prone today, always results in a distortion of our faith and hope. It results in an ignorance of the Scriptures, and a lack of a full knowledge and experience of God's power also results in spiritual ignorance.

At least the Pharisees were able to acknowledge the reality of the end-time resurrection. Scripture passages such as Isaiah 26:19; Ezekiel 37:12–14; and Daniel 12:2 had rightly convinced them of a future resurrection. The Sadducees, however, did not acknowledge the full authority of such Scriptures. Therefore Jesus quoted to them one of their own key Scriptures as proof of the resurrection: "I am the God of Abraham, the God of Isaac, and the God of Jacob" (Mark 12:26; see Ex. 3:6). He then continued, "He is God not of the dead, but of the living; you are quite wrong" (Mark 12:27). William L. Lane summarizes the thrust of Jesus' argument:

> In citing Ex. 3:6 Jesus showed how resurrection faith is attached in a profound way to the central concept of biblical revelation, the covenant, and how the salvation promised by God to the patriarchs and their descendants in virtue of the covenant contains implicitly the assurance of the resurrection. It was the failure to appreciate the essential link between God's covenant faithfulness and the resurrection which had led the Sadducees into their grievous error.[77]

Likewise for us, if "for this life only we have hoped in Christ, we are of all people most to be pitied" (1 Cor. 15:19). But Christ *is* risen. And

---

[77] William L. Lane, *The Gospel According to Mark* (NICNT; Grand Rapids: Eerdmans, 1974), 430.

our glorification is so certain that Paul could say in Romans 8:30 that we are "glorified"—past tense! Our resurrection is as certain as God's sovereignty!

Jesus' words concerning the resurrection were unequivocal:

> Very truly, I tell you, the hour is coming, and is now here, when the dead will hear the voice of the Son of God, and those who hear will live. For just as the Father has life in himself, so he has granted the Son also to have life in himself; and he has given him authority to execute judgment, because he is the Son of Man. Do not be astonished at this; for the hour is coming when all who are in their graves will hear his voice and will come out—those who have done good, to the resurrection of life, and those who have done evil, to the resurrection of condemnation. (John 5:25–29)

His response to Martha's affirmation of the last day resurrection (John 11:24) is equally clear: "I am the resurrection and the life. Those who believe in me, even though they die, will live, and everyone who lives and believes in me will never die" (11:25–26).

The apostle Paul regarded the doctrine of the resurrection as essential to the gospel message itself (1 Cor. 15). He argues cogently for the necessity of both Christ's resurrection and ours (15:12–19) and explains by analogy how the resurrection body evinces both continuity and contrast with our present earthly bodies (15:35–49). Our spiritual bodies are the result of transformation and metamorphosis and will live forever—like our Savior (15:50–57). Therefore, we should "be steadfast, immovable, always excelling in the work of the Lord, because [we] know that in the Lord [our] labor is not in vain" (15:58).

The Great White Throne Judgment

The premillennial, posttribulational interpretation of Revelation 20 sees two resurrections: the resurrection of the righteous prior to the Millennium (20:4–6) and the resurrection of the unrighteous for judgment at the end of the Millennium (20:11–15). But all three millennial views acknowledge the final judgment. It is not death and taxes that are inescapable, but death and judgment (Heb. 9:27)! "Then I saw a great white throne and the one who sat on it; the earth and the heaven fled from his presence, and no place was found for them. And I saw the dead, great and small, standing before the throne, and the books were opened" (Rev. 20:11–12).

This is how John begins his description of the last judgment. Cosmic changes are indicated at the outset, and the universal nature of the event is highlighted. *We will all someday face this judgment.* Until the liberal experiment in modern theology, this basic tenet of the faith—found in all the ecumenical creeds and virtually every ecclesiastical confession—was unquestioned.

We will all someday face judgment before the throne.

The testimony of Scripture is strong; but once its authority was undermined, this doctrine, like many others, was challenged. H. Richard Niebuhr summarized well the "new" approach: "A God without wrath brought men without sin into a kingdom without judgment through the ministrations of a Christ without a cross."[78] In actuality, even apart from the extensive biblical teaching, the reasoning behind a final judgment is convincing. Liberal rationalism at this juncture is simply short-circuited. Life without ultimate accountability, history without a final tribunal, and evil without divine retribution constitute innate meaninglessness. Our sense of worth as human beings is tied up with this admittedly terrifying reality. Combined with the gospel, however, it provides the only adequate basis for the ultimate significance of life.

As has already been indicated through previous pages, Jesus Christ is coming to raise and judge the dead. He came the first time not to judge but to save, and he sacrificed his life for us (see John 3:14–17). He will come a second time as a conquering king to judge the world and to complete that saving work. As the Son of Man on his throne of glory, he tells us, he will one day separate the righteous from the wicked and assign them their ultimate destiny (Matt. 25:31–46). Christians who know him as the one "who is to judge the living and the dead" and who anticipate "his appearing and his kingdom" (2 Tim. 4:1) live differently. "For all of us must appear before the judgment seat of Christ, so that each may receive recompense for what has been done in the body, whether good or evil" (2 Cor. 5:10).

To pass judgment on one another now is vain in view of the fact that "we will all stand before the judgment seat of God" (Rom. 14:10; note the context). As individuals we cannot even adequately judge ourselves:

---

[78] H. Richard Neibuhr, *The Kingdom of God in America* (New York: Harper & Row, 1937), 193.

"It is the Lord who judges [us]" (1 Cor. 4:4; again, note the context). One day all our works will be tested by fire (3:12–15); thus, only our Lord's assessment ultimately matters! The apostle Paul warned the intellectual elite of Athens:

> While God has overlooked the times of human ignorance, now he commands all people everywhere to repent, because he has fixed a day on which he will have the world judged in righteousness by a man whom he has appointed, and of this he has given assurance to all by raising him from the dead. (Acts 17:30–31)

The apostle Peter told his hearers at Cornelius's house that Jesus was "the one ordained by God as judge of the living and the dead" (Acts 10:42). James, the Lord's brother and leader of the Jerusalem church, counseled patience "until the coming of the Lord" (James 5:7): "Strengthen your hearts, for the coming of the Lord is near. Beloved, do not grumble against one another, so that you may not be judged. See, the Judge is standing at the doors!" (5:8–9). The expectation of Jesus' return as Savior and Judge determines both our message and our manner(s)!

> *The last judgment has a different dynamic for believers from that of unbelievers.*

In alerting his Jewish readers to their need of the gospel, Paul made a strong appeal to the final judgment (which surely sobered his Gentile readers as well; see Rom. 2:1–16). He refers to "the day of wrath, when God's righteous judgment will be revealed" (2:5). He further depicts the contrasting states of the righteous and wicked, reminding all that "God shows no partiality" (2:6–11). According to Paul's gospel, "God, through Jesus Christ, will judge the secret thoughts of all" (2:16).

At the same time, the last judgment has a different dynamic for believers from that of unbelievers. It is surely a sobering reality to realize that one day our works are going to be judged and rewards are going to be given. Undoubtedly, this fact is a strong motivation for diligence in our Christian walk. Nevertheless, the judgment for us is not for the purpose of determining our eternal destiny. That has already been determined through our acceptance by faith of God's judgment of our sins at Calvary. "There is therefore now no condemnation for those who are in Christ Jesus" (Rom. 8:1). In addition, the Bible indicates that we will actually share with Christ, in part, in this process of judgment (Matt.

19:28; Luke 22:28–30; 1 Cor. 6:2–3; Rev. 3:21; 20:4). What precisely that will entail we are not told, but it is an exhilarating thought! Thus, the final judgment does not engender in the mind of the believer the sense of dread that inevitably haunts the unbeliever who contemplates this reality.

The works of all will be judged on that day—not because we are justified by works but because of the inseparability of faith and works. Works are ultimately revelatory of character, and the true character of all will be revealed on that day. W. T. Conner discerns a threefold purpose for the last judgment as depicted in the Scriptures. The first is revelatory: "to bring out into the light every man's character as revealed in his words and deeds in relation to his fellow man and in the effects of his deeds upon the lives of others." Sin is, in the final analysis, the failure to live together *in a community of love* (see Mark 12:29–31). Our refusal to love God and each other will be judged on that day. God reveals our character at the final judgment.

Second, God assigns our eternal destiny. This is, of course, based on our revealed nature. "Everyone who loves is born of God and knows God. Whoever does not love does not know God, for God is love" (1 John 4:7, 8). Those outside God's community of love will be assigned to that place of eternal lovelessness called hell.

Third, at the last judgment history will be brought to a proper fulfillment, and God will thereby be vindicated in all his ways.[79]

> If it were only to assign the individual, strictly speaking as an individual, his destiny in accordance with character, then the judgment might possibly not be a necessity. But God created man as a race, not as isolated individuals; the race as a race fell in the sin of the first man; God provided redemption for the race in the last Adam; he preserves and governs the race in him; and he will judge the race at his final manifestation. It is especially stressed in the New Testament that the judgment is to be universal (Matt. 25:32; Rom. 14:10; Rev. 20:13). All men will be there, and the affairs of the race in its history in time on the earth will be consummated. God's ways with man will be vindicated.[80]

This great Baptist theologian goes right to the core issues, stating them in plain, straightforward language!

---

79 Conner, *The Gospel of Redemption*, 340–41.

80 Ibid., 341–42.

Hell

At the great white throne judgment "the book of life" is opened, and those whose names are not found therein are thrown into "the lake of fire," which is also called "the second death" (Rev. 20:12–15). What John describes here is traditionally referred to as hell.

Because the Lord's thoughts and ways are not ours and are infinitely higher than ours (Isa. 55:8–9), it should not surprise us to discover that traditional concepts of heaven and hell are generally the antithesis of reality. God values just the opposite of what sinful humankind values. Therefore, at the end of the age, the prophetic voice tells us time and again, everything will be turned upside down. Mary, the mother of Jesus, exulted: "He has brought down the powerful from their thrones, and lifted up the lowly; he has filled the hungry with good things, and sent the rich away empty" (Luke 1:52–53). We are enamored with the rich and famous. "But," says Jesus, "many who are first will be last, and the last will be first" (Matt. 19:30).

In popular mythology all the good people go to heaven and all the bad people go to hell. God puts all our good deeds on one side of the scale and all our bad deeds on the other, and the tip of the scale determines our eternal destiny. But as Shirley C. Guthrie comments, "According to Jesus and the writers of the New Testament, the truth is just the opposite: *Heaven is for sinners and hell is for 'good' people.*"[81] Jesus talked about hell more than anybody, but it was always with the "church folk," not the "sinners." "I have not come to call respectable people [the righteous], but outcasts [sinners]," he said (Matt. 9:13 GNB). We must be aware that we are sick and need a physician (9:12). The bottom line is whether we want God to be God in his universe or whether *we* prefer to be. "The wicked man finds himself thus in the strange position of being in God's universe, and yet he is neither God nor God's servant."[82]

C. S. Lewis always communicated divine truth in pithy and powerful ways:

> There are only two kinds of people in the end: those who say to God, "Thy will be done," and those to whom God says, in the end, "*Thy* will be done." All that are in Hell, choose it. Without that self-choice there

---

[81] Shirley C. Guthtrie, *Christian Doctrine,* rev. ed. (Louisville: Westminster John Knox, 1994), 396–97 (Guthrie's italics).

[82] Mullins, *The Christian Religion in Its Doctrinal Expression,* 489.

could be no Hell. No soul that seriously and constantly desires joy will ever miss it. Those who seek find. To those who knock it is opened.[83]

Jesus informs us that hell was "prepared," *not* for humankind but "for the devil and his angels" (Matt. 25:41). Nevertheless, he is crystal clear about the peril of hell. There is no better book to turn to for his comments on the subject than Matthew's Gospel.[84] John the Baptist was as hard on the Pharisees and Sadducees as Jesus was. Calling them to repentance, he warned of an impending judgment of "fire." The one to come (Jesus) would "clear his threshing floor," burning the chaff with "unquenchable fire" (Matt. 3:7–12).

In the first of the "six antitheses" of the Sermon on the Mount (5:21–48), Jesus says that having a murderous attitude in our heart makes us "liable to the hell [*geenna*] of fire" (5:22). Behind the Greek *geenna* is the Hebrew *ge hinnom*, the Valley of (the son[s]) Hinnom, located south and southwest of Jerusalem, where during the evil reigns of Ahaz and Manasseh children were sacrificed in fire to the god Molech (2 Chron. 28:3; 33:6). Good King Josiah defiled this location to prevent further such sacrifices and turned it into a place where refuse was continually burned (2 Kings 23:10). It became a prophetic symbol for divine judgment (Jer. 7:30–34) and finally for the last judgment of hell.

Thus, later in this same sermon Jesus warns that, in relation to adultery, we should take drastic measures to avoid both the *attitude* and the *act*. Metaphorically speaking, it is better to lose a member of our body than for our whole body to go into Gehenna, into hell (Matt. 5:27–30). In a later discourse Jesus used similar imagery, warning of "eternal fire" and of "the hell [*geenna*] of fire" (18:8–9). The Semitic language of exaggeration suggesting tearing out an eye or cutting off a hand or foot is meant to impress on us the horrors of hell, not to commend a literal carrying out of these acts. Otherwise, there would be a lot of sightless males in our churches. Sin destroys. Those who cling to sin rather than to the Savior face eternal destruction. Jesus concludes his sermon by stating that every "tree that does not bear good fruit is cut down and thrown into the fire" (7:19), that those who refuse his will and word will experience a great "fall" (destruction; 7:21–27).

In the narrative section that follows the Sermon on the Mount, Matthew relates the dramatic story of the Roman centurion whose ser-

---

[83] C. S. Lewis, *The Great Divorce* (New York: Macmillan, 1946), 72–73 (Lewis' italics).

[84] I am indebted for this insight to Gordon R. Lewis and Bruce A. Demarest, *Integrative Theology* (Grand Rapids: Zondervan, 1994), 3:478–79.

vant was healed through Jesus' word (8:5–13). Jesus commended the centurion's faith and warned the "heirs of the kingdom" that without such authentic faith they would "be thrown into the outer darkness, where there will be weeping and gnashing of teeth" (8:12). This description of hell reminds us not to interpret Jesus' metaphors literally, since fire and darkness are mutually exclusive. Nevertheless, this fact in no way lessens the horrors of hell. In the next teaching section, Jesus tells the Twelve: "Do not fear those who kill the body but cannot kill the soul; rather fear him [God] who can destroy both soul and body in hell [*geenna*]" (10:28). On the positive side, our Lord is saying in this context that the fear of the Lord casts out all other fears. On the negative side, he is again depicting the destructive nature of hell.

The judgment parables of the wheat and the weeds (Matt. 13:24–30, 36–43) and the dragnet (13:47–50) both teach that at "the end of the age" (13:39, 49), the wicked will be separated out by the angels and thrown "into the furnace of fire, where there will be weeping and gnashing of teeth" (13:42, 50). In the parable of the wedding banquet (22:1–14), though the invitation to the kingdom of heaven is broad, the way is narrow. The man who tried to enter the banquet on his own terms was bound and thrown "into the outer darkness, where there will be weeping and gnashing of teeth" (22:13). The parable of the talents (25:14–30) ends similarly. Finally, the parable of the last judgment describes hell as "eternal punishment" and heaven as "eternal life" (25:46). It is important to note that the same word—"eternal" [*aionion*]—is used to describe both. This observation will be important later when we consider annihilation and conditional immortality theories of hell.

Jesus reproached Chorazin and Bethsaida for their refusal to repent (Matt. 11:20–22), saying that "on the day of judgment it will be more tolerable for Tyre and Sidon than for you" (see also his warning to Capernaum, 11:23–24), suggesting degrees of punishment or suffering in hell (cf. Luke 12:41–48). He further described hell (*geenna*) as a place "where their worm never dies, and the fire is never quenched" (Mark 9:47–48, quoting Isa. 66:24). Again, the picture of Jerusalem's city dump, infested with maggots and burning with fire, comes to mind. A. T. Robertson remarks, "No figures of Gehenna can equal the dread reality which is here described."[85]

---

[85] A. T. Robertson, *Word Pictures in the New Testament*, vol. 1 (Nashville: Broadman), 347.

The apostle Paul draws on these images when he refers to the time "when the Lord Jesus is revealed from heaven with his mighty angels in flaming fire, inflicting vengeance on those who do not know God and on those who do not obey the gospel of our Lord Jesus." He continues: "These will suffer the punishment of eternal destruction, separated from the presence of the Lord and from the glory of his might" (2 Thess. 1:7–9).

Jesus did not hesitate to speak about hell, especially among those self-righteous ones who were unaware of their spiritual blindness and were misleading others:

> Woe to you, scribes and Pharisees, hypocrites! For you cross sea and land to make a single convert, and you make the new convert twice as much a child of hell [*geenna*] as yourselves.
>
> ... You snakes, you brood of vipers! How can you escape being sentenced to hell [*geenna*]? (Matt. 23:15, 33)

What a contrast with much of our soothing, insipid preaching today. As William V. Crockett has observed, "Even Hollywood, with its movies like *Ghost*, has a stronger message of coming judgment than most preachers in the pulpits of America."[86] Jonathan Edwards, a key leader in the First Great Awakening, preached "Sinners in the Hands of an Angry God" with great results. My own mother came into a saving relationship with Jesus Christ through the fear of the Lord induced by a sermon on the second coming of Jesus Christ.

> *If heaven is the Community of the Redeemed, then hell is the Community of the Damned.*

Nevertheless, we have probably all heard over-zealous preachers describing the torments of hell in graphic and literal terms (and seemingly enjoying it), as if the *physical* aspects of the suffering of hell, rather than the relational and spiritual, were all-important. The biblical picture emphasizing the mental anguish, loss, destruction, loneliness, separation, and darkness of hell should be our emphasis. Such horrors and torment, like fire itself, are incentive enough to heed the gospel. As evil seemingly increases in the world, we have a continuing portrayal of hell right before our eyes. More than one lost person has informed a witnessing Christian, "I'm living in hell right now." If heaven is the Community of the Redeemed, then hell

[86] William V. Crockett, "The Metaphorical View," in Crockett, ed., *Four Views of Hell*, 54.

is the Community of the Damned. Picture a totally godless society with no restraints on evil; that is what hell will be like. In mathematical terms, it is our present fallen world to the infinite power.

A Good God and an Eternal Hell—Reconcilable?

In recent years, however, theologians of renown within the evangelical community itself have questioned the traditional portrait of hell just outlined. Theories of annihilationism or conditional immortality are being given more serious consideration than ever before. The issues and concerns raised by these respected leaders deserve a fair hearing.

How can the portrait of a God of grace and goodness and the Christ who conquers evil, as we have already seen in our study of Scripture, be reconciled with the traditional understanding of hell just considered? If we are honest with ourselves, isn't the biblical picture of hell somewhat of an embarrassment to us? Is it really *just* for someone to suffer for all eternity for even a lifetime of sinful living? Could not a good and all-powerful God find some way to save all of us ultimately or at least find a more humane and reasonable way to right all wrongs and punish the wicked? If hell exists throughout all eternity, do we not have only a *partial* victory over evil?

We have already encountered at least the beginning of a response to such questions in what we have explored in previous chapters. Anselm's poignant presentation of the seriousness of sin (necessitating the death of Christ) is a starting place. After all, we have sinned against an infinite, holy, and loving God. Then, we must not forget how much God honors our *choice* in responding to his loving saving initiative. Hell is God's ultimate compliment to our freedom to choose our own way rather than his.

Nonetheless, such abstract reasoning, plausible though it may be, does not assuage the pain and sorrow we feel when contemplating the eternal destiny of someone we know and love dearly, but who never, as far as we can ascertain, accepted God's saving gift in Christ. Thus, in modern times, one can observe a trend away from literalistic interpretations of hell to metaphorical ones—and sometimes even toward universalism, or, at least among some conservatives, annihilationism.

It is a mistake, however, to assume that the metaphorical view is only of recent origin and that belief in a hell of literal fire has predominated the traditional approach. To be sure, literalism has loomed large in conservative circles, and the result has been a reticence to talk or preach much about hell. But the metaphorical approach has had historical precedence, as seen, for example, in John Calvin's writings. Calvin saw the physical depictions of the torments of hell in the New Testament as figurative and the essence of hell's wretchedness as being "cut off from all fellowship with God."[87] The evangelical tradition in general, it appears, has usually opted for the metaphorical position, as seen in the writings and/or preaching of such stalwarts as Billy Graham, Carl F. H. Henry, F. F. Bruce, Leon Morris, J. I. Packer, C. S. Lewis, Millard J. Erickson, Kenneth Kantzer, Ronald Youngblood, Donald Guthrie, D. A. Carson, and Roger Nicole.[88] If, as we have already seen, much of the end-time scenario is depicted in highly symbolic language in Scripture—including heaven, which we will consider next—why should some so stubbornly resist acknowledging this fact in relation to the Bible's portrayal of hell?

If we really believed in hell, we would be moved to avert as many as we could from its horrors.

Yet, even among those espousing the metaphorical view there seems to be a reluctance to face squarely the reality of hell. I often shock my students by claiming categorically that no one in the class really believes in hell—because if we did, we would be moved to avert as many as we could from its horrors. Further, if we truly had the heart of God in this matter, we would be moved often to tears at the very thought of the judgment. It is this tenderness of heart, sensitivity, and compassion for the lost that has prompted the evangelical giant John R. W. Stott to be open to the conditional view—that is, that hell ultimately entails God's allowing the lost simply to go out of existence rather than to suffer for all eternity.

Stott first published his thinking in this area in a "liberal-evangelical dialogue" with David L. Edwards.[89] At that time, he described his embracing the conditional view as tentative. Later, in a featured inter-

---

[87] John Calvin, *Institutes of the Christian Religion*, 2 vols., ed. John T. McNeill, trans. Ford Lewis Battles (Philadelphia: Westminster, 1960), 2:1,007–8 (III.xxv.12).

[88] See Crockett, ed., *Four Views on Hell*, 44–45 (from Crockett's presentation, "The Metaphorical View").

[89] David L. Edwards and John R.W. Stott, *Evangelical Essentials* (Downers Grove, Ill.: InterVarsity Press, 1988), 312–29.

view in *Christianity Today*, Stott described his position in relation to this view as "agnostic," concluding that both eternal punishment or annihilationism have "awkward texts" in the New Testament and that tolerance is called for in this debate.[90] At least this wise and respected leader had the courage to broach the issue!

Annihilationism and conditional immortality actually can be differentiated. *Annihilationism* can be taken as God's destroying ("with his heavenly blowtorch," to use Dale Moody's facetious description) the immortal soul of the lost person in the lake of fire, the second death. However, the Bible says that God alone is *by nature* immortal, and that immortality must be given to us by God. Therefore, *conditional immortality* denotes God's simply withholding the gift of immortality from the wicked at the last judgment. Thus, in this view there still remains a belief in an intermediate state of suffering for the lost and a further terrifying punishment at the last judgment before passing out of existence.

The conditional view raises such interpretive questions as: What if perishing, destruction, and the like in the New Testament can be taken in their straightforward sense? If the soul is *not* by nature immortal, then doesn't conditional immortality make even greater sense? Doesn't the conditional view provide a much fairer judgment of the wicked than does eternal punishment? Cannot this perspective provide just as great an incentive for openness to the gospel in view of the terrifying prospects awaiting unbelievers? It should be pointed out that a number of respected evangelical leaders have opted for this viewpoint and have provided cogent biblical and theological argument.[91]

Surely Stott's counsel of tolerance is appropriate to this debate. As it is, I still opt for the metaphorical view, although emotionally I often am drawn toward conditional immortality. Either fate is terrifying. Perhaps

---

90 Roy McCloughry, "Basic Stott," *Christianity Today* (January 8, 1996), 28.

91 See Clark Pinnock, "The Conditional View," in Crockett, ed., *Four Views on Hell*, 135–66 (cf. also Pinnock's responses to the other views presented); Philip Edgcumbe Hughes, *The True Image* (Grand Rapids: Eerdmans, 1989), 398–407; Stephen H. Travis, *Christian Hope and the Future of Man* (Downers Grove, Ill.: InterVarsity Press, 1980), 134–36; idem, *I Believe in the Second Coming of Jesus* (Grand Rapids: Eerdmans, 1982), 196–99; Michael Green, *Evangelism Through the Local Church* (Nashville: Thomas Nelson, 1990), 72–73. John W. Wenham raised the issues early on for evangelicals in *The Goodness of God* (Downers Grove, Ill.: InterVarsity Press, 1974), 34–41. Finally, Edward William Fudge has provided the most complete defense of conditional immortality in *The Fire That Consumes* (Houston: Providential Press, 1982). For a book that offers an extended critique of conditional immortality as well as universalism, see Christopher W. Morgan and Robert A. Peterson, eds., *Hell Under Fire: Modern Scholarship Reinvents Eternal Punishment* (Grand Rapids: Zondervan, 2004).

Jean-Paul Sartre's *No Exit* provides as poignant a contemporary parable of hell as can be found. In this well-known play three characters—Inez, Estelle, and Garcin—find themselves together after death. All of them died under circumstances that are clearly disgraceful. In the room where all three are confined, it soon becomes obvious that each of them is interested in the others only as an audience for his or her own attempts at self-justification and displays of self-pity. None cares for the others for any other reason. None shows any sign of gratitude or penitence; all are resentful and bitter.

As the play proceeds, it becomes plain that these three persons are doomed to remain alone together throughout eternity. The unheeded arguments repeat themselves in endless circles, and the emotional tension becomes unbearable. No sympathy. No love. No community. As the curtain descends on the scene of never-ending and ever-mounting frustration, the inmates sum up the significance of the drama in two desperate exclamations: "We shall be together forever! Hell is other people!" Significantly, on other lips these sentiments might describe the joys of heaven. "We shall be together forever"—the communion of saints in the life everlasting.[92]

It is to this glorious community of God in the new heaven and new earth that we now turn our attention.

Heaven

> Then I saw a new heaven and a new earth; for the first heaven and the first earth had passed away, and the sea was no more. And I saw the holy city, the new Jerusalem, coming down out of heaven from God, prepared as a bride adorned for her husband. And I heard a loud voice from the throne saying,
>
> "See, the home of God is among mortals.
> He will dwell with them as their God;
> they will be his peoples,
> and God himself will be with them;
> he will wipe every tear from their eyes.
> Death will be no more;
> mourning and crying and pain will be no more,
> for the first things have passed away."

---

[92] Bruce L. Shelley, *Christian Theology in Plain Language* (Dallas: Word, 1985), 219.

> And the one who was seated on the throne said, "See I am making all things new." (Rev. 21:1–5)

Thus John begins the final vision that forms a fitting climax both to the book of Revelation and to the entire Bible. This is what the saints of all the ages look forward to after the final judgment.

The new Jerusalem comes "down out of heaven" (Rev. 21:2). Now the prayer our Lord taught us to pray has been definitively answered: His kingdom *has* come and his will now will always be perfectly done *on earth as it is in heaven* (Matt. 6:10). Now heaven and earth are one. Now we "inherit the kingdom prepared for [us] from the foundation of the world" (Matt. 25:34). Now we "inherit the earth" (5:5).

Long ago, the Lord promised his people through Isaiah that he would "create new heavens and a new earth" that would last forever (Isa. 65:17; 66:22). This is the new heavens and new earth we have been waiting for, a place "where righteousness is at home" (2 Peter 3:13). And not only we, but the creation itself has been eagerly awaiting this day (Rom. 8:19–23). Now we get to see the ultimate place Christ has been preparing for us (John 14:1–3).

Immediately, we recognize that heaven is a *place*. It is where God our Father is (Matt. 6:9). Jesus ascended there and will return from there (Acts 1:11). Now both heaven and earth are renewed. In other words, "the creation in which we now live has a future"; what will transpire is a "transformation and renewal rather than a re-creation *ex nihilo*"![93] John's portrait of the new Jerusalem is dazzling. Again, we can only imagine how wonderful it will really be—no, we can't even imagine! What makes it so wonderful is that *God* is there in all his glory, dwelling among his people in all his radiant splendor (Rev. 21:3, 23–25).

"Death will be no more; mourning and crying and pain will be no more" (Rev. 21:4). And "nothing unclean will enter" the Holy City (21:27). The earth has been cleansed (2 Peter 3:10).

> Nothing accursed will be found there any more. But the throne of God and of the Lamb will be in it, and his servants will worship him; they will see his face, and his name will be on their foreheads. And there will be no more night; they need no light of lamp or sun, for the Lord God will be their light, and they will reign forever and ever. (Rev. 22:3–5)

---

[93] Gale Z. Heide, "What Is New about the New Heaven and the New Earth? A Theology of Creation from Revelation 21 and 2 Peter 3," *JETS* 40 (March 1997): 55.

This is the city, the community, the family, the fellowship, the joy, the perfection, the kingdom, the commonwealth, and the paradise for which we have all been longing!

Jesus Christ has made it all possible! His words to us are, "Surely I am coming soon"; and our response, appropriately, is, "Amen. Come, Lord Jesus!" (Rev. 22:20).

10 | Love
What Is God's Plan for the Church?

And now faith, hope, and love abide, these three; and the greatest of these is love.

—1 Corinthians 13:13

The first of all the commandments is: "Hear, O Israel, the L*ORD* *our God, the* L*ORD* *is one. And you shall love the* L*ORD* *your God with all your heart, with all your soul, with all your mind, and with all your strength." This is the first commandment. And the second, like it, is this: "You shall love your neighbor as yourself." There is no other commandment greater than these.*

—Mark 12:29–31 NKJV

By this everyone will know that you are my disciples, if you have love for one another.

—John 13:35

Go therefore and make disciples of all nations.

—Matthew 28:19

I will build my church.

—Matthew 16:18

THERE WAS ONCE A FIRST-CENTURY JEWISH MAN, born in Bethlehem, raised in Nazareth, who changed the course of human history. He came to his own people, the people of God, but they did not welcome him. He spoke much about the kingdom of God and performed many miraculous signs that pointed to the reality of this kingdom. He gathered a small group of men around him, who became the nucleus of a worldwide movement that would turn empires upside down and change the lives of untold billions: the church

"I Will Build My Church"

In every chapter of this book we have mentioned two fundamental realities: the kingdom and the church. This kingdom/church leitmotif has unified all that has been presented. The concluding chapters, entitled "Faith," "Hope," and "Love," are designed to provide a progression toward the concrete expression of the Christian faith known as the church. This one doctrine confronts us daily, for good or ill, in almost every part of the globe.

> *Christianity is a community of faith centered around the person of Jesus Christ.*

Christianity is a community of faith centered around the person of Jesus Christ.[1] It is a Trinitarian community of hope, experiencing and confessing God as Father, Son, and Holy Spirit. Further, it is a community that, according to its founder Jesus Christ, is marked supremely (or *should* be) as a fellowship of divine love. This community, known as the church, is the focus of our final chapter.

Amazingly, the founder of the church, Jesus Christ, stated categorically that he himself would build this community (Matt. 16:18). The emphasis is clear in the original: "I will build *my* church"! It is his church. Yet he spoke most often about the *kingdom,* and never did any of the things one would expect of an entrepreneur of a new religious organization. (Jesus always seemed to make it a point to surprise everyone!) What is the nature of the movement he himself launched two millennia ago?

---

[1] See Dale Moody, *The Word of Truth* (Grand Rapids: Eerdmans, 1982), 1.

One thing is certain: The testimony of the New Testament is that true Christianity entails two things: (1) being in union with the person of Christ and (2) being in fellowship with the body of Christ, the church.[2] The notion of a churchless Christianity is a heresy, created by the TV generations that closed out the twentieth century. But what precisely is the church?

What Is the Church?

Because the term itself has so many popular usages, confusion has reigned in relation to this question. Saying "The church is on fire!" could easily communicate two profoundly different realities: (1) "The building is in jeopardy; call the fire department!" or (2) "Those people are really spiritually *alive*!" "Church" can refer to a worship service, a denomination, a local congregation, or the universal people of God. But what do the Scriptures say?

Our English word "church" is derived from the Greek term *kyriakos*, meaning "belonging to the Lord." Biblical terminology sheds further light. A well-known New Testament word is the Greek *ekklesia*. Behind this term stands both a secular and a religious usage. In classical Greek this word referred to the assembly of the citizens of the city-state. In the Septuagint, this word most often translates the Hebrew *qahal*, referring to the assembly (gathering, congregation) of God's people. Another important Hebrew term, *ʿedah*, is usually rendered in the Septuagint as *synagoge*. Remembering that the Septuagint, the Greek translation of the Hebrew Scriptures, was the Bible of the New Testament Church, we can draw the conclusion that these Hebrew terms have informed the significance of *ekklesia* in the New Testament. In the most general sense, therefore, the word "church" in the New Testament refers to all true believers in Jesus Christ, at all times and places, as well as to the local gatherings of these, God's people.[3]

Matthew portrays Jesus as using *ekklesia* in both of these nuances. When Jesus said, "I will build *my* church" (Matt. 16:18, italics added), he was referring to the church *universal*. Later, in Matthew 18:15–20,

---

[2] Compare esp. Paul's letter to the Ephesians, which, as we have already said, can be aptly titled, "Christ and the Church."

[3] See Millard J. Erickson, *Introducing Christian Doctrine*, ed. L. Arnold Hustad (Grand Rapids: Baker, 1992), 330.

Jesus describes how discipline should be carried out in the *local* church (cf. v. 17). Both concepts are crucial to an accurate understanding of the church. Paul, for example, gives the Ephesians a majestic portrait of God's plan for his church universal, but he also refers to local congregations as "the church" and not merely as *part* of the church (e.g., 1 Cor. 1:2; 1 Thess. 1:1). Most of the time the word "church" in the New Testament refers to the local congregation. *This fact emphasizes the eternal significance of what goes on in every local congregation*!

At the same time, we should never become myopic or parochial in our concept of the church, forgetting the universal dimension of God's people. Each local church, though complete in itself, is also merely a local manifestation of the church universal, which is composed of all true believers. A quick survey reveals that the New Testament presents the church in Trinitarian terms—a beautiful tapestry of concepts related to the Father, the Son, and the Holy Spirit.

Images of the Church

The New Testament is filled with rich images of the church.[4] Dale Moody has conveniently organized some of the most important of these concepts in the Trinitarian pattern in which they are found in the New Testament. I will utilize his outline in this section:[5]

1. The Church in Relation to God
   a. The People of God
   b. The Temple of God
2. The Church in Relation to Christ
   a. The Body of Christ
   b. The Bride of Christ
3. The Church in Relation to the Holy Spirit
   a. The Fellowship (*koinonia*) of the Spirit
   b. The Ministry (*diakonia*) of the Spirit

---

[4] Paul S. Minear has perhaps provided us with the most thorough survey of these images: *Images of the Church in the New Testament* (Philadelphia: Westminster, 1960).

[5] Moody published three editions of his survey of New Testament images of the church. In chronological order they are: *Review and Expositor* 51 (April 1954): 204–16; *What Is the Church?* ed. Duke K. McCall (Nashville: Broadman, 1958), 15–27; and *The Word of Truth*, 440–48.

(1) (a) The church is the *people of God.* As the Gaither gospel song asserts, "God has always had a people!" In actuality, the church is the continuation of all that God began to do through Abraham, calling out a people unto himself for the salvation of the world. When God established his covenant with his people at Sinai, he said, "Now therefore, if you obey my voice and keep my covenant, you shall be my treasured possession out of all the peoples" (Ex. 19:5). Tragically, God's people were not faithful to this covenant, so ultimately God began to speak of another and better covenant in the future (Jer. 31:31–34; Ezek. 37:26–27; Heb. 8:8–12).

The church is the continuation of all that God began to do through Abraham.

When Jesus came as Messiah, preaching the gospel of the kingdom, God's people, the Jews, again refused to acknowledge his saving initiative. Jesus referred to his being "sent only to the lost sheep of the house of Israel" (Matt. 15:24; cf. 10:6). He finally had to warn them, however: "Therefore I tell you, the kingdom of God will be taken away from you and given to a people that produces the fruits of the kingdom" (21:43). George Eldon Ladd summarized the situation well:

> They were the sons of the Kingdom because it was Israel whom God had chosen and to whom He had promised the blessings of the Kingdom. The Kingdom was theirs by right of election, history, and heritage. So it was that our Lord directed His ministry to them and offered to them that which had been promised them. When Israel rejected the Kingdom, the blessings which should have been theirs were given to those who would accept them.[6]

The apostle Paul agonized over this situation (Rom. 9:1–5), but he also saw a coming day of restoration (11:25–32). At that time the Lord will no longer say, "You are not my people and I am not your God" (Hos. 1:9). Rather, he will say, "You are my people," and Israel will respond, "You are my God" (2:23).[7] Paul asserts that these words apply ultimately to both Jew and Gentile (Rom. 9:22–26).

Thus, although the church can rightfully be called "the Israel of God" (Gal. 6:16), in contrast to "Israel according to the flesh" (1 Cor.

[6] George Eldon Ladd, *The Gospel of the Kingdom* (Grand Rapids: Eerdmans, 1959), 107.

[7] See David L. Smith, *All God's People: A Theology of the Church* (Wheaton, Ill.: BridgePoint, 1996), 314.

10:18 NAB), it cannot be said that God has jettisoned the Jews in terms of his saving purposes. Neither can it be said that Israel was the "church" of the Old Testament era. The roles of Israel and the church in God's plan of redemption are similar yet distinct, as Paul explains in Romans 9–11. The descriptive phrase "the people of God," however, can rightfully be applied to both. Echoing these Old Testament themes, the apostle Peter wrote:

> But you are a chosen race, a royal priesthood, a holy nation, God's own people, in order that you may proclaim the mighty acts of him who called you out of darkness into his marvelous light.
>
> Once you were not a people,
> but now you are God's people;
> once you had not received mercy,
> but now you have received mercy. (1 Pet. 2:9–10)

The apostle Paul ransacks his vocabulary to characterize God's people, the church, as "saints" (*hagioi*; e.g., Rom. 1:7; 1 Cor. 1:2; 2 Cor. 1:1; Eph. 1:1; Phil. 1:1; Col. 1:2), "the elect" (*hoi eklektoi*; e.g., Rom. 8:33; 2 Tim. 2:10; see Col. 3:12; Titus 1:1), "beloved" (*egapemenoi*; e.g., Rom. 1:7; Col. 3:12; 1 Thess. 1:4; 2 Thess. 2:13), and "called" (*kletoi*; e.g., Rom. 1:6–7; 8:28; 1 Cor. 1:2, 24; 2 Thess. 2:13, 14).[8] Ridderbos summarizes the significance of these terms as follows:

> The leading idea of them all is this, that God has chosen and called a people to himself out of all peoples, as Abraham was called out of Ur, and believers have been called by the gospel of God's grace and to himself. As such they are his beloved, and they are holy, placed on God's side and separated from the world.[9]

(b) Both Paul and Peter closely relate the concept of the people of God to that of *the temple of God.* In the same context in which Paul cites several Old Testament passages referring to the people of God, he also describes the church as "the temple of the living God" (2 Cor. 6:16). Earlier the apostle had warned the Corinthians against doing any harm to that temple. "Do you not know that you are God's temple and that God's Spirit dwells in you? If anyone destroys God's temple, God will destroy that person. For God's temple is holy, and you are that temple"

---

[8] See Herman Ridderbos's excellent treatment in *Paul: An Outline of His Theology,* trans. John Richard De Witt (Grand Rapids: Eerdmans, 1975), 330–33.

[9] Ibid., 333.

(1 Cor. 3:16–17). How many church fights and splits might be averted if God's people had this sort of reverence toward God and his temple?

Paul depicts the church universal, uniting Jew and Gentile, in these words: "Through him [Christ] the whole structure is held together and grows into a temple sacred in the Lord; in him you also are being built together into a dwelling place of God in the Spirit" (Eph. 2:21–22 NAB). Should not such a vision of the church alter radically our attitudes toward one another across denominational lines?

Peter also speaks of the church as God's temple:

> So come to him, to the living stone which was rejected by men but chosen by God and of great worth to him. You also, as living stones, must be built up into a spiritual temple, and form a holy priesthood to offer spiritual sacrifices acceptable to God through Jesus Christ. (1 Pet. 2:4–5 REB)

While Solomon's temple and Herod's temple were magnificent, they pale in comparison to God's temple!

(2) (a) One of the most important Pauline metaphors for the church is the *body of Christ*. As Moody states, "The body of Christ is nothing less than the presence of Christ himself in the life and service of the Christian community."[10] God has made Christ "the head over all things for the church, which is his body, the fullness of him who fills all in all" (Eph. 1:22–23). Further, Paul presents the sevenfold unity of the Church in both a triadic and trinitarian fashion (4:4–6):

> one body, one Spirit, one hope
> one Lord, one faith, one baptism
> one God

The middle term of each triad is key: The one Spirit creates the one body and one hope. Faith is centered in the one Lord and is expressed in the one baptism. And "one God and Father of all, who is above all and through all and in all" (4:6) undergirds all.[11] The apostle then describes God's program for the building up of this body (4:7–16). Christ is "the head of the church" and "the Savior of the body" (5:23 NASB).

Colossians, "the twin letter of Ephesians," provides a similar picture of the church. Again, Christ's headship is stressed (Col. 1:18). As the head, Christ is the source of the life and growth of the body (2:19). As

---

[10] Moody, *The Word of Truth*, 445.

[11] I owe the insight into the triadic structure of this passage to James D. G. Dunn, *Baptism in the Holy Spirit* (London: SCM, 1970), 161–62.

his body (1:24), we are to allow "the peace of Christ" to rule in our hearts, to which we were called "in the one body" (3:15).[12]

(b) The church is also *the bride of Christ.* It is this image of the church that perhaps comes the closest to expressing the heart of the love relationship God desires to have with his people. The marriage metaphor looms large in the Scriptures. Israel's relationship with Yahweh is often couched in these terms, as God's people time and again are seen to be unfaithful to the covenant. Still the God of grace reaches out to them (cf., e.g., Isa. 54:5–8; 62:5; Jer. 2:2; 3:1–5, 14; 31:31–34; Ezek. 16; Hos. 2:16–20; 4:13–14; 9:1).

John the Baptist contrasted his preparatory ministry to that of the Messiah himself with these words: "He who has the bride [Jesus] is the bridegroom. The friend of the bridegroom [John], who stands and hears him, rejoices greatly at the bridegroom's voice" (John 3:29). In our culture, John would roughly be comparing himself to the best man, thus pointing everyone to the Savior.

Jesus referred to himself as the bridegroom on a number of occasions (Matt. 22:2; 25:1–13; Mark 2:18–20), using the wedding banquet as a metaphor in his kingdom message (see also Luke 14:7–14). As we have already seen, the end of the age is marked by the joining of the bride and bridegroom (Rev. 19:6–10; 21:2, 9, 17). Finally, Paul makes beautiful use of the marriage metaphor. To the church in Corinth he wrote these moving words:

> I feel a divine jealousy for you, for I promised you in marriage to one husband, to present you as a chaste virgin to Christ. But I am afraid that as the serpent deceived Eve by his cunning, your thoughts will be led astray from a sincere and pure devotion to Christ. (2 Cor. 11:2–3)

Ephesians provides simultaneous insight into both the husband/wife relationship and Christ's relationship to his church (Eph. 5:21–33). There is no more appropriate way for God to communicate to us the relationship of love, intimacy, and faithful commitment that he desires for us to have with him. If only the bride of Christ would take his words to heart.

(3) We must also understand the church in relation to the Holy Spirit. As we have already seen, the Spirit is mentioned or implied in some way in every image of the church we have studied thus far. John

---

[12] Later we will take an in-depth look at Paul's "body life" teachings in Rom. 12; 1 Cor. 12–14; and Eph. 4. The metaphor of the church as Christ's body is central to these teachings.

culminates his Revelation in part with the words, "The Spirit and the bride say, 'Come'" (Rev. 22:17), thus indicating the close relation between the Spirit and the church, the bride of Christ. Repeatedly in the letters to the seven churches, we read the exhortation, "Let anyone who has an ear listen to what the Spirit is saying to the churches" (2:7, 11, 17, 29; 3:6, 13, 22).

The Spirit's role in the body of Christ is even more evident.[13] Paul argues for the unity of the body of Christ. "For in one Spirit we were all baptized into one body—Jews or Greeks, slaves or free—and all were made to drink of one Spirit" (1 Cor. 12:13 ESV). The church is "a dwelling place of God in the Spirit" (Eph. 2:22 NAB). The Spirit dwells in us both corporately (1 Cor. 3:16) and individually (6:17–19). We literally are the temple of the Holy Spirit. It is the Spirit's presence that marks us off as the people of God. God redeems us and brings us into his family by sending his Son into history and sending "the Spirit of his Son into our hearts" (Gal. 4:4–7). In fact, "Anyone who does not have the Spirit of Christ does not belong to him" (Rom. 8:9).

The Spirit dwells in us both corporately and individually.

(a) Moody aptly summarizes the relation of the Spirit to the church. "The Holy Spirit transforms the sociological phenomenon, subject to the laws of other social groups, into a spiritual fellowship (*koinonia*) with a ministry (*diakonia*) of service."[14] First, the Church is *the fellowship of the Spirit* (2 Cor. 13:13; Phil. 2:1). Luke tells us that the early believers "devoted themselves to the apostles' teaching and fellowship, to the breaking of bread and the prayers" (Acts 2:42). These four elements are essential to the life of any vital church, as will be demonstrated more thoroughly later.

Fellowship (*koinonia*) is much more than enjoying cookies and Kool-Aid in the church basement while discussing the football game of the previous evening (although we should not be so "super-spiritual" as to preclude having good, clean Christian fun). Fellowship is *participating* together in the very life of God through his Spirit. This includes prayer, praise, witness, and service—and most of all love (*agape*) for God, for each other, and for those outside the fellowship. All of our relation-

[13] This will be seen even more clearly when we study the ministry of the church often referred to as "body life."

[14] Moody, *The Word of Truth*, 447.

ships will be marked by "the fruit of the Spirit": "love, joy, peace, patience, kindness, generosity, faithfulness, gentleness, and self-control" (Gal. 5:22).

(b) The church also can be seen as *the ministry of the Spirit.* The Spirit equips the body for ministry through the spiritual gifts (1 Cor. 12:1–11). "All these are activated by one and the same Spirit, who allots to each one individually just as the Spirit chooses" (v. 11). He empowers the church for her mission. "But you will receive power when the Holy Spirit has come upon you" (Acts 1:8). Being "filled with the Holy Spirit" results in an empowered witness for Christ (Acts 2:4; 4:8, 31; 9:17), and the Spirit gives us victory in spiritual warfare through "the sword of the Spirit, which is the word of God" (Eph. 6:17).[15]

All of these images (and many others in Scripture) effectively communicate the nature of the church. We have already seen that the church is both universal and local. But there is more to the nature of the church, and there are various forms that the church has taken down through the centuries. It is to these subjects that we now turn.

The Forms of the Church

Perhaps the best way to begin to explore the forms of the church is to refer to its *eschatological* and *historical* dimensions. When the writer of Hebrews contrasts Mount Sinai, where God formed his covenant with the Israelites in a dramatic display of his presence and power (Heb. 12:18–21; cf. Ex. 19), with Mount Zion, "the city of the living God, the heavenly Jerusalem" (Heb. 12:22–23; cf. Rev. 21:2), one becomes immediately aware of the eschatological dimension of the church. The saints of the past, now in heaven, and the saints of all the ages reunited at the end of the age ("the church [*ekklesia*] of the firstborn" [Heb. 12:23 NIV]) comprise the church in its *eschatological* dimension.

The saints now living throughout the earth make up the *historical* church, which, as we have already seen, should be viewed from both the universal and local perspectives. Because God's kingdom unites heaven and earth, time and eternity, the church exists in these two dimensions simultaneously. It is helpful, however, to explore further the forms in which the church can be found both in biblical times and in its present structures.

---

[15] Ibid., 447–48.

First, whenever God's people worship corporately—that is, when they are "in church" (*en ekklesia*; 1 Cor. 11:18; 14:19, 28, 35), when "the whole church comes together" (14:23)—this is a primary dimension of the people of God. The actual worship gathering itself is designated as "church" in the New Testament. Then, there are various forms of the local church as described in the New Testament.

Luke, in his first descriptive summary (in Acts) of the life of the early church, writes:

> Awe came upon everyone, because many wonders and signs were being done by the apostles. All who believed were together and had all things in common; they would sell their possessions and goods and distribute the proceeds to all, as any had need. Day by day, as they spent much time together in the temple, they broke bread at home [or "from house to house," NRSV margin] and ate their food with glad and generous hearts, praising God and having the goodwill of all the people. And day by day the Lord added to their number those who were being saved. (Acts 2:43–47)

The Pentecostal outpouring of the Holy Spirit had resulted in a vital, growing church. The signs and wonders of the apostles inspired a great reverential fear among the people (2:43). Further, they generously shared their possessions with one another (2:44–45).

Then Luke mentions two contexts in which the early believers met together: (1) the temple and (2) from house to house (Acts 2:46). Finally, he describes their vital fellowship and their supernatural growth as "day by day the Lord added to their number those who were being saved" (2:47). Apart from the example they provided for believers of subsequent generations, we should also note their congregational life. The temple continued to have a significant role among the early believers until they were ultimately driven out. But perhaps the most important thing to notice is the "house church" phenomenon that developed early on.

> *The Pentecostal outpouring of the Holy Spirit resulted in a vital, growing church.*

In effect, this pattern of public, institutional worship (the temple) coupled with the home fellowship (house church) has perpetuated itself in subsequent revivals among God's people. One thinks of Spener and seventeenth-century Pietism, the early Methodism of Wesley, the great awakenings in America, and the contemporary Pentecostal/charismatic revivals. The apostles used both contexts for the proclamation of the gospel (Acts 5:42), and Saul knew exactly where to go as he sought to imprison the believers, "ravaging the church by entering house after house" (8:3). Later Paul's letters would contain numerous references to various house churches: (1) Aquila and Prisca: "the church in their house" (Rom. 16:5; 1 Cor. 16:19); (2) Nympha: "the church in her house" (Col. 4:15); and (3) Philemon (along with Apphia and Archippus): "the church in your house" (Philem. 2).

The apostle also saw the *city* as a context for the church. He addresses "the church of God that is in Corinth" (1 Cor. 1:2; 2 Cor. 2:1). In the process, he makes it abundantly clear that the Corinthian church is complete in and of itself as well as vitally related to the universal church.

> To the church of God that is in Corinth, to those who are sanctified in Christ Jesus, called to be saints, together with all those who in every place call on the name of our Lord Jesus Christ, both their Lord and ours. (1 Cor. 1:2)

Jerusalem, of course, became the first great center of Christianity. And "the whole church" there was seized with a reverential fear and awe of God at the deaths of Ananias and Sapphira (Acts 5:11). Later a "severe persecution" broke out against "the church in Jerusalem" (8:1).

Antioch also became a key center of early Christianity. When "the church in Jerusalem" learned of the reception of the gospel at Antioch, they sent Barnabas to check it out (Acts 11:22). Barnabas rejoiced in what he saw and brought Saul from Tarsus to Antioch. "So it was that for an entire year they met with the church and taught a great many people, and it was in Antioch that the disciples were first called 'Christians'" (11:26). Here also many vital lessons for the contemporary church can be learned, as Ken Hemphill has so effectively shown in his excellent volume, *The Antioch Effect.*[16]

Finally, Paul wanted the letter he wrote to the Colossians to be "read also in the church of the Laodiceans" (Col. 4:16). Jesus addressed his messages to the seven churches of Asia in the book of Revelation: "the church in Ephesus . . . Smyrna . . . Pergamum . . . Thyatira . . . Sardis . . . Philadelphia . . . Laodicea" (Rev. 2:1, 8, 12, 18; 3:1, 7, 14). Although, as

---

[16] Ken Hemphill, *The Antioch Effect: 8 Characteristics of Highly Effective Churches* (Nashville: Broadman & Holman, 1994).

we will see, the New Testament refers to a plurality of the churches in a regional or provincial context, it never does so in relation to the city. "It comes as a jolt, but it must be said again that the modern concept of a plurality of churches in one city is never found in the New Testament."[17] Perhaps this is the context at which ecumenical efforts should first be targeted. One of the powerful dynamics of the Billy Graham Crusades has been this cooperative effort of various, often disparate, churches in a given urban context.

The New Testament also recognizes a regional dimension to the church in terms of the Roman provinces of that day, referring to the "churches" (plural) of Asia (1 Cor. 16:19), Judea (1 Thess. 2:14; Gal. 1:22), Galatia (1 Cor. 16:1; Gal. 1:2), and Macedonia (2 Cor. 8:1). However, these should be viewed in the light of one of Luke's summary statements in Acts: "Meanwhile the church [*singular*] throughout Judea, Galilee, and Samaria had peace and was built up. Living in the fear of the Lord and in the comfort of the Holy Spirit, it increased in numbers" (Acts 9:31). Although there is a plurality of churches in a given region, the vision of their fundamental unity in Christ is never compromised. Application of this principle to the contemporary ecumenical context has proven to be exceedingly difficult. At this juncture, however, it will suffice simply to describe present church structures, leaving the question of the unity of the churches for a subsequent discussion.

Although there is a plurality of churches in a given region, the vision of their fundamental unity in Christ is never compromised.

Contemporary Church Polities

Although there is an "invisible" dimension of the church in terms of the saints in heaven, dealing with the "visible" dimension of the historic church is inescapable. Too often Christians have tried to evade these issues and neglect ecclesial responsibility and accountability by retreating to a so called "invisible church"—a church without "tares" (cf. Matt. 13:24–30), as it were. But as we have already seen, the New Testament

[17] Moody, *The Word of Truth*, 435.

simply does not allow for this. Down the centuries the church has developed several basic governing structures or polities. It is this unavoidable reality that often presents the greatest challenges to those intent on seeing the church as all she was meant to be. Therefore, it is helpful to explore these basic structures as they find expression in the contemporary church.

Among the various denominational and independent churches, we can observe four basic approaches to governance. We will begin with the most complex and move to the simplest. The *episcopal* form of church government derives its name from the Greek *episkopos,* meaning "bishop." Among these churches the number of levels of bishops varies, as well as the levels of ordained ministry within a given structure. By far, the most complex polity is that of the Roman Catholic Church. At the head of this hierarchy is the Bishop of Rome—the "Vicar of Christ," the Pope. (In our day the two most influential religious leaders worldwide are certainly the Pope and, interestingly, the Protestant evangelist Billy Graham!)

As do all the other forms of episcopacy, the Roman Catholic Church sees a line of descent comprised of bishops going all the way back to the original apostles—the authority of whom is passed on by ordination through the laying on of hands. The Pope himself is assisted by the College of Cardinals. But when he speaks *ex cathedra* (lit., "from the chair"), as the head of the church, he represents Christ himself and is infallible in all his doctrinal pronouncements.

The Eastern Orthodox and Anglican or Episcopal churches have similar, albeit simpler, hierarchies, with bishops overseeing churches in various geographical regions, the basic unit of which is usually called a diocese. The Methodist church has the simplest hierarchical structure of all. Bishops in these ecclesiastical traditions are authorized to ordain and oversee the priests or ministers under their aegis.

The *presbyterian* model of authority (Presbyterian and Reformed churches) parallels the form of representive democracy found in the United States. Derived from the Greek *presbyteros* ("presbyter, elder"), this church structure is comprised of a series of ruling bodies selected by those whom they serve. Local congregations select ruling (administrative) and teaching (pastoral) elders who lead the congregation in its various ministries. This board, consisting of lay elders and clergy, is known as the session (Presbyterian) or consistory (Reformed). In turn, the churches in a given area select representatives to the presbytery

(Presbyterian) or classis (Reformed) that governs the member churches. Lay elders and clergy from this body are then chosen for the regional synod. Finally, in the Presbyterian churches a general assembly, composed of ruling and teaching elders from the presbyteries, governs the churches nationally. Based on the leadership model of the Jewish synagogues and the early New Testament churches, both of which had elders, the presbyterian form of church government takes the further step of spreading out ecclesiastical authority among both clergy and laity.

The *congregational* form of church government emphasizes the authority of the individual church member and the autonomy of each local congregation. Baptist, Congregational, Lutheran, and various Free church traditions generally espouse this view. In congregational polity every member has a voice in church decisions, and each congregation charts its own course without the supervision of any higher governmental authority. Pastors and deacons (or similar such leaders) are elected by the congregation, and these leaders' authority is derived from that of the congregation, to whom they are accountable. Such congregations may cooperate voluntarily at local, state, and national levels, but these institutional entities possess no governing authority over the local congregations.

Nonetheless, participating churches at the various levels of cooperation may choose to "disfellowship" congregations deemed incongruent doctrinally or spiritually with the cooperating churches as a whole. (On a practical note, the elected deacon bodies of some [perhaps many] congregational churches have often functioned with a ruling authority similar to that of a Presbyterian session.) The biblical picture of *all* of God's people's being priests, often called "the priesthood of all believers," looms large in this model. In Baptist circles this principle is almost certainly derived from the belief in "soul competency," that is, that each person has direct access to God without any human intermediaries.[18]

It is evident from the fact that Paul addressed each of his congregations directly rather than their elders (bishops or pastors, viewed as coterminous at that time) or deacons, that God has delegated spiritual authority to each member of the congregation. At the same time, it is easy to politicize church life on the model of a representive democracy

---

[18] See Herschel H. Hobbs, *You Are Chosen: The Priesthood of All Believers* (New York: Harper & Row, 1990) for an engaging treatment of this doctrine; also, Herschel H. Hobbs and E. Y. Mullins, *The Axioms of Religion*, rev. ed. (Nashville: Broadman, 1978).

that "gets out the vote," rather than calling on the Lord and listening to one another.

But there is an even more radical model of church authority to be considered. Certain Quaker (Friends) and Brethren (e.g., the Plymouth Brethren) bodies *reject the idea of formal structures* altogether. Downplaying formal congregational membership and relying primarily on the indwelling of the Holy Spirit, these groups may hold congregational meetings for decision-making, but no formal votes are taken. Obviously, this is an idealistic approach that demands the utmost spirituality on the part of all participants. Is it too idealistic?

Since there are scriptural principles to be found in each of the above polities, and since the New Testament—reflecting a variety and development of structures among the early churches—provides only such principles, without a precise polity prescription as a standard or norm, decisions about church government are somewhat ambiguous. In actuality, almost any church polity will work if the attitudes of the participants are right. But the closer we conform to the biblical principles of the authority of each member of Christ's body and the servant-leadership of the churches, the more stable and vital our congregations will be. The older I get, the more I gravitate toward the congregational polity in which I grew up. As a pastor, I have found that giving the congregation a voice is a *protection* for the pastor. Nevertheless, there are excellent examples of healthy congregations among all the polities described above. Certainly, we should not spiritually shun one another for participating in churches with differing polities.[19]

> *In actuality, almost any church polity will work if the attitudes of the participants are right.*

What must also be factored into these considerations are the various *parachurch organizations* that serve the churches. Consisting of Christians who usually also participate in a local congregation, these ministries

19 For a helpful overview of the various church polities see Erickson, *Introducing Christian Doctrine,* 342–45; Smith, *All God's People,* 369–74. Ted Haggard's New Life Church in Colorado Springs, Colorado studied these polities and sought to incorporate the strengths of each into their own structure, which seeks to balance spiritual leadership with corporate responsibility. Haggard's leadership (as President of the National Association of Evangelicals, for example) and his vital, growing congregation are an inspiration to many. See *The Life-Giving Church* (Ventura, Calif.: Regal, 1998) for a depiction of the principles and structures they developed, including an annotated edition of their by-laws.

function best when based on the same sound (biblical) principles by which the churches themselves operate. In addition, it must be remembered that each believer is a member of Christ's body, connected directly to him (John 15:1–11). Thus, each parachurch organization can be seen as participating in the body of Christ. The principle of accountability of these organizations to the church, however, should not be lost. Later, we will explore some of these dynamics further in terms of the functions of the church.

The Marks of the Church

Thus far, we have studied the nature and structure of the church. What are its distinguishing marks or characteristics? What attributes set apart the authentic church of God? From the late patristic era (fourth century) on, four "notes" or "marks" have been delineated: one, holy, catholic (universal), and apostolic. Further, during the Reformation period a shorter list of essential characteristics emerged. But is there *one indispensable mark* of the Christian church according to the witness of Scripture?

The Nicene Creed confesses belief in one, holy, catholic, and apostolic church. Historically, this belief has taken different forms or conceptions, but it continues to provide a convenient outline of salient characteristics of the church.

> *I believe in one, holy, catholic (universal), and apostolic church.*

The first mark is surely the most difficult. What does it mean to confess the *unity* of the church? With some 22,000 denominations in the world today—unfortunately the Protestant Reformation did open Pandora's Box in this regard!—how can we make such a confession with integrity? First Corinthians reflects the ambiguities we face. "For in one Spirit we were all baptized into one body—Jews or Greeks, slaves or free—and all were made to drink of one Spirit" (1 Cor. 12:13 ESV). Paul wants "no divisions" among them (1:10) and yet acknowledges the necessity of "factions" in order ultimately to ferret out the "genuine" (11:19).

The same is true in Paul's correspondence with the churches of Galatia. He reminds them that their faith, expressed in baptism, points to their being "children of God," signifies their being "clothed" with Christ, and means that no matter what their former social divisions, they are now "one in Christ Jesus" (Gal. 3:26–28). Nevertheless, he warns the Galatians of those who are perverting the gospel and confusing the believers (1:7).

We have already seen Paul's vision of the unity of the church. But the realities he addressed then and which we face today force us to acknowledge the eschatological dimension of the church. We are still in process as God's people. The fullness of our redemption awaits Christ's return. Therefore, we inevitably face the ambiguity of an incomplete and imperfect church. This realism, however, must be balanced by a spiritual idealism. Jesus Christ himself prayed for our unity (John 17:20–23), and we have already encountered statement after statement in Scripture affirming our unity. Therefore, we must avoid at all costs the four "evasions" Hans Küng highlights. Our very witness to the world is at stake.

Küng relates that we often retreat to an "invisible" church in relation to our unity. Unfortunately, it is our very *visibilty* that is at issue in terms of our witness. Postponing our efforts toward unity until the eschaton is also a cop-out. These first two evasions are the easiest to critique. The last two are more stubborn. Some would see the church as merely one tree with many branches. But Küng's passionate response to this evasion is true to the mark:

> Only when we can pray together, hear the Word of God together, confess our faith together and share our meal together, can we speak of one Church. Only then do we confess one Lord and not many, one Spirit and not many, one God and not many.[20]

The Roman Catholic Church—mistakenly, according to Küng—has taken the fourth position of simply asserting one empirical church, to the exclusion of all others. None of these evasions can be reconciled with the New Testament's call for our pursuing authentic unity.

Efforts toward a doctrinal unity in terms of a "lowest common denominator" have failed dismally because so often the churches have departed from "the faith that was once for all entrusted to the saints" (Jude 3). A political or structural unity is also unrealistic at this juncture, given the complex global dimensions of the church. Surely a spiritual unity at the community level is our best strategy at the outset. Again, Jude, the Lord's brother, points us in the right direction.

---

[20] Hans Küng, *The Church*, trans. Ray and Rosaleen Ockenden (New York: Sheed and Ward, 1967), 281–83.

> But you, beloved, must remember the predictions of the apostles of our Lord Jesus Christ; for they said to you, "In the last time there will be scoffers, indulging their own ungodly lusts." It is these worldly people, devoid of the Spirit, who are causing divisions. But you, beloved, build yourselves up on your most holy faith; pray in the Holy Spirit; keep yourselves in the love of God; look forward to the mercy of our Lord Jesus Christ that leads to eternal life. And have mercy on some who are wavering; save others by snatching them out of the fire; and have mercy on still others with fear, hating even the tunic defiled by their bodies. (Jude 17–23)

It was a spiritual unity and empowerment that initially launched the church on her worldwide mission (Acts 1–2), and it is a similar outpouring that is our best hope for unity and authentic growth today. The Pentecostals have led the way in this regard.

The Pentecostal/Charismatic Revival

With all its blemishes—to be expected, since it is a movement comprised of people—the twentieth-century Pentecostal/charismatic revival best exemplifies how a revitalized church is more easily unified. Renewal in the Spirit has done more to break down the barriers between us than all of our ecumenical organizations combined. My own pilgrimage illustrates this point.

Growing up in a large Southern Baptist church, I often looked across the street at the large Roman Catholic church with a sense of sadness, assuming few if any of their members really knew Christ. Then as a college student I became involved in charismatic renewal, a fact not welcomed with enthusiasm by my own church. The Catholic church across the street, however, began to have charismatic renewal services. I often found myself looking longingly in their direction, wishing I could attend those services rather than my own! God has a way of turning the tables on us. (Once I had a slip of tongue at a charismatic worship gathering, greeting a beloved Catholic priest as "Brother Father"!) Only the Holy Spirit himself can create an authentic unity between a Catholic believer and a Baptist believer.

> *It was a spiritual unity and empowerment that initially launched the church on her worldwide mission.*

Saying these things in no way diminishes the importance of doctrinal issues—thus this book. Nevertheless, the urgency of the hour demands that we all prayerfully seek the outpouring of God's Spirit, which can remove like a deluge so many of the obstacles to our fellowship and our cooperation in the worldwide mission of the church. Perhaps the missionaries on foreign fields best know this truth.

"A Holy Nation, God's Own People"[21]

We confess not only our unity but our *holiness* as well. What does this mean? If our holiness means "holier than thou," then we are indeed in trouble. For that matter, the church of the New Testament era was replete with problems. Our holiness is God's gracious gift of righteousness. Indeed, it is Christ himself who is our "wisdom from God, and righteousness and sanctification and redemption" (1 Cor. 1:30).

We are the *ekklesia*—"saints" or holy ones, "the elect," "the called," "the beloved"—a people set apart for God's own purposes, not having a righteousness of our own, "but one that comes through faith in Christ" (Phil. 3:9). We are sanctified (set apart), but (hopefully) not sanctimonious. We are just as in need of God's grace as everyone else.

"Built Upon the Foundation of the Apostles and Prophets"[22]

Once it is understood that *catholic* in the confession refers to the *universal* dimension of the church, most of the stumbling blocks are removed. To confess belief in the universal church is to acknowledge our unity with all true believers worldwide. It is to remind ourselves of this scriptural truth, which is so crucial to an overcoming attitude as we tackle the challenges we perennially face at the congregational and community levels.

Then, to acknowledge apostolicity takes us back to our roots. Jesus chose the Twelve with both historic and eschatological purposes in mind, and their teaching and preaching serve as the touchstone of doctrinal purity in every generation. Are we referring to succession or Scripture here? My position obviously opts for the latter. We have the deposit of apostolic authority in the New Testament. Thus, we always aspire to be New Testament Christians.

---

[21] 1 Peter 2:9.
[22] Ephesians 2:20.

When we confess the *apostolicity* of the church, we also acknowledge historical continuity. This characteristic of the church needs greater emphasis in independent charismatic circles, where one often finds saints lacking such a historical consciousness and identity.

Thomas Oden summarizes well these four marks of the Church:

> The church is one, finding its oneness in Christ. The church is holy, set apart from the world to mediate life to the world and bring forth the fruits of the Spirit amid the life of the world. The church is catholic in that it is whole, for all, and embracing all times and places. The church is apostolic in that it is grounded in the testimony of the first witnesses to Jesus' life and resurrection, and depends upon and continues their ministry.[23]

Because the Roman Catholic Church had begun to compromise these characteristics, the Reformers found a different way to articulate the church's distinguishing marks.

The Marks of the Church According to the Reformers

John Calvin summarized the Protestant understanding of the true church:

> Wherever we see the Word of God purely preached and heard, and the sacraments administered according to Christ's institution, there, it is not to be doubted, a church of God exists [cf. Eph. 2:20]. For his promise cannot fail: "Wherever two or three are gathered in my name, there I am in the midst of them [Matt. 18:20].[24]

Fidelity to the Scriptures in general and to the gospel in particular was the hallmark of the Reformers. In addition, they also stressed obedience to our Lord's commands, including those related to baptism and the Lord's Supper. Thus, the authentic church, according to the Reformers, is found wherever the Word of God is rightly preached and the sacraments are rightly administered.

It is important to note the emphasis on preaching in this definition. The church owes a debt to the Reformers in this regard. From the New Testament times to the present, it has been the faithful preaching of the gospel that has grown the church and kept her vital and on course. We

---

[23] Thomas C. Oden, *Life in the Spirit* (San Francisco: HarperSanFrancisco, 1992), 303.

[24] John Calvin, *Institutes of the Christian Religion*, 2 vols., ed. John T. McNeill, trans. Ford Lewis Battles (Philadelphia: Westminster, 1960), 1023 (IV.i.9).

are a Great Commission people—which entails heralding the good news, discipling the nations, and teaching the *entire* written Word of God. Therefore, these so-called marks of the Reformers should characterize every church in every generation. It is here that we see that the church's essence is closely tied to her mission. More will be said about this later.

The One Indispensable Mark of the Church

We have yet to indicate the most important characteristic of God's people. Jesus Christ said, unequivocally, "I give you a new commandment, that you love one another. Just as I have loved you, you also should love one another. By this everyone will know that you are my disciples, if you have love for one another" (John 13:34–35). Furthermore, he prayed,

> I ask not only on behalf of these, but also on behalf of those who will believe in me through their word, that they may all be one. As you, Father, are in me and I am in you, may they also be in us, so that the world may believe that you have sent me. The glory that you have given me I have given them, so that they may be one, as we are one, I in them and you in me, that they may become completely one, so that the world may know that you have sent me and have loved them even as you have loved me. (John 17:20–23)

And the apostle John, who recorded these words, stated categorically that without this love we are a counterfeit church (1 John 3:11–24; 4:7–21). No more important words could be pondered by the church in these days.

Love is *everything*, according to Paul (1 Cor. 13). And if God's essential character is love (Gal. 5:22; cf. 1 John 4:8, 16), then surely his people should also be characterized by love. Francis Schaeffer wrote a classic book on this subject, *The Mark of the Christian*.[25] Leon Morris's careful biblical scholarship has demonstrated the centrality of love to the message of the Bible, the church's guidebook.[26] The one indispensable mark of the church is love.

> *The one indispensable mark of the church is love.*

We must always remember that Jesus commanded us to love God with our whole being and our neighbors as ourselves (Matt. 22:37–40;

---

[25] Francis A. Schaeffer, *The Mark of the Christian* (Downers Grove, Ill.: InterVarsity Press, 1970).

[26] Leon Morris, *Testaments of Love: A Study of Love in the Bible* (Grand Rapids: Eerdmans, 1981). See also Timothy George and John Woodbridge, *The Mark of Jesus: Loving in a Way The World Can See* (Chicago: Moody Press, 2005).

Mark 12:29–30) as the quintessence of God's Word and will. This is our very purpose for being. This is why, combined with the Great Commission, this unmistakable mark of the church defines both her form and her function. Rick Warren, in his classic book on church health and growth, expresses this truth in a memorable slogan:

> A Great Commitment
> to the Great Commandment
> and the Great Commission
> will grow a Great Church![27]

Thus, our next step in the study of the church is to explore the functions of the church that are derived from this purpose.

The Functions of the Church

The functions of the church can be summarized under the rubrics of (1) *martyria* ("witness"), (2) *koinonia* ("fellowship"), and (3) *diakonia* ("service").[28] The total mission of the church is expressed by these terms.

Our marching orders are clear:

> All authority in heaven and on earth has been given to me. Go therefore and make disciples of all nations, baptizing them in the name of the Father and of the Son and of the Holy Spirit, and teaching them to obey everything that I have commanded you. And remember, I am with you always, to the end of the age. (Matt. 28:18–20)

A careful study of the Great Commission makes it clear that our call is to make *disciples,* a process that involves the entire church: baptizing, teaching, equipping, maturing, and mobilizing the saints for ministry.

Thus, we see at the outset that *martyria* is the source or seedbed for *koinonia* and *diakonia.* This truth was brought poignantly home to me while pastoring in Texas. Our guest evangelist for our spring revival was Ken Hemphill, a dynamic Southern Baptist pastor, church growth specialist, and seminary president, who was putting God's vision for his church before us in a series of messages.[29] I had taught the three above-

---

[27] Rick Warren, *The Purpose-Driven Church* (Grand Rapids: Zondervan, 1995), 102.

[28] Cf., e.g,, Moody, *The Word of Truth,* 429–33.

[29] These messages and other related messages are available in Ken Hemphill, *The Official Rule Book for the New Church Game* (Nashville: Broadman, 1990).

mentioned functions of the church for years, but as Dr. Hemphill's messages unfolded, I began to gain insight concerning the priority of *martyria*. *Martyria* spawns *koinonia* and *diakonia*. *Koinonia* and *diakonia* become enervated and even artificial apart from the ethos of *martyria*. This can be visualized as follows:

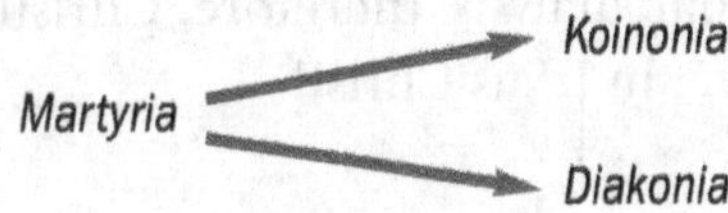

First and foremost, we have been sent out as witnesses to Jesus Christ and his saving work on our behalf. Our message, in a word, is the gospel. Millard Erickson states that the gospel is "the element which lies at the heart of all [the church's] functions"; it is the "heart of the ministry of the Church."[30]

Furthermore, the power of the Holy Spirit has been given to the church for this great purpose: "But you will receive power when the Holy Spirit has come upon you; and you will be my witnesses in Jerusalem, in all Judea and Samaria, and to the ends of the earth" (Acts 1:8). Luke's six summary statements (Acts 6:7; 9:31; 12:24; 16:5; 19:20; 28:30, 31), which provide demarcations of approximately five years in his historical account of the early church, depict the spread of the gospel and the growth of the church. These Spirit-empowered believers saw themselves simply as *witnesses to* the saving message of Christ's death and resurrection (2:32; 3:15; 5:32; 10:39–41; 13:31; 22:15; 26:16).[31] Jesus taught his disciples that the Holy Spirit was sent for this very purpose (John 15:26). When believers seek his power for any other purposes, they inevitably lose their way and often operate in counterfeit power.

> *In actuality, the church simply* continues *the earthly ministry of Jesus.*

The church has been given the two primary ingredients for success in her mission: authority (*exousia*; dominical authorization, Matt. 28:18) and power (*dynamis*; spiritual enablement, Acts 1:8). Culminating these provisions is the promise of our Lord's personal presence with us: "And remember, I am with you always, to the end of the age" (Matt. 28:20).[32] We are an *evangelistic* people. We are a *good*

[30] Erickson, *Introducing Christian Doctrine*, 340.
[31] See Moody, *The Word of Truth*, 429.
[32] Cf. Erickson, *Introducing Christian Doctrine*, 337.

news people. We come with a message that *lifts* people. In actuality, the church simply *continues* the earthly ministry of Jesus, as witnessed by Luke: "The first account I composed, Theophilus, about all that Jesus *began* to do and teach . . . " (Acts 1:1 NASB; italics added). Jesus said of his own ministry, "I came that they may have life, and have it abundantly" (John 10:10). In the final analysis, therefore, Christians are simply purveyors of *abundant life* . . . in Jesus Christ!

A Shared Life

Purveyors of and participants together in divine, eternal, and abundant life—that is what believers are. Our previous study of *koinonia* has already revealed this truth. This fellowship is a "sharing [*koinonia*] in the gospel" (Phil. 1:5). It is also a "sharing [*koinonia*] in the Spirit" (2:1). It entails all that transpires in our life together in the Christian community. Two key dimensions of this life are *worship* and *body life* (or the gifts/ministries of the Holy Spirit).

Even though as a race we have lost our way, there is still within the heart of every person the need for worship and community. We are worshipers by nature, and we also crave personal relationships. We need to know that we *belong*—first, to God our Creator, and then to one another. In a lecture on the ORU campus, Dr. Stanley J. Grenz pointed out that people in our postmodern culture are longing for community, having lost the sense of the *unity* of the human story. Only the Bible provides that overarching vision and story. Both the *message* (the gospel) and the *model* (the church) are crucial in these chaotic times.

First, it is imperative that we reflect on the meaning and importance of *worship*. Worship is God's gift to humankind, not something we have invented. God is not some cosmic ego in need of constant strokes. In the final analysis, worship is for *our* benefit. Yet when we worship for the sole purpose of our own personal blessing, we subtly move away from worship.[33] Perhaps this is why children so often can best lead the way (as they did in Jesus' day), because they are so unselfconscious and simply lost in delight!

In the broadest sense worship is any proper response to the revelation of our triune God. He has acted in history: Have we studied this? He has spoken: Have we listened? He has written: Have we read? He

---

[33] Franklin M. Segler, *Christian Worship: Its Theology and Practice* (Nashville: Broadman, 1967), 4.

speaks even now: Are we listening? To enter into a relationship with God, through Christ, in the Spirit, transforms all of life into an arena of praise! We can literally "do everything for the glory of God" (1 Cor. 10:31). We honor God with our lips and with our lives. Our individual daily walk, our family life, our congregational life, and our corporate worship are all important avenues for our worship of God.

Our often paltry, drowsy, and half-hearted worship services can mean only one thing: We are simply not in tune, not in touch, with the Creator of the universe. Everything in life ought to set us ablaze with love and gratitude to our giving God. The sun's rising in the quiet of morning, the lilting songs of the mockingbird, the crystal-clear shine of a baby's eyes, the tender sensitivities of a loving spouse—the list could fill myriad volumes! Do we spontaneously thank and praise our good God for these daily gifts? If not, then why not?

C. S. Lewis addresses these issues masterfully. He points out that our natural impulse is to praise that which brings us delight. I have lived in numerous contexts in which copious praise has been lavished on certain football teams—even at church (usually in Sunday school prior to getting down to the lesson). Lewis observes that "all enjoyment spontaneously overflows into praise."[34] We praise automobiles, dresses, suits, jewelry, athletes, actors, food, weather, books, and countless other things. Further, sharing this delight with others seems to *complete* our enjoyment.[35] So it is with God!

The *locus classicus* among the many relevant biblical texts on this subject is Isaiah 6:1–9. In Isaiah's majestic account of his prophetic calling we have the model of all authentic religious experience, including worship. The great prophet "saw the Lord sitting on a throne, high and lofty" (Isa. 6:1). God's holiness prompts him to exclaim, "Woe is me! I am lost, for I am a man of unclean lips, and I live among a people of unclean lips" (6:5). Then one of the seraphs touches Isaiah's mouth with a live coal from the altar and announces, "Lo [KJV] . . . your guilt has departed and your sin is blotted out" (6:7). When the Lord asks, "Whom shall I send?" Isaiah responds, "Here am I; send me!" (6: 8). And the Lord says, "Go and say to this people . . ." (6:9). Notice the three little words: woe, lo, and go. As Dale Moody preached it, it was the *woe* of conviction, the *lo* of cleansing, and the *go* of commission.

---

[34] C. S. Lewis, *Reflections on the Psalms* (New York: Harcourt, Brace & Co., 1958), 94.

[35] Ibid., 94–95.

Genuine worship of God always contains these dynamics. As we glimpse the grandeur of God, we immediately become aware of our sinfulness, our unworthiness. This leads us to repentance and cleansing. Finally, we are commissioned by God to go and tell others about his holy love, his grace and glory. William Temple's words concerning authentic worship have been quoted time and again. To worship is:

> to quicken the conscience by the holiness of God
> to feed the mind with the truth of God
> to purge the imagination by the beauty of God
> to open the heart to the love of God
> to devote the will to the purpose of God.[36]

In many ways worship is difficult to define. More often than not, we find ourselves describing its *effects* rather than its essence. One experienced pastor put it this way: "If you leave church with your faith stronger, your hope brighter, your love deeper, your sympathies broadened, your heart purer, and with your will more resolute to do the will of God, then you have truly worshiped!"[37] Ultimately, however, worship is an act of the *will*, apart from any perceived effects, or benefits.

The word "worship" in English is derived from the Anglo-Saxon "Weorthscipe," meaning "worth-ship." *šaḥah*, the principal Old Testament term, means to "bow down, prostrate oneself."[38] *Proskyneo* in the New Testament also means to "prostrate oneself, do obeisance."[39] For example, when Paul laid down his guidelines for public worship in relationship to prophecy and speaking in tongues, he elevated prophecy. When everyone speaks in tongues at the same time, the outsider might simply conclude that the worshipers are out of their minds (1 Cor. 14:23).

> But if all prophesy, and an unbeliever or an ungifted man enters, he is convicted by all, he is called to account by all; the secrets of his heart are disclosed; and so he will fall on his face and worship [verb: *proskyneo*] God, declaring that God is certainly among you. (1 Cor. 14:24–25 NASB)

These words beautifully capture the ethos of New Testament worship.

---

36 William Temple, *The Hope of a New World* (New York: Macmillan, 1942), 30; cited in Segler, Christian Worship, 4.

37 Cited in Segler, *Christian Worship*, 12.

38 Francis Brown, S. R. Driver, and Charles A. Briggs, *A Hebrew and English Lexicon of the Old Testament* (New York: Oxford Univ. Press, 1968), 1005.

39 Walter Bauer and Frederick Danker, *A Greek-English Lexicon of the New Testament and Other Early Christian Literature*, 3rd ed. (Chicago: Univ. of Chicago Press, 2000), 882.

In Spirit and Truth

But perhaps the most important passage in which *proskyneo* occurs is in John's famous account of Jesus' conversation with the woman at Jacob's well in Sychar. The Samaritan woman, perhaps as a defense mechanism, tried to engage Jesus in debate concerning the proper *place* of worship—the Samaritans arguing for Mount Gerizim, near Sychar in Samaria, rather than Mount Zion in Jerusalem. Jesus, however, identified the *person* as the key issue in worship. It is our attitude or manner of approach that matters in genuine worship:

> But the hour is coming, and is now here, when true worshipers will worship the Father in Spirit and truth; and indeed the Father seeks such people to worship him. God is Spirit, and those who worship him must worship in Spirit and truth. (John 4:23–24 NAB)

Notice the emphasis on the Father. We worship the Father; the Father seeks worshipers. Second, we worship "in spirit and truth" (one preposition governing both closely related terms). One immediately thinks of Paul's words to the Philippians, describing believers as those who "worship in the Spirit of God and boast in Christ Jesus and have no confidence in the flesh" (Phil. 3:3). True worship comes from the human spirit in union with the Holy Spirit. It involves both the heart ("spirit") and the head ("truth").

Truth is a key concept in John's Gospel. John describes Jesus as "full of grace and truth" (John 1:14) and as "the way, and the truth, and the life" (14:6). Therefore, it is likely that John would have us think of our worship as *Christocentric,* Christ-centered. Here John and Paul sound much alike in their Trinitarian pattern of worship: "for through him [Christ] both of us [Jew and Gentile] have access in one Spirit to the Father" (Eph. 2:18). To worship the Father in Spirit and Truth—this is *Christian* worship, and it is *Trinitarian* to the core! We should never forget that the Father is *seeking* such worshipers. This awesome reality lies at the heart of the biblical theology of worship.

Worship is also a *service* or *ministry* to the Lord. We offer our total bodily lives as a consecrated sacrifice to God; this is our "spiritual worship" (or "reasonable service" [*logiken latreian*]; Rom. 12:1). This encompasses our total daily life as well as our personal and corporate times of worship. It is both an *inward* ("spiritual") and a *rational* ("reasonable") worship. C. E. B. Cranfield clarifies for the contemporary reader what is meant by "rational":

> For Paul the true worship is rational not in the sense of being consistent with the natural rationality of a man ... but in the sense of being consistent with a proper understanding of the truth of God revealed in Jesus Christ.[40]

Again, we hear Jesus' words "in spirit and truth"!

Luke's account of the launching of Paul's first missionary journey also reminds us that worship is a ministry to or service of the Lord. It is also an occasion for the Holy Spirit to give directives for our mission! "While they were worshiping [*leitourgeo*] the Lord and fasting, the Holy Spirit said, 'Set apart for me Barnabas and Saul for the work to which I have called them'" (Acts 13:2). One quickly notices the early church's sense of the *immediacy* of the Lord's presence. Further, the attitude of awe and reverence toward God is evident. A *balance* was instinctively maintained between immanence (God's nearness: intimacy) and transcendence (God's mystery: reverence).

Today in our worship we tend to err in one of two directions. Either we put the total emphasis on intimacy, experience, and emotion to the neglect of reverence and awe, or we emphasize transcendence, mystery, and solemnity to the neglect of joy and celebration. A full-orbed experience of worship will always keep these celebrative and reflective dimensions in balance, as Robert Logan has pointed out in his excellent work on church growth.[41]

We have already seen how Isaiah was overwhelmed by God's holy presence. We should also be aware, however, that there is much in Scripture to commend raucous celebration as well. One classic example of this dimension of joy and rejoicing in worship is the occasion of King David's bringing the ark of the covenant to Jerusalem.

> Then David and the leaders of Israel and the generals of the army went to the home of Obed-edom to bring the Ark of the LORD's covenant up to Jerusalem with a great celebration.... So all Israel brought up the Ark of the LORD's covenant to Jerusalem with shouts of joy, the blowing of trumpets, the crashing of cymbals, and loud playing on harps and lyres.
>
> But as the Ark of the LORD's covenant entered the City of David, Michal, the daughter of Saul, looked down from her window. When she saw King David dancing and leaping for joy, she was filled with contempt for him. (1 Chron. 15:25, 28–29 NLT)

---

40 C. E. B. Cranfield, *The Epistle to the Romans* (ICC; Edinburgh: T. & T. Clark, 1979), 604–5.

41 Robert E. Logan, *Beyond Church Growth* (Tarrytown, N.Y.: Revell, 1989), 76–93.

I have seen contempt go in both directions: evangelicals despising the celebration of the Pentecostals, and charismatics despising the order and reverence of mainline believers. When will we grow up? In actuality, it appears that the Lord is doing just that—growing us up by bringing us together in a sort of cross-pollination process!

A virtual reformation is now going on in the worship of American churches. Jack Hayford has effectively laid down the guidelines for these exciting changes in his widely read volume, *Worship His Majesty*.[42] There is a *hunger* for worship across the body of Christ. Congregations are *demanding* that their leaders provide opportunities for new forms of worship—contemporary services with informal attire, contemporary praise songs, and the like. At the same time, many charismatics are developing a taste for the depth and beauty of liturgical forms of worship. What an exciting time to be alive![43]

> *There is a* hunger *for worship across the body of Christ.*

During a visit to Korea, I had the opportunity to observe firsthand how these vital Christians serve our Lord and reach their country with the gospel. In one Pentecostal church in which I preached and taught, I noticed that the Sunday morning worship was beautiful and majestic with its robed choir, glorious anthems, historic hymns, and printed order of worship. Their mid-week prayer meeting, however, was long and loud! In contrast to attitudes I have often encountered in America, the Koreans saw no contradiction between these services. They believed that God was just as much present in the quiet, ordered service as he was in the loud and less-structured one. The glimpses John provides us into the worship of heaven make it clear that both dimensions are appropriate (see, e.g., Rev. 4; 5; 8:1; 19:1–10).

All authentic worship contains ritual, symbol, and sacrament. *Ritual* is often despised, but it is inevitable. Indeed, all of life contains ritual—predictable patterns that provide order and meaning to life, including the way we start our days and even express romantic love in marriage. There is nothing intrinsically wrong with these patterns. They are even desirable and necessary. The same principle applies in worship: There must be a wedding of form and freedom. Note what Donald McCullough says:

---

[42] Jack W. Hayford, *Worship His Majesty* (Dallas: Word, 1987).

[43] See Robert Webber, *Signs of Wonder: The Phenomenon of Convergence in Modern Liturgical and Charismatic Churches* (Nashville: Abbott Martyn, 1992).

> Every service, whether a Pentecostal revival meeting on a sawdust trail or a Roman Catholic high mass with "smells and bells," has a structure, a pattern for praise. Even congregations that would never think of printing an Order of Worship because they consider themselves "free churches" nevertheless follow a predictable routine.
>
> The choice, therefore, is not between structured or unstructured worship, but between thoughtful or unthoughtful structure.[44]

In addition, the strength of the liturgical traditions is their recognition of the power of *symbol*, which is also inescapable in worship. The very words of the Scriptures are symbols. The manner in which the preacher handles his or her Bible speaks symbolically. The architecture and decor of the facilities in which we meet for worship are usually filled with symbols. Raised hands symbolize adoration and submission. Thus, it is better to be intentional in our use of symbols and to tap into the riches of our Christian heritage!

Finally, *sacrament* characterizes our worship. As visible expressions of invisible realities, the sacraments concretize the gracious actions of God's Spirit among us. For example, water baptism and the Lord's Supper provide us opportunity to put our faith in action, to give visible expression to our inward trust and expectations.

As these three dimensions converge, our worship becomes *incarnational.* We become one with God in our total persons. With our bodies we stand and kneel, clap and raise our hands. With our minds we meditate on God's beauty and truth and offer intelligent praise and prayer. With our spirits we unite with God's Spirit and are changed from glory to glory as we behold his glory (2 Cor. 3:18). We are in *dialogue* with the living God. We are "a holy priesthood" offering up "spiritual *sacrifices* acceptable to God through Jesus Christ" (1 Peter 2:5, italics added).

King David provides us, in the psalms he wrote, with a rich resource for our personal and corporate worship. Eugene Peterson masterfully captures the spirit of the psalmist and his honest and adoring relationship with God in his paraphrases of the Scriptures:

> God—you're my God!
> I can't get enough of you!
> I've worked up such hunger and thirst for God,
> traveling across dry and weary deserts.

---

[44] Donald W. McCullough, *The Trivialization of God: The Dangerous Illusion of a Manageable Deity* (Colorado Springs, Colo.: NavPress, 1995), 114–15.

So here I am in the place of worship, eyes open,
 drinking in your strength and glory.
In your generous love I am really living at last!
 My lips brim praises like fountains.
I bless you every time I take a breath;
 my arms wave like banners of praise to you.
I eat my fill of prime rib and gravy;
 I smack my lips. It's time to shout praises!
If I'm sleepless at midnight,
 I spend the hours in grateful reflection.
Because you've always stood up for me,
 I'm free to run and play.
I hold on to you for dear life,
 and you hold me steady as a post.
Those who are out to get me are marked for doom,
 marked for death, bound for hell.
They'll die violent deaths;
 jackals will tear them limb from limb.
But the king is glad in God;
 his true friends spread the joy,
While small-minded gossips
 are gagged for good.[45]

One senses a freedom and intimacy in this kind of worship—not unlike that of Pentecostal worship in our own day!

But the Pentecostals and charismatics do not have a corner on the Spirit. He belongs to the whole body of Christ, and the fellowship of all believers, by New Testament definitions, can rightly be called charismatic. We have all received the gift (*charisma*) of eternal life (Rom. 6:23). And in one Spirit we were all baptized into one body—Baptist or Methodist, Presbyterian or Pentecostal—and we were all made to drink of one Spirit (see 1 Cor. 12:13). Paul's twin letters, Ephesians and Colossians, depict beautifully this charismatic fellowship.

The Church—A Charismatic Fellowship

Closely tied to the worshiping ethos of the church is the charismatic dimension of church life. We are literally members of one another (Rom. 12:5). Out of our life as a worshiping community should also flow

[45] Psalm 63 in Eugene H. Peterson, *The Message: New Testament with Psalms and Proverbs* (Colorado Springs, Colo.: NavPress, 1995), 737–38.

a ministry of mutual edification. The apostle Paul provides two paradigmatic depicitions of the nature of this "body life."

> As God's chosen ones, holy and beloved, clothe yourselves with compassion, kindness, humility, meekness, and patience. Bear with one another and, if anyone has a complaint against another, forgive each other; just as the Lord has forgiven you, so you also must forgive. Above all, clothe yourselves with love, which binds everything together in perfect harmony. And let the peace of Christ rule in your hearts, to which indeed you were called in the one body. And be thankful. Let the word of Christ dwell in you richly; teach and admonish one another in all wisdom; and with gratitude in your hearts sing psalms, hymns, and spiritual songs to God. And whatever you do, in word or deed, do everything in the name of the Lord Jesus, giving thanks to God the Father through him. (Col. 3:12–17)

This one paragraph says it all in terms of how God intends us to live together in Christian community.

The apostle gives similar advice to the Ephesians—with words that, in our day, sound a much-needed note of urgency as we seemingly enter the eschatological woes as well as the exciting end-time harvest promised in Scripture. Here is my own rendering of Ephesians 5:15–21, with inserted comments and a sort of running commentary on this crucial passage:

Out of our life as a worshiping community should also flow a ministry of mutual edification.

> Consider [lit., look] carefully, then, how you are living [lit., walking]—not as unwise people, but as wise, redeeming [i.e., making the most of] the time, because the days are evil [how true of our own day!]. Because of this, do not be foolish, but understand [i.e., grasp firmly] what the will of the Lord is. And don't get drunk with wine, which is debauchery; but be filled[46] with [or in] the Spirit,[47] speaking to one another in psalms and hymns and spiritual [*pneumatikais*, i.e., having their source in the Spirit, therefore, supernatural] songs, singing and

---

[46] Present imperative passive, second person plural: (1) imperative—that is, a command, not an option; (2) present imperative—that is, continuous: go on being filled with the Spirit; (3) passive—allow the Holy Spirit to fill and control you; you are not merely "psyching" yourself; (4) second person plural—this command applies to all of us!

[47] What follows now is a string of participles with imperative force—speaking, singing, and making melody, giving thanks, submitting.

> making melody in your hearts to the Lord, always giving thanks for all things [*hyper panton*],[48] in the name of our Lord Jesus Christ to God the Father, [and] submitting yourselves to one another in the fear of [i.e., out of reverence for] Christ.

These words both *describe* a Spirit-filled community and *prescribe* how we can be a Spirit-filled community. If we can get church members to (1) *speak* to one another (which in itself is sometimes difficult), (2) *sing* God's praises, (3) *say thanks* for all things, and (4) *submit* to one another, they cannot help but be filled with the Holy Spirit! Speaking, singing, giving thanks, and submitting are God's recipe for a Spirit-filled community.[49]

Servanthood

The church is not only a worldwide missionary movement as well as a worshiping fellowship of believers; it is also a *serving* community (*diakonia*), continuing the ministry of her Lord and Savior. "For the Son of Man came not to be served but to serve, and to give his life a ransom for many" (Mark 10:45). With these programmatic words, Jesus himself summed up his ministry. He was the Suffering Servant of the Lord, who both preached and embodied the saving message of the kingdom of God.

Paul pointed to Jesus as the supreme example of a heart of servanthood. "Let each of you look not to your own interests, but to the interests of others. Let the same mind be in you that was in Christ Jesus . . . taking the form of a slave" (Phil. 2:4, 7). And what did Jesus do? His ministry included (1) teaching, (2) preaching, and (3) healing (Matt. 4:23). He "went about doing good and healing all who were oppressed by the devil" (Acts 10:38). He fed the hungry, delivered the demonized, healed the sick, raised the dead, forgave sins, and ultimately laid down his life for the salvation of the world. He was and is a *healing* Jesus, bringing wholeness to the whole person and to the whole of society. And the church is to continue this ministry throughout the world until he comes.

---

48 This phrase can also be translated "on behalf of all"; thus, "always giving thanks for one another"!

49 Parenthetically, it is interesting to note how the Spirit and speaking belong together in the New Testament. Whenever believers are filled with the Spirit, inevitably their speech is affected. They speak in other tongues (Acts 2:4), witness or preach boldly (4:8, 31; 9:17–20), praise God (10:46), or prophesy (19:6). We see the same phenomenon in this Ephesian passage.

His commandment to love (Mark 12:29–31) implies—more accurately, *demands*—a life of service to others. Every aspect of church life, including leadership, reflects this call to serve. When his disciples argued as to who was the greatest, Jesus responded, "Whoever wants to be first must be last of all and servant of all" (9:35). A short time later he expanded on this principle:

> You know that in this world kings are tyrants, and officials lord it over the people beneath them. But among you it should be quite different. Whoever wants to be a leader among you must be your servant, and whoever wants to be first must be the slave of all. (Mark 10:42–44 NLT)

Greatness in the kingdom and in the church is measured by *servanthood.*

Jesus taught the importance of *good works*—not as a means of salvation but as the expression of authentic saving faith. In the Sermon on the Mount he told his disciples, "Let your light shine before others, so that they may see your good works and give glory to your Father in heaven" (Matt. 5:16). In the same sermon, he did *not* say, *if* you give to the poor, but "When you give to the poor" (6:2 NCV, italics added). And in his Last Judgment parable, Jesus said we will be judged as to whether we have fed the hungry, given the thirsty something to drink, welcomed the stranger, clothed the naked, cared for the sick, and visited those in prison (25:31–46). "I assure you, when you did it to one of the least of these my brothers and sisters, you were doing it to me!" (v. 40 NLT).

> *Greatness in the kingdom and in the church is measured by* servanthood.

Ours is a salvation by grace through faith, "not the result of works" (Eph. 2:8–9). But Paul adds in the very next verse that we are "God's masterpiece" (2:10 NLT). "For we are what he has made us, created in Christ Jesus for good works, which God prepared beforehand to be our way of life" (2:10). "If a brother or sister is naked and lacks daily food," James adds, a living faith will do something concrete about it (James 2:15–22). Like the good Samaritan, we are to show mercy in concrete acts of service. Our neighbor is *anyone* in need (Luke 10:25–37).

Perhaps no one has exemplified this better than former President Jimmy Carter. Most people are aware of President Carter's active involvement with Habitat for Humanity. Many are not aware, however, of his active witness to heads of state while in office, his numerous substantive involvements with human rights efforts, his alleviation of suffering, and his educational endeavors throughout the world. The Carter Center is a world-class educational and service agency that impacts the lives of millions. At the same time, our former president continues to be active in his local church, including teaching his Sunday school class in Plains, Georgia.

Carter's pastor, Dan Ariail, and Cheryl Heckler-Feltz have written an enriching spiritual biography of Carter. They summarize his guiding philosophy, the key ingredients of his faith.

1. Jesus Christ is my personal Savior. I will serve him and maintain a pure relationship with him;
2. Scripture is my primary source for gaining clarity to God's will for my life;
3. The best way to serve God is by serving others, especially through the church.[50]

If the American church more faithfully lived out these beliefs, how different things would be!

Spiritual experiences are vital to our Christian walk, but they are no substitute for our active engagement with the moral and ethical social issues of our day. Jimmy Carter's life illustrates beautifully the balanced Christian life, in terms of *martyria, koinonia,* and *diakonia.* We often overlook this same dynamic in the lives of the New Testament saints. The same believers who participated in the outpouring of the Holy Spirit at Pentecost also shared their *material* goods with one another (Acts 2:44–45). We also know from his Corinthian, Galatian, and Roman correspondences that the same Paul who evangelized virtually the entire Roman Empire also headed up a major social project, a collection for the suffering saints in Jerusalem. Orthodoxy (right beliefs) also entails orthopraxy (right behavior). Faith without works is dead (James 2:17, 26).

The Holy Spirit himself superintends all of these ministries of the church. When we are truly sensitive and obedient to him, we will serve and disciple in *all* the ways described above. He structures the Spirit-filled community by the various gifts and ministries he has ordained.

The Gifts and Ministries of the Holy Spirit

The apostle Peter's words concerning the spiritual gifts and their end-time significance have a patently contemporary ring.

---

50 Dan Ariail and Cheryl Heckler-Feltz, *The Carpenter's Apprentice: The Spiritual Biography of Jimmy Carter* (Grand Rapids: Zondervan, 1996), 49.

> The end of the world is coming soon. Therefore, be earnest and disciplined in your prayers. Most important of all, continue to show deep love for each other, for love covers a multitude of sins. Cheerfully share your home with those who need a meal or a place to stay. (1 Peter 4:7–9 NLT)

Note how the service dimension of ministry comes to the fore. Peter continues:

> Like good stewards of the manifold grace of God, serve one another with whatever gift each of you has received. Whoever speaks must do so as one speaking the very words of God; whoever serves must do so with the strength that God supplies, so that God may be glorified in all things through Jesus Christ. To him belong the glory and the power forever and ever. Amen. (4:10–11)

Note several insights in these verses. First, everything is to be done for the glory of God (4:11). Second, we are to be "good stewards." What unifies us is that we have all received God's grace. This grace, however, is "manifold," variegated like a rainbow, resulting in a diversity of gifts and ministries among us (4:10). Third, Peter provides us with two convenient categories for spiritual gifts: speaking and serving (4:11). With this wise counsel, he echoes the salient themes of Paul's teachings on spiritual gifts, which can be summarized as follows: unity within diversity, and love and humility.

In our discussions concerning the spiritual gifts, we often miss the forest for the trees. We debate the nature of the individual gifts, dogmatic in our conclusions, when in all honesty there is little in the texts themselves to provide the precise definitions we defend. We also debate which gifts are still extant, assuming our lack has a theological explanation rather than a spiritual one. We disagree on the number of the gifts, when Paul clearly is giving us representative lists, not exhaustive ones. Most important, we too often are blind to the *attitudes* presented as the seedbed of all our gifts and ministries. To repeat, these character issues—foundational to all authentic ministry in the spiritual gifts—can be summed up with the slogan: *Unity within Diversity, Love and Humility.*

It should be pointed out that every believer receives a spiritual gift (or spiritual gifts) to equip him or her for service in the church. A false tradition has emerged in charismatic circles that believers do not receive the spiritual gifts, but rather those to whom they minister. Semantically, this teaching is quite appealing: The *sick person* receives a gift of healing, not the one serving him or her. Scripturally, however, this is simply not the case. We have already seen Peter's teaching. He says to "serve [*diakonountes*] one another with whatever gift [*charisma*] each of you has received" (1 Peter 4:10).

Paul speaks in precisely the same manner. The apostle wished that the Corinthian believers could live the single life as he did. "But each has a particular gift [*charisma*] from God, one having one kind and another a different kind" (1 Cor. 7:7). (This is a seldom-mentioned spiritual gift, incidentally, and few pursue it!) Paul begins his teaching on this subject in Romans with these words: "Having gifts [*charismata*] that differ according to the grace given to us, let us use them" (Rom. 12:6 RSV). Again, grace is our unity and the grace-gifts our diversity. God himself "gives" and "activates" the spiritual gifts (1 Cor. 12:4–11). We "receive" or "have" these gifts to serve one another, that is, "for the common good" (12:7). Thus, it is right to say, "I *have* a certain gift," despite what the charismatic tradition might say.

> *All authentic ministry in the spiritual gifts can be summed up with the slogan:* Unity within diversity, Love and Humility.

Further, Paul indicates that spiritual gifts, equipping us for ministry, can be imparted to us by the laying on of hands. He writes Timothy, "Do not neglect the gift [*charisma*] that is in you, which was given to you through prophecy with the laying on of hands by the council of elders" (1 Tim. 4:14). Later, Paul reminded Timothy to "fan into flame the gift [*charisma*] of God, which is in you through the laying on of my hands" (2 Tim. 1:6 NIV). Notice the gift was "in" Timothy. He "received" the gift; he "had" it. If these verses refer to Timothy's ordination, then we have a much more dynamic concept of the event than what is often practiced today. Prophetic utterances and the impartation of spiritual gifts evidently accompanied ordinations in New Testament times.

We must return to the bird's-eye view and our slogan, *Unity within Diversity, Love and Humility.* Paul uses the body metaphor to communicate the principle of unity within diversity. In Romans he points out that the body, both physical (the human body) and spiritual (the church), is one body with many members (Rom. 12:4–5). We "are members one of another," he adds, thus reinforcing our unity (12:5). But we "have gifts that differ according to the grace given to us" (12:6). Not "all the members have the same function" (12:4). Our unity is in the grace (*charis*) we have all received; our diversity is in the grace-gift(s) (*charisma*) we have each received. We are to express love and humility toward one another. We are not to think of ourselves more highly than we ought to think (12:3), and our "love must be real." "Love each other like brothers and sisters. Give each other more honor than you want for yourselves" (12:9–10 NCV). The entire Romans 12 provides a velvet setting for the sparkling jewels, the marvelous gifts, that God has bestowed on his church.

The apostle *expands* his treatment of these same principles in 1 Corinthians 12–14. With his demarcating words, "Now concerning" (*peri de*; see 1 Cor. 7:1, 25; 8:1; 16:1, 12), Paul begins another major section of his letter, this one devoted to "the things of the Spirit" (*ton pneumatikon*).[51] First, he gives the theological touchstone for all spiritual manifestations: the confession "Jesus is Lord" (12:1–3). Could it be that gnostic false prophets were prophesying, "Let Jesus be cursed!" (12:3) as a denial of the Incarnation? Certainly, Paul had to deal with such issues in Corinth, including the claims of the "super-apostles" (2 Cor. 11:5; 12:11) who challenged his authority. He desired that the Corinthians not be "uninformed" (1 Cor. 12:1) about these matters, a problem that persists even to our own day.

Paul then stresses unity within diversity. "Now there are varieties of gifts, but the same Spirit" (1 Cor. 12:4). The key words are "varieties" (diversity) and "the same" (unity). "And there are varieties of ministries, and the same Lord" (12:5 NASB). Completing the Trinitarian pattern, he writes, "and there are varieties of activities, but it is the same God who activates all of them in everyone" (12:6). These words would make a useful litany in congregational worship, while serving as a constant warning against a "cookie-cutter" Christianity that presses for *uniformity* rather than unity-within-diversity with regard to spiritual gifts and ministries!

"To each is given the manifestation of the Spirit for the common good" (1 Cor. 12:7). That is the controlling principle. The gifts are given, not for self-aggrandizement but for the edification, or building up, of the body—a theme to which the apostle devotes an entire chapter (ch. 14). Although the gifts, ministries, and activities vary greatly, they are all ultimately the result of the working of the one Holy Spirit,

---

[51] Gordon D. Fee, *God's Empowering Presence: The Holy Spirit in the Letters of Paul* (Peabody, Mass.: Hendrickson, 1994), 151–53.

as the phrases "through the Spirit," "according to the same Spirit," "by the same Spirit," "by the one Spirit," and "by one and the same Spirit" (12:8–11) clearly indicate. He "allots to each one individually just as the Spirit chooses" (12:11).

Using the body metaphor, the apostle continues the theme of unity within diversity (one body, many members) and integrates it with the theme of love and humility (1 Cor. 12:12–26). It is a false humility to feel inferior to any other member of the body (12:14–20). It is a denial of humility to feel superior to any other member of the body (12:21–26). In both cases Paul insists that God himself arranges the members of the body as he wills (12:18, 24). In fact, for the foot to feel itself not a part of the body because it is not a hand is in reality a case of *envy* (12:15). And for any member of the body to say to any other member of the body, "I have no need of you," is a case of *pride* (12:21). God has designed the body for mutual honor, care, dependence, and love. Chapter 13 describes this supernatural love in timeless words for all generations of believers.

Ephesians completes our portrait of the overarching ethos in which our gifts and ministries should function. We are to walk worthy of our calling "with all humility and gentleness, with patience, bearing with one another in love, making every effort to maintain the unity of the Spirit in the bond of peace" (Eph. 4:1–3). Paul then lists the seven great unities of the Church (4:4–6). Grace, says the apostle, has been given to each one of us (4:7)—which is our unity—but also some "apostles, some prophets, some evangelists, some pastors and teachers, to equip the saints for the work of the ministry, for building up the body of Christ" (4:11–12). Thus *together* we grow into maturity, and the body, "as each part is working properly," builds "itself up in love" (4:13–16).

Before we delve into the individual gifts, we should note carefully the atmosphere in which they should operate: *Unity within Diversity, Love and Humility.* Otherwise, as Paul warns, our works are hollow, and we gain nothing (1 Cor. 13:1–3). Since the apostle only gives us representative lists of the spiritual gifts, for the purposes of this study we will only look briefly at a select few of them.

Representative Gifts

Paul's list of gifts in Romans is a good place to begin our quick survey of representative gifts. Prophecy (*propheteia*) is mentioned first (Rom. 12:6). The apostle had a high regard for this gift. He wrote the

Corinthians, "Pursue love and strive for the spiritual gifts, and especially that you may prophesy" (1 Cor. 14:1). Wayne A. Grudem's *The Gift of Prophecy: In the New Testament and Today* is one of the most thorough and practical studies of this gift.[52] His position preserves the evangelical instinct to guard biblical authority while acknowledging the charismatic insight into the contemporary revelatory nature of this gift.

The following comment from Grudem's *Systematic Theology* points us in the right direction for understanding the nature of prophecy and its present-day expression:

> Although several definitions have been given for the gift of prophecy, a fresh examination of the New Testament teaching on this gift will show that it should be defined not as "predicting the future," nor as "proclaiming a word from the Lord," nor as "powerful preaching"—but rather as "*telling something that God has spontaneously brought to mind.*"[53]

Prophecy keeps us from "playing church." It disarms us as God directly addresses our present spiritual state. It is paired with and controlled by "the discernment [*diakriseis*] of spirits" (1 Cor. 12:10; see 14:29).[54] It is precisely at this point that the difference *in kind* between the inspiration of prophecies and that of Scripture is most clearly seen. Prophecies are to be judged by the Bible. In fact, one can better be used in this manner by the Holy Spirit by soaking oneself regularly in the Scriptures! In addition, it has been the experience of more than one preacher (including myself) that there are special moments when the Spirit of God seems to take over and we find ourselves speaking with an immediacy, urgency, and relevance that can only be the result of a manifestation of the gift of prophecy.

Paul continues, "If your gift is that of serving others, serve them well" (Rom. 12:7 NLT). More literally the apostle's words can be rendered, "if serving [*diakonia*], in our serving" (RSV) or, to expand this translation, "if it is a gift of practical service, let us devote ourselves to serving" (NJB). Paul is surely referring to "a range of activities similar to that which came to be the province of the deacon."[55] Thus, we are again reminded of

---

[52] Wayne A. Grudem, *The Gift of Prophecy: In the New Testament and Today* (Westchester, Ill.: Crossway, 1988).

[53] Wayne A. Grudem, *Systematic Theology* (Grand Rapids: Zondervan, 1994), 1049 (Grudem's italics). In other words, prophecy involves "speaking merely human words to report something God brings to mind"; Grudem, *The Gift of Prophecy*, 67, 89.

[54] See James D. G. Dunn, *Jesus and the Spirit* (London: SCM, 1975), 233–36.

[55] C. E. B. Cranfield, *Romans: A Shorter Commentary* (Grand Rapids: Eerdmans, 1985), 305.

the *charismatic* nature of *all* ministry in the church, including the practical service of various saints and of deacons.

Teaching (*didaskalia*) and encouraging or exhortation (*paraklesis*) are mentioned next (Rom. 12:7–8). How crucial these ministries are to the body of Christ today! Paul warned Timothy of the coming time "when people will not put up with sound doctrine [*didaskalia*]" (2 Tim. 4:3). If there were ever a need for *encouragement* among the saints, surely it is in the pressure-cooker days in which we now live. Luther commented on these gifts: "The teacher transmits knowledge; the exhorter stimulates."[56] Hopefully, of course, our teaching stimulates and our exhortations have solid content.

How crucial teaching and encouraging are to the body of Christ today!

Paul then refers to "the giver," who should give "in generosity" (Rom. 12:8). Evidently, some believers are gifted by the Lord specifically with making, and then generously sharing, money. It is the Lord who gives us the "power to get wealth" (Deut. 8:18). The apostle further comments to Timothy:

> As for those who in the present age are rich, command them not to be haughty, or to set their hopes on the uncertainty of riches, but rather on God who richly provides us with everything for our enjoyment. They are to do good, to be rich in good works, generous, and ready to share, thus storing up for themselves the treasure of a good foundation for the future, so that they may take hold of the life that really is life. (1 Tim. 6:17–19)

In all likelihood, the Lord cannot entrust this gift to many who would enthusiastically volunteer for it because of their impure motives and the dangers of riches (recall Jesus' and James's teachings on this subject)!

Paul rounds out his brief mention of specific gifts in Romans by referring to the one "who leads, with diligence" and the one "who shows mercy, with cheerfulness" (Rom. 12:8 NASB). If leadership is influence, as John Maxwell has defined it, then we all exercise a certain amount of leadership. The apostle, however, is referring here to those who are specifically gifted in this area for service to the body. "If God has given you leadership ability, take the responsibility seriously" (NLT). And "the compassionate" are to be cheerful. I once heard the dynamic pastor-teacher, Peter

---

[56] Cited in Leon Morris, *The Epistle to the Romans* (Grand Rapids: Eerdmans, 1988), 442.

Lord, share how he was initially intimidated by some persons in his congregation. They were more effective in hospital visitation in terms of bringing compassion, encouragement, and cheer than he was—and he had had seminary training. Finally, he learned to rejoice in how God had so gifted the body and to utilize fully their ministries!

The nine spiritual gifts listed in 1 Corinthians 12 are the best known *and* the most controversial. Some have tried to put these gifts in a separate category from those listed in Romans 12, but there is clearly no exegetical basis for doing so. The same terminology is used in both passages; we have here simply another representative list of gifts.

First, "the utterance of wisdom [*logos sophias*]" is mentioned (1 Cor. 12:8). Paul is referring here not to wisdom in general but to a *word* (*logos*), that is, a message or an utterance, of wisdom—an inspired speaking of God-given wisdom. From Paul's earlier moving words in this same letter (1:18–2:16), it is clear that the apostle has in mind a Christ-centered and a cross-centered message. Christ is "for us wisdom from God, and righteousness and sanctification and redemption" (1:30). We are to let "the word [or message, *logos*] of Christ" dwell in us "richly" (Col. 3:16).

The "utterance of knowledge [*logos gnoseos*]" is mentioned next. Again, an inspired utterance of a revelatory nature related to the contemporary situation of the hearers is in purview. Since the Corinthian believers were enamored by "wisdom" and "knowledge," often of a gnostic flavor, Paul seems to be seizing on these realities at the outset of his discussion of the *charismata*, the spiritual gifts. He contrasts authentic Spirit-given utterances of wisdom and knowledge with the false spirituality of the incipient gnosticism that threatened many of Paul's churches.

I have had the privilege of hearing Oral Roberts teach on each of the spiritual gifts and relate his personal experiences with them. One of the best examples of a word of wisdom came when Dr. Roberts was a guest at the Berlin Congress on Evangelism in 1996. A pastor from India, unaccustomed to praying for the sick, related how a dying child had been thrust at him for prayer. He prayed and the child recovered. This pastor asked the famed healing evangelist whether he had done right. Oral Roberts replied with this word of wisdom: "Why don't you ask the little boy?"[57]

---

[57] Oral Roberts, *The Call: An Autobiography* (Garden City, N.Y.: Doubleday, 1972), 121; David Edwin Harrell Jr., *Oral Roberts: An American Life* (Bloomington, Ind.: Indiana Univ. Press, 1985), 203.

Richard Roberts, Oral Roberts's son and his successor as president of Oral Roberts University, is a healing evangelist in his own right. Richard Roberts has been used dramatically by God in the word of knowledge. Don Dunkerley, a Presbyterian healing evangelist and educator, relates how he had the opportunity to observe firsthand how this gift operated both through Richard Roberts himself and his ORU student-team members in a crusade in Trivandrum, India, in 1993. Dunkerley was impressed with their genuineness and integrity.[58]

Once I was the personal recipient of ministry in this area from *both* Oral and Richard Roberts. Standing before a crowd of about six thousand, I heard Oral ask Richard if he had sensed a God-given heat in my right hand for a healing ministry. Richard confirmed the same revelatory word of knowledge. When I was asked directly whether I had sensed this myself, I could only answer in the negative. However, a few days later I experienced dramatically what had been revealed that day. I was serving as chaplain of the University at ORU at the time and was counseling a student in my office in Christ Chapel. While praying for the student, I felt heat in my right hand as I placed it on her head. I immediately asked the student if she had felt the same heat. She confirmed that the heat had gone through her entire body and that she was healed! These kinds of things occur often at this university, which is known to continually Expect a Miracle!

In fact, it is just such a miracle-working faith that the apostle Paul next mentions in his list of gifts in Corinthians. It is useful to list the next three gifts together: "to another faith by the same Spirit, to another gifts of healing[s] by the one Spirit, to another the working of miracles" (1 Cor. 12:9–10). Clearly, the word faith here refers to extraordinary *faith* "so as to remove mountains" (13:2), as it were—that is, faith related to healings and miracles.

By personal experience I know that when the gift of faith is in operation, one is *emptied* of doubt and moves out with boldness. Once in Cordova, Argentina, in a basketball arena seating about five thousand people, I prayed a bold prayer of faith for the healing of the people in the arena. Shortly thereafter my wife, the ORU seminarians with us, and I were being rushed to the bus station to catch an overnight ride to Buenos Aires. Before we exited the building, someone rushed up to us and related how a woman who had had a paralyzed hand was instantly

---

58 Don Dunkerley, *Healing Evangelism* (Grand Rapids: Chosen, 1995), 190–91, 195.

healed when I prayed that bold prayer of faith. Her hand just shot open. Being among people of such great faith and anointing had encouraged my own faith, and the gracious Holy Spirit had given a gift of faith!

No one has stood for—or for that matter *demonstrated*—the ministry of healing and miracles more than Oral Roberts. His son, Richard Roberts, moves in the same anointing for healing evangelism. The whole Pentecostal/charismatic stream that has come to dominate the church on mission into the twenty-first century has also exemplified the effective use of these gifts. God still offers us "gifts of healing[s]" (plural: *iamaton*; 1 Cor. 12:9) for the myriad needs we face today. Miraculous faith, healings, and miracles serve as signs of the kingdom and should be a natural and normal part of the church's end-time ministry. These ministries should no more be stopped because of abuse in some quarters than should the ministry of evangelism, which has sometimes suffered similar abuse. Western Christianity is having to revise its Enlightenment worldview these days in view of the overwhelming evidence of the miraculous and in the face of the pressing needs of our times.[59]

Finally, Paul lists two pairs of gifts that work in tandem in corporate worship: "to another prophecy, to another the discernment of spirits, to another various kinds of tongues, to another the interpretation of tongues" (1 Cor. 12:10). We have already seen how the discernment of spirits serves as the "control" gift on prophecy. The apostle John wrote:

> Beloved, do not believe every spirit, but test the spirits to see whether they are from God; for many false prophets have gone out into the world. By this you know the Spirit of God: every spirit that confesses that Jesus Christ has come in the flesh is from God, and every spirit that does not confess Jesus is not from God. And this is the spirit of the antichrist, of which you have heard that it is coming; and now it is already in the world. (1 John 4:1–3)

Apparently, Paul addressed precisely the same situation in his churches (1 Cor. 12:1–3). Prophecies and prophetic ministries in general are to be judged by the *theology* of their messages, that is, by the Scriptures. The Spirit will never contradict the Scriptures!

Tongues and interpretation belong together as well. If *all* churches would simply follow Paul's guidelines in 1 Corinthian 14, there would

---

[59] See Charles H. Kraft, *Christianity with Power: Your Worldview and Your Experience of the Supernatural* (Ann Arbor: Vine Books, 1989).

not be nearly as much confusion and controversy. The apostle strikes a beautiful balance between form and freedom in corporate worship in this important chapter. Bottom line: "So, my friends, be eager to prophesy, and do not forbid speaking in tongues; but all things should be done decently and in order" (1 Cor. 14:39). Of all the spiritual gifts, speaking in tongues has been the most controversial. When believers argue militantly *for* or *against* tongues, problems inevitably emerge.

Speaking in tongues, as generally practiced by the millions of Pentecostal/charismatic Christians in the world today, is neither a satanic counterfeit nor a panacea for the church's ills. Paul saw a limited use for tongues and interpretation in corporate worship, but he valued the gift highly as an aid to private prayer. Widely respected Pentecostal New Testament scholar Gordon Fee concludes the same. "As a gift for private prayer, Paul held it in the highest regard (14:4, 5, 15, 17–18; cf. Rom. 8:26–27; Eph. 6:18)."[60] In view of what we saw earlier in the theme *Unity within Diversity, Love and Humility,* the biblical posture towards speaking in tongues is clear. No one should feel superior or inferior with reference to this experience. There are no first and second class citizens in the kingdom. No member can say of another, "I have no need of you." Finally, we should note that in his directives Paul *regulates,* rather than *exterminates,* the rampant tongues at Corinth.

The Spirit will never contradict the Scriptures!

I have heard Oral Roberts say many times that speaking in tongues, though available to all believers as a means of prayer, should never be mandated. Paul would only say, "Now I would like all of you to speak in tongues" (1 Cor. 14:5)—it was Paul's *wish,* not his command. At the same time, we should seek continually the Spirit's presence, power, and help in our prayer, praise, and service. It is time for Christians to exercise greater acceptance, tolerance, and esteem toward each other, whether speaking in tongues is a part of our walk with the Lord or not. *We all need each other.* I personally long for the day when this gift, along with all the other wonderful gifts of God's gracious Spirit, can be accepted as a normal part of our personal and corporate life together—with love as our ultimate theme (1 Cor. 13)!

There is one other list to consider within this context. In 1 Corinthians 12:27–31, Paul culminates his depiction of the unity within the

---

[60] Gordon D. Fee, *Paul, the Spirit, and the People of God* (Peabody, Mass.: Hendrickson, 1996), 169.

diversity of the body with these words: "Now you are the body of Christ and individually members of it. And God has appointed in the church first apostles, second prophets, third teachers" (12:27–28). The apostle goes on to mention miracles, gifts of healings, helps, leadership, and tongues (12:28). With the initial ranking of the *persons* of apostles, prophets, and teachers—as contrasted with the *gifts* that ensue (miracles and the like)—we are immediately reminded of the list of Christ's "gifts to his people" listed in Ephesians 4:8–11).[61]

Apostles, Prophets, Evangelists, Pastors, and Teachers

In actuality, Paul's list in Ephesians 4 should probably be understood as fourfold: apostles, prophets, evangelists, and pastor-teachers. Since, however, teachers are singled out in 1 Corinthians 12:28, it is also beneficial to consider separately the ministries of pastors and teachers.

Who were the apostles of the New Testament church? First and foremost, the Twelve, hand-chosen by our Lord himself, should be mentioned (Matt. 10:1–4; Mark 3:13–19; Luke 6:12–16; Acts 1:15–26). The circle then widens to include Paul and Barnabas, Andronicus and Junia, James the brother of our Lord, and possibly others (Acts 14:14; Rom. 16:7; 1 Cor. 15:7; Gal. 1:19). These undoubtedly are the foundational apostles referred to by Paul in Ephesians 2:20. James D. G. Dunn lists the following essential characteristics of their apostleship:

> (1) they had been commissioned personally by the risen Jesus in a resurrection appearance (1 Cor. 9:1; 15:7; Gal. 1:1, 15f.; 1 Thess. 2:6/7—"apostles of Christ"); (2) they were missionaries and church founders (Rom. 1:5; 11:13; 15:20; 1 Cor. 3:5f., 10; 9:2; 15:9ff.; Gal. 1:15f.); (3) theirs was a distinctively and decisively eschatological role (Rom. 11:13ff.; 15:15f.; 1 Cor. 4:9; 15:8; Eph. 3:5).[62]

The term *apostle* was also used in the sense of messenger, envoy, or delegate (2 Cor. 8:23; Phil. 2:25)—much in the same way that local congregations of the Southern Baptist Convention send messengers to their national conventions.

---

[61] The issue of cessationism—the belief that certain miraculous, or "sign," gifts (such as healings, miracles, tongues, and prophecy) have ceased—deserves a separate treatment beyond the parameters of this volume. My own presentation here of spiritual gifts parallels the bridge-building position of Craig Keener's *Gift and Giver: The Holy Spirit for Today* (Grand Rapids: Baker, 2001). For an excellent brief overview of the subject with a helpful bibliography, see Wayne Grudem, *Bible Doctrine: Essential Teachings of the Christian Faith*, ed. Jeff Purswell (Grand Rapids: Zondervan, 1999), 402–6.

[62] Dunn, *Jesus and the Spirit*, 273.

Paul reminded the Corinthians, "For though you might have ten thousand guardians in Christ, you do not have many fathers. Indeed, in Christ Jesus I became your father through the gospel" (1 Cor. 4:15). Later he added, "If I am not an apostle to others, at least I am to you; for you are the seal of my apostleship in the Lord" (9:2). Paul never "pulled rank" as their apostle, but rather appealed to them and exhorted them as their spiritual father. He addressed his letters to the entire congregation rather than to the established leadership within the church. He based his authority on the gospel he had been given divine commission to preach and on the fact that he had founded that particular congregation.

There are many today who continue to carry on apostolic work. They are missionaries and church planters who further the gospel across the globe and establish ongoing congregations. They do not have the same authority as the original apostles, who formed the foundation of the church, "with Christ Jesus himself as the cornerstone" (Eph. 2:20). But they have been entrusted with leadership over the particular congregations they have established.

I was privileged to observe firsthand the apostolic work of Omar Cabrera of Argentina. Cabrera would go into a village or a large city and fast and pray for a number of days. Then he would hold public meetings in which many signs and wonders occurred and the gospel was preached with great power. A new church was formed from the converts, and a trained pastor was put in charge of the fledgling congregation. Cabrera's church, called Vision de Futuro (Vision of the Future), consisted of a string of congregations across central Argentina, with membership numbering about 160,000. I have also been the founding pastor of two churches, and there is no more delightful a task!

Prophets also exerted significant authority in the New Testament churches. Perhaps providentially, the apostles and prophets of this era loomed large precisely because the canon of the New Testament was not yet complete. Thus, the Holy Spirit could preserve the words of our Lord through these leaders and ultimately through the New Testament, the authority of which was based on what the apostles preached and taught. Prophets were known as such precisely because the Holy Spirit used them consistently in prophetic utterances. Again, their authority was derivative of the gospel as well as based on the inspiration of the prophecies themselves. Prophetic ministry is emerging afresh in our own day with admittedly uneven results because of abuses in some quarters. Nonetheless, this scriptural ministry is essential to the vitality of churches today.

The twentieth century saw some of the most powerful *evangelists* in the history of the church. Their very title is indicative of their work—the evangelization of the world. These are the anointed gospel preachers who sow the seed of God's Word across the globe. Working in tandem with the other ministries of the church and in cooperation with local congregations in general, these heralds of the good news aid tremendously in the growth of the church. Billy Graham and Oral Roberts have been perhaps the two leading evangelists of this century, although an entire phalanx of gospel preachers has blanketed the globe with the gospel.

Pastors are shepherds or overseers of the congregations (see Phil. 1:1). Perhaps theirs is the most challenging task of all—especially since today they are often expected to be great orators, dynamic motivational speakers and leaders, powerful evangelists, skilled administrators, professional counselors, biblical and theological scholars, and social workers all wrapped into one. These expectations are unrealistic. There is solid evidence that there is a crisis in this regard across America right now, causing pastors and congregations both to suffer immensely. The biblical vision of the members of the body working together, each with a limited number of responsibilities, must be recovered in our day before there are thousands more casualties. When deacons actually take care of the practical needs of the congregation (see Acts 6:1–7) and others fulfill their ministries, then pastors can more effectively teach, equip, and nurture the flock.

Finally, *teachers* round out what have often been called the fivefold ministries. This function of the church has come to the fore again during the last few decades. The importance of the teaching ministry of the church in general has been reemphasized with positive results. Pastors are rediscovering their *teaching* responsibilities. And teachers in myriad contexts from Sunday schools to seminaries to various traveling ministries have done much to revitalize the church. Correlating with these developments has been the rediscovery of the importance of the ministries of *women* in the life of the church.

Women loomed large in the ministry of the early church. Most healthy congregations today owe their vitality in large measure to the faithful service of women. At this very moment, the church is in the midst of a painful reexamination of the role of women in the ministry of the

Church, and there is much progress yet to be made. Donald G. Bloesch has provided a sane, sage, and strategic perspective with his volume, *Is the Bible Sexist? Beyond Feminism and Patriarchalism.*[63] Perhaps it is the new appreciation for the importance of the doctrine of the Trinity that will pave the way for the church's full recovery of her vital ministries.

Trinitarian Ecclesiology

We have already seen the Trinitarian nature of the church in our previous study of New Testament images. Clearly the church is vitally related to each person of the Godhead. It is equally important, however, to see the church as a reflection of the *relations* among the Father, the Son, and the Holy Spirit. Our God is a *community* of persons. God is *relational* to an infinite degree. He defines what is meant by person—that is, persons are beings in relationship, not merely "Lone Ranger," independent individuals. Thus, the church is communal "to the max." Catherine Mowry LaCugna observes that "the truth about both God and ourselves is that we were meant to exist as persons in communion in a common household, living as persons from and for others, not persons in isolation or withdrawal or self-centeredness."[64] Kevin Giles adds, "The church is therefore not something extra in the Christian life, but of the very essence of life in Christ."[65]

> *The church is a reflection of the* relations *among the Father, the Son, and the Holy Spirit.*

Further, just as Father, Son, and Holy Spirit are coequal, so there is an inherent *egalitarianism* within the life of the church. There is to be a mutual submission (Eph. 5:21) and humble service one of another. We are to be interdependent and to transcend all the social barriers the world would foist on us (Gal. 3:28).[66] Every voice is important in this

---

[63] Donald G. Bloesch, *Is the Bible Sexist? Beyond Feminism and Patriarchalism* (Westchester, Ill.: Crossway, 1982).

[64] Catherine Mowry LaCugna, *God for Us: The Trinity and Christian Life* (San Francisco: HarperCollins, 1991), 383.

[65] Kevin Giles, *What on Earth Is the Church* (Downers Grove, Ill.: InterVarsity Press, 1995), 223.

[66] See Gilbert Bilezikian, "Hermeneutical Bungee-Jumping: Subordination in the Godhead," *JETS* 40 (March 1997): 57–68; also idem, *Community 101: Reclaiming the Local Church as a Community of Oneness* (Grand Rapids: Zondervan, 1997).

model. Women and men are equal. Racial barriers drop. A more democratic spirit replaces domination and authoritarianism. Divisive denominational pride is transformed into a cooperative spirit and mutual respect among the churches. Millard Erickson aptly summarizes this insight:

> Thus, the type of relationship that should characterize human persons, particularly believing Christians who have accepted the structure of intratrinitarian relationships as the pattern for their own relationships to others, would be one of unselfish love and submission to the other, seeking the welfare of the other over one's own.[67]

This inclusive approach would extend outside the church to a world in need of God's liberating love.[68] The perichoretic understanding of the Trinity, which we studied earlier, is the ultimate foundation for this perspective: What one person of the Holy Trinity does, all do; there is an *inseparable* unity—and so it should be with the church!

Catherine Mowry LaCugna puts this Trinitarian ecclesiology in its broadest biblical and theological perspective:

> Ecclesial life is a way of living in anticipation of the coming reign of God. The church makes a claim that civil governments do not: that it is the People of God, Body of Christ, and Temple of the Holy Spirit. The life of the church is to be animated by the life of God; the church is to embody in the world the presence of the risen Christ, showing by its preaching and by its own form of life that sin and death have been overcome by Jesus Christ. The church also claims to embody in its corporate life the presence, fruits, and work of the Holy Spirit, to be the visible sign of God's reign, of the divine-human communion, and the communion of all creatures with one another.[69]

Jesus himself instituted the two ordinances that mark both our entrance into (baptism) and our ongoing participation in (the Lord's Supper) this divine-human community. Our consideration of these ordinances will culminate our study of the doctrine of the church.

---

[67] Millard J. Erickson, *God in Three Persons: A Contemporay Interpretation of the Trinity* (Grand Rapids: Baker, 1995), 333.

[68] See Leonardo Boff, *Trinity and Society* (Maryknoll, N.Y.: Orbis, 1988).

[69] LaCugna, *God for Us*, 401.

Baptism

In the Great Commission Jesus Christ told us in part to *baptize* "in the name of the Father and of the Son and of the Holy Spirit" (Matt. 28:19). When Peter was asked by his hearers on the day of Pentecost what they should do, he replied: "Repent, and be baptized" (Acts 2:38). And the entire book of Acts makes it clear that the early church obeyed her Lord in this matter.

The practice of water baptism keeps the *corporate* dimension of becoming and being a Christian constantly before us. The church preaches the gospel to us, baptizes us, disciples us, and nurtures us. God is our Father, and the church is our mother (Calvin). Just as the marriage ceremony is the public declaration of a mutual belonging and devotion, so water baptism signifies our public and permanent commitment to Christ and his church. We are entering into the divine-human community of persons—the Tripersonal God and his church!

Water baptism was meant in part to express our unity in the church.

Water baptism was meant in part to express our unity in the church (Eph. 4:5). Ironically, it has become in many quarters an occasion for division in the body of Christ. Honest differences of interpretation of Scripture, theological outlook, and ritual practice set various groups apart. Many see water baptism as a sacrament, an outward and visible sign of an inward and invisible grace. Baptism is viewed as mediating God's saving grace to us. Others see baptism as a covenantal sign, marking us off as members of the New Testament community (similar to circumcision under the old covenant). Still others view this rite as a means of expressing our faith and obedience to Christ, who himself ordained (thus the term "ordinance") this practice. Perhaps there is a kernel of truth in each of these positions.

Water baptism can be seen as a sacrament in that it can be the concrete occasion (through faith) of experiencing the transforming presence of God's Spirit (grace). Because it is a public event, practiced within the believing community, it certainly serves as a sign of our covenant relationship with God and one another. And the Scriptures clearly point to the symbolic significance of baptism as a means of expressing our union with Christ in his death and resurrection as well as our obedient faith. From my own perspective, the baptismal rite is a means of faith and the Spirit himself is the means of grace. Baptism enables us to express authentic repentance and faith. The Holy Spirit is present, all along enabling these realities and saving us thereby—which is what grace signifies in the New Testament.

The term *baptize* is actually a transliteration of the Greek word that means to dip or immerse, which was clearly the prevailing practice of the church during the first two centuries. Other modes, such as pouring and sprinkling, emerged early in the patristic era and continue to be practiced today. No New Testament text ever directly states that infants were ever baptized, and, therefore, baptism should be seen (from this interpreter's perspective) as the occasion for a believer in Christ to express his or her obedient faith—be that person seven years old, as I was, or seventy-seven.

All of these matters are still hotly debated among the churches. What does the rite signify? What actually transpires at baptism? Who should be baptized, and when? Certainly tolerance of diversity of opinion is called for—as well as the ongoing attempt to rightly interpret the Scriptures and practice what they teach.

Baptist theologian Dale Moody observed that there have been many, baptized as infants in the church, who have gone on to live sterling Christian lives, while there have been many others who received "believer's baptism," yet turned out to be unbelievers.[70] Again, humility is the order of the day. At the same time, our quest for biblical precedent and doctrinal precision should continue—and we should never at any price compromise the central gospel doctrine of justification by grace through faith.

Because it is literally a "washing," baptism serves as a fitting symbol for our salvation. As Ananias instructed Saul, "Get up, be baptized, and have your sins washed away, calling on his name" (Acts 22:16; see also 1 Cor. 6:11; Eph. 5:26; Titus 3:4–7). But it is what Christ has done that saves us, not what we do. Only as an act of Spirit-enabled repentance and faith is baptism efficacious. We call on the Lord and are saved (Rom. 10:13). Water baptism beautifully expresses this reality. "And baptism ... now saves you—not as a removal of dirt from the body, but as an appeal to God for a good conscience, through the resurrection of Jesus Christ" (1 Peter 3:21). It is not the physical washing that counts, but the spiritual. The physical merely represents the spiritual.

[70] Moody, *The Word of Truth*, 460.

Further, through baptism we identify with our Lord in his death, burial, and resurrection (Rom. 6:1–11; see Col. 2:11–12). It is, in addition, an impetus toward sanctification, as Paul indicates in Romans 6. Actually, however, the water rite itself is only in the background of this chapter, and the apostle is developing the spiritual reality itself, in much the same way as he does our unity in Christ in Galatians 3:28. Again, it is the spiritual dimension that is primary. The rite may or may not be an actual occasion of spiritual significance, depending on whether authentic faith is being expressed. It is the initiatory *Spirit baptism*, to which Paul refers in 1 Corinthians 12:13, that is of ultimate significance. Water baptism is only a symbolic depiction of this spiritual reality. And this reality is also a human reality of solidarity with God's people, as Paul argues so congently in that context.

Baptism points us, therefore, to the importance of church membership. One cannot be in fellowship with a Christian book or television program; one can only be in fellowship with flesh and blood human beings. Such a statement was not necessary in previous generations. But in our consumer age of shallow commitments and selfish pleasure-seeking, it needs to be said. No one has confronted this disease—perhaps plague—more poignantly or effectively than Charles Colson and Ellen Vaughn in their classic book, *Being the Body*.[71] No matter how it is practiced (and, again, from my perspective the correct mode is immersion, and the appropriate candidate is the professing believer), water baptism has its effects.

The new believer is ushered into a new life with new loyalties, a new family of faith, and a fulfilling, eternally significant mission in life. The gospel is acted out in symbol and pageant—which impacts both observing believers, who are freshly reminded of their own baptismal vows, and unbelievers, who vividly encounter the concrete reality of Christ's having saved someone.[72]

The Lord's Supper

Observing the Eucharist—or Holy Communion (the biblical title is Lord's Supper)—was not a meaningful part of my life growing up in the Baptist church. It did not seem to be an important event, since we observed it only about four times a year. There was such a stern warning

---

71 Charles Colson and Ellen Vaughn, *Being the Body* (Nashville: W Publishing Group, 2003).
72 See Stanley J. Grenz, *Created for Community* (Grand Rapids: Baker, 1996), 234–38.

against partaking of the meal in an unworthy manner that I associated fear with this rite more than faith, hope, and love. My memory is simply that of being told that we do this because Christ commanded it and because it reminds us of his death. I knew there had to be more to it than that, but I was mystified as to precisely what that "more" would be.

Then I became a student at Oral Roberts University. Bob Stamps, the chaplain of the university, took me under his wing and began taking me to various liturgical services around the city of Tulsa and giving me a quiet running commentary during the services as to the significance of the various practices of the churches we attended. I saw how vast and variegated the body of Christ really is as we attended a Roman Catholic mass one Sunday, a Lutheran service the next, a United Methodist service the following Sunday, and so on.

On campus Stamps had established noon communion services each weekday, a Friday evening communion service, and a Sunday night vespers—all liturgical in nature with processionals, lectionary readings, and communion, and all charismatic in nature, with prophecies, tongues, prayers for healing, and the beautiful singing of "spiritual songs." I learned firsthand that form and freedom are not antithetical in worship. I learned too that the Lord's Supper is a beautiful and powerful means by which God's people commune with God and each other. It is literally a table fellowship of the saints with their Savior!

Christ himself instituted the meal at the last Passover supper he shared with the disciples before his Passion (Matt. 26:26–29; Mark 14:22–25; Luke 22:14–20; 1 Cor. 11:23–26). Thus, the covenantal context looms large (and unites the Old and New Testaments): "For our paschal lamb, Christ, has been sacrificed" (1 Cor. 5:7). Jesus' words of institution were straightforward enough, but they have been variously interpreted through Christian history. Perhaps the real dividing line came with the introduction of Aristotelian philosophy into Roman Catholic thought during the Middle Ages, and the insertion of the concept of *transubstantiation* into the church's theology.

In this view the elements of communion literally become the body and blood of our Lord. Luther was convinced that this amounted to the introduction of a foreign substance into the church's traditional teaching, and he was equally sure that the average believer was incapable of grasping the significance or importance of the concept.[73] Probably the same is true

[73] See his "Babylonian Captivity of the Church" (1520).

of the entire debate today. Many are just as baffled by Luther's *consubstantiation* view of Christ's body and blood as "incarnate" in the elements. Calvin moved the church in the right direction with his concept of the *spiritual* presence of Christ in the elements, but the focus was still on the elements. Finally, Zwingli perhaps overreacted with his *symbolic* interpretation of the elements, which came down to me as a Baptist in the phrase "mere symbol." How could the elements be a mere anything? As with baptism, the key lies in our doctrine of the Spirit.

In the Lord's Supper believers enjoy intimate personal fellowship with the risen Lord through the presence of the Holy Spirit.

The Lord's Supper as practiced by the New Testament church was the ritual by means of which early believers enjoyed intimate personal fellowship with the risen Lord *through the presence of the Holy Spirit.* The focus was on the Lord and not on the physical emblems of his passion. They regularly and faithfully "devoted themselves" to "the breaking of bread" (Acts 2:42) because the Lord made himself "known to them in the breaking of the bread" (Luke 24:35; see vv. 30–31). Earlier Jesus had said, "It is the Spirit who gives life; the flesh profits nothing" (John 6:63 NASB). Gary Burge's summary of the Johannine view of communion could also be applied to Paul's theology:

> In that the Spirit draws the believer into union with Christ, who was truly incarnate and who died, eucharistic participation serves to usher the believer toward eternal life (6:53, 54). As in baptismal water, bread and wine are simply our Godward expression of faith. But within this worship, the movement of God toward us involves the Spirit, who accomplishes both the rebirth and the union through his transforming of our worship and material expressions. It is what we might term pneumatic worship (*chrisma*, 1 John 2:20; etc.) that John hopes for in the eucharist as the Spirit actively leads us to Christ.[74]

In commenting on the spiritual (*pnematikon*) food, drink, and rock Paul refers to in 1 Corinthians 10:3–4, Gordon Fee summarizes

> how Paul understood the food of the Lord's Table as the place where the Spirit regularly applies the benefits of the cross, as represented in the

[74] Gary M. Burge, *The Anointed Community: The Holy Spirit in the Johannine Tradition* (Grand Rapids: Eerdmans, 1987), 189.

> food, to the life of the believer. Paul's understanding of the Table, therefore, falls not on the side of a kind of sacramentalism, where the food is regarded as conveying grace in some way, but, on the side of the Spirit as present at the Table, freshly appropriating the benefits of Christ to the believers' lives. Thus, the food of the Table is the Spirit's food in the sense that the Spirit, as the real presence, once more appropriates the provision of the cross to the one who eats by faith, in celebration with others.[75]

Thus, Fee further corroborates the univocal voice of the New Testament as to the significance of this meal.

We will, therefore, guard with all diligence our sharing (*koinonia*) in the body and blood of our Lord (1 Cor. 10:16–17). We will eat and drink together, "discerning the body" and guarding its unity (11:29). We will always examine ourselves in these matters and thus avert God's judgment (11:27–32). Most important, we will see this meal as proclaiming "the Lord's death until he comes" (11:26). Our focus will be on remembering him and on celebrating the new covenant in his blood (11:24–26). There are three dimensions to these actions: (1) We relive the past—our Lord's passion; (2) we commune with the risen Lord and one another in the present; and (3) we joyously anticipate his return in his Father's kingdom.

The Church and the Future

The twenty-first-century church faces rapid change and stark contrasts. The world is getting darker, and the church is shining brighter. Postmoderns seem to value both tradition and innovation. Both the individual and the community are viewed as all important. Congregations are getting larger (megachurches) and smaller (metachurches). They are getting older (Boomers) and younger (Busters, X-ers, and the like). New models for doing church have emerged, and the one constant is *change.*

Traditional models for church life—be they mainline, evangelical, or charismatic—are flourishing in some quarters, languishing in others. The *Saddleback model* (purpose-driven) is perhaps the most transferable model, applying the biblical purposes for the church in various settings. The *Willow Creek model* (seeker-targeted) has kept the focus on reaching

---

[75] Fee, *God's Empowering Presence,* 144.

the unchurched, a needed emphasis. The *apostolic model* (apostolic leaders) has sought to liberate young megachurch entrepreneurs to be all that they can be in leading the church on mission. The *Toronto model* (revival orientation) promotes revival and awakening, a perennial need of the church. The *metachurch model* (cell-based) has rightly emphasized the need for small-group interaction, care, and discipleship. And the *emerging church model* (mindset) has sought to more effectively contextualize the church in the postmodern setting.[76]

God is building his church,[77] and he graciously lets us in on the action. These are both perilous and promising times. There has never been a better time to be joined with the church on her end-time mission. God's kingdom *will* come in all its fullness, and the church *will* triumph through her Lord and Savior Jesus Christ. Ablaze with God's Spirit and God's truth, the church will one day shine like the sun. Her cry of "Maranatha" will be fulfilled, and the universal confession will be "Jesus is Lord!" Lord, hasten the day!

---

[76] See Larry Hart, "Models for Ministry in the 21st Century," *Ministries Today* (November/December 2001), 55–59.

[77] See Bob Russell, *When God Builds a Church* (West Monroe, La.: Howard, 2000), for one astounding local church example (with many transferable principles).

Subject Index

Person Index

Scripture Index

2 Corinthians

Galatians

Ephesians

Philippians

Colossians

Copyrights of Bible Versions Used